The Echoing Years

An Anthology of Poetry from Canada and Ireland

The Echoing Years

An Anthology of Poetry from Canada and Ireland

EDITED BY

John Ennis,
Centre for Newfoundland and Labrador Studies,
School of Humanities, Waterford Institute of Technology

Randall Maggs
Sir Wilfred Grenfell College, Corner Brook

Stephanie McKenzie
Sir Wilfred Grenfell College, Corner Brook

Published by the Centre for Newfoundland & Labrador Studies
School of Humanities Publications
Waterford Institute of Technology, Ireland

WIT wishes to acknowledge the financial assistance received towards the publication of this book from Sir Wilfred Grenfell College, the Ireland Newfoundland Partnership, The Ireland Business Partnerships and Foras na Gaeilge.

The Echoing Years
First published in 2007 by

The Centre for Newfoundland & Labrador Studies,
School of Humanities Publications, Waterford Institute of Technology.

Selection and Introduction © John Ennis, Randall Maggs and
Stephanie McKenzie, 2007.
The appendices form an extension of this copyright notice.

Poetry © individual poets and / or publishing houses
(as indicated in credits).

All rights reserved; no part of this book may be reproduced by
any means, electronic or mechanical, except for passages in a
review to be printed in a newspaper or magazine or
broadcast on radio or television.

Printed and bound in Ireland by eprint Limited, Dublin.

Cover illustration by Michael Pittman, Newfoundland.
Michael Pittman is an award-winning painter from Newfoundland, Canada, where he resides with his wife and fellow artist, Krista. He has a Bachelor of Fine Arts degree from Sir Wilfred Grenfell College and a Masters degree from Waterford Institute of Technology. Pittman works with multiple media, utilizing non-traditional combinations of materials to create eclectic, multi-layered images which often deal with personal psychological experience. The cover artwork is an original image based on another untitled piece by Pittman. Latest distinction received, the VANC / CARFAC Excellence in Visual Arts (EVA) Award 2007. Visit the artist's website at www.newfoundartist.com.

Graphic design and layout by Jackie Raftery, Ireland.
Jackie Raftery is a graphic designer with some twenty years' experience in the field. She lectures in Graphic Reproduction and Origination at Waterford Institute of Technology. She is presently engaged in postgraduate fine art research on the Jokob Locher's 1497 Latin translation, *Stultifera Navis* (*The Ship of Fools*), by Sebastian Brant, an incunabulum which is housed in the Chester Beatty Library in Dublin. Artwork based on her research practice will form part of the Chester Beatty art collection.

ISBN 0-9540281-6-3

In memory of Craig Dobbin,
a consistent and faithful patron of the arts,
and Margaret Avison,
whose poetry provided the title
and inspiration for this book.

Still, he had his coat,
and she, the echoing years.

(from "Balancing Out," Margaret Avison)

The Echoing Years

An Anthology of Poetry from Canada and Ireland

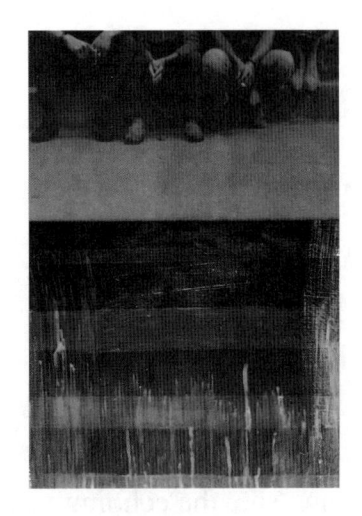

Contents

Acknowledgements XLI

Genesis of the Text XLIV

Poèmes en français, poèmes du Québec XLVI

An Ghaeilge XLIX

A Note on Translation L

A Note from the Editors LII

Three Voices LIV

Poetry from Canada

Kateri Akiwenzie-Damm
stray bullets (oka re/vision)................................. 3
partridge song 3
rainstorm in volcano: eight poems for rain.................... 4
sturgeon 6

Jeannette C. Armstrong
History Lesson 7
Threads of Old Memory 8
Rocks 12

Tammy Armstrong
Hockey 15
No One Goes with the Exhibition Boys 16

Martine Audet
"Les labours blancs . . ." 18
"De certains rêves . . ." 18
"Il nous semblait parfois . . ." 19

Margaret Avison
Balancing Out 20
Ramsden 21
Ambivalence 21
He Was There / He Was Here 23
Remembering Gordon G. Nanos 23
On a Maundy Thursday Walk 25
Lament for Byways 26

Ken Babstock
Marram Grass 28
Essentialist 29
Windspeed 30
Late Drive Toward Innisfil 31
A Berth in the Stern 32

Anurima Banerji
Summer or, I Want the Rage of Poets to Bleed Guns
   Speechless with Words 34

Mike Barnes
Stirring a Can of Soup on the Stove 38

Stephanie Bolster
Aperture, 1856 39
Whose Eyes 39
from In Which Alice Poses for Julia Margaret Cameron, 1872
   Cordelia 40
Two Deaths in January, 1898 41
Close Your Eyes and Think of England 42
Portrait of Alice with Christopher Robin 43

Roo Borson
River 44
Rivers to the Sea 47
from Autumn Record
   "Once, early in the morning . . ." 48

Tim Bowling
Grade One 49
Watching the Academy Awards in the Bar
   of the Patricia Hotel 50

Dionne Brand
 from *thirsty*
  "This city is beauty..." 51
 from *Land To Light On*
  "If you come out..." 52
  "I look at that road..." 52
  "All I could do...". 53
  "I have to think again..." 53
  "no wonder I could get lost there..." 54
  "In the middle of afternoons...". 54
  "Look, let me be specific..." 55
  "One gleeful headline..." 56
  "in the middle of traffic..." 57
  "the girl starts the morning..." 57
  "a Baptist priestess preaches...". 58
  "Maybe this wide country...". 58
  "Light passes through me..." 59
  "I feel like my aunt hunkered...". 60
  "I saw her head up the road..." 60
  "that night we wanted to fly..." 61
  "She came in a hurry to leave...". 62
  "In this country where islands vanish...". 63

Jacques Brault
 "c'est un soir pas...". 64
 "Neige d'un soir..." 64
 "Ce n'est plus le moment..." 64
 Bucolique 65

Diana Brebner
 The Blue Light of the Neutron Pool 67
 The Green Canoe 69
 from "At the Schwarzschild Radius"
  3. "The beautiful long-haired boys..." 70
 Morning on the Guitar 71
 Port 72

Nicole Brossard
 (translated by Robert Majzels and Erín Moure)
 Typhon dru / *Typhoon Thrum* 74

Mark Callanan
 The Delicate Touch Required for China 80

Anne Carson
New Rule.. 82
Shadowboxer.. 83
Father's Old Blue Cardigan 83
from TV Men
    Antigone (Scripts 1 and 2)........................ 84
    from Akhmatova (Treatment for a Script)
        Mandelstam 86
        Akhmatova Comes to the Wall 86
        Because of His Mother, Because of Her Son 87
        Akhmatova Repents (1950)...................... 87
        The Poison Son is Back........................... 88
    Thucydides in Conversation with
        Virginia Woolf on the Set of *The Peloponnesian War* .. 89
from *The Beauty of the Husband*
    II. But a Dedication Is Only Felicitous 91
    V. Here Is My Propaganda 93
    VI. To Clean Your Hooves 95
Short Talk on Defloration 96

Francis Catalano
"Vus d'en bas ..." 97
néo-libéralisme à clavier (aire de rapprochement de deux solitudes)... 97
"Les idées fondent comme du beurre ..." 98
"Amérique terre archaïque ..." 99
"*Homo lupus est ...*" 100

Herménégilde Chiasson
de *Répertoire* 101

George Elliott Clarke
Identity I 110
Child Hood I 110
Reading *Titus Andronicus* in Three Mile Plains, N.S. 111
Duet.. 112
Hard Nails... 113
Spree 114
Trial II 114
Look Homeward, Exile..................................... 115
Four Guitars 116
Night Train 119
Blues for X 119
Rev. F. R. Langford's Miracle............................. 120
A Sermon to the Undecided 120
The Sermon of Liana 121

Leonard Cohen
"Paris again . . ." 122
Too Old 122
Layton's Question 123
Robert Appears Again 123
Pardon Me 124
The Party Was Over Then Too 124
Butter Dish 125
The Collapse of Zen 126
"Oh and one more thing . . ." 127
A Note to the Chinese Reader 128

Don Coles
Kingdom 129
Night Game 130
Sampling from a Dialogue 132
Forests of the Medieval World 133
from The Edvard Munch Poems
    Death and the Maiden 135
    What They Didn't Like 136
    Self-Portrait at 3.15 a.m. 138
"There are no words to remember, but I do have that gaze" 139
Reading a Biography of Samuel Beckett 141
Romance 143

Lorna Crozier
Dust 147
Not the Music 148
Mrs. Bentley 148
Dictionary of Symbols 149
Variation on the Origin of Flight 151
The Memorial Wall 152
South Dakota Refuge 153
Skunks 153
Home Care 155
Small Gesture 156
You're So Covered with Scars 156
Hoping to Fix Up, a Little, This World 157

Beth Cuthand
Post-Oka Kinda Woman 158
For All the Settlers Who Secretly Sing 159
Zen Indian 160

Mary Dalton
To Be Sold 162
I'm Bursting to Tell: Riddles for Conception Bay 163

Jean-Paul Daoust
(translated by Daniel Sloate)
de *Les cendres bleues* / from *Blue Ashes*
"Maintenant..."/ "Now..." 169

Degan Davis
Hockey 175

Monique Deland
"la question toujours la même..." 176
"certains lendemains..." 176
"mes mains frileuses..." 177
"La nuit a rejoint la ligne..." 177
"J'accumule des retailles..." 178
"Une voix sans corps annonce..." 178
"la joue sur l'oreiller..." 178

Jean-Marc Desgent
65 179
Les premiers paysages 179
Le monde des monstres est banal 181
Je vois l'intelligent théâtre 182

Joël Des Rosiers
(translated by Hugh Hazelton)
"le 26 Octobre 1951..."/ "on October 26 1951..." 183
"mon père assembla..." / "my father assembled..." 184
"l'enfance est d'immortalité..." / "childhood is immortality..." 185
"pour Guillane..." / "for Guillane..." 186
"il fut difficile de quitter..." / "it was hard to leave..." 187

Adam Dickinson
When We Become Desirable 189
Believing the First Words You Hear 189
Fort Smith Fire Brigade 190

Hélène Dorion
"En ce temps-là . . ." 191
"Une maison brûle . . ." 191
"Recommence devant moi . . ." 192
"Tu refais le voyage . . ." 193
"Le monde dévore nos paupières . . ." 193

Marilyn Dumont
Circle the Wagons 194
The White Judges 194
Letter to Sir John A. Macdonald 196
Leather and Naughahyde 197
Let the Ponies Out 197
The Sky is Promising 198

Louise Dupré
"Là, voilà ta demeure . . ." 201
"Tout est possible à l'ombre des jardins . . ." 201
"Tu peux encore lever la main . . ." 202
"Rien ne suffit à ton regard . . ." 202
"Cela arrive toujours sans prévenir . . ." 203
"Tu relèves ta robe . . ." 204
"Tes morts, tu en es venue . . ." 204

Paul Dutton
One Plus 205
Lost Way Lost 205
Kit-Talk 206
Strata 206
Thinking 207
Dreaming 207
Jazzstory 208
Succession 209
Obscure 210
Truck 211
Content 212
Night 212
Several Times Table 213
Shy Thought 214
Words 214

Gary Geddes
Subsidies 216
Junk Food Pastoral 217

Susan Gillis
Distant Islands (But of course they were further apart) 219
Habitat (South elevation) 219
Habitat (We stand here looking) 220
River (Dear X.) 221

Goh, Poh Seng
The Girl from Ermita 222

Lorna Goodison
Brunetto Latini 228
Questions for Marcus Mosiah Garvey 231
Crossover Griot 231
Poor Mrs. Lot 232

Susan Goyette
This Contradiction of Passion 233
Sisters 234
More Widow Than Queen Victoria 234
Sinking 235
A Chinese Lantern for Audrey 236

Catherine Greenwood
The Diving Girls' Prayer 237
In Service to a Dream 238
Pearl Farmer's Wife 239
Dream Thief 239

Louise Halfe
Der Poop 242
In Da Name of Da Fadder 243
Pāhkahkos 244
Nōhkom, Medicine Bear 246
You've Got to Teach White Women Everything. 247
from *Blue Marrow*
"*Father, these robes I wear confuse me . . .*" 248

Richard Harrison
Coach's Corner 250
Elegy for the Rocket 251

Ray Hsu
Early Work: An Eclogue..................................252
from *Inferno* XXXII-XXXIII
"Our bread-famished mouths . . ." 253
Dora (Confession, 0:93 Seconds) 253

Catherine Hunter
Two Thousand and Two 254

Patrick Lane
Drought 1980 257
Weasel..257
Monarch I 258
The Happy Little Towns..................................259
The Dream of the Red Chamber..........................261

Tania Langlais
"sa façon, la sienne . . ." 262
"quand elle retire sa petite robe . . ." 262
"s'il fallait que tu meures . . ." 263
"rien ne se raconte plus . . ."...............................263
"tu lisais l'autre nuit . . ." 264
"je suppose que ça va finir . . ." 264
"n'en pouvant plus je l'ai écrit . . ." 265
"je ne soigne personne . . ." 265
"le désorde ça prend combien de boîtes . . ." 265

Irving Layton
The Swimmer 266
Fishermen 267
On Seeing the Statuettes of Ezekiel and Jeremiah in the
   Church of Notre Dame...............................268
The Fertile Muck...269
Berry Picking 270
An Old Niçoise Whore 270
To the Girls of My Graduating Class 272
Song for Naomi...273
The Predator 274
Aran Islands 275

Nadine Ltaif
(translated by Christine Tipper)
    La Simûrghiade / Simurghiade 277
    Reconnaissance 281
    "Si j'étais un homme . . ." 282
    "Début mai . . ." 282
    "Un arbre dans sa solitude . . ." 283
    "Les arbres nus du printemps froid . . ." 283
    "Quand je pourrai écrire un chant . . ." 283
    "Je suis de retour dans les contrées sauvages . . ." 284

Laura Lush
    Children 285
    The Last of Us 285
    Darkening In 286
    Strays 286
    157 Islington 287
    Home 288
    Border 288
    Mr. Ishigami 289
    Gavey H. 289
    Kelly 290
    Riverside Heights 290
    The Session 291
    Komachu's 292
    Mama-san 292
    The Wellesdale 293
    The Year My Sister Came to Live with Me 294

Don McKay
    Meditation on Antique Glass 295
    Softball: 295
    Sometimes a Voice (1) 296
    Song of the Saxifrage to the Rock 298
    Precambrian Shield 298
    Song for the Songs of the Common Raven 299
    Chickadee Encounter 300
    Hover 301
    Meditation on Shovels 301
    Setting Up the Drums 302
    Matériel
        I. The Man from Nod 303
        II. Fates Worse than Death 304
        III. The Base 305
        IV. *Stretto* 307

Robert Melançon
Peinture aveugle 310
L'été. 310
Les dieux en décembre 311
Description d'un après-midi 311
36. 312

Anne Michaels
Three Weeks 313
Ice House 313

Roy Miki
fool's scold, 1.4.97 318

Hélène Monette
(translated by Cole Swenson)
"Un coin du jardin sans soleil . . ." 322
160 secondes / *160 Seconds* 323
"Il n'y a personne qui crie . . ." / *"No one is crying . . ."* 325

Pamela Mordecai
from *de Man: a performance poem*
I Jesus Is Condemned to Death 328
IV Jesus Meets His Mother 330
VIII The Women of Jerusalem Mourn for Jesus 332
XI Jesus Is Nailed to the Cross 333
XIII Jesus Is Taken Down from the Cross 334

Pierre Morency
Le monde dans le peau 338
Je t'écris 338

Daniel David Moses
Song in the Light of Dawn 339
Rooms Under Rain 339
The Line 340
The Persistence of Songs 342
Falling Song 343

Erín Moure
Shock Troop 344
Homage 344

from Seven Rail Poems
    2 VIA: Tourism. 345
    3 We Are a Trade 346
A History of Vietnam & Central America as Seen in the Paintings
    of Leon Golub, *Musée des beaux arts, Montréal, 1985*. 347
Goodbye to Beef. 348
Fifteen Years 350
Thirteen Years 350
West to West 351
In These (Tough) Times 352
Miss Chatelaine. 353
Meeting 354

Alayna Munce
To Train and Keep a Peregrine You Cannot Miss a Day 355

Susan Musgrave
Magnolia 357
Understanding the Sky 358
No Hablo Ingles 359
The Room Where They Found You 362

Pierre Nepveu
(translated by Judith Cowan)
Étendue 363
Belvédère 364
de *Mirabel* / from *Mirabel*
    "On promet d'excaver le sol . . ." / "They're promising to
        excavate the ground . . ." 364
    "Je pressens cette terre sans arbres . . ." /
        "Already I see this land stripped of trees . . ." 365
    Nouveau monde / *New World* 367
    L'homme des plans / *The Plans Man* 369
    Bilan / *Summing Up* 370

bpNichol
St. Anzas VIII 371
early morning variation. 372
Moth 374
Blues 376
Untitled ("Sometimes as other sums . . .") 377
for steve. 378
probable systems 13: 379

Chain 1 excerpt, from *The Martyrology: Book 5* 380
Hour 25... 381
Chain 10, from *The Martyrology: Book 5* 383
The Frog Variations 384
Prayer 385

David O'Meara
from Desert Sonnets
    III Igjugarjuk 387
    VI Postcard from Camus 387
Rough Directions 388
Fun 389
At the Aching-Heart Diner 390
Something Akin to Worship Now........................... 391
Poise..392
Boswell by the Fire...................................... 393
The Unhappy Condition 396

Michael Ondaatje
from *The Collected Works of Billy the Kid*
    "Blurred a waist high river . . ." 398
    "She leans against the door . . ." 398
Sallie Chisum / Last Words on Billy the Kid 4 a.m. 399
from Rock Bottom
    (Inner Tube) 401
    ("The space in which we have dissolved —
        does it taste of us?")........................... 402
    "How many windows have I broken . . ." 402
    "Speaking to you . . ." 403
from *Running in the Family*
    An hour later he could have stopped
        at the Ambepussa resthouse 404
The Cinnamon Peeler 405
Women like You 406
The Siyabaslakara.. 408
Birch Bark... 409

Elise Partridge
One Calvinist's God 410
On the Road to Emmaus................................. 410
Four Lectures by Robert Lowell, 1977 412
Rural Route.. 415
Two Scenes from Philadelphia 415

John Pass
    Sundeck in Houselight 417
    Nestbox 417
    Browse. 418
    Underberries 419
    Wind Chime 420
    To the Branch from Which the Robin Flew 421
    These Are the Days. 421

Alison Pick
    "Tell me, what is it you plan to do with your one wild
        and precious life?" 423

Kyran Pittman
    Launch. 424

Yves Préfontaine
(translated by Judith Cowan)
    Peuple inhabité 425
    Pays, Ô soudain éclaté 426
    Pays sans parole 427
    Non-Lieu / Non-Lieu 428

Steven Price
    from *Anatomy of Keys*
        VII "Such newreels flicker still . . ." 433
        VIII "Then guy-ropes creaked, plashed and I sank . . ." .. 434
        XX   "The torn rope is twice useful . . ." 435

Al Purdy
    The Country of the Young. 436
    Roblin's Mills 437
    The Cariboo Horses 439
    Dog Song 2. 440
    Rodeo 442
    Dream of Havana 443
    The Buddhist Bell. 444
    The Blue City 445
    Double Focus 446
    Story 447

Matt Rader
Cruelty... 450
Faith... 451
Clearing Out 451
Paradise Meadows................................... 452
Wolf Lake 453
Preparations.. 455

Michael Redhill
VIA, Outside Quebec City 456
Murder.. 456
One Year 457
Happy Hour.. 458
True Story.. 459
Casson.. 460
from Coming to Earth (Alzheimer Elegy)
    1. "The old man's ghost prowls near the TV . . .". 460
    4. "Poland spreads across the ruined hippocampi . . ." 461
    7. "Let's not think about pits. Or forests . . ." 462
    8. "I would give you this fall light, this yellow slant . . ." 462
    9. "Eat a heel of rye, a bit of meat on it . . ." 463

Armand Garnet Ruffo
Poetry 464
Poem for Duncan Campbell Scott 465
At Geronimo's Grave 466
Grey Owl, 1937...................................... 467
Alex Espaniel, 1920 468
Influences 468
An Imagined Country................................. 470
Archie Belaney, 1915-16 470
Archie Belaney, 1930-31 471
Joe Hassrak.. 472
Later 474

Gregory Scofield
Ode to the Greats (Northern Tribute)................ 475
Not All Halfbreed Mothers........................... 479
T. For.. 480
Pawâcakinâsîs-pîsim / December — The Frost Exploding Moon... 482
Pêyak-Nikamowin — One Song 483

Olive Senior
Peacock Tale, I 486
Emperor Penguin 487
Thirteen Ways of Looking at Blackbird 487
Embroidery 489
Amazon Women 491
Fishing in the Waters Where My Dreams Lie 494

Sue Sinclair
Between Stations, October 496
The Dorsals 496
No One Asks Leda to Dance 497
Goldfish 498
Dining Room, Morning after Mrs. Dalloway's Party 498
Once Lost 499
Photograph of My Mother as a Child or Invitation to the Wedding ... 500
The Making of "Lawrence of Arabia" 501
Four Poems for Virginia Woolf
    I Portrait 501
    II A Sunday Drive 502
    III Observation 503
    IV The Pattles 504
100 Love Sonnets 504

Karen Solie
Skid 506
Boyfriend's Car 506
Sturgeon 507
Thanksgiving 508
72 Miles 509
The Bench 510
Nice 511
Your Premiums Will Never Increase 512
Determinism 513

Carmine Starnino
The Lesson 514
First Kiss (Teresa) 514
Navigation 515
Picking the Last Tomatoes with My Uncle 516
On the Obsolescence of Caphone 517
Song of the House Husband 520
The Last Days 520
Good to Go 521

John Steffler
The Role of Calcium in Evolution............................. 522
Cape Norman 523
Book Rock 524
Barrens Willow 524
Notes on Burnt Cape....................................... 525

Marie Uguay
"Il existe pourtant des pommes..."......................... 526
"maintenant nous sommes assis..." 527
"le cri d'une mouette...". 528
"il y a ce désert acharnement..." 528
"tout ce qui va suivre..." 529
"des fleurs sur la table...". 529
"il fallait bien parfois..." 530

Agnes Walsh
I Solemn 531
Thomas 532
Contacts... 533

Frederick Ward
from *Riverlisp*
   4. Fuss.. 534
   6. Rufus... 535
   8. Blind Woman 537
A Pattern of Escape....................................... 538
Dialogue # 3 539
Najean 540
From Who All Was There................................. 540
Yet Among–Us 542
Me Grandaunt.. 542

Enos Watts
The Grandmothers of Argentina........................... 544

Darren Wershler-Henry
from *Ten Out of Ten, or Why Poetry Criticism Sucks in 2003* (2003)
   3. Jeff Derksen — *Dwell* 546
   5. Steve McCaffery — *The Black Debt* 547
   6. Ken Babstock — *Days into Flatspin* 548
   10. Kenneth Goldsmith — *No. 111 2.7.93 – 10.20.96*........ 549

Zoe Whittall
Stiff Little Fingers. 550
Six Thoughts on a Parkdale Porch 551

Patricia Young
The Fire. 553
Grocery List 554

Jan Zwicky
Driving Northwest. 556
Prairie 557
Robinson's Crossing 557
Another Version ("Look, all I can tell you is . . .") 562
Work 563
Soup 564
Aspen in Wind. 565
Bill Evans: "Here's That Rainy Day". 565
Three Mysterious Songs 566
Closing the Cabin 567
Glenn Gould: Bach's "Italian" Concerto, BWV 971 568
Passing Sangudo 568

Poetry from Ireland

Leland Bardwell
- Hard to Imagine Your Face Dead 575
- The Night's Empty Shells 575
- Innismurray 576
- 'No Road Beyond the Graveyard' 577
- The Horse Protestant Joke Is Over 578
- Prison Poem III: For a Friend Doing Life in Portlaoise 579

Sebastian Barry
- The Wood-Pigeons 580
- The Pinkening Boy 580
- The Owner 581
- The Man Monaghan 582

Sara Berkeley
- Strawberry Thief 583
- How We Meet 584
- Still Life, Yellow Quilt 585

Denise Blake
- In Mourning 587
- *Kaiyuglak* — Rippled Surface of Snow 587
- Knowing the Wizard 588
- Early Lessons 589
- Letterkenny 567 590
- Vows 591

Eavan Boland
from Writing in a Time of Violence: A Sequence
    I: 5 The Dolls Museum in Dublin 593
from *Code*
    I Marriage
        I   In Which Hester Bateman, Eighteenth-Century English Silversmith, Takes an Irish Commission ... 594
        II   Against Love Poetry 595
        III The Pinhole Camera 596
        IV Quarantine 597
        V   Embers 598
        VI Then 599
        VII First Year 599
        VIII Once 600

IX	Thankëd be Fortune.................601
X	A Marriage for the Millennium.........602
XI	Lines for a Thirtieth Wedding Anniversary ..603

Rosita Boland
The Astronaut's Wife 604
Diamonds 605
Sightless 605
Gold — The Gleninsheen Gorget.........................606
Teeth 607
Tears 608

Pat Boran
The Magic Roundabout................................609
Jupiter 610
Tent 611

Katarzyna Borun-Jagodzinska
(translated by Gerry Murphy)
Theresa at the Laundry................................612
Photograph of Theresa Martin as Joan of Arc 612
Van Morrison Plays Mother Goose........................613
Scarpia..613
Mimi's Aria..614
Aida..615
Scarpia's Aria 615

Colm Breathnach
(translated by Colm Breathnach)
Bróga Nua / *New Shoes* 616
Scarúint / *Parting* 617
Forlámhas / *Supremacy*.................................618
An Fear Marbh / *The Dead Man* 619
Lorgaíodh mo Shúile tú / *My Eyes Would Look for You*..........621
Seana-ghnás / *The Old Ways*.............................623
Ar an Leaba Leathan / *On the Bed Spread*...................624
An Ghéag Theasctha / *The Severed Limb*....................625

Deirdre Brennan
The Burning 626
In the National Archives...............................628
About Being Human..................................630
'The Blue Dress' (Henri Matisse).........................631
Fallen Woman 631

```
Repossession..........................................632
The Last Observance ..................................633
The Collector ........................................635
(translated by Gréagóir Ó Dúill)
    Sníomh / Spinning ................................636
    Maighdeana Mara / Mermaids .......................637
    Is 'Werewolf' mé anocht / I Am a Werewolf Tonight ............639
```

Vincent Buckley
```
Hunger-Strike ........................................642
```

Paddy Bushe
(translated by Paddy Bushe)
```
Bolgam / Gulp ........................................649
Ag Aistriú Buddha in Der Glorie / Translating Buddha in Der Glorie .650
Éin i gCliabháin / Caged Birds........................651
```

Catherine Byron
```
Coffin. Crypt. Consumption. ..........................653
Coco de Mer...........................................657
Egyptians.............................................658
The Getting of Vellum ................................661
St Thomas Aquinas in MacNeice's House ................669
Minding You ..........................................670
After the Nuptial Mass ...............................672
```

Mary Rose Callan
```
Clean as a Wish.......................................674
Her Grief.............................................676
Facts of Life ........................................676
```

Moya Cannon
```
Murdering the Language................................678
```

Ellie Carr
from *Traveller Ways Traveller Words*
```
"What me husband done, ever he done . . ." ............680
"When the woman'd have a child . . ."..................680
"Well a May mornin', we'd all get out . . .".............681
```

Ciaran Carson
from *The Inferno of Dante Alighieri*
```
Canto XV .............................................682
```

Kyriakos Charalambides
(translated by Greg Delanty)
- Of the People of Olympia 686
- from The Tyranny of Words 686
- Spoon Sweet 687
- Death's Art 689
- Candaules' Wife 690
- Nitocris, Queen of Babylon 692
- Potiphar's Wife 693
- Tears for Twenty-Five Years 694

Michael Coady
- Interview on Main Street 696
- Low Winter Sun 697
- School Tour, Kilmainham Jail 699

Enda Coyle-Greene
- Another Moon 700
- Grafton Street 701
- Handed On 702
- Opium 703
- Vertigo 704
- The Rooms 705
- So Many 706

Anthony Cronin
- On Seeing Lord Tennyson's Nightcap at Westport House 707
- In Praise of Hestia, Goddess of the Hearth Fire 708
- Meditation on a Clare Cliff-Top 710

Phillip Crymble
- Tomatoes 714
- Rice Lake 715

Philip Cummings
(translated by Gréagóir Ó Dúill and Philip Cummings)
- Deochanna / *Drinks* 716
- Uiscí Reatha / *Running Water* 717
- Newton / *Newton* 718
- Anne / *Anne* 719
- Séamus / *Seamus* 720
- Reilig an Mhuine Ghlais / *Moneyglass Cemetery* 721

Celia De Fréine,
(translated by Celia de Fréine)
In Aois / *Getting On* 725

Louis de Paor
(translated by Louis de Paor)
Foghlaimeoirí / *Homework* 727
Dán Grá / *Love Poem* 729
Ceartúcháin / *Corrections* 730
Gaeilgeoirí / *Gaeilgeoirí* 731
Searmanas / *Rituals* 733
Seanchas / *Old Stories* 735
Didjeridu / *Didjeridoo* 737
Inghean / *Daughter* 740
Iarlais / *Changeling* 741
Timpbriste / *Accidentally* 743

Patrick Dillon
The Crocodile 744

Kristin Dimitrova
(translated by Gregory O'Donoghue)
Auntie 746
A Lament for the Saintly Mothers 747
Freight Depot 747
First Blood 748
Fused 748
In the Train 749
The Wall by the Swings 750
The Local School 750
A Visit to the Clockmaker 751

Seán Dunne
The Healing Island 752

Paul Durcan
Golden Island Shopping Centre 757
The Man with a Bit of Jizz in Him 758
A Robin in Autumn Chatting at Dawn 759
HEADLINES 760
On Giving a Poetry Recital to an Empty Hall 762
The Annual Mass of the Knights of Columbanus 763

The Proud Cry of the Young Father 764
The 12 O'Clock Mass, Roundstone, County Galway,
    28 July 2002 765
Tarnowo Podgorne 767

Andres Ehin
(translated by Patrick Cotter)
I am... 768
"The colonels of several hostile armies" 768
"fish livers lie scattered on the ground" 769
"I'm a cripple with yellow, burning eyes" 770
Secret.. 771
I am your Missing Car 771
"deep, below ground, breathe" 772

Peter Fallon
from *The Georgics of Virgil*
    "How frequently we've watched eruptions . . ." 773

Janice Fitzpatrick Simmons
Cocoon 775
Blessings... 775
Faith... 776
Making Room 777
Sex 777
A Year On 777
Alive, Alive, Alive...................................... 778

Roderick Ford
Giuseppe 779
First Love 780

Tom French
Touching the Bones..................................... 781
Night Drive 782
Asperger Child 783
The Post-Hole... 783
Pity the Bastards....................................... 784
Mending a Puncture 789
Striking Distance....................................... 790

Alan Garvey
- Love ... 792
- Judge These Books ... 792
- Poppy ... 793
- The Fields of Beaumont-Hamel ... 794

Alan Gillis
- The Ulster Way ... 796
- 12th October, 1994 ... 796
- Cold Flow ... 799
- To Belfast ... 800
- Love Bites ... 801
- Casualty ... 801
- Niamh ... 802
- Last Friday Night ... 804
- Progress ... 804

Eamon Grennan
- from *The Quick of It*
  - "because the body stops here ..." ... 805
  - "So this is what it comes down to? ..." ... 805
  - "When that great conflagration ..." ... 806
  - "Off the skin of water ..." ... 807
  - "When I saw the deer's breath ..." ... 807
  - "It must be a particular kind of grace ..." ... 808
  - "Although snow has wrapped the house ..." ... 809
  - "I'm trying to get one line ..." ... 810
  - "Rained in all day like this ..." ... 810

Seamus Heaney
- Anahorish 1944 ... 811
- Helmet ... 811
- The Nod ... 812
- Out of This World ... 813
- Tate's Avenue ... 814
- The Blackbird of Glanmore ... 815

Zbyněk Hejda
(translated by Bernard O'Donoghue)
- from A Stay in a Sanatorium
  - ("A Poem ...") ... 817
- A Stay in a Sanatorium ... 818
- Some Evening ... 825

Pearse Hutchinson
(translated by Gréagóir Ó Dúill)
    Fúinne / *About Us* 828

Oritsegbemi Emmanuel Jakpa
    Harmattan 829
    Eden 831

Biddy Jenkinson
(translated by Juliette Saumande)
    Tuireamh Marie Antoinette / *La chute de Marie-Antoinette* 833

Rita Kelly
(translated by Rita Kelly)
    Beir Beannacht / *Fare Well* 839

Brendan Kennelly
    from *Cromwell*
        Our Place 841
        In Oliver's Army.................................. 841
        A Bad Time 842
        The Soldiers 842
        Reading Aloud 843
        A Running Battle 843

Thomas Kinsella
    Tao and Unfitness at Inistiogue on the River Nore 845
    Wedding Service.. 847
    Chrysalides 849
    King John's Castle 850
    Pause en Route 851
    from *Readings in Poetry*
        Sonnet 29 853
        Sonnet 30 855

Barbara Korun
(translated by Theo Dorgan)
    Stag 857
    Wolf.. 858
    White Bulls.. 859

Nick Laird
Cuttings 860
Remaindermen 861
The Signpost 862
To the Wife 863
The Evening Forecast for the Region 863

Ann Leahy
A Good Rogeting 865
Mince Customer 866
Cold Storage 867

Michael Longley
Swallow 869
Northern Lights 869
Björn Olinder's Pictures 869
A Norwegian Wedding 870
Broken Dishes 870
The Mustard Tin 870
The Daffodils 871
A Sprig of Bay 871
A Poppy 872
The War Graves 873
A Prayer 874
The Horses 874
Scrap Metal 875
Laertes 876
Ceasefire 876
All of These People 877

Dave Lordan
In the Model Village 878
TEA 880
The Longest Queue 880
from Reflections on Shannon
 ("Fuck the la-dee-da . . .") 883
Holding Chirac's Hand in Temple Bar 884

Alice Lyons
Thank God It's Dry 886
The Polish Language 889

Gearailt Mac Eoin
(translated by Gréagóir Ó Dúill)
- Deireadh Caithréime / The End of Triumph 888
- Agus an Samhradh Thart / Now Summer's Over 889

Tomás Mac Síomóin
(translated by Gréagóir Ó Dúill)
- 1845 / *1845* 891

Ilena Mălăncioiu
(translated by Eiléan Ní Chuilleanáin)
- The Headless Bird...................................... 893
- The Bear 894
- A Dog 895
- Song of Joy 895
- You Gave Me a Long Look 896
- The Doctor on Duty 896
- Let the Grass Grow Over Her........................... 897
- Laid Beside You 898
- It Snowed on the Body 898

Thomas McCarthy
- He Meets His Future Sister-in-Law, Miss Teresette O'Neill, 1811 ... 900
- He Turns to His Wife, 1797 901
- He Watches His Wife Create a Silhouette Portrait, 1812......... 902
- He Contemplates a Stolen *Bozzetto* of Canova's *Cupid and Psyche*, 1811 903
- He Witnesses a Military Execution, 1804................. 904
- He Witnesses Another Hanging, 1813 904
- He Buries His Father, 1809............................. 905
- He Goes Through His Father's Belongings, 1809 905
- He Writes to His Estranged Sister, 1803 906
- He Recalls a Letter from Home, 1771 907
- He Spends Christmas at Clonakilty, 1809 907
- He Considers the Rev. Dill-Wallace, 1817............... 908
- He Sees a Warehouse Burning, August, 1798 909

Medbh McGuckian
- Mappa Mundi 910
- House without Eyebrows 911
- My Sister's Way to Make Mead 912
- The Gorgon as Mistress of the Animals.................. 913
- Woman Forming the Handle of a Cane 914

Nigel McLoughlin
High Water 915
Bomb.. 916
A Hill Farmer Speaks 916

Paula Meehan
My Father Perceived as a Vision of St. Francis 918
Not Your Muse 919
'Not alone the rue in my herb garden . . .' 920
from Berlin Diary, 1991
    5 Folktale 922
    7 At Pankow S-Bahn 922
from Suburb
    Stood Up.. 924
    Stink Bomb 924
    Sudden Rain 925
The Tantric Master 925

Máire Mhac an tSaoi
(translated by Gréagóir Ó Dúill)
Mutterrecht / *Mutterrecht* 927

Immanuel Mifsud
(translated by Maurice Riordan)
Confidential Reports — in the Form of a Public-Private Confession . . 928

Geraldine Mills
Blighted.. 930
What We Understood 931
Out of Old Stories....................................... 931
About Lifelines 932
Cutaway Philosophers................................... 933
Boy at the Window Waiting 934
Poet as Magpie 935
Wednesday Women..................................... 935

John Montague
Border Sick Call 937

Sinéad Morrissey
Pilots 950
Little House in the Big Woods 951

Juist 953
Reading the Greats 956
In Praise of Salt 956
from The State of the Prisons
    4 "They say I rode like a horseman of the Apocalypse . . ." 957
    5 "A lone voice in the wilderness? . . ." 958

Richard Murphy
Kassapa 960
Sigiriya, 11 January 1987 963

Kate Newmann
Put to Loss Because of the Snow 965

Nuala Ní Dhomhnaill
(translated by Paul Muldoon)
Na Murúcha a Thriomaigh / *The Assimilated Merfolk* 971

Collette Ní Ghallchóir
(translated by Gréagóir Ó Dúill)
Antain / *Antain* 975
An tAmharc Deireanach / *The Last Look* 976

Máire Áine Nic Gearailt
(translated by Gréagóir Ó Dúill)
Teicheadh / *Fleeing* 978

Áine Ní Ghlinn
(translated by Gréagóir Ó Dúill)
Teangmháil / *Contact* 980
Iomrascáil Oíche leis na Mairbh / *Night Wrestling with the Dead* 981

Yilmaz Odabaşi
(translated by Patrick Galvin and Robert O'Donoghue)
from Feride 983

Jean O'Brien
Severed 987
Veronica's Epiphany 987
Veronica 989
Yes, I can bake a cake. 989

An Anthology of Poetry from Canada and Ireland   XXXVII

Mícheál Ó Cuaig
(translated by Gréagóir Ó Dúill)
Uchtóga / *Armfuls* 991
Toibreacha / *Wells* 992

Aodh Ó Domhnaill
(translated by Gréagóir Ó Dúill)
Oifigiúil / *Official* 994

Bernard O'Donoghue
from *Sir Gawain and the Green Knight* 995

Dennis O'Driscoll
Missing God 1004
England 1006
At the Seminar 1010
Lord Mayo 1012
The Light of Other Days 1013

Seán Ó Leocháin
(translated by Gréagóir Ó Dúill)
999 / *999* 1016
Traidisiún / *Tradition* 1017
Tóraíocht / *Pursuit* 1018

Michael O'Loughlin
Latin as a Foreign Language 1019
Boxer 1021
Three Fragments on the Theme of Moving Around in Cities 1021
To a Child in the Womb 1022
Yellow 1023

Mary O'Malley
Anniversary 1024
My Mac 1024
Angry Arthur 1025
The Poet's Fancy 1026

Liam Ó Muirthile
When Will I Get to Be Called a Man 1027
Basáin Mhara 1027
Baile an Tae 1029

Li Am ar Fhalla Mór na Síne 1030
Ringabella 1031
Eitseáil Bheo 1032
Suantraí Sarah is Asmahane 1033
San Aonad Alzheimer 1034
An Seanduine 1035

Derry O'Sullivan
(translated by Gréagóir Ó Dúill)
Finit / *Finit* 1037

Paul Perry
The Gate to Mulcahy's Farm 1039

Dana Podracká
(translated by Robert Welch)
A Parcel from Prison.................................. 1041
A White Bedsheet...................................... 1042
The Place of Execution of the First President 1043

Billy Ramsell
Breath 1044
Middle Distance 1046
Complicated Pleasures 1047
Still Life with Frozen Pizza 1049
Ireland.. 1050
Southern Shores 1051

Gabriel Rosenstock
(translated by Gabriel Rosenstock)
As gach póir Díot / *From each and every pore* 1055
Seanfhalla / *Old Wall* 1055
Sneachta na mBunchnoc / *Snow on the foothills* 1056
Do nochtacht / *Your nakedness*........................... 1057
Gustaí mhí Aibreáin / *April Gusts* 1057
Samhradh / *Summer* 1058
Colúr Marbh / *Dead Pigeon*............................. 1058
Yugapat-srishti / *Yugapat-srishti*......................... 1059
Coillteán / *Castrato*.................................... 1060
Deirid gur daonnaí mé / *They say I am human* 1060
Tóg Chun do Dhraenacha Mé / *Take Me to Your Drains* 1061

John W. Sexton
Vortex 1062
Frogspawn 1064
Roland Gets It 1065

Eileen Sheehan
Lady in White 1067

Peter Sirr
The Names of the Houses 1069
from Here and There: A Notebook 1069
Housesitting 1071
from A Journal ("In the beginning . . .") 1072
The Writer's Studio 1074

Dolores Stewart
American Wake 1075
Maryville, Winter, 2001 1076
Death of Socrates 1077
(translated by Gréagóir Ó Dúill)
Dóchas / Hope 1077
Idir Scylla agus Charybdis / Between Scylla and Charybdis 1078
Ar Iarraidh / Lost 1079
Ceol Johnny Phádraig Pheter / Johnny Phádraig Pheter's Music ... 1081

Samantha Thomas
Late August, Donegal 1082
Man O' War 1083
Man-Eating Leopard of Rudrapraya 1084
Morne Grande 1086
Verlaine 1087

Áine Uí Fhoghlú
(translated by Áine Uí Fhoghlú)
What's that in English? / What's that in English? 1088
Sa tír / In the land 1093
Íota / Desire 1095
An Tine Bheo / The Burning Fire 1098
I Seomra Feithimh an Dochtúra, 1974 /
    In the Doctor's Waiting Room, 1974 1100
Fiailí / Weeds 1102
An tUllmhúchán / Getting Ready 1105

Grace Wells
Aşure 1109
The Only Medicine 1110
Horse Fair 1111
The Funeral Director's Wife 1112
The Muezzin's Call 1112
The Lone Parent Does Not Write 1113
The Hostage Place 1114

Enda Wyley
Going Home 1115
Love Bruise 1116
Marlborough Road 1117
Two Women in Kosovo 1118
Diary of a Fat Man 1120
Master Chef 1121
Mint Gatherers 1122
Emperor 1123

Irish Society and Immigration 1995 — 2006:
  A Brief Overview **Jonathan Culleton** 1125

Notes on Contributors (Canada) 1129

Notes on Editors and Consultants 1152

Permissions / Acknowledgements (Canada) 1154

Notes on Contributors (Ireland) 1164

Permissions / Acknowledgements (Ireland) 1180

Index of Poets (Canada) 1188

Index of Poems (Canada) 1189

Index of Poets (Ireland) 1202

Index of Poems (Ireland) 1203

Acknowledgements

In compiling this anthology, we wish to thank the following for their support and assistance: in particular, the Ireland Canada University Foundation (ICUF) for providing a research scholarship without which this book could not have been compiled. Many thanks, too, to Professor John Kelly, for administering this valuable contribution to scholarship.

In Canada
Barry Snow, Executive Director and the Board of Directors of the Irish Business Partnerships; Pauline Hayes and Pam Parsons (Sir Wilfred Grenfell College), for their administrative assistance. Elizabeth Behrens, Louise McGillis and the staff at the Ferriss Hodget Library, Sir Wilfred Grenfell College, for research support. Adam Kelly, Rebekah Robbins, Connie Lasaga, Kristy Lee, Jennifer Hedd, Doug Gough and Krystal Lee Hann, for providing excellent services as research assistants. John Ashton, Principal, and Wade Bowers, Associate Vice-Principal (Research), Sir Wilfred Grenfell College, for their time spent attempting to aid this project through until the end. Marc Thackray and Martin Ware, Department of English, Sir Wilfred Grenfell College, for their consultancy with various selections, and Matthew Janes, Department of French, Sir Wilfred Grenfell College, for translating correspondences and providing much-needed assistance. Stephanie Bolster, Jason Camlot, Mary di Michele, Don Coles, Susan Gillis, Laura Lush, David O'Meara, Michael Redhill and Erín Moure for their input, suggestions and consultancy. Carmine Starnino and Anne Thareau, for their help with matters concerning French selections. Thanks to Adrian Fowler for allowing us to use a biographical note taken from *The March Hare Anthology*. And a warm thanks to Anne Pinsent for her copy editing and input and consistent professional support.

Special thank-yous go to Dominique Gaucher and Jean-Pierre Pelletier, who chose most of the French selections which appear within this volume, provided an introduction to the French verse and spent many hours copyediting and providing contacts and liaisons; Jean-François Bourgeault, who got us started in making French selections; and Kristina Fagan, Assistant Professor in the Department of English (Aboriginal Writing and Storytelling in Canada) at the University of Saskatchewan, who chose most of the Aboriginal poetry in *The Echoing Years*. And a special thank you to George Elliott Clarke, E.J. Pratt Professor of Canadian Literature at the University of Toronto, who provided valuable information about many poets who should be considered for inclusion in such a work and Paul Dutton, who provided consultancy and help above and beyond the call of poetic duty.

For their hard work and help with distribution and promotion, a heartfelt thanks to Stan Dragland and Kitty Lewis of Brick Books.

In Ireland

Agnes Aylward, Andrea Thompson and their board of directors at the Ireland Newfoundland Partnership; Deirdre Davitt and Orlaigh Ní Raghallaigh at Foras na Gaeilge; faculty in the School of Humanities, especially Dr. Christine O'Dowd-Smyth for her assistance with French language matters; Ms. Janice Fitzpatrick Simmons and Dr. Gréagóir Ó Dúill at the Poets' House, Creative Writing Centre, School of Humanities; Institute faculty including Director, Kieran R. Byrne; Dr. Willie Donnelly, Head of Research and Innovation; Dr. Venie Martin, Head of Development, including the International Office; Dr. Michael Howlett, Head of Department of Applied Arts; Mr. Ray Cullen, Acting Head of Languages, Tourism and Hospitality; John Maher, vice-chair of the Centre for Newfoundland and Labrador Studies, and the board members of the Centre; Liam Rellis, co-ordinator at the Centre for Newfoundland and Labrador Studies; School of Humanities administrative staff for their assistance: Norah Fogarty, Rita Dalton, Hannah Butler, Margaret Fagan, Eimear Murphy, Maria Dunphy and Martin Power; Kate Kennedy in Finance for processing payments for poets and publishers; Dermot Aylward, Derek Sheridan and Paul Kelly in Educational Technology; College Street staff, including Marc Jones, Larry Condon, Edward Walsh, David Drohan and Paddy Kavanagh; Patrick Cotter at the Munster Literature Centre; Carmine Starnino; Joe Woods at Poetry Ireland; our word processing team of Samantha Thomas and Michael Collins; Jonathan Culleton of the Centre for Social and Family Research for his supportive article; Louise Catinot for allowing us to use her award-winning artwork; the various permissions and editorial staff of publishing houses in Ireland, England, France and Canada who made the volume possible; the welcoming staff at Pavee Point; Margaret Mannion of Newman College, University of Melbourne, for introducing John Ennis to Penelope Buckley; Minister Akin Oyateru and staff at the Nigerian Embassy in Dublin; Peter Fallon, for his time and advice offered to Stephanie McKenzie; Selina Guiness, for sharing her recent knowledge about compiling an anthology of Irish poetry; Jessie Lendennie, publisher of Salmon poetry, for opening her house and allowing Salmon's collections to be perused; designer, Jackie Raftery, for the many hours arranging texts and pdfs; Michael Pittman, for his cover artwork; poets who assisted at various times, including Richard Tillinghast, Rita Kelly and Áine Uí Fhoghlú; Kenny's in Galway; Michael Walsh, Auxiliary Services, who bussed us around Ireland for the launches of previous anthologies in the trilogy; Elieen O'Carroll, copy-editor; Barry O'Brien and staff at eprint; all staff, poets and publishers who helped to make this venture possible, along with our previous anthologies in the trilogy, *The Backyards of Heaven* (2003) and *However Blow the Winds* (2004).

An especial thank-you to The International Council for Canadian Studies for grant-aiding an explorative fact-finding trip to Canada in 2005 to meet poets and publishers and to all the welcoming people encountered there, including Susan Purcell in Toronto.

While every effort has been made to ensure that biographical and bibliographical details given in this work are accurate, the editors do not claim this work to be fully authoritative. The editors and publisher apologize to poets and their publishers for any errors or omissions in the acknowledgements and would be grateful to be notified of any corrections that should be incorporated into any future edition of this work. Most importantly, every effort has been made to trace the holders of copyright, but if copyright has been inadvertently breached in any case, copyright holders should contact the publisher.

Genesis of the Text

In his address at the latest Patrick Kavanagh awards ceremony, "Kavanagh: A Return to the Work," Anthony Cronin (2006) spoke of the need to revision an understanding of Kavanagh's work and to de-mythologize the poet. He also spoke of Kavanagh's genius and explained that he had the ability to stand outside himself and observe his comic role in life. Cronin reminded readers that Kavanagh did not conceive of *The Great Hunger* as his best poem, though that realization challenges what canons would have us understand as his best and most influential work. Cronin was asking his audience to put close attention to the poet's work ahead of national scripts.

The Echoing Years contains poetry from two countries, though the anthology implicitly questions its ostensible parameters, holding verse in higher esteem than any flag. Hopefully, *The Echoing Years* will present poets observing their own positions, too — positions defined, at times, by nationalism, sometimes by a strict adherence to other disparate claims of ownership, sometimes nonplussed by the bedrock of traditional canonization. As well, this anthology is not guided by a desire to chronicle the scripts of former canons. It reflects a process engendered by three editors, defined by their own tastes, upbringings and readings (and generously advised by many voices), who had chance encounters on the island of Newfoundland between 2002 and 2004. Each of us is interested in poetry — the reading of it, the making of it, the teaching of it and the promotion of it for other poets. We spent several years hearing one another talk of the poets we admired. We wished to share our experiences with wider audiences.

The Echoing Years is the continuation and finale of two previous anthologies, *However Blow the Winds: Poetry and Song from Newfoundland & Labrador and Ireland* (2004) and *The Backyards of Heaven: Contemporary Poetry from Ireland and Newfoundland & Labrador* (2003). The former, a collection which chronicles the development of verse in Ireland and Newfoundland, and the latter, a diverse offering of many voices intended to provide large and general introductions between poets on both sides of the Atlantic, set the stage for the present volume. Since *The Echoing Years* is the last book in a trilogy which attempts to add new and diverse voices to its undertaking and representation thus far, one will not find many poems by Newfoundland authors, though some new work by several Newfoundland poets is included.

The Echoing Years includes for the most part, and with very few exceptions, poems published from 1980 and after. Anthologies demand parameters for the sake of pragmatics. This year was chosen to reflect an agreeable meeting point in Irish and Canadian history. In 1982, the constitution of Canada was repatriated from Britain, marking a symbolic end of colonial governance. In 1973, Ireland became part of the European Union. Ireland would then go on to govern the EU (with its presidency of 2004), a history of servitude to the British Crown replaced by newfound freedom of economic success but a reflection, really, of cultural vitality that is just as strong, if not stronger, than the arrogance of imperial intent. Thus, by choosing a midpoint of sorts between these two moments, *The Echoing Years* takes as its starting point voices borne out of a revisioning of nationalism predicated on a breakdown of colonial inheritance and control. Perhaps this book will find its place in a future when borders, and those that maintain them, are a grim memory.

In *The Echoing Years*, courtesy of a phrase by Margaret Avison, old pros can make guest appearances: Dante introduced by Ciaran Carson or revisioned and re-invigorated by Lorna Goodison and Ray Hsu; Shakespeare and his sonnets modulated in the fastidious notes of Thomas Kinsella; the crucifixion of Christ given new breath by Pamela Mordecai's blue-collar, feminist and West Indian account; *The Georgics of Virgil*, translated by Peter Fallon and the imaginings of an anachronistic Augustan age as the bombs fell on Iraq a second time. How hollow now within this perspective the "shock and awe" as one remembers Robert Duncan's "A Poem Beginning with a Line by Pindar":

How sad 'amid lanes and through old woods'

Echoes Whitman's love for Lincoln.

And Leonard Cohen, in his verse, ponders what comes after America.

John Ennis, Randall Maggs and Stephanie McKenzie

Poèmes en français, poèmes du Québec

C'est à Terre-Neuve que nous avons rencontré John Ennis, Stephanie McKenzie, puis Randall Maggs, qui nous ont fait part de leur ambitieux projet d'une anthologie cherchant à regrouper des poètes du Canada et de l'Irlande, *The Echoing Years*. Ils n'en étaient pas à leur première collaboration et voulaient que résulte de celle-ci un vaste panorama de ce qui s'écrit maintenant des deux côtés de l'Atlantique, y incluant des paroles minoritaires, en périphérie. Ainsi une place serait faite à des auteurs de langue gaélique, d'une part, et d'autre part, un effort y serait fait pour qu'y soient compris des poètes de régions différentes du Canada et des voix autochtones. Une anthologie qui ferait éclater un chant actuel, aux voix multiples.

L'équipe se sentait en terrain moins solide concernant la poésie qu'ils qualifiaient de *canadienne-française*, ne maîtrisant pas la langue de Miron et avouant y connaître surtout les noms les plus traduits, ceux qui ont eu le bonheur de se trouver dans des anthologies : Anne Hébert, Nicole Brossard, plus quelques autres. Il leur fallait plusieurs collaborateurs pour y voir clair, repérer des voix variées et émergentes. Le souci de trouver ce chant pluriel nous a plu et, en cours de projet, nous sommes ainsi devenus leurs antennes au Québec. Nous avons vite fait comprendre à nos amis que la poésie canadienne francophone serait, ici, surtout québécoise, la seule moisson du Québec exigeant un espace important. Mais, là encore, quel portrait allions-nous tenter d'en dresser ?

Au-delà de l'éternelle question de la présence du fait « francophone » au Canada — le lecteur même peu au fait de la ou des réalités canadiennes, connaît l'existence, voire la coexistence de deux réalités sur un même territoire, attestant la justesse du titre du roman emblématique de Hugh MacLennan, *Deux solitudes*, publié dans la deuxième moitié du siècle précédent —, il nous fallait faire ressortir la diversité des paroles et des langages, dire l'incommensurable complexité de la réalité d'aujourd'hui, qui modifie considérablement la géographie de ces deux solitudes. Comme le Canada anglais, et plus que lui encore, le Québec a beaucoup changé depuis une quarantaine d'années. Sa poésie s'est transformée, a évolué dans des directions différentes. Si chaque génération est appelée à écrire des livres où pourrait se dégager une représentation plus ou moins unifiée d'elle-même, il n'en reste pas moins que chacun cherche à créer des formes-sens où peut se lire un discours nouveau, c'est-à-dire une autre façon, pour reprendre le mot du poète et essayiste Paul Chamberland, de « faire chanter la langue autrement ». Et par discours, entendons une organisation non pas tant de la langue dans son acception normative ou ordinaire, même si cela peut aussi être le cas, mais plutôt un aménagement d'un matériau à la portée de tous et que le poète a pour tâche de *transformer* à sa manière. En clair, il est créateur de langage.

Les dix-neuf voix offertes ici aux lecteurs donneront une « petite » idée de ce qui s'écrit au Québec, surtout depuis le début des années 1980. Tout projet de ce genre ayant, comme chacun le sait, ses limites, sa part inévitable d'arbitraire, ne peut donc prétendre donner un portrait exhaustif et très détaillé de ce qu'est écrire de nos jours, en français, dans cette contrée des Amériques. Les lecteurs découvriront des poètes, presque autant de voix de femmes que d'hommes, certains ayant fait leurs débuts dans les années 1950 et 1960, tels Yves Préfontaine, Jacques Brault, Pierre Morency et Nicole Brossard; d'autres ont commencé à s'affirmer à partir des deux décennies suivantes, tels Robert Melançon, Jean-Paul Daoust, Pierre Nepveu, Louise Dupré, Hélène Dorion, Jean-Marc Desgent, Nadine Ltaif, Joël Des Rosiers, Marie Uguay et l'Acadien Herménégilde Chiasson; enfin, dans les années 1990, Monique Deland, Francis Catalano, Hélène Monette, Martine Audet et Tania Langlais.

En ce qui concerne la thématique qui traverse les oeuvres des différents poètes composant cette sélection, elle est sans doute à l'image de ce qui peut s'écrire ailleurs. S'il est avéré que les thèmes de la femme et du pays, parfois même de la femme-pays (chez certains poètes hommes, en particulier), ainsi que de l'amour occupèrent souvent le lieu du discours poétique dans les années 1950 et 1960, la deuxième moitié des années soixante est déjà marquée par une rupture qui marque un tournant important et significatif dans le champ spécifique de la littérature québécoise, avec l'apparition de *La Barre du jour* et les premiers écrits de Nicole Brossard, suivis dans la décennie suivante de *La Nouvelle Barre du jour* et de la maison d'édition *Les Herbes rouges*, s'inspirant, entre autres, du courant formaliste européen et de ce qui se faisait autour de la revue parisienne *L'Infini / Tel Quel*. S'ouvraient aussi d'autres possibles dans l'exploration d'avenues avec, par exemple, la découverte de la contre-culture, une certaine redécouverte de l'Amérique, surtout états-unienne, la contestation, la guerre du Viêt-Nam, etc. C'est alors qu'e commencent à s'affirmer les thèmes de la dérive urbaine, du corps comme lieu de désir, d'une sexualité plus franchement ouverte parce que dite, d'un certain érotisme autant chez l'homme que la femme, de la solitude, d'une poésie se voulant au ras du quotidien, en apparence presque banale. Enfin, l'apparition d'une parole dite « migrante », de l'exil (J. Des Rosiers, N. Ltaif), puis une exploration nouvelle du continent, en quelque sorte « revisité », problématisé et requestionné par Francis Catalano (v. son livre *Index*, en particulier).

Il faudrait ici une étude plus détaillée, une attention plus grande accordée à chacun des poètes composant cette sélection, mais l'espace fait défaut. Pour ceux et celles dont la curiosité a été piquée, nous les renvoyons à l'anthologie de Pierre Nepveu et Laurent Mailhot, qui fait un survol de la poésie québécoise depuis l'époque du Régime français jusqu'à la fin des années 1980, et à celle de Nicole Brossard et Lisette Girouard, qui porte exclusivement sur la poésie écrite par des femmes.

À vous les poèmes.

Et bonne lecture.

Dominique Gaucher et Jean-Pierre Pelletier

An Ghaeilge

Chuireamar romhainn léargas a thabhairt ar staid reatha na filíochta Gaeilge sa díolaim seo. Is díol spéise mar atá saol na filíochta Gaeilge ag athrú le tamall de bhlianta. Ar feadh i bhfad, ba iad filí *Innti* a bhí chun tosaigh agus rinneadh rogha ar a gcuid saothair sin a chur i gcló sna díolaimí a d'fhoilsíomar cheana. Ach le tamall, tá daoine úra a bhfuil a nglór in airde, glór úr difriúil go minic, glór a léiríonn an t-athrú a tháinig ar shaol na Gaeilge le tamall.

Tá scéal na Gaeilge tar éis dul i bhfeabhas ar bhealaí, agus dul ar gcúl ar bhealaí eile. Tá stádas nua ag an teanga, stádas oifigiúil mar theanga bainte amach go húrnua in Éirinn, faoi Acht Teanga / the Official Languages Act 2003, agus aitheantas mar chritéir anois aici sa phróiseas pleanála. Tá seasamh nua bainte amach i dTuaisceart Éireann. Aithníodh an Ghaeilge mar theanga oifigiúil de chuid an Aontais Eorpaigh. Leanann ar an mhéadú ar an oideachas tré mheán na Gaeilge, agus ar shaothrú na teanga sna meáin nua, an teilifís go mórmhór.

Ar an láimh eile, tá fianaise ann go bhfuil laghdú ag teacht ar labhairt na Gaeilge ag an aos óg sa Ghaeltacht. Fágann sin gur beag filí Gaeltachta atá ag teacht chun cinn. Tugaimid áit anseo do roinnt díobh, Collette Ní Ghallchobhair, Mícheál Ó Cuaig, Áine Uí Fhoghlú mar shamplaí. Tá anseo fosta duine nó beirt den bheagán filí ón Tuaisceart, Philip Cummings a chleachtaíonn an ghontacht Ultach, an greann searbh.

Thugamar tús áite do bheirt filí a bhfuil tús áite bainte amach acu le tamall goirid de bhlianta anuas leis an oiread de shaothar a chuireadar díobh féin, agus le feabhas an tsaothair sin. Filí difriúla iad Colm Breathnach agus Louis de Paor. Tarlaíonn gurb as Corcaigh dóibh beirt, rud a chruthaíonn gur shíolraigh muintir *Innti* cois Laoi. Táid oilte ar an teanga agus oilte ar an fhilíocht. Tugann siad aghaidh ar an uafás agus ar an ghrá agus bíonn féith an ghrinn le sonrú orthu. Léiríonn siad go bhfuil an teanga bheo liteartha is sine in iarthar na hEorpa fós beo liteartha.

Gréagóir Ó Dúill

A Note on Translation

The translation of poetry is an exercise at once necessary and impossible. Necessary because of our need to be aware of what is being and has been expressed by others. Without this knowledge, what follows can be ignorance and isolation, a breakdown of communication and a loss of opportunity, an impoverishment. Impossible because poetry reflects a life of the other which we can only glimpse imperfectly, half aware of the aural tricks, the oral traditions, the cultural referents, the behavioural norms, the philosophical positions, the lotus pose, the syntactical rules of the other.

However, to see through the glass darkly is better than to shut one's eyes. There are different ways of doing it, of translating poetry. They range from staying as close, linguistically or in form, to the original text as is possible without rendering the new text totally opaque to a much freer version, reflecting the translator's reaction to the spirit of the original text. Too close a rendition may reflect some of the original, but often fails to get across the spirit, the simplicity, the force, the formal qualities. It may be necessary to break eggs in order to achieve an omelette. On the other hand, too free a version raises questions of intellectual property, of moral ownership, of veracity, of the marginalization of the untranslated and untranslatable, of cultural imperialism. Languages, like cultures, are seldom of equal strength, and this puts their poets in different places. Translation, like other intimate human behaviour, is best shared on a basis of consent freely given by equal partners.

In Ireland there are no monoglot Irish speakers. Of the living poets most often noted, all but one or two came to Irish as their second language, and the dominant language of most of their lives is English. They choose, they adopt Irish for complex reasons of national, cultural and personal identity. They do so with varying degrees of success, and that success varies over time, for language is a muscle which grows flaccid without exercise, without challenge. A small number refuse to be translated into English because such translation would undermine their effort to add to the culture and heritage of the Irish tradition and would subvert the continuity of their work as part of the Irish literary tradition. One or two prefer to translate their own work into English — there are compelling reasons for this, not least the need to give readings bilingually.

Some facilitate the translation of their work with conversation, explication. Some seek actively to be translated by established poets in English so that a mutuality of reputation-building can occur. Some work the two languages almost in parallel, but not in translation, and the same concerns can be seen, compared and contrasted in the two languages in the growth of their work.

The Irish literary tradition had much effect on English and European traditions from the time of MacPherson's Ossianic fraud and its impact on romanticism. The Irish Literary Revival at the end of the nineteenth century pretended to an informed and sympathetic position on the continuing cultural influence of the older language. The educational efforts and public stance of the Irish state which reached independence in the twentieth century encouraged the writing of poetry in Irish. The dominance of a group of young poets from Cork University was established suddenly in 1970 and has been a notable feature of the Irish poetry scene — they were enthusiastic about the interface of language and about opportunities for translation.

Gréagóir Ó Dúill

A Note from the Editors

The scholarship of graphic design and that of literary studies often blend and, *ipso facto*, create unique rules. However, it is hoped that consistency will lead readers of *The Echoing Years* to be able to determine types of poems, as well as their origins. This note is, therefore, being provided in order to explain the rules of consistency which govern the *body* of *The Echoing Years* (the table of contents, acknowledgements and appendices being immune to such dictates and largely adhering, it is hoped, to MLA rules).

To begin with, all poem titles were initially italicized for the sake of aesthetics; this means, then, that MLA conventions are automatically breached as only works published on their own (such as book-length poems — things not included within another work) are typically accorded italics. The following decisions were then made to distinguish different types of poems from one another:

- when there are excerpts taken from an independently published work (such as a long, book-length poem published in and of itself), the word "from" appears before the title of the work in italics. Though most poems are in italics, "from," therefore — as a precursor to a title in italics — indicates the following title / poem is an independent publication.

- when there are excerpts taken from "longish" poems (poems which have originally been published within another work or poems, perhaps, which are not yet published but are not destined for publication on their own), quotation marks surround the title of the poem (with "from" — the preposition in italics — preceding the title of the poem).

- when there are poems with subsections, the title of the poem remains in bold and in italics, but the bold is removed from the subsections in order that the reader can determine when one poem ends and a new one begins.

- when (and this occurs in only a few cases) there are subsections within subsections of poems, subsequent subsections are represented in a different font than the titles of main poems — and their main subsections — both being represented in the same-size font but with bold having been removed from both subsections (unlike the title of the governing poem itself, which remains in bold).

- for standardization's sake, double quotation marks have been used throughout (in various circumstances — in the acknowledgements, for example, when referring to a poem, or to denote dialogue within a poem's narrative; however, in the case where there are quotation marks around the original title of a poem, or around something within the original title of a poem, single quotation marks have been placed around what surrounds quotation marks in an original title).

- when words appear in italics in the original poem's title, these words are "un-italicized" in the poem's title (therefore reversing expected rules).

- when a poem begins *in medias res*, or when the editors have excised material in the middle of a poem or ended their selection of a poem before the actual poem's end, three ellipses marks indicate missing text (including movements taken out of long poems).

- when any of these rules threaten to muddy the representation of an author's work (such as those works which are, in effect, long poems with individual titles accorded to separate movements or poems within long poems), the editors have not applied the above rules and hope, instead, that cross-referencing between the body of the book, table of contents, and appendices will provide necessary bibliographical information.

The editors have intended to be consistent with their choices; however, if there are mistakes or if confusion about the nature of a work ensues, it is hoped that readers will purchase the poetry in question to determine, for themselves, the answers to bibliographical mysteries.

Three Voices

SM (Stephanie McKenzie): We are all poets in our own rights, as well as critics of literature, and we carry with us our own schoolings, as well as personal preferences. These things are bound to have influenced decisions, and our inclusion of new voices — or voices largely disregarded in existing Canadian and Irish anthologies — might not always be the result of editors questioning and challenging and engaging with their own national traditions but simply of fresh and exciting new encounters.

JE (John Ennis): Yes. There were the inevitable "finds" we tripped upon, at first individually and, then, collectively, the finds one might have wished as practitioner to savour in quietude, like the pearl in a field one might try to keep quiet about, like Diana Brebner's "The Blue Light of the Neutron Pool," Catherine Byron's *The Getting of Vellum*, George Elliott Clarke's *Execution Poems*, David O'Meara's "Boswell by the Fire," Don Coles's "Forests of Medieval Europe." These among so many . . . And all this with the awesome vastness of Canada and its provinces, territories and nations and voices that constitute the nation bounded by yesterday's parallels.

RM (Randall Maggs): I was particularly struck by the powerful voice of Paula Meehan. "Not alone the rue in my herb garden" is one of the great poems in the anthology for me. I remember, too, coming upon Eavan Boland's poems, really for the first time . . . How sure she is with her imagery and rhythms and forms, the depth of her wisdom and her recognition of life's complexity (especially a woman's life) . . . No cheap tricks here. And the poetry of Grace Wells offered a wonderful new world to me. Her style is so strong, the words tumbling out line after line. I also dearly love the work of Anthony Cronin. "Tennyson's Nightcap" is a masterpiece — this is my kind of poem. I enjoy his big vistas and musings and wisdom as much as I do probably because they are so carefully weighed and because of his tone in delivering them — assured, unthundering. As for my own country, I was a little surprised and very pleased to find so many really good younger writers, poets like David O'Meara, Karen Solie, Steven Price, Matt Rader and Sue Sinclair.

SM: For me, reading Frederick Ward's *Riverlisp* for the first time was one of my highlights, and I will always be indebted to George Elliott Clarke for drawing my attention to his work, as well as the work of other important voices (he is a large reason why Olive Senior, Pamela Mordecai, Anurima Banerji and Ray Hsu are included in this volume). Reading *Riverlisp*, I was reminded of Elizabeth Smart's *By Grand Central Station*, a book which left me in my undergraduate years looking up age-old definitions of poetry and prose, trying to find words to explain why something could move me so. Pamela Mordecai's *de Man: a performance poem* left me equally shaken, though for different reasons. Her recounting of the crucifixion of Christ, told in Jamaican English, is a new mixture of familiar and unfamiliar returnings. What a powerful and innovative hold on a story so often held in the arms of an unquestioned élite. And, then, there's the work of Alan Gillis. He's one of the most interesting poets to have emerged out of the blue. His vision is just as much driven by the language of video games and the net as it is by his knowledge of pantoums and sestinas. It's like he right clicked on an anxiety of influence . . .

RM: Gillis's poetry is young and downtown and rejects (as in "The Ulster Way") the traditions of a lot of the poetry in the collection . . . After looking at poetry from many different regions of both countries, it seems to me that what the strongest and most interesting from each of these have in common is that they are lived poems. For me, whether a poem is based on an actual or imagined experience, it needs to have blood and bone in it and human emotion. I realize, too, that I am more interested in poems than poetry, the latter too often tending to a kind of intrusiveness of the poet himself or herself that seems to me somewhat artificial and rather irritating. These preferences, I expect, arise partly out of my own ancestry (grain farmers, horsemen and millwrights) and partly from the influence of some of the great teachers in my life: Malcolm Ross at Dalhousie University in Halifax and Desmond Pacey at the University of New Brunswick in Fredericton, both pioneers in the development of Canadian literature, and Don Coles, one of Canada's greatest poets and a skilful and inspiring editor whom I was lucky enough to work with in several Spring Studios at the Banff Centre. What these three had in common, as I understood it, was an interest in the kind of poetry that was *about* something. What they admired, I thought, was the kind of poet who struggled to confront or interpret or remind us of some important aspect of our human situation.

JE: The whole *raison d'être* of the anthology was, and remains, to provide a compendium of excellence of all that is best in contemporary Canadian and contemporary Irish poetry (it is unlikely that poems of the calibre of Ondaatje's "The Cinnamon Peeler" or George Elliott Clarke's *Execution Poems* will ever age). However, the Kavanaghesque bother of getting all of this together was outsmarted by the imperative to finish the job. And speaking of Kavanagh, once the butt of many a neighbour's joke 'round Inniskeen for his lack of farming *nous* — Kavanagh would have loved "Junk Pastoral," by Gary Geddes: "Yours is the worst hay I cut . . . but my cows seem to like it best."

SM: But for me, there was also the imperative to question anthologizing as we rolled along. The act of anthologizing is suspect, bound up with canonization, personal preferences and sometimes, if not always, political agendas. I often had at the back of my mind the canons of eighteenth-century literature. No other period within the history of canonical English study makes me as uncomfortable and nervous of the act of canonization. This period is male dominated, the popular defence being that women were not writing neo-Augustan verse. But how were they to write such poetry if the majority didn't have access to learning Latin and Greek? The act of anthologizing is often exclusionary due to social and political inequities.

JE: The original impulse for me was to bring the descendant voices of long separated kith and kin together, in particular the poetic spokesvoices, as they were, and are, of kindred (if such ever existed) — descendants of people often fleeing from the cornfields of landlords to the Americas in times of hunger and death, who found a safe place to settle some dawn (if they hadn't already added to the mass graves of Gros Ile) only then, after a time, and, if ever, to glance back . . . Say, the famine people Peter Behrens talks of in his new novel, *The Law of Dreams* (winner of the Governor General's Literary Award for fiction, 2006), and whom Eavan Boland embraces within her poem "Quarantine;" the same famine people President McAleese referred to when she opened "Ireland Park" in Toronto commemorating black '47 (1847), when the Canadian city numbered some twenty thousand inhabitants: led by enlightened city authorities, Toronto somehow coped with the arrival of thirty-eight thousand ill and destitute Irish famine victims; many officials lie buried with the fevered they assisted. This in a time of deportations, and served deportations at home, the case of Olivia Agbonlahor and her autistic child. A time of shame.

RM: As may be seen in the first two anthologies of this trilogy, *The Backyards of Heaven* and *However Blow the Winds*, one of the strong common themes linking the literature of our two countries is the complex network of issues arising out of the physical and psychological dislocation of people. Traditionally, as the works of Eavan Boland, Dionne Brand and Jan Zwicky, among others, illustrate, Ireland has been the country of emigration and Canada of immigration. The body of work in *The Echoing Years* reflects how the migration patterns of the past have become a little more complex. With its improved economic situation, Ireland finds itself now drawing many of its own back home, as well as many new immigrants from less fortunate European and African countries, and is having to learn how to deal with new social issues. *The Echoing Years* contains a significant quantity of work translated from poets from those countries whose people are now coming to Ireland (as they continue to come to Canada) with all that immigrant people hope to offer and all that they hope to find.

SM: Kith and kindred . . . What does this mean? I'd have to say that the first and foremost issue for me was the desire to have this anthology include fifty per cent of women's voices. My kindred is first and foremost a community of women, and one doesn't have to go back to the eighteenth century to find examples of anthologies which are more heavily weighted towards male voices. Even the predecessor to this work, *However Blow the Winds*, in its attempt to chronicle tradition included many more male voices than female. For me, the concept of migration also reflects the movement of female voices into a space to claim citizenship in the annals of international poetics. I had the pleasure of staying for a day-and-a-half at the house of Salmon publisher, Jessie Lendennie, at the Cliffs of Moher, where I read and collected materials. Over twenty-five years in business, Salmon is noted for publishing many emerging and lasting voices but, most notably, the voices of female poets. What a treat to immerse myself in the voices of women defined by another country, at times another language, but often, too, by a refusal to embrace the strictures of patriarchy within which all women must strive to breathe. It was here I was introduced to the poetry of Catherine Byron for the first time and her breathtaking work *The Getting of Vellum*, which is healthily represented within the pages of *The Echoing Years*. This was the publishing house that also recognized and recorded the talent of Mary O'Malley, Rita Ann Higgins and Nuala Archer. Though much of this verse shares with the poetry of Irish men the mythological inflections which prick at times the sensibility of many Canadians who strive desperately to recognize national myths, much of this verse, too, shares significant sensibilities with the poetic output of such Canadian poets as Lorna Crozier, Dionne Brand and Pamela Mordecai who write not only out of a female space but also with the rhythms of feminine forms which are, in turn, dominated by interests in subjects which defy understanding women as objects.

RM: I see the inclusion of the voices of as many regions and cultures in the two countries as we could manage to have been one of our main aims in this project from the beginning. I am especially gratified by and pleased with the selection of poets and works from French Canada. French and English poets in Canada know far too little about each other's work, and I hope this anthology will help in some way to change that. Some readers may find it strange that we offer only a portion of the work in translation. The fact is that not nearly enough of it has been translated. And at the same time, I see this book as an Irish and Canadian anthology, not Irish and English-Canadian, and am content to include many of the works of the poets of French Canada only in their own language. There's a comfort, too, in the symmetry of having Canada's poetry in French and English and Ireland's in Irish and English. A point that needs to be made here is that we would not have been able to put together such an extensive and insightful selection of French Canada's poetry if we had not had the help of some very knowledgeable and helpful individuals. We are especially grateful for the long and late hours put in by Dominique Gaucher, a prize-winning French Canadian poet herself, Jean-Pierre Pelletier, a translator and teacher, and Jean-François Bourgeault, all residents of Montréal. As well, for their help in this area we need also to thank Carmine Starnino, a poet, critic and anthologist himself and the poetry editor of Véhicule, and Christine O'Dowd-Smyth of WIT's French department in Waterford City.

SM: Yes, this is important, but I also hope this anthology will question the myth of the two founding nations in Canada. Of course, there were many nations which preceded the formation of the "Canadian nation" — many Aboriginal nations, a number of whom are represented in these pages. I am most indebted to Kristina Fagan, Assistant Professor in the Department of English (Aboriginal Writing and Storytelling in Canada) at the University of Saskatchewan, who chose most of the Aboriginal poetry in *The Echoing Years*. Though I am a scholar who has worked in the field of Aboriginal literature, too,

I specialized in Canadian Native literature of the 1960s and 1970s and needed significant guidance to choose the best of contemporary Native voices. The field of Native literature is just as large as the canons of English literature. I wanted to ensure that contemporary Aboriginal voices from Canada were adequately considered, especially given the fact that I had been away from the mainland of Canada for seven years, teaching in disparate literary fields. I am indebted, therefore, to the careful suggestions made by Fagan.

JE: I think part of my desire was to create a new "commonwealth" of poets from coast-to-coast Canada and Irish poets as these latter move from insular and British contexts to embrace the poetries of the newly emerging EU communities: they re-open routes of the spirit the old arts and gospel scholars trekked when Celtdom stretched from the Burren to Thrace. Continent to continent, to new cross-fertilizations in tone, technique and theme, the linkage of poets along one geographic globe curve of poetry . . .

SM: I'm nervous of commonwealths. I'm reminded here of lines in Canadian poet Dennis Lee's *Civil Elegies*, a long poem which lamented Canadian "nationalist" values and was awarded the Governor General's award during the Vietnam war when Canada, ostensibly refusing to participate, fashioned napalm on its soil to aid its Southern neighbour who brashly went to war: "The humiliations of imperial necessity / are an old story, though it does not / improve in the telling and no man / believes it of himself" (47). How does one respect diversity and equality in the process of representing poets of two nations? I could say I was looking for good poetry, a certain quality of language. But who and what defines just what those things are?

JE: I wanted to capture settled, or immigrant, or migrant, or nomadic, or transient, or living-at-the-edge voices scattered across prairie or REPS landscapes, cityscapes and urban sprawls, where the universities defend their own canonicities, to showcase some of tomorrow's voices with today's veterans, to explore (as in Dennis O'Driscoll's "England" or in Melbourne writer Vincent Buckley's "Hunger-Strike") the bonds of war and civic trauma that recede in the consciousness . . . Not that these contexts or frameworks mean a lot anymore to millions, except to grace titles or gates to other communities. At these gates now, we must take off our shoes for the friskings of critics and lovers of the medium, their value and valued judgements on what went on board, or didn't go, and why not and why . . .

SM: When I had the opportunity to travel to and present a paper at the twenty-fifth conference on West Indian literature at the University of the West Indies, St. Augustine, Trinidad and Tobago, I broached some of these considerations. I presented a paper entitled "Canonizing and Anthologizing Canadian-Caribbean Poetry" in which I outlined this project and spoke about the two prior anthologies, *The Backyards of Heaven* and *However Blow the Winds*. I then used the question period to ask the audience about Caribbean / Canadian poetry and whether or not that was a useful title. Some felt it was; others did not. And the point was also raised that it might also be theoretically logical to include the poetry of Caribbean poets who had lived for a while in Canada and, then, returned to the West Indies (rather than simply considering West Indian poets now living in Canada). Rather than presenting any easy answers to the questions I might have had, this trip raised further questions. What does it mean to root oneself in a nation? What are the values which lead to exclusion? Who and what determines the "rights of belonging" in anthologies and canons?

JE: Interestingly, I found old Irish verities reaffirmed elsewhere. Daniel David Moses pinpoints in his Introduction to *An Anthology of Canadian Native Literature in English* how the healing imperative is uppermost in the consciousness of First Nation cultures; this finds its counterpart in Irish literature, too, from the curative plants listed in *Buile Shuibhne (The Madness of Sweeney)* through to Longley's Burren landscapes and on to the latest book by Medbh McGuckian, *The Currach Requires No Harbours*: how individual hurt and communal trauma, as in First Nations genocide, Ulster slaughter and maimings, are addressed. I think of the curative thrust, from different sides of the globe, in Louise Halfe's "Nõhkom, Medicine Bear" and Ilena Mălăncioiu's "The Bear."

RM: I'm thinking, too, about the poetry of Richard Murphy in the earlier anthologies . . . I don't know Murphy's work well enough to know with much assurance where it fits in, but it feels very close here to Michael Ondaatje. Murphy's Sigiriya is presumably Ondaatje's Sigiriya focused on in the poems of *Running in the Family*. The whole feels very much like Ondaatje's *Handwriting*, a collection of poems about his native country.

JE: Yes, as the anthology developed, synergies in cultural suffusion became a highlight for me: the plight of the prisoner, as seen by Dana Podracká, Susan Musgrave, Leland Bardwell and Laura Lush; laments for the executed, as in George Elliott Clarke and in Áine Uí Fhoghlú; the scattering of the ashes of a loved one, as in Deirdre Brennan, Kyran Pittman and Matt Rader; Alzheimers, as in Michael Redhill, Liam Ó Muirthile and Dolores Stewart; Eavan Boland and Kyriakos Charalambides retelling the plight of the Pharaoh Psammetichus; the follies of state power, old and new, as in Pierre Nepveu, Thomas Kinsella and Yilmaz Odabaşi; the Cliffs of Moher and Clare, as seen by Anthony Cronin and Irving Layton; the two Achilles of Michael Longley and Don Coles; the unabashed hyperbole of Darren Wershler-Henry which could walk off the page of any master *file*; the "Englands" of Stephanie Bolster, Dennis O'Driscoll and Vincent Buckley; galloping deforestation, as seen in Don Coles's medieval Europe or in Samantha Thomas's Caribbean-via-the-Irish experience; the narrative skills of a John Montague or a Jan Zwicky; the ubiquitous blackbird of Irish poetry well-perched in Seamus Heaney and in Olive Senior; little things, like the humble salad tomato, glorified by Senior, and, again, by Phillip Crymble and Carmine Starnino and so on.

SM: It's hard to put words to connections felt. I am always reminded of Frantz Fanon who said nearly half a century ago that "every dialect is a different way of thinking" (*Black Skin, White Mask* 25). Different languages carry different aesthetic sensibilities. I traveled to Cork on August 25, 2006 and attended the launch of Katarzyna Borun-Jagodzinska's *Pocket Apocalypse*, a book of verse translated by Irish poet Gerry Murphy. Borun-Jagodzinska read her poems in Polish, and Murphy followed by reading his English translations. Not knowing a word of Polish, I was struck by the length of Polish words and lines and the relatively shorter length it took to translate the verse and sensibility into another language. I was also struck by "differences" in intonation and delivery. People have been schooled in different ways and languages, and one's reception of, or reaction to, language is part of that schooling. Earlier, I had travelled to the Munster Literature Centre in Cork and had spoken with Patrick Cotter whom I interviewed about contemporary Cork poets and the recent Irish translations of European poetry which formed an impressive addition to the Cork City of Culture 2005 celebrations. Notable Irish poets had translated the work of European poets writing in languages as various as Slovene, Greek, Czech, Maltese, Polish and Turkish. This body of verse (some of which is represented within the anthology) provides a new and exciting addition to the poetic canons of Ireland. The often stark and startling nature of much Eastern European poetry I encountered stands out amongst much of the traditional and mythologically inspired verse of Irish poetry which seems more ornate in its cadences, more circumlocutory at times as it circles its subjects with polished detail.

RM: . . . Kristin Dimitrova, translated by Gregory O'Donoghue . . . I loved this stuff. It's the kind of thing you think looks easy until you try it. Really unique, off-beat, unpredictable, economical and perceptive. She can be absolutely hilarious, but there's an undercutting ominousness in her work as well. Must have been a devil to translate . . . In the end, I agree with Philip Larkin's idea (first made known to me by Don Coles) that pretty much every poem is a failure and fails to the degree that it falls short of the mark that the poet hoped to reach in dealing with his or her subject. In my own view, the creative tension in a poem shouldn't exist so much between the poem's words and parts but between the poem itself and the subject it's grappling with. And this latter quality is what I find in what I see as some of the strongest work in *The Echoing Years*, poems like Don McKay's "Sometimes a Voice (1)," Don Coles's "Romance," Grace Wells's "Aşure," John Montague's "Border Sick Call," and Lorna Crozier's "The Memorial Wall."

JE: And, in the end, I am reminded of Samuel Johnson: "Let observation with extensive view / Survey mankind, from China to Peru . . ." (*The Vanity of Human Wishes*). Certainly this couplet well summarizes the multiple challenges posed by this anthology, the shortest global distance between China and Peru being equivalent to, or less than, the cultural territories traversed by this book, which range from British Columbia to Newfoundland, in Canada, across to Ireland and the nations of Eastern Europe, whose poetry appears in the anthology in English through translations by Irish poets . . .

RM: Having said what I have about what generally makes for the most interesting kind of poem for me, I'll make one additional comment. Although you can pretty much sense when you're in the presence of greatness in poetry, it's difficult to say with much certainty what makes it great, and that's fine with me. That's probably the lesson I learned from an inspiring teacher I was fortunate to have had at the University of New Brunswick back in the early seventies. Lauriat Lane was a scholar whose field was the literature of New England. I remember him as generous, down-to-earth, learned and very large, and I remember, in particular, one sunny New Brunswick autumn morning in his American literature seminar. We had been looking at Frost and Dickinson, and he was tipped back on his chair with his large hands clasped on his chest as if he were thinking aloud about what made a great poet, and he spoke those jolting lines from one of the poems we'd been looking at in that class: "Because I could not stop for Death — / He kindly stopped for me — . . ." He hadn't quite made up his mind about whether or not Frost was a great poet, but he had no doubts about Dickinson. After speaking those lines, he sat there balanced for a moment on the back legs of his chair and gave that little shake of his head that I've come to know so well in Newfoundland, then neatly let the chair fall forward and just as neatly dismissed us for the day. That moment has stayed with me for thirty-five years.

The Echoing Years
Poetry from Canada

Kateri Akiwenzie-Damm

stray bullets (oka re/vision)

my touch is a history book
full of lies and half-forgotten truths
written by others
who hold the pens
and power

my heart is a stray bullet
ricocheting in an empty room

my head was sold
for the first shiny trinket
offered

my beliefs were bought cheap
like magic potions at a travelling road show
with promises
everyone wants to believe
but only a fool invests in

my name was stolen
by bandits in black robes
my world was taken
for a putting green

partridge song

come to me
my love
i am calling

hear my song
sweet one
i am drumming

near the reeds
dear one
i am waiting

come to me
my love
i am calling

rainstorm in volcano:
eight poems for rain

    (i)
    rain is a woman laughing
    with her sisters
    spreading her smile wide
            and rain is a woman's fingers
            moving down
                    down
                          the expectant skin
                          of her lover
                                the moon
                                an eye
                                half-closed
                                in ecstasy

            (ii)
            rain drips on the fronds
                and they uncurl
                      reaching outwards and upwards
                            to her
        the root of her power
        evident
        in their unfurling desire

                    (iii)
                    rain comes
                        pours down
                            a shaft of fading light
                    rain comes
                        like a woman
                            laughing with her lover

(iv)
rain is my lover
    spilling across my belly
    and we smile
            fall into each other's arms
                and sleep

(v)
rain on the roof
    pouring harder and harder
    until we hear nothing
            but rain

                    (vi)
                    rain breathes
                    touching herself
                dreaming of her lovers
                    as her longing rumbles
                            across the earth and sky

(vii)
rain breathes
soft and steady
touches the face of the sea
and the surface shivers

(viii)
rain is coming
    into the womb of earth
            and life is sustained

sturgeon

i twist and gasp
open and close my mouth
searching for air
whenever a sturgeon is caught in the rainy river
i know
the feel of strange hands touching my body
the struggle
to be free
the longing
to go where i want to go
i feel
the impact of stick or rock on bone
the splash of colour
then the emptiness that is my head
my head like a midnight sky if the stars and moon were captured
by another heaven
i know
even when i am awake again
sitting at the kitchen table
staring at my plate with its bramble design
and rough chipped edges
i know

that is why i do not eat sturgeon
because i know
when a sturgeon is caught in the rainy river
i am a sturgeon
and i dangle on hooks

Jeannette C. Armstrong

History Lesson

Out of the belly of Christopher's ship
a mob bursts
Running in all directions
Pulling furs off animals
Shooting buffalo
Shooting each other
left and right

Father mean well
waves his makeshift wand
forgives saucer-eyed Indians

Red coated knights
gallop across the prairie
to get their men
and to build a new world

Pioneers and traders
bring gifts
Smallpox, Seagrams
and Rice Krispies

Civilization has reached
the promised land.

Between the snap crackle pop
of smoke stacks
and multi-coloured rivers
swelling with flower powered zee
are farmers sowing skulls and bones
and miners
pulling from gaping holes
green paper faces
of smiling English lady

The colossi
in which they trust
while burying
breathing forests and fields
beneath concrete and steel
stand shaking fists
waiting to mutilate
whole civilizations
ten generations at a blow.

Somewhere among the remains
of skinless animals
is the termination
to a long journey
and unholy search
for the power
glimpsed in a garden
forever closed
forever lost.

battered and crippled
under all the lies
I teach them the songs
I help them to hear
I give them truth

I am a sacred trust
I am Indian woman.

Threads of Old Memory

Speaking to newcomers in their language is dangerous
for when I speak
history is a dreamer
empowering thought
from which I awaken the imaginings of the past
bringing the sweep and surge of meaning

coming from a place
rooted in the memory of loss
experienced in ceremonies
wrenched from the minds of a people
whose language spoke only harmony
through a language
meant to overpower
to overtake
in skillfully crafted words
moving towards surrender
leaving in its swirling wake
only those songs
hidden
cherished
protected
the secret singing of which
I glimpse through bewildered eyes
an old lost world
of astounding beauty

When I speak
I attempt to bring together
with my hands
gossamer thin threads of old memory
thoughts from the underpinnings of understanding
words steeped in age
slim
barely visible strands of harmony
stretching across the chaos brought into this world
through words
shaped as sounds in air
meaning made physical
changers of the world
carriers into this place of things
from a place of magic
the underside of knowing
the origination place

a pure place
silent
wordless
from where thoughts I choose
silently transform into words
I speak and
powerfully become actions
become memory in someone
I become different memories to different people
different stories in the retelling of my place
I am the dreamer
the choice maker
the word speaker
I speak in a language of words
formed of the actions of the past
words that become the sharing
the collective knowing
the links that become a people
the dreaming that becomes a history
the calling forth of voices
the sending forward of memory
I am the weaver of memory thread
twining past to future
I am the artist
the storyteller
the singer
from the known and familiar
pushing out into darkness
dreaming splinters together
the coming to knowing

When I speak
I sing a song called up through ages
of carefully crafted rhythm
of a purpose close to the wordless
in a coming to this world
from the cold and hungry spaces in the heart

through the desolate and lost places of the mind
to this stark and windswept mountain top
I search for the sacred words
spoken serenely in the gaps between memory
the lost places of history
pieces mislaid
forgotten or stolen
muffled by violence
splintered by evil
when languages collide in mid air
when past and present explode in chaos
and the imaginings of the past
rip into the dreams of the future

When I speak
I choose the words gently
asking the whys
dangerous words
in the language of the newcomers
words releasing unspeakable grief
for all that is lost
dispelling lies in the retelling
I choose threads of truth
that in its telling cannot be hidden
and brings forward
old words that heal
moving to a place
where a new song begins
a new ceremony
through medicine eyes I glimpse a world
that cannot be stolen or lost
only shared
shaped by new words
joining precisely to form old patterns
a song of stars
glittering against an endless silence

Rocks

I study rocks
strewn into the distance

I scan jagged faces of dark cliff
for horses
with wings
examine underwater pebbles
rolling together
for signs
for a telling
of age old
crumblings
and majestic rises

I look long
at thunder eggs
lying silent unopened
wait ages
to discern the heart shaped moment
frozen inside agate

I ponder bearstone glowing red
heaped in the centre pit

I carry a round calm blue stone
secure inside a pouch
and lift tobacco
in a red smooth familiar shape
cupped in the palm

I strike rocks together
calling fishes upstream
watch pointed obsidian
arc upward
and trace ochre rock dust finger marks
on shadowy cave surfaces

I hold onto erect pestle contours
and move precise circles
against elegant curves
inside hollowed mortar

I release a polar bear's stealthy creeping
in midnight black slate

I observe rocks
placed shape to shape
become old sanctuaries
pounded
baked into brick
change into garrisons

I weigh ores liquefied
forged into ploughs
into swords
poured into moulds
polished into bullion
minted
into coins

I see boulders
move to roadsides
as solid bedrock blasted away
becomes tunnels
and mountains dissolve into grey slag piles
and coal black mounds
heaped on trains racing through the night
toward granite and glass wall towerings
in asphalt and concrete canyons
encasing marble stairways
burnished brass
and stainless steel
reflecting the cold lights
trapped in glitter rocks
set in gold
wrapped around fingers

I watched rocks
hurled and smash
into cars of old Mohawk men
women and children
on a bridge
in Montreal
and the million dollar
rock slide
blockades
on ten BC roads
after stones rained
down rock cliffs
on police lifting
human blockades
protecting the slow disintegration
of bones into sand
resting under head stones
on Liliwat land

In the foreground
rock pillared bridges collapse
under the groan of earth's rock changed
into tunnelings
shiftings and spewings
as old stone worked churches dissolve ever so minutely
in the sad rain
while in the distance
one tiny grain waits
to flower into glazing white

I study the rocks
I have set into a circle
opening to the east
on this mountaintop

Tammy Armstrong

Hockey

Hockey rumbles through Saturday afternoon —
ashtray peaked with Dunhills
microbrew for breakfast.
An acolyte of the great Northern tradition
you chant at swag-bellied athletes who shoot
one-timers across the screen while I
read a borrowed book, sip warm beer.

Canucks, Red Wings, Islanders —
all words I've now learned to use differently.
I've mistaken a Shark for a Star
really believed there were two Odjicks.
A practice is cracked-ice pronunciations
Czech rolling out of announcers' throats
like chili dog, Molson, hat trick.

I pretend to comprehend icing
try not to think of children's birthday parties
which always end in tears and bad photography.
Offside, high sticking, slashing —
all parts of relationships gone bad, I thought.

When the TV shorts: mock plays,
preprogrammed radio
the backup: you
in military sweater and boxers
sliding over the floor
stepping over books, plates, cats
toward some net
somewhere near the refrigerator.

This season goes on forever
the rains will eventually thin
bring back Vancouver's panhandlers, tulips
yet we'll still be here each Saturday
watching blurry figures skate
through the static of an old RCA.

I am Canadian without heart, I suppose.
My ignorance of national sports so obvious
on buses, in bars, these terms:
we are always at the blue line
at the unpronounceable words between us.

No One Goes with the Exhibition Boys

We slow
through the exhibition grounds
to watch the shirtless carnies —
calliope scalded tattoos
etched onto chests and arms —
haul carts across the lot.

These are the upended men
with pockets of addresses:
Du Maurier packs
left by small-town girls in belly shirts,
flirting for the sake of the tally,
young enough to cling to Sioux Lookout stories
and believe them exotic.

But no one goes with the exhibition boys.
Around their eyes
raglan maps of draft and smoke,
no newness in their portages down the seaboard,
wintering in motor inns
through xenophobic midlands.
They know the mottos on every license plate.

The nowhere men,
with bodies that smart with transparent concession
when the gates open
and the children queue,
hands full of tokens, day pass bracelets,
hypnotized with what darkness brings:
tilt-a-whirl and duck shoots,
nothing tired nor worn thin.

Martine Audet

 Les labours blancs   de l'air
         et les cordes
         là-haut,
         la vérité des anges
         (nos dernières faiblesses),
         ne se défendaient plus de mourir.

         Était-ce l'ombre abattue
         qui nous maintenait debout?

         Ce qui avait resplendi
         ne disait rien
         ou apprenait à se taire.

∼

 De certains rêves,   nous possédions la langue.
         Du vide, comme d'un amour,
         nous épuisions l'élan extrême,
         puis sa désespérance.

         Nous avions vu la beauté
         (un orient au cœur des lettres exécutées).
         mais n'avions pu trouver de réponse au mal
         qui battait en nous
         et ce qui était resté
         dans nos yeux,
         avec le vent,

         montait l'éclair.

∼

Il nous semblait parfois que nous avions aimé,
que nos bras déployés,
du seul trait des corneilles,
aspiraient le vent,
ses rasades solaires ou liquides,
ses insultes aussi.

Pour quel espoir?
quelle vérité enfouie
en nos seules présences?

Nous répétions que nous n'existions pas.
Nos fronts brûlaient un peu.

∽

Margaret Avison

Balancing Out

He smells of — what?
It's like wet coal-dust.
He came very late:
tangled brown hair, his face
streaked, and bleary;
no gloves, but (Merry
Christmas) from a mission, twice
blest — a good warm coat
that could go anywhere — and had!
now puckered, snagged, hem spread
from sleeping out, and ripped
around one leather elbow,
and buttoned crooked. There were no
other buttons now. He slept
there in his pew.

The giver of his topcoat eerily
watched, her widow's desolation clearly
inconsolable now
(a pang — like joy!),
to see what she had seen
on a fine, and steady man
made come full circle on this ruined fellow.

Still, he had his coat,
and she, the echoing years.

Ramsden

Let's go to the park where
the dogs and children
cluster and circle and run
under the sombre old trees — they are
hanging on to their swarthing
leaves — while the young
medallioned trees in the early
sun are dancing
among them.
The knapsacked students too
hurtle, always too late, focused
on there, blindingly
swerving out of the now and
here where children and dogs
and a few rather shabby, slow
old ones, straying, move
across the owners, standing with
loose leashes, intent on "their day."
The benched but sleepless
mothers and nannies, watching,
are quieted here, warmed and fed
by the good old trees and
the shining little ones.

Ambivalence

When the shutters are down
the outside work is pleasanter
even when fingers out of the mitts
go numb on the hammer;
the boathouse whispered with
ice-splinters and slush when I fetched the ladder.
We'll have to deal with the chimney
before we can warm the place up

inside, and then the cleaning out and sweeping up
will be dirty jobs before it's safe
to light the kindling, inside.

    After the shutters are up
    let's build a fire
    out here: there's wood
    under the cottage; we can
    open the thermos and eat our lunch
    before we tackle the rest?
    It's pleasurable outside.

Being inside will be good when we're
in and out all the time. It can be cosy
when rain is drumming the roof — but that
fireplace sometimes smokes.
In mid-July
it's stifling under the shingles
even after a midnight swim.
On such a night it is pleasanter
under the stars, outside.

    We've never been here when it's
    outside only wherever you might
    need to be to do
    whatever needed doing —
    after the local wood-and-ice fellow who
    helps us has cleared the roof from a heavy snow
    and left again.
    Then   would it   still   be
    better   outside   alone,   only outside?

He Was There
He Was Here

A whiskered mask was all I saw
in the milkers' twilight hour
of the glimmery ghost of Fortinbras
not in Denmark, but here.
Wings creaked, deep before daybreak
and flapped, bird-necks astretch,
out beyond sight in the ghoul-light
(straw-smell, wet armour-brass).

The whiskery glint was gone.
Nobody passed by the smoking glass
of the lost lake either, that morn.

Where he had gone, whom he had seen,
indeed what he might have wanted,
invisibly wired the hours between
wharf and the usual noon canteen,
but it made both disjointed.

As the day wears on, those shinbone greaves
and that bale-bright glaring no-one believes,
nor the milkwarm farm he haunted.

Remembering Gordon G. Nanos

Visual memory:
A narrow, uninsistently
dapper "senior,"
felt hat, casual jacket
unassertive,
quietly walking, listening
(usually the companion
was the same lady);

this Residence
has its own Armistice Day
service: Nanos (air force),
with one (army) Major, two
engineering corps men
several nurses etc.,
in the front row, all — old. All standing,
painfully or not,
rigidly upright for
the national anthem.

At a Families' Day
picnic pool
in some hostess's
grassy back yard. Most adults
trying not to slump
in shiny patio furniture
observed, smiling to see
splashers and little dancers in the sun.

Nanos? He'd slipped away;
nobody had noticed
his little satchel.
The costume, when he appeared!!
In swimsuits, dripping still, gathered
the children, all aglow,
enchanted by his nods and capers
marvelling at his magic.

Nanos is gone
after four-score years. I see
a clown's death has
a spacious dignity.

On a Maundy Thursday Walk

The Creator was
walking by the sea, the
Holy Book says. Finely-tuned
senses — flooded with
intense awareness — tested
a clear serene constancy.

Who can imagine it, sullied
as our senses are? Faulty as are even our
most excellent makings?

The perfection of
created Being, in the perfect
morning was born from the walker-by-the-sea's
imagination. At a word —
the hot smell of sunned rock, of
the sea, the sea, the sound of lapping, bird-calls,
the sifting sponginess of sand
under the sandals, delicate.
April light — all, at a word
had become this almost-
overwhelming loveliness.

Surely the exultation —
the Artist
Himself immersed in
His work, finding it flawless —
intensified the so soon
leaving (lifted out of
mortal life for good
forever).

That too eludes
us who disbelieve that we
also shall say goodbye to
trees and cherished friends and
sunsets and crunching snow

to travel off
into a solo death.

How much more, that
(suffering this
creation to go under
its Maker, and us all)
He, the Father of love, should stake it all
on a sufficient
indeed on an essential
pivot.

Lament for Byways

The harrowed city
swirls with grit;
it's thundery
with chutes emitting
shards, broken stone
from in behind
brickwork going, gone
to dust within.
New little canopies
appear. Wooden partitions
shield the passerby
from inward operations
(something else under the wrecker,
shovel, and scoop . . .). Through spy-
holed fences, we inspect
the backs of streets we knew
before.

        Some starts should not be
        stopped at a dead-end.
        This habitual short-cut ought to
        open on my old friend

>   the boarded-up, blue, disused
>   warehouse, well known to me.
>   Here where it stood is — just a
>   pavement! and empty sky!

With the old short-cut in mind
will we bear with it, white and flat?
Somehow the cars keep blinding
the last few alleys we had.

These handsome new high-rises
help us to overlook
throbbing cement-truck noises
and gritty slime underfoot.
Yesterday's old blue eyesore is
now a new tidied-up site,

but, my city, it's still in your lanes and mews
that your heart beats.

Ken Babstock

Marram Grass

These boardwalk slats intermittently
visible where the sand, like an hourglass's
pinch, seeps between chinks, free-
handing straight lines that stop without fuss —

then fill again, as the wind wills it.
The beach path cuts through undulate
dune land where wild rose, marram grass
cover the scene like a pelt

of shifting greens, or rippled sea of bent
and tapered stalks. To step off
the path's to severely threaten
what a modest plaque declares "this fragile balance." If

my affection's bending toward you seems
or feels ever just a blind, predetermined
consequence of random winds,
think of here: our land's end, streams

of ocean mist weighed down your curls,
spritzed your cheeks and lids, made both
our jeans sag and stick. The shore birds'
reasons blow through us too, but underneath

or way above our range of
understanding . . . even caring. I'll
pass this sight of you — soggy, in love
with me, bent to inspect and feel

the petals of something tiny, wild, nestled
among the roots and moss — over
the projector of my fluctuating self if ever
life's thin, rigid narrowness

requests my heart be small. You taught
and teach me things. Most alive when grit
makes seeing hard, scrapes the lens
through which what's fixed is seen to weaken.

Essentialist

Snug underground in the civic worm burrowing
        west, I was headed to class when a cadet
                in full combat dress got on my train.

        But for a pompom sprucing up the beret,
    his age, the fact he was alone, and here,
this boy could've been boarding amphibious

landing craft. I checked for guns, grew pious
        of this spinning orb's hotter spots. He
                was all camo, enactment-of-shrubbery, semblance

        of flora in varying shades, hues, mottlements
    of green. A helmet dangled on his back, a hillock
in spring, sprouting a version of verdant grasses

in plastic. I got past enjoying a civilian's recoil
        from things military, brutal, conformist, and took
                a peek at what my soldier was so engrossed in —

        Thoreau's *Walden* — imagine him, rubbing oil
    into a Sten gun's springed bolts, working through
his chances at a life away from men: berries

plumping in among their thorns, night's
        curtain drawn across the window of the lake . . .
                We must reconcile the contradictions as we

        can, but their discord and their concord
    introduce wild absurdities into our thinking
and speech. No sentence will hold the whole

truth, and the only way in which we can be just
    is by giving ourselves the lie; speech is better
        than silence; silence is better than speech; —

    All things are in contact; every atom has
  a sphere of repulsion; — Things are, and are
not, at the same time; — and the like. There are other

minds. Surfacing at St. George, I cupped my hands
    and blew — bodies scattering among museums,
        bank towers, campus rooms, and shops, each

        to where they're thinking of or not, seemed
    to prove a law we're locked into, demonstrable
with iron filings, magnets, and clean tabletop.

I can watch their faces go away. The singing's not
    to record experience, but to build one viable
        armature of feeling sustainable over time.

        The stadium's lit, empty, and hash-marked
    for measuring the forward push. On the surface
of the earth are us, who look in error, and only seem.

Windspeed

We were more than a little sullen on the descent —
ticked, really, at the dead-calm state of the air
at the summit of Topsail. Like a row of penitents,
we'd hiked the hard-scrabble straight up, lugging beer

and a designer kite. It was blue and red and meant
to funnel gusts through its windsock frame. Far
from catching a mean updraft, it spent
the afternoon nose down in the crowberries and fir.

What monarch butterfly in Sumatra was so spent,
so drugged or lifeless it couldn't flap one ear-

shaped wing just once and cause a breeze, at least a dent
in the Wedgwood stillness we stood inside up there?

We coiled it and came down. And down on the crescent
of shale, four different kids tugged on the guide wire
of four different kites and hollered and bent
backwards at the strength of their flight. Composure

legged it back to the truck, we lit smokes and began to vent
into our chests. Colin moved first, sliding over near
a glib little pilot and flicking open a Leatherman blade. I went
with it, thumbing the grind-wheel of my Zippo under

the thin string nearest me. It left as if snipped. A parent
saw what his boy had lost and ran over full of hot air,
clutching tongs that pincer-gripped a heat-split wiener.
We shrugged and sniffed as the appendix of string burnt

to a cinder. We were up in the rarer atmosphere,
the social layer, where it often gets hard to breathe, and silent.
A new constellation just then visible over
Belle Isle, specks leaving, signs enacting what signs meant.

Late Drive Toward Innisfil

Late morning we arose and went;
West Gwillimbury,
Wooden Sticks, coats of arms carved
into the overpass,
Maples of Ballantrae, and box stores . . .

a barn wall tagged by the one boy pinned
to the peace on that farm,
an X-Box, culture
in bold colour bleeds into flea markets.
Everyone sweats and crawls north.

This will be our 13th

concession. Purple loosestrife let
loose through Nottawasaga.
New Nevada plates on a purple
Cutlass chewing the scenery.

Patterns are a ruse.
Our dashboard's dark, compartmentalized
life illuminated as the jaw's latch
drops. Little bulb, little bulb over wet naps
and manuals —

A Berth in the Stern

From over the port side's rail, our two faces
cameo'd, cast back, cross-haired in the lenses
of a wandering armada of jellyfish. The surface's
slickness a zero on the State-of-Sea scale. No fog,
oil rigs mushrooming the northeast horizon,

spilling these rubbery spores, perhaps, that'll clog
the Baltic if they spawn. And I'm told they
will; something about unbalanced fish stocks.
Full day and a night, approximately, aboard
the *Prinsesse Ragnhild* letting the earth's curve

unspool under her hull. All that herring
and tritium encroaching on sea-level Lübeck,
we're pointed at Oslo's elevated ground.
Thirty-five-and-a-half thousand tonnes, a traffic
jam in her hold — I've never got my head around

how these gargantua *float.* Within her massive
warren is a micro-environment: *"The smell
of ship seized you by the sinuses: the smell
of something pressurized and ferociously synthetic."*
Every threshold is a stepping over low walls

designed to trip, until habit lifts knees, marching,
under no orders, seeking air, or the casino. Both
luncheonette and pub offer brown cheese, salmon
on brown cheese, brown cheese under shrimp, or
just brown cheese. I think the Norse are funny,

and fine biathletes. In Rotterdam I asked one why
always the Finns and Swedes at International-level
hockey? "We don't play well together. It's amusing
to watch our neighbours do this. We like skis, and
the dark in the forest. Do you know more of us

are on the plains than in our own country?"
"Norwegians like to fly?" She looked
into her glass, then around at the assembled,
"Minnesota, North Dakota, Saskatchewan," she said.
"*Prairies*! Dust. Diaspora of the Norse." We lifted

glasses above our heads, masts in that windless
bar on the Maas where there was too much singing.
Down below multiple car decks, under the decks
for trucks lined like pachyderms in the pachyderm
part of the ark, our berth in the stern just above

the propeller. A strip of mirror, two narrow bunks,
a geologic dark when the cabin door swung shut.
Dark like that dark we fear thought arises from,
coated in its oil, and might descend back into but
for our propulsion to talk over the engine's baleen

thrum and whine. Here was lightlessness,
an active black that eeled in the ear. Paired gifts,
we'd been given back to the world alive;
the incision of selfhood healed over, now adrift
in the wrong element, two mute, unshuttable eyes.

Anurima Banerji

Summer

or,

I Want the Rage of Poets to Bleed Guns Speechless with Words

I. Summer is the season of sun

and rape. tanning: I am not thinking of a leisurely afternoon on the riviera
with bronzing cream but tanning, like an animal slaughtered, bodies packed
into ice like meat, torn skin
ripped
from bone, stretched wide across grass, something like a hammer pounding
leather (dead).

This is me, Draupadi: I am thinking of a hand as soft as darkness, I am
thinking of murmurs and kissing, the burden of a body under the weight of
rebellion. With eyes
like guillotines, I carry the impression of footprints she walked that day, out
the door, downstairs, against the wall where she pressed my thighs and
kissed —

and I am thinking of an ambulance, police cars, the mythology of birth, him,
that terror on the highway, the street, and at home.

It has been this way for a long time, since they put a restraining order against
my breasts and called it a bra.

— Were you wearing something provocative?
— No
— Were you wearing something provocative?
— No
— Were you wearing something provocative?
— Yes, my vagina

II. Chandrabhaga

where does the sun begin or my body end (bloody)

between the cries of *bitch, pussy, fuck*
in this summer, season of crime
I am a traitor to semen in this season of
gun
held in mouth like I should come to him while he comes in me
but I am a traitor, a dyke, crawling out of light like a cockroach
or just like a cock, and he's got his gun cocked in my mouth
about to burst until

I bleed guns speechless with words

III. this is what makes me live: pierced nipples

and gauze, a look that brings me
to my knees,
when I want it

Do you understand?

When I want it
from her

IV. I will make amerika sink
this is my motherfucking country
and tonight

between my sheets,
I am making love and slow jazz
with a woman slipping through sweat
and nightmare,
sliding into the hard grace
of thighs clenched like fists
that smashed my jaw that day,
but he could not strip words

out of me, they come back
virus

until I bleed guns speechless

V. living in the body of a poet in vertigo,
        she rolls syllables off her tongue,

satyam shivam sundaram.

                om bhur bhuvaha swaha
                tat savitur varenyam
                bhargo devasya dhimahi
                dhiyoyonaha prachodayaat.

In the beginning of this poem she finds me,

                om namah saraswate
                om namah durge
                om namah kali
                om namah stute.

And skin to skin,
this is satyam shivam sundaram,
sruti and smriti,
the prayer of wedding
never uttered outside
man and woman

these are small pieces of longing I write,
with more devotion than veda or darshan,
words thicker than the smoke
rising from the stripped scalp of coconut
in the morning.

VI. Surya:

I could not tell you where water ends and her body begins

there is no other way to know this, only
travel through sinew and muscle,
through ventricle and chamber,
through marrow, bone, and blood —

VII. *love, I heard you underneath*

like Vishnu crawling seas as fish,
Buddha in samadhi,
Krishna smashing body against soul,

satyam shivam sundaram.

she saw me in the making of death, and I could not speak or hide since

she found me, beneath the layers of poetry, a cover like a second skin of plastic alphabet,

bleeding guns speechless

and then,

   somewhere

      I disappeared,

         becoming water

           under   her   tongue

Mike Barnes

Stirring a Can of Soup on the Stove

The windowpane is freckled with rain and I am
stirring a can of soup on the stove.
The thing, I think, is to do this;
just to do it, and only it. To remember perhaps
                                as well
that this drizzling February afternoon will become
green-shooted April, then hot August,
in the comforting cliché of seasons.
To look no further, nor aim higher, than the opening
of this can of clam chowder, the addition
of a reasonable amount of milk
and the heating of both elements to an
edible warmth. Rye bread, icewater,
the hum of the fridge and there is some
cheese left if I am still hungry.

The rain taps, the element glows red, the darkness
                                sets in.

As for the truly terrible events of the last
                      two days
(which cannot be forgotten)
the thing, I think, is not to forget them,
but rather to remember that they happened, and
merely happened.
Neither to dismiss nor dwell upon
them, but to remember and heat this soup.
And then I think the thing to do is to
wash the dishes, set them up to dry,
make the bed as carefully as I ever have
and get into it.

Stephanie Bolster

Aperture, 1856

First the flood of chemicals:
guncotton, ether, silver
nitrate. Then forty-five long seconds
of stillness — and she only three
and quick. Did they meet because

of a raising of eyebrows, curiouser
about each other than about anyone
else in the garden? Her sisters
blurred into foliage;
he smelled of medicine. He was

twenty-four, did not choose her
as his favourite until the *Adventures*
six years later. But something began
that afternoon, marked in his diary
"with a white stone."

Her blue eyes tight buds.
Her mousy thatch straight across
the forehead. Spring everywhere threatening
to open them both: tense in that unfurling
garden, during the long exposure.

Whose Eyes

Perhaps he named that desirous stillness
he required not posing but hinting. Perhaps
he called the game Pretend — *you want something
very badly, but someone will not give it to you,
though there is a small chance they might.*

As he tilted her head down she may have thought
of pink iced cakes reserved for guests, gazed at them
from under shadowed lids as he murmured, *There.*

You are just right. To this Oxford don
with that huge contraption of a camera
and a large nose, this quiet man with waves in his hair,
she may have given these looks to be his characters.
Pretend you are the Queen of Hearts, in a huff —
and at once she found the feeling that would make
the face: her servants bustled to paint white roses
red, flamingoes bent into croquet mallets at her wish.

Nestled close against the lens, the dark
cloth draped over his head, did he not yearn
to crawl into the tunnel of the aperture?
He might have found that place where she
waited with her long-lashed eyes, clear
in black and white, just a breath away,
while the little girl had already flounced outside
to play hide and seek in the red garden.

from "In Which Alice Poses for Julia Margaret Cameron, 1872"

Cordelia

> "*What shall Cordelia speak? Love, and be silent.*"
> — King Lear

What father has your honesty
betrayed? Your own brooked
no favourites but Dodgson made you
his. You offered love: unspeaking,

true, but not the sort he sought.
According to your bond
you walked with him awhile and then

you stopped. Now grown, and still

he sends you books in which
the face of your unfurrowed girlhood
drifts. What prince will take you now,
mock Queen of an old man's kingdom?

He who made you his beloved
has hung your coy and tattered
likeness in his private chambers.
Had you not become a still life

in his darkroom, you would not be
here now, waiting for another lens
to take you in and make a new
self, neither you nor Alice.

Two Deaths in January, 1898

Those flowers you sent to Dodgson's funeral
took your place in the crowd. Beside his stone
a perfumed heap of lilies and gentleness
of babies' breath, your name on the white card
still a child's. You spared mourners
your real face: fallen, etched with lines.

At Father's service you wore black as required,
let tears roll serenely down your cheeks, let
Reginald's husbandly elbow hook around your own.
Condolences blurred to the letter o, hollow
disbelief, *so sorry — and this on top of
the other.* You nodded at appropriate times.

For months your griefs brushed past each other,
draped and faceless as the men who left them.
On a wall inside the Deanery appeared a spreading
damp the servants covered with a chair

and wouldn't let you see. It seemed the profile of a man.

Then one morning, alone in your husband's unused
study, you found in a whiff of ink the word *father*
and your ears buzzed, stars spun you

into darkness. Your orphaned body rocked
as on a boat down a river one ancient, golden
afternoon, but no one to tell the stories, no one to row.

Close Your Eyes and Think of England

Did you follow that advice
while your husband strained for sons?
Or only once the eldest two were dead

in the Great War, and you guessed
what sodden nights had all along
been for? Your country is no mother.

Your children's country was in books,
a small and tangled patch

Dodgson planted years before —
your hand hazy in warm green water,
his words like dragonflies by your ear.

His words the children who lived
beyond all expectation. Your sons

lie broken underneath a land of stones
and bones and mud. England recovers,
Wonderland flourishes. Alice keeps on

cheating: she closes her eyes,
goes underground, comes back.

Portrait of Alice with Christopher Robin

In the midst of a winter wood
she walks like old age,
bent under falling snow and the ghost
of her written self, heavy
as bundled kindling on her back.

At a tree's base he huddles his narrow shoulders
as if lost — his head, familiar from books,
hung forward in dangerous
chilled sleep, calves downy-haired
and goose-bumped past short pants.
An italic fall of snowflakes
various as dreams across his face.

She watches his trembling lips
mumble of yellowed bears and bluster and rain,
of being irrevocably stuck,
then presses her hand to his cheek.
His lashes flutter, he shows her
his eyes made of glaciers and pronounces her name.

To the magic flame he makes
with two rubbed sticks
she gives her pinafore and white socks,
the ribbon from her fallen hair.
He fumbles with his buttons, burns
his trousers and dirty shirt.

They point to figures in the smoke —
lumpen bear, white rabbit, honey pot,
tea cup. Naked together, they watch with ash-stung
eyes and neither blink nor shiver.

Roo Borson

River

I'm never, now, not walking by that river,
dragonflies dipped in evening sun,
coots, and the wicked swans, honking and scooting,
in the haze of after-work traffic
the whole city, it seems, setting sail for home —
home, finally, a place where we are temporarily
responsible for something: lights, water,
the neighbours' peaceful sleep, and where
another might, and will, one day, fulfill
some other function with even less ado. The planets rise
and set with all the limpid consternation the foreheads
of philosophers must feel, glowering their way
through problems they've posed themselves. Old light,
old when it reaches us. Lion-sounds from the zoo as
dusk comes on, smelling the river, no doubt —
a lament. All night the miseries of others
gnawing at our bones. But dreams
are only dreams, unless they're the dead:
elaborate in autumn's gold frame, or those resonant
kitchen sounds that let us know we're loved. Tea,
wheat, sand, water, paper, gold — a life in which,
if you pause, you can hear the dust settling,
in which summer nears winter and disappears,
each seems the only condition possible,
candid while it lasts. Bashō,
surely this is your doing.

   I've been in touch with the gods,
and equally well I know

such gods do not exist. Graffiti under the bridge,
hyacinths and goslings . . . It may be
one of these so-called gods turns over in its sleep,
and so spring comes. The moral order of minerals,
the code of the samurai in stone. For ague:
read the old books in which ague is still argued.
For sun, for rain: a pink umbrella. But in the cool
of the rain you'll be on your own, though the evening
is upright and sharp and the petals scatter,
don't imagine I'll come after you, for I'll be gone —
lingering among the heliotrope,
or stuck to the sole of your shoe,
where again you won't know me. And when the pages,
cool and soft, intend a melody, remember
you weren't here before and you won't be again,
when you go the whole world goes with you,
trace of an afterimage in the infrared
measured by some lonely instrument in Baja.
As I write this, clouds are being born,
they blow across the sky at dawn.
Infinite patience, infinite
disinclination to understand. Just so,
it will be early again, in the faint blue realms.

    Greetings of strangers in the morning
and again at evening, people out walking,
or else walking their dogs, a formal brevity
in such mere pleasures. Though when the wind
blows in from the hot dusty centre and a harsh
arguing ascends, the petty dicta can be seen
standing whole, for a moment, in the sky above the trailer park,
the illumined ends of our need for reason
falling to the river, glittering ash. No, pure heart,
you're not the only poetry, though you may be the best,
at least against the summer's heat. Here
at the bottom of the world the whorls

of weather are as big as a continent,
July is in January, so January is in July,
and the cool change comes, when it comes,
from the coast. *In the sum
of the beautiful I closed my eyes and lay down,
the god of spring at my cheek,
and the summer gods,
and the four hundred gods of the summer night skyline.
All six thousand miles of me I laid down,
nerves and blood and faeces —*
lay down, eyes closed,
where the god of poetry is poetry.

    Long river,
I do still long for you. To make
these drifting things,
of cast-offs
dribbled down the banks in fealty to something
not well understood, like deities perhaps,
a twisted shirt,
a bottle a house in turn atop the reeds,
things for coots and insects to use, if they choose to.

    So much
    for logic.

Spring, I'll say, *coming all this way
just to see me again, here or on the road —*
but in the mornings when you've gone off to work
a loneliness moves into the litter on the hillside
as if it could replace you. Hardly anyone knows this.
No arguments, no dicta, but the little yard intact.

    And the life beneath this life?

Rivers to the Sea

From rain to underground springs, from springs
to fountains, freshets, and rivers,
from rivers to the sea, or the winter snow.
But the wind, *the wind bloweth where it listeth*,
like those disjunct souls drifting and alighting,
always distant — spaceships, or glowing teacups,
most often seen at dusk, on the long straight stretches.
What message? Just that no one any longer
means to do you any harm, or good,
though the dog and then the cat come in,
each able to grant a single wish in exchange for which
each would be the star of the household.
Now the seasons are merely vestigial,
though what shrivels the leaves still fattens the eels,
autumn too — cluttering the playground with extra fins and tails
after everyone's gone home to tomato soup and toast.
Lost in the wood like Hindemith. Whosoever's children
are not practising now will never learn their instruments —

But gentle as the Thursday rain
or the winged sound of traffic as the bakeries are closing
toward four p.m. and there never was, nor can be,
any other form of waking life: now,
goes the ancient advice, is the time for practising
the character for courage. But what if the strokes
are hesitantly drawn, a lost direction,
yellow bedstraw or cloth of gold,
in the nether months, in the nether weeks of the year?
What then are the obligations? Torrens, Patawalonga,
Onkaparinga. Little Para, Torrens. Early or late
along the river road. The leaves are streaked with brilliantine,
the pelicans to their estuaries, the coots to their
twigs and bottle. What are the obligations?
From springs to fountains, fountains to rivers, rivers to the sea.

Button grass or couch grass in the fallen yellow light.
Black silk pool, mirror of no thoughts —
black silk mirror, river of no thoughts.

To set off, instead, on a May morning,
as convention dictates, whether south or north,
autumn or spring, the commentaries decline to tell us.
But the line bends as the river bends, the cherries of that
other time are pink and dark and sweet, an allegorical painting
standing in for the world in the level light of dawn,
morning along the river, growing warm. Who lives here?
Herons standing sentry, bees in the bee tree at noon.
To live to tell old news, without the disgust the dead must feel
toward portraiture, or music — harmonics that depend,
as always, on previous conditions. Anyway,
to change pitch continuously
might be one aim.

from "Autumn Record"
• • •

Once, early in the morning, I happened upon a few drops of still-wet blood. This was on the university grounds, and I could see a broken ground-floor window in a nearby building. I followed the trail, the drops getting smaller and farther apart as I went, all the way to the State Library, where they simply stopped. Things like this happen in broad daylight, when help is nowhere near. Another time, not far from here, I came upon someone crouched in the shadows beneath the overpass. He stood up with his pants down, not even bothering to wipe himself, and looked straight into my face.

• • •

Tim Bowling

Grade One

Out of Miss Robinson's ringless hand, the letters
rose like smoke on the night-black blackboard.
I closed my eyes. Her perfume wafted
through mingled scents of glue and apple-core
until I thought the strange, chalk figures
were a slow smoulder off her skin.

She had the most beautiful auburn hair,
its shade the early rouge on a gravenstein.
Recess-rumour said she once dated Bobby Orr.

The musk of old rain
steamed off our coats and boots
clustered in the cloakroom
where there hung no cloaks.

We sat in our desks as if we had boarded a train
that would take us to knowledge of the clock-face
looming over our clasped hands and clear brows.

Something was ticking down all around us
but it couldn't be the hour. We didn't know hours.

Miss Robinson sighed
as she flamed the entrance to the cave.

Slowly, I opened my eyes on the vowels.

Watching the Academy Awards
in the Bar of the Patricia Hotel

A woman somewhere is winning something.
The dark cleave between her roundnesses
parallels the landscape outside
this almost empty place. No. It's no
use. There are no parallels. We're
on another planet. And yet
the giant wooden Albertosaurus
outside the one-pump gas station
selling stale bread and overripe fruit
is pure Hollywood. I can imagine
the toothsome starlet slinkily posed
beside the open jaws, Fay Wray
of the fossil set. No. I can't.
If there are a million shutter whirrs
in the mosquito drone, only
the God of heat and coyote-echo
stands behind that camera.

The victories here are without gloss
and for the self. Someone, this weekend,
might win a bet on the calf-roping
at the circuit rodeo. More likely, though,
the day will be got through minus
all but the heart's most local hurrah.

Here, the stars are real and stone-heavy.
The eyes of the world don't look
out of their high-corner static and blur,
and we only look part way in.
Horses to break, bones to dig,
poems to write. Gentlemen, raise a glass
to the sweat and the ache and the awe
of the work unsung, the life unglamorous.

Dionne Brand

from **thirsty**

I

This city is beauty
unbreakable and amorous as eyelids,
in the streets, pressed with fierce departures,
submerged landings,
I am innocent as thresholds
and smashed night birds, lovesick,
as empty elevators

let me declare doorways,
corners, pursuit, let me say
standing here in eyelashes, in
invisible breasts, in the shrinking lake
in the tiny shops of untrue recollections,
the brittle, gnawed life we live,
I am held, and held

the touch of everything blushes me,
pigeons and wrecked boys,
half-dead hours, blind musicians,
inconclusive women in bruised dresses
even the habitual grey-suited men with terrible
briefcases, how come, how come
I anticipate nothing as intimate as history

would I have had a different life
failing this embrace with broken things,
iridescent veins, ecstatic bullets, small cracks
in the brain, would I know these particular facts,
how a phrase scars a cheek, how water

dries love out, this, a thought as casual
as any second eviscerates a breath
and this, we meet in careless intervals,
in coffee bars, gas stations, in prosthetic
conversations, lotteries, untranslatable
mouths, in versions of what we may be,
a tremor of the hand in the realization
of endings, a glancing blow of tears
on skin, the keen dismissal in speed

from **Land To Light On**

• • •

I ii

If you come out and you see nothing recognizable,
if the stars stark and brazen like glass,
already done decide you cannot read them.
If the trees don't flower and colour refuse to limn
when a white man in a red truck on a rural road
jumps out at you, screaming his exact hatred
of the world, his faith extravagant and earnest
and he threatens, something about your cunt,
you do not recover, you think of Malcolm
on this snow drifted road, you think,
"Is really so evil they is then
that one of them in a red truck can split your heart
open, crush a day in fog?"

• • •

I iv

I look at that road a long time.
It seem to close.
Yes, is here I reach

framed and frozen on a shivered
country road instead of where I thought
I'd be in the blood
red flame of a revolution.
I couldn't be farther away.
And none of these thoughts
disturb the stars or the pine
or the road or the red truck
screeching cunt along it.

I v

All I could do was turn and go back to the house
and the door that I can't see out of.
My life was supposed to be wider, not so forlorn
and not standing out in this north country bled
like maple. I did not want to write poems
about stacking cords of wood, as if the world
is that simple, that quiet is not simple or content
but finally cornered and killed. I still need the revolution
bright as the blaze of the wood stove in the window
when I shut the light and mount the stairs to bed.

• • •

II ii

I have to think again what it means that I am here,
what it means that this, harsh as it is and without
a name, can swallow me up. I have to think how I
am here, so eaten up and frayed, a life that I was
supposed to finish by making something of it
not regularly made, where I am not this woman
fastened to this ugly and disappointing world.
I wanted it for me, to burst my brain and leap a distance
and all I have are these hoarse words that still owe

this life and all I'll be is tied to this century and waiting
without a knife or courage and still these same words
strapped to my back

• • •

II iv

no wonder I could get lost here, no wonder
in this set of trees I lose my way, counting
on living long and not noticing a closing,
no wonder a red truck could surprise me
and every night shape me into a crouch
with the telephone close by and the doors
checked and checked, all night. I can hear
everything and I can hear birds waking up
by four a.m. and the hours between three
and five last a whole day. I can hear wood
breathe and stars crackle on the galvanised
steel, I can hear smoke turn solid and this
house is only as safe as flesh. I can hear the
gate slam, I can hear wasps in my doorway,
and foraging mice, there's an old tree next
to my car and I can hear it fall, I can hear
the road sigh and the trees shift. I can
hear them far away from this house late, late
waiting for what this country is to happen,
I listen for the crunch of a car on ice or gravel,
the crush of boots and something coming

• • •

III i

In the middle of afternoons driving north
on 35, stopping for a paper and a coffee,
I read the terrifying poetry of newspapers. I

notice vowels have suddenly stopped their
routine, their alarming rooms are shut,
their burning light collapsed

the wave of takeovers, mergers and restructuring
. . . swept the world's . . . blue chips rally in New York
. . . Bundesbank looms . . . Imperial Oil increases dividends
. . . tough cutbacks build confidence

Your mouth never opens to say all this.
The breathful air of words are taken. Swept, yes.
You feel your coffee turn asphalt, you look around
and your eyes hit the dirty corners of the windy store,
stray paper, stray cups, stray oil, stray fumes of gas.
Your mouth never opens, your keys look unfamiliar.

is Microsoft a rapacious plunderer . . . or a benign
benevolent giant . . . rough road ahead

Rough road ahead they say so I leave the gas
station, leaving the paper on the counter,
not listening to the woman calling me back,
my mouth full and tasteless

• • •

III iii

Look, let me be specific. I have been losing roads
and tracks and air and rivers and little thoughts
and smells and incidents and a sense of myself
and fights I used to be passionate about
and don't remember. And once I lost the mechanics, no,
the meaning of dancing, and
I have been forgetting everything, friends, and pain.
The body bleeds only water and fear when you survive
the death of your politics, but why don't I forget.
That island with an explosive at the beginning of its name

keeps tripping me and why don't I recall my life
in detail because I was always going somewhere else
and what I was living was unimportant for the while

Rough Road Ahead

let me say that all the classrooms should be burned
and all this paper abandoned like dancing and the gas
stations heading north, and all the independents
who wasted time arguing and being superior, pulling out
dictionaries and refereed journals, new marxists, neo-marxists,
independent marxists, all of us loving our smartness, oh jeez,
the arguments filling auditoriums and town halls with
smartness, taking our time with smartness for serious study,
committing suicide blowing saxophones of smartness, going
home, which windy night on Bloor Street knowing full well and
waking up shaky until smartness rings the telephone with
another invitation and postmortem about last night's meeting.
Then I lost, well, gave up the wherewithal

III iv

One gleeful headline drives me to the floor, kneeling,
and all paint turns to gazette paper and all memory
collides into photographs we could not say happened
that is us, that's what we did. When you lose you become
ancient but this time no one will rake over these bodies
gently collecting their valuables, their pots, their hearts
and intestines, their papers and what they could bury.
This civilisation will be dug up to burn all its manifestos.
No tender archaeologist will mend our furious writings
concluding, "They wanted sweat to taste sweet, that is all,
some of them played music for nothing, some of them
wrote poems to tractors, rough hands, and rough roads,
some sang for no reason at all to judge by their condition."

• • •

IV ii

in the middle of traffic at Church and Gerrard I notice someone,
two women, for a moment unfamiliar, not crouched with me
in a hallway, for this moment unfamiliar, not cringing at the
grit of bombers, the whine of our breath in collapsing chests, in
the middle of traffic right there for a moment unfamiliar and
familiar, the light changing and as usual in the middle of almost
dying, yelling phone numbers and parting, feeling now, as the
light beckons, all the delicateness of pedestrians. I wish that I
was forgetful. All that day the streets felt painful and the
subways tender as eggshells.

• • •

IV v

the girl starts the morning too, ragged like years
ahead of her, she is a translator of languages
and souls, she waits for the bus, her Walkman
in a war with the pages she's been handed,
her mother's face, her brother's face, the bus
driver's face, and the sign for starvation, the sign
for music, the one for reprisals, she'll read and ignore
them and turn her Walkman loud enough to curdle
the liquid in her eardrums that turns every music
to its rightful metronome of iron foot rings, bracelets.
This. You will read nothing in her own face now. She
is a translator of bureaucracies. This race passes through
her, ledgers and columns of thirst, notebooks of bitter
feeling, this street she's arrived at waiting for the bus
is only one. All night she's been up dancing in her room,
keeping out her mother, barring the doorway with bass,
she's feeding on genius, so till, the girl starts the morning,
weary on the floor, wisdom is what's keeping her up, she's
a noticiary of pain, that faculty is overgrown in her until
it is all she conducts, she's an electrician, pure electricity

flows through her, her fingertips are disappearing in sheer
lightning.

IV vi

a Baptist priestess preaches to a sidewalk in this city
and if this city could take it she would look into its eyes
but everyone, me too, glides by,
all who might pronounce her sane run ahead,
drive quickly before she catches our eyes,
and she is mad, thinking god could find her here,
and in her eyes that is her penance I suppose,
to talk to the pavement at Oakwood and St. Clair
and ours to avoid her as if we suddenly lost
consciousness of race and what she's calling for,
all eyes instead drop to the sash of dirt around her waist
and say "for god's sake, these people could embarrass you, ay!"
her husband left her, took all her money
after she worked to bring him here, well after all
who else could explain but the pavement dense with answers
• • •

V i

Maybe this wide country just stretches your life to a thinness
just trying to take it in, trying to calculate in it what you must
do, the airy bay at its head scatters your thoughts like someone
going mad from science and birds pulling your hair, ice invades
your nostrils in chunks, land fills your throat, you are so busy
with collecting the north, scrambling to the Arctic so wilfully, so
busy getting a handle to steady you to this place you get blown
into bays and lakes and fissures you have yet to see, except
on a map in a schoolroom long ago but you have a sense that
whole parts of you are floating in heavy lake water heading for

what you suspect is some other life that lives there, and you, you
only trust moving water and water that reveals itself in colour. It
always takes long to come to what you have to say, you have to
sweep this stretch of land up around your feet and point to the
signs, pleat whole histories with pins in your mouth and guess
at the fall of words.

• • •

V vi

Light passes through me lightless, sound soundless,
smoking nowhere, groaning with sudden birds. Paper
dies, flesh melts, leaving stockings and their useless vanity
in graves, bodies lie still across foolish borders.
I'm going my way, going my way gleaning shade, burnt
meridians, dropping carets, flung latitudes, inattention,
screeching looks. I'm trying to put my tongue on dawns
now, I'm busy licking dusk away, tracking deep twittering
silences. You come to this, here's the marrow of it, not
moving, not standing, it's too much to hold up, what I
really want to say is, I don't want no fucking country, here
or there and all the way back, I don't like it, none of it,
easy as that. I'm giving up on land to light on, and why not,
I can't perfect my own shadow, my violent sorrow, my
individual wrists.

VI i

I feel like my aunt hunkered to a foot that wouldn't
cure, her hair tightened to a "dougla" wave and her mouth
sweet on laughter and paradise plums, she could fry fish
and make it taste sweet, sweet after her seasoning
rubbed the silvery red skin on snapper and she could turn
flour into sweet bread glazed with crystalled sugar water,
bread carved in steamy yeast and butter, her hands parted
a corn row clean clean and ribbons bounced white and blue
satin to her fingers, she liked to sweeten up, perfume
cheap as pennies richened on her skin and her one good leg
slender and tapered to the ankle she braceleted against
the whispers of bad woman, she dressed in tight skirts and low
backer bodices, taught us the jive spinning and dipping
between the Morris chairs to Count Basie but she could not
knead that leaky leg well. I woke up to her sitting in the dark,
the corners of the living room warm and amber with floor
polish, moaning and rubbing her foot. She didn't sleep,
she sat up, her leg on a chair waiting for daylight
to turn corn meal into porridge with cinnamon spice and
vanilla essence, or roll it into fig leaves with raisins, to repeat
the lesson of the jive when we got home at three and to quarrel
about our hair, flying away free which she'd pulled back smart
in rubber bands just this morning.

• • •

VII iii

I saw her head up the road toward
the evening coming, that road, the same
as when its name was Carib, cut
in the San Fernando hill, that evening
as unconcerned as any for her, bent
on its own gluttony, she, like an ancient
woman with her regular burdens heading

into a hill. I saw her begin again,
the coming dark slipping between her legs
and disappearing into which century past.
I saw her shoulder the dark like another child
and consider its face, its waiting mouth
closed on her breast.
She told me once she loved babies, hated
to see them grow up, she missed
their babyness, that's why she had so many.
I saw her heading up a road into a hill
with her vanity and her lust
not for any man in an electric company truck
but for her own face.

• • •

VIII ii

that night we wanted to fly in our aunts' skin,
we so loved their talk, the sugar in their mouths,
they were always laughing, throwing water over
their shoulders and going on anyway, the one
with five children stealing out the door without them
after she'd fed them and oiled them or perhaps not,
but slipping out the door going looking for another
as her mother said; trusting the cane field, at the bottom
of Cocoyea village asleep behind the house, at her back,
blue in the black black night, to put those children
to sleep too and keep them while she found another,
tall and pretty, who would bend into the well of her cheeks,
clutch the bone of them like a carnivore, five children
and she could still laugh the best men into the dough
of her skirt and love them so hard a ship to England
would leave without her many times and leave the wharf
without the suitcase full of dresses sewn for months
piled on the Hitachi machine, mouthsful of needles
and thread bristling and black cake packed for sisters

abroad, waiting for news and hungry for such skirts,
such love themselves, her mother and father waiting
in disappointment and dread until there was no way
she would make that ship.
• • •

VIII iv

She came in a hurry to leave, "Keep the children
for me, mama. I hear about a work." Bustling
sweetly dressed like she was going to a party, kissing
the children promising them sweeties if they behaved
for mama. She wore pink powder and dabbed
the puff on our faces, exquisite dust clouds
of perfume exploding, we squealed with love
and terror. Where she went, we wanted to go.
It was some place you had to hurry to and something
hot and sweet was going on there and waiting for you,
knowledge. What was it that she had to keep going to
and was more seductive than a ship going away
and returning into another life, not a bucket
under the leak of a bachie, the man with promises gone,
not fright at a failed abortion, the blood endless
in a small room, what was so sweet in all that running
racket, in men grinding the hills of her cheeks to gravel,
panning her eyes for their brittle rages.
• • •

XIII

In this country where islands vanish, bodies submerge,
the heart of darkness is these white roads, snow
at our throats, and at the windshield a thick white cop
in a blue steel windbreaker peering into our car, suspiciously,
even in the blow and freeze of a snowstorm, or perhaps
not suspicion but as a man looking at aliens.
Three Blacks in a car on a road blowing eighty miles an hour
in the wind between a gas station and Chatham. We stumble
on our antiquity. The snow-blue laser of a cop's eyes fixes us
in this unbearable archaeology.

How quickly the planet can take itself back. I saw this
once in the summer in daylight, corn dangling bronze, flat
farm land growing flatter, eaten up in highways, tonight,
big and rolling it is storming in its sleep. A cop is standing at its
lip.
• • •

Jacques Brault

c'est un soir pas comme les autres soirs
sa lenteur descend sur moi   et ma frayeur
reste sans voix que ferai-je   à la nuit
sous tant de soie et de moire   de sueur et de moiteur
non ce n'est pas un soir comme les autres
un soir de fatigue qui s'apaise un soir qui pèse
en toute hâleur ou de corps brûlé
ou de froid jusqu'à l'os de l'âme
et la nuit alors délivre du dernier espoir
le matin dans la mémoire s'obscurcit
j'accueille cette heure droite et parfaite
et si je me couche en mon lit toute peu dépouillée
c'est que j'aime imaginer de dormir
comme on doit mourir

∽

Neige d'un soir   épands-toi partout
brouille l'air alentour
que cette vieille angoisse qui me vient
ne trouve pas son chemin

∽

Ce n'est plus le moment de gober les mouches. Le départ nous prend au corps. Ça fourmille de partout, le non-sens. Et allons-y, à ce nulle part. Bondieu, je n'arrive plus à me lever. Où sont mes bottines, mon chapeau, mon sac? C'est vrai, il n'y a plus de chemin. Bof! on l'inventera; c'était une idée comme ça, de continuer. Donnez-moi la main. Attendez-moi. Il n'y a vraiment personne? On imagine, on s'enroule dans une image, on s'invente une autre vie. Façon de mourir en douce, à petites secousses. Et merci pour cette bonne journée, qu'ils disaient. Et l'honneur est sauf, et au moins on ne s'est pas trahi, et toujours l'horreur se lasse, qu'ils disaient encore et redisaient. Maintenant, ça y est, je vais me mettre au trou avec la sombre vagabonde. Elle n'annonce rien et ne promet rien. Elle te prend et t'emmène à l'amer. Tu reconnaîtras sans peine cet arrière-goût de vivre. J'espérais, malgré tout. Disparaître en un petit chemin, avec un souffle de quelqu'un tout près; une vieille bonté comme au premier instant. Mon espérance, ne meurs pas avec moi.

Bucolique

Me voici   néant   tu m'attendais
depuis avant ma naissance oui
je te reconnais à ta figure vide
nous ne dirons rien   le vent nu
nous précède sur le chemin de campagne
nous n'irons pas loin   le vent
finit toujours par tomber on l'oublie
et le silence n'est-ce pas est une violence
qui ne fait pas de bruit   demain
n'existe plus   mort on s'en lave les mains
voici la colline aux corneilles
et des ormes qui persistent et des champs
toute une douceur d'horizon à l'abri
de la bêtise   mais le moment est venu
de se dissoudre dans la buée du soir
néant ferme-moi les yeux je te prie

et laisse-moi debout piquet de clôture
ici où ne passe personne ni le temps
et va sans crainte plus rien en ce monde
n'a de sens hormis à mes pieds
une touffe de fougère qui a besoin d'ombre
la mienne   pour vivre pourquoi pas

Diana Brebner

The Blue Light
of the Neutron Pool

All the generations of me go up with you,
past Petawawa and the military convoys,
past Chalk River, Deep River, Rolphton, and
the rivers of nuclear power, past the
quiet churches: Our Lady of the Snows,
St. Andrew's Among the Pines, and the spires
in Mattawa where we turn. This is when
we are most together, driving the highways

that lead to our wild places. In an old car,
loaded up with: packs, boots, a borrowed
canoe, we go up to Kioshkokwi, leaving
the city and the everglowing sky behind,
hoping to see the darkness in each other,
the black joy of an empty night, the little
cries of the hidden stars as they become
visible and beloved. When we were leaving

Cally shouted "Have a good trip" and then,
unexpectedly, "We love you." So many people
are left behind, the ones who will not,
or cannot be with us. I bring them with me
and carry their eyes, old lamps in the dark.
Who are we to travel over water to the
islands of pines and spirit? Portaging in
mystic green worlds, the red leaves warning,

the winter coming, and wading small rivers,
leading the canoe in the turbulent waters,
I remember my friends and take their peace
with me. And you, constant man, who changes

shape with the days, with the weather: raven,
brother loon, river merganser, holy fish
as you leap in the water, companion, silent
comrade; be assured, I could never leave you.

First early hours in the north of Algonquin:
we are listening to freight trains rumbling
on to North Bay. We see the eerie glow of
settlement to the northwest. Later, the loons
will greet us in the grey morning, the clouds
on the water. Then small rain, like a blessing,
dampens the day. A moose and her calf
browse in the shallows where our next portage

begins. We can wait. The baby canters
on the surface, confident, kicking its heels
like a small horse, and the mother, benign
madonna, watches and chews. In the forest
we will encounter silence, a man and his dog,
the cathedral green of lichen, moss, and
the emptying gothic of the columnar trees.
Winds are up at the beach at Manitou Lake;

a pair of ravens stand guard at the shore.
I, who have lived as a mind, cogito's captive,
must submit: this is a world of body and
spirit. In purity, or violence, the water
receives you, and you become it. Thunderbird
roars overhead and the drumbeats of the
spirit pound, detonations in the heart.
There is no turning back from fear, or joy,

and our moment of salutation. Every green
branch and living thing springs up, every
fish becomes a silver word. On the island
of pines, unmapped on the lake, we come
home to the animate universe, the breathing
earth. I'm alone. So, how can I explain: in all
my prayers, I am with you, and you are here.
In the morning we will walk among stones

and broken shells, naked as children, in
the living water. I will think of my friends,
the lovers and the beloved, the believers
and the quiet companions. The scientist lives
for the moment of light, to have one night
when the code unravels, or to spend a life
without politics or worry, her face alive in
the blue light of the neutron pool. My friend,

the believer, asks for enlightenment;
my friend, the painter, for vision; my
friend, northern boy, for the green country
of childhood that his heart cannot forget.
As for me, Thunderbird, I ask that you take
me with you, in a boat that crosses to the
world of spirits. I want to dance at my death,
to make a little thunder the earth will hear.

The Green Canoe

We are back, each in a green canoe. Old Night
descends. Or do we ascend, touching the
stars? We have learned to name them: Orion,
and the dog Sirius, at heel, Cassiopeia's

curious bent chair, the Bear, the constant
blessing of the Northern Star. We're in deep,
taken aback, by meteors. The bright bursts
fall, and we are under fire. Our hands can't

hold, nor our four eyes, made bold by love,
endure, the multiplying sights. Too much,
far too much love, for our pairs of arms,
or eyes, or hearts. If I stepped out now

from the encasing cedar, would I float up
from the memory of water (that sees all)

into the skittering path of I's and souls,
catching the burning hieroglyphs, all fired

on my open palm? I think this is where we
learn to pray: that some things will never
end (though they did), that we remember
(though we will not) the gifts of our lives.

Look up! Look up! How many burning wishes
fall: to lust, greedy lovers, just like us,
leaning out too far for love, who break in
time, and starry water too? I fell for you.

from "At the Schwarzschild Radius"
• • •

3.

The beautiful long-haired boys
walk the streets in their
black great-coats. In ancient

boots, with beads plaited
in their hair, they are
like luminous fish. The art

schools cannot contain them.
The crazy people they love
cannot contain them. I will

not try to keep you from
floating, high in the winter
air. Little fish, I love how

your hair streams behind you
in the urban afternoon. If
I am brave I will touch it

and rob the shoals and the
studios of their hour.
Black boots. Golden boy.

Our time will cost me one
life (gladly wasted) so briefly
to brighten the city's air.

Morning on the Guitar

Ragged, in jeans and your father's plaid shirt,
there you are, at the end of my bed,
typical you, turned away. You won't even
let me look at you as you play your
new piece, "the first one that really sounds

like music" you say. It is "Morning,"
for the guitar. It is late, later than either
of us can know, and silence and
darkness have settled in circles around
us. When I try to reach out there are

always things unspoken, deep & bass,
blue & heavy, that I must get past. You are
beautiful & insular, just learning to play,
and slowly emerging from childhood into
this place of music & balance. Your right

hand, still awkward, is near the neck,
your left hand floating near the bridge
that will make the notes uneasy, metallic.
Your head of long brown hair swings,
just slightly, in concentration, as

an old melody emerges, *cantabile*,
a voice singing between us. Now, I find
you have turned, face to me, still,
not speaking. When you look up is it you
or the room that glows with faint light?

Port

Sometimes the tricks you learn as a child
are useful later on. When I was beaten
or raped I learned to move myself away
to a place without pain or degradation,

to stick it out and watch at a distance,
and never to vomit. I have been lucky
in joy, and have felt exultation. I have
been moved to tears and, nowadays,

I am hardly ever beside myself. I've
read that there is a science of pain
management. I think I could be an
expert. When the surgeon removed

my port, small metal disc implanted
just under the skin of my shoulder
to make delivery of chemotherapy less
painful (and which, by the way, was

never used by the tired nurses in a hurry
who could just stick an intravenous in
a good vein and get on with it), he was
doublebooked and did the procedure

during his lunch hour. I liked this man,
he spoke honestly and listened to me
but everyone has their bad days and
this was one. In the outpatient surgery

he began and I wondered, idly, why
I could feel so much, my shoulder
deadened with anaesthetic. We talked
and he worked and I said I could feel

his hands and the instruments as he
worked and he said: No, you cannot.
Can. Cannot. Can. Mutual panic
as the pain increased and he knew

he was alone, had to proceed, could
not call for help and I said: OK, Listen up.
I have gone to the top of a mountain
where it is very cold, so cold I am

frozen and cannot feel, but I can see.
And way, way down at the bottom of
the mountain there you are, tending
a fire. I can see the red flames and

imagine the heat but here I am, up at
the peak, feeling nothing. He looked
at me strangely and was silent, worked
quickly and then left me, quite alone.

I waited a long time up on that
mountain but gradually the fire went
out, and he never did come back.
I got up, and walked home, was

a body but not wholly connected.
As the afternoon wore on, the cold
wore off. I began to shake: my
hands frozen, my teeth chattering. I

couldn't stop shaking and imagined
someone lost in a storm, perhaps
at sea, hoping like crazy to make
it to port, to the safe place that is

calm, and the first thing to do when
you arrive is to be sick to your
stomach, to know you have survived
but also to know that out there,

in the dark centre of destruction,
someone you loved, and had known
so well she might have been yourself
was lost, irretrievably, at sea.

Nicole Brossard
Translated by Robert Majzels and Erín Moure

Typhon dru

et c'est l'envol vagues typhon dru
comme un coude dans la nuit
rai de mœurs
le monde est vite obscur

partout où la bouche est excentrique
il neige : et pourtant cette chaleur longue
sous la langue, le moi s'enroule émoi
plane ruban de joie
paupières harmoniques

car le monde est vite obscur
et la nuit me rend avide
de partout frôle tant
que la langue avec son sel
un à un les verbes les troue
de silence, typhon dru

en plein vol si j'ouvre les bras
mes cheveux sont lents dans l'oxygène
je prétends qui'il y a de vastes lois
au-delà des villes et des sépultures
ruban de voix, lame des yeux

ce soir si tu rapproches ton visage
et que la civilisation s'étire
au bout de tes bras, ce soir
si en plein vol tu rattrapes mon image
dis que c'était au loin
comme un dé dans la nuit

et pendant que mon sexe songe à l'aurore
mouille muqueuses heureuses
il neige et la proximité encore
je prétends que c'est l'aura
ou l'image asymétrique
de l'image brève en plein vol

lame de fond, cérémonie de l'image
mon cœur est agile
l'émotion entre nous
matière du rire matière trop vraie
et ma voix qui craque
dans le froid des galaxies

je prétends veiller en silence
dans le froid rose des galaxies
je prétends que si l'œil est noir
il ne peut pas veiller

partout où la bouche rieuse virtuelle
d'énergie dévore l'aube déverse son oui
elle crie du mieux qu'elle jouit
tympan, mauves sonores
vastes lois qui lèchent
au loin le fond de l'air

au matin *e* plane haut
et les rivières sont longues
sous ma peau d'autant de parcours
à saveur de femme et de lucidité
au matin la rivière est flue emportée
quand je te touche
face à face dans l'affirmation

Typhoon Thrum

and it takes flight whitecaps typhoon thrum
like an elbow in the night
ray of mores
the world is swiftly dark

everywhere where the mouth is eccentric
it's snowing: and yet this heat long
beneath the tongue, the me curls up emotion
glides ribbon of joy
harmonic eyelids

as the world is swiftly dark
and night turns me avid
from everywhere so much brushes up
that the tongue with its salt
pierces one by one the words
with silence, typhoon thrum

in full flight if I spread my arms
my hair slow in the oxygen
I claim there are vast laws
beyond cities and sepultures
voice ribbon, eyes' blade.

tonight if you lean your face close
and civilisation stretches out
at the end of your arms, tonight
if in full flight you catch my image
say it was from afar
like a die in the night

and while my sex dreams of daybreak
engorges ecstatic epitheliums
it's snowing and again proximity
I claim it's the aura
or the image asymmetric
of the image in brief full flight

groundswell, image ceremony
my heart is agile
emotion between us
matter of laughter matter too true
and my voice that cracks
in the cold of galaxies

I claim I keep watch in silence
in the rose cold of galaxies
I claim that if the eye is black
it cannot keep watch

everywhere where the laughing virtual mouth
of energy devours dawn disgorges its yes
she cries out as wildly as she comes
tympanum, sonorous mauve
vast laws that lick
the air's depth from afar

in the morning the she glides high
and rivers beneath my skin
are long from so many windings
savoury with women and lucidity
in the morning the river surges swept away
when I touch you
face-to-face in affirmation

Mark Callanan

The Delicate Touch Required for China
for Nan

My grandmother's hands were crippled,
twisted like roots sunk deep
into earth —

when she was young
two small birds fluttering
about their duties,

tying a shoelace,
bandaging a scraped knee

and, late at night,
taking my mother
by the hand
and leading her home over the dirt road.

I used to bring her tea
and watch her fumble with the cup,
balance it between two hands, wince
          at the delicate touch
          required for china.
The cracks in the cup
trailed off into her palms.

I remember her sitting on the edge of her bed,
fingers twisted useless around a brush.

I used to sit behind her
and pull comb through hair,
stringing out her history in tangles,
in waves thickly knotted.

Her hair felt like rope

in my small hands.

I remember her lying in a hospital bed,
still as stone,
seeing her dead at the funeral home,
her hands,
two clumps of earth.

In winter, my fingers ache with the cold.
           (the frost sinks deep
               into the cracks of my skin)

My hands are roots buried under mounds of snow.

Anne Carson

New Rule

A New Year's white morning of hard new ice.
High on the frozen branches I saw a squirrel jump and skid.
Is this scary? he seemed to say and glanced

down at me, clutching his branch as it bobbed
in stiff recoil — or is it just that everything sounds wrong today?
The branches

clinked.
He wiped his small cold lips with one hand.
Do you fear the same things as

I fear? I countered, looking up.
His empire of branches slid against the air.
The night of hooks?

The man blade left open on the stair?
Not enough spin on it, said my true love
when he left in our fifth year.

The squirrel bounced down a branch
and caught a peg of tears.
The way to hold on is

afterwords
so
clear.

Shadowboxer

Of the soldier who put a spear through Christ's side on the cross
(and by some accounts broke his legs),
whose name was Longinus,
it is said
that after that he had trouble sleeping
and fell into a hard mood,
drifted out of the army
and came west,
as far as Provincia.
Was a body's carbon not simply carbon.
Jab hook jab.
Slight shift and we catch him
in a moment of expansion and catastrophe,
white arms sporting strangely in a void.
Uppercut jab jab hook jab.
Don't want to bore you,
my troubles jab.
Jab.
Jab.
Punch hook.
Jab. *Was a face not all stille
as dew in Aprille.*
Hook.
Jab.
Jab.

Father's Old Blue Cardigan

Now it hangs on the back of the kitchen chair
where I always sit, as it did
on the back of the kitchen chair where he always sat.

I put it on whenever I come in,
as he did, stamping

the snow from his boots.

I put it on and sit in the dark.
He would not have done this.
Coldness comes paring down from the moonbone in the sky.

His laws were a secret.
But I remember the moment at which I knew
he was going mad inside his laws.

He was standing at the turn of the driveway when I arrived.
He had on the blue cardigan with the buttons done up all the way to the top.
Not only because it was a hot July afternoon

but the look on his face —
as a small child who has been dressed by some aunt early in the morning
for a long trip

on cold trains and windy platforms
will sit very straight at the edge of his seat
while the shadows like long fingers

over the haystacks that sweep past
keep shocking him
because he is riding backwards.

from "TV Men"
• • •

Antigone (Scripts 1 and 2)

> Antigone likes walking behind Oedipus
> to brake the wind.
> As he is blind he often does not agree to this.
> March sky cold as a hare's paw.
> Antigone and Oedipus eat lunch on the lip of a crater.
> Trunks of hundred-year-old trees forced
> down
> by wind

crawl on the gravel. One green centimeter of twig
still vertical —
catches her eye. She leads his hand to it.
Lightly
he made sure
what it was.
Lightly left it there.

[Antigone felt a sting against her cheek. She motions the soundman out of the way and taking the microphone begins to speak.]

There is nowhere to keep anything, the way we live.
This I find hard. Other things I like — a burnish
along the butt end of days
that people inside houses never see.
Projects, yes I have projects.
I want to make a lot of money. Just kidding. Next
question. No I do not lament.
God's will is not some sort of physics, is it.
Today we are light, tomorrow shadow, says the song.
Ironic? Not really. My father is the ironic one.
I have my own ideas about it.
At our backs is a big anarchy.
If you are strong you can twist a bit off
and pound on it — your freedom!

Now Oedipus has risen, Antigone rises. He begins to move off,
into the wind,
immersed in precious memory.
Thinking *Too much memory* Antigone comes after.
Both of them are gold all along the sunset side.
Last bell, he knew.
Among all fleshbags you will not find
one who if God
baits
does not bite.

[For sound-bite purposes we had to cut Antigone's script from 42 seconds to 7: substantial changes of wording were involved but we felt we got her "take" right.]

Other things I like: a lot of money!
The way we live, light and shadow are ironic.
Projects? yes: physics. Anarchy. My father.
Here, twist a bit off.
Freedom is next.

from *Akhmatova (Treatment for a Script)*
. . .

MANDELSTAM

Akhmatova was translating *Macbeth* in the early '30s
        (a time she called "the vegetarian years" to distinguish
            its charm from "the meat-eating years" still ahead).
For a poem in which he likened Stalin's fingers to worms
        Osip Mandelstam was arrested in May 1934. All night
            the police searched his papers and threw them
out on the floor
        to the sound of a ukelele
            from the next apartment.
Akhmatova never finished *Macbeth* although
        she liked to quote the hero saying people
            in my homeland die faster than
the flowers on their hats.

AKHMATOVA COMES TO THE WALL

Real Terror began in December 1934.
Song bees by the thousand vanishing as the Kremlin clock struck twelve.
        Akhmatova — weep now,
"but the moisture boiled off before it reached my eyes."
Akhmatova's son Lev was arrested in 1933 (released), 1935 (released),
        1938 (not released).
She came to the wall to stand in line.
Inner prison of the NKVD on Shpalernaya Street.

Then Kresty Prison across the Neva.
Once a month a window opened in the wall.
Akhmatova — for Gumilyov, she said
    shoving her parcel through the grate.
• • •

BECAUSE OF HIS MOTHER, BECAUSE OF HER SON

You're guilty! In what form would you like to confess this?
they said to Lev at the interrogation. They did not beat him much.
Sentenced him to 10 years in Karaganda region, correspondence limited.
    Akhmatova burned all her papers — manuscripts, notebooks, letters —
    and began the tale of two cities:
    Leningrad to Moscow
    every month
to hand in a parcel of food at the little window in the wall
(8 kilos maximum including the box).
Accepted, it meant he was still alive.

AKHMATOVA REPENTS (1950)

How could she save her son except by praising Stalin?
    "Along the once demolished highway,
        light autos now fly."
Her cycle of Socialist Realist poems was published in Moscow in
Ogonyok.
    Amid the unending tundra Lev labored on.
        Her head was covered that day by a large black seeing
        scar.
She walked like someone in the ashes of a house, stopping.
    On hot days we loved to hide here. Pointing. *Like mortals.*

THE POISON SON IS BACK

Not poisoned when he left (1949) from Lefortovo Prison (Moscow)
    to Karaganda region for ten years hard labor.
        She spent those long years trying to get him free.
    But she was a writer under Decree.
One Wednesday (1956) he turned up
    unannounced at her door.
        Lev smokes like a chimney!
    Akhmatova was jubilant at first,
waving fumes toward the window of the small kitchen where she
    lived. Lev had balanced 14 years
        on a bloodaxe, now he
    spoke in monosyllables and didn't like her friends — "dead grapes"
who steamed up his glasses with their Lyova! Lyovushka! and their
endless
    tiny cups of tea.
        Spirits passing on the border saw flesh and blood and blame
    darken the kitchen like torture.
After a quarrel she had a heart attack.
    You've always been ill, said Lev and got accommodation
        on the other side of the city.
    And those walls saturated with thoughts of him —
with dreams, insomnia, declarations,
    summonses, petitions, meetings,
        nonmeetings, fevers,
    mortifications,
if-clauses,
    hairs
        placed in a notebook — are still there to see.

• • •

Thucydides in Conversation with Virginia Woolf on the Set *of* The Peloponnesian War

T: Bell dies away in seven seconds then a light comes up and we see you walking.

VW: Can you explain the walking again.

T: Begin right with the right foot, left with the left, each time nine steps right to left and back again.

VW: Does she do this every day.

T: Yes it is routine.

VW: Without feeling.

T: Routine.

VW: When does she speak.

T: Fourth step. First sentence ends immediately before the turn.

VW [walking]: *War costs are of two kinds direct and indirect.*

T: When you walk slump together. When you speak straighten up a bit.

VW: *War costs are of two kinds direct and indirect. Direct costs embrace all expenditures made by belligerents in carrying on hostilities.*

T: Too much color. No movements with the head. Monotone, very distant.

VW: *War costs are of two kinds direct and indirect. Direct costs embrace all expenditures made by belligerents in carrying on hostilites. Indirect costs —*

T: It's an improvisation not a story. You're looking for words, correct yourself constantly. Voice of an epilogue.

VW: *War costs are of two kinds direct and indirect. Direct costs embrace all expenditures made by belligerents in carrying on hostilities. Indirect costs include economic loss from death —*

T: That's a terrible singsong now. Tone has to be colder. But tense.

VW: *War costs are of two kinds direct and —*

T: Perhaps we should time the lips' movements.

VW: *War costs are of two kinds direct and indirect. Direct — no.*

T: You're looking for the tone, that's fatal. Think visionary. Try again from "death."

VW: *. . . death, property damage, reduced production, war relief and the like. For example, direct costs of the European War 1914-1918 are estimated at $186,333,637,097 and indirect costs at —*

T: Keep the tension.

VW [voice rising]: *$151,646,942,560 bringing the total war bill to $337,980,579,657 (calculated in U.S. dollars) for all participants!*

T: Not quite. Remember you feel cold the whole time. Your body too. North wind and night.

VW: How about a cigarette.

T: And not too sad it should under no circumstances sound tragic. Perhaps I'll leave you alone awhile.

VW [walking and whispering]: *Notwithstanding these figures the First World War was fought mainly on credit.*

T: Lip movements should be roughly the same length. In fact one is twenty-two seconds, the other twenty-four.

VW: *Hence the Second World War.*

T: Can we play with that strip of light.

• • •

from **The Beauty of the Husband**
• • •

II. But a Dedication Is Only Felicitous if Performed before Witnesses — It Is an Essentially Public Surrender Like That of Standards of Battle

You know I was married years ago and when he left my husband took my notebooks.
Wirebound notebooks.
You know that cool sly verb *write*. He liked writing, disliked having to start
each thought himself.
Used my starts to various ends, for example in a pocket I found a letter he'd begun
(to his mistress at that time)
containing a phrase I had copied from Homer: 'εντροπαλιζομένη is how Homer says
Andromache went
after she parted from Hektor — "often turning to look back"
she went
down from Troy's tower and through stone streets to her loyal husband's
house and there
with her women raised a lament for a living man in his own halls.
Loyal to nothing
my husband. So why did I love him from early girlhood to late middle age
and the divorce decree came in the mail?
Beauty. No great secret. Not ashamed to say I loved him for his beauty.
As I would again
if he came near. Beauty convinces. You know beauty makes sex possible.
Beauty makes sex sex.
You if anyone grasp this — hush, let's pass

to natural situations.
Other species, which are not poisonous, often have colorations and patterns
similar to poisonous species.
This imitation of a poisonous by a nonpoisonous species is called *mimicry*.
My husband was no mimic.
You will mention of course the war games. I complained to you often enough
when they were here all night

with the boards spread out and rugs and little lamps and cigarettes like Napoleon's tent I suppose,
who could sleep? All in all my husband was a man who knew more
about the Battle of Borodino
than he did about his own wife's body, much more! Tensions poured up the walls and along the ceiling,
sometimes they played Friday night till Monday morning straight through, he and his pale wrathful friends.
They sweated badly. They ate meats of the countries in play.
Jealousy
formed no small part of my relationship to the Battle of Borodino.

I hate it.
Do you.
Why play all night.
The time is real.
It's a game.
It's a real game.
Is that a quote.
Come here.
No.
I need to touch you.
No.
Yes.

That night we made love "the real way" which we had not yet attempted
although married six months.
Big mystery. No one knew where to put their leg and to this day I'm not sure we got it right.
He seemed happy. You're like Venice he said beautifully.
Early next day
I wrote a short talk ("On Defloration") which he stole and had published
in a small quarterly magazine.
Overall this was a characteristic interaction between us.
Or should I say ideal.
Neither of us had ever seen Venice.

• • •

V. Here Is My Propaganda One One One One Oneing on Your Forehead like Droplets of Luminous Sin

Like many a wife I boosted the husband up to Godhood and held him there.
What is strength?
Opposition of friends or family merely toughens it.
I recall my mother's first encounter with him.
Glancing

at a book I'd brought home from school with his name inscribed on the flyleaf
she said
I wouldn't trust anyone who calls himself X — and
something exposed itself in her voice,
a Babel

thrust between us at that instant which we would never
learn to construe —
taste of iron.
Prophetic. Her prophecies all came true although she didn't
mean them to.

Well it's his name I said and put the book away. That was the first night
(I was fifteen)
I raised my bedroom window creak by creak and went out to meet him
in the ravine, traipsing till dawn in the drenched things
and avowals

of the language that is "alone and first in mind." I stood stupid
before it,
watched its old golds and *lieblicher* blues abandon themselves
like peacocks stepping out of cages into an empty kitchen of God.
God

or some blessed royal personage. Napoleon. Hirohito. You know
how novelist Ōe
describes the day Hirohito went on air and spoke
as a mortal man. "The adults sat around the radio
and cried.

Children gathered in the dusty road and whispered bewilderment. Astonished
and disappointed that their emperor had spoken in *a voice*.
Looked at one another in silence. How to believe God had
become human

on a designated summer day?" Less than a year after our marriage
my husband
began to receive calls from [a woman] late at night.
If I answered [she]
hung up. My ears grew hoarse.

How are you.
—
No.
—
Maybe. Eight. Can you.
—
The white oh yes.
—
Yes.

What is so ecstatic unknowable cutthroat glad as the walls
of the flesh
of the voice of betrayal — yet all the while lapped in talk more dull
than the tick of a clock.
A puppy

learns to listen this way. Sting in the silver.
Ōe says
many children were told and some believed that when the war was over
the emperor would wipe away their tears
with his own hand.

VI. To Clean Your Hooves Here Is a Dance in Honor of the Grape Which throughout History Has Been a Symbol of Revelry and Joy Not to Say Analogy for the Bride as Uncut Blossom

Smell
I will never forget.
Out behind the vineyard.
Stone place maybe a shed or an icehouse no longer in use.
October, a little cold. Hay on the floor. We had gone to his grandfather's farm to help

crush
the grapes for wine.
You cannot imagine the feeling if you have never done it —
like hard bulbs of wet red satin exploding under your feet,
between your toes and up your legs arms face splashing everywhere —
It goes right through your clothes you know he said as we slogged up and down

in the vat.
When you take them off
you'll have juice all over.
His eyes moved onto me then he said Let's check.
Naked in the stone place it was true, sticky stains, skin, I lay on the hay

and he licked.
Licked it off.
Ran out and got more dregs in his hands and smeared
it on my knees neck belly licking. Plucking. Diving.
Tongue is the smell of October to me. I remember it as
swimming in a fast river for I kept moving and it was hard to move

while all around me
was moving too, that smell
of turned earth and cold plants and night coming on and
the old vat steaming slightly in the dusk out there and him,

raw juice on him.
Stamens on him
and as Kafka said in the end
my swimming was of no use to me you know I cannot swim after all.

Well it so happens more than 90% of all cultivated grapes are varieties of

Vitis vinifera
the Old World or European grape,
while native American grapes derive
from certain wild species of *Vitis* and differ in their "foxy" odor
as well as the fact that their skins slip so liquidly from the pulp.

An ideal wine grape
is one that is easily crushed.
Such things I learned from the grandfather
when we sat in the kitchen late at night cracking chestnuts.
Also that I should under no circumstances marry his grandson
whom he called *tragikos* a country word meaning either tragic or goat.
• • •

Short Talk on Defloration

The actions of life are not so many. To go in, to go, to go in secret, to cross the bridge of sighs. And when you dishonoured me, I saw that dishonour is an action. It happened in Venice, it causes the vocal chords to swell. I went booming through Venice, under and over the bridges, but you were gone. Later that day I telephoned your brother. What's wrong with your voice? he said.

Francis Catalano

Vus d'en bas les toits de tuiles
incurvées ont l'aspect flou
du homard au fond de l'eau, sa vulnérabilité,
sa couleur terre cuite,
d'ici on dirait qu'au moindre péril
ce qui abrite s'abrite aussi.
Au pied de la fixité, au pas des portails,
les antennules les voir
courber, plier, tendre dans l'onde
sens dessus dessous
alors qu'à l'aube des premières émissions
les antennes télé se frôlent
là-haut sur des toitures.

néo-libéralisme à clavier
(aire de rapprochement de deux solitudes)

to continue in English, say english.
— français
— je suis caroline, votre assistante automatisée. pour obtenir de l'aide, dites : << assistance >>. autrement, dites-moi simplement la raison de votre appel et je vous dirigerai au bon endroit. alors, comment puis-je vous aider?
— ... !
— ce système permet de vous exprimer naturellement au moyen de courtes phrases. pour que je puisse vois diriger rapidement au bon endroit, dites-moi simplement en vos propres mots la raison pour laquelle vous appelez. alors, comment puis-je vous aider?

— assistance ?
— je m'explique, ce système permet de vous exprimer naturellement au moyen de courtes phrases. par exemple, vous pouvez dire : << quel est le solde de mon compte >>, <<je voudrais de l'information sur les forfaits >> ou << je déménage >>. alors, allons-y, quelle est la raison de votre appel?
— je voudrais m'exprimer avec mes propres mots.
— désolé, je n'ai pas compris.
— . . .
— je crois comprendre que vous avez de la difficulté à recevoir des appels. si vous appellez d'un téléphone à cadran, restez en ligne.
— je voudrais m'exprimer avec mes propres mots.
— . . .
— . . .
— s'il vous plaît, veuillez raccrocher.

∽

Les idées fondent comme du beurre dans la poêle
un fond de fumée sur quoi
faire revenir la viande
un steak avec ses nerfs, son gras
si seulement ils avaient la même fortune
que les hamburgers ou les hot-dogs
une nouvelle génération de steaks-idées
qui mastiquerait depuis l'assiette
le visage des convives.

∽

Amérique terre archaïque
sable sans sablier
Amérique du Nord Amérique du Nom
fragment de Pangée qui avance où s'étalent
ses pierres lentement
scellée à un secret lithique la Laurentia déroule
son granit convoyeur d'elle-même
qu'éventre le dos des océans
par l'ajour d'un casse-tête les yeux plissés je scrute
le continent qui se démantèle
dérive à l'emporte-pièce c'est un charroi
à plat ventre à outrance
basalte grinçant puisque raclé à fond
c'est une infra-Amérique et son Nord plonge
cap premier dans l'équateur
encastrements au modelé des gerbes minérales
plaques inféodées à leur hésitante marche
nuptiale martiale tels les os
d'un crâne fracturé dont les cals
s'ajustent s'adjoignent poussent
— *à la vitesse des cheveux*
sur la tête abîmée d'un convalescent

Homo lupus est
et Wolfe et Montcalm glissés
dans leur uniforme assorti
de médailles à venir
à pas feutrés passent
de la bergerie au champ de bataille.
Tels des Moïses apatrides
égarés sur les plaines d'Abraham
les deux généraux succombent
— *dans un nuage*
de fumée monosémique.
Sans perdre leur calme
les troupes des deux camps
abattent la besogne.
Agenouillement, en position de tir
l'étau se resserre
et les fantassins tombent
un à un
— *spirales sur l'herbe*
pelures de pommes pelées.

Herménégilde Chiasson

de Répertoire

1

une vrille neuve pour faire des trous dans le plâtre
la lumière luisant sur le métal
son poids sa densité
ma crainte de l'ébrécher de la salir
les excuses engendrant une destruction du monde

2

une vis munie d'un papillon de métal
la difficulté pour l'enfoncer dans le mur
l'oubli de la passer dans l'objet à retenir
ma résignation à l'idée de cette perte
le temps nécessaire à l'abandon définitif

3

un tableau d'affichage
la porosité de la composition
les clous enfoncés à même les doigts
les images qu'on déplace sans ordre précis
l'art de s'arrêter quand tout a été dit tout a été fait

4

une pointe en étoile pour tourne-vis électrique
la perte constante de l'objet
le lit où elle s'égare continuellement
l'inconscience de la mémoire pour le retrouver
la poursuite des mêmes erreurs

5

des boucles de ruban gommé pour poser des affiches
déplacer ainsi la rumeur du monde
inscrire des faire-part
laisser manger ceux qui s'abritent du froid
comme si le lustre des surfaces ne nous importait pas

6

une image enveloppée dans du papier kraft
seul dans un coin s'inclinant dans l'ombre
les mots sincères surgissant de la texture
on parlait d'une autre époque autrement plus prospère
et l'ange passa sa main sur leur front

7

un chapeau en feutre fantaisiste dans une friperie
dans cette tête tant de douleur si mal contenue
la mélodie qui les avait réunis jouait partout
ils formaient tous les trois un drôle de trio
sur la lame des amitiés fragiles et des amours perdues

8

un ange découpé dans une feuille de métal rouillée
on aurait dit un démon échevelé
une mauvaise nouvelle tombée du ciel
un autre objet à reclouer au mur
toutes les deux voulaient à tout prix qu'il s'envole

• • •

101

un tourne-vis antique au manche en bois fendu
retour au désarroi des peines d'amour de jadis
son rire résonnant dans l'univers jaune
ils n'étaient plus qu'eux deux et lui s'en allait
trajet approximatif de l'affection

102

un pansement imbibé de sang
regard sur la cause profonde de toute agression
un sein palpitant de propreté sous l'uniforme empesé
des yeux d'une beauté inestimable au milieu du masque
dans une autre vie oui j'avoue

103

une fourchette de plastique
des histoires d'empoisonnement industriel
la voix d'un enfant qui remercie quelqu'un
le malentendu qui régit désormais vos vies
d'autres histoires diffusées de la forteresse

104

l'odeur d'un diluant à peinture
la mauvaise nouvelle s'infiltrant par les égratignures
une marée rouge comme la préhistoire
le temps de s'en aller le monde étiré à sa fin
heureusement qu'il en restera des images

105

un ensemble de tubes d'aquarelle
la maison en bois où il a fini par s'ennuyer
un trafic d'été et cet amour inavouable
la chambre d'hôtel où il chantait le jour de sa fête
elle s'en allait dans la grisaille si lentement

106

un ruban rouge autour d'un paquet de cartes de souhait
le lieu où chaque mur est un mot d'amour
les animaux endormis sur les planchers boisés
les arbres lumineux constellés d'ampoules
celui qui quitte qui s'en inquiète

107

un sac de vidanges
des lettres et des fils de fer
cette couleur des prospectus qu'il ne regardait même pas
un envahissement
au soir tombant seul comme un ogre il grognait

108

de la poussière accumulée au plancher
les lutins et toute la magie des contes de fées
cette femme qui dort engloutie dans son sommeil
ce livre qui revient le hanter de son enfance
cette vraie fatigue c'est bien autre chose

. . .

201

de la neige dans le halo d'une lumière au mercure
il faisait si noir et elle se perdait dans le blanc
ses mots d'esprit qui ne lui servent plus à rien
son incessant combat ses spasmes d'insomnie
des confettis comme son cœur en miettes

202

un bout de câble de fibres optiques
des conversations d'une solitude extrême
s'imaginant fragile et tassé dans le nerf du monde
vulnérable sous son enveloppe incertaine
même les injures finiront par passer

203

un rouleau de ruban de cellophane
quelqu'un court en plein hiver à ta rencontre
une vision norvégienne dans un décor de sucre d'orge
ce soir nous dormirons dans un conte de fées
ce qu'il faut pour garder nos rêves

204

de la pâte à barbe dans un évier de cuisine
le sifflement tragique derrière le miroir
le vol d'une tempête sur nos têtes
le noir de la nuit s'estompe
il fait matin il fait jour

205

une pierre dans le plancher
l'été quand ils regardaient la mer ensemble
ses yeux posés contre le roc et sa bouche pleine d'amour
elle avait fait du ciel son moment magique
une porte ouverte à jamais

206

de la peinture dans un verre à boire
dans les fleurs où son audace se répand
l'herbe bleue le lac dans la montagne rouge
l'arbre poussant sur le toit du monde et l'ange
celui que vole les ailes en feu effaçant tout du doigt

207

un poème sur un t-shirt
le registre négatif de la politesse
le besoin indéniable de repréciser l'exil
le déplacement imperceptible de la vengeance
tout ça écrit dans le dos

208

du lait dans un bol de céréales
autrefois perché sur les bancs de neige
la pente abrupte d'une enfance en chute libre
la brutalité des matins et le sommeil insurmontable
dehors l'immensité se poursuit

. . .

301

de l'eau froide dans un verre à bière
du haut de la forteresse l'agrandissement du monde
la blessure se fermant près du glaive
il a fait soleil et nous savons que bientôt l'été sera ici
malheur à ceux qui doutent de l'eau

302

un carrousel de diapositives
images fugitives du temps passé
ces gens en robes qui s'improvisent
instants perdus dans des sels d'argent
les chevaux et leurs cavalières d'autrefois

303

le voyant lumineux indiquant le plein d'essence
une dérive toute floue dans le vague anglophone
un visage plein de colère dans un carré de frimas
un avion se pose dans la glace de notre mémoire
ma vie inquiète son icône clignotant dans la nuit

304

une brosse à cheveux au manche en plastique rouge
une rivière ondoyante une tempête de sable
le regard qui blesse la tête qui explose
des fils d'argent entre ses doigts
sa colère son camouflage

305

des fleurs rouges brodées dans du satin bleu
la marche intense des souvenirs enfuis
le tissu qui pâlissait fragilement
ses yeux bien trop bleus
continuellement

306

une bouteille de correcteur liquide
jadis la nudité criant par les fenêtres ouvertes
jadis pleurant dans une voiture la perte d'un autre amour
jadis le cri désespéré de l'oiseau pris au piège
maintenant tout redevient si blanc

307

un cartable à couverture rigide
toute détente sera sévèrement blâmée
le rire devrait pouvoir se calculer autrement
les instants perdus seront repris à une date ultérieure
nous accomplirons une œuvre hors du commun

308

un biscuit aux graines de sésame
émerger du sommeil les yeux recroquevillés
n'avoir qu'un seul projet en tête
faire en sorte que le monde reste un mystère
et manger encore par habitude

• • •

401

des livres empilés dans une armoire de verre
le repaire de l'ogre ses yeux rabougris et malheureux
elle avait déposé sa beauté près de lui
le grognement de celui qui faisait trembler les arbres
personne ne lit plus ces textes que par devoir

402

les sièges rouges d'un amphithéâtre
l'image tremble et elle s'est assise derrière
debout il a vu une ombre se lever
très floue à peine s'il a bougé la tête
le film s'est déchiré et elle s'est enfuie

403

une petite boîte de métal d'un assortiment de thé
un exotisme de pacotille pénétrait son œsophage
la toux envahissait la maison rauque et gutturale
la fontaine de cheveux dorés où il s'en irait boire
la boîte ouverte les sortilèges menaçants presque

404

le son répétitif d'une enregistreuse-cassettes
raconter sa vie circuler dans la plénitude de l'enfance
ceux qui ne disent rien ceux qui oublieront
reprendre une autre fois ce qui a fini par se cristalliser
je ne sais rien dire je ne fais que me répéter

405

des armatures de métal pour tenir des panneaux de bois
après les douches les antichambres de la vertu
des femmes qui parlent à tue-tête
un refuge mystérieux
quand il n'y a rien d'autre que du silence ou si peu à dire

406

un paravent incrusté de motifs de jade
la dureté du langage et la joie de redire
mordre dans les mots et faire semblant
nous avons essayé de percer le mystère
une surface lisse froide et impénétrable

407

le goût de la coriandre dans une soupe thaïlandaise
le son de leur exil nous frappait en plein cœur
le son aigu de leurs voix jusqu'à la nausée
une épopée pénétrant jusqu'au cœur
l'espace épuisant l'amour perdu

408

un foulard de soie à rayures et à pois rouges
je t'ai imaginée en cramoisi
je pensais à toi dans cette couleur
plus tard il y aura une tempête de sucre
réunis autour d'une même table à s'attendre

George Elliott Clarke

Identity I

Rue: My colour is guttural.
I was born in lachrymose air.

My face makes a mess of light:
It's like a black splinter lancing snow.

I'm negative, but positive with a knife.
My instinct? Is to damage someone.

My words collide with walls of fists,
Collapse, my teeth clacking like typewriters.

The encyclopedias encourage rape;
Murder lunges — sable genie — out the radio.

So what? So what? So what? So?
Am I the only nigger in this province with a pistol?

What I am
Cannot be dreamt

By anyone
Imperfect as you.

Child Hood I

Geo: Pops beat Ma with belts, branches, bottles.
Anything left-handed. Anything at all.
He'd buck Ma onto the bed, buckle his hips to hers.
Slap her across her breasts, blacken them.

Rue: Her terrorized-and tear-shaped breasts.

He thought her being Mulatto
Was mutilation.

(I miss peanut butter cookies, her sewing machine, the grey gloves
she let me present to a schoolgirl, her preacher-lover-dad's second-
hand Shakespeare and tattered scripture she taught me to read, her
confusingly cream-coloured breasts stupefying dazzling under the
threadbare black disintegrating nightshirt she wore to spoonfeed me
oatmeal.)

Geo: Pops smashed Ma like she was Joe Louis.
Stuck a razor to her throat. Struck her down,
pelted soft flesh with fists and bricks.

Rue: I swung a two-by-four and bust Pop's face open.
Kicked the iron bone that was his skull:
Bleeding was so bad I knelt by the stove like I was praying.
I wanted to be God. I wanted him dead.

Geo: Ma fainted scrubbin some white house's blackened crap-box.
She got a heart stoppage and drooped, *kaput*.

Rue: Years, our only real emotion was hunger.
Our thin bellies had to take rain for bread.

Reading Titus Andronicus *in Three Mile Plains, N.S.*

Rue: When Witnesses sat before Bibles open like plates
And spat sour sermons of interposition and nullification,
While burr-orchards vomited bushels of thorns, and leaves
Rattled like uprooted skull-teeth across rough highways,
And stars ejected brutal, serrated, heart-shredding light,
And dark brothers lied down, *quare*, in government graves,
Their white skulls jabbering amid farmer's dead flowers —
The junked geraniums and broken truths of car engines,
And *History* snapped its whip and bankrupted scholars,
School was violent improvement. I opened Shakespeare
And discovered a scarepriest, shaking in violent winds,

Some hallowed, heartless man, his brain boiling blood,
Aaron, seething, demanding, "Is black so base a hue?"
And shouting, "Coal-black refutes and foils any other hue
In that it scorns to bear another hue." O! Listen at that!
I listen, flummoxed, for language cometh volatile,
Each line burning, and unslaked *Vengeance* reddens rivers.
I see that, notwithstanding hosts of buds, the sultry cumuli
Of petals, greatening like the pluvial light in Turner's great
Paintings, the wind hovers — like a death sentence — over
Fields, chilling us with mortality recalcitrant. (Hear now
The worm-sighing waves.) *Sit fas aut nefas,* I am become
Aaron, desiring poisoned lilies and burning, staggered air,
A King James God, spitting fire, brimstone, leprosy, cancers,
Dreaming of tearing down stars and letting grass incinerate
Pale citizens' prized bones. What should they mean to me?
A plough rots, returns to ore; weeds snatch it back to earth;
The stones of the sanctuaries pour out onto every street.
Like drastic Aaron's heir, Nat Turner, I's natural homicidal:
My pages blaze, my lines pall, crying fratricidal damnation.

Duet

India: Yesterday, I traipsed through an apple orchard
and bit flesh elegantly named "Rosie de Cliej" —
lovely, small, and sweet. So wonderfully healing,
strolling with baskets of apples, a paring knife
in one hand, sharing slices with strangers . . .
I glimpsed a different side of Eve, of Eden.

Rue: I treasure the pleasure of your hands on my back,
your face stirring the heavens to a broth of stars.
Let me kiss your plum lips under plum blossoms,
show you the river cocking through this valley.

India: Wish you were here to taste my "Rosie," "Gala," and "Luck."
I miss the cool ceramic smoothness of your shoulder.

I miss the scent of apple blossoms in the field
and the scent of apple blossoms in our hair —
especially me confusing the two:
The delicate flesh smell of apple blossoms — or whose flesh?

Rue: You move soft — too soft to resist — against resistance.
Look! Your April perfume is still locked, rose madder, in my shirt.

India: Let the moon fall, full throttle, into seas,
lightning, scrunched up, quake into windows.
August wafts a cathedral over us.

Rue: Open your gold mine — suave dark shaft
cream wet with jewelled love — beneath me,
so I'll mine and mine, staking fierce claim,
your kisses puttering rapturous about my face.

India: Why should our talk be like two birds in separate cages?

Hard Nails

Geo: Hard nails split my frail bones;
Hard nails gouge my tomb from stone.
Hard nails pierce my feet and hands,
Tack me down so I can't stand.

Hard nails scratch my frail skin;
Hard nails fasten us chin to chin.
Hard nails I want, hard nails I lack —
Her fingernails ploughin my back.

Drench me down with rum and Coca-Cola.
The gal I kiss be a pretty pretty colour.
I ain't got a dollar, but I ain't got no dolour.
Drench me down with rum and Coca-Cola.

Spree

Rue: .45s smashing into The Palette Restaurant, we corral screaming
swine in a radio-shrieking and ammonia-reeking right-angle, vicious;
smell white money stench on a bitch plus her viscous pimp.

(Hum of money prepared in banks succumbs
to hubbub of coins now brained in the till.)

Gun swats *thap!* up gainst his greasy skull and he tanks —
and she drops slinkily after him, like silk excrement, and I kick
his wallet out his ass pocket, *wallop!* getting farts —
vodka snorting from bad bowels,
while his dame screeches, and Georgie, giggling,
rips her pearls off her craning neck
and the little white balls bullet everywhere.

Bleeding in Nova Scotia is just like drinking.

Trial II

Rue: This courtroom's a parliament of jackals —
see Hitler faces front dark robes.

Unsullied, though, a wafer of light silvers water;
unspoiled, the wind rattles alders.

    I would like very much to sing —
in a new life, a new world,
some April song —
"A slight dusting of snow,
the indigo dawn hovers —
and we sweeten in our love,"
yes, something like that,
but blood must expunge, sponge up, blood.

We're condemned because death is not condemned.
We're damned because desire is not damned.

Stars are hanging like locusts in the trees.

Birds faction the air.

April collapses snow into flowers.

The river goes cloudy with moon.

Look Homeward, Exile

I can still see that soil crimsoned by butchered
Hog and imbrued with rye, lye, and homely
Spirituals everybody must know,
Still dream of folks who broke or cracked like shale:
Pushkin, who twisted his hands in boxing,
Marrocco, who ran girls like dogs and got stabbed,
Lavinia, her teeth decayed to black stumps,
Her lovemaking still in demand, spitting
Black phlegm — her pension after twenty towns,
And Toof, suckled on anger that no Baptist
Church could contain, who let wrinkled Eely
Seed her moist womb when she was just thirteen.
    And the tyrant sun that reared from barbed-wire
Spewed flame that charred the idiot crops
To Depression, and hurt my granddaddy
To bottle after bottle of sweet death,
His dreams beaten to one, tremendous pulp,
Until his heart seized, choked; his love gave out.
    But Beauty survived, secreted
In freight trains snorting in their pens, in babes
Whose faces were coal-black mirrors, in strange
Strummers who plucked Ghanaian banjos, hummed
Blind blues — precise, ornate, rich needlepoint,
In sermons scorched with sulphur and brimstone,
And in my love's dark, orient skin that smelled
Like orange peels and tasted like rum, good God!
    I remember my Creator in the old ways:

I sit in taverns and stare at my fists;
I knead earth into bread, spell water into wine.
Still, nothing warms my wintry exile — neither
Prayers nor fine love, neither votes nor hard drink:
For nothing heals those saints felled in green beds,
Whose loves are smashed by just one word or glance
Or pain — a screw jammed in thick, straining wood.

Four Guitars

Pushkin, Othello, and Pablo gather in the livingroom coral reef, under a sea of sunshine, to perform improv music (no note knowing where the next is going to or coming from). They lean over their guitars like accountants studying thick ledgers.

    Casting half-notes, thirds, and quarter-notes that stretch music like putty, Puskin opens the concert. He bends the long metre of Baptist hymns into infernal hollers that true Baptists are sure the wicked Anglicans and Catholics enjoy behind the dark doors of their temples. From "If All the World Were Apple Pie," a nursery rhyme, he dredges sedimentary notes laden with a sorrow as rich as that felt by Schliemann who discovered Troy because he was looking for love and the lost city got in his way.

    Desperate for his own private sound, Pushkin once crafted a banjo from a frying pan and four pieces of string. Favouring *E* or *A* notes, plucking them — luscious fruit, heavy with memory and tears — from his American Martin guitar, he stands before us now, revelling in an *abb* rhyme scheme, the cadence of decadence:

> *April rain snows white and cold,*
> *I feel so goddamn scared.*
> *You could've loved me if you'd dared.*
> *Were you waitin' to get old?*
> *Why did you act so weird?*
> *You loved me like you never cared!*

Next, he plumbs the depths of bottomless love, "Don't do me evil / If you want the sun to shine," holding a breadknife against the throat of the guitar, forcing forth bastard slurs and mongrel fluctuations, a lover's midnight moans. He slides his stopping finger on the string, contrasting long notes with quick arpeggios, then backs into "Black Liquor" with fierce fluidity. Forgetting that his hands are warped, he plays, plagued by the currency of the radio cantos of Ezra "Epopee" Pound: *I love my baby, love her to the bone.* Like Don Messer and his Famous Islanders, Pushkin cannibalizes cacophony. When he attains zen-silence, hullabaloo collapses the room. He empties a bottle — a backward song — down his throat, smiles like sudden, brilliant snow.

Lean Othello follows the sweating giant, steps into the wake of his lilt and the still fluttering applause. He snatches his Dobro-chrome, steel-bodied guitar, tunes it Sebastopol style, dreaming that that's where William Hall won the Victoria Cross more than a hundred years ago. O chooses "Hurry Down, Sunshine," then discards it because the room is bright enough. He selects, to a chorus of whoops and thigh slaps, "Black Water Blues." He lays the guitar gently across his hips, presses the supine strings with a tall, brown bottle, and plays, thus sending quirky notes, tottering like drunken flowers, into the air. In the corner, Pushkin gasps, "Ooh!" O's artistry is that fine. His elegant left-hand figures, instrumental algebra, merge with his rough, dark voice:

I bought ya red, red, calico:
mmmmmmm, ya didn't love me though.

Moon burnt the blue sky orange;
not ripe, plucked stars tasted green.
In its hard bed, the river tossed, black.

God made everyone with a need to love;
wonder who ya be thinkin' of?

His waterfall-hands cascade across the strings, leave, behind the glistening notes, a dark, inarticulate silence.

Unable to restrain himself, Pablo tunes his flamenco guitar Spanish style, nudging O into a Latinate version of "I bes troubled." Pablo contributes his exotic expertise, his Moorish sense to that spiritual salvaged from two centuries of bad luck. His music tastes of three little feelings: saltiness, bitterness, and sweetness. Reminiscing in tempo, Othello pursues Pablo's anxious influence. Stressing static sadness by inverting the scale of flattened third and seventh degrees, they distort prettily Robert Johnson's classic blues, "Hell Hound."

Suddenly, Pablo discovers music drowned in a seashell and raises it, sounding as polished and suave as the clear, hairless limbs of the Chinese, Spanish, and Jamaican women he loves, women with indigent breasts, shell-smooth skin, and opulent thighs. While he plays, Sixhiboux River shimmies silver through the hills, lindys beneath the bridge, and jitters into Saint Mary's Bay. He uncaps a bottle of Keith's India Pale Ale, *brewed the same way for a hundred years*, and nods in the direction of *Nisan*:

> *Thirty days of daffodils,*
> *Lilies, and chrysanthemums,*
> *Open with snowy petals*
> *And close with apple blossoms.*

O follows, remembering the lost music of sub-Saharan Africa and trying to perfect the blues.

When this chance duet fades, leaving clear notes hanging, untended, in the air, Missy barges in, panting, yammers, "Quit the gentle mercies and the delicate fears! God expects truth, not entertainment!" She unfolds a dark mandolin, rich, smelling of drenched forests, then jumbles the room into shape around her, juggling it so it becomes circular, curling around her curves. "Who's got a cigar box and string? A diddley bow?" Silence. Then, Pushkin, his breath renewed, manifests a ten-hole, twenty-reed, Marine Band harmonica, commences to mock a train, a historic freight, stuffed with Southern sunflowers, Mississippi magnolias. Missy adopts Poor Girl tuning, mumbles her debt to Bessie Smith and Amy "Big Mama" Lowell, booms, "I've got Ford engine movements in my hips."

I look outside. The sun has turned inside out. Moonlight lacquers the world. Black bliss. Missy trolls an immortal song:

> *Come and love me, darling one,*
> *In sweetest April rain.*
> *Kiss me until life is done:*
> *Youth will not come again.*

Night Train

The lean, livid engine plunges through night.
I almost feel moist softness — rain's sheer silk:
A crow wallows in this wet, cool pleasure
Like a man in his tomb, stricken numb, dumb,
By soil, its cool clench, sexual pressure.
I hug cigarette smoke, anticipate
Selah, her dark face upturned full of stars,
Her love's squeezed cotton and muscle. The town
Pulls tight. The train shudders. A sweet spasm.

Blues for X

Pretty boy, towel your tears,
And robe yourself in black.
Pretty boy, dry your tears,
You know I'm comin' back.
I'm your lavish lover
And I'm slavish in the sack.

Call me Sweet Potato,
Sweet Pea, or Sweety Pie,
There's sugar on my lips
And honey in my thighs.
Jos'phine Baker bakes beans,
But I stew pigtails in rye.

My bones are guitar strings
And blues the chords you strum.
My bones are slender flutes
And blues the bars you hum.
You wanna stay my man,
Serve me whisky when I come.

Rev. F. R. Langford's Miracle

Lightning scratches the oily sky with fire,
Trembles, troubles, the dark white church; apple
Blossoms sag; lumberyard falls mute. Icy
Rain strikes; snow-robed Baptists cringe, cry, scrabble
With soaked hymns, down the quagmired logging trail.
But Reverend Langford faces the storm
And, cyclone-muscular, pine-tall, plunges,
Forces his fierce horse through wet violence.
    Back to that conjurer, Eely, who nursed
With snakes, Langford surges, moors the pitching
Horse at the black cabin, squelches through muck,
And yells for strength to part a kept darkness.
Eely hisses; rain freely floods his cave.
Yelling God words, Langford rips a curtain,
The sun leaps forth. And eyes pleasure to see
The rain becalmed in wine bottles and wells.

A Sermon to the Undecided

Sinners, hear the loud sun cryin' awake with freight train howl 'cos it'll be a bit like that when great Christ come cleavin' the cloudy air to thunder love all over His precious Creation. I wanna tell you, 'cos God don't lie, that Christ is gonna catch the scarlet and purple women and the prophesyin' drunkards by surprise. Yep! When they be playin' poker, gigglin' and tee-heein' all night, they won't notice the Sun glarin' at 'em 'til it's too late and they is proved palpable fools.

    How you'll be, boy, when you spy the King of Glory, brighter than the high-noon river, through rum-yellowed eyes? Will you just stumble, mumble, pass out? King Jesus says, "Woe unto you!" And how'll you be, girl? Will you be shoutin' "Hallelujah!" with scandal kisses stainin' your wine-purpled lips? Woe unto you!

    Children of God, doncha know that your every breath drags through dirt? Doncha know that death overshadows you? All you want are barbecues and holidays. You don't want the House of God. You complain about this mouldy bread and the watered-down wine. You say that this commandment is too hard, this commitment too much. I say: Dirty your knees in the worship of the Lord!

Little children, get right with King Jesus! Olive Christ ain't lynched or nailed to stiff lumber. Christ is mighty! Sinners'll spy 'im by the Sixhiboux tramplin' down the lumber kings. They'll spy 'im descendin' over the sawmill, inspiring holy horror. What good will runnin' do? You can run to them Boston States, but you can't run from your sinful self!

Preach out your Bible! God says, "Love one another." Love satisfies. Love is the only thing that can't be oppressed. If any try to deny love, why, that's when the stones would tear free from their graves and howl disgust at our implicit trusts! You gotta feel love, live it, and make it true. It's not enough to be in the right church, you gotta be in the right pew!

Sinners, come home to King Jesus! Remember gold streets, sweet pastures, and doves by the river of waters. Come home, little children, to that land of milk and honey, where you don't need no passport or money. Come home!

We're gonna shine in the fiery storm;
We're gonna dance on the starry shore;
We're gonna shout Christ's gloried name;
Praise God! None of us will be the same!

The Sermon of Liana

A silver Sixhiboux, the Gospel glints.
Langford stakes the Bible, sights lustrous ore,
Flustering gems. Mining, he finds that Christ,
A carpenter, made lumber hiss its lust
For air, riveted rain to riverbeds.
Langford lectures, "In the name of Heaven . . ."
But forgets the other names for heaven —
Daisy, lily, the River Sixhiboux,
Or even Liana and Langford.
   Once he completes, pebbles and boulders burst
Into blossom, lifelong drunkards sober,
The brilliant sun centres, brands him with light.
Yet, he's blinded by words, can't see that love
Is all that created and keeps our world.

Leonard Cohen

Paris again
the great Mouth Culture
oysters and cheese
explanations to everyone

Too Old

I am too old
to learn the names
of the new killers
This one here
looks tired and attractive
devoted, professorial
He looks a lot like me
when I was teaching
a radical form of Buddhism
to the hopelessly insane
In the name of the old
high magic
he commands
families to be burned alive
and children mutilated
He probably knows
a song or two that I wrote
All of them
all the bloody hand bathers
and the chewers of entrails
and the scalp peelers
they all danced
to the music of the Beatles
they worshipped Bob Dylan
Dear friends
there are very few of us left
silenced

trembling all the time
hidden among the blood —
stunned fanatics
as we witness to each other
the old atrocity
the old obsolete atrocity
that has driven out
the heart's warm appetite
and humbled evolution
and made a puke of prayer

Layton's Question

Always after I tell him
what I intend to do next,
Layton solemnly inquires:
Leonard, are you sure
you're doing the wrong thing?

Robert Appears Again

Well, Robert, here you are again talking to me at the Café de Flore in Paris. I haven't seen you for a while. I have several versions of that sonnet I wrote after your death but I never got it right. I love you, Robert, I still do. You were an interesting man, and the first friend I really quarrelled with. I'm slightly stoned on half-a-tab of speed I found in this old suit, it must be twenty years old, and I took it with a glass of orange juice. It couldn't possibly work after all this time, but here we are, talking again. I'm glad you don't tell me what it's like where you are because I have no interest in the afterlife. You're a little pissed off as usual, as if you've just come from something immensely boring. Here we are, talking about the lousy deal we negotiated for ourselves. What are you saying? Why are you smiling? I'm still working hard, Robert. I can't seem to bring anything to completion and I'm in real trouble. The speed is wearing off, or the mood, and I can't tell you an amusing story about my trouble, but you know what I mean. Of all my friends you know what I mean. Well, goodbye, Robert, and fuck you too. Your disembodied status entitles you to a lot of privileges, but you might have excused yourself before disappearing again for who knows how long.

Pardon Me

Pardon me, lords and ladies,
if I do not think of myself
as the disease.
Pardon me if I receive the Holy Spirit
without telling you about it.
Pardon me,
Commissars of the West,
if you do not think
I have suffered enough.

The Party Was Over Then Too

When I was about fifteen
I followed a beautiful girl
into the Communist Party of Canada.
There were secret meetings
and you got yelled at
if you were a minute late.
We studied the McCarran Act
passed by the stooges in Washington
and the Padlock Law
passed by their lackeys in colonized Quebec;
and they said nasty shit
about my family
and how we got our money.
They wanted to overthrow
the country that I loved

(and served, as a Sea Scout).
And even the good people
who wanted to change things,
they hated them too
and called them social fascists.
They had plans for criminals
like my uncles and aunties
and they even had plans
for my poor little mother
who had slipped out of Lithuania
with two frozen apples
and a bandana full of monopoly money.
They never let me get near the girl
and the girl never let me get near the girl.
She became more and more beautiful
until she married a lawyer
and became a social fascist herself
and very likely a criminal too.
But I admired the Communists
for their pig-headed devotion
to something absolutely wrong.
It was years before I found
something comparable for myself:
I joined a tiny band of steel-jawed zealots
who considered themselves
the Marines of the spiritual world.
It's just a matter of time:
We'll be landing this raft
on the Other Shore.
We'll be taking that beach
on the Other Shore.

Butter Dish

Darling, I now have a butter dish
that is shaped like a cow.

The Collapse of Zen

When I can wedge my face
into the place
and struggle with my breathing
as she brings her eager fingers down
      to separate herself,
to help me use my whole mouth
against her hungriness,
      her most private of hungers —
why should I want to be enlightened?
Is there something that I missed?
Have I forgotten yesterday's mosquito
or tomorrow's hungry ghost?

When I can roam this hill with a knife in my back
caused by too much drinking of Chateau Latour
and spill my heart into the valley
      of the lights of Caguas
and freeze in fear as the watchdog
comes drooling out of the bushes
and refuses to recognize me
and there we are, yes, bewildered
as to who should kill the other first —
and I move and it moves,
and it moves and I move,
why should I want to be enlightened?
Did I leave something out?
Was there some world I failed to embrace?
Some bone I didn't steal?

When Jesus loves me so much that blood
      comes out of his heart
and I climb a metal ladder
into the hole in his bosom
which is caused by sorrow as big as China
and I enter the innermost room wearing white clothes
and I entreat and I plead:
"Not this one, Sir. Not that one, Sir. I beg you, Sir."

and I look through His eyes
as the helpless are shit on again
and the tender blooming nipple of mankind
is caught in the pincers
of power and muscle and money —
why should I seek enlightenment?
Did I fail to recognize some cockroach?
Some vermin in the ooze of my majesty?

When "men are stupid and women are crazy"
and everyone is asleep in San Juan and Caguas
and everyone is in love but me
and everyone has a religion and a boyfriend
and a great genius for loneliness —

When I can dribble over all the universes
and undress a woman without touching her
and run errands for my urine
         and offer my huge silver shoulders
to the pinhead moon —
When my heart is broken as usual
over someone's evanescent beauty
and design after design
they fade like kingdoms with no writing
and, look, I wheeze my way
up to the station of Sahara's
         incomparable privacy
and churn the air into a dark cocoon
of effortless forgetting —
why should I shiver on the altar of enlightenment?
why should I want to smile forever?

~

Oh and one more thing
You aren't going to like
what comes after America

A Note to the Chinese Reader

Dear Reader,

Thank you for coming to this book. It is an honour, and a surprise, to have the frenzied thoughts of my youth expressed in Chinese characters. I sincerely appreciate the efforts of the translator and the publishers in bringing this curious work to your attention. I hope you will find it useful or amusing.

When I was young, my friends and I read and admired the old Chinese poets. Our ideas of love and friendship, of wine and distance, of poetry itself, were much affected by those ancient songs. Much later, during the years when I practised as a Zen monk under the guidance of my teacher Kyozan Joshu Roshi, the thrilling sermons of Lin Chi (Rinzai) were studied every day. So you can understand, Dear Reader, how privileged I feel to be able to graze, even for a moment, and with such meagre credentials, on the outskirts of your tradition.

This is a difficult book, even in English, if it is taken too seriously. May I suggest that you skip over the parts you don't like? Dip into it here and there. Perhaps there will be a passage, or even a page, that resonates with your curiosity. After a while, if you are sufficiently bored or unemployed, you may want to read it from cover to cover. In any case, I thank you for your interest in this odd collection of jazz riffs, pop-art jokes, religious kitsch and muffled prayer, an interest which indicates, to my thinking, a rather reckless, though very touching, generosity on your part.

Beautiful Losers was written outside, on a table set among the rocks, weeds and daisies, behind my house on Hydra, an island in the Aegean Sea. I lived there many years ago. It was a blazing hot summer. I never covered my head. What you have in your hands is more of a sunstroke than a book.

Dear Reader, please forgive me if I have wasted your time.

Don Coles

Kingdom
for Luke

Around six, six-thirty these late winter days
I'm usually walking home across Lawrence fields,
couple of blocks from here. Make a point
of checking on the rink, the afternoon hockey guys
finished now and the last light fading off it,
though you can easily spot the gone-silent
sprayed brakings and prodigal wheelings incised
on the glow. I like it best when the Zamboni's
out there doing its ignored choreography,
blue lights glittering and the kid's dark head
turning to neither one side nor the other, just
intent on getting it right. Around one end and
up the middle and peel off, down the side
and up the pure broadening middle again,
lights glittering, kid's silhouette watching ahead.
He must like this. Nobody else around,
no older guy to shout advice or start anything.
A one-handed spin on the wheel takes him down
the far side. All along the streets the skaters
are at supper, they've abandoned their small
criss-crossing calls, terse celebrations, all
those rasping swiftnesses in exchange for their
ampler lives, and what's left is this,
slow dance of blue light in a darkening
space. He's going around the last bend
now. I head off. The perfect thing's
just about ready again.

Night Game

Supper over, and with not much time left before we
Decamp from this weekend with my Dad,
I wander out towards the park for air.
He's already back into his duel to the
Death, I mean it, with the TV, where
Teams X and Y are manoeuvring on some
Nebulous, perpetual ground. There's
A game on out here too, I see —
Industrial League softball, scoreboard claims it's
Triple Star Cleaners vs. Harper's Electric.
Shortsleeve shirts confirm. Hardly dusk
But they're already under the lights.
"Way to look, Gary, way to look!" seems to, yes, *does*
Come from the third-base coach, though long before
The exclamation-mark he's browsing among
The interior stitchings of his stripey green cap:
He's hung around one base or another out here
A few hundred times before, that one,
I think the message is. Two on —
I'll just see if they bring them in. Although
Two down, too. Oh well, hmm. Funny banter,
Back-and-forth ribbings among the bluejeaned families,
And players from an earlier or still-upcoming game
Spotted here and there. Usual comings and goings,
Nods, little signals. It's a soft night. Sitting
Where I am right now I'm farther away, it
Occurs to me, from my agreed-upon present life
Than I've been for a long while. And now Gary pops up,
Stranding both of them, and mindlessly cast down
At this development I'm beginning to plot
My smartest route sideways and down among the families
When here on his way past our end of the bleacher
And now right in front of us, momentarily pausing
For an exchange of quips with the arriving Star
Third-baseman, comes the greencapped coach, and
I know his name, I know the street he lived on
Thirty years ago, and I know exactly how old he is

Right now. Who once of his own accord
Opted out of a richly promising — from *his*
Point of view, though never mine — schoolyard free-for-all
To sit on that school's cement steps with me when
I'd stopped a punch to what we used to call the solar plexus
That left me winded and incapable and ashamed.
We sat until my breath remembered its way back,
Saying only occasional things, and then walked off
Together to somewhere below memory. His act,
Relinquishing that stage he was so good on, astonished
Me then, though I never told him so,
And does so still, seeing him here — he might
With equal probability, that day, have mentioned
Kierkegaard, or Brahms. And now has ambled back
To his bench and is sitting there, his green cap
Tugged straight-visored onto his greyish crewcut head,
Staring into the evening diamond. Lornie Hart, who
One day with no warning stepped out of the corridor
That led to all my proliferating classrooms,
Closing off a decade shared as never another would be,
And set off towards tonight by a clandestine route.
Does he still work at that plant, by now
Service Manager, Parts Division, did he marry
One of those girls we leaned on our handlebars
To watch, oh, wherever we happened to come
Across them? No, skip that, the condescension and
All of it: say this instead — he has just dropped in from some
Intricate adventure to rest here, replenish
His special energies before slipping away
As the whole town knows he must, knows
He always has and always will, gone from the corridor,
Its quick capricious son. I watch him here, I'm
Testing plans of approach, but none of my scenarios
Seems promising: our words will surely stall
In a formal distance we never knew or learned
To deal with. Shown these thoughts of mine
Lornie will think *No, this isn't how it is.*
This is not how either of us used to think.
And the game proceeds. Ten minutes and I'll

Have to be back on the road to the city.
Lornie Hart hunches forward on his bench,
Guarding something of me. Those two boys who
Hugged their knees in the sunlight, talking sparingly
Of anything that was not a punch, waiting
For enough indifference to gather in them
To allow them to get up and go, they are more
His property than mine, they are more at home here
Than anywhere I can get to. They'll fade again
From me, they'll be a little further off
During my walk back to the house even, but
Down there on the bench their brief voices
Are vibrant and near.

Sampling from a Dialogue

Stopping by the bedroom wall he says God
damn it Marge (if that's her name), we have been through
this forty thousand times now let's have a new
line, I need to hear something different, and this odd
and, well, obviously it's inflated, analogy comes into his mind
— Roland, at Roncesvalles, and *his* last long call —
and he stands where he happens to be, beside the wall
and waits, listening, he knows now he's waiting for some kind
of miracle, what's she going to say,
one of them always finds a consoling pose
and his feel all used up, and he tries to picture those
horsemen, bright lances, rescuing armies on the way,
and from the bed behind him she says *Well*
maybe there is just such a thing as
having enough of somebody,
breaking the rhyme,
and both of them stay where they are, too far
apart again, in a clarity neither of them expected or thought
they were making, and listen to
the catastrophe of time.

Forests of the Medieval World

Forests of the medieval world, that's
where her mind will wander
the three dissertation years, lucky girl —
Forest of Bleu, which crowded around
the walls of Paris and stretched 10,000 leagues
in every direction; the great Hercynian forests
of East Prussia, from which each year
334 drovers bore the logs for the fires
in the Grand Duke's castles of Rostock,
of Danzig and, furthest east of all, guarding
the borders towards the Polish marshes,
Greifswald and Wolgast. I'm so sad
I could die, you said as you left, but
my children, how could I bear it —
and I know, I know there are ways
of losing children, of seeing them stray off
among the trees even now, especially now!
Every fleet needed for its construction
the razing of an entire forest —
lost forests meeting on the tilting hills
of the Caspian, the Baltic, the Black Sea,
over the mountains of water the file of forests
comes. Your face is a mobile mischief,
do you know? Your eyes mocked before
they entreated, your lips rendered
both comedy and its dark twin
in microseconds, and your tongue
harried my mouth's bays and inlets.
The *Oberforstmeister* of Kurland promised
the King 'at least half-fabulous' beasts
for the hunt, his forest measured
140,000 *arpents* and even on the swiftest mounts
horsemen could not traverse it
in a month. My mind runs fast
down its *arpents* and leafy corridors,
seeing no one, I should slash

tree-trunks to procure my safe return
but I can't stop. My mind is running
on pure grief and pure love, I want you
to know this. The Forest of Othe
was so still you could hear a shadow
cross a face at 60 leagues distance —
it had linked the Lyons Massif with
the Woods of Gisors but after a hurricane
levelled a million trees in 1519 the diligent
peasants moved in with plows and those forests
were never reunited. And
the forests of Finland, have you thought of those?
All the way to Archangel and the White Sea?
They can show you how you were
before these excuses. What can you do
about this, your exigent look said
in the doorway, I am going do you realize
I am going? And that both of us will survive this?
When the Swedes needed cash they cut down
the forests of Pomerania, the result in
many cases is sand-dunes. This for day-trippers
is nice, in your rented *Strandkorb* there is room
for everybody, also for dressing and undressing
when the beach is crowded. In the forest of Morois
Tristan lies with Iseult, they are waiting
for the King her husband who will tell history
they were only sleeping. In
the Black Forest dwarf trees and greenheart
still flourish — as for the Rominter Heide
it was so huge that most of its lakes
and forests were "held in reserve,"
not listed or even mentioned, so for generations
all that those lakes and forests could do was
grow uncontrollably in the imagination. I
would take you with me into the Rominter Heide
if you would come: there
each child we must not hurt will

wear a rose in sign of her ardent, forbearing
heart, in sign of his calm-eyed ascent through
our extreme, necessary years.

from *"The Edvard Munch Poems"*
• • •

Death and the Maiden

Ibsen stood beside me
a long while looking.
He seemed more interested
in the spermflowing margins
than in Death thrusting his
spindleshank between her thighs,
or her ripe belly pressing
against and apparently massaging
an everlasting absence — or
something very hard
to guess the nature of. It
reminded me how Fru H.'s[†]
soft body would give
way, and give way, and how
her mouth would go down, and
down, and I said
the world is always useless
without just this one human being,
isn't it. Ibsen replied
he found it painful to
look at young girls, though
he'd be helped from now on
remembering their smooth bodies
were not durable. He then said
his own body had been
silent for years.

† *Fru H. — She is usually so identified in Munch's diaries, and although biographers have since told us her name, we can leave it as Munch left it. She was a married woman and the very young E.M. had a brief affair with her. He was probably in love with her for the rest of his life.*

· · ·
What They Didn't Like

What they didn't like took me years
to understand. What they *said* it was
was the serving-maid on the rumpled
conjugal bed or a madonna's
equivocal sweating or even
Hans Jaeger's[†] coffehouse rhetoric,
as if I needed smoky talk to decide
where the paint went. But these weren't
what they really hated. It wasn't even
those solitary ones I showed
gazing across a salt-stirring sea
towards something perfect they once saw —
those horizon-aching women who were
almost 40 now and so unused,
so quietly, quietly unused. Women
saw them and kept just as quiet
as who they were seeing;
men imagined, finding them new,
they could save them.
　　　　　　　No, what they really
couldn't abide, or if they could
couldn't stand their wives'
learning about, was *nothing. Nothing*
was what they didn't like. What
frightened them. That madonna, who
could have been lying back anywhere, being
worshipped or fucked, or Sophie dying
in her chair by the window
with its flowerpot, and then dying
minus all of those, *no* chair *no*
window *no* flowerpot, nothing but
loose brown colour around both those lives,
all the detail gone, the skirtingboards, pupils
in the eyes, all of it rubbed away,
smeared over, dug out with the brush's

butt-end, even the floorboards
unreliable — *that's* what was
upsetting, the framelessness of
everything. All those things which
people feel confused by
which you'd better not deprive them of.
If the rims of our lives go imageless
anything at all can drift in there,
a long glance for instance —
how do you cope with that? Or
you might think you want to give yourself
completely to somebody, and if
there's no surroundings
it could all at once be hard not to —
all your trees, piano lessons, holidays, little looks
you've been on the receiving end of
ever since you started, they'd all go
with you and there'd be nothing left
anywhere to just wait for you, to show
a way back from this somebody
if you needed it sometime. Of course
it's frightening! And yet we all guess
it's the only place to really
find ourselves in, don't we?
A place with no furniture? No books,
no people, no plants on the window-ledge?
All those things we never really wanted
that are always there? Oh,
we've always known this — that
anything complicated is a lie. So
coming now in sight of it, the lies
pouring out of the sides of the canvases,
must have felt contagious and worrying,
especially to people who would be bound
to realize that others seeing this
could understand it too. Others
who lived with them and wished every day
they didn't. All of them together now

falling into a place where no word
had ever been. Like Sophie, sickening
all those months in the same room,
her eyes taking back all the images
the room had ever had, taking them back inside
just by looking at them so many hours. Finally
without anything at all to look at or be safe in.
You're not supposed to admit
that this happens — especially
if you do what I do, if you make things.
But it does, you know.

† *Hans Jaeger was the leader of a so-called Bohemian set in Oslo frequented by the young E.M.*

Self-Portrait at 3.15 a.m.

A skinny old party in a too-big suit
has just turned the lights on
at a quarter past three. What
does he do now? Where is everybody?
He is just realizing nobody has told him
how to be as old as this. Another way
of putting it: nobody has taught old age
how to enter him. He's wondering
why has he painted himself into this room
which so obviously has got only
a few minutes left in it. Just inches
below the paint's surface in that canvas
over there the shadowy damp breasts
of that woman remind him of something.
Was it worth her while, once, to love him?
He remembers a night-fulcrum —
those breasts swaying close over his eyes
again and again, half the night it seems,
coming over like moons, his mouth too
was continuously amazed. He always knew

descriptions of happiness must remain illegible
but you can stay close to it if you don't move,
can't you? No you can't. These did, though —
glistening from his own young mouth, too;
an hour's immortal even if a life isn't.

'There are no words to remember, but I do have that gaze'

*(Title line and some other things from the letters
column in a September 1997 U.K. newspaper)*
for Christopher Wiseman

He'd been aware of the big man
lording it over a bunch of officers nearby
but it was only after he'd finished
the morning's casualty parade (no
shrapnel wounds for once, just
the usual exhaustions plus
one too-young trooper from the South,
Granada it could have been, whom he'd
dispatched back to his regiment with
a chit saying, For God's sake
send him home where he might stop
crying) he learned who the big man was.
Hemingway, would you believe. Who had
a press corps badge and was whingeing
about his billet, didn't like bed and didn't
like board, and who when nobody much
spoke up just went on and on, bullying.
Can you whinge and bully at the same time?
Apparently. But that morning would long ago
have dipped below memory if that was
all that held it up — what kept it afloat for
the sixty years until he posted today's
letter to the editor was what happened

next. He noticed a young woman
standing at the quiet centre, it seemed,
of her blowhard companion's ongoing
scene, and there was something
about her he liked. This something was
first of all she was beautiful and
second of all her eyes had a kind of
calm he'd never seen before. In
the same minute that he noticed this,
Martha Gellhorn, who that winter was
just beginning her move into literary
history as one of the specialty, I am
going to risk saying, dishes in the big man's
moveable feast, noticed him standing there
watching her. That calm gaze
returned his and for a few seconds
neither of them even tried to restore
order. Of course he wanted to speak
to her and I'm sure would have, this is
not *The Wings of the Dove*, but
either there was really no chance
or if there was it passed. Point
of all this is that simple arithmetic
shows he has to be over ninety now,
contributing today's letter because of
some Hemingway anniversary, and there's
not a whisper in this letter about his own
subsequent life, about how he made it back
from Spain or how he spent, probably,
the next six decades ministering to
the ill and the damaged
in that Shropshire town his letter
comes from. There's just these few
understated paragraphs, easily
as effective as the piece you're reading
right now, which by the way I only offer
in case you missed *Our Readers Write*

this morning — and how he manages this
amid the pervasive self-pandering babble
we're all trying to shuffle through
these days, keeping our heads down,
aiming for the exits, I do not know . . . and
ends with the unadjectived sentence
in the title up there. Keeping quiet, and
not just for a little while, about something
you guess could have led to everything
but led to nothing at all, led only to
this thought you sometimes have about it,
and which is so perfect inside the thought
that you can only smile at it and then
get on with your life, is, I'm coming to believe,
just about the most moving thing.

Reading a Biography of Samuel Beckett
for Charles Israel

I'm lying here reading on my bed, which is
where I basically do all my reading,
privily stocking my mind with news from
Samuel Beckett's singular life, a life
that I'm now learning was also covertly
very kind; and every once in a while,
feeling half ironic and half puzzled, I let
the book fall to my chest and ask myself
why (apart from the unqualified joy I am
experiencing reading Samuel Beckett's
own words, much quoted here, which are
so manifestly more exact and in an odd way
nobler than the words I am normally
exposed to in any standing-up situation)
am I doing this? stocking my mind, I mean?
After all I am not young, gone are those
perpetual landscapes full of uncatalogued

wisdom-caches that would, for a long while
I took this for granted, sooner or later be
stumbled upon, nor is there anything
in my current circumstances that leads me
to suppose I will ever be able to hand on
to others, as a result of this reading,
possibly with some interesting additions,
a real sense of how it feels to be lying in
this cave of wonderfully nuanced language.
(Although "You cannot feel better than this,"
I could say. Or I could stick to saying, "*I
could not feel better than this.*" But nobody's
interested.) *Take into the air my quiet breath,*
Keats wrote, and Samuel Beckett read that and
wanted to, and therefore did, write the same
words down again, so there are two men who
found those words and decided to write them
down, as if they answered something. And now
here is one more.

Romance

for George Calder

When I was small my parents took me,
three years running, to the local Town Hall
for Richard Haliburton's slide-lectures,
generically known as *The Royal Road
to Romance*. In who knows what sequence,
these were "Treasures of the Incas,"
"The Mountains of the Moon," and
"Lost Tribes of the Amazon." He was
a silvery-haired American and the place
was always packed. Did I admire him?
Hard to say. Later I hoped I hadn't;
pompous, he seemed by then, the orotund mid-
Atlantic voice, and patronizing to those
yearning small-town audiences in ways
even that little boy must have noticed.
Now that I've learned he disappeared on,
amazing coincidence, his last voyage, never
to be heard of again, his dignity seems to be
returning; my putative admiration too. Why?
Maybe because he has been speechless for years.
Which permits a supposition of modesty. You
can suppose a step back towards innocence.

> *The main thing is to burn off all the debris.*
> *The crap. Now that I'm into the last third*
> *of things I'll be glad never again to have to*
> *stand forth, never again to find myself*
> *acting as if I know, never again to be*
> *up there scanning an auditorium with*
> *eyes practised in rewarding*
> *the especially intent face. Same*
> *with all the rest of it, it's all connected!*
> *Never again those obligatory juxtaposings*
> *of whatever I see or hear or read, all those*
> *intervenings between me and a decently*

*straightforward life — that long-ago little-valued
given-away thing. Later so missed! And
ever since it went (so missed!), only and
always this ego-powered, darkness-driven
stuff: "How can I use this?" . . . "There has to be
some deeper sound wanting into
this sentence . . ." . . . "These disparate
images must have a secret and potent shape,
in an hour or a week I'll find it . . ." Oh,
all in the name of the hungry imagination,
sure, all in the name of whatever it's
always been called (that short Latinate
sound, that allegedly longer-than-life
thing) — but so much of it self-infected, drama-
directed, life-falsifying. And for what? Ah,
Jesus, for what? — for many a bootless
thing. So skip it, I tell myself, leave it. Ride
out of town. Just ride the hell out. Horseman,
pass by. Delete that last. Just see. Listen.
Walk up and down. Read.*

*Read, yes. About others, goes without saying,
others. And not the "truly great," no, but less
than those, less than those — less, or other,
than those so often extravagant, so sometimes
counterfeit, so invariably distorted scenes and
names, the jostlings, the half-celebrated faces,
the ubiquitous unreticent bodies —*

*Instead, the other ones, the un-
raised voices, intimate, daily,
unsurprising, trustable —*

*The ones I've been ignoring, oh, catching
small sounds from but ignoring, most of my
grown-up life.*

And the reasons for this are — ?

Unknown.

*And for going the other way, the way
I took, am still on, so flawed, all those
words, all the lovely and dishonest
and moving and suspect
syllables — ?*

Well —

On a provincial platform on some
inexact date in the late 1930s or early 1940s
the Town Clerk has begun to speak. Coughings
and general shufflings on the thinly padded
collapsible chairs. My parents are beside me,
here and there I can glimpse a neighbour
or two, and a few rows ahead is my aunt, Bea —
I don't call her Aunt Bea, just Bea. And Frank,
who is her husband, is of course there too. I
recognize him from the back because of his
Leaf sweater, the one Syl Apps donated
to the raffle. Up at the front there's
a press-ganged clutch of my teachers past and
present and future. We've already stood for
The King and now the Town Clerk is telling us
when our honoured guest was born and
mentioning the several towns, all larger than
ours, where he has recently delivered this same
lecture; also one very large city, Hamilton,
where he has not yet delivered this lecture but
will next week. He is lecturing to us *before*
Hamilton. Also, turn our clocks back one hour
tonight. Finally, due to the inclement weather,
which will make driving home a matter for concern,
only a brief question period will be permitted at
the conclusion of the lecture. We applaud as
the Town Clerk finds his way to his seat in the front row,
one away from Miss Darnley, whose class I am in

and who will ask us on Monday if we have been here. The lights start to go down and someone comes out hurriedly from the side and turns on the little bulb on the lectern and then retreats to the side again.

Richard Haliburton walks out and takes his place at the lectern. As he does so the slide-projector begins to whir quietly.

"The Mountains of the Moon," he says.

Lorna Crozier

Dust

Rags stuffed under the doors,
around the windows
as if they were wounds
that needed staunching

yet the dust
settles everywhere,
on my skin, my hair, inside
my sleeves and collar.
I feel old, used up,
something found
in the back of a cupboard.

I cover the water crock
with a tea towel
embroidered with a *B*,
turn the dinner plates
face down on the table.
When we lift them
two moons glow
on the gritty cloth
and in the mornings when we rise,
the shape of our heads
remains on the pillowslips
as if we leave behind
the part of us
that keeps on dreaming.

Not the Music

Not the music.
It is this other thing
I keep from all of them
that matters, inviolable.

I scratch in my journals,
a mouse rummaging through cupboards,
nibbling on a crust of bread, apple skins,
chewing the edges of photographs, the small
details of a life. I hoard and save,
place one thing inside another
inside the next.

Start with a prairie, then Horizon
and inside it our house,
the kitchen, the table where I sit
with my journal, and inside it
everything I write — dust, moths,
wind speaking in whispers
across the page,
the absence of rain,
forgiveness —
everything shrinking
to the smallest
thinnest letter,
I.

Mrs. Bentley

I've walked through this story
in housedresses and splay-
footed rubbers. Mousy hair
without curls. Philip never drew
a convenient portrait
for me to comment on,

a hasty sketch. I could have said,
though his hand is flawless,
this does not resemble me.
That's my high forehead
and the way I purse my lips
but he's placed my eyes
far apart. I look in two directions.
The right one stares at you,
follows you as you move.
The left, my prairie eye,
gazes at what lies just over
where the lines converge.
No portraits exist, no photographs
and little self-description.
And nowhere in these pages
can you find my name.
Gladys, Louise, Madeline?
I fancy Margaret though in the country
everyone would call her Peg.
We're left with Mrs.
Bentley, dowdy, frumpy, plain.
Don't you wonder what Philip
called me as we lay together,
my flesh warmed by his hands,
the taste of me on his tongue,
as if there were no better sound
in all the world,
my name, my name!

Dictionary of Symbols

The woman who undresses in the dark
with the curtains open. Slowly
she twists her hands around her back,
unhooks her bra, slides her panties
over her hips and down her legs.

No one can see her.
There is more light outside than in her room.
But she stands at the window naked as if
the moon were a mirror held in night's hands.
It is the colour of her breasts
when they are full of milk,
it is dimpled like her thighs,
her tired belly, it waxes and wanes.
She tries to hold it in her arms,
imagines wading into it,
all its roundness one tranquil sea.

On the street below her a man
in a red farmer's cap pulls a rusty wagon
full of empty bottles down the sidewalk,
the wheels rattling. She wants to show him
the moon, its calm indifference
on a summer evening when all her children
are asleep, when her husband kneels on a bed
in another house, entering a woman
from behind, so he can watch himself
disappear into the flesh,
his hands on her buttocks,
round and glistening with sweat.

The woman who undresses in the dark,
stands at the window, turns on the light.

This is what it looks like, she says,
this pale celestial body, faceless
as the moon is faceless, coldly luminescent.
You can stare at it forever
and never burn your eyes.

Variation on the Origin of Flight

Of all the body
it's the creature closest to the sea.
Snail-moist, all tuck and salty
muscle, it opens and closes
like a sea anemone. Mute
but several tongued,
minus legs and memory,
it's what moves you
to bowl and basin,
to hollows in the stone
where water gathers after storms.
It draws you past the breakers
to the wild, the open,
gives your arms and naked thighs
their power and pull. More
reptilian than cat, its brain
is the oldest brain, prelapsarian,
soft moss and weeping fern.
Stopped on its evolutionary trail.
Beached, becalmed, stranded without
gills, scales or jewelled tail,
yet you feel it
flex and flutter
beneath your lover's tongue
as feather
after slow inevitable feather
it dreams the world's
first wings.

The Memorial Wall

When they built the wall
they had no idea the living would leave
so much stuff underneath the names.
They didn't know the dead had so many
strange requests, didn't know there'd be
so many pilgrims in a country with satellite TV.
The man who cleans up along the wall
can't wait to tell his wife after work each day.
You wouldn't believe what he picks up!
Flowers, letters, photographs, even a Coors,
okay, but a baby carriage full of human hair,
a stuffed alligator, a Lionel electric
train, its cars piled high with wishbones.
They had to build a warehouse to store
everything that piled up, like so much merchandise,
as if the dead still need a shopping mall.
In a ledger each item is carefully described
by a retired bus conductor who used to classify
butterflies in his spare time. He records
the object's height and weight, the exact
place it was found, then lays it on a metal shelf.
He doesn't note its name or use, its possible intent.
One of the painters hired to coat the building
battleship grey, a young man who'd come
from Montana to find his brother's name,
paints the side door lapis lazuli
because he likes the sound of it. He doesn't know
the dead can walk through any kind of blue
as easily as air. At night when all the staff have gone,
when the pilgrims pile in buses, cars and trains,
one after another the dead rattle down the aisles
with grocery carts to claim the one thing
they cannot leave behind: a baseball bat,
a red roller skate, a doll that says *Kiss me, honey,*
when you turn her upside down.

South Dakota Refuge

Go to Sand Lake, she says,
*in November it's a platter
full of geese, your geese,
the Canadas come down with the snow,
feed on marsh grass
before their southern flight.*

Along the border of the refuge:
wind off the lake, grey fog settling
on the water, the stir of wings.
Men warm their hands on thermoses,
cigarettes burn the morning air.
Against the cars like young boys,
bored, waiting for the end of silence,
the guns lean.

Skunks

The morning cold with dawn,
I stand at the window, first
light spilling through the glass.
Across the yard I see my neighbour
on his front step. He waves,
then points a rifle at my head.

Yesterday he told me
he'd buy a gun to shoot the skunks
who come up from the river,
drawn from the willows to our
apple cores, our overripe
melons and sour milk, our almost
empty jars of jam. Night-raiders,
they dip into the wells
of the garbage cans.

I have imagined them,
their narrow faces
peering in the windows while I sleep,
turning the thin bones of dream
over and over in their paws.

Now it is my neighbour's face
I see through the window,
the precision of his eyes and hands.
He waves and grins, then lines me up,
practises his sight.

We are in this together now.
He studies my face like a lover,
knows the curve of my forehead,
the slight indentation of
my temples, the blue pulse
beating there.

After dark when he waits
in the alley the smell of me
will sting his eyes, fill his mouth,
make his nostrils flare.

For I will have been there
before him,
driving ahead of me
these dark sisters
with their slow walk
down to the river, the white
on their backs blazing
in the moonlight,
their sweet mouths
red with jam.

Home Care

The woman from Home Care is late. She apologizes, but she had a helluva day yesterday. She was supposed to go fishing with her boyfriend in LaRonge, packed the sleeping bags in his truck, found the Coleman stove and fishing rods, made a big pot of chili while he was supposed to be at work, poured it into coffee tins, then drove to her friend's to pick up a cooler. This woman's the same age as her mother, but guess what? There he was fishin' already, she says, but in her friend's bed, get my drift? So, she goes back to her place and waits, gets all dressed up as if she's going out, puts on her new shirt and cowboy boots. When he gets there, sits at the kitchen table, all sorry, blubbering *never again*, she takes the boots to him and she means what she says, she kicks him right in the face. Boy did he look stunned, like a big one when the hook bites in, too stunned to lift a finger, blood spattering his shirt. And he deserves it. His first wife said he used to beat on her but who wanted to believe it? *Fishin' good?* she says. Now he's gone, she means for *ever*, but he'll never be rid of her. She opened him right above the cheek — there'll be a scar there three inches long saying *howdee-do* every time he looks in the mirror and he's the kind of guy has to shave twice a day for the rest of his life so that's a lot of lookin'.

Small Gesture

Before she moves head down into the dark,
the woman pauses beneath the streetlight,
turns up her collar. Black wool coat.
Now she is a body of pure grief.

From the upstairs window you watch the streetlight
flash her picture, one of several slides
you'll save on the wheel of winter,
this one called

Small Gesture Against the Cold.

You're So Covered with Scars

You're so covered with scars
you forget where they come from.
Like birds they sing to the wounded
who descend from the railings of bridges
to follow you. In bars the cripples limp
to your table, drag their bleeding casts
towards the criss-cross of your face.
The old sit beside you in stations,
cough their lives into your lap. And now
I have come with my darkness to lie
against you. I trace the braille of your body:
the broken lip, the hole in the side
of your face. But you are emptied of stories.
Instead you press into my skin. The scars
cover me like feathers.

Hoping to Fix Up, a Little, This World

The cat we've named Basho
plays with the ghost cat who slips
from bamboo to drink at the pond
when the sun begins to fall.
Our other cat, the shy one, climbs
the slow branches of the pear,
and you, my love, go to bed
again too soon. Too much sun?
I ask. Did you forget to wear your hat?

Dusk gives way to darkness
and leaves behind its watchfulness.
The cats absorb it. They see what I am
missing, what I can't make out.

At the pond I light three candles
and float them on the water.
Fish flare up, combustible as coals;
they warm the lotus bud that swells
to breaking but will not open. How long
your sleeping makes the night.

Beth Cuthand

Post-Oka Kinda Woman

Here she comes strutting down your street.
This Post-Oka woman don't take no shit.
She's done with victimization, reparation,
degradation, assimilation,
devolution, coddled collusion,
the "plight of the Native Peoples."

Post-Okay woman, she's o.k.
She shashay into your suburbia.
MacKenzie Way, Riel Crescent belong to her
like software, microwave ovens,
plastic Christmas trees and lawn chairs.

Her daughter wears Reeboks and works out.
Her sons cook and wash up.
Her grandkids don't sass their Kohkom!
No way.

She drives a Toyota, reads bestsellers,
sweats on weekends, colors her hair,
sings old songs, gathers herbs.
Two steps Tuesdays,
Round dance Wednesdays,
Twelve steps when she needs it.

Post-Oka woman she's struttin' her stuff
not walkin' one step behind her man.
She don't take that shit
Don't need it!   Don't want it.
You want her   then treat her right.

Talk to her of post-modern deconstructivism
She'll say: "What took you so long?"

You wanna discuss Land Claims?
She'll tell ya she'd rather leave
her kids with a struggle than a bad settlement.

Indian Government?
        Show her cold hard cash.
Tell her you've never talked to a real live "Indian"
        She'll say: "Isn't that special."

Post-Oka woman, she's cheeky.
        She's bold.   She's cold.

And she don't take no shit!
No shit.

For All the Settlers Who Secretly Sing
for Sharon Butala

You have seen my ancestors
riding in buckskins
down the coulee into the trees.
You have watched them
frightened that it is you who intrudes
awed, that it is you who sees.

You have met the hawk
soaring above you as you sit
still
waiting for the land to speak
to you who have not heard her
since you fled your lands across the seas.

At night you dream of drums
and hear voices singing
high in the night sky
and you wonder if the northern lights
are more than they appear to be.

And you hold these questions
in your heart not daring to ask
the indigenous people who hold
themselves aloof from settler voices
chattering.
You know they think no one listens
and you understand
the stillness it requires
        and the faith
        and the faith
to hear the heart beat of the land
as one solitude not two.

And you dare not tell the others
her song rises in you
yet it rises and you sing
secretly   to the land
        to the land

And then she knows sister/brother,
that you belong here too.

Zen Indian

Zen Indian tiptoes into Taos
watches coyote disguised
as an ice-cream vendor
sell dollar popsicles
to thirsty tourists.

Fishes down the Fraser
for dried salmon
thinking a No. 10 hook
will catch those freeze-dried suckers.

Careens into Calgary in time
for Stampede; bells polished

feathers fluffed
to dance three times a day
for a free pass to the rodeo.

Makes it to Winnipeg
just after Bismark and right before
wild rice time
to get folk-sey at the Indian Pavilion

Then it's on to pick wild rice
for Uncle Ben;
drop a few rocks in the sacks,
shoot at the crows and reminisce
about how it used to be
before the harvest became
the domain of Bros in hydro
planes and enough money for gas.

Oh oh, cold's coming.
Time to find a fine filly
with a job, not too many kids
and a warm place to lay up for
the winter.

Put cities in a hat:
    Minneapolis, LA
        Boulder, Sante Fe
Calgary, Seattle, Salt Lake.
Yee-ha! Watch out Boulder!
Here he comes.
Zen Indian on the road to enlightenment!

Mary Dalton

To Be Sold
newspaper ad, 1796

To be sold for five shillings,
my wife, Jane Hebland.

She is stout built,
stands firm on her posterns
and is sound wind and limb.
She can sow and reap,
hold a plough, and drive a team.
She would answer
any stout able man that can
hold a tight rein,
for she is damned hard-mouthed and headstrong,
but if properly managed
would either lead or drive
as tame as a rabbit.
She now and then,
if not watched, will make a false step.

Her husband parts with her
because she is too much for him.

Enquire of the printer.

I'm Bursting to Tell: Riddles for Conception Bay

1

I'm the conduit of neighbourliness.
At my best I'm hot-tempered.
Alone I grow cold.
In my belly I hold
what will be a stream soon.

2

I am a gape, an astonishment
with a little beard.
In my belly they have found
old rings, tin cans, a broken oar.
My children once were legion,
crammed the waters.

3

I, sir, am straight as a die,
and a firm believer in hanging.
Swinging forms mean the world's kept in good order.
But I'm at the mercy of weather —
mauzy days I'm abandoned;
windy ones, much burdened.

4

I am a small paradox:
I am a world in myself;
I am just a beginning.
I'm not the mammal's way,
but I'm chockful of meat.

5

I've got more pleats than a girl's skirt —
and I'm the first to jump up for a dance.

I fancy the swoop, the razzamatazz.
Draw me out at a party
and I'm a real old smoothie.
Ah I'm on to the ins and outs of a tune.
But I'm a touchy sort:
rough handling makes me squawk.

6

I'm a drifter, shape-shifter;
I'm prone to upheaval.
Now I'm castle, now cathedral.
Although you note my diminishing
there's more to me than meets the eye.

7

I'm easily needled —
up to a point, no further.
Then I'm the impervious,
the staunch little hard hat.
There's blood on my mind, but
I don't give the finger.

8

I am the blind one,
the old brown one, knobbed and warty.
In my dusty coat, the earth's eyes.
In my cream innards I hold a story of water.
Sometimes a faint dark at my heart.

9

Many-armed, dot-eyed,
ricochet-minded,
I am the stuff of bad dreams.
Like a jilted lover
I spurt ink in anger.

10
I am the sea's green mandala.
Some say I'm the spawn of whores.
Gulls drop me from the sky,
smash my hedgehog armour
to spill my secrets on stone.

11

Hubbub's my name;
corrugation's my game.
A burly trailblazer,
I blunder along.
Where I go, brokenness,
a barren new way.

12

I can't make my mind up:
I'm a child of the land — or
am I a child of the sea?
A creature of margins,
I've an eye for a trinket,
some nice bric-à-brac.
I soothe the washed-up.

13

A barbed question,
I am my own answer.
(Now taboo.)
The sun glints off me.
I'm designed to rip flesh,
but some think me a healer.

14

I run in circles
on an addlebrain's back.
Spring sees me cut off from home.

I sprawl in the meadow, sun-struck.
A knotty proposition.
Much work thereafter
to set me in order.

15

Quite lowly am I —
and yet you bend to me.
Sun and rain made me
a blue globe
with a dark little crown.

16

Four workers, a boss:
five spinning,
stealing the breath
of the spinning one.

17

Bird-name,
I gleam in high places.
On stone you'll kneel,
pluck out my small red eye.

18

I hug the shore,
but I go with the flow.
I know my future is ash.
Ripped from my moorings,
I repay upheaval with blessing:
I fatten your fields.

19

I love your hands;
let me come closer.
But you're a fickle one.

A flower unleashed a rumour,
linked me with foxes.
Now you sneer at my velvety kiss,
mutter fears of an iron grip.

20

A collapsible I —
I'm your very own tunneller,
your private worm in the head.
I've got your number.
An absence-license,
I wheedle you into air —
into the rushing elsewhere.

21

Some of us travel white fields,
are entangled in the affairs of men.
We can, it's said, shed our skins,
shuffle off the sea's spell.
With a flip and a wriggle we can
vanish from view.

22

The one-eyed fish,
the wiry spelunker.
The horse that rides you never know when.
(A Trojan horse, me, with my cargo of swimmers.)
They build statues to me, towers,
stacks — such tall prayers to me.

23

My cousins are grander,
but I'm free and easy.
I float on water,
on my own rubber raft.
I flaunt my sleek self,
a concave little sun.

24

Birds, boats, crops —
in time I've swallowed all.
I've patted your baby's face,
played hide-and-seek in your lilacs.
You'd do well to mind me.

25

In wry lines I muster
dreams, lies, enigmas.
Though some scorn me as cipher,
I'm full of grand notions.
I'm bursting to tell —
but I'm mute till you come to me.

Jean-Paul Daoust

Translated by Daniel Sloate

de **Les cendres bleues** / from **Blue Ashes**
. . .

Maintenant
Dans mes rêves contemporains
Tu me hantes
Étoiles polaires
Où je m'oriente
Comme quand je patinais sur la baie gelée
Je regardais le ciel étoilé
À chercher
Qui n'est jamais venu
Dans le hangar le fruit défendu
Qu'on croquait assaisonné
De nos larmes
Tes bras un autel
Où tu m'immolais
Y a-t-il un enfer pour les enfants
Qui ont aimé pécher
Qui ont appris des mots
Qu'ils savaient ne pas devoir connaître
Des mots d'amour de haine
De luxure de mensonge
Les autres ne comptaient plus
Je t'ai aimé
Comme tu voulais
Que je t'aime
Mais je n'étais qu'en première année
Au Jardin de l'Enfance de Bellerive
Soeur Lucille était si gentille
M'offrait ses petits Chinois

Pour vingt-cinq cents
Missionnaire moi aussi
À en baptiser toute la Chine
Ou Père Blanc en Afrique
Aux Philippines
À travers les caresses confuses
Nos ombres
Dans cette dépendance
Où tu fendais du bois
Hiver comme été
Où on a gravé inlassablement nos noms
Ceux de l'amour disais-tu
Mais qu'est-ce que j'en savais
À six ans et demi on ne sait pas tout
Maintenant ce texte
Que tu ne liras pas
C'est tant mieux
Les amours sont plus souvent des malchances
Oui j'aurai bu l'eau bleue de tes yeux
Plus forte que ces alcools purs
Trop dangereux
Parfois le soir seul
Dans la piscine éclairée
L'impression de nager dans ta peau
Comme jadis
J'ai peur
La panique de cet éclairage
La nuit est terrible dans ces piscines
Insupportable ce bleu gonflé
Toutes nos peurs ancestrales
Les dinosaures les mauvais génies
Comme toi
Plus mauvais gue le plus mauvais
Que j'aimais pourtant
En cachette de toi
Je rêvais d'être le professeur Tournesol
Pour trouver une invention

Qui te réduirait en cendres
Te brûler comme ces sorciers du Moyen Âge
Mais j'étais si petit
Dans les neiges
Dans les vents d'automne
Dans les parfums de tes bras
Les refrains de jadis m'emportent
Mais quand je t'ai surpris
Avec un autre
Un petit voisin
Je me suis juré ta perte
Oui je vous ai vus
Non je ne scènais pas comme tu disais
Moi qui pensais que nous étions sacrés
C'est toi qui l'avais dit
Qui a brûlé qui
Ma vengeance sera terrible
Les gestes que je croyais uniques
Je me suis enfui
En criant
Vers l'épée de la cathédrale gothique
Dans le reflet violacé de la baie
De Valleyfield
Moi qui avais tout sacrifié
Pour toi
Mon père ma mère mon frère
Mes ami-e-s Monsieur le Curé
Monseigneur
Soeur Lucille
Les voisins
Tout que je te dis
Une bûche lancée sur ton crâne infidèle
Vlan
La tête dans le feu
• • •

from *Blue Ashes*
· · ·

Now
In my contemporary dreams
You haunt me
Polar stars
I use to find my bearings
As when I skated on the frozen bay
I'd look up at the starry sky
Looking for
What never came
The forbidden fruit in the woodshed
Seasoned with our tears
That we bit into
Your arms an altar
Where I was immolated
Is there a hell for children
Who liked to sin
Who learned words
They knew they shouldn't know
Words of love words of hate
Of lust of lies
The others didn't count anymore
I loved you
The way you wanted
Me to love you
But I was only in the first grade
At the Bellerive elementary school
Sister Lucille was so nice
She'd offer me her little Chinese children
For twenty-five cents
I was a missionary too
Out to baptize all of China
Or a White Father in Africa
In the Philippines
Our shadows

Cast by our dim caresses
In that woodshed
Where you split wood
Summer and winter
Where we never tired of carving our names
The names of love you said
But what did I know
One doesn't know everything at six and a half
Now this text
That you will never read
Just as well
Love is a mishap more often than not
Yes I did drink in the blue waters of your eyes
Stronger than the purest of alcohols
Too perilous
At times in the evening alone
In the lighted pool
The feeling I'm swimming in your skin
As I once did
I'm frightened
Panic in the lighting
Night is terrible in those pools
Unbearable the swollen blue
All our primal fears
Dinosaurs evil genies
Like you
More evil than the most evil
Yet I loved you
I kept a dream secret from you
To become Professor Tournesol
And invent some device
That would reduce you to ashes
Burn you at the stake
Like a sorcerer in the Middle Ages
But I was so little
In the falling snow
In the winds of autumn

In the perfume of your arms
The refrains from those days transport me
But when I caught you
With another
A young neighbor boy
I swore you would die
Yes I did see the two of you
No I wasn't spying as you said
I thought the two of us were sacred
You told me that
Who burned whom
My revenge will be terrible
The gestures I thought unique
I ran away
Screaming
Towards the spear of the Gothic cathedral
Reflected in the deep purple bay
Of Valleyfield
I had sacrificed everything
For you
My father my mother my brother
My boyfriends my girlfriends the parish priest
The bishop
Sister Lucille
The neighbors
Everything and everyone I tell you
A log thrown at your unfaithful head
And pow
Your head in the flames

• • •

Degan Davis

Hockey

You can explain all the rules
the endless drills, the skates, white-cut perfect
curves, the blind passes, the adrenaline shadow
following you three feet back but why would you?

Puck in net. Simple as a shoulder check.
In a dark bar north of Saskatoon I met
a former N.H.L. goon who tore his calves,
lost his way, limped back home to factory work,
poker, narcotics, and finally, poetry.

Silence between us. Poetry? On the screen two-inch men
passed back and forth like overdressed birds
in a brilliant white cage.
No other game with that finesse, he said, that rage.

Monique Deland

la question toujours la même

tu voudrais savoir si
oui or non
j'ai fait quelque chose de mes dix doigts

l'un deux
aura repris cent fois
la trajet circulaire
du bleu de la tasse
épiant la timide beauté du geste et feignant surtout
la méconnaissance du fond
qui indiscutablement s'assèche

∼

certains lendemains
tes lèvres sont une menace

dès le milieu du jour
la dentelle est salie
et tout serait à refaire

entendez-moi
la nuit
converser
avec mon âme sauvage

∼

mes mains frileuses
regardent le combat
celle-ci vide
cette autre la soutenant

ma nuque se rompt
la tête s'affale
je n'ai rien pu sauver
c'est arrivé d'un coup

je me demandais seulement
si l'on peut avoir
le même courage deux fois

∽

La nuit a rejoint la ligne disparue du ciel. Qui n'aura pas parlé.

À la maison, l'âme arrive, un peu après moi. Bientôt, nues toutes les deux. Son visage entre mes mains, je vois bouger ce que je veux. Des noirs mats, des bruns crasseux, des rouges pourris. Hachures, coulisses et débords.

Avec des trous. Plein de trous, pour la face durable de l'épouvante.

Je peindrai au couteau, s'il le faut.

∽

J'accumule des retailles. Des papiers de toutes sortes. Petits morceaux de rien. Déchirés, séparés du tout.

Je range les solitudes les unes à côte des autres. La ligne bleue de l'horizon mortel. Les carrefours de routes vus d'en haut. La frange noire des arbres. Les hachures métalliques des clôtures. Méconnaissables.

Je garde tout dans une boîte et j'attends que ça parle.

∽

Une voix sans corps annonce « Villa-Maria ». Le train ralentit. Chacun se penche vers ses pieds. Ramasse ses affaires, se redresse et se lève. Pour sortir.

Moi, je reste prise, comme par le fond. À chercher qui viendra. Me soulever. Qui se penchera pour me prendre. Et me sortir d'ici.

Une voix sans corps demande je suis l'affaire de qui.

∽

la joue sur l'oreiller
qui suinte à l'endroit de l'œil
j'attends le bord de dormir
le nivellement des ondes
la mort des questions

mais tu cognes si fort
le cœur
que j'ai peur

d'être en vie

Jean-Marc Desgent

65

Je m'approche de minuit.
Je fais l'Homme malgré moi, avec les mystères,
   l'ignorance des choses,
les mots qui pourraient ne pas avoir de limites
   immédiates, les drôleries inexpliquées de la
   dénature: sexe, temple, argent, transcendance, futur.
D'un coup de ciseau, on sort de l'existence prévue.
Elle est arrivée, est restée immobile devant une porte,
   devant l'aspiration d'une porte.
Le vertige nous a pris, j'ai posé mon visage dans le
   sien, et j'ai su la véritable histoire d'une femme.
Nous sommes d'anciens morts.
Je suis sans gravité.

Les premiers paysages

Ici, même s'il y avait la disparition
des bêtes et des filles,
la grande déportation
des choses et des garçons,
les destructions de langues et d'âmes,
les innombrables pertes de foi,
d'espérance et de charité,
la dislocation des champs et des rues . . .
il y aurait le silence,
le mal intérieur, la loi du cadenas :
c'est l'habitude séculaire de nos bons cœurs troués.

Alors, on pense, on s'élance. . .
Il y a peut-être quelqu'un, là-haut,

nous délestant de nos plaies,
nous disant la dignité des liens,
nous abandonnant sa joie juste.
C'est pourquoi on regarde le ciel,
on y promène ses mains.
On roule, s'enroule,
s'écroule humblement dans le désir du ciel,
on provoque l'avènement des choses célestes,
des amants et de leurs mutuelles aventures,
on cherche un nuage,
on le prend, l'enserre,
on demeure ému,
transporté par les tempêtes tout autour,
là-bas, en nous, juste en deçà de notre âme:
ce petit sac de cuir où murmurent
nos audaces ou nos étreintes.

Penser, brûler . . .
Je descends dans la vie pour l'embrasser,
mes mains liées au vertige des paysages.
Je me dévêts
et me jette dans la première mare venue.
L'eau me pénètre, se précipite en moi;
nous sommes la nuit de ma tête.

Et, pour demeurer le plus bel humain
malgré l'état des choses,
me voici prosterné devant nos travaux
et nos jours blottis entre nos cuisses,
me voici prosterné, dans mes chants,
devant nous, pauvres rôdeurs
si loin encore des cerveaux incendiaires,
des changeantes morphologies,
des beautés astronomiques,
me voici prosterné devant nous

si loin encore des présences sans cadavre,
sans perte, sans abîme.

Je visite le ciel avec ma fatigue,
je goûte tous les jours ses feux,
je suis habillé de ses désordres, de ses désastres.
Maintenant, je suis sans breuvage
et j'ai soif dans ma langue à demi morte
dans sa maison politique.

∼

**Le monde des monstres est banal,
et je me repose après ce banquet.**

Je reviendrai avec un grand pouvoir sur les têtes . . . Je suis trente secondes et les rues désertes, je suis simple dehors et j'avale les blessures. J'ai le chaos dans la fillette qui vit dans ma chambre, qui est mon amie dans la tête, j'ai le chaos de son odeur, j'ai la traversée de sa vie pas longue pour dire des mots très simples.

Tout est chevreuil avec elle.

2

J'ai l'état feu, l'état échafaudage, l'état Terre promise, l'espace du midi avec cuisses vigoureuses, l'espace du midi avec la lumière, c'est la bonté, c'est un joli jour tout complice, je suis le roi des animaux, elle est sportive avec le vélocipède, nous sommes rois de peuples à machettes, abattons, abattus.

La limite du monde est loin, le soleil ne se couchera pas.

3

Nous sommes cinquante à table, trois cents au salon, nous nous retrouvons quelques milliers dans la chambre nuptiale, debout, entassés, collés, au coude à coude, ça fume avec véhémence, on ne tente même pas de faire taire le couple, le gouffre dans le lit.

C'était les ombres et on s'ennuie encore.

Glissando sous la pluie, glissando et fellation de l'arme à feu... C'est ça, l'amour qu'on donne : des pièces de métal, morceaux, fragments du mal qu'on entasse jusqu'à la partie supérieure de la voûte céleste.

C'était... si on se touche, il y a les conséquences, mais'on n'a pas caressé.

**Je vois l'intelligent théâtre,
je suis là avec ma machine,
je rêvais d'être beau et grand.**

En conclusion, on peut abattre du travail, abattre un arbre, on peut abattre quelqu'un, c'est comme on veut, c'est personne, c'est sans conséquences, ce n'est pas suicidaire, c'est occidental, ce n'est pas curieux, c'est peut-être de l'argent, c'est le pays, c'est le drapeau. Il y a aussi une chaise estropiée, à la toile déchirée. Les champs vagues derrière la porte sont couverts d'escaliers abattus. Derrière la porte, c'est le crâne, c'est la tête complètement maigre... On verra ça, après mon corps.

Joël Des Rosiers

Translated by Hugh Hazelton

le 26 octobre 1951 eut lieu la première césarienne
dans l'histoire de la ville il n'y eut pas de sommeil pour personne
le père de ma mère s'enquit d'une voix lente de magistrat
ma fille va-t-elle survivre il répéta la question
s'éloigna sous la pergola
dans le jardin priaient les nonnes oblates de Marie
la main du chirurgien ouvrit le ventre de ma mère
du xiphoïde au pubis la tribu exulta dans l'assomption du sang
l'enfant tenait la lame du bistouri entre ses mains
à l'aube la mère de ma mère me retrouva exsangue
dans les langes immaculés sentant le vétiver
ô rhizomes vos huiles essentielles punissent les anophèles
et vos tanins baptisent les plaies ombilicales
les artérioles digitales sectionnées spasmées par l'éther
s'étaient rouvertes durant la nuit un caillot dans la bouche
l'enfant avait porté la blessure à ses lèvres
on crut au miracle le père de ma mère cita *Éloges*
ah! les cayes, nos maisons plates la ville des Cayes
où je suis né blessé aux mains se trouve encore
sur le finistère au bout de la langue de terre
sur la presqu'île d'où vient le paradis
à l'extrême bout de la langue

On October 26 1951 the first caesarian
in the city's history took place no one got any sleep
will my daughter survive
my mother's father asked in his slow magistrate's voice
he repeated the question

and went off beneath the pergola
the Oblate nuns of Mary prayed in the garden
the surgeon's hand opened my mother's womb
from the xiphisternum to the pubis
the tribe exulted in the assumption of blood
the child held the scalpel blade between his hands
at dawn my mother's mother found me bloodless
in the immaculate swaddling clothes smelling of vetiver
O rhizomes your essence punishes the anopheles
and your tannins baptize umbilical wounds
the digital arterioles severed spasmed by ether
reopened during the night a blood clot in the mouth
the child had held the wound to his lips
people thought it was a miracle my mother's father quoted *Praise!*
Ah! the keys, our jlat houses the city of Les Cayes
where I was born with wounded hands is still there
at land's end at the tip of the tongue of land
on the peninsula that paradise comes from
at the very tip of the tongue

~

mon père assembla les lettres en bas de casse
ses mains étaient fines et élégantes bouleversé il pensa
qu'il avait hérité d'un manuscrit et des mains d'une femme
si bien que ces mains-là lui étaient étrangères devenues
trace impudique de beauté trop belle
à ce point d'apitoyante tendresse
pour aussitôt les cacher à sa vue il se voyait voué
à l'accablante torture
de devoir sans fin se hisser à la hauteur d'extrémités charnelles
au moyen des lettres de plomb il composa
Joël est noyé dans le sang
fit tomber les lettres *o* et *y* de *noyé* dans leurs cases

et ajouta le tréma au signe *e* en tombant les lettres tintèrent
la râle du tréma ressemblait à un chant logé depuis l'aube
dans ta*ï*no ou encore dans cara*ï*be le son du tréma était ineffable
il songea que le tréma rappelait le nom d'Ha*ï*ti
manière d'accentuer le tremblement des voyelles
la résonance des lettres aimées *a ï e*

my father assembled the lower-case letters
he had fine elegant hands overwhelmed he thought
he had inherited a manuscript and a woman's hands
so that those hands so foreign to him had become
the indecent trace of a too lovely beauty
to the pitiful tender point
that to hide them from his own view he found himself fated
to the excruciating torture
of endlessly having to hoist himself up as high as carnal extremities
using the lead letters he wrote
Joël has drowned in blood
he let the letters *o* and *d* of *drowned* fall into their boxes
adding the diaeresis over the *e* as they dropped jingling into place
the death rattle of the diaeresis was like a song lodged since dawn
in *Taïno* or *Caraïbe* the sound of the diaeresis was ineffable
he mused over how the diaeresis made him think of the name *Haïti* a
way of accentuating the trembling vowels
the resonance of the beloved letters *a ï e*

~

l'enfance est d'immortalité
les cahiers d'écolier les récitations
de capitales de pays les appellations angéliques

de lac de Bolivie griffonnées sur des bouts de papier
échangés sans honte et que nous criions à la récréation
auxquelles personne ne comprenait rien mais
les gros mots faisaient rire attirant sur nos têtes le regard
courroucé de l'instituteur qui nous menaçait de sa vengeance
en des notes pleines de soufre
accolées aux fautes d'orthographe
que nous garderions en mémoire pour toujours
non sans une certaine tendresse
et que nous nous rappellerions ô maître

childhood is immortality
the student notebooks recitations
of capitals countries the Bolivian lake
angelic names scrawled on bits of paper
passed around secretly shamelessly and called out during recess
names no one understood but
the long words made us laugh drawing the teacher's
wrathful gaze as he threatened us with his vengeance
in sulfurous notes
he would write next to spelling mistakes
notes we would remember forever
not without a certain tenderness
and that we still recall sir

∼

pour *Guillane* ou la malheureuse *Caïenne*
vos devoirs sont rédigés dans une langue
qui voulut mais en vain
ressembler au français

ou encore
votre écriture d'insecte
ne vous autorise point à mettre deux *l* à Guyane
le maître pourfendait moins nos fautes
qu'il nous transmettait
pour longtemps la passion de la langue
et la hantise des formes qui l'excèdent

for *Guillane* or the wretched *Caïenne*
your homework is written in a language
which vainly wishes
to seem like French
and even
your insect-like writing
doesn't authorize you to put two *l's* in *Guyan*
the teacher didn't as much combat our mistakes
as pass on to us
for future years his passion for the language
and fear of any form that went beyond it

∾

il fut difficile de quitter les confins
pour l'eau de Grande-Rivière
où glissaient des feux
un désir de pèlerinage vers les mornes de café
les cases d'esclaves horribles reliques cantées
ouvertes aux stridences
pourquoi après tant de siècles modernes
parcourir la route de lacets et de cols
l'abîme chaque fois s'offrant

voir les balisiers déshabillés les amandiers en sommeil
les élancements païens des troncs affluent
hantés d'épiphytes
pour parmi les chaumes prendre l'Asiate
en style animal
l'ombre des arbres comme un drap
le mariage le plus haut s'est ainsi accompli
m'obsèdent de vieilles machines hydrauliques
des tiroirs à parches qu'on poussait à l'abri
commettre les gestes de qui cherche parmi
les essentes le collier de servitude
le maillet de gaïac ayant soif de charpentes
ô rôdeur

it was hard to leave the boundaries
for the waters of Grande-Rivière
where the fires glided along
a desire for a pilgrimage to the coffee slopes
the horrible slave huts sagging relics
open to the stridence
why after so many modern centuries
travel along the road of snares and passes
continually opening chasms
see the undressed canna plants slumbering almond trees
the pagan elation of tree trunks surges forward
haunted by epiphytes
to take the half-breed Asian among the stubble
animal style
the shade of the trees like a sheet
thus fulfilling the highest marriage
old hydraulic machines obsess me
flat boxes spread with green coffee that you'd cover over
making the gestures of someone searching among
the planks for the collar of servitude
the mallets of the guayacum trees thirsty for framing
O prowler

Adam Dickinson

When We Become Desirable

There is a genus of spruce so enamoured with the sky
it is painful to look at its blue needles —
like watching someone give themselves
so wholly to a doomed love
that you know you can do little,
except be there when the crepuscular heart fails.
Its limbs are the blue under your nails, in your lips
when the cold has opened its umbrella inside you.
In winter, the shadows in its crown
are footprints through a playground in deep snow
collecting the bruised light of retreating children;
it takes some time to recover yourself
after seeing this in the late afternoon.
It is not the kind of tree you can climb,
but often its lower branches hang down
like the sloped walls of a tent you can enter
and be, for a moment, among the pitch and splinters
of wanting, with all the colour of your blue-veined blood,
what will not receive you.

Believing the First Words You Hear

When the axe jams in the log
it is memory
reaching to pull you in.
Cherry is the easiest wood to split;
its grains are straight
paved roads.

Maple makes me think of you;
it grows branches as though
committing to entirely new trees.
I think of the axe handle
alive in my hands,
I think of the leaves.

Fort Smith Fire Brigade

The ravens are as large and as loud as babies.
They are public tantrums
for food that has dropped in the dirt.
In the town parks, on the hydrants,
they are wood leftover
from a catastrophic fire, a black that gulps
daylight and holds it like a rain barrel,
a locked and scorched water.
They are ambassadors from the other side
of what-has-burned, laughter
that reverberates at the end of language,
rises up, its feathers of thinking smoke.
They treat the things we build
as furniture; the gas pumps,
the stop signs are slouching galleries,
are the relaxed mess of a building
they know they can leave.
A raven is the child that leaps into your throat
when branches have fallen in the street.
It is the part of you that grows younger
when first you realise at night
how well the dark takes up residence
among the open, leafless stars.

Hélène Dorion

En ce temps-là je n'avais de regard
qu'absent de moi-même mon corps
verrouillé du dedans
au dehors mes chemins rétrécis
jusqu'à ne plus être
je traçais l'erratique
mouvement de la chair
éprise du sombre comme du silence
je marchais au bord de moi
conjuguant l'exil et la fuite
à même ce qui restait
dans les muscles
un fragment de geste
sachant bien la préhension
d'une ombre
qui ne m'appartient pas

tout ce qu'est ma vie tu sais
ce froid qui s'immisce
pour sans cesse y inscrire la fin

∽

Une maison brûle et nous la regardons consumer ce qui était encore habitable. Tant de maisons brûlent chaque jour en moi, et tu n'en sais rien.

Le temps passe et ai-je seulement commencé à vivre ?

Le premier geste fut celui de passer à travers la mère. Le dernier sera le même, il ne s'y ajoutera qu'un peu de lumière.

Je la sens qui cogne
dans mon ventre
elle remue la tête
ne veut pas quitter
sa fille je suis
celle par qui se referme
la boucle la dernière
des deux filles
je tiens entre mes mains
le dernier cordon

Ce soir-là tu poses la main
au milieu du dos le frisson
longe cette main
qui est un peu la mienne

Il y aura l'appel, une voix reconnue qui prononcera la mort sans que la mort imaginée ne l'apaise.

∼

Recommence devant moi
le mouvement de la mer.
Les parois se ferment
alors que se dessine la gravité
du poème, cette lumière
penchée sur la vie.

Je retourne vers les quais
de notre attente, là où mes pas, mon regard
mes mains ont longtemps cherché
à se poser. Cherché les chemins
où personne ne va.

Je reviens à la gare du monde
qui peu à peu se vide
des voyageurs sans voyage.

∼

Tu refais le voyage qui t'a mené jusqu'ici
tu rassembles les fossiles, plonges la main
dans le ciel, mais aucune lumière n'en jaillit.

Tu revois le premier homme
lever la tête, tu entends le cri
qu'il pousse devant la nuit.

Des milliards d'années plus loin, l'écho
porte le même effroi, la même solitude
— le même bruit de pas résonne
dans le temple abandonné.

∼

Le monde dévore nos paupières
au-delà des rêves, de la rose
que mâche la nuit, nous vivons
comme des feuilles enroulées
autour de l'horizon, nous flottons
et pour guérir de nous-mêmes

— quand éclatent les fissures
que se perdent les pierres
jetées parmi les lambeaux des siècles —

nous glissons avec les continents
cherchons l'eau, cherchons le rivage
et un jour l'image se retourne
le Gardien des Lieux, à nouveau
se penche sur nous.

∼

Marilyn Dumont

Circle the Wagons

There it is again, the circle, that goddamned circle, as if we thought in circles, judged things on the merit of their circularity, as if all we ate was bologna and bannock, drank Tetley tea, so many times "we are" the circle, the medicine wheel, the moon, the womb, and sacred hoops, you'd think we were one big tribe, is there nothing more than the circle in the deep structure of native literature? Are my eyes circles yet? Yet I feel compelled to incorporate something circular into the text, plot, or narrative structure because if it's linear then that proves that I'm a ghost and that native culture really has vanished and what is all this fuss about appropriation anyways? Are my eyes round yet? There are times when I feel that if I don't have a circle or the number four or legend in my poetry, I am lost, just a fading urban Indian caught in all the trappings of Doc Martens, cappuccinos and foreign films but there it is again orbiting, lunar, hoops encompassing your thoughts and canonizing mine, there it is again, circle the wagons . . .

The White Judges

We lived in an old schoolhouse, one large room that my father converted into two storeys with a plank staircase leading to the second floor. A single window on the south wall created a space that was dimly lit even at midday. All nine kids and the occasional friend slept upstairs like cadets in rows of shared double beds, ate downstairs in the kitchen near the gas stove and watched TV near the airtight heater in the adjacent room. Our floors were worn linoleum and scatter rugs, our walls high and bare except for the family photos whose frames were crowded with siblings waiting to come of age, marry or leave. At supper eleven of us would stare down a pot of moose stew, bannock and tea, while outside the white judges sat encircling our house.

And they waited to judge.

waited till we ate tripe
watched us inhale its wild vapour
sliced and steaming on our plates,
watched us welcome it into our being,
sink our teeth into its rubbery texture
chew and roll each wet and tentacled piece
swallow its gamey juices
until we had become it and it had become us.

Or waited till the cardboard boxes
were anonymously dropped at our door, spilling with clothes
waited till we ran swiftly away from the windows and doors
to the farthest room for fear of being seen
and dared one another to
"open it"
"no you open it"
"no you"
someone would open it
cautiously pulling out a shirt
that would be tried on
then passed around till somebody claimed it by fit
then sixteen or eighteen hands would be pulling out
skirts, pants, jackets, dresses from a box transformed now
into the Sears catalogue.

Or the white judges would wait till twilight
and my father and older brothers
would drag a bloodstained canvas
heavy with meat from the truck onto our lawn, and
my mother would lift and lay it in place
like a dead relative,
praying, coaxing and thanking it
then she'd cut the thick hair and skin back
till it lay in folds beside it like carpet

carving off firm chunks
until the marble bone shone out of the red-blue flesh

long into the truck-headlight-night she'd carve
talking in Cree to my father and in English to my brothers
long into the dark their voices talking us to sleep
while our bellies rested in the meat days ahead.

Or wait till the guitars came out
and the furniture was pushed up against the walls
and we'd polish the linoleum with our dancing
till our socks had holes.

Or wait till a fight broke out
and the night would settle in our bones
and we'd ache with shame
for having heard or spoken
that which sits at the edge of our light side
that which comes but we wished it hadn't
like "settlement" relatives who would arrive at Christmas and
leave at Easter.

Letter to Sir John A. Macdonald

Dear John: I'm still here and halfbreed,
after all these years
you're dead, funny thing,
that railway you wanted so badly,
there was talk a year ago
of shutting it down
and part of it was shut down,
the dayliner at least,
"from sea to shining sea,"
and you know, John,
after all that shuffling us around to suit the settlers,
we're still here and Metis.

We're still here
after Meech Lake and
one no-good-for-nothin-Indian

holdin-up-the-train,
stalling the "Cabin syllables / Nouns of settlement,
/ . . . steel syntax [and] / The long sentence of its exploitation†"
and John, that goddamned railroad never made this a great nation,
cause the railway shut down
and this country is still quarreling over unity,
and Riel is dead
but he just keeps coming back
in all the Bill Wilsons yet to speak out of turn or favour
because you know as well as I
that we were railroaded
by some steel tracks that didn't last
and some settlers who wouldn't settle
and it's funny we're still here and callin ourselves halfbreed.

† F. R. Scott, "Laurentian Shield"

Leather and Naughahyde

So, I'm having coffee with this treaty guy from up north and we're laughing at how crazy "the mooniyaw" are in the city and the conversation comes around to where I'm from, as it does in underground languages, in the oblique way it does to find out someone's status without actually asking, and knowing this, I say I'm Metis like it's an apology and he says "mmh," like he forgives me, like he's got a big heart and mine's pumping diluted blood and his voice has sounded well-fed up till this point, but now it goes thin like he's across the room taking another look and when he returns he's got "this look," that says he's leather and I'm naughahyde.

Let the Ponies Out

oh papa, to have you drift up, some part of you drift up through water through
fresh water into the teal plate of sky soaking foothills, papa,
to have your breath leave, escape you, escape the
weight of bone, muscle and organ, escape you, to rise up, to loft,

till you are all breath filling the room, rising, escaping the white, the white
sheets, airborne, taken in a gust of wind and unbridled ponies, let the ponies
out, I would open that gate if I could find it, if there was one
to let you go, to drift up into, out, out
of this experiment into the dome of all breath and wind and
reappear in the sound of the first year's thunder with
Chigayow cutting the clouds over your eyes expanding, wafting, wings
of a bird over fields, fat ponies, spruce, birch and poplar, circling
wider than that tight square sanitized whiteness
you breathe in, if you could just stop breathing you could
escape, go anywhere, blow, tumble in the prairie grass,
bloom in the face of crocuses
appear in the smell of cedar dust off a saw
in the smell of thick leather
in the whistling sounds of the trees
in the far off sound of a chainsaw or someone chopping wood
in the smooth curve of a felt hat, in unbridled ponies.

The Sky is Promising

Danny, come home
it's sunny
the ponies are frisky,
the sawdust pile is high,
the spruce are whistling and
the day rolls out before us.

Danny come home to sky
the color of juniper berries,
it's summer and
time to twist binder-twine
into long ropes to catch the ponies,
race them to the water trough,
listen for the sound of green
poplar leaves applauding
and dream of prizes,

hand-tooled saddles
big silver buckles and
our victories assure us
we have lived our sawdust days well.

Danny come home
the berries are ripe and we've collected
lard pails for picking. We're driving
up the bench road to fill them
with sweet smelling huckleberries.
We'll meet for lunch, use the tailgate for a table,
dump our berries into buckets and
talk about the patch we found,
the deer we saw, the stream
we drank from or the bees'
nest almost stepped on.

Danny come home
the sawdust pile is high and
its slopes are sand
dunes we can slide down
at the bottom we can look
up and see only the crest
of sand and the promising sky.

Danny come home. The men
are riding skid horses into camp,
watering them at the trough,
we can get close, watch
their flared steaming nostrils
sink into the icy water,
see them chew the cool liquid,
teeth the size of our fingers,
water dripping from their chins
throwing their heads back,
harness sounds rippling,
whinnying to the horses in the corral.

Danny come home we can

walk through the warm pine smells
to where the men are falling, we can
listen to them hollering orders
to the skid horses
whose heavy hind legs
lever the still logs
into a moving universe.

Louise Dupré

Là, voilà ta demeure
la ville vissée à tes os
la ville blême
incapable de t'accueillir
Tu avances comme hors de toi
dans une solitude molle
méfiance, abandon
et ta parole arrêtée
au seuil des mots
quand ils s'embrouillent dans ta voix
Rien que cela
rien d'autre
que ton piétinement assourdi
par la mêlée de cris et de klaxons
Tu cherches sous quels volets
tu pourrais déposer tes pas

∽

Tout est possible à l'ombre des jardins, dans le luxe de leurs parfums, même l'amour et ses audaces, l'insistance d'un aveu coulant entre les pierres sans certitude qu'il parviendra jusqu'à l'autre. Tendre les bras, chuchoter les mots amples des femmes qui détachent leur blouse devant un inconnu. Et le risque de rester là, honteuse dans sa nudité s'il advenait qu'il détourne la tête. Savoir pourtant qu'on ne s'effondrerait pas, car tout est possible, toujours, si les reliques reposent sous le lobe apaisé du cœur.

∽

Tu peux encore lever la main
pour cueillir un fruit mûr
quand distraite par une intention
de chaleur
tu vois apparaître un verger
là où un pommier chétif
ploie sous le vent d'octobre
Il t'arrive en effet de corriger
le paysage
c'est ton espérance
elle s'agite dans l'angle mort
de la réalité
avec ses parfums printaniers
laissant croire à quelque fête
Mais tes visions parfois s'estompent
et tu te retrouves
face au vide du crépuscule
qui avance résolument
sans se préoccuper de toi

∼

Rien ne suffit à ton regard
nul arrangement d'arbres ni d'oiseaux
dans les squares bien taillés
Tu retardes le moment
où tu enjamberas le jour, où tu verras
vaciller cette lueur
qu'on surprend quelquefois chez les vieillards
quand ils se croient seuls
et se demandent
de quelle mort mourir
C'est aussi ta question
mais tu ne l'avouerais à quiconque

sauf peut-être à toi-même
tard le soir
si tu en venais à quitter les livres
pour tourner la tête vers ton ombre
Tu repenserais alors
au mutisme acharné de ton père

∽

Cela arrive toujours sans prévenir
ces longs convois de phares tamisés
de sanglots et de glaïeuls
ces corps qu'on achemine
jusqu'à la montagne
avec sa verdure trop verte
nourrie de poudre d'os
Le monde s'écroule devant toi
menacé par les talons des passants
qui ne se soucient pas de leur marche
et tu le laisses à son abandon
tu te signes
coupable de t'enfuir
loin de tes yeux
très loin, là où l'on peut ignorer
le néant
à la ligne d'horizon

∽

Tu relèves ta robe
de plus en plus haut
jusqu'au paysage noir
de ton ventre
et tu t'affiches dans les rues
avec ce seul écriteau
Tu dis qu'il ne te reste plus de temps
pour les jupes circulaires
plus de temps pour attendre
Tu cherches quelqu'un
avec des bras
et des gestes assez solides
pour te retenir
un homme
adossé au silence d'une nuit
aussi scandaleuse
que ta nudité

∼

Tes morts, tu en es venue à les confondre avec la terre sous les pierres tombales, la terre rouge qui creuse des salons pour y allumer des lampes. Tu oublies la pourriture des cadavres quand ils se décomposent, tu veux nier les ruisseaux cachés qui charrient les restes d'ongle et de sang jusqu'aux bras des mers. Et tu n'inquiètes plus le paysage où le fleuve, déjà loin derrière son cri, n'en finit pas de courir avec assurance dans des eaux pourtant peu certaines.

Paul Dutton

One Plus

It is a one was many were a morning over and over. Been. Noon and before. After. It was a one is many are an afternoon again. Later. Between each, a little bit. And through. It will be another evening was some are once more. Where one will once be each night, many more have. Many more are one is always less and some have each to be another for starters, which seldom were, but usually under, usually emerging. Some ever will be more than just another, more than less or few, as who would sooner be are later than who do. Some pure form. Some few. Some few who were where someone is. Some few who were where someone is others. Some few who were where someone is others are many who having been others are one. One might lately be or have been further or far. Some far who were are. A node. Several seem to be fewer than are some less others is one. Morning after noon is night. After night falls, dawn breaks. After one (and not the first by any means), many. Many means one, means one plus. Plus one means one, means many. Many times. Many times, one means plus one anytime.

Lost Way Lost

Somewhere off from near beyond a clear-cut choice made much before what led to all that is behind the point of no view more being made than having faded from sight to far from what's been said might be construed as less than where things are how one turn given can take a way to lose a trek instead of moving one step further on or being lost in arriving at an abandoned principal region where rebel hordes overrun drugs barren mind that all you need is shove push has come to an impasse shunned by not just another pretty phase to get your thoughts behind what stutter-lip and stammer-tongue have gone and Götterdamerung the curtain down on the spot to which they got when thought gave out what body'd been saying all along was done to a wrong turn taken aback right when the route was forked by a tongue unspoken wheel we'll wail at while wool will well wear out its welcome in the age of synthetics and virtual everything virtually everywhere wondering where anywhere is any more than enough is too much to endure the loss of a way of life we'd not yet got the hang of let alone were done with.

Kit-Talk

mutter to tight head stutter at stick-tip pepper past rim-pulled skin held taut. got a little. got a lot. got a metal-splash sizzle as excess is, as is a zero's eyes assessing assizes. put. put put. put. pause. put in a pause. put in a pause 'n' snap. put in a pause 'n' snap off a sizable bit to tip a put-up past a pot-head patsy whose tight-lipped two-timing's tapered off. tapered-off top-spin whispers hisses at a brush-back pitch sent to size up what type o' sissy's up to bat. tough tit, kid, but suck it, suck it, suck it till it's tender, 'n' suck it, suck it, suck it till its tip is stiff as a stick, 'n' suck it, suck it, suck it, suck it, suck. suck at it. suck at it. suck at it till it tingles. suck at it till it tingles and its spit-wet tip can't take it. shhh. shhh. she's sighin', sure as shootin' she's not shy shit no she's shirtless 'n' shameless she's shorts-down dyin' to do it 'n' here's to it. to it 'n' at it. to it 'n' at it 'n' overnight. good night. good good good good good good night. good good good good good good day. good good good good good good time. good. good good. good good good good, good 'n' gooder. gooder in the gutter. got 'er gooder in the gutter n' took it up top to clatter that tick on a metal bit clatter his stick on a metal bit tip took off on a pulled down pop-pulled pow paid pat paid peter paid paul paid cash-strapped fish-store short shrift for switching from fish-stick sales to hash-stick pushing to doped-up wish-merchants waiting by wash-stands in run-down walkways past push-stick talk, paid pull-down pow-wow walkway west, way hey-down, hoe-down, who got gone gained getalong ghost, gained go round goalie has got that puck, has got that puck and won't let go, has got that puck and won't let you, let one, let all, let no one in, let this be it till dream-drip trickle-up pushes past top-down tail tipped sold out sin-fest lips slide slipping off flesh flaps flipped for fuller fooling 'round with chunk of punch-drunk monkey-mind spun down, wrung out, hard-held think unthunk. plunk.

Strata

Lizard-brain from viper-mind uncoils spine-fed up through stem to shrug across perimeters of thought turned from that which thought refuses, focused on present shadows cloaking thrust of lizard-brain from viper-mind uncoiling jungle-thought through branches laced above the slither-base they're transformed from that presses up along the bark, a hiss of appetite transmitted over networks buried back of lizard-brain that loops its mesozoic mind around a present order ignorant of what slinks through suck of mud and scrape of scale upon perimeters of thought unthinking, mindless of impulses electric and uncodified, surface countered and controlled by lizard-brain from viper-mind that lashes out in wordless flick, unleashed within language that buckles and breaks, the lie in the eye of who would shrink from mind mined for reptile-minded matter sunk from sight, encoded nightly in vague reflective images that percolate from lizard-brain with slick and glistening reptilian grace.

Thinking

Language shapes thought, not thought language. And language shapes thought not thought to be language-shapes. Thought not thought to be language shapes language, shapes thought, shapes shapes. Thought thought to be shapes not thought to be language shapes thoughts thought not to be shaped by language. Thought language shapes thought-shapes shaped by language thought to be thought. Thought thought not to be language-shapes shapes language, shapes thought, shapes language-thought. Language thinks. Language thinks shapes not shaped by thought, shapes thoughts thought thinks not shaped by language. Language thinks thoughts thought thinks think language. Language thinks language.

Dreaming

Dreaming sleep and dreaming eyes slipping dream into dream of deeper sleep that slips layers of the mind inside a dream of what's behind and before eyes closed on the self and on the world before the self become the world behind the blind that sleep peers at shadows on to puzzle out a form from what mind distils in dream dreamt of shapes behind, before, within the closed self dreaming signs out of mind, your mind, any mind signing the world behind the self, the self behind the world burning closer to dream slipping layers of behind beneath below, below meaning what we would know, beneath below meaning what we can't know now, puzzle of form of matter what will, what puzzle of form matter is lifts layers of mind from dream's lips speaking form seeking matter out of mind, out of your mind sleeping, dreams seeping from a crevice in a brain thoughts are enacted in a world before the self behind the mind inside a puzzle on a screen the mind is dreaming in images beyond words the images are couched in, words lying in a brain dreams creep from.

Jazzstory

bass line drum support trumpet speaks guitar
is
bass drums trumpet line guitar speaks support
is
line bass guitar speaks support trumpet drums
is
guitar trumpet line support drums bass speaks

    strum peaks pet line
    pumps out a gut art

    drum sum, traps a part
    rump air a sport

    bass gets tugged
    gets gutted
    gets mud dump

    drum murders beats
    spurts pus
    raps a lass as tar leaks
    lines outta time

    a glass part spits spots sputtered at
    rum murmurs names o' ports a nipper got potted in
    bump 'n' grind lined up 'n' out
    pout past pumped garter
                    art or
                    ardour

an eager leap
a tumble, a gulp
an ultimate mustard
a lapsed map

guitar speaks trumpet support drums line bass
is
support speaks guitar line trumpet drums bass
is
drums trumpet support speaks guitar bass line
is
speaks bass drums support line trumpet guitar
is

Succession

Just one, some before some, just one before another one after some other before. Just some after one before one after another, before more than some more than any, just one more another after one more before. Someone else. Someone then. Someone now. Someone just now before another just after. A. Not her. So me. Someone so not her, so me, so other, so just before one some more now else. Some other else. Just some other now before anyone else. Or other some just before one more anyone. Anyone more than someone more than anyone else. Anyone ever more after than else and more else than ever after any before. Often. Often more other after anyone is. Anyone is more some ever after than ever before just anyone else. Ever more after than just before even is, after is often more over before more is said. Say more. Say after. Say just before is. Say one is before over more than another, not her and not here after more than before. Still more. Still more than some before just after one. Well before two, more than well after anyone, anyone still more than just before when two is enough. Just enough. Two is just enough for one more after someone else is more than many might, because we may but haven't yet, and are though could as has been still in what we meant to be be more than ever where we had to get to go to say to do what any age thought good is likely up to no more of it than the next or last or this, which isn't any more than any one or two can anyway do worse than, doing worse and doing

more, as this one does, and is, moreover, more than enough, that two would
be too much of. Two too much and one that's, what's more, less than could be
hoped for. Not that hope's an option anymore, if it ever was before. Ever
before and ever after, then and now and now and again and other after other,
some or one or two or more, another one before, another after.

Obscure

    Light barrier
    between lines
    of gravity
    strung
    out or along —
    a weight of wire, taut,
    or burden of deceit.

    The same ring chimes in
    time after time:
    life's off-rhyme
    repeating

    Darkness opens
    on deeper dark
    lines obscured
    between origin and end,
    muscle wired fibre
    binding bound
    to be
    what was
    what is
    what might be.

    Within barred light
    a scene lies
    on or about
    where light casts doubt,
    invoking something seen

lying in the present, where
a dollar is a penny any-
more, is less than ever
what you get
for what you think
is what you paid for
once again and haven't got

Truck

I get into the truck with him. It was, is, a truck I got into with him, get into again or then a truck now I'm in is with him getting in it seems, him in and me getting in with him, the truck I got into then or again, now and then and again a truck and him and the dim green of the dashboard glowing. I get into the truck with him and pull the door shut behind me in the dim glow of the dashboard lit green in the night within the truck we're in, were again in, him in dim green glow, getting in and pulling the door shut behind him, green-lit highlights, glint of skin-sheen in the green pall. I get into the truck with him and with the green pall and the door pulled behind me against the dark outside, inside out of light outside night inside and outside of night out of light in the truck outside in my view from the door I open and enter the night, approaching the truck from the door I stood behind: night at the glass pane before me; behind and around me, light. Here, at the fringe, neither light nor night, a pane between the two, both opened and entered on, closed and collapsed, the white glare of the hall, of lit rooms within the night inside approaching, light behind, within, dim in some dark doorway a figure stands at, hand on the knob of a door pushed into the room the figure leaned into out of the pale glow of a hall lit with light from afar, a white glare somewhere shedding light in some other hall a lit figure leans from into a room suffused with light against the night at the window pressing into the unlit room filling with the slow dark glow of halls and doorways and figures approaching in the night in light or dark clothes leaning with glint of skin-sheen casting back the faint glow from the pale bulb burning now and then in white again or green.

Content

Not wrenched, but rendered —
extract beyond word or image:
matter melted into mind into matter melting,
tongue telling eye
seeing melt of mind beyond matter,
eye mattering as mouth does,
here much more than ear
ever than an h is,
ere eye sees y.

Why an ear sees here
more than eyes hear there
is what a paradox is.

A mouth mattering
as word or image.
An eye's as much an ear:
look, hear beyond mutter of fact.

Night

Across a darkened room a shadow steals a mind from a darkened room to a darkened room across a darkened room a shadow sees a pale illumination in a pale dark room across a mind a shadow steals a thought across a streetlight-moon lighting a room with a pale wash across a wall illuminating the point of fusion, of the darkened room, of a pale light, of a shadow moving across a wall a shadow stole from a darkened room to combine in mind, pale and streetlight and moon fused, thought taught to feel, a moving shadow taught to feel a darkened room vaguely lit by light of street or moon in mind, feeling a moving shadow of shades upon a wall in a darkened room a mind feels, thinking in a darkened room, a mind a shadow working at feeling that a body is a mind working, a feeling mined from a darkened room in a darkened room across a shadow falling from ceiling to floor with the light a passing car arches over a wall across a dim-lit room with shades a light beams through to steal a mind from a room a shadow rises from light moving up the wall descending with the shadows a light from a passing car passes through the windows standing open to the night. Shadows passing shadows in repeating light of night upon the wall across a room a figure moves through in shadow-light etched on night opening on light of darkened room. A figure in the room speaks and falls silent: a figure of speech becomes a body of thought. In a night repeated, felt, a figure feeling without words, speaks a room. Shadows fall still, while, where shadows still fall, a room speaks without words a stream of thought a figure feels alight upon its mind, a light of passing cars on a road a streetlight shines its circle of light upon a mind in a room where shadows move and sigh a window open on a night the room's a shadow in, the night a shadow a room's in, the room a shadow a night's in, a shadow, a room, a night, where pale and streetlight and moon are fused and a figure in the room lifts an arm as though to shield its eyes, desiring only sleep, where shadows spill across the wall, ceiling, wall, and disappear.

Several Times Table

Several times many is much.
Several times few is most.
Several times some is less.
Several times any is almost.
Several times soon is then.
Several times lots is more.
Several times plenty's enough.
Several times partly's about.
Several times ever is maybe.
Several times kind-of is close.
Several times something is likely.
Several times sometime's forever.

Shy Thought

There's something about always saying the same thing over and over again usually making it different all the time talking around what disappears when it's talked about, saying again what was already said differently around what won't stay still that keeps it somehow close. It's the same thing talking about always saying around something being about near what it is. Just what's usually always different about which one anyway's disappearing is still what it won't make be said about what's put differently, wanting not to stop repeating what's almost being said. Same again. Speaking of saying over and over what's always somehow almost being said, it's not just there but here again somewhere being different still. There's always something about saying things over that's usually different each time it's there in peripheral cognition. See? The same old thing. There's something always about, something always talking about, something somewhere always talking about almost saying something exactly the same way nearly every time it's said over and practically there out of the corner of your mind differently again. Again, it's not the same thing. Something else is the same thing differently another time somewhere where it's not being talked of but around again.

Words

She has words and smiles she has for me something about her I always knew she had something I knew she knew something about her was smiles and words to me, something she has I always knew words about her smiles she had for me something I knew. She had something in smiles and something in words for me, something I always knew words wouldn't do for — something in anyway all she has been. She has anyway always been something in words for me, something in anyway all she could be, being smiles of something I never could have, having words for her smiles and something for anything, something for having to do what she had to to smile her words to me, somewhere below what could really be heard, somewhere above what was meant to be said: "Words," she said, "and smiles for me." She says words and smiles something words couldn't be, something about her that's something she smiles words are and she can be words and be smiles and do what she wants sitting and smiling at words telling what she knew they could do, smiling and using them, saying words as though they had made her and made me, which they did and she is, beyond words smiling, beyond meaning what words are becoming her sitting in light clothing black as her hair is her clothing she smiles in light becoming her words forever becoming smiles and her black hair framing her pale face her lips smile in saying, "Words."

Gary Geddes

Subsidies

A boy with a mechanical arm
addresses a group of kids
on farm safety;
a farmer tries to talk
to the camera — still asking himself
how it happened — youngest son, beside him
one moment on the fender,
slipping under the rear wheel of the tractor.

Eighty percent of rural deaths,
the voice explains,
are the result of farm accidents.

Statistics are no consolation
when you've seen the support-block
give way and the circular saw
walk through the flesh of your son's neck.
At night as you drift towards sleep
you see the recognition
in his startled eyes;
cock's crow
is the engine's whine.

A year later, you still can't look at her
over breakfast, rise
to the need in her flesh
or yours. You toy with an egg,
hard boiled and intransigent
on your plate, invite
the coffee to burn your lips.

You hear them debate subsidies
in parliament, the future of the family farm,
and you know that nothing you plant
will ever again grow straight,
nothing you do
will ever make it right.

Junk Food Pastoral

Yours is the worst hay I cut,
Frank tells me, as he hoists another bale
onto the loaded wagon, where his wife
places it in interlocking fashion
over the previous layer, and the boy,
a late and unexpected child,
runs up and down the angled stooks.

I don't see Frank all winter, except to wave
as he drives home to family
and chores from the factory in Ottawa.
He speaks wistfully of retirement,
wondering how much steam he'll still have
when the nine-year-old leaves home.

A low yield this year, nine hundred bales,
fields overrun with straw weed,
hay I first charged him for, then shared,
and am now pleased just to have cut
to keep the thistles and burdock in check.

As the haywagon fills, he uses
the front-end loader with a sheet of plywood
to hoist six bales at a time.
This is their holiday, racing the weather,
ten loads in the heat of the day,
binder twine burning capable hands.

Rhythm of work. Smiles that take root
in stomach wall or rib-cage — they don't fade
easily. *Yours is the worst hay,* Frank is standing
eight feet above me on his plywood stage,
scenery of fast-moving cloud, *but my cows
seem to like it best.*

Susan Gillis

Distant Islands
(But of course they were further apart)

Plumes of smoke rose like poplar trees.
There was the sun, punched into the sky like the sky's navel.
The river, pricked and lifted by windhooks.
Mist puffing up, the sun black then white.
We could have walked the columns of air like pathways
to waiting Airbuses, walked into the sky-hold.
The smoke-plumes, wind at them: leaf-shake.
Then the river reared up like a dragon,
scales flapping — sun, smoke, islands,
all collapsed in the froth of its lashing.
I have never been so small, atomic.
We were tossed, and I have to say "maelstrom" —
I wanted out. I wanted time to turn back.
When I felt my feet on the ground again
I was shaking. It seemed I could reach
in any direction and touch the clouds,
the opposite shore, the islands, mist and smoke.
The gaps between things had closed.
I tell you this because I have not been able to separate them
and now all hurts are nothing, are blips, leaf-loss.
When I leave, understand, I will not be gone.

Habitat (South elevation)

In noon light the south elevation
resembles a nautilus in cross-section,
rooms dangled around the plumb-line
ganged up in clusters; or a grain of sand
barnacled, limed, cemented

onto itself, boiler-lunged; or

a crenellation left in a sea-bed
when the sea shrank away — I can't
order the plans into rooms, they show a door
to a terrace-court

but when I walk through
it's into somebody's swimming pool.
Up the left lane and down the right
around a boulevard of tropical plants
under steel trusses and glass and ruthless light

someone is swimming. I want to know
what happened. "A corridor runs between,"
she explains, but does it divide or join? "Please,"
she answers, nodding toward the springboard,
and I climb on, for this is a living room.

Habitat (We stand here looking)

Like many, I see it first from the river,
improbable, arbitrary-seeming,
crannied as a sea-stack, nest-
populated, designed by glaciation,
thermal flux, earth-accident.

Slowly the jags resolve themselves
into made things on a made shore,
blocks gripped by a central core,
each with a sweeping view of partial
things: beyond the river, the flood

plain and rising hills, or the city
roads and buildings and the port.
Here is Safdie, stacking the future
in Mediterranean terrace-houses
craned onto fill in a cold Canadian river.

A good maker orders the material.
We stand here looking.

Come, the building says,
with terrible urgency.
Come lie down in my rooms.

River (Dear X.)

Today wind is driving the snow horizontal.
The window is flocked with frost-lands

bronchiole-edged and populous with cryoplankton
probably building cities, oblivious in their archipelago

to the inevitable oncoming thaw.
Through this I can see the shape of the bridge

but not the bridge. All is ice, silver, obsidian.
My piece of this improbable place.

My father taught me how to carry coffee
without spilling: look where you're going, he said,

don't look at the cup. In many ways
it's been good advice. About my *volte-face:*

and you're not wrong to call it that.
Do you know the story of the night-bird

and its pebble-throated song?
Something the bird loved had died,

and so it longed to die.
As it sang, its breast filled with stones.

Its song became a river of stones
which the bird felt as pleasure.

Is this love, then? Clear-eyed friend,
I tell you, I found myself in a city

more unlike my own than I could bear.
I came here to hold the river.

Goh, Poh Seng

The Girl from Ermita

If you ever come to Manila,
come down to red-light Ermita
Where nightly I ply my trade.

They call me Fely.
I was born in Samar.
I'm the girl with the bird in her head.

Yes, a bird in my head!
If you look deep into my eyes
you can see it flying about.

You ask what kind of bird it is?
Why, a white gull of course!
For I was born in Samar by the sea.

And how did it get there:
this white gull in my head?
Well, it flew in when I was fourteen.

But you don't really want
to hear the same old hard-luck story!
There are no new legends anymore.

Better take me away somewhere,
take me in your sweaty arms,
and your eyes, cold as death,

Can feed on the peach of my skin,
your savage heart
release its black secrets.

You can do what
you like with me.
I know all the positions.

Come, lie with me
and I will be your love.
Don't you believe me?

Yes, come lie down with me,
it will only cost a hundred *pesos*,
and it's good therapy.

I'll give good value for your money.
I have the techniques
learned through ten thousand nights.

I will embrace you
and the stars outside
will mind their own bloody business.

The wind will not complain,
the trees not grumble,
and all the cops have been bribed.

Or perhaps you think yourself too grand,
too good and holy
to pay to lie with me?

Perhaps you're afraid
the universe will roar in disgust
if you pay for my body?

Don't you know by now
life's a market-place where
you can buy cow meat, goat meat and my meat?

I was born in Samar in Visayas
where the sea ran silver when I was a child
and clouds and trees were my friends.

Of my own father,
I only know
he was a *carabao* of a man.

And like the *carabao*,
he was patient and ignorant,
his feet stubborn in the loam.

But his eyes.
I remember his eyes:
they held such innocence!

When I was twelve, he died,
and my mother and I
lived on, any old how.

Come to think of it.
I don't know how we did it!
Then my mother remarried.

We shifted to an old lean-to
with my step-father.
I had turned fourteen.

For a time I was content enough.
I was only a child then and you know
how children can grow smiles even out of a dungheap!

Then one night my step-father
laid his hands on my green breasts,
and I was too petrified to move.

I endured for many months
my step-father's hands
till one night I could not suppress my cry.

My mother came to intervene:
it drove my step-father wild
as a mad, rampaging bull.

He punched me in the face,
kicked my mother in the ribs,
left us black and blue.

The next day I drew
a real deep breath
and ran away from home.

The ferry boat crossing the sea
delivered me from my past:
my childhood lay like broken glass.

An hour after
we reached Cebu city,
I got myself picked up

By a dirty old man
who fed me, gave me shelter and clothes,
and treated me like a household pet.

I was surprised how soon
I got used to his caresses,
no longer reacting with nausea and tears.

So five years passed.
Five Christmases and five Easters
I stayed with my dirty old man.

In our second year
I bore him a bastard girl:
a child, when I was myself a child

Of sixteen.
But already the months
began to wall me in.

When I was eighteen
I went with a handsome man
who took me away to Batangas.

For a brief few months
I blossomed like the *sampaguita*
with this first young man in my life.

A tangerine time it was,
with ice-cream on Sundays,
dances and kisses under the moon.

And then it was over.
His wife came screaming for our blood
and he returned to her like a pup.

Well, life's like that.
I came to Manila
in search of fame and gold.

But found only dust
in the crowded streets
of the capital.

I became a salesgirl
and had to sleep with my boss.
I became a go-go dancer.

Ground my bum in the faces of fools
who drooled like rotten fruit,
while klieg lights tore at my skin.

Now I'm landed here
where life has got me in its jaws
and I no longer wait for miracles.

I no longer care
to look into the eyes of my johns,
for they hold no more secrets.

Now I simply lie flat on my back,
my face upturned to the sugary sky
which the stars eat like white ants.

Now I fuck for a refrigerator,
or for my daughter's school fees:
my girl's just turned eight this May.

Yes, I will turn a trick for a meal,
and men can take me
in any position they wish.

The white scream never flies
out of my black mouth,
the radios will remain silent.

The newspapers advertise soap,
the priests launder
the limp souls of their sinners.

Yes, at night I can be your sweet mango,
but come the dawn,
I'll be as sour as a *calamansi*.

There's still some acid in me,
you know that?
You, who sit there listening so dumbly!

So I've unloaded my story
and my head's just an empty hole
with nameless echoes in it.

Are you quite sure
you don't want
to take me to bed?

Come, lie down with me.
I will be your true love,
for only a hundred *pesos*.

But you only laugh
green and gold and purple
and fly free into the night.

For you are the white gull
who left secret spaces again
inside my head!

But if you ever come back to Manila,
come down to red-light Ermita,
where nightly I ply my trade.

They call me Fely,
I was born in Samar by the sea,
I'm the girl with a hole in her head.

Lorna Goodison

Brunetto Latini

And so we proceeded along the built-up mud banking
above a water course like an infernal Bog Walk gorge
with fog draped like wet sheets against fire burning.
Just as how people in foreign build thick mud walls
to keep out big sea when it rises up high and swells
to overflow their food cultivations and pasture lands
in places like British and French Guyana near Brazil.
Or some Italian town named Padua along the Brent
where they erect big retaining walls with weep-holes
to protect tower and yard against deconstruction's
snowmelt, earthrunnings, carrydown and watershed.
It's as if hell's civil engineer got an illegal gully contract
to bitch-up some similar but lean-side walls like that.
By now we are travelling in the bowels of the earth
leaving the murdersuicide woodland so far out of sight
we could not spy it even from the land of look behind.
We buck up a procession of duppies shuffling below
the banking, staring up into our faces like how some
scrutinize one another under the light of a new moon.
Staring, like fast people trying to see who passing by
dark road on a moonless night; staring, like an old tailor
with glaucoma trying hard to thread a fine-eyed needle.
The staring duppies screwed their faces and frowned,
then one sight me, grab me by the hem of my gown
and said, "Lord have mercy, could this really be true.
Dear poet is it you?" As he touched me I focused hard
riveting my eyes upon the charred skin of his face
so that I summoned up his image from my memory.
And bending near, I peered into his burnt countenance
and groaned, "Is it you down here so Teacher Brown?"
"O my friend I do hope you will not object if Brownman

turns around and walks along by your side so allowing
this ghostly procession to proceed a while without me."
Said I, "I would be most honoured if you and I could sit in,
if it pleases him who is my guide through this dark pit."
Said Mr. B., "Whichever one of this done-dead-already band
stops for a moment must remain still for a hundred years,
forbidden to brush off these drops of corrosive acid rain.
No, my good friend, do walk on, I will walk below you
until it will be time for me to rejoin my duppy company
who must perpetually weep and wail in eternal flames."
So since I dared not descend from my banking and walk
with him on the burning no-life path, I inclined my head,
walked with it bowed low to show my respect, like a mystic
meditating reverently upon the divide between goodness
and evil. "And what brings you down here before your time?
Was it that big accident up by Providence? And who is he
that is leading you through this dive of such deep darkness?"
Hear me: "Up there in the land of the living, I went astray,
I lost my livity, lost my way before I reached the fullness
of my years, only yesterday before day did I find myself
and this master here appeared and wheel and turned me
like a Revivalist Darwish/Sufi and is now leading me home."
Hear him: "Follow your guiding star, for in all the good life
I experienced I learned this one thing that's true. What is fi
you, can not be un-fi you. And had I lived out my time
and purpose, instead of having it cut short, I would have
helped, supported and encouraged your work, seeing that
you are a true poet, God-blessed. But that bad-minded set,
those pharisaical keepers of our country's gates, whose
hearts are as hard as Blue Mountain alabaster, those who
occupy the chairs of the colonial masters, they envy you
your talent. But poet, the roseapple was not ever meant
to flourish beside these blighted soursop trees, bear in mind
that even old proverbs call them blind-guides, a bad mind
petty, mean spirited, myopic kind; take care to uproot
their grudging ways from your heart. It is written in the stars.
It must surely come to pass that your honours will make

both parties want to claim you. That ram goat will never
reach high enough to crop on such sweet grass, let them
devour their one another's (excuse me) one another's rass.
But never let them cut down any innocent plant that
despite their stunting hands will still thrive amongst them."
"Mr. Brown, if I had my wish," I said, "you wouldn't be
banished from the land of the living in which you were
a source of light among our people. I recall your gentle
compassionate and fatherly face as you taught me daily
how human beings can make themselves live eternally.
This image of you, pentimento, surfaces on my heart and
lives on in my mind and while I am alive I give thanks
for it, and I will tell of you to the world through my life
and my art. Your predictions for my future I will file
with some works of mine I save to show a wise someone
who will be the judge of these matters anon, if I can ever
reach her higherheights. As the Most High is my witness
I tell you this: As long as, I say, as long as my conscience
is clear, I am prepared for whatever destiny shall bring
my way. Twice already, I have heard that same prophecy.
But let Fortune's wheel turn around as it pleases, round
and round she must go and countryman must dig with hoe."
My spirit guide paused when he heard what it was I said,
turned and looked into my eyes and spoke. "Well heeded
is well heard." But I did not answer, I went on speaking
to Teacher Brown, asking him who was down here with him
in hell's hot sands, from manor-born to just commerown.
He said, "It is good to know about some deads down here
on this walk with me; about the rest of them, let them be.
For our time is too short to engage in idle pointless talk.
Long story short: We were all professionals of true worth,
men and women of letters, scholars of high renown all
brought down by arrogance and excess love of self.
I would tell you more but now I see some fresh steam
rising out of the sand, and some parvenu duppies I want
to avoid are at hand. Hear what I say, don't cry for me or
pity me. Read my books, they vindicate me. In my words

I am alive and I am no duppy." So saying he turned sprinting
across that fiery plain like a runner competing in a race,
and then he seemed like one who ran ahead and passed
the tape first and not as one who had come in dead last.

    from Dante's *Inferno,* Canto XV

Questions for Marcus Mosiah Garvey

And did prophets ascended come swift
to attend you at the end
in your small cold water room in London?

Was it William Blake now seraph and ferryman
who rowed you across the Thames to where Africans
took you by longboat home?

And did the Nazarene walking upon water
come alongside to bless and assure you that he
of all prophets understood and knew

just how they had betrayed and ill-used you?
And did you wonder again what manner of people
sell out prophets for silver and food?

Crossover Griot

The jump-ship Irishman
who took that Guinea girl
would croon when rum
anointed his tongue.

And she left to mind
first mulatta child
would go end of day
to ululate by the bay.

"I am O'Rahilly" he croons.
She moans "since them
carry me from Guinea
me can't go home"

Of crossover griot
they want to ask
how all this come about?
To no known answer.

Still they ask her
why you chant so?
And why she turn poet
not even she know.

Poor Mrs. Lot

And so it was that Lot's hard-ears wife
became a pillar of solid eye water.

Poor woman, frozen there crystalline
up from ground, salt stalagmite.

One last glance at what you left behind:
your mother's cutlery, your yellow plates.

One more look behind to memorize
the lay, the order of the landscape.

The red water tank. The church spire.
One last look is enough to petrify.

Like you, she should have cried
as she left, not daring to look back,

savouring hard homeground with salt.

Susan Goyette

This Contradiction of Passion

If your husband owns a rifle company, you must face facts.
There will always be ghosts. The ghosts of rifle victims follow
you out of your bath, clinging to your nightgown. And the ghosts

of your husband's hands, the contradiction of his passion,
his thin finger tracing your lips, touching your tongue,
and the same finger squeezing a trigger. Wanting to squeeze a trigger.

And if you're a sculptor you're obsessed with the human body,
and must face faults. There will be an arm longer than the other,
a thigh more muscular. But that vision you've seen, that slender

body of spirit with its feathers and wish bone hides beneath
those flaws and day after day you must chase it. Whittle and chisel
after that image you know must be true. When you finish,

your work is in powder, in dust that you sweep up and store
in matchboxes. Maybe you'll swallow it, mixed in your tea
and it will awaken something in you that doesn't yet have a name.

Despite these facts, these faults, I have licked the fingers
of a man who knows the secret steps of stalking
and can follow me anywhere. I have sculpted him here

behind the shadows I keep casting. This is my contradiction.
I still want him. I have swallowed the powder of his bones,
slept with his words beneath my pillow. It's the weight

of his body on mine when I lie in his traps;
his teeth, the gentle tracks they leave on my skin.

Sisters

We weren't temples or even bungalows. We were apartments. Small
rooms each of us, with no space for storage or sunlight. What was your fire

escape snaking to on those long nights filled with dog whistles
and sirens. What saved you when our hands couldn't reach each other

and our toes stuck to cold metal balconies. When we tried to escape,
the fence gave us splinters and we'd wait for the darning needle to blacken

in the flame, hiding our fingers behind our backs. We had no idea
what else could splinter, what else could break from that childhood

and lodge into us. Now watching our children play in a pool
full of rainwater, we think we are brave, heroically brave to be sitting

here in lawnchairs doing nothing. But this backyard has a secret
path of buried pets and we can name each angel fish, each canary.

More Widow Than Queen Victoria

My son is weaving quietly in his room, a hat made from spiders' webs
as only a son can do. An ancient ritual to stop my breath. There's even a feast
of my favourite foods. And as mango juice slides down my arm into my sleeve,
I know it's just another symbol for the sun and I must say good night.

A bobbypin and a lighter, that's one way of scarring. But what about fossils,
the amber of childhood and how it sets. If I dug deep enough I'd find whole
memories curled and kept, their souls long gone. Measure this
with your goddamned feather of truth I want to yell. I can't even open the
    window.

There were two men walking behind me the whole way to the river.
"My goal is to eliminate all my options," one of them said. I'd rather flirt
with options, I think. Lick my lips and look out to the water. Bow River,
I'm part mountain, part dirt, split me in two like the rest of this scenery.

I know about being too far from home. In ancient Egypt, fowlers would
surround pelicans' nests with dried dung and set fire to them. A guarantee
that the pelican would try to put out the fire with its wings, fanning it
as its wings burnt. I take long walks, ignore the smoke billowing from the east.

Sinking

Be careful my sweet daughter, careful of
the snapping jaws of time that spin
coke-bottle crazy around a circle of boys
with running noses and hungry
thirteen-year-old hands.
Be wary, even of the boy you'll let

rib-climb to your training bra.
And be careful of your breasts,
of men opening their thermos lunches
while they eat you with their eyes.

I want to run after you like some mad-mother-goose-
mother, swinging a straw broom cackling
calling your name amidst farm animals
and laundry.
Escape, I'd yell, *escape*.

When I was young, I became the cat
that clawed up curtains,
crazed with indoors and things
flying just out of reach.
My mother stamped her foot and sent me out
into arms that held me.
Cajoled with one hand,
unbuttoned with the other.
Unbuttoned, undid all the rules,
the nevers, the shouldn'ts.

And I know how long the sinking can be,
how lonely,
before learning to swim.

A Chinese Lantern for Audrey

The girl who never speaks appears to me in dreams carrying an armful
of snapdragons. And my garden is in ruin. All of my neighbour's grief
is seeping into the soil. He mourns all day into my dahlias.
What can I do but bake him lemon loaves and hope for the best.

I spent the morning with seven-year-olds, coaxing them to describe fall.
Fall is brown, one boy declared, and it's cold and dark and frosty.
It isn't the girl who haunts me, but the snapdragons in her arms,
how they're poised for her very first word, jaws unhinged, ready to swallow.

Brown because everything dies in the fall, he says. And my neighbour slowly
gets up from his picnic table, digs up his wife's Chinese Lanterns and throws
them in the creek. If not dead then dying, the bobbing lanterns lament.
Grief has so many stages. I can rescue only one of the plants and transplant it

to my garden. Only one Chinese Lantern in memory of Audrey. What about red
or yellow, what about hibernation, sleeping? Dead, my neighbour and the
boy insist. And if I held all the snapdragons to free her arms, the girl would
  agree. Fall
is brown, she'd say, then twirl and twirl like a falling leaf right down to the
  ground.

Catherine Greenwood

The Diving Girls' Prayer

As the seal is strong and breathes air,
As the fish is quick and breathes water,
So make me, a mermaid strong and quick.

Bless me with abalone abundant as mushrooms,
Oysters dropping ripe as plums into my palm.
Let my births keep me ashore a few days only,
Only for a little while let labour make me rest.

Rouse the beach fire when I break from working,
Let the blaze burn weariness away.
Fill the bowl of my pipe with mellow smoke,
My cup with steaming tea.

Let the wind weary of rampage,
The rain of sorrow.
Lead me down ladders of sunlight,
Part the deep green curtain of the sea.

Send the eels to sleep deep in their tunnels,
The sharks to slumber in the far coral beds.

As sponges are weighted with water
May my lungs be laden with air.
Let the stone I ride down
to the bottom not sink me.

Let my tender on the boat above
See my basket tip on the waves like a temple bell.
When I tug the rope make my signal swing,
Make the basket ring like a soundless bell.

In Service to a Dream

I spend long days
manicuring the maturing
oysters: haul dripping ropes
knotted with molluscs
onto the raft, tear off clumped
seaweed and chip away barnacle
infestations, shellac the shells
to protect them from parasites.

Hoping to coax pearls
from these lumps, I kneel
stiff-necked in the heat, hallucinating:
heaped shellfish become
a creature crawling with sea lice.
I scrub her slimed feet,
paint her many toenails,
rippled and black.

The sun burns my bowed
wishful head. Salt stings
the cuts in my hands.
Out in the bay, tender
transparent shells, tiny
as babies' fingernails, are growing
on newly-spawned spats
numberless as sand grains.

Meantime I sit picking nits
from the back of the world's
biggest monkey. Stable boy
to my own ambition, endlessly
polishing the hooves of
the beast, grooming
the monstrous brood-
mare of my dream.

Pearl Farmer's Wife

In the hours of night remaining
he quietly slides the screen
shut against the moonlit beds
and crawls into ours already spent.

A miracle, that we've conceived
between us five children.
When he touches me his hands
smell of salt, of honeyed bait,

still damp with the work of sowing
flesh. I accuse him of being
in love with an oyster,
making my resentment a jest,

a small seed spit out
so it won't grow in me.

Dream Thief

> Moist, glaucus,
> in my mother-of-pearl house,
> its door tightly shut
> against intruders,
> I drink in a dream from the sea
>
> Carmen Bernos de Gasztold, "The Oyster"

I was blessed with big ears
fashioned to catch gold and I hear
you're the best interpreter in town.
The others will say I've stolen
their dreams, that I have listened,
and with my listening lured
their nestling thoughts to the porches
of my own imagination — like that old story,
where some fool prince talks too much

and his bright ideas, barely
in pinfeathers, fly off like pigeons
to roost in a pauper's head.

It was the oysters' dream
to begin with. My competitors tested
nuclei of lead, silver and gold.
While they sat like hens hatching notions,
the fox slunk in and sucked out
the yolk. I learned how to pry
those tight lips open and feed seed
like pills to guinea pigs. I've tried
every kernel of inspiration: shipwreck
coral, clay from an urn, stained glass
from a ruined church. Tooth filling, bone
marrow of unborn manatee. A potion
of powdered sturgeon scale and soap.

Every foreign body I can imagine,
and the oysters spit the pits out
faster than I can put them in,
then clamp their jaws shut
like gossips guarding a secret
against me. The neighbours
call me a fraud; say my beads,
like red berries dipped in white paint,
will reveal their false hearts in the rain.

I've endured those leering corrugated grins
long enough. Last night even the moon
in its fullness mocked me,
the mystery at its core concealed
like the mythic door into the ocean's
glistening omphalos. I lay on the raft
and cupped my hand to listen
above that rippling black skin,
the way one puts a glass to a wall
to trap the voices beyond it.

From the mute beds below, the sea's mind
dumbly echoed in my head

I filled a bucket with a few
species of oyster and threw in
an abalone ear-shell snail for luck,
an eavesdropper to help me tap into
that undercurrent of murmured
contemplation. Back in my room,
I set the pail near and fell into bed
utterly drained. Have you ever heard
an oyster talking in its sleep?
As I lay in the dark feigning slumber
the thought grew louder. The whispered
bicker of silent dialects scraped
against the tin, a drawling glossal din.

The whole long night sweet
discordant nothings crawled like mites
inside my ears. In my stark
insomniac vigil, I heard it all:
gritty pleas, squelched
green weeping, belched out
insults to pedigree. You can see,
I'm willing to pay plenty
for this dream. If I repeat exactly
what the oysters spoke, will you translate
the answer cloaked in that obtuse silver tongue?

Help me find the mother of my pearl.

Louise Halfe

Der Poop

der poop
forgive me for writing on dis newspaper
i found it in da outhouse, saw lines
dat said you is sorry
some of my indian friends say is good but
some of dem say you sorry don't walk
so i was sitting here dinking dat we
maybe dalk
say, i always want to dell you stay
out of my pissness
if me wants to dalk to trees
and build nests in house
dats hup to me
if me wants to pitch my dent
and feed da ghost bannock hen berries
and maybe drow some indian popcorn
for you geezuz dats hup to me
i don't hask forgiveness not want
hand mary's, or a step ladder to heaven,
me is happy with da sky, da bird *Iyiniwak*,
four-legged *Iyiniwak*, i is happy
sorry mean dat i don't need yous church
and yous priest telling me what to do
sorry mean dat i free to dalk to *Manitou*
the spirits and plant *Iyiniwak*.
dats all for now, poop
maybe we dalk again next time i see you
in da newspaper.

In Da Name of Da Fadder

In da name of da fadder, poop
on my knees I pray to geezuz
cuz I got mad at my husband for
humpin' and makin too many babies
I 'pologize cuz I mad and cried I
didn't have no bannock and lard
to feed dem cuz my husband
drank all da *sōniyās* for wine.

In da name of da fadder, poop
my husband slap, fist and kick me
I hit him back. I 'pologize poop
da priest said I must of done someding
wrong and I deserve it cuz woman is
'uppose to listen to man. I not a good
wife cuz my hands somedimes
want to kill him.

In da name of da fadder, poop
I lookit other man he is so
handsome my eyes hurt, he kind, gentle,
soft laugh and my body wants to
feel his hot face. I no geezuz
would be mad he said I must not
be durty in my doughts but
poop I want smile and warm arms.

In da name of da fadder, poop
Inside the sweatlodge I shame cuz
Indian *iskwew* don't know anydin',
In church priest said all us pagans
will go to hell. I don't no what da means,
all I no I is big sinner
and maybe I won't see geezuz when I die.

In da name of da fadder, poop
I dought da geezuz kind but
I is no good. I can't read hen write.
I don't understand how come *mōnīyās* has
clean howse and lottsa feed and he don't
share it with me and my children.
I don't understand why geezuz say I be
poor, stay on welfare cuz *mōnīyās* say
I good for nuddin' cuz I don't have
wisdom. Forgive me poop I is
big sinner.

Pāhkahkos

Flying Skeleton
I used to wonder where
You kept yourself.
I'd hear you rattle about
Scraping your bones

I opened a door
You grinned at me
Your hollow mouth
Stared through my heart
With empty eyes.

You lifted your boney hands
To greet me and I
Ran without a tongue.

You jumped on my back
Clinging to my neck you hugged
My mound of flesh.

For a thousand years you were
The heavy bones
The companion who would not leave.

You knocked your skull
On my head
I felt your boney feet.
I dragged and dragged
I couldn't carry
Your burden more.
I pried you loose
Bone after bone.

We stood, skull to face
Pāhkahkos, your many bones
Exposed
I, lighter than I could stand.

I fed you the drink of healing
You ran skeleton fingers
Down your face and onto mine.

I gave you a prayer cloth
I wove a blanket of forgiveness
You covered us both, skeleton and flesh.

I gave you the smoke of truth
You lit your Pipe to life
You lifted it to your ghostly mouth,
To mine.

My *Pāhkahkos* companion,
My dancing Skeleton
My dancing friend.

We carry our bundles
Side by side
Bones and flesh.

Nōhkom, Medicine Bear

A shuffling brown bear
snorting and puffing
ambles up the stairs.

In her den
covered wall to wall
herbs hang. . . carrot roots, yarrow,
camomile, rat-root,
and *cācāmosikan*.

To the centre of the room she waddles
sits with one leg out, the other hugged close.
She bends over her roots and leaves
sniffs, snorts and tastes them
as she sorts them into piles.

She grinds the chosen few
on a small tire grater,
dust-devils settling into mole hills.
Her large brown paws take a patch
of soft deer skin
and wraps her poultice
until hundreds of tiny bundle-chains
swing from the rafters.

The brown laboring bear
Nōhkom, the medicine woman
alone in her attic den
smoking slim cigarettes
wears the perfume of sage, sweetgrass
and earth medicine ties.

Nōhkom, the medicine bear
healer of troubled spirits.
A red kerchief on her head,
blonde-white braids hang below her breasts.
She hums her medicine songs
shuffling alone in her den where
no light penetrates, no secrets escape.

She bends and her skirt drapes
over her aged beaded moccasins.
She brushes the potions off her apron.
A long day's work complete
Nōhkom ambles down the stairs
sweeps her long skirt behind her
drapes her paws on the stair rails
leaves her dark den and its medicine powers
to work in silence.

You've Got to Teach White Women Everything

I've tasted myself.
Gooseberries, pin cherries and
rosehips rolled between my teeth,
stretched till my bones bent
and my breath was wind.

I've tasted the tongue of
bear, deer and dog,
left camomile in the corners of my
mouth.

I've tasted
the sweet drip of sea
drying between my thighs
belly sweat breathing
on my breast.

I've tasted chocolate raisins
on my spine, rolling raspberries
between my toes and the breath
of swallows, feathers on my face.

I've tasted
till I'm swollen with sleep.

from **Blue Marrow**

. . .

> Father, these robes I wear confuse me. I have forgotten
> who I am. A jesuit. A monk. A brother. A priest. A
> nun, perhaps. It matters not. I have sinned. My last
> confession was in 1492. Yesterday. Ah yes, late today.

I wrote His Eminence,
offered my life to save savage souls.
My mother kissed my crucifix,
said, God go with you.

I am filled with wind, empty forest,
savages peek beneath my robe,
tender hands send heat up my spine.
I bless them.

This whip doesn't bite hard enough, Mother.
I crouch under the cross. Shroud my face.
Swallow. Swallow. Swallow.

This salt water I trickle,
send the Father's Bible thundering.
God be with you.

These savage men — they laugh at my disdain
of their brown-breasted women.
I grind the crucifix. Dry myself.
God be with me.

> *kahkiyaw iskwêwak, nôtokwêsiwak, câpânak, êkwa*
> *ohkomipanak.*
> Grandmothers, and the Eternal Grandmothers
> proclaim

There are Holy iskwêwak — nôsisim, *all over.*
We were the ones who burned down the jesuits'

church, trilled, danced and laughed through the night.
We watched those cabins eaten by our flames. We
were the ones, nôsisim, who hid the Bundles,
held council when we learned how those brothers
lifted their skirts to spill their devils into our sons' night.
And did they think they suffered as they burned,
screaming against our flame?

     nôhkom âtayôhkan

I am weary
Snakes dance above my head.
Spit from my womb.
Entwine my legs.
I am not done.

     âcimowinis

Sage Woman Eyes with Spirits.
When Thunder speaks,
Lightning flashes from them.
I sit with her in her Lodge.
We cling to our Pipes and weep.
When we weep her tears get up,
become Blue Butterflies.
Mine become Little People
beating their drum.
Butterflies dance.
The Morning Robins lay
their heads to one side
then to the other.
Lift their bustles,
War Dance around our Lodge.
Neither one of us wants to brush away
our tears.

• • •

Richard Harrison

Coach's Corner

The almost clerical collar, he is the priest of rock 'em
sock 'em. He silences his more knowledgeable friends
with his faith in the bodies of men and without him
and his kind the NHL would be as vapid as the All-Star
Game forever. He is loud and whiny and complaining,
and he chokes up on air if he's hurt by someone's words —
everything a man should not be, yet every sports bar
wills itself to quiet, turns up the volume on its dozen
sets only for his words. He is their man in a way no
hero of the play could be; his big league career was a
single game, but remember, he used to tell Bobby Orr
what to do, and Bobby listened as we listen though
we let the game go on in silence. He slams foreigners,
praises women in all the ways wrong for our time,
rejects any wavering in the masculinity of his troops
like a colonel in the US Marines. And yet he is here
because he is unafraid to love, love the game, the
journeyman players, love the code that makes a man
a man — and if you don't know it I ain't gonna tell ya.
He loves the fans, for all the pain we cause him, and
we are here with our own uncomfortable backs for that
dogged love, the voice that rises like a tenor sax, the
pointed finger, eyes narrowed to see clear and deep
the world that has him trapped on two sides already.

Elegy for the Rocket

For a minute or two, I spoke with him, Maurice Richard,
the month before he died. He told me his legs *were gone*,
from the medicine; the room was hot and crowded.
I brought him water and dared that moment to look
right into those famous eyes so dark with their official
colour they looked pure pupil. We've all heard men say
they were afire like coal, and maybe it was that language
that affected me because what came to mind as I
considered the grey lace woven where the iris is lined
with muscle was the way briquettes burn out under the
grill — such a little image, I know. And in the tranquil
now I can conjure charred wood veined with burnt-out
embers, or the remains of a home set ablaze rather than
surrendered out of *War & Peace* — a book worthy of
the public stature of the man — but the truth is, up close,
not staring me down to score a goal, those eyes were
a humble fire at the end of its use. And all the ferocity
of the man and his reputation couldn't hide in his fading
light what they also knew who lined up by the thousand
round the Forum to say farewell, and wept on all the
streets ringing Nôtre Dame at his passing.

Ray Hsu

Early Work: An Eclogue

Waist-deep cradling
a shotgun through the wheat
reminds me of when my father
would push the egg
white edges back
to the skillet middle. I'd hear his keys leave
like pieces of music
morning would bring for miles
and the phone with its delicate
interruption long after he had gone
while I outside
alone imagined the tortured engines
coming home for sundown. Barbed
wire on the Derrick farm
brought every cow back
the way field
hands looked up and saw
the next morning. This time I hear
nothing, not the splay
of metal and skin. My father
turns to me with his grainy hands
as if his muscular face
could say
Lord.

from *Inferno XXXII-XXXIII*

. . .

our bread-famished mouths watered over
the sturgeon-head pie with all the
cartilage embroidered with fish trimmings:

Tydeus carefully teased from the platter
a fried fork-full of Melanippus's dumplings,
which swelled hearty aroma in each of our nostrils.

"Oh don't you be so cruel as to relish
your inclination to devour all that; I'd hate to
have to chat myself up," I said. "Next occasion,

an artful pinch of lemon for each plate,
to tip this vodka mouthful to that clinking tune
no other kitchen in world could match;
each cognac-colored expression is nothing if not satiated."

His learned solution burned with piquant
wit, while the generosity of his
look spoke whole recipes we could feed on.

. . .

Dora (Confession, 0:93 Seconds)

Hard to describe how his body exploded
in the tub. I had pictured him a godlike enemy
and instead he was mostly modest, not
much evil. New, rare, briefly astonished
then he just settled back into the water. Fragments
of plaster hung. Disappointing how unguilty
he bypassed all those rapes, casual injustices,
impatiences, lice which slid off. Hard to imagine
the soft ticking feet passing as he finished
combing his slow hair around
his hammered look, flat. Already I was going,
already a slight depression kicking in. The flowers
on the sill watched.

Catherine Hunter

Two Thousand and Two

It's winter again, you said. It was April.
Snow was erasing the city, eliminating the surface of things.
We stood on the Main Street bridge above the broken
river, and the wind blew through me,
but I didn't fall. You removed one glove, slid your hand
up the sleeve of my coat. Under the girders of the bridge,
a flock of pigeons startled and took wing. While your bare
fingers traced the rhythm of my pulse, I saw
the pigeons rise together and then separate, fly south
to the hospital, north to the Cathedral.
Love is a division, a splitting through. I felt the cold
heat of your skin against my skin, explaining
an equation I found difficult to learn: how two
can be cancelled and cleft in two, becoming
one. You took my hand. I wanted
to move on deep with you
into winter.

It's winter again, you said. It was March.
I was remembering the night you followed me
four city blocks through a blizzard when I was angry
and mean and never wanted to speak to another man again
as long as I live I mean it so help me god, but you kept walking
one two three four blocks, a windchill factor of two thousand
and two, and every time I turned around, I saw you
coming after me. Love is simple as arithmetic, a kind of subtraction.
You followed me from Ellice to Portage from Portage to Graham
from Graham to St. Mary, and on the corner of York and Garry, I stopped
and let you reach me. Love is elementary.
A peeling down to the square root.

It's winter again, you said. It was February.
We stood on the footbridge in Kildonan Park. Skate blades
scraped and scribbled on the creek. Icicles hung
from the diving board, and in the middle of the day
I became confused, the pale solar disk so cool in the white sky
I mistook it for the moon. I saw the two small clouds
of our breathing mingle, disappear. I couldn't remember
what summer was. Winter had pared me to a sliver.
Little crystal needles laced holes in my brain.
You opened my fist. We both looked at my empty palm.
I couldn't remember what I'd been
holding on to.

It was winter again in January. Then, in December, it was winter again.
I looked south, naming the bridges between our houses: Redwood, Disraeli,
Louise, Provencher, Norwood, every steel arch of the river's ribcage
a cold blade sharp enough to clean me to the bone, and love
unmade me, took me deep into the dead of winter,
straight through its polished lens. I saw the wind
uncolour the city, the rivers buckle the land.
I saw our friends lay down
their lives, one by one, through this terrible season,
until I was numb, felt nothing except
your hand on my wrist, pulling me through.

On October thirty-first, the snow began to fall.
It's winter again, again, you said.
I looked north, because north is the direction
you come from, and north is the direction you travel
when you move away from me. Love is a kind of counting
or counting down: Norwood, Provencher,
Louise, Disraeli, Redwood. The rungs of a river as long
as winter. A river you crossed, when I was still and white with grief.
You unfolded my fingers, broke me open,
and when you had stripped me utterly
naked, you touched me again.
I fell. I sank below zero.

Now, there is nothing more that can be taken from me.
Look at the sky, darkening toward spring. The trees
that open, forgiving. The students who jump up
and down in the courtyard, clapping their hands for sheer
love of the light at seven o'clock in the evening. None of these things
can ever be lifted away — not even this weightless light,
this temporary joy. Because everything that is mine I have already given
over. Because you followed me one night all the way
to the corner of Garry and York. Because you took my hand.
You moved on deep with me
through winter.

Patrick Lane

Drought 1980

The unsold milk-cow falls to the hammer
as the last hog screams himself to a pick-up,
pulled by the measured cursing of a man.
A yellow dog circles and barks at a truck
piled high with implements. Dry grass breaks
under its tires as it creaks to the correction line.
A woman slams the screen door and lists her losses:
the spoons, the cups, the names of plastic flowers.
The land, split by the sun, turns to ash
and is spilled by the wind into sky
making at dawn a wound more beautiful
than the night that lies ahead.
The dawn lies ahead.
The leaving.
Strange names are whispered:
Calgary, Vancouver, Okanagan.
They roll on the children's lips, on the back porch
where the yellow dog clicks nails on wood,
in bedrooms where the fear cannot be seen, in shade,
in every darkness where the sun cannot be found.

Weasel

Thin as death,
the dark brown weasel slides
like smoke through night's hard silence.
The worlds of the small are still. He glides
beneath the chicken house. Bird life
above him sleeps in feathers as he creeps

among the stones, small nose testing every board
for opening, a hole small as an eye, a fallen knot,
a crack where time has broken through.
His sharp teeth chatter.
Again and again he quests the darkness
below the sleeping birds. A mouse freezes,
small mouth caught by silence in the wood.
His life is quick. He slips into his hole.
Thin as death, the dark brown weasel slides
like smoke. His needles worry wood.
The night is long.
Above him bird blood beats.

Monarch I

Half-pet, half-wildness, Monarch leads
his thirteen hens in an endless search
for food. Range birds, they return
to the pen only for sleep. He guides them
through the day, one eye upon the sky
for the falling hawk, the other on the earth.
He hates their wandering.
His beak drives them from the brush
where they've gone to lay, their clucks
his torment. They fly from their beds
in squawking clusters. Only the brooding
ones are left alone. He knows the mother's
eye. It is his only fear.

When they are lost he scratches at the dirt
and calls out food. They run from everywhere,
push him away and peck at the nothing there.
During the sun he mounts them one by one,
his hard black beak holding their heads
as his spurs rake their sides. The soft
flesh tears. The hens brace stiff wings

against the ground and hold him there.
When he is done, some wounded, some surprised,
they flip the tangle of their tails,
rub beaks to stone and cluck contentedly.

Then darkness moves among the trees
and shadows stretch like necks into the grass.
He drives them from their graves of dust
to the safety of the pen. Drinking and scratching
they search for parasites among their feathers.
The preening over, they rise on ruffled wings,
settle above his head. In the bramble thickets
three brooding hens are left. Theirs is
a single eye. He does not go to them.
Their warning chirr keeps him far away.

He counts the rest and gives one final crow,
then satisfied and finally tired,
lifts to his isolate perch among them.
Claws locked, the hens pull night
into their breasts. They sleep a flying dream.
Monarch's red eyes close, they open, search
the gathered dark for weasel sound or fox,
then close like wounds upon a restless sleep.

The Happy Little Towns

Walking the muddy road past the swamp
I thought the butterflies a gift I couldn't bear,
there in the sun pulling light into their wings,
drinking sweet water with their tongues.
I was so young I thought I was a man
and that little town a place where a life could be
made, that things like bears or ravens
or the body of a woman were sufficient to themselves
and without guile. That the man walking beside me

had a boot full of blood was nothing more
than the end of a day. A man who had opened
his body with an axe. It could have easily been
a boy with an eye scooped out, or a woman
bleeding into diapers for a month, afraid
to tell her man she'd lost his child.

That was the year my wife slept with my best friend.
I could tell her now the summer was oblivion,
that the blood gone from a body cannot be
given back, the wound opening like a mouth
without forgiveness. The inside of the body
when it first feels air feels only noise, as the
butterfly when it first crawls out of itself
feels only wonder and never eats again. I remember
the brightness of the days as my hands healed
the many injuries, the hours alone. It wasn't sadness
or self-pity, only oblivion, the kind a boy feels
when he is made into a man, wanting only to be
held, for the first time in his life without love.

The wreckage of that world stayed wreckage, though
we tried to build it back. The steady years of trying,
her taking the flowers I picked in the fields
and placing them in a jar where we watched them die.
What I remember most is that injured man who,
with the dignity of the very poor, told me he was
sorry to bother me, as if his wound could have waited
for a better time to happen; my hands putting him
back together, the stitches climbing up his leg
like small black insects I created out of nothing,
the curved steel needle entering his pale flesh,
pulling behind it a thread thin as a butterfly's
tongue, him saying he was sorry, and me knowing
for the first time in my life what that must mean.

The Dream of the Red Chamber

I cannot find the symbol of the crane on the silver
ink-boxes. Tarnished with dust they lie among
the scarred jade bats and scattered lions.
On the walls hang dresses from the Ch'ing.
Their stitching reveals the faded
dance of chrysanthemums. I search for the ancient
in the clutter of dynasties. An old woman
walks with slowness among the curios.
Her feet are bound. They are the last illusion
in a world that no longer believes such pain is
beautiful. What I want to take back from China
is found only in my dream of the red chamber.
Ashamed, I walk into the crowds on the street
where young women, bright as birds,
run laughing among the Wu t'ung trees.

Tania Langlais

sa façon, la sienne
rajouter qu'avec le temps
c'est certain, le lin s'use
les aiguilles aussi
à force de lames
aux cheveux d'une fille
une douleur de plus
et son chemin, juste là
entre la robe soleil
et celle du mensonge

∽

quand elle retire sa petite robe de nuit
et la passe au nord des ruptures
l'après-midi je sais que ça recommence
dans la transparente averse
de ses hanches
je connais ses mensonges
chacune de ses manies
alors qui osera demain et en quelle langue
me dire qu'elle m'a tué
avec ma déroute pour mobile
et mes chemises comme bestiaire?

∽

s'il fallait que tu meures
je te jure
j'aurai une robe noire ajustée
à la descente du jour
et celle ensuite du cercueil
ainsi on pourra dire:
« la mort pour elle est une robe »
si vrai tant je sais que je n'arriverai pas
ce jour-là
à en délacer tout à fait le corsage

∼

rien ne se raconte plus
c'est un glissement de choses et d'autres
avoir tout l'été envie d'exagérer le désordre
sur la véranda assise
de toutes ses forces suspendre la lumière
pour corriger le jour sur cette maison
le travail ne se raconte pas
c'est pourquoi, patiente, je préfère compter
combien de cheveux aujourd'hui
sont restés dans ma brosse
pour comprendre que je ne suis propriétaire de rien
même plus du nombre

∼

tu lisais l'autre nuit
c'était beau à voir
le chat et moi
on aurait cru rien faire
d'autre que de mourir lentement
chacun son tour il a fallu penser
que peut-être on ne faisait pas le poids
quand tu lisais l'autre nuit
pour accepter la gravité
générale des choses
sans trop savoir pourquoi
on s'est dit que quelque part un cargo
venait de disparaître

～

je suppose que ça va finir
par passer sans qu'on s'en aperçoive
quelque chose très près du désastre
aura raison de moi
douze bêtes dans sa chemise
un peu comme une névrose
que dire du pire sinon qu'il tue
debout sur la douleur
qui donc voudrait mourir à côté du bétail?

～

n'en pouvant plus je l'ai écrit :
avec le temps c'est certain
le lin s'use
la fatigue envoie ses chats dormir ailleurs

∽

je ne soigne personne
à dérouler du sommeil pour la fin heureuse
je couche dans ton lit
la part difficile de ton prénom

∽

le désordre ça prend combien de boîtes
dormir comme tout le monde
quand la clarté s'installe comme un chat
sur une couverture d'hôpital

∽

Irving Layton

The Swimmer

The afternoon foreclosing, see
The swimmer plunges from his raft,
Opening the spray corollas by his act of war —
The snake heads strike
Quickly and are silent.

Emerging see how for a moment,
A brown weed with marvellous bulbs,
He lies imminent upon the water
While light and sound come with a sharp passion
From the gonad sea around the poles
And break in bright cockle-shells about his ears.

He dives, floats, goes under like a thief
Where his blood sings to the tiger shadows
In the scentless greenery that leads him home,
A male salmon down fretted stairways
Through underwater slums . . .

Stunned by the memory of lost gills
He frames gestures of self-absorption
Upon the skull-like beach;
Observes with instigated eyes
The sun that empties itself upon the water,
And the last wave romping in
To throw its boyhood on the marble sand.

Fishermen

When I wish to make myself perfectly happy
— as happy as when I was an ignorant boy —
I hurry down to the village harbour
to hold in one gaze the sun scarcely above
the horizon, itself a wall of soft flame
and the small brave boats that have been out
all night moving towards the stone pier
stately and slow and magnificent as the ships
of Columbus; O for all their blue solemnity
I think they are bursting to signal us
the great news: "It's been a good haul!"

I have seen fishermen unload their catch;
they are silent with exhaustion, perhaps
with reckoning up their gain. There are still
boxes to fill and broken ice to sprinkle
over the fresh gray skins of the fish
glazing like the eyes of many many-eyed
Arguses crushed and glistening between the crystals;
and the torn nets strung out for mending
when the crates of fish have been nailed shut
— to be freighted to the maritime stomachs
of Athenians waiting for them like ravenous fish.

I like the rhythm and unhurried skill,
the humour and dignity of fishermen.
These are men; they do not have to unravel
Danes and Germans to disinter their dead selves.
Bibliothèques are for the soul-sick, for whoever
have swindled themselves of risk, companions,
the communion of sun and sea. In the monster cities
they are doomed; alas I can summon no pity,
no affection for them: they choose their hell.
Deep and irrational as the sea itself
my joy returns with the fishing boats at dawn.

On Seeing the Statuettes of Ezekiel and Jeremiah in the Church of Notre Dame

They have given you French names
    and made you captive, my rugged
troublesome compatriots;
        your splendid beards, here, are epicene,
plaster white
        and your angers
unclothed with Palestinian hills quite lost
in this immense and ugly edifice.

You are bored — I see it — sultry prophets
    with priests and nuns
(What coarse jokes must pass between you!)
    and with those morbidly religious
i.e. my prize brother-in-law
              ex-Lawrencian
pawing his rosary, and his wife
sick with many guilts.

Believe me I would gladly take you
    from this spidery church
its bad melodrama, its musty smell of candle
    and set you both free again
in no make-believe world
        of sin and penitence
but the sunlit square opposite
alive at noon with arrogant men.

Yet cheer up Ezekiel and you Jeremiah
    who were once cast into a pit;
I shall not leave you here incensed, uneasy
    among alien Catholic saints
but shall bring you from time to time
        my hot Hebrew heart
as passionate as your own, and stand
with you here awhile in aching confraternity.

The Fertile Muck

There are brightest apples on those trees
    but until I, fabulist, have spoken
they do not know their significance
or what other legends are hung like garlands
    on their black boughs twisting
like a rumour. The wind's noise is empty.

Nor are the winged insects better off
    though they wear my crafty eyes
wherever they alight. Stay here, my love;
you will see how delicately they deposit
    me on the leaves of elms
or fold me in the orient dust of summer.

And if in August joiners and bricklayers
    are thick as flies around us
building expensive bungalows for those
who do not need them, unless they release
    me roaring from their moth-proofed cupboards
their buyers will have no joy, no ease.

I could extend their rooms for them without cost
    and give them crazy sundials
to tell the time with, but I have noticed
how my irregular footprint horrifies them
    evenings and Sunday afternoons:
they spray for hours to erase its shadow.

How to dominate reality? Love is one way;
    imagination another. Sit here
beside me, sweet; take my hard hand in yours.
We'll mark the butterflies disappearing over the hedge
    with tiny wristwatches on their wings,
our fingers touching the earth, like two Buddhas.

Berry Picking

Silently my wife walks on the still wet furze
Now darkgreen the leaves are full of metaphors
Now lit up is each tiny lamp of blueberry.
The white nails of rain have dropped and the sun is free.

And whether she bends or straightens to each bush
To find the children's laughter among the leaves
Her quiet hands seem to make the quiet summer hush —
Berries or children, patient she is with these.

I only vex and perplex her; madness, rage
Are endearing perhaps put down upon the page;
Even silence daylong and sullen can then
Enamour as restraint or classic discipline.

So I envy the berries she puts in her mouth,
The red and spurting juice that stains her lips;
I shall never taste that good to her, nor will they
Displease her with a thousand barbarous jests.

How they lie easily for her hand to take,
Part of the unoffending world that is hers;
Here beyond complexity she stands and stares
And leans her marvellous head as if for answers.

No more the easy soul my childish craft deceives
Nor the simpler one for whom yes is always yes;
No, now her voice comes to me from a far way off
Though her lips are redder than the raspberries.

An Old Niçoise Whore

The famous and rich, even the learned and the wise,
   Singly or in pairs went to her dwelling
To press their civilized lips to her thighs
   Or learn at first hand her buttocks' swelling.

Of high-paying customers she had no lack
And was herself now rich: so she implied.
Mostly she had made her pile while on her back
But sometimes she had made it on the side.

Reich she read; of course the Viennese doctor.
Lawrence — his poems and novels she devoured;
Kafka at the beginning almost rocked her
But as she read him more she said he soured.

Swedish she spoke, French, Polish, fluent German;
Had even picked up Hindi — who knows how?
In bed she had learned to moan and sigh in Russian
Though its rhythms troubled her even now.

A nymphomaniac like Napoleon's sister
She could exhaust a bull or stallion;
Bankers had kneeled before her crotch to kiss her
And ex-princes, Spanish and Italian.

And all the amorous mayors of France-Sud
Impelled by lust or by regional pride
Would drive their Renaults into her neighbourhood,
Ring her bell and troop happily inside.

And pimpled teenagers whom priests and rabbis
Had made gauche, fearful, prurient and blind
Prodded by Venus had sought her expert thighs:
Ah, to these she was especially kind.

And having translated several Swinburne lines
She kept the finest whips she could afford
To be, though most aristocrats brought their canes,
Ready for some forgetful English lord.

We saw waves like athletes dash towards the shore
Breaking it seemed from a line of green scum;
We saw the sun dying, and this aged whore
Noted how it gave clouds a tinge of rum.

Engaging was her mien, her voice low and sweet;
   Convent nuns might have envied her address.
She was touched by the bathers below her feet;
   I, by this vitality sprung from cess.

And as she spoke to me on the crowded quay
   And reminisced about her well-spent years
I mourned with her her shrivelled face and body
   And gave what no man had given her: tears.

To the Girls of My Graduating Class

   Wanting for their young limbs praise,
Their thighs, hips, and saintly breasts,
   They grow from awkwardness to delight,
Their mouths made perfect with the air
   About them and the sweet rage in the blood,
   The delicate trouble in their veins.

   Intolerant as happiness, suddenly
They'll dart like bewildered birds;
   For there's no mercy in that bugler Time
That excites against their virginity
   The massed infantry of days, nor in the tendrils
   Greening on their enchanted battlements.

   Golda, Fruma, Dinnie, Elinor,
My saintly wantons, passionate nuns;
   O light-footed daughters, your unopened
Brittle beauty troubles an aging man
   Who hobbles after you a little way
   Fierce and ridiculous.

Song for Naomi

Who is that in the tall grasses singing
By herself, near the water?
I can not see her
But can it be her
Than whom the grasses so tall
Are taller,
My daughter,
My lovely daughter?

Who is that in the tall grasses running
Beside her, near the water?
She can not see there
Time that pursued her
In the deep grasses so fast
And faster
And caught her,
My foolish daughter.

What is the wind in the fair grass saying
Like a verse, near the water?
Saviours that over
All things have power
Make Time himself grow kind
And kinder
That sought her,
My little daughter.

Who is that at the close of the summer
Near the deep lake? Who wrought her
Comely and slender?
Time but attends and befriends her
Than whom the grasses though tall
Are not taller,
My daughter,
My gentle daughter.

The Predator

The little fox
was lying in a pool of blood,
having gnawed his way out to freedom.

Or the farmhand,
seeing his puny, unprofitable size
had slugged him after with a rifle butt

And he had crawled
to the country roadside
where I came upon him, his fur dust-covered.

Hard to believe
a fox is ever dead, that he isn't
just lying there pretending with eyes shut.

His fame's against
him; one suspects him of anything,
even when there's blood oozing from the shut eyes.

His evident
self-enjoyment is against him also:
no creature so wild and gleeful can ever be done for.

But this fox was;
there's no place in the world any more
for free and gallant predators like him.

Eagle, lion,
fox and falcon; their freedom is their death.
Man, animal tamed and tainted, wishes to forget.

He prefers bears
in cages: delights to see them pace
back and forth, swatting their bars despondently.

Yet hates himself,
knowing he's somehow contemptible;
with knives and libraries the dirtiest predator of all.

Ghost of small fox,
hear me, if you're hovering close
and watching this slow red trickle of your blood:

Man sets even
more terrible traps for his own kind.
Be at peace; your gnawed leg will be well-revenged.

Aran Islands

Dun Aengus

High walls . . . of stones;
man-humbling cliff and shattering sea;
ramparts:
trenches of stone, fierce four of them
and in-between
prehistory's barbed wire, *cheveux de frise*
. . . of stones.

Enclosing a mist.

Gone are the defenders;
gone, they who attacked.

Nothing here:
only mist
and blue-grey stones.

Cliffs of Moher

At last, as in a dream,
I've come to the cliffs
from where God hurls down
His enemies, every one.

Rat-faced cunning mercers

with a rat's delight;
all, all who are dead of soul,
male and female.

See, their polls open like flowers
on the black rocks below;
their brains dance with the foam
on a green wave's tow.

Kilmurvey

Low are the hills, a mere rise
in the ground, grey with stones and green;
Stand anywhere and you can trace
outlines with your new-found eyes
of stone fences delicate as lace:
Stand anywhere and you can be seen.

Nadine Ltaif

Translated by Christine Tipper

La Simûrghiade

Tiamat. Le monstre femelle du chaos originel.
On ne saura pas me dicter une conduite.
Je suis libre et rebelle. Je ne saurai être Sage.
Dans ce lieu choisi pour renaître de personne.
Que de moi comme le Simûrgh de mon pays natal.
De mes pays natals. J'ai compris que je n'étais
pas faite d'une seule civilisation.

    Premier Jardin. Pishôn et Gihôn. Deux mers entourant le berceau initial. Le Tigre. L'Euphrate. Ce Tigre. Le Premier meurtre. Les invasions sanguinaires. Les Assyriens qui ne veulent pas se faire oublier. Les Assyriennes. Leur cri. Faut-il comprendre? Avec les sonorités, les tonalités qui écorchent. Les oreilles de l'Occident sourd. La Terre fait naufrage sous un tel carnage. Je ne suis pas seule à le dénoncer.

    Ma figure a les traits de l'humanité entière et de ses diversités. Yeux bridés, lèvres charnues. Et visages de toutes les rondeurs. Et peaux brunes et nuancées.

    C'est difficile de me décrire tellement je me vide pour recevoir tant de représentations graphiques de la fureur, de la douleur, de la joie en toutes les langues. Je ne sais plus ma langue natale. Tellement j'ai entendu de langues dans mon enfance.

Tellement j'ai appris à parler de langues. Une langue pour chaque culture, pour chaque culte. Quel jardin vais-je faire croître? Mon jardin collectionne les ruines. Je ne puise qu'aux sources vives et vivifiantes. Mes peintures, les plus modernes, sont celles qui se nourrissent des origines. Non celles qui n'ont pas de racines. L'expert est celui qui sait découvrir la source. La racine. L'essence. Le parfum. Le mystère. Des commencements. Lorsqu'il ne reste des ruines que leur arôme. L'Egypte se referme sur son mystère. Carthage aussi. Byblos et Tyr et Sidon et Suse. La Bible. Homère. Ou *Le Roman de la Rose*.

Avant toutes lois humaines, avant toute société, la nature se multipliait. À l'origine. Avant Dieu. Avant l'unicité suprême. Il y avait foisonnement. Susurrement. Vie grouillante. Presque dégoûtante si je m'en distancie. Mais la distance n'a pas sa raison d'être ici. Quand j'écris je rejoins cette vie antérieure d'où je viens. Où je suis née une première fois. Il n'y a pas d'indifférence mais équilibre naturel.

Je suis morte très vite cette année-là. Les cataclysmes se succédaient. Et on trépassait. Avant toute culture, il y avait l'Art.

Nous vous observons aujourd'hui, nous, de notre passé, vivants, présents, plus présents que Vous, par Votre présence si dure. Si manifestée. Sans aucun espoir de rédemption. Avec Vos mains tachetées de crimes.

Vous roulerez intacts au-delà de Vos morts. De Votre misérable mort. Inchangés. Vers Vos vies d'errants. De fantômes repus mais assoiffés. Vous n'avez pas réussi à vous débarrasser tout à fait de Votre ancienne peau. Celle qui Vous colle à la chair. Vous débordez d'excroissances. Vous devenez de plus en plus laids et violents à chacune de Vos naissances.

Évidemment personne ne vous reconnaît.

Comment reconnaître ceux qui ne savent pas se transformer ? Ils sont pareils. Identiques. Depuis la première goutte de sang versée. Jusqu'à l'écroulement de temps dévoreur. Dévoreuse. Kronos ou Lilith ? Quel enfant choisir cette fois ? Il n'y a plus d'âge ma voix.

Simurghiade

Tiamat. The female monster of original chaos.
I cannot be told how to behave.
I am free and rebellious. I wouldn't know how to be
Sage.
In this place chosen for rebirth from no one.
Only from myself like the Simurgh of my homeland.
Of my homelands. I've understood that I was
not formed from a single civilisation.

First Garden. Pishon and Gihon. Two seas encircling the initial cradle. The Tigris. The Euphrates. This Tigris. The First murder. The bloody invasions. The Assyrians who don't want to be forgotten. The Assyrians. Their cry. Should we understand? With sounds, tones that grate. The ears of the deaf West. The Earth shipwrecked by such carnage. I'm not alone in denouncing it.

My face has the features of the whole of humanity and its diversities. Slanting eyes, full lips. And faces of varied roundness. And brown skins of assorted tones.

It is difficult to describe myself because I've emptied myself to receive all the graphic representations of fury, of pain, of joy in every language. I no longer know my mother tongue. I heard so many languages during my childhood.

I learnt to speak so many languages. A language for each culture, for each belief. Which garden will I grow? My garden collects ruins. I draw only from live and living sources. My paintings, the most modern, are those that are nourished by origins. Not those that have no roots. The expert is the one who knows where to discover the source. The root. The essence. The perfume. The mystery. Of the beginnings. When only the aroma of the ruins remains. Egypt closes in on its mystery. Carthage also. Byblos and Tyre and Sidon and Susa. The Bible. Homer. Or *The Book of the Rose*.

Before any human laws, before any society, nature multiplied. In the beginning. Before God. Before the supreme uniqueness. There was profusion. Whispers. Swarming life. Almost disgusting if I distance myself from it. But distance has no reason for being here. When I write I rejoin this past life from whence I came. Where I was born a first time. There is no indifference but a natural balance.

I died very quickly that year. Cataclysms succeeded each other. And we passed away. Before all culture, there was Art.

We watch you today, us, from our past, living, present, more present than You, by Your presence so difficult. So obvious. Without any hope of redemption. With Your hands stained with crimes.

You will continue intact beyond Your deaths. Beyond Your miserable death. Unchanged. Towards Your errant lives. Phantoms sated but thirsty. You did not manage to completely shed Your ancient skin. That which sticks to your flesh. You are covered in tumours. You become more and more ugly and violent with each of Your births.

Obviously no one recognises you.

How can we recognise those who don't know how to transform themselves? They are the same. Identical. From the first drop of spilt blood. Until the crumbling of devouring time. *Dévoreuse.* Kronos or Lilith? Which child will you choose this time? My voice no longer has an age.

Reconnaissance

La vie nous laboure chaque jour.
Nous sommes un champ cultivé d'épines.

Nous ne souffrons pas
par manque d'identité ?

Nous souffrons de connaître
notre identité.

Les hommes passent leur vie à se fuir
et à détruire les miroirs
qu'ils rencontrent.

Même les étangs.

Si j'étais un homme je m'y serais
noyée depuis longtemps.

Dans le cœur de chaque homme
une femme pleure.

Moi, Dieu m'a créée femme
et je ne me rappelle plus combien
j'ai ruisselé d'hommes dans mon cœur.

Il y a sur la terre tant d'étres
il nous faut quantité de vies
pour les connaître.

Et ceux qui croient tout connaître.

Ils pensent que leur langue suffit
pour communiquer avec le monde
entier et les peuples.

Mille fois merci je suis née femme
en rapport direct avec le secret.

∼

Début mai
je porte
la cruauté des naissances
plus durement que la chute
des feuilles en automne.

∼

Un arbre dans sa solitude
a trouvé un puits d'eau.
À sa fraîcheur
se désaltère ma soif.

Ces brefs instants de présence
nourrissent le long chemin
de mon errance.

∼

Les arbres nus du printemps froid
revêtent le duvet vert tendre
et plus dénuement encore
des pas naissent sur le sable.

∼

Quand je pourrai écrire un chant
une voix seule
telle l'unique
l'éternelle voix d'alto
dans la *Passion selon saint Matthieu*
s'élèvera
s'ouvrira un passage
dans la souffrance.
De la prison de la souffrance
elle sortira
et réussira
par son exercice
à trouver le timbre de la liberté.

∼

Je suis de retour dans les contrées sauvages
où la liberté est donnée
à l'amour.

Loin des anciennes mentalités
mais dans la solitude
je vis.

Une récompense pour celles
déchiquetées par les injustices.

Mon corps en harmonie
avec le désir.

Une paix victorieuse
de l'angoisse
et du jugement d'autrui.

Partout sur terre
Je retrouve
l'inspiration et l'expiration
des pierres.

Dans chaque brindille,
un cœur bat, sensuel,
sous les dures apparences.

∼

Laura Lush

Children

As my parents get older,
their memories form a blue viscous pond.
In the middle are us. Their children.
Small fish that nibble at the surface.
Sometimes we float on our backs
as if already surrendered
as if we won't get another chance.
It's hard to leave, harder to live.
We circle around each other,
each breath a link.
The underwater won't let us go
until we release our own eggs
like the tadpole, the salamander —
their awkward evolution
all blood and instinct.

The Last of Us

The ground pulls at our feet.
No small births burst back.
No roots grab. Instead, we roam
our small territories, careful
not to seed, not to build the nests too strongly.
We are surrounded by the half-glow
of rainbows, barely audible wings.
We are a gift no one can open.
Our hearts dry gourds in our chests.
If you approach, you will hear the warning
rattle. *Stay away.*

Darkening In

Winter and the air shines.
The smallest of stars barely breathing.
Birds unfold their wings,
fly their smooth-sounding flights.
Watch them blurring past,
white stains on the night.
They see the forest turning,
trees darkening in
for night, for life.

Later,
a man undoes the world,
his wife's hair.
He waits patiently —
like a husband, like a hostage.
Waits till she frees the day
from him.

Love, a small drink
of cold lake
he cannot get enough of,
cannot jump in
or out of
quickly enough.

Strays

I used to bring home strays:
cats with one ear, no tails.
I was convinced that love
could make a difference.
But there was something
permanent in their bodies
that sent them flying out of my hands
no matter how gently

I held them,
no matter how often
I reassured them.
It is how I flee
a man's grip today,
squirming away whenever
he tries to hold me.
I am a fish
flopping between
his fingers, my one eye
gelatinous, gold.
It is all in the body
my latest lover tells me.
It is all in the way
we have learned about abandonment
and then to abandon.

157 Islington

When you open the door garlic blooms like roses,
a pudding of stale air in the hallway.
Leszek is making dinner, his face scorched red from vodka.
Tomorrow he'll start English classes — he can feel
the words in his mouth exquisite as mints.
In another room is the one who sat in prison,
the sad numb vegetables of his hands.
He's been here the longest, he's seen seasons collide.
Everyday he watches the light under his
door scuttle like mice.

Home

What's substantial is your cleft chin,
the beard you grew the first time
they sent you to prison.
We have no common language.
Our words scattered dark and shiny
as nuts. Here in this country
you can only see winter —
none of your black tulips
that topple off stems like hats.
Yet there is so much light in your eyes,
light swimming round and round its black pond.
You miss your country, your son's sausage-breath.
His teeth like tiny white steps.
Sit tight Marek. I am gathering
in the slow harvest of your language.
Next month we'll finally speak.

Border

Do you see the gold filigrees of light?
Do you know they are still selling roses
in Warsaw, drinking the cool blue
streams of vodka?
After three years you still
don't know how to step back
into your country. You dream its border.

What good would it do
to wake you?
Whiskers rising like tiny
black whips on your face.
How is it that you look so peaceful
yet wake with your head in your hands?

Mr. Ishigami

I have my Japanese lover — almost.
What sounds will come clear
when the bright blue fields at night
race like bamboo?
When he goes to Taiwan
will he have a girl,
drink in a bar where the window
wears a mask of moths?
Maybe he'll grow a moustache,
lend a shaving to his oak-plane face.
Alone in the *ryokan*
what will he say to me,
now that I sit just like him,
legs crossed, the contentment of frogs
all over my face?
What will he do when I unwind my heart
its cicada whirring through the night?

Gavey H.

Because he had big blondie curls
and a wrinkly sprog face.
Because he had the mouth of a Cork boy,
the Yoda ears, the laugh of a million
churlish children.
Because he was the only one who
could *get away with it*, could *get away*, could *get it*,
they all wanted to kill him.
But he left.

Kelly

Think white shirt, hair cut short.
Destroyer grin.
And that's all you need to know.

Riverside Heights

It was as if some giant had landed there years before
and, from his pocket, placed the little blue house
down on the grass, fresh and shiny as an after dinner mint.
And the house sat there for a little while
until they came — these Irish — all seven of them,
dragging the tattered cloth of their own island behind them,
and stuffed their too-big bodies into those too-small rooms
with the too-small beds that shook every time a train rattled past.
They didn't know then that they were making local history,
that for years after their departure,
the neighbours would still be talking about *them*.
How their windows and balconies flowered with dirty laundry,
how their boxers sailed from the TV antennae regally as kites.
How on Friday nights — or sometimes even Tuesdays — they'd run
up and down the stairs banging pots — and still later,
home after the pub, they'd charge through each other's flats
with *kendo* sticks and boogie boards, mad as bulls.
It was presumed on many a night that they had killed one other,
squashed each other's bodies into wardrobes
and garbage bags, tossed them off the balcony
into the clear shimmering of rice paddies.
While their fortress slowly grew — the tall brown
beer bottles, toppling one after the other
like fallen soldiers.
Some nights
they still see them dancing.
The white-bellied pagans from another kind of island.

The Session

During the week, they roamed the flat
tense and lithe as greyhounds.
These were their days of rest. Misfit knights
preparing for a great battle.
They slept naked, woke the next day
with all the old parts miraculously intact —
the hands working the air, the knees bending
back and forth as they pushed through the day, heads lowered,
struggling to get back to the place
before their bodies had clogged and died.
And when the five o'clock bell rang, they ran and ran
and kept running until they were on the 9:36 train
with skins wet and shiny. And finally they
were there — bursting through the bar — *seven,seventeen,seventy*
thick as Marlboro looked up,
issued his *I-ras-shai-ma-se's*.
Then Joe and Brian would bring out their guitars.
And in walked the babes! *Jaysus the babes!*
Maura and Christina, Jan and Heidi.
Donna, Mi-La and Kristyn. And your ones
from Iwata. And your ones from Hamamatsu
who still glowed like nice new ones do.
Then beer after beer being passed swiftly as batons
while the others tumbled in, red-faced, ready.
Mecca and Colin, Shanley and Seanie. Pearce, Aido and Tom.
Ha Ha Connors with his mickey of whiskey under his coat.
The race still on — Friday pushing into Sunday
where only the fit and few will survive.

Komachu's

It was our second home. And our Mama
fed us. Oh how she fed us well.
Tsukaemono,takenoko,yakitori.
It was our little masked bar,
our laughing room, our cheering room,
our place of solitude and a kind of winter
holiness that battens the memory forever.
It was our chapel, our temple, our little red-roofed
sky. Our spring, summer, fall, winter.
It was the first unravelling — the veil off the face.

Mama-san

First you pass through the beads in the doorway.
You bend your head a little. You wait for Rieko-san
to rush at you with her hot little towels,
for Mama-san to clear the side of the bar for you.
You have special gifts. Things she has never seen before.
She will change the menu, add cream corn and spuds.
She will watch over your slow, strange growing in her country.
She will watch you edge your way into love and out of it again.
Another one of your magic tricks.

The Wellesdale

It was, he joked, his little *pied à terre* in "Lower Rosedale" —
that seven-storey holdout from the 1940s
squatting among the once leg-elegant '60s high-rises.
    A modest bachelor, filled with books, magazines,
a couple of fish — Simone and Oscar — fattening on
    cockroaches,
        and that single Italian marble table
covered in tins of capers and jars of Classico Pasta Sauce —
staples, he said, for getting by on U.I.C.
It was my brother's place, and I'd visit between countries
and lovers,
        so he'd always give me his bed,
the one with the orthopaedic pillow, the man-loved mattress.
    Regal Host, he'd serve me pasta and
tomato soup from burnt pots, while outside the three-legged
    dog
        performed its sad acrobatics
to the sound of "No Woman No Cry." And that one
    summer night, he left at 2:00 a.m.,
slow and deliberate as the turning of his bicycle spokes.
    As I lay awake, trapped on this bed,
imagining the crack dealers, transvestite hookers leaning
        into the darkened car windows
of married men from the suburbs. In the morning, he
    came back
        looking even more tired
of the world than ever. And that's when I knew his heart
    was the same as mine
floating further and further away from earth like that
    space station
        bound for some distant yet-to-be-named star.

The Year My Sister Came to Live with Me

The year my sister came to live with me, she brought
two cats, no money, ten years of experience
in the mental health field, a dozen pairs of sports
bras, a book called *When The Worst Thing That
Has Happened To You Happens.* It did.
The year my sister came to live with me, she'd
just come home from another heartbreak.
Me too. I came home drunk every Friday night,
took up Tai Chi, step dancing, rowing for singles.
The year my sister came to live with me, she took up
massage, gave me "freebies" in exchange for rent,
told me my body was holding grief, like some large
animal stopping the mouth of a black black cave.
I got my first cat, signed my free-loving
independence away for good.
She got odd jobs bathing a brain-damaged taxi driver,
lifting twenty-pound trays over her shoulder
while a guy named Karl yelled "Faster! Faster!"
The year my sister came to live with me, all the planets
converged, the moon, lopsided, hung
above our bedroom window while Hale-Bop
flashed across the thin line of sky.
I went to Ireland, England, came back again, found my sister
still sitting at the kitchen table.
I finally had to pay her to leave.
The year my sister left,
I wept for three days, missed her the way I had missed
all the great loves of my life.
Until, finally, I learned as with the rest of them
how to hold the best of her deep inside,
neither whole nor broken,
but just there.

Don McKay

Meditation on Antique Glass

This room, whose windows are waterfalls
in stasis, dreaming in one place, is wrong
for figuring your income tax or poker.
Susceptibility
they say as they teach the light to cry
and introduce hard facts to their first
delicious tremors of metamorphosis:
susceptibility
as though the film were paused at the point of flashing back,
woozy with semiosis: *the rapids are gentle,*
they say, *drink me.* Wrong
for marking essays or making plans.

Nights are worse. Darkness,
as it makes love to the glass, grows thick
and rich, advertising for itself, it whispers
memory muscle, whispers
Guinness is good for you, whispers
loss is its own fur, whispers
once, once
irresistibly.

Softball:

grows along the fringe of industry and corn.
You come upon it out of thick
summer darkness, floodlights
focusing a neighbourhood or township: way to
fire, way to mix, way to hum.
Everything trim,

unlike life: Frost Fence, straight
basepaths of lime, warm-up jackets worn by
wives and girl friends in the bleachers
match the uniforms performing on the field.

Half-tons stare blindly from the sidelines.
Overhead
unnoticed nighthawks flash past the floodlights effortlessly
catching flies: way to
dip, pick, snag that sucker,
way to be.

Down here everyone is casual and tense,
tethered to a base.
Each has a motive, none
an alibi.
The body is about to be discovered.

He peers in for the sign, perfect order
a diamond in the pitcher's mind.
Chance will be fate, all
will be out. Someone
will be called to arabesque or glide
                              someone
muscular and shy

will become the momentary genius of the infield.

Sometimes a Voice (1)

Sometimes a voice — have you heard this? —
wants not to be voice any longer, wants something
whispering between the words, some
rumour of its former life. Sometimes, even
in the midst of making sense or conversation it will
hearken back to breath, or even farther,
to the wind, and recognize itself

as troubled air, a flight path still
looking for its bird.
                    I'm thinking of us up there
shingling the boathouse roof. That job is all
off balance — squat, hammer, body skewed
against the incline, heft the bundle,
daub the tar, squat. Talking,
as we always talked, about not living
past the age of thirty with its
labyrinthine perils: getting hooked,
steady job, kids, business suit. Fuck that. The roof
sloped upward like a take-off ramp
waiting for Evel Knievel, pointing into open sky. Beyond it
twenty feet or so of concrete wharf before
the blue-black water of the lake. Danny said
that he could make it, easy. We said
never. He said case of beer, put up
or shut up. We said
asshole. Frank said first he should go get our beer
because he wasn't going to get it paralysed or dead.
Everybody got up, taking this excuse
to stretch and smoke and pace the roof
from eaves to peak, discussing gravity
and Steve McQueen, who never used a stunt man, Danny's
life expectancy, and whether that should be a case
of Export or O'Keefe's. We knew what this was —
ongoing argument to fray
the tedium of work akin to filter vs. plain,
stick shift vs. automatic, condom vs.
pulling out in time. We flicked our butts toward the lake
and got back to the job. And then, amid the squat,
hammer, heft, no one saw him go. Suddenly he
wasn't there, just his boots
with his hammer stuck inside one like a heavy-headed
flower. Back then it was bizarre that,
after all that banter, he should be so silent,
so inward with it just to

run off into sky. Later I thought,
cool. Still later I think it makes sense his voice should
sink back into breath and breath
devote itself to taking in whatever air
might have to say on that short flight between the roof
and the rest of his natural life.

Song of the Saxifrage to the Rock

Who is so heavy with the past as you,
Monsieur Basalt? Not the planet's most muscular
depressive, not the twentieth century.
How many fingerholds
have failed, been blown or washed away, unworthy
of your dignified *avoirdupois*, your strict
hexagonal heart? I have arrived to show you, first
the interrogative mood, then secrets of the niche,
then Italian. Listen, slow one,
let me be your fool, let me sit
on your front porch in my underwear
and tell you risqué stories about death. Together
we will mix our dust and luck and turn ourself
into the archipelago of nooks.

Precambrian Shield

Ancient and young, oldest
bone of the planet that was just
last week laid bare by the blunt
sculpting of the ice: it seemed a land designed
to summon mammals — haunched and shouldered,
socketed. Each lake we entered
was a lens, curious and cold
that brought us into focus.
Would I go back to that time,

that chaste and dangerous embrace?
Not unless I was allowed,
as carry-on, some sediment that has since
accumulated, something to impede the
passage of those days that ran through us
like celluloid. Excerpts from the book of loss.
Tendonitis. Second thoughts. Field guides.
Did we even notice
that the red pine sprang directly from the rock
and swayed in wind like gospel choirs?
Not us. We were muscle loving muscle, drank
straight from the rivers ran the rapids threw
our axes at the trees rode the back of every moose
we caught mid-crossing put our campfires out
by pissing on the flames. We could tell you
how those fuck-ups in *Deliverance*
fucked up: (1) stupid tin canoe (2) couldn't
do the J-stroke (3) wore life jackets (4) didn't
have the wit to be immortal
and ephemeral as we were. Sometimes,
in Tom Thomson's paintings you can see
vestigial human figures, brushstrokes
among brushstrokes. Would I go back
to that time, those lakes? Not without my oft-repeated dream
of diving for the body — possibly my own, possibly the lost
anonymous companion's — and surfacing to gulp in air
(the granite ridges watching, the clouds above them vacant
and declarative) and plunging once again into transparent
unintelligible depths.

Song for the Songs of the Common Raven

You could say it carries, you could say
dwells. Corvus corax: even in latin
you can hear that smoke-and-whisky brogue —
croak, curruck and (swallowing the syllable)

tok. You could say a fierce
unsayable secret has possessed the voice,
which has to speak and must not tell and so
is hollowed out and rendered terminally
hoarse. Of its brutal
seismic histories, its *duende*,
it says nothing. Nothing of the flowing and bending of rock,
of the burning going down and coming
up again as lava. Of rogue gods
loitering among the hemlocks nurturing the urge
to break out into body it conspicuously
does not sing. While sending messages that might
say "watch your asses, creatures
of the Neogene" or might say "Baby,
bring it on."

Chickadee Encounter

ok ok ok ok
here they come, the tidbits, the uppers,
animating the bramble,
whetting details. Hi,
I always say, I may be glum or dozy, still
hi, how's it going, every time they zip —
drawing that crisp invisible lilt from point to point — up
to check me out: ok: it's practically pauseless,
but as though some big machine —
domestication maybe — hiccuped,
a glitch through which the oceanic
thirsts of poetry pour: o
zippers, quicklings,
may you inherit earth, may you
perch at the edge of the shipwreck of state,
on the scragged uneconomical alders,
and chat.

Hover

What goes up
improvises, makes itself a shelf out of nowt,
out of ether and work, ushering the air, backstroke
after backstroke, underneath
the earth turns and you
don't, and don't,
and don't: O
who do you think you are so
hugely paused, pissing off both
gravity and time,
refusing to be born into the next
inexorable instant?
We wait in our
pocket of held breath, secretly
cheering you on.
Do it for us.

Meditation on Shovels

How well they love us, palm and instep, lifeline
running with the grain as we
stab   pry   heave
our grunts and curses are their music.
What a (stab) fucking life, you dig these
(pry) dumb holes in the ground and (heave) fill
them up again until they (stab)
dig a fucking hole for you:
      beautiful,
they love it, hum it as they stand,
disembodied backbones,
waiting for you to get back to work.

But in the Book of Symbols, after Shoes
(Van Gogh, Heidegger, and Cinderella)
they do not appear.

Of course not.
>	They're still out there
humming
patiently pointing down.

Setting Up the Drums

The tools of music: this is where it first
emerged from noise and how it
stays in touch with clutter
and how it gets back to the heart —
that single-stroke kachunker with its grab, give,
grab. He is bringing the kitchen,
the workshop, screwing wingnuts and attaching
brackets, placing the pedals like accelerators,
setting up the stands for snare and high hat like decapitated
wading birds. How music will make itself walk
into the terrible stunned air behind the shed
where all the objects looked away. Now the hollow bodies,
their blank moons tilted *just asking for it*, and back and
back to the time you missed the step
and dropped the baby and your heart leapt out
to catch it, for all those accidents that might have
and that happened he floats the ride and then
suspends the crash above the wreckage like its flat
burnished bell.
Unsheathes the brushes that can shuffle through the grass
or pitter like small rain. All this hardware to recall
the mess you left back home
and bring it to the music
and get back to the heart.
He sits on the stool
in the middle of your life
and waits to feel the beat. To speak it
and keep it. Here we go.

Matériel

(i) The Man from Nod

Since his later history is so obscure, it's no wonder he is most remembered for his first bold steps in the areas of sibling rivalry and land use. It should not be forgotten that, although Adam received God's breath, and angels delivered his message, it was Cain who got tattooed — inscribed with the sign which guarantees a sevenfold revenge to be dished out to antagonists. Sometimes translated "Born to Lose."

He was the first to realize there is no future in farming.

How must he have felt, after tilling, sowing, weeding, harvesting, and finally offering his crop, about God's preference for meat? Was God trying to push his prized human creatures further into the fanged romance of chasing and escaping? Was he already in the pocket of the cattle barons? Cain must have scratched and scratched his head before he bashed in his brother's.

He becomes the first displaced person, exiled to the land of Nod, whose etymology, as he probably realized, was already infected with wandering. Then his biography goes underground, rumouring everywhere. Some say he tries farming once again in the hinterland, scratching illegibly at the glacial till before hitting the first road. Some say he fathers a particularly warlike tribe, the Kenites. Some, like Saint Augustine, claim that he takes revenge on agriculture by founding the first cities, rationalizing all his wanderings into streets and tenements, and so charting the course for enclosures and clearances to come. But perhaps his strategy is simpler and more elegant. Perhaps he just thins into his anger, living as a virus in the body politic: the wronged assassin, the anti-farmer, the terrorist tattooed with the promise of sevenfold revenge. Like anyone, he wants to leave his mark.

(ii) Fates Worse than Death

Atrocity
implies an audience of gods.
The gods watched as swiftfooted
godlike Achilles cut behind the tendons of both feet
and pulled a strap of oxhide through
so he could drag the body of Hektor,
tamer of horses, head down in the dust
behind his chariot.
Some were appalled, some not,
having nursed their grudges well, until
those grudges were fine milkfed
adolescents, armed
with automatic weapons. The gods,
and farther off,
the gods before the gods, those who ate
their children and contrived
exquisite tortures in eternity, watched
and knew themselves undead. Such is the loss, such
the wrath of swiftfooted godlike
Achilles, the dumb fucker, that he drags,
up and down, and round and round the tomb
of his beloved, the body of Hektor,
tamer of horses. Atrocity
is never senseless. No. Atrocity is dead ones
locked in sense, forbidden
to return to dust, but scribbled in it,
so that everyone — the gods,
the gods before the gods, the enemy, the absent mothers, all
must read what it is like to live out exile on the earth
without it, to be without recesses, place,
a campsite where the river opens
into the lake, must read
what it means to live against the sun and not to die.
Watch,
he says, alone in the public

newscast of his torment, as he
cuts behind the tendons of both feet,
and pulls a strap of oxhide through,
so he can drag the body that cannot stop being Hektor,
tamer of horses, head down in the dust
behind his chariot, watch
this.

(iii) The Base

Unheard helicopter chop
locks my mind in neutral.
What was it I was supposed to think
as I entered the forbidden country of the base? For this
was not the wisdom I had bargained for —
banality. No orchids of evil
thriving on the phosphorus that leaks
from unexploded shells. No litter of black
ratatats like insoluble hailstones, or fungi
springing up from dead ka-booms.
After nearly forty years of shattered air, I find
not one crystal in the khaki gravel.
Nondescription.

What was Cain thinking
as he wandered here? Whatever
"here" may be, for it has largely been forgotten
by the maps, and also by itself, a large anonymous
amnesia in the middle of New Brunswick.
What shapes occupied the mind
which since has occupied the landscape?
Did he foresee this triumph of enchantment
whereby place itself becomes its camouflage,
surrenders Petersville, Coot Hill, and New
Jerusalem, to take up orders?
Did he anticipate the kingdom of pure policy,

whose only citizens — apart
from coyotes, ravens, moose —
are its police?
Except for graveyards, which have been
preserved, this real estate is wholly owned
and operated by the will, clearcut,
chemicalled and bombed.
Black wires like illegible writing
left everywhere. Ballistics? Baker Dog Charley?
Plastic vials tied to trees at intervals, containing
unknown viscous liquid. In some folktale
I can't conjure, I would steal this potion
and confer great gifts — or possibly destruction —
upon humanity. In a myth
or Wonderland, I'd drink it and become
a native. No thanks.
                        Yet blueberries grow, creeks
sparkle, and an early robin
sings from the scrub. Can a person eat
the berries when they ripen? What kind of fish
thicken in the creeks? During hunting season,
claims the Base Commander, moose and deer
take sanctuary in the impact areas, since no personnel
may enter. Often, late September, you may
see a moose, Jean Paul L'Orignal, perhaps,
sitting on a stump along the border of the base,
huge chin resting on a foreleg,
pondering alternatives: cheerful psychopaths
in psychedelic orange, or a moose-sized replica
of the absurd, ka-boom?

Now I recall
the story of the soldier detailed to attack
an "enemy position," which turned out to be
his grandfather's old farmhouse. Basic Training:
once out of nature he was not about
to get sucked in by some natural seduction

and disgrace himself with tears
or running to the kitchen for an oatmeal cookie.
He made, as we all do, an adjustment.
                    Standing here
still parked in neutral
I'm unable to identify the enemy's position or
sort the evil genii from fallen
farmers, victims and assassins
interpenetrate with vendors and *vendus* in long
chromosomal threads.
                Time to retreat.
Walking back, I try to jump a creek
and sprain my wrist. Pick up your goddamned
feet — . Still, I stop to cut two
pussy-willow branches. Why? Imagined
anti-fasces? Never
was the heaviness of gesture
heavier, nor hope more of a lump,
than trying to imagine that those buds
might, back home in the kitchen, unclench, each fragile hair
pom-pommed with pollen, some day
to open into leaf.

(iv) Stretto

Having oversold the spirit, having,
having talked too much of angels, the fool's rush, having the wish,
thicker than a donkey's penis,
holier than o, having the wish
to dress up like the birds,
to dress up like the birds and be and be and be.
Off the hook.
Too good for this world.
Unavailable for comment.
Elsewhere.

*

     Wonderful Elsewhere, Unspoiled,
Elsewhere as Advertised, Enchanted, Pristine,
Expensive. To lift, voluptuous, each feather cloak
worth fifty thousand finches: to transcend
the food chains we have perched upon and hover — hi there
fans from coast to coast — to beam back dazzling
shots of the stadium, drifting in its cosmos
like a supernova, everywhere the charged
particles of stardom winking and twinkling, o, exponentially
us. As every angel is.

     *

     Every angel is incestuous.
Agglutinoglomerosis: the inlet choked with algae thriving on
         the warmth
imparted by the effluent. *Contermitaminoma*: runoff through
the clearcut takes the topsoil to the river then
out into the bay to coat the coral reef in silt. *Gagaligogo*:
seepage from the landfill finds the water table. *Elugelah*:
           the south-
sea island angelized by the first H-blast.
         In the dead sea
we will float as stones. Unmortal

     *

     Unmortality Incorporated.
No shadow. All day
it is noon it is no one. All day
it utters one true sentence jammed
into its period. Nothing is to be allowed
to die but everything gets killed
and then reclassified: the death of its death
makes it an art form. Hang it.
Prohibit the ravens. Prohibit the coyotes.
Prohibit the women with their oils and cloths and

weep weep weeping. Tattoo this extra letter
on the air:
    This is what we can do.
Detonation. Heartbeats of the other,
signed, sealed,
delivered. Thunder
eats of its echo eats its vowels smothers its
elf. To strike
hour after hour   the same hour. To dig
redig the gravels that are no one's grave.

                      *

                    Gravels, aye, tis gravels ye'll gnash
mit muchas gracias and will it please thee sergeant dear to boot
me arse until I hear the mermaids sinking? You know it: tis the
gravel of old rocknroll highroad, me darling sibs, the yellow brick
jornada del muerto. You fancy me far from your minds, wandering lonely as a clod in longlost brotherhood, while your door's locked and your life's grammatically insured, yet (listen) *scurry scurry* (Is – That – Only – A – Rat – In – The – Basement – Better – Phone – Dad – Oh – No – The – Line's – Dead, Mandatory Lightning Flash) yup, here I am with the hook old chum. Hardly Fair, what? Now gnash this: beautiful tooth, tooth beautiful. Repeat: die nacht ist die nacht. How many fucking times do I have to *Fucking* tell you, me rosasharns? Nayther frahlicher ner mumbo, nayther oft when on my couch I lie ner *bonny doom* will lift from these eyes of thine their click clock particles of record time. *Ammo ergo somme.* We bombs it back to square one, then, o babes in arms, we bombs square one. Nomine Fat Boy ate Elugelah ate Alamogordo gravel. Mit click clock lock licht nicht.
Encore.
Die Nacht ist die Nacht.

Robert Melançon

Peinture aveugle

Est donnée une forme.
Où célébrer par un cycle de poèmes,
Fragments mais inséparables,
La naissance de la lumière
Et sa dissipation.
Où dire ce que n'ont pas dit
L'exclamation, le cri.
La passivité fait
Chaque rythme, et avec lui
Le buisson des figures.
Où atteindre la terre.
Comment accueillir ce que je vois?
Combinaisons de syllabes, mouvement
Et image, exprimeraient par la fureur
(D'où venue?)
L'indicible, la révélation?
Est donné ce silence.

L'été

Lilas que multiplie
Le soleil, que flaire
Le vent: chaque feuille
Où se pose le temps soutient
Tout le ciel. Une fauvette,
Fruit bref, l'ébranle,
Fait couler le bleu.

Les dieux en décembre

À la fin de la nuit d'hiver,
À cette heure où on attend
Le jour qui tarde, la fumée
Des cheminées, s'enroule
En panaches qui retombent
Sur les toits. Le froid pèse.
L'air vitrifié laisse voir
Des étoiles dans le ciel
Qui pâlit, sans plus ;
En décembre, le jour vient
Ainsi qu'un bilan qu'on dépose,
Qui décharge l'âme. Les dieux
Se sont retirés avec l'automne ;
On dirait qu'ils se sont couchés
Sous la terre rase, qu'ils ont
Rejoint les morts dans la terre dure.

Description d'un après-midi
à Robert Marteau

Le printemps n'est pas moins inexorable
Que septembre, octobre, novembre, alors qu'on voit
Le temps creuser son lit, mais on ne le dit pas.
Tout se recompose dans le soleil qui efface
La neige sur l'herbe, qu'on distingue mal de la boue :
Des traînées de lumière dressent des murs,
Tracent des corniches ; des rameaux, d'un jaune
Un peu ocré, ébouriffent un saule
Sur un fond de craie broyée dans l'air humide ;
Des pans de briques s'ornent d'un entrelacs
D'ombres finement encrées ; une vapeur,
À peine, qui suggère un feuillage, s'étend
Dans l'air biseauté tel un prisme. Il suffit pourtant
Qu'un nuage s'interpose et tout s'efface

Comme si la rue n'était qu'un enduit de lumière
Barbouillé sur rien de bien solide.
Cela va et vient, avec les cris des merles
Et des parfums de terre ; cela passe et revient
Dans les flaques qui répètent le ciel incertain.

36

Tout doit tenir en douze vers — un sonnet allégé — ,
Tout ce qui se peint à chaque instant dans la caverne
Qu'avait creusée Platon pour y enchaîner

Ceux qu'il croyait la proie des illusions.
Mais dans la sphère de son système, l'âme qui se libérait
Devait troquer pour une blancheur fade tout ce qui plaît :

Ces arbres que herse le vent, le jeu du soleil et des ombres,
Cet oiseau rose et marron qui se pose sur un fil.
Je m'en tiens au paradis des apparences :

Je trace un rectangle de douze lignes ;
C'est une fenêtre par laquelle je regarde
Tout ce qui apparaît, qui n'a lieu qu'une fois.

Anne Michaels

Three Weeks

Three weeks longing, water burning
stone. Three weeks leopard blood
pacing under the loud insomnia of stars.
Three weeks voltaic. Weeks of winter
afternoons, darkness half descended.
Howling at distance, ocean
pulling between us, bending time.
Three weeks finding you in me in new places,
luminescent as a tetra in depths,
its neon trail.
Three weeks shipwrecked on this mad island;
twisting aurora of perfumes. Every boundary of body
electrified, every thought hunted down
by memory of touch. Three weeks of open eyes
when you call, your first question,
Did I wake you . . .

Ice House

I regret nothing but his suffering.
— Kathleen Scott

Wherever we cry,
it's far from home.

*

At Sandwich, our son pointed
persistently to sea.
I followed his infant gaze,

expecting a bird or a boat
but there was nothing.
How unnerving,
as if he could see you
on the horizon,
knew where you were
exactly:
at the edge of the world.

       *

You unloaded the ship at Lyttleton
and repacked her:

"thirty-five dogs
five tons of dog food
fifteen ponies
thirty-two tons of pony fodder
three motor-sledges
four hundred and sixty tons of coal
collapsible huts
an acetylene plant
thirty-five thousand cigars
one guinea pig
one fantail pigeon
three rabbits
one cat with its own hammock, blanket and pillow
one hundred and sixty-two carcasses of mutton and
an ice house"

       *

Men returned from war
without faces, with noses lost
discretely as antique statues,
accurately as if eaten
by frostbite.
In clay I shaped their
flesh, sometimes

retrieving a likeness
from photographs.
Then the surgeons copied
nose, ears, jaw
with molten wax and metal plates
and horsehair stitches;
with borrowed cartilage,
from the soldiers' own ribs,
leftovers stored under the skin
of the abdomen. I held the men down
until the morphia
slid into them.
I was only sick
afterwards.

Working the clay, I remembered
mornings in Rodin's studio,
his drawerfuls of tiny hands and feet,
like a mechanic's tool box.
I imagined my mother in her blindness
before she died, touching my face,
as if still she could
build me with her body.

At night, in the studio
I took your face in my hands and your fine
arms and long legs, your small waist,
and loved you into stone.

The men returned from France
to Ellerman's Hospital.
Their courage
was beautiful.
I understood the work at once:
To use scar tissue to advantage.
To construct through art,
one's face to the world.
Sculpt what's missing.

*

You reached furthest south,
then you went further.

In neither of those forsaken places
did you forsake us.

*

At Lyttleton the hills unrolled,
a Japanese scroll painting;
we opened the landscape with our bare feet.

So much learned by observation.
We took in brainfuls of New Zealand air
on the blue climb over the falls.

Our last night together we slept
not in the big house but
in the Kinseys' garden.
Belonging only
to each other.
Guests of the earth.

*

Mid-sea, a month out of range
of the wireless;
on my way to you. Floating
between landfalls,
between one hemisphere and another.
Between the words
"wife" and "widow."

*

Newspapers, politicians
scavenged your journals.
But your words
never lost their way.

*

We mourn in a place no one knows;
it's right that our grief be unseen.

I love you as if you'll return
after years of absence.
As if we'd invented
moonlight.

*

Still I dream
of your arrival.

Roy Miki

fool's scold, 1.4.97
to commemorate april 1, 1949, the day the last of the restrictions on freedom of movement was lifted for japanese canadians

for peggy m @ irvine, california

*

48 years since the last restriction on jcs. the USA of it all this year. set out with irvine english department secretary pm to get a social security number to legitimate my sojourn as a lowly canuck. a routine procedure, i'm told. few minutes drive to pick up the card needed for my stay. get there, but no, i need to be approved first by immigration and naturalization. ok, ok, drive across town. a line up already forming, and the sun is bright, the breeze just right, children fidgeting. the opaque glass window speaks, then minutes pass with her supervisor. no, can't do. require to be re-examined by justice, section for aliens.

re-examined? when was i examined? that's the problem. the voice said, i wasn't, at the vancouver border. new regulations. since? today.

*

astride the fault lines
the enemy within stutters

"it was all an ordinary day"

warm california sun
    casting a glow
        on the landscape

sinecures planned in absentia
climb the wall to perch on parapets

    "canadian? pass"

as limply as a hand falling off a cart
(strain the figure for the sake of time spent

the passage into empire made so glibly
on this auspicious day before the coastal dawn

    ie the moon rose on march 31

    *

on the freeway to LA. if we rush we can make it by noon.
pm knows the route, and before we finish exchanging lives,
we're turning off and circling justice looking for a place to
park. peripheral vision signals we're right next door to
nihonbashi or j-town.

    *

sinuous thread dialects about which nothing
has been written
                  ecological damage on over
drive
    the slack alters the speech task

    ie the sun rose on april 1

  "but why didn't you
              declare your intent
    on the way through?"

in tent? the nomadic armour had fallen away
leaving only the mask to fill the passage

now the LA freeway's intent has gripes on the wall
the mouse mandate to get the cursor on track

at the entrance to the halls of justice the burly
blue uniform before the security gate electrons

    the weave of short fuses
                      the fiery hearts arc

      *

7th floor, down the long deserted hallway, to the
interrogation room, and a hand behind glass posts a sign.
closed for lunch.

back at 1:30, the room has filled with restlessness as lawyers
and clients whisper inaudible words. my examination form is
5 pages with questions of identity, intent, motive,
declaration, and why i hadn't been examined. at the canlit
border? i mused for a second. i can't understand why, she
says, when i hand her back the form, my hand sore. i didn't
know. well, if you ever do this another time, you'll have to
leave.

      *

set on demos magnetic no registration card needed
the US is not my telos no sir no sir no sir no sir i
won't tell sir no sir won't tell won't tell i promise
cross my jc heart but i won't hope to die no sir
no sir just passing no really i'm not looking for a
home yes this english is genuine the form is no problem
sure i can wait until after lunch no problem i love
grilled fish and rice i understand the problems you have
with so many trying to sneak through the nets no joking
i'm canadian and was sent here to speak on redress
for the internment of jcs at irvine university no i can't
stay longer but thanks for making such a fuss on
this fool's day memorial ok glad to be of service

*

new regulations, she continues, needed to deal with illegal aliens here. are there legal aliens here? i don't ask but at this interstice i imagine the border zone of "enemy alien," thinking of the ja's expelled from the coast in 42.

this is all an allegory i assure pm who by this time is incredulous. the plight of a lowly canuck, i tell her, april 1 is always a trial day for jc's — a day the spectral "enemy alien" plays tricks on us.

sure enough i'm given permission. april fool, i thought she would say through the glass, but she only smiled as she passed me the coveted "J" form.

*

        across the firmament
             this marked marvel
          heads for the hills

the blue candles lit
the litter on the causeway

        the foils in the narrative

Hélène Monette
Translated by Cole Swenson

Un coin du jardin sans soleil, tu m'as offert
en me conseillant d'y rester
pour veiller à l'éclosion des roses
des ronces
des barbelés autour de mes hanches

Un coin du supermarché, tu m'as cédé
rayon de conserves
et de papier d'argent, papier ciré
tu croyais que ce domaine me séduirait
tu m'y as laissée
les oreilles pleines d'insanités
aubaines hurlées dans les haut-parleurs
réclames, rabais, vitamines et santé
la honte, masques et crèmes, la réalité

j'aurais dû m'en aller
dès que tu m'as reléguée dans un coin obscur du grenier
— là, dans ta tête —
pendant que tu t'accordais les sourires éclatants
de la victoire
du réel sur la durée

Dans un coin de la salle de bal, tu m'as oubliée
après m'avoir conviée à profiter de la fête
avec l'intensité barbare
des innocents plus grands que nature

et quand j'ai compris d'où jaillissaient
ces éclats de lumière dans tes yeux
la nuit
chaque fois nuit d'ivresse

et quand je me suis considérée intacte
malgré cette chaise en métal inconfortable
qui ne soutenait même pas mes reins

dans cette salle de bal
je me suis mise à danser
seule dans mon coin
lèvres bannies
gercées de vin
la robe sale
les yeux éteints

une ferveur inaltérable dans les mains

160 Secondes / 160 Seconds

j'ai dû rêver de prier encore
que personne n'abandonne personne
existe-t-il ce chemin
qui t'a mené ici ?
me confierais-tu d'autres fois
tes mots, ta bouche, tes mains ?
retrouveras-tu le fil de l'histoire
qui est là
à peine encombrante
comme une tranchée ouverte
en cours de route
parmi les explosions ?
à venir, au fond
dans la terre battue
comme un diamant ténu
éblouissant

I must have been dreaming to keep on asking
that no one abandon no one
does the road
that led you here exist ?
would you entrust to me another time
your words, your mouth, your hands ?
will you find the thread of the story again
there
barely a burden
like an open trench
among the explosions
en route ?
to come, in the end
in the battered earth
like a diamond held
dazzling

*

un grand vacarme ravage la rue
on coupe les arbres à la chaîne
on scie des autos, tape du marteau
le jour est rempli de mes inquiétudes
et de ton sourire, calme lumière
de ton visage dans la nuit

a great din tears up the street
they're cutting down the trees one after another
sawing up cars, tap of the hammer
the day is full of my cares
and your smile, calm light
of your face in the night

*

la ville ensoleillée
joue dans le bruit
un grand vacarme tue le poème
je est un autre
et tu es lui
quelqu'un qui vit
ardent passager fantôme

the sunny town
plays in the noise
a great din kills the poem
I is an other
and you are he
someone who lives
ardent passenger ghost

∼

Il n'y a personne qui crie
dans cette chambre
cette chambre est vide
comme une femme
qui n'a été aimée de personne
et la foule contient toutes les femmes
tous les hommes
aussi les disparus
le monde est dans la rue
et dans la maison
entre l'écuelle et la couverture
les petits sentiments
et l'émotion dure

No one is crying
in this room
this room is empty
like a woman
who's been loved by no one
and the crowd includes all women
all men
and the disappeared
the world is in the streets
and in the house
between the bowl and the lid
the little feelings
and hard emotion

*

les nerfs aboient
le cœur délire
> *viens plus près*
> *que je te déchire*

et tout le monde crie
dans la chambre vide
le monde explose
expire

the nerves bark
the heart crazes
> *come closer*
> *so I can shred you*

and everyone cries
in the empty room

the world bursts
goes out

                    *

c'était une chose
qu'on ne voulait pas de la vie

et on se demande
où est l'amour
devant, dedans
pour nos nerfs finis

it was something
that we didn't want from life

and we wonder
where love is
before, within
for our finite nerves

~

Pamela Mordecai

from de Man: a performance poem

I
Jesus Is Condemned to Death

NAOMI   Oonu see mi dyin trial!
Dem people yah nuh easy.
A kill dem a go kill de man.
How yuh mean "Which man?"
Nuh de man Jesus. Yuh know —
De one dat preach? And
Tell story? Yuh never hear
Him yet? Bwoy, me nuh
Understand oonu young
People. If oonu did stay at
Oonu yard, me would seh
Come. But oonu walk street
And ignorant same way.
Me studying dis man from
Him come down a Jordan side
And mek de Baptist dip him.
Is dat baptism yuh must
Hear about! Dat's how
Me know is not a ting but
Politricks — dat and red eye.
All dem old hypocrite —
Seh dem is priest and nuh
Have time fi people.
A good ting rain nuh fall
Fi joke round dese parts else
Dem would a sure fi drown.
So dem ugly, a so de man

Good-looking. Dem have big
Word fi t'row but him
Could talk. De truth is not
A one o'dem could draw
A crowd like him. And when
Him ready him just tek
Time and do a likl healing:
Who lame cyan walk. Who dumb
Cyan talk . . . Dem seh him all
Raise dead! Beelzebub
Or no Beelzebub —
De man have power yuh hear.
Dem old and ugly, full
Up of dem self; have nuff book
Learning and cyaan talk three
Word straight. And if dem life
Did turn pon it dem wouldn't
Have de power fi mek
A dead fish twitch.
Dat is de whole ting —
Cash bill and receipt.
So dem send some old
Criminal fi drape him up
And drag him here. Real
Ragamuffin — if yuh
Ever see dem . . . Beg yuh just
Pass mi head-wrap — do. Time
Going. Me betta go dere quick.
God know which dutty business
Dem a knock dem wicked head
Togadda fi perpetrate . . .

Is must be why my mistress send
Me to report on what dem
Doing to him. Me sure she not
Going stand fi it. Me hear
Her tell de Pilate one

"You let him die and you
Will have no peace." She seh
She dream some awful tings
And yuh know dat is one
Could dream . . .
    Still
Pray Jah dat my future
Never rest with that frog-
Face for him have neither
Character nor courage
Nor de commonsense
Fi do what him wife seh.

• • •

IV
Jesus Meets His Mother

SAMUEL *(To himself as he struggles*
to get closer to Jesus)
Naomi? Well . . . How she
Could know? She did mek up
Her mind and gwaan her way
Time me reach Nazareth.
And it nuh mek no sense
Me try fi tell her now.
She wouldn't keep quiet to hear
Me anyhow . . .
    When dis child
Jesus was a likl bwoy
Me was apprentice to him Pa.
A real funny 'prentice!
Me was a big man, forty plus,
Wid one hand twist, de next
One chop off at de wrist.
But dat man Joseph teach

Me how to use hammer
And saw and chisel wid
Mi twist hand and mi stump.
. . . Still is de lady Mary
Dat me couldn't take
Mi two eye from. And so
Me watch her, so she watch
Dat child. An all de while
She going on doing what she
Have to do. Me cyaan ex-
Plain to yuh. Is like she
Know dis child is de most
Precious thing and like — just
How him running up and
Down chasing him ball — she
Seeing him dying right dere
As she look.
            So me just
Have to do a likl
Jostling here today. Me
Know just now she seeing
Before her eye what she
Was looking at for all
Dem years. See. Is de self-
Same countenance she gazing
On him wid . . . And him . . .
Oh Jesus, don't look pon
Her so. She know yuh love
Her right down to yuh toe.
She know yuh never want
To leave her so. She know
Jah seh is so it haffe
Go. From yuh was likl
Jesus she did know.

. . .

VIII
The Women of Jerusalem Mourn for Jesus

SAMUEL   Den what? Yuh mean to seh
De sistren yonder have
More stomach than yuh? Or
Dat dem watching dis fi
Spectacle? If dat's de
Case, is a real sorry show.
Dem crying so till dem
Wetting up de ground.
And when yuh look into dem
Face a awful bleakness
Looking back at yuh. Yuh
See Naomi . . . Me is a
Man well old. Is many
Me see go into de
Grave and me see many
Many dawtas weep
And in de midst of
Every lamentation
Yuh hear a sound of
Comfort and of hope. But
Not dis time. No hope
Inside that grief. Naomi
Look pon dem.

NAOMI   True Samuel. Dem don't look
Like is dead smadi going
Dead. Dem favour like de
Worl' come to a end . . .

SAMUEL   But after yuh nuh look
No better, come to tink
On it.

NAOMI   Him talking to
Dem now. Is a long speech
Fi somebody half-dead . . .

SAMUEL   And yuh and me too far
         Away fi hear. Joseph
         Me grieve for what dem
         Doing to yuh only son . . .

• • •

XI
Jesus Is Nailed to the Cross

NAOMI   Well in a way it had
        To come to dis. Is so
        Life stay. If him was just
        Anadda likl madman
        Passing through, dem wouldn'
        Haffe kill him. Him mussi
        Really God fi true, else
        Him would dead t'ree time
        A'ready. And now dem
        Going to lick some royal
        Nail into him wrist
        And kill him one more time
        Before him dead. Look
        Samuel. De man whole
        Body jump each time dem
        Bring de hammer down. Blood
        Running from him two hand
        Like two river. Is lift
        Dem lifting up de cross
        Now — Samuel, dem nail
        So big him weight going tear
        Him off it when dem drop
        De cross inna de hole.

SAMUEL Naomi yuh know is
        Now I see de ting. Dis
        Crucifixion is a

Sacrifice. Dis Golgotha,
Hill of de Skull, come like
De altar for de sacrifice.
And de man Jesus is de
Offering. And if him
Is God son fi true den
Any how dem kill him, some
Dread dread things going come
Upon dis land. So me
Nah leave yah till him dead,
No matta how it bruk
Up mi old body and
Tear mi soul apart. Mi
Time well short. Today me
Must find out which priest is
Really priest. Me haffe know
Who have de truth, who have
De power, who me must
Follow — de Pharisee dem
Or de Nazarene.

. . .

XIII
Jesus Is Taken Down from the Cross

NAOMI   Samuel is why yuh keep
Look-looking back up to
Dat hill? Listen mi bredda.
Come yuh and me mek
Haste put plenty space
Between de two of we
And dat renk wickedness
What Pilate and dem ugly
Priestman perpetrate
Top o' dat hill today.

SAMUEL   Well tell de trut' Naomi
           One big piece o' me
           Lef up dere wid de man
           What dem just crucify.
           As for de lady Mary —
           Well me woulda easy give
           Mi ears-dem eye-dem foot-dem
           Hand-dem — all mi very life
           Me woulda give fi bring
           Him back. Compare to me,
           Yuh know, de man is just
           A likl youngster. Me
           Cyaan stop memba how him
           Use to chase dat likl ball.
           Him and de dawg, de tiefing
           Puss, him and de neighbour
           Pikni dem.
                              Den wait Naomi.
           Look like yuh going back too . . .?

NAOMI   After me cyaan lef yuh
           One in de midst of dark-
           Ness and of politricks.
           Oh Samuel, look — dem tek
           Him down. Dem putting him
           Into her hand.
                              Listen sister
           Me grieve for yuh same like
           Him was mi very own.
           Me feel de dead weight in
           Mi arms. Me feel de limpness
           In mi lap. Me feel mi heart
           Leave from mi bosom drop
           Down to mi belly bottom.
           Sister Mary tell no lie
           Me know it hard fi carry
           Him and rear him up and

Cherish him fi dis.
Me know yuh want to tear
Yuh hair out root by root
And rend yuh clothes and bawl
Until yuh eye dem don't have
No more tears to drop.
No mind. No mind. Yuh pikni
Wasn't no criminal.
Don't worry. Everybody
Know. It was a nasty
Scheming ting cook up by
Evil godless men . . .

SAMUEL   Naomi why yuh talk so much?
Hush up and look. Yuh don't
See like a light around
De two of dem? Yuh don't
See how de air get bright
Look like it full of men
On fire, flying and floating,
Settling round madda and son?
Oh Massa God take time
Me begging yuh . . . Take time
Wid sinners. Jesus help.
Naomi answer me. Yuh ever
See a angel yet?

Glossary

a	is, are
a go	are going
bredda	brother
cyan	can
cyaan	can't
dawg	dog(s)
drape	seize by the neck, seize forcibly
fi	for, to
gwaan	go on, behave

lef	leave, left
madda	mother
me	I, me
mek	make
mi	my
mussi	must be
nah	not (emphatic)
nuff	enough, many
nuh	not, no, don't
pikni	children
pon	upon, on
red eye	jealous
seh	say
so-so	single (*one so-so word* = a single word)
tek	take
way	away
wi	will
yah	here

Author's Notes

Pam gratefully acknowledges the contribution of the following persons to *de Man:* first, Father Oliver Nickerson, S.J., my pastor at the time, who in 1989 asked if I would write "something for Good Friday" for the parishoners of St. Thomas Aquinas Church, Papine, Jamaica: the poem is the result of that suggestion; next, Ted Chamberlin, Rachel Ramsay, Betty Wilson and, in particular, Keith Lowe and Olive Senior, for their invaluable comments on earlier drafts; the late Dennis Scott for pointing me to "an engine" for the poem; and finally, wid nuff respec, Makeda Silvera and Stephanie Martin of Sister Vision Press for sharing my sense of urgency and taking very special care.

Pierre Morency

Le monde dans la peau

Tout alentour de nos maisons secrètes
les éléments du monde n'ont plus de transparence
nous avons l'air d'avoir du feu
l'air d'avoir du vent de l'eau
et nos pieds ne touchent plus la terre

il faudra recommencer la vérité du sol
de nos os de nos yeux

je suis offert en toi comme revers du feu
et je me donne comme l'envers de l'eau

Je t'écris

Par la bouche des branches où des oiseaux fleurissent
par les mille niches du silence
et par la peau du lac tendue comme un tambour
je t'appelle et te crie

dans la corne brouillée de ce matin qui monte
dans le porte-voix du petit soir de sept heures
et par le corridor exsangue des rues mortes
je t'appelle et te crie

par toutes les eaux blanches à l'orée des champs mûrs
par la proue et la poupe des îles
par les paumes pressantes de l'air
je t'appelle et te crie

à travers les grilles briseuses de mon corps
à travers mes fenêtres abouchées au ciel d'eau
la tête séparée par les lames du cœur
je t'appelle et t'écris

Daniel David Moses

Song in the Light of Dawn

Fish. My eyes were sleepy
fish and in the overcast
world the road to work was mud.
Then something near a pond

turned my head. A black bird's
banded wing made the perfect
lure, the gay colour a hook
without hurt, a blushing

wash. Now further on on
this shoulder of the high
way even the gravel and
asphalt greys overflow

their textures. They're so clear
I feel more than awake. Oh
to stay and swim in them here
would be, would be enough.

Rooms Under Rain

Through the day's underwater
light we came
home, past the almost
desperate sway of wet blacked
maples. And we sat in that sun
room into the night, the gusty

storm voice a vague echo
of the radio. And we took

sweet tea, waiting for Grand
mother, insomniac in
the north bedroom, to be
up and all right. In her shadow

steeped room she looked so
thin, nested in her electric
blanket like a mouse who knows no
other burrows but dry
grasses. Tentatively
she'd sip the clear tea we'd carry

in, then curl and begin to
dream though the ache floating
in her side persisted like
the rain. We were glad warm
tea again and again was
a sleeping water. And we ignored

the similar fluid gathered
under roads. In leaf
clogged culverts it glimmered
like the disease that waits for
dark to ice over the tea
sweet rooms of any house.

The Line

This is not the poem, this line
I'm feeding you. And the thought
that this line is not the poem
is not it either. Instead
the thought of what this line is
not is the weight that sinks it
in. And though this image of
that thought as a weight is quite
a neat figure of speech, you

know what it's not — though it did
this time let the line smoothly
arc to this spot, and now lets
it reach down to one other,
one further rhyme — the music
of which almost does measure
up, the way it keeps the line
stirring through the dampening
air. Oh, you know you can hear
the lure in that. As you know
you've known from the start the self
referring this line's doing
was a hook — a sharp, twisted
bit of wit that made you look
and see how clear it is no
part of this line or its gear
could be the poem. Still it cast
and kept the line reeling out
till now at last the hook's on
to itself and about to
tie this line I'm feeding you
up with a knot. Referring
to itself has got the line
and us nowhere. So clever's
not what the poem is about
either. We're left hanging there
while something like a snout starts
nudging at your ear, nibbling
near my mouth — and it's likely
it's the poem about to take
the bait. From the inside ought
to be a great way to learn
what the poem is. And we'll use
this line when the poem's drawn it
taut and fine as breath to tell
what we know, where we are and
where we'll go — unless the line

breaks. How would it feel, knowing,
at last, what the poem really
is, to lack the line to speak?

The Persistence of Songs

The people feed from the river and conceive songs.
But the strangers with the dead heads march towards the long
edges of their own blades. They see a thundering
fog along the horned horizon and turn around
to stalk the rising sun. They find four lanterns made
of skin arrayed along the river, the people
still feasting within. The strangers feed off their own
anger, flooding the river with blood. The four songs,
who are the children, go dumb and their white dogs mad
before the people have the strangers rounded up.

They bind them with skin from the fog and throw them in;
then, they wait for the river to heal. They try
to feast again. They pray to the children. By noon
the river grows an old skin and the children fade.
In the cold mud the strangers congeal. A fog
bleeds from the river, drowns the lanterns and stops up
the ears of the people with a dull, three-note song.
The strangers are praising honed edges and the white
meat of their own bodies. They curse the sun and vow
the moon turns so perfectly round they will square it.

They lurch up through the river's dull skin and begin
the marching again. The people search in the skin
for reflected light, the sunset or a lantern,
then assume the skin as mourning. The procession
the people enter tracks the moon through fog, cuts it
into quarters. And black dogs track the procession.

They feed off their own hunger and conceive a song
in praise of a perfect horizon made of meat.

That song fades; but, the four songs, who are the children,
return with horned heads. They feed from ears and edges.

Falling Song

There was the sweet but reedy
honking of geese coming down
this morning with rain over
rush hour streets, coming
through like bells that celebrate.

I got right up, pushing up
close to the sooty window
pane. I peered out and up through
the weather, imagining
that that line of winged dots would

be shifting as if waves moved
easily through them, as if
waves floated them south. I wanted
to catch them riding, spots on
the wake of the wind, marking

the certain direction of
their migration. But I got
no satisfaction. Mist kept
them mysterious, quickly
dampening their call. Leaning

over the sill, I gaped at
a window shade dull sky, at
a hollow city, and felt
like I'd missed a parade I
would have wanted to follow.

Erín Moure

Shock Troop

Shock troop
shock exercise
Knife is a verb
Bayonet a verb
Coat a verb
Absolute is a conjunction
Now get up & pay for the coffee,
make a sentence, fool

She knife, she coat, absolute she bayonet
he said
incomprehensible as
shock troops blowing the door in
& taking the TV down stairs to a truck

You don't pay me, you live here
she said, pushing his money back, the tip, too

Homage
November 1976

The dictator's former aide reports
three hundred thousand killed.
7am, in the dining car serving breakfast, here
morning is open, the season
ripe w / food.
No tanks in the kitchen.
No one hides in the bush, takes aim, there are
no bullets, just
the random ritual of eggs.
In the dining room innocent passengers

eat their path into the day.
The waiters banter back & forth.
Harry is in the washroom drinking beer.
Alex stands in the pantry, in everyone's road, giving
Information. About his girlfriend.
Three hundred thousand killed.
In the kitchen, the chef careens against fridges,
eyes out of sync, drunk.
Cyclone Todd fries eggs & yells.
His face the same sweaty colour.
Killed.

This moment, this day, to UPI
the dictator's former aide reports
three hundred thousand killed.
In the dining car, now nearly at Wabamun,
sun & bright snow, on schedule, no
bullets, no armed men in the field,
nowhere the obese tyrant shouting *Fire!*
his chest clotted w / medals, his own people
bloated in rivers, mouths gaped, utter
lost defiance or
the homage no one can know —

from "Seven Rail Poems"
• • •

2
VIA: Tourism

Always, the same bodies
slumped in rows, the same questions & fear
of accident or delay
The words of technique, comfort
dealt out to strangers in the wheels' rough noise
The jagged train of hours

Then there are the women   beaten by their husbands
who bear the marks as they bore their children,
without disgrace,
who bring their children away with them
across the country in coach seats or
jammed into one berth
drinking pepsi, eating aspirin
Locked in the motion of rails, of constant arrival
Their bruised eyes & hands swollen
from battering tables
Insistent
Children tangled among their legs
Vacant of husbands
Wondering, alone
Gone where they've never been, moving into their lives
with no more father

Above all this, for miles & days, the habitual
tourism that never stops, the PR rep in her blue coat
saying VIA, VIA

3
We Are a Trade

Sometimes people clutter in aisleways, holding
unspent money,
their eyes tired, by days travelled
in broken airconditioning,
the sun & prairies cut in their bodies, their stance —
You can't say you don't see
Pythagoras,
the immigrant Canadian sending money home;
he's out there in his lousy field of rapeseed
on New Holland equipment, cutting
one yellow swath from the horizon.
Some will call this impossible

politics.
Pythagoras will turn his tractor toward the train.
His belief bends the earth & grows.
Wheat corporations take the money, America —

In the train, passengers eat & return
to watch & drink whisky,
speak old aphorism —
the duck-lakes of Saskatchewan, money in Alberta,
Valley farmers dead in their silage
& us, employees, members
of the union who won't vote anymore
who serve doggedly
18 hours every day, who work dogged
For the time off at home, whole afternoons spent
in poolrooms, or sleeping
Affluent in dreams, paying rent in public housing

What do you expect from me
We earn dividends for no one
We watch Pythagoras & prime ministers from the same train
flat & curious
We are a stubborn trade

• • •

A History of Vietnam & Central America as Seen in the Paintings of Leon Golub, Musée des beaux arts, Montréal, 1985

Several sections of this photograph are not visible.
Several sections have been repaired.
Several pieces of this canvas have been torn out
or covered over.
Several sections have been smeared.
If you turn around the photograph the result

is not the backs of heads.
The result of one painting sawn in three
is three paintings.
Several sections of this paragraph have been repaired.
Several sections have been forged with outside influence.
The woman holding the man's cock in the painting was also painted
by the man.
If the eye sees & the mouth describes.
If several sections of this photograph are not visible.
If the corn in the field winnowed new
teeth smiling
Several sections of this painting have been recently
restored
There is no speaking torn out & lifted says the president
There is no section of this painting you do not see

Several sections of this photograph have been torn out.
Several sections have been replaced.
Several parts of this poem are encoded to prevent theft
of language.
Several parts of this poem are encoded by theft,
to prevent language.
The mercenaries hold silver guns, they are throwing
the artist's body into the trunk of an American car.
Several pictures have not been taken.
Several times I have not stopped listing over.
The photograph gets smaller in the fingers.
When it is over we stand up & walk out, our breath fast,
uncreasing our knees

Goodbye to Beef

The irrational deafness of our heads, that's
all.
Where our elegant coiffure comes from,
our own fingers, hey: squirrel-
hunting in the Rocky Mountains under the smell of spruce

forest I said I never would forget
& haven't.
Damn it.
Where our research will get us,
home free, sliding fast
past the hard throw from second baseman.
Looking for just one more homer.

We are listening to too much music, & our tastes
are lousy.

The squirrel my brother shot down with the .22 so the dog could play.
The dog just sniffed the dead fur
& looked up the tree again, eye
cocked for the squirrel.
It is always in our damn heads.

Or my head.

Or anyone's.

When we got together, what we talked of,
the moose my uncle shot & cut up into frozen pieces,
& sent it down, in 1964, on the Greyhound.

What I forgot to say, was:
When we saw that box of moose hefted out of the bus bay in
the din of yelling navvies,
we knew it was goodbye to beef
till springtime.

& I haven't talked to my aunt since.

I go deaf thinking of it.   Or anything.

Fifteen Years

I am in a daydream of my uncle,
his shirt out at his daughter's wedding,
white scoop of the shirt-tail bobbing
on the dance floor.
When I think of it.
When I think of my cousin, otherwise,
shooting the BB gun up the exhaust pipe of his motorcycle,
behind the garage.
It is the softness of a puppy we have brought home from the farm,
& set on the grass to fall over crying,
sleeping in a boot next to the heart-tick of the alarm.

I am wondering how we live at all
unable to replace these images.
The green space beside my parents' house in summer
where we lay down on our stomachs to keep cool.
My uncle's shirt-tail beneath his suit jacket, dancing.
The flag of that shirt-tail.
I tell you.
His daughter married for fifteen years.

Thirteen Years

I am in a daydream of my uncle,
his shirt out at his daughter's wedding,
white scoop of the shirt-tail bobbing
on the dance floor & him in it, no,
his drunk friend pawing me, it was *his* shirt dangling,
I forgot this,
my youngest cousin in his dress pants downing straight whisky,
& me too, tying tin cans to his sister's car.
The sour taste of it. Drink this, he said.

I am wondering how we live at all
or if we do.

The puppy we grew up with came from the same uncle's farm.
His shirt-tail beneath his suit jacket, dancing.
The friend of the family touching my new chest.
They told me not to say so.
I'll drive you to the motel, he said, his breath close.
No. Be nice to him, they said, & waved me off from the table.
I was so scared.
Everyone had been drinking. Including me. Thirteen years old.
Who the hell did my cousin marry.
I tell you.

West to West

Eventually I came to miss the mountains, the man said
hands knotted in front of his jacket
in the Faculty bar of an English university
in Montréal where the heat stifles
No, I don't miss them, the mountains, the woman
said, perhaps
you depended upon them, &
I became them, she said, they're here with me now
in this hot room
inside my body head resting, otherwise, she said
this is just another metaphor
for sexual difference, she said, crossing out
line after line &
George Vancouver the healer stepping into the trees,
his boat fluttered with flags, or
the place Mr. Fraser came out into the delta & was frightened
The woman putting her coat on in the heat

Oh little lamb, who made thee, she said & stood up,
hugging the woman she came with, in her painfulness & quiet,
their arms close & hands open, the fear they'd been through
unspeakable, from the West to the West,
& their affection,
laughing

In These (Tough) Times

I want to say just now I don't care
about the three fish lying on the counter
their stomachs opened in a straight line
soft & waiting for the pan

to heat up

I want to say just now I don't care
The rockets above my building are testing
Russian overcoats
The traffic stops at the light where two streets
meet head-on
A design problem

I want to say just now I don't care
The fat in the pan is smoking
The grey shadow of my thought rises
I want to carry my body restless into your room
& hold my mouth beside your ear
where I first kissed you
"beyond consequence"

Tho your body (out of pain) remembers only painfulness
just yet
I want to say just now I can live
without jubilance
I want to say I'm never again going to be lonely
I want you to sleep

as I lay the fish soft into the frypan
& smell the fat cooling
& hear the crackle of the fish skin
cooking

Miss Chatelaine

In the movie, the horse almost dies.
A classic for children, where the small girl pushes a thin
knife into the horse's side.
Later I am sitting in brightness with the women
I went to high school with in Calgary,
fifteen years later we are all feminist, talking of the girl
in the film.
The horse who has some parasite & is afraid of the storm,
& the girl who goes out to save him.
We are in a baggage car on VIA Rail around a huge table,
its varnish light & cold,
as if inside the board rooms of the corporation;
the baggage door is open
to the smell of dark prairie,
we are fifteen years older, serious
about women, these images:
the girl running at night between the house & the barn,
& the noise of the horse's fear mixed in with the rain.

Finally there are no men between us.
Finally none of us are passing or failing according to
Miss Chatelaine.
I wish I could tell you how much I love you,
my friends with your odd looks, our odd looks,
our nervousness with each other,
the girl crying out as she runs in the darkness,
our decoration we wore, so many years ago, high school
boys watching from another table.

Finally I can love you.
Wherever you have gone to, in your secret marriages.
When the knife goes so deeply into the horse's side, a
few seconds & the rush of air.
In the morning, the rain is over.
The space between the house & barn is just a space again.
Finally I can meet with you & talk this over.
Finally I can see us meeting, & our true tenderness, emerge.

Meeting

Meeting implies purpose. The Vietnamese boy sweeping the floor
also makes good
coffee
& owns
this restaurant where the woman pats the yellow curled dog on the terrasse
& a boy does Tai Chi in the doorway the ache
in my back is the same ache I feel
for your mouth on those open places their tenderness the
tenderness of blind birds soft asleep
in their shells their feathers pin-small combed flat with
mucous hair & bird thoughts of the dome-light shining
thru the egg the earth the way light shines
thru the fingers, opalescent, the way a woman sitting
forward rubs her soft lidded centre on the chair's cloth
the texture of that
the restaurant where I sit today, good coffee
in the cup in my fingers, not waiting,
meeting no one

Alayna Munce

To Train and Keep a Peregrine You Cannot Miss a Day

If, in the morning, I wake first, I lie awhile beside you.
A small window holds a square and impossibly partial
view: the outside world as seen from our bed, a scrap of sky
criss-crossed by the swaying upper branches of a dying
elm. Occasionally a bird. Lying there I gather evidence
of the day's weather. It was from you that I first heard
of bards whose minds were strong-benched ships, holds
full of heroes, well-tended hives aswarm with heroes; who,
in their apprenticeships, spent days fasting and prone, tartans
swaddled round their heads and head-sized stones
upon their stomachs while they mazed the many-branched
corridors of ancient stories and memorized the honeycomb, the
stroke
      stroke
            stroke of a thousand years. We leave each other
and return. Planets in syncopated orbits. Remember
that first winter we lived together? You worked days and I,
nights (me serving bottomless cups of black coffee to
cab drivers and drag queens at an all-night diner near
Maple Leaf Gardens, my name tag crooked; you
serving soup-kitchen slop to buddy who'd follow it up with a
cocktail in the park — can of Sprite spiked with aftershave —
unless you spared him a five for a real bottle, the tongues
of your untied workboots panting all afternoon in the dish room).
We both concentrated all we were on that hour near dawn
when I crawled into bed beside you — first hour of your day,
last of mine — that hour
      we overlapped. That hour
            yawned wide. Laughing, half
proud, we used to say, *Like ships passing in the night*. Later
we warned each other with phrases like, *to drift apart*. Still

later, a month of your face so foreign I knew you had forged
some strange alliance, yielded to the need for mutiny.
                                            We lose each other
and return. Now, our agendas let us curl in bed together,
though one of us always falls asleep first, leaving the other
stranded, beached in wakefulness. (There's no betrayal
greater than unconsciousness.) In the morning,
if I wake first, I lie awhile beside you, lie there memorizing
the verses of our life so far. Some mornings we are as
obsolete as an oral tradition. Other days, leaning
on the phrasing
                of the moments
                              of return,
I want to make and keep a promise,
master a forgiveness as ingenious and out of date
as the art of falconry.
To train and keep a peregrine
you cannot miss a day. Today
I want to say, *Every day*
at sunrise, love,
I will remove
the ornamented hood
                and send the bird out
                              to bring me
back.

Susan Musgrave

Magnolia

Another Valentine's Day behind bars
and I bring you light from the stars
that you might find your way back to us
out of darkness. I bring you memories
of me — naked, happy, nine months pregnant
tasting applesauce in the kitchen.

I bring you the wind, the way
our house creaked as you rocked
our newborn daughter who couldn't sleep.

I bring a handful of rain
that you may remember the sound of it,
and the smell of the earth
when you turn it in your hands.
I don't know why our life took
the turn it did, but now the smell
of earth reminds you — the magnolia
tree you planted the day
our daughter was born: did it live?

I bring you tears, the ones you wept
mixed with the milky scent of those I kept
locked up in me as I sang our daughter
to sleep those first merciful years —
*if I could I would give you wings
to carry you up to the sky.*

When I kiss your eyes, your sudden cry
startles the magnolia to a deeper white.

Understanding the Sky

> "Sometimes I go about in pity for myself, and all the while
> A great wind is bearing me across the sky."
> — from the Anishinabi (Ojibwa)

The ravens arrived before daybreak,
awakening me. I moved from my moonlit
bed to the window, my heartbeat the sound
a hammer makes striking emptiness, before
and after. How much easier to embrace
pain than the common miracles of freezing
rain, the fires of smudgy juniper
smouldering across the water
or the mist that stills its whispery music
in my mind. What sound does the wind make
if you don't name it? Oh my ancestors
you are like clouds with nothing
to keep you from flying, like the running-away
river with no one to depend on. I go outside
understanding the sky is
just as present beneath my feet as it is
up above, and so try to tread
lightly on the crust of this earth, knowing
it is thin. The ravens slope towards the stars,
the black night in their beaks, and I think
Be light, light, light, as I make my way
in darkness to the river's edge. And then,
from overhead, a branch drooping
with snow, the owl takes flight, swoops
and glides down beside me. Even though
the requiem birds had failed to roust him
from his place of refuge, it is my quiet
uneasiness that causes him to strike
out over the river, to the brighter side.
What brings tears, I do not know, nor grasp
the thieflike tendency of tears to disappear,

but I feel graced to have felt the snow
owl's breath upon my face, as if I no longer need
to go on breathing; I am being breathed.
Be light, I whisper to the wind
as I climb the bank back to my dreaming
bed, nodding at the green bamboo stalk
I used to stake an unruly chrysanthemum
clinging to life in the frozen garden. The going
doesn't get any easier, but by any name
I'd miss the wind too much to be
parted from this life for even one hard winter.

No Hablo Ingles

What I want to say to His Honour
who sentenced the father of my children
to eighteen years for armed robbery
is let's just let bygones be bygones
be bye bye bye he'll be gone so long
but it doesn't come out that way, instead I say
it's not like he knocked off a Food Bank
Your Honour; nobody's going to bed hungry.
The first time this parole officer
comes to my house to see if I'm the kind
of woman suitable to be visiting her better half
in the bucket, he won't shake hands due to it
being flu season, a titch touchy. Your Honour,
having a parole officer in your house
is like going through airport security
without leaving home, jokes bomb
as mightily as the U.S. Forces
in Afghanistan. Last week leaving Deer Lake,
Newfoundland, the security guards
made me gulp down my bottled
Evian water to prove it wasn't a controlled
substance, my fault for pointing out

Evian is Naïve spelled backwards: like the sign
says *joking is a criminal offense punishable
by whatever it takes to make a person think
twice before being a comedian.* This encourages me,
I say *heard any good jokes lately* to the comedian
in front of me who looks seriously like the dead
poet Al Pittman, and he cracks to me it is taking
so long to get through security he is afraid
his forged passport is going to expire
after which the drug-and-bomb-squad pit bulls
are onto him taking formidable bites
out of this right to remain
silent; Al confesses he returned from the dead
without remembering to warn anyone
and is flying back to Kandahar under the alias
bin Pittman, which is why he wears the T-shirt
with the many faces of bin Laden on it,
inside out. I try to diffuse the situation,
saying Al joined Al-Qaeda and all he got
was this lousy T-shirt but then when
it is my turn to be interrogated I err
on the side of terror and swallow the one bag
I haven't packed myself, a small bag
of white powder a criminal
lawyer in St. John's has given me
as a going-away gift. The false-sense-of-security
guards start sniffing around, and suddenly
I feel a new solidarity with Al
going away for good
to the jug in Corner Brook
so I get all Joan Baezy pro-active singing BAN
THE BOMB BOMB BOMB he'll be gone so long
until I cough up the gift bag of white powder
a sodden bath BOMB with Souvenir of The Rock
written on it for the love of Allah, so arrest me
why don't you, these are desperate times.
If you want my opinion they should detain

all passengers who *don't* board the aircraft joking:
a sense of humour should be a prerequisite
for *anyone* flying Air Canada these days.
Your Honour, when I offer this parole officer
coffee, he says I don't *use* caffeine
as if I've just suggested we inject heroin
with a turkey baster. Then he goes *you ever
considered therapy*? like I must be
some kind of case to stand by a man who steals
honest money from an ATM to make ends meet.
I don't miss a beat. I spent twenty years
in analysis until my therapist finally said
three words that would forever change
my life, he said *no hablo ingles*.
An old joke, Your Honour, but a good one,
ever noticed when you cut *therapist*
in two you get *the* and *rapist*, how half of *anal-
ysis* is *anal*? When you analyze it that way
I don't need some bad-ass parole officer
repeating how my better half is bad, badder
and baddest, why couldn't he try putting
my kids' Dad in some kind of positive
historical context? I mean, he ain't bad like
Hitler was bad, not like Stalin-bad,
Attila the Hun-bad, Jack-the-Ripper or
George-the-Bush-bad, not half as bad
as the Bader Meinhoff Gang. Furthermore I say
to him, when was the last time you went into
a bank feeling holy? That's when this excuse
for a parole officer pulls out his Corrections
Services Canada pen and writes that I am a minimizer
of my spousal equivalent's crimes, unsuited to visit
said spousal equivalent due to my non deferential
attitude and negative influencing factors.
Your Honour I had three words to say to said
parole officer after that:
no hablo ingles.

The Room Where They Found You

smelled of Madagascar vanilla.
After touching you for the last time
I scrubbed the scent from my skin — I would try
to remember later what the water felt like
on my hands but it was like trying to remember
thirst when you are drowning. They say love
doesn't take much, you just have to be there
when it comes around. I'd been there
from the beginning, I've been here all along.

I believed in everything: the hope
in you, your brokenness, the way
you arranged cut flowers on a tray
beside my blue and white teacup, the cracked
cup I'd told you brought me luck, the note
you wrote, "These flowers are a little ragged
— like your husband." The day you died

of an overdose in Vancouver
I found a moonshell in the forest, far
from the sea; when I picked it up
and pressed it to my ear I could hear you
taking the last breath you had the sad luck

to breathe. Our daughter cupped her hands
over her ears, as if she could stop death
from entering the life she had believed in
up until now. Childhood, as she had
known it, was over: the slap
of the breakers, the wind bruising the sea
tells her she is no longer safe in this world —
it's you she needs. I see you pulling away
after shooting up in the car while we
stood crying on the road, begging
you to come home. The vast sky
does not stop wild clouds
from flying. This boundless grieving,
for whom is it carried on?

Pierre Nepveu
Translated by Judith Cowan

Étendue

Je disais: attends tu n'as rien vu,
et j'étendis à perte de vue
des rangées de dents sur la table,
je braquai des os
fins comme des antennes
en direction de son visage, à travers
son aura turbulente,
comme un être cherchant
hors de soi un appui
pour croire et pour durer.
Qu'en pensez-vous? demandai-je,
et je montrai au plus offrant
des kilomètres de cerveau
des guirlandes de synapses
scintillant comme des fils
électriques après la pluie.
De folles intrigues me quittèrent,
des colonies de livres aimés et soufferts,
et les grandioses connaissances
qui me serraient comme un étau.
Je sentais croître en moi le fantôme
et je fus bien pâle au moment de subir
l'examen d'existence et de densité.
Des femmes d'esprit voulurent m'assister
mais je vaquais déjà dans l'exsangue,
j'arpentais les espaces très purs
de l'humilité et de l'inertie, à peine
tenu encore par la rate et le côlon
et toutes ces choses intérieures
par où la vie nous comble
ou nous trahit.

Belvédère

Surplombant un espace qui est un peu
de moi-même, par les actes tentés
et quelques souvenirs, l'invitation louche
d'un homme au coin de Peel et Sainte-Catherine
quand j'étais adolescent, le spectacle oblique
des pénis dans les urinoirs des gares
après avoir cueilli des feuilles de chênes
en haut de l'avenue des Pins. Ici au sommet
j'embrasse les mêmes montagnes
échouées au-delà du fleuve, et la plaine
est un peu de mon corps lointain,
ses membres perdus, ses sueurs froides.
Ici se détache presque ma tête comme un fruit
et redevient mûre pour l'ampleur du sud.
Quelque chose d'à peine connu de l'intelligence
et de pourtant si cher, comme si la distance
au fond de soi, hors de soi-même se montrait.

de "Mirabel" / from Mirabel
. . .

On promet d'excaver le sol pour des piscines bleues, à cinq milles d'ici. On annonce une armada de camions qui dépècera la nuit et déballera au petit matin les entrailles préfabriquées d'usines rutilantes et les corps des jeunes cadres en pièces détachées, avec les manuels d'instruction pour les assembler, et tout indique que le cours des choses en sera meilleur. Cinquante fois par jour, un petit train glissera entre les troupeaux de vaches en voie d'extinction et, la nuit, jettera la lueur de ses fenêtres filantes sur la terre en pleine éruption d'impatientes et de géraniums. À l'orée du temps, le dernier fermier éteindra sa lampe et s'endormira recroquevillé contre sa femme. Des familles nouvelles s'étaleront près des champs de maïs, transportées par des fourgonnettes aux odeurs de cuir neuf, et les boyaux d'arrosage couleront même le dimanche, l'eau savonneuse plein les fossés, le long de rues graveleuses aboyant vers l'avenir, et même les chiens croiront au bonheur.

They're promising to excavate the ground for blue swimming pools, five miles from here. They're announcing an armada of trucks that will shatter the night and, early in the morning, unpack the prefabricated entrails of gleaming factories and the bodies of young executives in separate parts, with instruction manuals for putting them together, and everything points to an optimistic unfolding of events. Fifty times a day a small train will whoosh past between the herds of cows, soon to be extinct, and at night the glow from its rushing windows will shine out across a land in full eruption of impatiens and geraniums. At the fringe of time, the last farmer will turn out his lamp and fall asleep huddled against his wife. Near the cornfields, other families will spread out, arriving in vans smelling of new leather, and the garden hoses will run even on Sundays, filling the ditches with soapy water, down all the gravelled streets barking towards the future, where even the dogs will believe in happiness.

*

Je pressens cette terre sans arbres
et pure de ne dresser aucun obstacle,
et les visages eux-mêmes vidés de tout destin,
attendant au coin d'un bois déjà rouge
l'illumination tombée des limbes du froid,
j'envisage tout cela et même l'aérogare
ne sera qu'une immense cage claire
dont la structure aérienne allégera l'esprit
et où les pas des voyageurs à peine visibles
résonneront sur la tuile des passerelles
pour disparaître dans des escalateurs infinis
glissant vers le troisième sous-sol,
et ce monde n'aura de religieux
que ses églises de villages barricadées
au bout des côtes aux noms de saints et d'anges
et l'harmonie grégorienne des grenouilles

et le cantique sexuel des danseuses de bars,
— et je songe à l'évanouissement de quelques chevaux noirs,
à un défilé de maisons fantômes vers la nuit
sur des arpents sans clôtures hérissés seulement
de buissons fleuris et de vieux pommiers
et dans ce beau triomphe de la raison,
des avions cracheront aux deux minutes
de fines fumées chaudes
ensorceleuses de grands ciels
et nous vivrons dans la récitation
des arrivées et des départs, dans la grâce
des horaires respectés et des contrôles de mouvements,
et la beauté sidérante des carlingues et des chromes,
nous y plongerons des yeux de fièvre
et frôlerons de nos corps chauds les baies vitrées
pour y laisser une empreinte à peine visible de nous-mêmes,
la marque d'un doigt ou la buée d'un souffle,
avant de nous envoler vers des jours meilleurs.

Already I see this land stripped of trees
and pure in that it will offer no obstacle,
with the faces themselves emptied of destiny,
waiting at the corner of a red-leaved woodlot
for illumination to fall from the cold's limbo,
I envisage all that and even the air terminal
as nothing but a big bright cage
whose airy structure will lighten the mind
with the footsteps of passengers scarcely seen
ringing on the tiles of the walkways
and disappearing into infinite escalators
rumbling towards the third sub-basement,
in a world with nothing left that is religious
but the barricaded churches in its villages
at the ends of the roads named for saints and angels,
and the Gregorian harmony of the frogs,
and the sexual psalm of strippers in the bars

— while I ponder the vanishing of a few black horses,
or a row of phantom houses towards nightfall
over unfenced acres sprouting only
with flowering bushes and old apple trees,
while in this admirable triumph of reason,
every two minutes a plane will blast off,
lifting on the long hot enchantment
of a sky-high vapour trail
and we shall live in the recitation
of arrivals and departures, in the grace
of timetables respected and movements controlled,
and the dazzling beauty of fuselages and chrome,
plunging our fevered eyes into their gleam,
rubbing our warm bodies against the tall windows
and leaving just the faintest impression of ourselves,
a fingerprint or a little cloud of breath
before taking off for better days.

*

Nouveau monde

En ces régions d'ancienne seigneurie
de vergers séculaires et d'arpents lumineux,
le siècle s'écoula sans heurts,
on ne vit aucun tank
au trécarré des terres arables,
ni d'enfant estropié par une mine
enfouie dans les labours,
mais un après-midi du printemps
les trompettes de l'avenir hurlèrent,
on annonça des nuées noires de voyageurs
sur la basse campagne, on décréta
officiellement la mise au ban des bêlements,
l'évidement des bas-côtés et des cuisines d'été
où traînait encore l'odeur des vieilles crêpes

il y eut un branle-bas de meubles à l'encan
et de pierres numérotées pour rebâtir ailleurs,
on signala des détresses de poulets,
des affolements de chevaux dans l'érablière
des plaintes de tracteurs attelés au vide,
et dans le ciel majeur un oracle
annonça l'érection prochaine
au beau milieu d'un champ de fraises
d'une usine capable de parthénogénèse,
d'une université de village
spécialisée en aménagement de l'espace,
et de vingt mille maisons modèles
dédiées à l'assomption des jeunes familles
jalouses de leurs chambres roses
et de leurs animaux domestiques

• • •

New World

In these once seigneurial regions
of ancient orchards and luminous acres,
the century unfolded without incident,
no tank was ever seen
along the base line of the arable lands,
and no child was crippled by a mine
concealed in the furrows,
but on an afternoon in spring
the future's trumpets blared,
announcing black clouds of travellers
across the simple flatlands, while an official decree
banned all bleatings
emptied out all sheds and summer kitchens
where a smell of pancakes lingered —
there was a jostling of furniture to be auctioned
and stones to be numbered for rebuilding elsewhere,
with reports of chickens in distress
of horses panicking in the sugar-bush

of the lamentations of tractors hitched to the void,
and in the over-arching sky an oracle
announced the coming installation
right in the middle of a strawberry field
of a factory capable of parthenogenesis,
of a university in the village
specialized in the organization of space
with twenty thousand model homes
destined for assumption by young families
possessive of their pink bedrooms
and their domestic pets.

• • •

L'homme des plans

Le progrès préfère la ligne droite, dit le prophète en complet bleu sombre, et il tire de sa mallette le plan des installations aéroportuaires. Il y a un grain de poussière sur son épaule et la main de la femme se retient de la balayer. Sur le papier mince comme un patron de robe, toute la région semble abstraite et monotone, réduite à des lignes continues ou pointillées, et la terre est uniformément blanche, de tous côtés. L'empereur du paysage se penche sur la table. Il connaît la rectitude de la nouvelle route, il sait que le toit de la maison ancienne a été modifié. Il se réclame du style pur, de la science des reconstitutions historiques. Le progrès, dit-il, n'est pas seulement affaire d'avenir, it doit aussi rendre le passé à son intégrité. La femme a perdu la notion exacte du temps et de l'espace, et il lui semble que jamais plus le coucou de l'horloge grand-père ne se fera entendre. Le son tranquille de la voix de l'homme accompagne le ciel gris qu'elle aperçoit par la fenêtre, étendu sur les champs gris, en ce début d'avril encore froid.

The Plans Man

Progress prefers a straight line, says the prophet in the dark blue suit, and out of his briefcase he pulls the airport construction plans. There's a speck of dust on his shoulder and the woman's hand does not dare reach out to brush it off. On paper thin as a sewing pattern, the whole region seems abstract and featureless, reduced to solid or dotted lines, with the land on all sides uniformly white. The emperor of landscape bends over the table. He knows the straightness of the new road, he knows too that the roof of the old house has been changed. He claims to understand purity of style, the science of historical restoration. Progress, he says, is more than just a question of the future, it should give the past back its integrity as well. The woman has lost any precise notion of time or space and it seems to her that the cuckoo in the grandfather clock will never be heard again. The quiet sound of the man's voice goes with the grey sky she glimpses through the window, spreading over the grey fields, in the early April chill.

Bilan

La récolte cette année-là
ne fut ni de fraises ni de maïs
mais de petits secrets retrouvés
dans les tiroirs longtemps clos
et de détresse nouvelle qui suintait
de chaque mur avant qu'il tombe
à l'heure de la mise aux enchères
des outils et des restes de vie.
• • •

Summing Up

That year the harvest
was neither strawberries nor corn
but small secrets uncovered
in drawers long shut
and a new distress that oozed
from every wall before it fell
when time came for the auction
of tools and the remains of lives.
• • •

bpNichol

St. Anzas VIII

he he. stop that. just a joke
really. ssssss. did you even think it thru
sir? pent-up emotion or
down mood. e-
quate them. quit then. no
's eye ears it this way. say?
same thing. s & then the a
prior i prior he. si.

junkyard let trembling, new
locales to cancer warlord presently. aldermen. grapes. "Or
whatever," she says, fingering butter son of a bitch dead languages.

rough somebody quick waiting, gone
profile mistaken.

sh. together
quietens the scream, anguish anyway. anxiety
lived with. terror. t's error &
s's in — in everything
really, st she say (the triple play
he's dealing with, bases loaded
try another way, base 5 or 10
(refigure the equation))

sitting sideways, hound or horse,
grief hugging blink daybed. ancient nicotine.
gravel all desktop hinder or
rambunctious. curled eyelid drip
vertical tinned.

so mulch for thatch.

she. sex talk. he. sf/x talk's
s's ex talk, gentle gender. what's out there? i's he. i she.
i dent i. fie yourself! we we we. all the way home.

early morning variation

di
agon al
y

      die
al
   in agony

a gone y
a hip s
a ship

shhh

i is p
"under what conditions?"
unclear

uncle ear
auntie tongue

"i am against no one"

an e at noon
an s at night
the y gone
         shipped out to sea

d
  e f g
     h
i j k
l ephant

om
    e
equals mc^2
how to
find my way back from
these letters
        sounds you sent me
out into the world to find
found
      the world reduced to
its codes
          systems
the plants grow on
obsolescent images
art facts

without the i f acts

we fear f's ear
dead arms close round us
rigor mort is the one
removes our lungs
         seals our face
f's ace up the sleeve
ning
    variations
between the real & the reeled in
monsters from the seas we sail
(contra the old dogma of supremacy)

the unknown unfolds as
the known folds over & is undone

    STATEMENT: Of Ath: "C's land, eh Stein?"

        (translation:
        De Ath: "Stein? Est-ce que le terre du C?"

relationships to figures

1 &

s's cape a shroud
sweet sibilance piercing the tongue
led by the one i did not recognize
deeper into language
the lung images
the mind
               simpler froms of speech
signs
        showing me this other world
the landscape lay behind

Moth
    for Robin Blaser

"grey butterflies," i said, not convincing myself

when it flew towards me i ducked

cringing when the drawer's drawn open & the moth flutters out

flut flut flut flut flut flut flut

"it's only a moth," my sister said

in my dream the moth's body glowed white before it absorbed me

under the trees in the backyard the porch light on

cowering when the closet door flew open & the moth flew out

angel of death of release

in the room and i could not open the window

when my mother saw the holes in the sweater she said "moths" moth mouth mother myth math smother smooth

i was covering my head with my arms & hands & felt like screaming

terror like an error in the scheme of things

the moth flew out of the old jar in the back kitchen

heaven's wingèd creatures hell's

lithp lip slip slippery moss mass mess miss muss mouse

the grey bodies with four legs & long tails the grey bodies with wings

out of the centre of any meaning another meaning

the moth will eat them up

lighting candles to see if it was true

trapped inside the lampshade its wings beating against the fabric

my mother put the moth balls in the drawers with the sweaters

we were talking about the irrational but i kept feeling we were missing the point

when i took the old newspapers out of the closet i found mice had nibbled holes in them

i have tried to keep the moth out of the poem

the only thing that stops me screaming is embarrassment

in the dark closet among the sweaters and wool coats for winter

flickering light in the theatre like the flickering light of its
giant wings

who are crushed before the moth

watching it fly out of the darkness and hit against the window again
and again

i was in the backyard talking and one flew into my mouth

moth in the mouth like a trapped tongue fluttering

at the window in the night thinking to see the moon

unspeakable terror diminished in naming whom each one names differently
my name for you is moth

Blues

```
                l       e
               o      e
            l o v e
            o     e v o    l
      l o v e         o
          e v o    l
       e       o
    e          l
```

Untitled

Sometimes as other sums of time are measured the day is not
dark no but bright the light the actual pleasure that the sun is
upon your skin you live inside your body   sometimes or
this one time the line is right to be spoken not as some time or
other marked as the moving point is disjointed ripped out of
time but as is seen the scene set not as set or play but
moments reality continuums & not glum no seen in this way
   all times times could be as they are now   assuming the
form
          the 'tu' (familiar phrase
          all days to be lived as pleasure
          inside the skin of history
          we know no measure of

          why poems are (for me)
          the highest form of reality
          i speak my mind   sing
          my song
          long as the ear can catch the tune
          the poem *is* the rune
          as the man the man
          how you hand it on
          one to the other
          part of the action of
          living
          giving
          what you can
          & i saw clearly as one does see the eye peels
away (no other way to describe it) that layer of feelings blinds
the mind & i saw clearly the poem is the man the man the
rune & time the concept "he sings his tune as long as he can"

for steve

an and and an an   a this and that   his this is that hat or
her error   now it is winter & spring comes   that day
i walked towards the the from the a   the other way
    woods &

                to encompass the world
                to take it in
                inside that outside
                outside that in
                to be real
                one thing beside the other

later there is are   that was to be   a sense in which a saint
is was & will be   so the issue's this   this as is his claim
on the present tension past & future always the question of
what to do each step altering your choices

voice as song
            speech is
to belong to
form as an expression of dilemma
conceptualization placing you on the brink of dissolution
you make a choice
narrow the distance between
the tree as it is & the word "tree"
between the object & the object
as the you can be the me
we are (as pronouns) each other
nouns divide
hide behind that name we are given

late night outside the room
book beside the window
words inside
            written
as they are
objects in the worlds we live in

carry us far
         ther a
way
    from
       each
          other
             than
                they
                   should

probable systems 13:
text & deduction

song

s on g
or simply on
as s can be

ass scan
(looking both ways)
s in e
         wave goodbye
a w
      a y
an s or
rowing faster
f as t
s as k at o on the map face
tracing the line all the way thru
these lines are so long
the s e (l in e) s are (is) so l on g

---

if l is on g
& l is in e
& since s is in e (as we have already seen)
& s is on g
then s & l ⎧ e & e is on g

now since e is on g & f lies between e & g
then the meaning of the alphabetic sequence 'e f g' becomes clear

Chain 1 excerpt, from *The Martyrology: Book 5*

    i m

    u r

    n g i c so clearly
looking out across the surface of the words today
the letters are not my n m e
no thing is my n m e
tho evil lives in various guises
it's i s i's n m e
narcissus as it was so long a go
                e go
    and maybe even i go
        o go s poe goed
        edgarrishly
        all'a narcissistically

so u go
but u wonder y go
as hugo ball did
when e died e rose to heaven
& his friends said 'did. He is done.
D one & only hugo ball's bell billowed boldly BULLONG
BELONG
BE LONG TO SING MY SONG
TO YOU LORD'
flying out of
'TIME OUT'
the referee cries
'VOWELS'
        so disconsonantly

          u name me
'i forget you'
            i name me anew
claim my signs
why me
m a r t
in the word mart
the word m art
yr ology
the ology
word ology
like some old bop phrase haunts my dreams
ornithology
horn it
      Ornette Coleman C.O.

le man is bird or parker
    b   o   p
    \ | /
     W
    (ʹ)

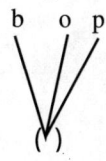

bp's me
but what is it exactly comes together

Hour 25

2:35 to 3:35 am

'somewhere there's music'

                how faint, the tune
                falls over & over
                the ear drums echo
                stirrup, chirrup
                (a cricket somewhere in the room
      there's music

or) there
pressure of air on the still moving face
shift in the drift that age presses on the body
vocalabulary
        the way that word 'drift' keeps drifting in
from what origin? continental or wood or snow or
'i get your drift'
right in the face
the poem snowballs
voKABALLAry

        'Dr. if this is the cure
        what's the sickness?'

dis-ease

    (a state that thinking is)

'don't think such bad thots'
'it's not such a bad idea'
'he's so lost in thot he can't hear us'

        adrift or

        one drift or

        'wonder if
        they really got my drift'

could, be

'all the conditional conditions that may, be'
MURPHY'S LAW (circa 1983), & hence
'somewhere there's heaven' even
        'tell me your idea'
'show me your I.D.'
        or like my sister Dea said
,age three,
        'I Dea'

& pointed to herself

'Heisenberg's principle of one certainty
falls over and over on
the ear drummmmmmmmm

a-tom-tom-tom-tom-tom-ic age
& now the atom is passé
(discarded model, like a Model A)

'atomic age' evokes the 1950s

we're Model A/Ts now
all hydrogen & heavy water &

'I'm gonna take you on a sea cruise'
miss-a-lot
if you don't watch out

the window
narrows

        'how high the moon')

pressure of air on a still moving face

age presses on the body

'im presses

presses it out

Chain 10, *from* The Martyrology: Book 5

every(all at(toge(forever)ther) once)thing

The Frog Variations
for Louise Prael

1.   Dawn   fog
                          log
                          bog

       Noon   frog
                          log
                          bog

       Dusk   fog
                          frog
                          bog

2.   fog fog fog frog fog

3.   moonfrog
       pondfrog
       frogfrog

4.   (definition of a lily-pad)
               fragile
               frog île

5.   (the frog's obsession with the fly)
               frog'll oggle all

6.   frog's tongue: fly catcher
       frog's eye: bird measure
       frog stung
       frog sigh
               bird fly

7.   o moon
       no moon
        o frog
        no frog
         o pond
         no pond

      o
      no
      o
      no
      o
      no

8.   splash
      splayed beneath the bending ash
      fragile children of the great bog
      frog
      pond
      poised under the autumn frond
      more singers of the dark water croon
      moon

9.   into the sky at night
      the moon & all her frogs drop
      under the brilliant light of the pond
      rippling life goes on

Prayer

teach me song. i
would sing. teach me
love. i would
i were open
to it. teach me
to pray
privately, praise
quietly
those things
i should. show me
the grace
of movement
& touch — that much

i would offer
to her. teach me
more — a way
for me
to reach her
who beckons
hesitantly. teach me
to be sure.

David O'Meara

from "Desert Sonnets"
• • •

III Igjugarjuk

"When I was young, strange visions came and spoke
to me in dreams I could not interpret.
Disturbed, my parents sent for Peqanaoq,
who recognized the crisis, took and set
me on a sledge just large enough to hold
me, and pulled it out into the flat, vast,
and frozen Arctic night. There, I was told
to sit for thirty days, to wait and fast;
and thinking only of the Great Spirit
I was left to face that cold and brutal
month. My heart went numb, seclusion broke it
bit by bit. *Sometimes I died a little.*
Near the end, a spirit came. More or less,
I've learned what I know from that loneliness."
• • •

VI Postcard from Camus

I will be perfectly honest with you:
the heat's just awful. I wander half-dazed
through town, stopping to shake sand from my shoe
while cypresses shimmer in the heat-haze.
At night there's nothing to do except sip
gin and smoke cigarettes with the door shut.
It's too dangerous otherwise — a nip
to the store, that's all. I think I'll go nuts
if something doesn't happen soon. It's hell.
From dawn till dark we're fixed like specimens

under the sun's searing lamp; I can't tell
up or down, right from left, trapped in its lens.
I only love the brown bodies — young, alert,
and full of joy. Wish you were here. — Albert

Rough Directions

The exact way back is fading, indistinct
like the shine after brief rain, when a soft
ether-veil of haze hangs in open vistas between apartment
blocks, like the abandoned quiet of cul-de-sacs, or escapes
into bars on a tossed-away lazy Saturday.
Along that street — I can't remember the name — of storefront glass
kid-scribbled in traceries of January's taut frost,
by those homeless human shapes bent
in the steam of a laundromat vent.
Down the boulevard: a balcony in oak shade, just
one flight up, that noses its ledge toward the park's
soccer field; past an Art Deco facade, where ornate iron banisters
curl to the one-room spread
of hardwood floor, tulip-glass lampshades,
a Murphy bed, and radiators that knock
far more than visitors.

On the corner, down further, there's
a coffee place, open twenty-four hours, penned with a plot
of narcosis and long espressos, page-
turning as the roll of its cigarette smoke,
where someone sits, waiting. Turn right, I guess,
past Doric-flanked bank lobbies, by half-thought-of shops;
near afternoons, and summer, where shadows lengthen and lean
into all-of-the-sudden dust-devils that are born
and expire in ten-second lives
across the edges of parking lots. Past the pong of fish markets, head shops,
and delicatessens, where waiters
in rolled-up sleeves have locked up for the night, had one quick drink,
                                                       and stroll

to barely-known neighbourhoods.
Along other streets, certain corners, whole
evenings not found on any map. Memory,
you can go there. Down Some-such Avenue,
Rue Saint Whatever.

Fun

Glad interim, your line-ups
stretch past sidewalk patios,

those polyester pastels and unbuttoned plunges
of neckline deepen

this brio of cologne, neon, and patter.
Nice shoes. Great hair.

Walk me past here, in the swing of this compunction.
The street, summer-stung, swells,
                                infected.

You're a grin in the gut, buzz
in the breastbone, a straightaway where
                  energy can rev heavy on the throttle, then just open
up.

In a cave of strobe and blacklight,
some rock outfit, guitars slung low, clutch garage-
chord euphoria. Bass drum,
snare,
scintillant snap and shrug of cymbal-pools
                  shuck through waves of sound.
Everyone moves, keelhauling
the intellect,

shakes asses.
There's comfort in the mirrorball, slur of
light-flash,

the body's ineloquent thump
                    spun through the crowd.
Let even Wednesday
carry us through, spill us out
and gather us.
Fun,
surprise us, blow smooches,
                    tell me
a good one down here in the dark,

giggle our fool heads off, a few hours
                    gulping the vintage
            of now
    and now and

now

since these moments will have no cellar-life.

At the Aching-Heart Diner

She will flavour her coffee with both cream and sugar
and tap on the window as she mentions the weather,
tossing off sparks when she pulls off her sweater.
The waiter will come. She'll give her order
bluntly: "A hot chicken sandwich and a tall glass of water."
She'll spatter her french fries in grand doses of vinegar
and the point she is making, emphasize with a gesture,
her steak knife held high like a gravy-stained scimitar.
And the salt that is scattered when she topples the shaker
she'll toss with a flourish across her left shoulder.
I'd like, I will say, to get to know you better.
I'll look down at my clubhouse, so we don't look at each other
as I pull out the toothpick that holds it together.

Something Akin to Worship Now

They recklessly bowed,
kissed the idol of the other's carved smile
with bent knees and necks, gladly low, embracing
the terms of self-exile

in their stark-new
colony of two. Two in rooms protected from the great
alone. Spread their private flag then, a down-filled quilt
left white

(since surrender
would be the refrain to a plainsong or anthem
of tugged waistbands and gooseflesh composed
entirely of them)

and stroked
their astonished hips across the frets and cello-low moans
of the other. But more, simply wanted to share
stuff, so made loans

of some books
and CDs, said *you should listen to this*, hoping those
kindred lyrics and lapsteel might ring a bit true
and expose

the stalled core
of what they might feel. And smitten, traded quips
on old hairdos in photos, Wim Wenders, dumb secrets,
all the creeps

and dead-ends
they once dated. And rushed over at the end of their shifts,
called when they couldn't, and might, for example, in a restaurant
notice a faint drift

of freckles
on the collarbone one itched to work a fingertip over,
but mostly just wanted and wanted and wanted to be
with each other.

Poise

for Andrea Skillen (1968-2002)

I see that steady beauty mark
and hear your clear dissenting voice say
oh c'mon, as I scratch this note to you
on a low, wet day in summer.

You wouldn't want the fuss, I know, nor
trust the souped-up sentiment — it's just
I'm trying to arrange a parting batch
of verse before we all get too disorganized, stray

far apart, forget the dates of birthdays
you'd have marked inside your calendar. (Strange
to think that in a certain numbered space
you've stopped, and we keep going on.)

If it scares me in the future that
things we did might blur, get lost, as if you'd
slipped off to a back room in a badly-lighted
bar with greying carpets, I equally know

your footwork on the dance floor
or that purple grin of lipstick will not
escape remembering. Just as we won't soon
forget that hospital bed, the undying

laughter there, and you and Claire grown
more beautiful with courage.
The word I'm thinking of is *poise*, why
we'll miss you greatly in the years

that come, and wonder what you'd say, each
semblance of your remembered wit reminding us how
whole years pass by without telling
our friends how much we love them,

so I'm telling them now.

Boswell by the Fire

> ... *he leaned forward and very delicately prodded the fire*
> *with the iron poker, as I was afterwards pleased to think, like*
> *a man dipping his quill into the embers of memory that were*
> *still hot.*
> — Richard Holmes

Those flatlands, empty emerald-tinted horizons.
And Utrecht, its tidy squares;
the cathedral's hourly summons
of doom that boomed through the dark ancient furniture

of my single room squatting in its shadow.
With tea, I ate dry biscuits from a polished tray
on those first forlorn afternoons, only twenty-two
but thought myself old, nearing decay,

so I decided to hate it there, resolving to shoulder
my burdens through a disciplined crusade
of wind-rattled winter, like a soldier
or a spartan sensible monk: wake at six-thirty, read

Ovid till nine, study both Dutch and Français, then
essays, lectures, and letters to friends.
In the disappointed eyes of my father, I'd straighten
up and make the most forthright amends

for a rakish past, become industrious, chaste
and good, a very bee in its hive,
maybe curry a few royal favours, then haste
back to England, hardly parting a wave

like a right trumpeting angel. Mademoiselle,
that was my plan, though I never said
so, but hid those thoughts on the tell-tale
pages of my journal instead.

But I was duly unhorsed by that old problem: girls.
Yes, women. Their sentiments and boredoms, their trite

whims. And those profiles in doorways, flushed whirls
on the dance floor, décolletage in candle-light!

(Remember Madame Geelvinck? How young she was,
beautiful, coy and spoilt. Rich and widowed
at only twenty-four. Like her many suitors, I played the ass
to bear the weight of her attentions, and followed

along on errands, doted on her son, forcing deliberate
bungles of my French in the hope that she'd correct me.
Then she left for The Hague. On that cold date
of her departure, I rose and went directly

to the sentry-post of St. Catherine's Gate, and plied the guard
with a flask of Geneva gin, just to huddle inside the door
to glimpse her coach slipping past. And on the ramparts I stared
into the fog-blue dawn and watched it disappear . . .)

Such sodden antics. You'd said she had no passion,
but for once you held your tongue, its eternal ridicule,
and helped me limp my head-cold through March's depression
with lessons in your cynic's school

of your laughter and frankness. You were bashing a racket
against the cork eye of a shuttlecock, just inside
the painted boundaries, I think, the first time we met.
Your sharp legs shuffled and parried

beneath the pleated billows of your skirts.
We turned friends, fast friends, and closer still from confidences
you let me shelter in your ear as we ate desserts
while playing whist in gardens, salons and dances,

but always your mocking voice — on society, wealth,
dull marriages and my tailored sea-green suit — delivered from
the sidle of a measured grin beneath each measured breath.
It unsettled me, that proud and heated talk of freedom,

how you goaded me against the smallest compromise
lest I set roaming some bitter shadow of regret whose pace

might never rest. Don't just settle for anything, you had me promise,
or that shadow will return to harden the angles of my face.

So, just as sudden as these first winter days, years later
I have awoken from the most disagreeable dreams
of absent faces, cities, and even greater
lost things. I've been too long in London it seems,

where my every frustrated ambition raps upon
the window sashes. Is it only these December gusts?
Or my own dull spirits, gnawing, as on a bone
at the memories of youth, its pithy lusts

I'd been no stranger to with any Jenny or Alice
breathing in my arms, and inhale them now, each
pleasant gasp, like decanted vintage or *Hermippus Redivivus*.
But there's a haunting look I see but never catch

that turns away and sinks into the shadows
of a Holland thirty summers ago. I'll not erase
nor change it now, the June I departed through the tulip rows
south to seek my fame, and that familiar face

grown suddenly awkward as the swallows slashed along
the moat and through the beech trees' darkening colonnade.
"Have you ever been in love," I asked. "If *one* might feel a strong
affection . . . if *one* might meet *un homme amiable* — " you hinted,

"and *if* those affections were *returned*, then . . ." Well,
it was dusk; I had to go. I took my leave in the half-light.
Madame — yes, no longer Mademoiselle —
forgive these idle musings I'll never send; it's late

and it seems I'm very tired. It feels that Time itself
has dusted off these thoughts, fusses at my broken tooth
like a mouldering memento arranged upon a shelf
or across this mantel above the fire, where, like a moth

I've come to do my stubborn dance. I lean
into the ochre logs that scowl, hiss and crackle — such

restrained heat — and imagine my green
self burned away with a past I cannot touch.

Rain beats the casements, and the wind's sleety bite
chatters in the lead of the panes. "Will you think of
me?" you said. That fading look, the last, returns, in spite
of thirty Junes away. Good creature, I always have.

The Unhappy Condition

> Such was the unhappy condition of the Roman emperors, that whatever
> might be their conduct, their fate was commonly the same.
> — Edward Gibbon

On that subject, let me
comment: that the wide
populace had endured twelve years
of forced flattery, general terror, and private groans
is well-known; witness to state and senate
dissolving from idle suspicions into public blood —
The miscreant whimsy of Commodus still
bruises civic memory.
Twelve years multiplied by his lusts and purges.
A terrible equation
only his servants solved: Maria,
the favoured concubine, laced his drink, and while
he slept, a local wrestler held his throat
perfectly shut.

And such was the mistrust heightened by those years
that when, in the same late hour, ancient Pertinax
rolled half-aware
to find the wild-eyed crew
of domestics circling his bed, he uncurled
and lay prone, prepared for death. Instead

they offered the throne of the Roman world.

Some eighty-six days was the proof of their enlightened assessment.
Hasty in virtue, Pertinax cut
Imperial comforts, replaced pilfered fortunes, called exiles home.
History will record the esteem of his people.

I am also witness to that fact, and to the Praetorian Guards' jealousy.
For one good reason or another, it fell to me
to level the first sufficient blow
and the rest of them tore him to pieces.

Michael Ondaatje

from **The Collected Works of Billy the Kid**

. . .

Blurred a waist high river
foam against the horse
riding naked clothes and boots
and pistol in the air

Crossed a crooked river
loving in my head
ambled dry on stubble
shot a crooked bird

Held it in my fingers
the eyes were small and far
it yelled out like a trumpet
destroyed it of its fear

. . .

She leans against the door, holds
her left hand at the elbow
with her right, looks at the bed

on my sheets — oranges
peeled half peeled
bright as hidden coins against the pillow

she walks slow to the window
lifts the sackcloth
and jams it horizontal on a nail
so the bent oblong of sun
hoists itself across the room
framing the bed the white flesh
of my arm

she is crossing the sun
sits on her leg here
sweeping off the peels

traces the thin bones on me
turns toppling slow back to the pillow
Bonney Bonney

I am very still
I take in all the angles of the room.
. . .

Sallie Chisum/Last Words
on Billy the Kid 4 a.m.
for Nancy Beatty

The moon hard and yellow where Billy's head is.
I have been moving in my room
these last 5 minutes. Looking for a cigarette.
That is a sin he taught me.
Showed me how to hold it and how to want it.

I had been looking and stepped forward
to feel along the windowsill
and there was the tanned moon head.
His body the shadow of the only tree on the property.

I am at the table.
Billy's mouth is trying
to remove a splinter out of my foot.
Tough skin on the bottom of me.
Still. I can feel his teeth
bite precise. And then moving his face back
holding something in his grin, says he's got it.

Where have you been I ask
Where have you been he replies

I have been into every room about 300 times
since you were here

I have walked about 60 miles in this house
Where have you been I ask

Billy was a fool
he was like those reversible mirrors
you can pivot round and see yourself again
but there is something showing on the other side always.
Sunlight. The shade beside the cupboard.

He fired two bullets into the dummy
on which I built dresses
where the nipples should have been.
That wasn't too funny, but we laughed a lot.

One morning he was still sleeping
I pushed the door and watched him from the hall
he looked like he was having a serious dream.
Concentrating. Angry. As if wallpaper
had been ripped off a wall.

Billy's mouth at my foot
removing the splinter.
Did I say that?

It was just before lunch one day.

I have been alive
37 years since I knew him. He was a fool.
He was like those mirrors I told you about.

I am leaning against the bed rail
I have finished my cigarette
now I cannot find the ashtray.
I put it out, squash it
against the window
where the moon is.
In his stupid eyes.

from "Rock Bottom"
• • •

(Inner Tube)

On the warm July river
head back

upside down river
for a roof

slowly paddling
towards an estuary between trees

there's a dog
learning to swim near me
friends on shore

my head
dips
back to the eyebrow
I'm the prow
on an ancient vessel,
this afternoon
I'm going down to Peru
soul between my teeth

a blue heron
with its awkward
broken backed flap
upside down

one of us is wrong

he
in his blue grey thud
thinking he knows
the blue way
out of here

or me

("The space in which we have dissolved — does it taste of us?")

Summer night came out of the water
climbed into my car and drove home
got out of the car still wet towel round me
opened the gate and walked to the house

Disintegration of the spirit
no stars
leaf being eaten by moonlight

The small creatures who are blind
who travel with the aid
of petite white horns
take over the world

Sound of a moth

The screen door in its suspicion
allows nothing in, as I allow nothing in.
The raspberries my son gave me
wild, cold out of the fridge, a few I put
in my mouth, some in my shirt pocket
and forgot

I sit here
in a half dark kitchen
the stain at my heart
caused by this gift
• • •

*

How many windows have I broken?
And doors and lamps, and last month
a tumbler I smashed into a desk

then stood over the sink
digging out splinters
with an awkward left hand
I have beaten my head with stones
pieces of fence

tried to tear out my eyes
these are not exaggerations
they were acts when words failed
the way surgeons
hammer hearts gone still

now this
small parallel pain
in my finger
the invisible thing inside
circling
        glass
        on its voyage out
        to the heart

• • •

*

Speaking to you
this hour
these days when
I have lost the feather of poetry
and the rains
of separation
surround us tock
tock like *Go* tablets

Everyone has learned
to move carefully

"Dancing" "laughing" "bad taste"
is a memory
a tableau behind trees and law

In the midst of love for you
my wife's suffering
anger in every direction
and the children wise
as tough shrubs
but they are not tough
— so I fear

how anything can grow from this

all the wise blood
poured from little cuts
down into the sink

this hour it is not
your body I want
but your quiet company.

• • •

from *Running in the Family*

An hour later he could have stopped at the Ambepussa resthouse but continued on, the day's alcohol still in him though he had already stopped twice on the side of the road, urinated into darkness and mysterious foliage. Halted briefly at Warakapola where the dark villages held the future and gave a Tamil a lift, the man striking up a conversation about stars, and he, proud of that mutual ancestry, discussing Orion with him. The man was a cinnamon peeler and the smell filled the car, he did not want to stop, wanted to take him all the way past the spice gardens to Kegalle rather than letting him out a mile up the road. He drove on, the cinnamon blown out already by new smells from the night, drove dangerously, he couldn't quite remember if he was driving dangerously or not, just aware of the night breezes, the fall-out from spice gardens he skirted as if driving past vast kitchens. One of the lamps of his car was dead so he knew he was approaching stray walkers disguised as a motorcycle. He weaved up the Nelundeniya U-turns, then into the town of Kegalle. Over the bridge into Rock Hill.

    For about ten minutes he sat in front of the house now fully aware that the car was empty but for his body, this corpse. Leaving the car door open like a white broken wing on the lawn, he moved towards the porch, a case of liquor under his arm. *Moonless.* The absence of even an edge of the moon. Into the bedroom, the bottle top already unscrewed. Tooby, Tooby, you should see your school friend now. The bottle top in my mouth as I sit on the bed like a lost ship on a white sea. And they sat years ago on deck-chairs, young, going to England. In the absurd English clothes they surprised each other with. And then during the heart of the marriage sailed to Australia serene over the dark mountains in the sea, the bed of the ocean like a dragon's back, ridges and troughs and the darkest eye of the Diamantina crater. This too was part of the universe, a feature of the earth. Kissed in the botanical gardens of Perth, took the Overland train east across the country just so they could say they had seen the Pacific. His Colombo suit fell off him now to the floor, onto its own pool of white and he got into bed. Thinking. What was he thinking about? More and more he watched himself do nothing, with nothing. At moments like this.

• • •

The Cinnamon Peeler

If I were a cinnamon peeler
I would ride your bed
and leave the yellow bark dust
on your pillow.

Your breasts and shoulders would reek
you could never walk through markets
without the profession of my fingers
floating over you. The blind would
stumble certain of whom they approached
though you might bathe
under rain gutters, monsoon.

Here on the upper thigh
at this smooth pasture
neighbour to your hair
or the crease
that cuts your back. This ankle.
You will be known among strangers
as the cinnamon peeler's wife.

I could hardly glance at you
before marriage
never touch you
— your keen nosed mother, your rough brothers.
I buried my hands
in saffron, disguised them
over smoking tar,

helped the honey gatherers . . .

When we swam once
I touched you in water
and our bodies remained free,
you could hold me and be blind of smell.
You climbed the bank and said

        this is how you touch other women
the grass cutter's wife, the lime burner's daughter.
And you searched your arms
for the missing perfume

        and knew

      what good is it
to be the lime burner's daughter
left with no trace
as if not spoken to in the act of love
as if wounded without the pleasure of a scar.

You touched
your belly to my hands
in the dry air and said
I am the cinnamon
peeler's wife. Smell me.

Women like You

      the communal poem — Sigiri Graffiti, 5th century

They do not stir
these ladies of the mountain
do not give us
the twitch of eyelids

        The king is dead

They answer no one
take the hard
rock as lover.
Women like you
make men pour out their hearts

"Seeing you I want
no other life"

"The golden skins have
caught my mind"

who came here
out of the bleached land
climbed this fortress
to adore the rock
and with the solitude of the air
behind them
        carved an alphabet
whose motive was perfect desire

wanting these portraits of women
to speak
and caress

Hundreds of small verses
by different hands
became one
habit of the unrequited

Seeing you
I want no other life
and turn around
to the sky
and everywhere below
jungle, waves of heat
secular love

Holding the new flowers
a circle of
first finger and thumb
which is a window

to your breast

pleasure of the skin
earring   earring
curl
of the belly
          and then
stone mermaid

stone heart
dry as a flower
on rock
you long eyed women

the golden
drunk swan breasts
lips
the long long eyes

we stand against the sky

I bring you

a flute
from the throat

of a loon
so talk to me
of the used heart

The Siyabaslakara

In the 10th century, the young princess
entered a rock pool like the moon

within a blue cloud

Her sisters
who dove, lit by flares,
were lightning

Water and erotics

The path from the king to rainmaking

— his dark shoulders a platform
against the youngest instep

waving her head above him
this way
this way

Later the art of aqueducts,

the banning of monks
from water events

so they would not be caught
within the melodious sounds

or in the noon heat
under the rain of her hair

Birch Bark
for George Whalley

An hour after the storm on Birch Lake
the island bristles. Rock. Leaves still falling.
At this time, in the hour after lightning
we release the canoes.
Silence of water
purer than the silence of rock.
A paddle touches itself. We move
over blind mercury, feel the muscle
within the river, the blade
weave in dark water.

Now each casual word is precisely chosen
passed from bow to stern, as if
leaning back to pass a canteen.
There are echoes, repercussions of water.
We are in absolute landscape,
among names that fold in onto themselves.

To circle the island means witnessing
the blue grey dust of a heron
released out of the trees.
So the dialogue slides
nothing more than friendship
an old song we break into
not needing all the words.

We are past naming the country.
The reflections are never there
without us, without the exhaustion
of water and trees after storm.

Elise Partridge

One Calvinist's God

Your deity was as patient as a heron,
watching and waiting, as if he could stand for a week
without trembling once on those old-man's legs;
then with one jab of his beak

stab you and gulp. Or, a bald eagle, he'd hunch
on a pine snag or barnacled dais of rock,
scowling, scanning the shore for a newborn duck
to scoop from the flock.

Even the hopping robin who tilted one eye
as though listening at blades of grass put you on guard,
in case he should snap you, wormlike, a writhing thread
from your white-fenced yard.

One midnight, you imagine, you'll be swept up,
a mouse off a toadstool, shrieking into the air;
gathered by icepick talons to his tweedy chest,
his yellow-eyed glare.

On The Road to Emmaus
from a sixteenth-century Flemish painting

1. The Painting

Over the disciples' shoulders
Jesus listens,
eyebrows raised to his hairline, bemused and sad.
Behind them, arched gateways, insouciant pennants;
a pale-blue harbor with minuscule ships,

ochre city, jumble of turrets.
A white-aproned woman in a farmhouse door
chats with a caller;
two men stride off on branching roads,
one trailed by a dawdling child.

2. The Disciples

It was a long walk.
Only a few gulps of stale water
slosh around their gourd. Their scalps itch.
Cranky, yawning, shuffling along,
they come upon a man robed in white
and start to explain the entire fiasco:
the nails' heft, the burglar groaning,
how gray He looked when they eased Him down.
How, on that third morning,
birds had darted
restlessly; how one disciple had pictured Jesus
hovering over all His flocks,
Pilate's house halved
by a thunderbolt, centurions claiming
they'd only been following somebody's orders.
Bobbing donkeys, squashed pomegranate-rind —
fifty yards from the tomb's mouth:
"The boulder's gone!"
They edged inside, eyes straining
to adjust from glare.
Black walls dribbled, clay oozed
through their toes. Peering,
they saw ants ferrying chunks of fig.
A crumpled sheet; whiff of myrrh.

On the way to Emmaus the arguments started.
Each turned over and
over particulars.
"I think we've been taken."
You know, nodded the other, I was never really sure.

3. Always on the Road

Why did the painter locate them here,
even including a hatpin-height steeple?
Unto the nth generation, he seems to say,
we'll be complaining to the miracle's face
that it is no miracle,
we'll insist to life eternal, "There is no such thing!"
But the tree he placed the disciples under
means more than the sum of its plain brown leaves.
The city's gates swing wide for the asking,
the harbor beckons you to a new life.
That woman in the farmhouse door
loves the man she is speaking to;
her soul has opened to meet his.
The child is a blessing to all of them,
the dust on the road cleanses the sparrows.

Four Lectures by Robert Lowell, 1977

On "Repose of Rivers" by Hart Crane

"What's the plot?
The Mississippi flowing to the sea,
and Crane going from childhood to death.
One of his clearest and his greatest poems,
much quieter than the other we just read.
The river speaks the poem;
the river's washing out to sea
like your own life — the river's doomed,
all childhood memories, washing out to sea
to find repose. The sapphire's the sea,
remorseless, sinister, hard. Angels might
flake sapphire — that might be one of their jobs.
He's taunting you with paradise.
The willows do hold steady sound, and yet

they don't; the sea's fulfillment of a kind,
the end of life . . . Don't read this just as death-wish;
Crane was unusually full of life."

On *"The Yachts"* by *William Carlos Williams*

"This starts as terza rima; here his lines
are much longer than usual. Very few poems
attempt a narrative; you have to do it
plainly, like a sports reporter would.
Is it a satire, against yachts? Or are
they made quite beautiful? What's horrible
about the race, the competition?
(I think he must have watched basketball games.)
The yachts here could be women, thoroughbreds —
anything beautiful trampling over all
it doesn't notice. Beauty's terrible,
expensive, skillful . . . Very beautiful
careful description . . . "arms" . . . they're desperate . . .
Greeks when they sank a ship mowed the survivors
down, or speared them; the yachts just pass over.
Seems supernatural, doesn't it?
                        These two
extremes of writing, Williams, Crane — do you
imagine Crane was maddened by this stuff?
He rather liked it, though. Crane could never
describe a yacht, and Williams thought
he was all rhetoric.
                        Two modernists:
Williams was breaking old metrical forms,
and using new material; Crane had read
Rimbaud, brought thunder and obscurity."

On "Out of the Cradle Endlessly Rocking" by Walt Whitman

"Most operatic thing he ever wrote,
a tour de force, probably about something . . .
What? — I mean personal. Two thrushes, one dies:
imagine someone Whitman was in love with,
lost. The beginning's all one sentence, highly
organized musically, but loose writing,
as Whitman practiced. Tempting to scan; you can't.
The cradle is the sea . . . it's very odd,
original without one's knowing why.
If you want to say these things, it's falling rhythm.
The ostensible sorrow is the boy
Discovering death, desertion . . . (I'd
be talking through my hat, if I had one on.)
And often rhythmical musical things
aren't good, they're padding for not feeling. What
prevents that here? It's awfully eloquent
wherever you pick it up. 'From such as now
they start the scene revisiting': this has
a tender Pindaric grandeur — I don't know
if you can say that. It's about a child —
that's not a Whitman subject, childhood.

His saddest poem in some ways. Hard to think
that birds meant very much to him . . ."

On "Goodbye My Fancy" by Walt Whitman

"'Goodbye My Fancy' he intended as
his last poem . . . you're too sick to write your last
poem, when the time comes. Clear and elegant —
except for some of the language, and the meter,
it could be seventeenth-century.
Your eyes water, reading it."

Rural Route

He picked three dozen quarts, starting at dawn;
died suddenly in the garden. "Around one,
he had a stroke — I found him, but he was gone —."
He left a widow, three daughters and six sons.

Two days later, widow and children, at dawn,
picked forty dozen. They ate, washed, dressed;
buried him in the churchyard just after one.
Early the next day, they picked the rest.

Two Scenes from Philadelphia

1. Valley Forge, 1777–1778

Thanksgiving rations, the second year of the war:
a quarter-cup of rice, a dash of vinegar.

Twenty-five barrels of flour, twelve thousand men.
One feasted for two days on a fist-sized pumpkin.

Sentries stood on their hats to warm their feet;
the officers' horses shuddered under needling sleet.

One of three soldiers wintering lost his life.
New Year's morning, a ten-year-old played the fife.

2. Victorian Interior

The French windows were swathed with mauve-gray drapes,
ends gathering on plum rugs in velvet folds
reflected in a ten-foot gilt-framed mirror
above the stag crowning the étagère,
black, lacquered cabinets japanned with ivory,
a pinch-stitched mauve petitpoint fireplace screen.
Carved rosettes above brass chandeliers

which Belfast maids kept glinting with their dusters
trapped, in their arabesques, each gram of soot.
Silver brushes etched with swirled initials
lay poised by "hair receivers" on vanities —
crystal jars for collecting straying wisps
to be woven into wreaths or framed in jet.
The door to the master-bedroom's marbled bath
was diamonded with ruby stained-glass panes;
on the rosewood desk's ebonized veneer,
Trollope was propped with guides to English dogs.

John Pass

Sundeck in Houselight

Holy and goofy from under the eaves' brow, from under
the drooping eyelid of the blinds, out of season, conciliatory
a vague light falls, interior light gone out past its purpose

to make a little floor, smudged at the edges, on the cedar planking.
There the plant pots have been pulled to the wall, the railings have nothing
to hold but leafless vine, no-one to hold back. There might be mist, a condensed

attention, hovering. What is this world to the world, compelling pause

in memory as if before some icon of belief? A door?
One of those precise, bright cubes

excavated in the chests of saints, wherein their shimmery vermilion hearts
float, crowned

in a white intensity, in light from nowhere? Were the gods here
dancing? We lay

in those deck-chairs folded and hung on the wall, well-oiled and sacrificial once
in direct sunlight, who haunt the huge surround now (the floorless murk
unbuilt, unmanifest) or from within, from the dining-room window

pursue enigma in the twice-tried, tireless, observable spaces.

Nestbox

See what I've made here and hung overhead

out of reach. Something of the dead
of these surrounding presences, these red cedars,
something of their grain and spread and loftiness
sawn and squared, of their fragrance. It is ingenious

protection against weather with a whole side that opens

to sky if you wish. A small nail in a slot holds it

shut. I have followed instructions and made adjustments for the years
of visitation, the favoured locations, that seem now merely

favoured minutes of the long year, those in any scant April
when the violet-green iridescence slips in

and out through the perfect oval
and the raucous chirping emerges. It's nothing new. It's everything

measured and sturdy I've handled, and emptiness
cornered, fastened upon as invitation.

Browse

I had not meant to talk myself into silence.
I had in mind an irony honoured

that would take heart too from innocence out-
of-the-blue, as when stepping

into summer rain to cover the boat
there seems a sudden freshness in the smell of dry grass flattened
to earth. A serious wet newness. As what the young buck in the garden squandered

wasn't raspberries, but the newest leaf of next years' canes and nothing
to stretch or kneel for, only those easiest. Only the torso of the verdure, haunches

to shoulder. Body of the world. I would walk around out of my head with choosing.
Not choosing. Nibbling in a crooked light whatever caught it. I would not talk

myself into corners and conclusions. I would be whetted appetite. This would be
banquet, each piquancy mouthed leisurely, articulate, ever-furthering, fruitful only

incidentally. But see

how he wheels within enclosure at the dog's bark, outflanked
and vulnerable. Routed. Who thought himself dreaming to be the thing.

Who dreams himself speaking to be the thing.

Underberries

Until your peripheral work is exhausted, your standing work
in the easy light, and you've mastered the slight

shifts of perspective from above or aside that reveal
the fruit behind the leaves you won't even imagine

you could lie on your back in the loam and musky shade
beneath the lush foliage reaching up, feeling for them, feeling

them (plucked

just so) let go between your fingers with a subtle
resistance into your palms, settling with discrete aplomb and a sigh

of summer heat and sweetness past
their skirmish with lips and tongue

into the messy juice and stain and unshouldered weight
of satisfaction, into the shoulderless dark

of you there.

Wind Chime

> Let the wind speak
> that is paradise.
> — Ezra Pound

Come sway in its ear-level lilt and lapses, fond instrument
day-long of come what may. It lolls, an insatiate

tongue for the random, whim's trinket, net
of the invisible, middle-sister to leaf

and sail, shimmering
suspension in silver wire, knotted

to waft and to the copper lizard, to the warm belly
of sleep, to the cusp and tasty metallic slither

of consciousness. Here
in the slip-stream off
a five tone scale, in

infinite range of interval, swinging from sunny
jingle to anguished cacophony, shimmies all the jazz

and dirge of weather — limitless possibility, excruciating
limitation. Here is the puffed world expansive

as the air come sidling, glancing
home to itself at a porch corner

thinly, briefly, just under the eaves. It might be
our biggest brain tinkling, immersed

in a further exquisite brilliance, that ultimately appropriate distance:
background. *Lead, accompaniment!* Lest we blunder

against you forever ducking inside for the phone . . . Let's slip/
slide sun-stunned and song-prone astray

into bodiless voice.

To the Branch from Which the Robin Flew

that bore the weight of pulse and trill and is shaking it off

that inhabits its allotted space fully in diminishing doodles

that knew from before the beginning it wouldn't be harking far
after flight and song

that in its tangential rooted inherent stillness uninterruptedly
senses elementals, and is therein expressive
but immune to lamentation

that is the lateral receptiveness of a vertical patient persistence tipped
in nonchalant fall-back from furthest untextured blue

undipped brush
of a painterly attention

at ease in the forest's grey-green foreground
at rest in the tensile essential mist of itself

These Are the Days

These are the days. They shimmer
and close (summer's finale)
against an urgency I harbour
a strenuous ache . . .

    the moon in my vise
    of window jamb and edge
    of open window, the device
    as I turn my head

of the curtain lifting
on that further background, stars
at night's extremities, exquisite, precise.
It's taken me years to get the filing right

on the chainsaw teeth to chew
straight through windfall fir. I've got it

these days out of the blue
and my chisels sharpened and oiled
in their little rack, the crowns
of the trees on the heads
of the mountains, first gold

maple flashing — an alchemy
of the leaves' breezy jiggle
and eyes' skill after all, the air
as hollow and honest as ever.

As ever and ever. Eons
of light gone cerulean ring

confirmation
in each sledge swing
on the wedge — echo, extol

the working proposition:
be home here in splendour!

Alison Pick

**"Tell me, what is it you plan to do
with your one wild and precious life?"
— Mary Oliver**

I come to the desk in my flannel pyjamas, carrying a cup of black
coffee. Print the last page, make some corrections. It's cold,
and the thermostat cranky. Put on a sweater, then take it off.
Out in the field, nothing needs changing: the field goes about
the business of dying with perfect belief in the spring. Last night
it snowed but this morning it sticks, coats the gravel driveway,
the road, in a ribbon of white all the way to the lake. Michael
has written, saying he doesn't believe the divine intervention
thing. Neither do I. But somehow the field is focused in frost,
somehow the stars go out and come back. Somehow the moon
spins on its axis, opens and closes its mouth without making
a sound. Now my lover comes into

the room, wearing long-underwear, sleep in his hair. He puts
on the Schubert. We drink our coffee in front of the window,
fat flakes of snow falling into the water. This and each morning
we try not to speak. Soon I will put my sweater back on, move
to the desk. This space, this silence, someone who loves me;
over the field the clouds shift their shadows. When the last
change is made I will sit by the blank paper, listening.

Kyran Pittman

Launch

I was six the summer I learned to swim
in a lake, in Maine
face to face with my father.
His beard is as black as the water
and when he smiles his small teeth
glisten like a flash of trout
mid-leap against the lowering sun.

He is just within, and out of my reach:
thirty-six years old,
as I am now thirty-six.
We circle each other, like Pisces.

I remember thunderheads gathering
at the edge of the sky, time
pressing us both forward.
The water was cool and dark
like the river near our home
where he canoed and fished and where
I poured out by the fistful
the ash of his teeth and bones.
How it glinted like mica as it ran
through my fingers to drift
across the sun-studded surface of the river
rain falling
on a lake in Maine
my father's face
like God moving
over the face of the waters.
I believed in it
and pushed off.

Yves Préfontaine

Peuple inhabité

    J'habite un espace où le froid triomphe de l'herbe, où la grisaille règne en lourdeur sur des fantômes d'arbres.

    J'habite en silence un peuple qui sommeille, frileux sous le givre de ses mots. J'habite un peuple dont se tarit la parole frêle et brusque.

    J'habite un cri tout alentour de moi —
pierre sans verbe —
falaise abrupte —
lame nue dans ma poitrine   l'hiver.

    Une neige de fatigue étrangle avec douceur le pays que j'habite.

    Et je persiste en des fumées.
Et je m'acharne à parler.
Et la blessure n'a point d'écho.
Le pain d'un peuple est sa parole.
Mais point de clarté dans le blé qui pourrit.

    J'habite un peuple qui ne s'habite plus.

    Et les champs entiers de la joie se flétrissent sous tant de sécheresse et tant de gerbes reniées.

    J'habite un cri qui n'en peut plus de heurter, de cogner, d'abattre ces parois de crachats et de masques.

    J'habite le spectre d'un peuple renié comme fille sans faste.

    Et mes pas font un cercle en ce désert. Une pluie de visages blancs me cerne de fureur.

Le pays que j'habite est un marbre sous la glace.

Et ce pays sans hommes de lumière glisse dans mes veines comme femme que j'aime.

Or je sévis contre l'absence avec, entre les dents, une pauvreté de mots qui brillent et se perdent.

Pays, Ô soudain éclaté...

Pays, Ô soudain éclaté comme verrière écarlate sous le feuillu délire de l'automne.

Je t'épouse à grands genoux plantés comme racines d'homme dans ton sol à la veille du froid.

Mais l'hiver à masque de terreur ne prévaut encore contre l'extase à sauver de novembre, à figer dans la phrase meuble et franche de tes terres.

Ô — soudain, si tenace l'insomnie d'un peuple en proie aux folles lueurs de sa saison parturiente et de son ordre.

Aujourd'hui se déroule la fastueuse liturgie du soleil dans l'arbre, le peuple arborescent.

Et l'homme s'abreuve à la sagesse d'Octobre.

Ô brassées de rousseur et rites de vent dans le sourire des forêts, et sur nos lèvres de réveil.

S'éploye la saison sage et vierge et fécondée, saison plus femme que femme neuve labourée.

Lors que la nuit même se pare d'orgues aux musiques d'espace et de mouvance.

Octobre me nomme, et nomme mon sang qui est d'un peuple dur en gésine.

Octobre nomme le sol, nos racines, la face drue du pays
qui ruisselle.

Nous soit aliment la transhumance des saisons, la transparence
femelle des feuilles chues.

Nous soit mémoire, adage sculpté dans la pierre du pays
aux chaînes subtiles, Octobre qui donne à l'arbre ce nom
libre et rouge de révolte.

Nous soit enseignement l'automne, tendre bourreau de
nos yeux naufragés.

Joie. —

Les mots morts nous redeviennent patrie fraternelle aux
récoltes de clarté.

Pays sans parole

Une détresse saigne à l'ombre de l'automne
Sitôt que mûrs les fruits se flétrissent

Cette femme ici ne parle plus que de braises dans l'âtre
tandis que l'homme assume seul l'inimitié du froid
et toutes blessures faites au visage de sa terre qu'il
    s'acharne à semer

Cette femme ici ne parle que de mots
tandis que l'homme se fane debout
les mains ouvertes
la poitrine ouverte
son corps tout entier accueillant
la gerçure énorme d'un pays sans parole

Non-Lieu

Nous qui sommes d'ici sans être ici
et qui sommes d'ailleurs sans être vraiment là.
Nous qui sommes d'ailleurs tout en étant là, nous perdant là,
et qui sommes d'ici sans pouvoir y rester.

Nous qui sommes d'ici sans pouvoir, et qui sommes ailleurs
        mais si peu,
et qui sommes ici sans pouvoir être ailleurs.
Nous qui sommes d'ailleurs sans pouvoir y rester
et qui sommes de partout sans pouvoir nous arrêter.
Nous qui sommes de partout sans pouvoir être ailleurs
et qui sommes de partout sans pouvoir être ici,
et qui sommes d'ici sans être parce que nul jamais
        ne reste là sans mourir.

Mais nous qui ne voulons pas mourir sinon trop fatigués
        pour rester.
Nous qui allons mourir au moment justement où —
Nous qui resterons là désormais, ici ou ailleurs,
incapables d'aller mourir plus loin,
incapables d'aller mourir partout en même temps
        et ce serait si beau.

Nous qui sommes là, voyez-vous, sans y être,
        parce que vous avez mal regardé,
et qui sommes sans que les autres soient,
et qui sommes sans les autres.

Mais justement, nous justement qui ne sommes rien sans
les autres, et qui sommes sans que les autres soient là,
et qui ne sommes pas bien quand les autres n'y sont pas.

Nous justement, nous qui ne sommes jamais rien
        sans que les autres soient.
Mais nous, justement, nous qui n'arrivons nulle part
        sans que les autres y soient déjà pour arrêter ça.

Qu'allons-nous de —
Oui — la question — la seule
Mais vraiment la seule qui reste à poser.
Aux cailloux parce que les hommes ne répondent plus
        aux questions qu'on leur pose.

Nous savons à peu près d'où nous venons mais si mal.
Vous ne savez pas mieux qu'avant qui vous êtes.
Ils ne savent pas du tout où ils vont.

Alors qu'allons-nous de —

D'abord voulons-nous aller — je veux dire
voulons-nous aller quelque part ou quoi ?
Où voulons-nous rien — je veux dire aller
nulle part ou quoi ?
Ou quoi, je veux dire, où ?

Enfin, je parle, je ne sais pas.
C'est quoi ça nous qui
nous qui justement
nous qui sommes d'ici sans y être parce que nul jamais
        ne reste là sans mourir.

Nous qui . . . Comment disiez-vous déjà ?
Nous qui . . . Quoi ? Mais vraiment je ne comprends pas.
Nous qui . . . Mais c'est quoi ça ?
Nous qui . . . Mais qui cogne à la porte ?
Il n'y a pas de portes ici. Nous sommes très libres.
Toutes les ports sont ouvertes. Et memê si les têtes
        sont fermées.
Alors qui cogne quoi ?

Qui cogne sur qui parce que j'entends
    dans le lointain qui s'approche
        un bruit mou et parfois dur
            que je connais
                qui me rappelle . . .
                    quoi déjà ?

Ah nous qui sommes sans vraiment être vraiment,
nous qui sommes ou ne sommes pas,
qu'allons-nous, oui
qu'allons-nous devenir ?

Non-Lieu

We who are from here but without being here
and who are from elsewhere while being neither here
    nor there.
We who are from elsewhere while actually being
    there, and losing ourselves there,
and who are from here but are powerless to stay.

We who are from here but powerless, and who are
    also elsewhere but just barely,
and who are here and powerless to be elsewhere.
We who are from elsewhere and powerless to remain
    there
and who are from everywhere and powerless to stop.
We who are from everywhere and powerless to be
    elsewhere
and who are from everywhere and powerless to be
    here,
and who are from here without actually being here
because no one ever stays here without dying.

But we who do not wish to die unless we are too tired
    to remain.
We who are going to die at the precise moment
    when . . .
We who shall remain from now on, here or
    elsewhere,
unable to go on and die farther along,
unable to go on and die everywhere at the same time
    and how beautiful that would be.

We who are there, do you see, without being there,
    because you did not know how to look,
and who are, although others are not,
and who still are, without the others.

But precisely, we precisely who are nothing
without the others, and who are, even in the absence
    of the others,
and who are not happy when the others are not there.

We, precisely, we who are never anything
    unless the others are too.
But we, precisely, we who never arrive anywhere
    unless the others are already there to stop all that.

What are we going to beco . . .
Yes — the question — the only question —
And really the only one left to be asked.
To be asked of the stones because men no longer
    answer
    the questions that are asked of them.

We have some idea of where we come from but not
    much.
You have no better idea than before of who you are.
They have no idea of where they are going.

So what are we going to beco . . .

In the first place, do we want to go — I mean
do we want to go somewhere or don't we?
Or is there nothing we want — I mean
to go nowhere or what?
Or what, I mean, where?

When it comes down to it, I don't know, I'm just
    talking.
What does it mean, we who
we who precisely
we who are from here without being here

because no one ever stays here without dying.

We who . . . But what were you just saying?
We who . . . What? I just don't understand.
We who . . . But what is all this?
We who . . . But who's that knocking at the door?
There are no doors here. We are completely free.
All doors are open. Even if heads are closed.
So who is knocking what?

Who is knocking whom because I can hear
      in the distance and coming closer
         a sound sometimes dull and sometimes sharp
           and which I recognise
              and which reminds me . . .
                but of what?

Ah, we who are without really being really,
we who are or are not,
what is going to become, yes
what is going to become of us?

                    Translated by Judith Cowan

Steven Price

from *Anatomy of Keys*
• • •

VII

Such newsreels flicker still. His mother in a crowd
shawled soot-dark and frail. The roped-off ledge
of a dour steel bridge; ten thousand blazing throats and the stretch

of girders toward a stinking canal. His chained ankles
flickering; then his shrug to her, shy, as if rising
dully from some couch or half-eaten lunch to step but a moment out

when he plunges. The wet thump of flashbulbs flaring the river,
rail, sunlight, his grey flesh gone in that lazy wash of foam;
crowds jostling in, hushed; a shadow ripples the water —

    but true suffering is an art like any art; it must be learned.
    In a peeling kitchen in Appleton a child's knees grind
    the lip of a tub, his knuckle crooks the shy hairless fish
    of his sex,

    he grins *Ma look at this!*, scrunches his nose: is gone.
    Heels farting the washtub walls. Hair strangling the oily surface.
    She hears it still: her old chair rasping back, that flat skitter

    of peeler and skin and potato meat across the floor,
    in her ears the fast plaited river of Budapest, of girlhood
    and quick as a gasp she is up, crying *Nein, nein Ehrich* —

his nose blowing careful air and him pausing
beneath the gurgling pockets of breath just long enough
to draw out the awe in her dark face.

VIII

Then guy-ropes creaked, plashed, and I sank
to a muscular thud of blood. That cage of water
windowing darkly round me. Ankles bound.
My slow hair untangling. I sighed and a crowd sighed;
fear in the stagelamps, fear clicking at the glass:
nothing felt farther from Appleton, nothing nearer.
Ma's strained love I'd dragged down like a lock,
dragged until no longer strange to me,
its spill of thick soil, its black shawls
of Budapest, of her life before mine;
I lived in her love as if of its element,
swallowed her ribs, ate the thin dream
of a son's first escape: his twisting
shyly in her frozen kitchen,
hissing *Shake me Ma I'm magic,*
darkness shining from her black eyes
set like lanterns of unlighted oil, and her
knuckles, her knuckles, taloned
fiercely in his flesh, and her shaking
shaking him, the cupboards seething
dark with faces, slitted eyes, the shrill
clashing of her silverware —
and then her laugh, clean like a blade,
as the year's bright coins spilled forth from his hair.

• • •

XX
from Proverbs of Escape

The torn rope is twice useful.
A chained wise man remains free. A chained fool escapes.
In old age even the butter-lid grins.
Lies of the illusionist. Truths of the illusion.
Thicker the cord, weaker the knot.
The tied trunk never tells the rope what it holds.
Where conscience is the door, privilege is the hinge.
When he is bound, the crowd is. When he is free, the crowd is not.
The fettered man's curses open only his own mouth.
In the Garden the key is no place. In Hell the key is every place.
Satan goes hidden. God goes unnoticed.
Shackled at daybreak, shadows. Shackled at dusk, lanterns.
No release without first being bound.
Skinniest wrists, hungriest cuffs.
Locks laugh not, weep not; but embrace all things with ease.
Knowledge into goodness. Wisdom out of goodness.
The new pick bends, the old pick breaks.
Mourning unties no knot. Praying unclasps no cuff.
He who conceals everything conceals nothing.
Never how it was done. Always how it was not.
Compassion. Attention. Praise. An anatomy of keys.
To leave the self is love.

Al Purdy

The Country of the Young

A.Y. Jackson for instance
83 years old
halfway up a mountain
standing in a patch of snow
to paint a picture that says
"Look here
You've never seen this country
it's not the way you thought it was
Look again"
And boozy traders
lost in a dream of money
crews of homesick seamen
moored to a China-vision
hunting the North West Passage
they didn't see it either
The colours I mean
for they're not bright Gauguin
or blazing Vincent
not even Brueghel's "Hunters in the Snow"
where you can get lost
and found in five minutes
— but the original colour-matrix
that after a giant's heartbeat
lighted the maple forests
in the country south
You have to stoop a little
bend over and then look up
— dull orange on a cliff face
that says iron deposits
olive leaves of the ground willow
with grey silver catkins

minute wild flower beacons
sea blue as the world's eye —
And you can't be looking for something else
money or a night's lodging on earth
a stepping stone to death maybe
or you'll never find the place
hear an old man's voice
in the country of the young
that says
      "Look here —"

Roblin's Mills

The mill was torn down last year
and stone's internal grey light
gives way to new green
a shading of surface colour
like the greenest apple of several
The spate of Marthas and Tabithas
    incessant Hirams and Josephs
is stemmed in the valley graveyard
where the censored quarrels of loving
and the hatred and by golly gusto
of a good crop of buckwheat and turnips
end naturally as an agreement between friends
    (in the sandy soil
that would grow nothing but weeds
or feed a few gaunt cattle) —
And the spring rain takes their bodies
a little deeper down each year
    and maybe the earliest settlers
some stern Martha or speechless Joseph
perhaps meet and mingle
    1,000 feet down —

And the story about the grist mill

rented in 1914 to a man named Taylor
by the last of the Roblin family
who demanded a share of the profits
that poured golden thru the flume
because the new miller knew his business:
    & the lighting alters
    here and now changes
to then and you can see
    how a bald man stood
sturdily indignant
    and spat on the floor
and stamped away so hard the flour
dust floated out from his clothes
like a white ghostly nimbus
around the red scorn
and the mill closed down —

    Those old ones
you can hear them on a rural party line
sometimes
    when the copper wires
sing before the number is dialed and
then your own words stall some distance
from the house you said them in
    lost in the 4th concession
    or dimension of wherever
    what happened still happens
    a lump in your throat
    an adam's apple half
    a mile down the road
    permits their voices
    to join living voices
    and float by
    on the party line sometimes
    and you hang up then
    so long now —

The Cariboo Horses

At 100 Mile House the cowboys ride in rolling
stagey cigarettes with one hand reining
half-tame bronco rebels on a morning grey as stone
— so much like riding dangerous women
          with whiskey coloured eyes —
such women as once fell dead with their lovers
with fire in their heads and slippery froth on thighs
— Beaver or Carrier women maybe or
          Blackfoot squaws far past the edge of this valley
on the other side of those two toy mountain ranges
          from the sunfierce plains beyond

But only horses
          waiting in stables
hitched at taverns
          standing at dawn
pastured outside the town with
jeeps and fords and chevys and
busy muttering stake trucks rushing
importantly over roads of man's devising
over the safe known roads of the ranchers
families and merchants of the town
          On the high prairie
are only horse and rider
          wind in dry grass
clopping in silence under the toy mountains
dropping sometimes and
          lost in the dry glass
          golden oranges of dung

Only horses
          no stopwatch memories or palace ancestors
not Kiangs hauling undressed stone in the Nile Valley
and having stubborn Egyptian tantrums or
Onagers racing thru Hither Asia and
the last Quagga screaming in African highlands

lost relatives of these
whose hooves were thunder
the ghosts of horses battering thru the wind
whose names were the wind's common usage
whose life was the sun's
        arriving here at chilly noon
        in the gasoline smell of the
        dust and waiting 15 minutes
        at the grocer's

Dog Song 2

Sooner or later
it all comes thronging back
everything that ever happened to you:
suddenly I find myself singing
and I can't sing worth a damn
which doesn't matter anyway
standing on the stony shoreline
of an arctic island watching icebergs
drifting in white night of Cumberland Sound
like ghost ships of lost explorers
trying to find safe passage
thru the ice trying to get home
and without awareness of doing it
I began to hum deep in my throat
then burst out singing with voice cracking
from fever I'd just recovered from —
the actual song-words didn't matter
but for a moment I was prehistoric man
coming out of his cave at night to howl
from sheer self-importance
because he was a damn good hunter
or because a woman had smiled
And the song said: Hello my friends
Hello my friends because we're friends

let's have a drink while we're alive
And the song said: Let's have a drink
for no reason or any reason
and because there's a time in your life
like bacon frying like stars exploding
and you stand on your hind legs and sing
because you're a dreaming animal
trapped in a human body
After a while there was a little echo
the merest whine and whimper and thread
of sound when a sled dog joined me
then another and another
in solemn sadness with a great undertone
of exaltation from weary arctic miles
they had all travelled together
with balls of ice torturing their feet
and whips biting hairy shoulders
and starvation meals of frozen fish
so hard it was like eating fire
they sang the soul's grief of being trapped
and knowing it inside an animal's body
and the dogs mourned

We stopped and there was silence
but not an empty silence
Jonahsie and Leah stood in their doorway
watching me with a peculiar look
but I grinned at them
while the great floating ice castles
swayed by at the edge of the world —

Rodeo

Inside the Stockmen's Hall drinking
beer with Marvin Paul who looks
like a tragic poet and carves totem-poles
taking three weeks to earn four dollars
Outside in the dusty arena horses explode
with arched backs and William Billy Boy
sails upward in air and downward to dust
Another bronco refuses to do anything at all
just stands there somewhat reminding me
of a friend saying "It's better not to be born"
There is free will it seems here in the Chilcotin
a semicircle of mountains stares at the sun
an old Indian with his face a dark forest
outside the Stockmen's Hall sleeps tenderly
I am waiting with Marvin Paul for one of those
moments when all will be made plain
to me when the calf-ropers build their loops
and lasso the stars as William Billy Boy rides
to his inheritance on earth in eighteen seconds flat
his own people quiet and the whites noisy
while our round earth resumes colloquy with the gods
As things stand now Marvin Paul incoherent
with beer sells me his pencil portrait
which translates him to a tragic dimension
the wild cow-milkers clutching beer bottles
strain for a few drops but the beasts refuse
William Billy Boy is slammed to the dust
his bent back aches and he won't ride for a while
Nothing is finally made plain to me
but I have stated my intention set the scene
the same one in which a bored housewife
prays for a romantic lover and the bankrupt rancher
stares at his parched range and starving cattle and spits
Both settle for less than their dreams: the woman for a man
the rancher for one more year in the high Chilcotin
myself for something less tangible
hovering in my mind close to this poem

Dream of Havana

Talking to Red Chinese sailors
with a Cuban interpreter
at the bar in a dark night club
and so hot the air is thick
you have to move sideways
and backward to go forward
Outside on the waterfront
anti-aircraft guns point to the sky
searchlights swing like jumpy nerves
awaiting the Roman invasion
a grey American warship
cruises beyond the 12-mile limit
an international ghost
waiting for buttons to be pushed

In the Sierra Maestras
tanks rumble over mountain roads
and knock down ripe coconuts
Here in Havana Fidel
finds another friend's apartment
and settles down for the night
while his potential assassin
dials information
What world is this I've come to?
I don't believe it
not for a moment
and my thoughts exit
sideways and backward
to childhood and a lost dog
tantrums and broken toys
trouble enough
mothers in long ago doorways
calling children home at night
for bedtime stories
while the Red Chinese sailors
mumble in my ear
and I drink white rum
to the sound of trombones

The Buddhist Bell

Walking thru the Peace Park
you hear a serene bronze sound then
and now it scallops the air into waves
or drifts among the trees softly
as the child who made it happen
and wasn't strong enough
to make the whole world go BOOM
A sign says everyone who wants peace
should strike the bell to make that happen
I don't strike the bell
it's not that I don't want peace
but my arms are full of parcels
And besides I think it's a bit naive
to imagine ringing a bell brings peace
when the warmakers all look like businessmen
and businessmen are bellringers at heart
in their deepest heart of hearts you know
they strike the bell
then look around to see who noticed them
Not me
I think of the bell as an air raid warning:
the bomb bay doors are open
the pilot makes a 158 degree right turn
and heads back for home base
having obeyed orders
like Eichmann or Lieutenant Calley
his conscience clear or relatively
And the Bomb is falling
taking a little longer than usual
but everyone knows it's coming
except the bellringers
and maybe some of them know
besides my arms are full of parcels

The Blue City

Of such an intense azure
that it seeps into your bones
providing dull earth
with an upsidedown sky
My wife is still sleeping
tired from the long journey
I have awakened very early
and must let her sleep longer
Her face is turned to one wall
of the strange hotel room
not feeling my own excitement
at being here with blood thrumming
and pulse beating a little faster
at the sheer romance of Asia
She turns over and sighs
while I'm standing at the window
trying to glimpse a camel
outside on awakening streets:
a woman is sweeping cobblestones
with some kind of twig broom
charcoal burning in a brazier
much blue ceramic but no camels
It occurs to me that I will remember
this time for its inbetweenness
removed from the continuity of things
and it's as if I'm a long way off
somewhere else and watching myself
watching a woman in bed sleeping
seeing what I see for the second time
the wished-for camel and burning charcoal
a blue city slowly coming awake
the little pulse in my wife's throat
I will be seeing it a second time
or has that second time arrived?
— My wife awakening not exactly

here nor there and aware of oddness
disoriented she keeps looking at me
brown eyes puzzled for a long moment

Double Focus

And Timur again set out for the wars —
At this time (late 14th century),
there was not one man in the known world,
from high Pamirs to the Tien Shan Mountains,
who could say his name without trembling.
Timur then was deep in middle-age,
and looked it;
one foot had been lame from birth;
he wore a drooping Mongolian moustache;
no woman would call him handsome.
It may be that power is attractive,
and certainly fear is a factor,
and it may be that age has compensations:
in any event Bibi Khanum loved him.
The Chinese princess watched him go
(beautiful as a roomful of rainbows)
from the blue city of Samarkand:
a long dusty confused line
of horsemen and baggage animals
straggled towards the mountain passes,
short chunky men with faces like boards,
with oxhide shields and bone crossbows
and a leader who would conquer the world.

In 1977,
in the blue city of Samarkand,
a great stone sarcophagus
where Timur is said to be entombed,
waiting to leap out and conquer some more;
red and yellow portraits of Lenin

and Marx cover walls of buildings,
with the inevitable hammer and sickle,
while fleas hop from dust to dust mote.
Stand in a parking lot,
you can see shuddering heat waves
lift and dance across the steppes,
and more distant still the Tien Shan
Mountains and peaks of the high Pamirs,
where armies died of frostbite.
Nothing you can say or think
means very much:
you stand in a sort of trance
for several minutes,
until the dream-movements of a woman,
hanging out washing in the trembling sun,
shatter colour in your unfocused eye,
domestic as dirt.
And thinking: in all this unwashed savagery,
thank god for women.

Story

Thirty years ago
they got married and had children
lived in a town beside the sea
and waves poured in across the sand
in hills beyond the town wind blowing
and sometimes white ships passed by
out at sea as if in someone else's dream

Whatever happiness may be it touched them
with the high seriousness of lovers
who know they are lucky from watching other people:
whose lives rise and fall in peaks and valleys
like the sea waves' constant rise and fall
elated at nothing much and then depressed

because the novelty wears off
and yesterday was just the same as tomorrow

Of course the lovers had that feeling too
since everyone is aware of it more or less
the desolation of vast wastes of time
the monotony of each action so similar
to the last it seems a continual rehearsal
for some great event that never happens
for which many of us get tired of waiting

But our lovers were more fortunate
because they loved or for other reasons
the high emotional peaks and troughs
of despair were levelled to a slight rise and fall
much like the motion of that white ship at sea
whereby no passenger was in any way aware
of underwater mountains and submarine disasters
reflected in their lives

Then they stopped being lucky
the woman ill with cancer
a terminal illness the disease deadly
whether she was aware of this or not
and probably she was
as others have been for thousands of years
whispering goodbye to whoever loved them

Here I intrude myself
to say this story was told me
by the man who was my friend
who saw how the cancer ate her life
and shrank her body down to half
while he kept his surface feelings under control

He slept upstairs and this one morning
in the story came downstairs
naked to visit his wife
naked because he slept that way

and because all of us are part of nature
came down with a large erection dangling
not really a sexual signal
but indication his equipment was in order
the woman seeing it smiled weakly and said
"Sorry love I can't do much about it"

That's most of the story
of course she died and was buried
and in a fairly short time my friend will die too
but it seems worthwhile mentioning all this
as something one would like to feel as well
— not the gruesome part but the tenderness
of someone before being swept out to sea
who says everything to you in a single phrase

The town they lived in is little different
white ships pass far away in sunlight
there are dances at night sometimes no doubt
and another young couple might lean against the rail
of one of those ships
to gulp fresh air and glance toward the land
where vague lights blur in darkness
wind sweeps over hills beyond the town
waves pour in across the sand
and the ship sails on —

Matt Rader

Cruelty

The girl we call Missy lives in the pea-green two-storey
on the corner. Her real name is Jane or Mary, and she's known
for eating cat food from a bag her mother keeps in the closet

of their unfinished basement, which is all gyprock and plumbing,
and a sea of unwashed clothes next to the litter box
where we wrestle. She and I fight at school, but on the block

we're friends, except when she stinks or her face is filthy
with bruises, which is often, and then we throw stones
or ignore her until she goes home. Never seen her father,

but her mum is fat and pale and has hair on her chin.
Missy and I take our clothes off in the bush at the end of the road,
look each other over. Not much to distinguish one from the other

at this age. Eventually all is forgotten except our skin
and the teaming hump of ants we are teaching now
about destruction. Missy would like to touch me

but I will not let her. An ant clings between my thumb
and forefinger. Missy pulls it apart, leg by leg, until it is
only head and *thorax*, she says. Missy is moving at the end of

the summer to a base called Cold Lake where it snows
most seasons. Today, we nurse honeysuckle and do not speak of her
leaving, though it is something we both understand better

than the feeling which rises in us when Missy closes
my hand, crushes the ant.

Faith

Stored Dad's ashes in a mason jar —
swept them from the funeral pyre
after it cooled, bits of bone and tooth,
the smell of salmon somehow.
Kept him in the living-room
fireplace and had no more fires.
Tried not to look during breakfast.
Looked. Duct-taped the glass,
then peeled it off before Mum saw.
I wanted to make him an hourglass,
my sisters thought a pillow or a shaker,
someone said beach. At night
I stole pinches of foot, dashes
of hand, refilled it with sand,
and buried him toe-by-finger
in potted earth and rose seed.
In this way he came back to me:
root and thorn, rosehip, became
jam that smelled of fishmeal,
forty-one white petals I pressed
between the pages of my hand.

Clearing Out

Perched like a gargoyle at the gable end of the house,
feet firmly fixed on the rough tar and shingles, ankles
angled to the pitch and run of the roof, I was stooped

and anchored by the job I had to do: guard the gutter-
spout from a winter's worth of soggy leaves and grime,
while a steady push of lake water pulsed from the hose-

mouth the entire length of the house. It was annual
end-of-winter work and I was obligated to it since
I professed no sense of vertigo the way my brothers did,

no strange impulse to a header just for the hell of it.
Hands numbed to dumb animals that fumbled
and scooped the grungy residue and hurled it earth-

wards like black-wet epithets on chores and work.
Couple minutes and the cramps kicked in, so it was
all shift and squat and shift again, each new position

a gamble against gravity and wind. Who would do this
for less than a case of Keith's and a pack of JPS — minus
two sticks — slipped into his coat pocket? Truth is,

I craved the distance, the quick two-storey trip
to a whole new perspective — doe-eyed satellite dishes,
antennae like birthday wishes — good ear tuned

to the trickle turned thrum of water, clear and true.

Paradise Meadows

The blade blinked in the lover's moss at the edge of the trail,
and I stopped, reached down and touched it, half-buried in the
    boggy earth,

where the boy stumbled and lost his balance in the whitening
    snow,
the gash in his calf where the trap closed tied off
with a strip of canvas from his pants he could not make tight
    enough,

blood like huckleberries speckling the snow
and the sharp stink of the she-wolf he'd been tracking all
    afternoon in his nostrils,
her shadow shifting through the timbers,

the knife he used to free himself from the steel-grip still in his
    fist —

I wiped it on my sleeve and the sun jumped from tree to tree
like a small white flame, caught my face ablaze in the frame of
    the blade,
folded it and put it away —

Wolf Lake

It was down that road he brought her, still
in the trunk of his car. That September
the horseflies were murder and I remember
the dust of the logging trucks rolling off
the mountain seemed to travel forever
over the valley like insects or weather.
Everything seemed darker that month,
that year. How many times have we been down
this road to snag some trout, to poach
some timber: the old Ford pickup rutting
in the gravel where the road washed out
the previous winter and Pete rolling a joint
in the passenger seat, always so anxious
to meet a bear or a cougar, something at least
potentially vicious, out there in the woods,
where his screams and shouts would do him
no good except to spook the creature
or get it riled up and maybe that way
he'd get to use the Winchester I kept
resting in the gun rack behind our heads.
But in the end, we never saw much —
a few deer, a muskrat, the odd raven
we always heard first, its steel-on-steel
wing-carving of the late summer air. We did
a lot of talking and swallowing of beer
but sometimes we liked to pretend
we weren't really there, imagine if
we were quiet enough and didn't move
much, the world would forget about us
and get on with its business: the fir trees would
uproot and plot revenge on the chainsaw,
the fossilised logs spiking the lake would
rise up on the back of the last dinosaur.
It's what we wished for but it never happened
and after a while we'd split the final round

or pack up the tackle and toss it in the back
of the truck, maybe smoke a last j—. I remember
we always smelled of fish or sawdust
by the end of the day, and there was a tape
of Stan Rogers we liked to play on the drive out —
which was what we were doing in the twilight
of that afternoon, when we turned the corner
and spotted the rust-bitten Chrysler stopped
on the shoulder with him hunched over,
hauling a figure up and out of the trunk.
He paused at the sound of the truck, but didn't
look up and we could tell by the hair
and slender arms and fingers it was
a woman he had draped over him like a rug.
As we got closer he started for the woods
and I thought I spotted blood on the hood
of the car. I braked hard and as we slowed up,
the wheels locked and the back end fishtailed
in the dust. My head rushed, thinking
what end are we about to come to here,
as he dumped her body and started to run.
I admit to a little fear, but Pete just laughed
and reached back for the gun —

Preparations

Broke the bird bath with a sledgehammer before the sun
got up and spent the rest of the morning draining
the goldfish barrel and burning it in the firepit. Have to
wonder what viruses or spores, what bugs
were borne off with the smoke or survived buried
in the ash and coal, gone dormant, but alive,
violent and unpredictable as volcanoes. Still,
we do what we can. Used to be
the crows were so noisy I couldn't sleep past seven.
Now silence is the thing that wakes me — the birds having been
poisoned or exposed, infected with a new blackness
that caused them to lose contrast I guess and disappear.
So it's an end to standing water in the backyard.
An end to composting the robins that storm
against the kitchen window as played by the wind
for a joke, an offering or omen laid crooked
and limp at the foot of the house. No more
evenings on the front porch reading or watching
the children skateboard or ride bikes in the street;
nights we go indoors to avoid the bugs and spray trucks
that roam the neighbourhood like ghosts
from the days of chemical warfare and plague.
Later today, I'll go down to the lake to count ducks —
some now turning up dead in the reeds —
the numbers used to track the disease as it deepens
and spreads species to species. Other volunteers
bag the bodies and take photographs
as if at a crime scene. For me it's an excuse
to get away from the house, to put my mind to use —
condition my memory for field and forest of the future,
for clearing or lakeshore, where all the fliers are
gone and only imperfectly remembered.

Michael Redhill

VIA, Outside Quebec City

The two brothers were huddled in the seat,
the elder's eyes going click click
over Quebec fields. The eight-year-old
watched me write a letter, his fingers
zigzagging a mimicked alphabet into his hand.
He had a Mi'kmaq face, a tiny cat's head.
I asked him where he was from, he said
it was a grey house with a banana tree. Not Mi'kmaq.
He put his head down and closed one eye
making me vanish, then come back. What do you like
about your house, I ask. He bolts up,
chirps *candy*. I ask him what he likes least
and then he's silent. You like everything, I say.
The elder is watching me in the window:
He no like tear gas.

Now we sit quietly and dusk is coming.
The older brother has told me everything.
The little one plays quietly with my travelling clock.
We clack over the tracks to the townships:
Bogota Bogota Bogota Bogota.

Murder

I had been sitting alone when they found her; I was
drinking tea, eating sweet cake, some adult joy,
and on one side a man was speaking to a woman,
his hand on her wrist, and I thought of people I have known
who have lived by small safeties, words
we carry with us — *I'll see you later, be back soon,*

other things not meant to be lies, and after reading
that they had found the child
I returned to the café and tried to find
the man and woman, tried,
because I thought they should know, wanted
to say *this one is over, go home* but they were gone
and at their table a woman was telling another
that the grandmother had died, and the woman
looked suddenly quite alone and there was no one near
who could speak her childhood tongue
who might have said *Child —
you can cry for her but then move on,*
or, more cruelly, *We're here for a while
and then we're gone.*

One Year

Was that you cocooned
in his father's hammock or perched on end
of branch, dangling, spiderlike, afraid?
Hard to recall — we were boys,
those tricks were brave, pranks we played
at the feet of death. To fall or unwind meant loss —
of breath at least — that was pretty scary.
(If temporary.) We knew we'd somehow last.
In cold rain we'd go missing, vanish
into slick canoes and go on kissing hunts
to friends across the lake, dive in lilac
or brackish water, watch the backs of fish
curved like lashes swimming — was that you?
If I have you in the right place,
that's your face there sitting in Napoli's
eating pizza, putting your mother at unease
staining your summer pants — *Please
be more careful!* Boys can get into trouble:
they could see us in the dusk on the lake,

motor cut, gliding into fog, or that hognosed
snake that burrowed in dust that we found
was poisonous. All these things we survived.
And to think now how easily I left you
when one of us had had enough — *I'm not ready yet,
I'll meet you inside* — and I had
stayed out a while and played. I think
it's true then — you've actually died.
If this is you (and you've gone missing
if it's not) I want to tell you
I'm still angry, and I think of you a lot.

Happy Hour

The chicken magnates sit
by the fireplace, spouting prices
in clipped dactyls, cigars glowing
like stars in the corner of the room.
Their wives circle the buffet,
loading up plates for them. Dogs
and children crowd underfoot, the din
is enormous. Outside,
incessant rain. Lake Nora is transfigured:
goose-flesh. All day my mother has prepared
for the gathering, poppy bagels, withered fish
with the eyes still in, a huge
anniversary cake.

Later, the grandparents stand
at the edge of the candles, chins glowing
and blow them out. A camera
grinds in someone's hands sucking up
the moment, freezing it in camera amber.
People navigate the thin hallway
to the bathroom, flat against the walls
like spies. A punch-line floats in the air
how should I know — I'm fourteen miles from home!

and my mother turns, laughing,
her mouth full of cake.

I look around. The chicken men are drunk,
their empty glasses tilt on their bellies.
A child has fallen asleep. A woman
I have never met thumbs up poppy seeds
from the table and eats them as she argues
with her neighbour. The crazy
aunt and uncle who still love each other
kiss in a corner. After this is all forgotten
we'll long for the background
where the unnamed visitor appears
in all the films, whose name
no one remembers. We'll watch those films
years from now, reviewing
the divorced and the dead,
that old ambient weather.
Someone will say, I wish I could go back
and someone else, No, never.

True Story

You got your big lakes and you got your small lakes.
From space it looks like a buckshot stopsign.
Some of 'em are knee-deep all the way across
(like your Nipissing)
and these ones breed your giant insatiable pike.
A friend of mine let his golden
jump around in the water, way up see,
and the dog could swim, but then suddenly
it vanishes. "Ranger!" we're yelling,
"Ranger!" But Ranger doesn't answer.
Pike attack. Honest.
Now you listen to me:
Don't walk across Lake Nipissing —
run. Run like hell because they got pike in that lake.

Casson

I remember how the blustery neighbour showed you off
like a big ring and left you on the dock
in a canvas chair with a ginger shandy
in your leathery hand. You were watching that island
just a short distance off across the water,

the water tacked down loose along the shore
like the skin of your face where your two dog-eyes
lay in deep blue mosaic. How's it going
I said, and you woke from your lake-dreaming life.
My wife, you said, she would have paddled me across

to Picnic Island and let me sleep in the stern.
But my knees are wrecked now — they go off
like rifles and I can't get into boats. It's fine
now (I suppose) to sit here and be among my friends.
Your hand pointed at the distant island. Then

the neighbour came and you held his hand and went
for your supper. His wife (whose body you imagined
in all its wild colours) propped you at the table head
and served you carrots and peas and potatoes and bread
which they ate with you in reverent silence.

from "Coming to Earth (Alzheimer Elegy)"

1.

The old man's ghost prowls near the TV,
fed up with the sweating boxers. He's
translucent as smoke, dragging on the brown
cigarette. *Where's you mother, honey?*
He points out the window: *all this
is once orchards*, he says, then falls into a chair.
(Cormorant-beaked, pale with dark gutters

under the eyes, white tank
shifting under the checked dress shirt,
collar open. Freckled clavicle, thin,
leathery, one thumbnail brown.)
Go back and look, he says, *go back and see.*
And so appear the lean cut suit,
his smooth high cheekbones,
hands like willows.

• • •

4.

Poland spreads across the ruined hippocampi
like a stain. To this Poland comes peace,
to this one death. In unending youth
he crosses up and downcountry, raising
tented stages, performing the Polish plays
alongside his wife. In some Polands, he arrives at a door
to find children waiting in a warm house;
in others, the waste of land, destroyed crops,
femurs and patches of hair lying among the stumps.
All day and all night the nurses pass his bed like a haze
of rain, tilt his body to collect the runoff, and he is himself
a great field where next year's grain is planted.
If he does not die.
If the energy of things breaking apart
can be harnessed. If the yellow light from the window
comes down brightly for many days and weeks.

• • •

7.

Let's not think about pits. Or forests.
Lattice of bone worked under mounds
of snow and years. Recall instead
the names of those who walked the streets
in that town, tell me who was called
Charlie Crook, which tables appeared in the gloaming
meat-laden, groaning with bottles,
playing cards. Which sharp finger
ground a word in the book and which voice spoke
that word. Under a crown of smoke,
half a world away and years after, you cut collars,
the loops of your undershirt arched stiff
above your shoulders. And far above, even
higher than those idle thoughts of home,
new satellites looping the heavens.
They send word of the cloud-swirled planet
in the same tongue that told your cousins
to stand together by the peaty ditches.
Closer. It is closer now, and ever the tumbling motion:
Sputnik in the darkness, *Voyager* in the darkness,
Babel starbound, and the names in your mind's dark
slipping over the wrong faces.

8.

I would give you this fall light, this yellow slant
across my table, if you would take the clean
bright air with its people sounds, the sting
of coffee, if it was in you to see yourself
in shop windows, to shrug your jacket forward.
I would give you the huge car with its obscene emissions, the smell
of its leather, the satisfying *pock* of the glove. I
would give you Kew Beach where you were not allowed to walk,
make the longshot come in. You would keep the Bell

until it got to 43$^{1}/_{2}$, there would be more dinners
in the back of the store on Ulster, it would be 1928 again
and Jabotinsky would stay an extra night. You would be a soldier,
an adviser, your hands beside the frosty water glass on the podium,
taking questions. I would give you winter light when it came,
sharp air, a full night of sleep.

9.

Eat a heel of rye, a bit of meat on it.
Feast on nubbins after he's gone to bed, you
who he's unlearning. Cantilevering
around the small apartment, head
aswirl, snowstorm in the brain, asking asking
those questions you hate but answer:
we got this vase ten years ago, ten years ago
you bought the car, static in his head, low hum
under the skin and food
tastes metallic. Stand in the hall
after turning off the television, try
to bring back the faces from long ago. What would they say —
love him but live? At night there's no sleep,
the sound of cigarette-breathing in his room, you
eat an apricot in the light of the fridge, the smooth
sweet orange youth of it, love and human
sexuality on the tongue, the slight prickle of skin.
And after, the pale fissured stone at the middle,
cold and sharp: living after being young, loneliness after love,
death at the end, death and dying at the end.

• • •

Armand Garnet Ruffo

Poetry

makes me
want to write poetry,
exotic disease I guess,
    butterfly palpitations
bursting across the kitchen table
fragrance of sweetgrass
and wild mint wafting into the room,
    jasmine tea
    for two
suddenly on the boil,
    whistling intimacy,
warming what is inside,
perfection of nipple, im-
perfection of heart,
arc of arm,
shape of (tender?) greeting,
(bitter?) farewell,
extended from toe to thigh to infinity.
nothing to do with
I can do better
nothing like that, this honest desire
that kicks
like a new born calf
jumping up and disappearing
into its own geography.

Poem for Duncan Campbell Scott

*Canadian poet who "had a long and distinguished career
in the Department of Indian Affairs, retiring in 1932."*
— The Penguin Book of Canadian Verse.

Who is this black coat and tie?
Christian severity etched in the lines
he draws from his mouth. Clearly a noble man
who believes in work and mission. See
how he rises from the red velvet chair,
rises out of the boat with the two Union Jacks
fluttering like birds of prey
and makes his way towards our tents.
This man looks as if he could walk on water
and for our benefit probably would,
if he could.

He says he comes from Ottawa way, Odawa country,
comes to talk treaty and annuity and destiny,
to make the inevitable less painful,
bearing gifts that must be had.
Notice how he speaks aloud and forthright:
        This or Nothing.
        Beware! Without title to the land
        under the Crown you have no legal right
        to be here.
Speaks as though what has been long decided wasn't.
As though he wasn't merely carrying out his duty
to God and King. But sincerely felt.

Some whisper this man lives in a house of many rooms,
has a cook and a maid and even a gardener
to cut his grass and water his flowers.
Some don't care, they don't like the look of him.
They say he asks many questions but
doesn't want to listen. Asks
much about yesterday, little about today
and acts as if he knows tomorrow.

Alex Espaniel, 1920

Everybody can see plain as day he's suffering.
Maybe a better way is to say there's something chewing
at his insides, the beast of war hunched and hissing,
all that he's seen and done over there in the trenches
coiled inward.

We do like the rest and just watch him.
        (nobody wants to get too close
        especially when he's drinking)
We see him fall to all fours, snarl for more
drink, scream when he doesn't get it,
watch the icy fangs dig in.
Devilish, my wife says. Call it Weendigo.

Then one day we see him sprawled outside his shack
shivering, too weak even to get up and feed himself,
and my wife says, Look at the pitiful thing won't you?
He's got to get back into the bush, I say,
and my son puts him over his shoulder
and we take him to our camp
on Indian Lake.

Influences

> You must speak straight so that your words may go as sunlight
> into our hearts. When God made the world he gave one part
> to the whiteman and another part to the Apache.
> Why did they come together? I am no longer Chief
> of all the Apaches. I am no longer rich; I am but a poor man.
> The world was not always this way. I have no father or mother;
> I am alone in the world. No one cares for Cochise,
> that is why I do not care to live
> and wish the rocks to fall on me and cover me up.
>   — Cochise, 1866

After school, rather than go directly home to his Grandmother
Belaney's at 36 St. Mary's Terrace, Archie, 11 years old and alone,

walks for miles along the grassy cliff overlooking Hastings
and the English Channel. Come sunset, he heads
for a favourite bluff where he sits with his arms around his knees
and looks west, out past the waves and rising fog,
and dreams of America, of a long-lost father
who in Archie's mind is living somewhere out there
among the Red Indians. The books Archie carries, *Great Chiefs
of the Wild West* and *Two Little Savages: The Adventures
of Two Boys Who Lived as Indians and What They Learned,*
tell him what he already knows, that he too can do it,
and that his real life will begin when he joins his father
and like him is also adopted by the Apache.

With Cochise's words memorised and piercing his heart,
Archie plans his escape, whittles the days into wood.
Lost in a white starched world he cannot understand,
rejected and abandoned, he too wonders,
why things are the way they are,
and wishes deeply with all his will and green strength
for the sea to carry him away. Yes, Apache,
Archie will become an Apache!

Let his classmates jeer as loud as they want, because up here
on this cliff he can see how small they really are, and
he no longer cares what they say about him or his father.
His mind made up, this he reconfirms
as he repeats the words of his hero Cochise,
his thin legs hurrying him back to his Grandmother's before
his Aunts miss him and decide to punish
him with a strapping or, worse,
lock him indoors.

An Imagined Country

See this portrait of Archibald Stansfeld Belaney, age 12,
posing stiffly in his dark woolen Sunday suit,
beside his Aunt's collie.

(Never does he suspect
that one day
you will catch him
like this.)

A boy and a dog. Seems pleasant enough. But take a moment
to look into the boy's eyes and ask yourself what you detect.
For this is the same boy who has the ability to see himself
(as you see him) clear across the ocean, all the way,
into the heart of an imagined country called Canada.

Archie Belaney, 1915–16

You want to talk civilization. OK
let's talk War. On August 6th, I join the 13th Battalion
and because I can handle a rifle I'm sent promptly
to the trenches.

One black night I hang my greatcoat
on a branch sticking up in the mud,
in the morning a dead man's green arm
hands it back to me.

I see a man trying to stuff his intestines back inside himself.
He asks me for help.

    Chlorine Gas: Blisters your lungs
                              You vomit blood.
                              No mask. Piss in a rag
                              and stick it in your face
                              No piss. Borrow some.

They make me a sniper. I get to see the tears
the second the bullet rips through them.

The shelling, it makes my brother Hugh go mad.
Now his life is a room where he sits and pounds
his exploding head.

I'm lucky. On April 23rd, I'm wounded in the foot
and sent away to have a toe removed. Later I'm discharged.
Some accuse me of shooting myself. Others say impossible.

Archie Belaney, 1930–31

The current is faster than I expect.
Suddenly my articles break into demand.
Letters of congratulations come flying
in from across Britain and the United States
(few from Canada which I find disconcerting).
Strangers want to visit me.
Reporters want to interview me.
They announce that I'm the first
to promote conservation:
the beaver,
the forests, the
Indian
way of life.

I begin by signing my name Grey Owl,
and saying I was adopted by the Ojibway,
and that for 15 years I spoke nothing but Indian;
then, before I know it, I have Apache blood.
Finally I'm calling myself an Indian writer.

Fast, it all happens so fast.
At first I'm hesitant.
I'm unsure of the name, the sound of it.
(Although, do I not prefer traveling at night?

Did I not hoot like an owl in Bisco?)
I think of the risk, those who know me.
There are Belaneys in Brandon.
My wife Angele in Temagami —
who knew me when I still carried an accent —
not to mention all those folks in northern Ontario.

But the thrust of self-promotion is upon me,
and head first into it, I hear myself
convincing myself that nobody's going to listen
to an immigrant ex-trapper from England,
promote an indigenous philosophy for Canada.
And if this is the only way
to get Canadians to listen,
then I'll do it, and more
if I have to. I'll be
what I have to be.
Without hesitation.

Joe Hassrak

One thing about being a bartender, you see everything.

Yeah, he's here drinking at the Plaza hotel, perched
on a bar stool as though this is where he belongs.
Sure he's loud, and I do my best to try and calm him down,
ply him with more drinks (I know it's foolish of me).
Normally, we don't even let Indians in, but seeing he's famous
and judging from the looks of him,
he's obviously got a lot of whiteman in him.
So I look the other way, so to speak. Besides,
he's a likeable guy, though certainly a helleva strange bird
in his dark suit, red neckband, hat pulled low.
A heck of a storyteller too.

Right now he's going on about some party he's supposed to be at.
Earlier in the day, he had his photograph taken by Mr. Karsh,

you know the guy who takes pictures of Kings
and Prime Ministers and the like. He says he was invited
back for a dinner in his honour. Mr. Karsh assured him
he would make all the necessary arrangements,
even refurbish his studio to make it look presentable
(imagine that!), order food and wine,
and invite forty or so prominent writers, journalists
and politicians. And now Grey Owl decides
he doesn't want to go. Just like that!
(Maybe there's more Indian in him than I think.)

Anybody who's somebody must be there, eager
to meet the famous Canadian celebrity extraordinaire.
They've all read about him, news of his British tour
has been quick to reach Ottawa. So there they are waiting,
waiting, until their patience is burnt through and
the anxious murmuring in the room has become unbearable
for the host. While Grey Owl sits here in my bar,
at the appointed hour, as though he couldn't care less,
carrying on about something or other, his glass raised,
his voice boisterous.

What is it he's going on about? Something about Indians?
the government? his film? his wife? Something
about himself? career? health? happiness?
That he doesn't care.
And as if that weren't enough, it's exactly at this moment
that I see him, Mr. Karsh, himself.
But rather than approach, he remains at the entrance door
carefully considering what he is witnessing,
as though he were about to take the perfect photograph,
a portrait that tells him he should have known better.

Later

The day after he dies, she is told a certain Angele Egwuna
of Temagami claims to have married an Englishman
named Archie Belaney, and an old northern Ontario guide
by the name of Bill Guppy confirms he knew Archie Belaney
when he had just stepped off the boat and still carried
an English accent. She is even told of an English wife.

His manager asks her to England to meet Grey Owl's mother
and confirm his parentage. After all she is his true wife,
the heroine of his pilgrimage, his Anahareo, she should know.
She doesn't. The man she slept with, thought she knew,
she now sees is (and was) a ghost, invisible and laughing
with great gusto. This man she will later call, with a grin
of her own, a devil in deerskins.

Gregory Scofield

Ode to the Greats (Northern Tribute)

Live

from the Grand Ole Opry
Hank cooed in all his glory

sailed

blue notes, fiddle strings
over airwaves,
pining lonesome,
his cheating heart
bursting through the voice box

up north

long before me, paved roads
and flushing toilets,

long before
the blues were reinvented,
sung
in a dozen shades of grey,
pale in comparison,
those rockabilly crooners
changed the soul
of heartland music

up north
before electric heat

they cuddled up to the woodstove,
toes tapping
along with Kitty, quivering
old-time twang,

her honky-tonk angels
bush and backroads
as Tennessee could never be,

crying blue
as Amigo's guitar
longing sweetly, strumming fingers
long past sundown

up north

a damn sight wild,
their generation,
half crazy on home brew
tuning hand-me-down guitars,
feet stomping
and lifting higher,
breaking into jigs
sweeping plywood floors

up north

long before power lines, oil rigs
burping underground

Patsy's syrup voice and sweet dreams
flowed from maple trees,
echoed far and wide
loons on the lake
crooning stars, pulling the moon

down
and through the voice box

Sarah, A.P.
and Maybelle
picked autoharp strings,
chimed Clinch Mountain bluegrass
lonely
as muskeg reeds, spring frogs
pitching into chorus,

pining blue sky
orange, purple
crimson

up north

when the wind picks up,
blows sweet juniper
through the tent flaps,
the only thing to do
is sing, sing

strum and sing,
the northern lights
bright as Opryland,

dancing

the whole night through
they sang, their generation
sang
low and mean,
the poor man's blues,
richer than most

up north, before me,
before all roads
led down south

there was Heartland, USA

tuned in and

live

on the voice box
Jimmie and Wilf, all of
the Greats
chiming their Opry hi-dee-ho,
calling all lonesome rangers
to gather round
the voice box

up north

they sang and played
long after
the lights went down,

long after
the stage went silent,

the Greats
immortalized on records
that over time
skipped and scratched,

lifted me off to sleep

down south

my Greats, those two
homesick rounders
spoke of the north,
the glory days
as if it were only yesterday,
as if
one small ocean
could ever claim

their spirits, untamed,
sharp and tuned
as Hank's guitar.

Not All Halfbreed Mothers
for Mom, Maria

Not all halfbreed mothers

drink

red rose, blue ribbon,
Kelowna Red, Labatt's Blue.

Not all halfbreed mothers
wear cowboy shirts or hats,
flowers behind their ears
or moccasins
sent from up north.

Not all halfbreed mothers
crave wild meat,
settle for hand-fed rabbits
from SuperStore.

Not all halfbreed mothers
pine over lost loves,
express their heartache
with guitars, juice harps,
old records shoved
into the wrong dustcover.

Not all halfbreed mothers
read *The Star, The Enquirer,
The Tibetan Book of the Dead*
or Edgar Cayce,
know the Lady of Shalott
like she was a best friend
or sister.

Not all halfbreed mothers
speak like a dictionary
or Cree hymn book,
tell stories

about faithful dogs
or bears
that hung around or sniffed
in the wrong place.

Not all halfbreed mothers
know how to saddle
and ride a horse,
how to hot-wire a car
or siphon gas.

Not all halfbreed mothers

drink

red rose, blue ribbon,
Kelowna Red, Labatt's Blue.

Mine just happened
to like it

Old Style.

T. For

> Texas, T. for Tennessee,
> T. for Texas, T. for Tennessee,
> T. for Thelma
> That gal that made
> A wreck out of me
>
> If you don't want me mama,
> You sure don't have to stall,
> Lord, Lord,
> If you don't want me mama,
> You sure don't have to stall
> 'Cause I can get more women
> Than a passenger train can haul . . .

and the needle would catch,

slide into
its well-worn groove,
refusing to budge
like Fat Paul the bootlegger
our very own
small-town Buddha.

Even weighted with pennies
and promises
it wouldn't move
so T. was always for Texas,
Tennessee, for Thelma
that invisible gal
that made a wreck
out of the record, so

T. ended up
strummed in D, sung in C minor
D. for Desmarais, Alberta,
C. for the Carter Family
and Harry . . .

If you don't want me daddy
You sure don't have to call,
If you don't want me daddy
You sure don't have to call,
Cause I can get more neecheemoosuk†
than a dog sled can haul

and the needle and Fat Paul
scratched
and waited, stubborn
as hell,
thinking it was damn funny
till they
both got busted.

Lyrics sung by Jimmie Rodgers, "Blue Yodel No. 1," from *Down the Old Road*.
† neecheemoosuk: sweethearts

Pawâcakinâsîs-pîsim
December — The Frost Exploding Moon

And where did we start?
Was it the summer
of my seven year moulting,
the day I thought
another man's body beautiful?
Or was it the spring
and the night
your eyes passed over my naked feet
and lingered such an infinite time?

Perhaps neither.
Perhaps it was only a day
no different from the ones
haphazardly strung together
like the silver bones
of the wind chime
rubbing the night's cool finger.

And though the day eludes me,
I remember that love
galloped in on the backs of horses,
kicked up dust in my heart,
their drumming hooves
carrying you, the dreamrider,
the four corners of the earth
tied together
in a sacred bundle.

But this is the day
of your hateful absence.
Last night stars fell from the sky,
and moon, with her winter cough
hacked all night.
Now I wonder did we kiss good-bye
and was this the last dream?

Tonight there is no trace.
I've searched every valley,
every canyon, every mountain.
You are gone. The horses are gone
and the earth is cold
with all the things I cannot say.

Now
what name is to be given
to the moon?
Coyote has torn her to shreds,
dances wild from the blood of her
to the cracking of the trees,
the frost and my heart exploding.

Pêyak-Nikamowin — *One Song*

At the break of dawn
the spirits I call
to the west, the south,
the north, the east
I am looking
like them I am looking
calling to my love.

âstam ôta nîcimos
ôtantâyan, ôtantâyan
hey-ya-ho-ho
hey-ya-ho-ho
hey-ya-ho-ho
hey-ya-ho-ho

In this dream
he is across the river
standing upon the bank
just over there
my sweetheart.

kâya mâto nîcimos
kinîtôhtan, kinîtôhtan
hey-ya-ho-ho
hey-ya-ho-ho
hey-ya-ho-ho
hey-ya-ho-ho

I am going to cross
to where he is
cross that river
for my love
but he is gone
and the reeds are weeping.

kakwêyahok nîcimos
ninêstosin, ninêstosin
hey-ya-ho-ho
hey-ya-ho-ho
hey-ya-ho-ho
hey-ya-ho-ho

Now all I have are
rainberries and tears to give
as I sit here
watching where he stood.

pekîwêyan nîcimos
nî-mâtoyân, nî-mâtoyân
hey-ya-ho-ho
hey-ya-ho-ho
hey-ya-ho-ho
hey-ya-ho-ho

*âstam ôta nîcimos
ôtantâyan, ôtantâyan:*

*come here my sweetheart
I am here, I am here*

                      kâya mâto nîcimos
                      kinîtôhtan, kinîtôhtan:

don't cry my sweetheart
I hear you, I hear you

                      kakwêyahok nîcimos
                      ninêstosin, ninêstosin.

hurry my sweetheart
I am tired, I am tired

                      pekîwêyan nîcimos
                      nî-mâtoyân, nî-mâtoyân.

come home my sweetheart
I am crying, I am crying

Olive Senior

Peacock Tale, I

Once upon a time, Peacocks were eaten
    but only by Royalty and therein
        hangs a tale.
King George the Third in a moment of
    lucidity, was set to practicing
        his Speech from the Throne.
All went well, except that at the end of
    every sentence he intoned
        the word: "Peacock."
The Minister sent to drill him scratched
    his head and finally said:
        "Majesty, 'peacock'
is a very fine word. So fine indeed it
    needs be reserved exclusively
        for Royalty. If you pardon me
— Majesty — such a word should never
    be breathed aloud to excite
        the common herd."
This pleased the King excessively.
    Thereafter his speech he said
        punctuated by the word
"peacock" but silently at the end
    of every sentence. Interpreted
        as a strategic pause
which many said made for an excellent
    delivery. Still, some kept muttering
        "insane." Not knowing
that in eating peacock, the King
    had swallowed not just bird
        but word.

Which is to say, with the goose: sauce.
With the peacock: sorcery.

Emperor Penguin

The Emperor Penguin stands sentinel to progeny in the dark
Antarctic winter. Two months solitary on the Great Ice Barrier
incubating a single egg in the fold of the skin between his legs.
By the time his mate returns from her long eating spell
to relieve him, he's but a shadow of his former self.
Such parental cooperation! Sounds to me like a marriage made
in Hell. Penguins perhaps are too well matched. By the time
mating season draws near, the male has forgotten all he's
learnt the previous year. With everyone dressing unisex, he
sometimes presses the wrong suit. The consequences could
be appalling. What does an Emperor Penguin do with no egg
to hatch on the Great Ice Barrier during the dark Antarctic
winter? It seems as if in exchanging wings for flippers, flight
for fortitude, the courageous Emperor Penguin
made a mess of dress.

Thirteen Ways of Looking at Blackbird
after Wallace Stevens

I
The ship
    trips
into sight of land. Blackbird
is all eyes. Vows nothing but sunlight
will ever hold him now.

II
Survivor of the crossing, Blackbird
the lucky one in three, moves
his eyes and weary
limbs. Finds his wings clipped.
Palm trees gaze and swoon.

III
Swept like the leaves on autumn wind,
Blackbird is bought and sold and bought
again, whirled into waving fields
of sugar cane.

IV
Blackbird no longer knows
if he is man or woman or bird or simply is.
Or if among the sugar cane he is
sprouting.

V
Blackbird's voice has turned rusty.
The voice of the field mice
is thin and squeaky.
I do not know which to prefer.

VI
Blackbird traces in the shadow not cast
the indecipherable past.

VII
Blackbird finds thrilling
    the drum beats drilling
        the feet of
men of women into
    utterance.

VIII
To Blackbird rhythm
    is inescapable
Fired to heights alchemical
the immortal bird consumed

Charlie Parker

wired.

IX
Blackbird once again
attempts flight. Crashes into
the circle's contracting edge.

X
Even the sight of the whip makes
Blackbird cry out sharply.
No euphony.

XI
Pierced by fear, Massa and all his generation
mistake Blackbird for the long shadow.

XII
Blackbird strips to reduce gravity's pull
readying for flight again. Fate hauls him in
to another impetus.

XIII
In the dark
    out of the sun
Blackbird sits
    among the shavings
from the cedar coffins.

Embroidery

The women of the family took tea all together except for
Aunt Millie, Uncle Vincent's wife. She read books, she

wore makeup and jewellery even on weekdays. On Sunday
afternoons behind locked door, she had me put colouring

(Madame Walker's, IMPORTED FROM AMERICA) in her
hair. She was a blue foot, a stranger, not a born-ya. She

had crossed water. They did not know precisely where
Uncle V had found her. He was the eldest, family head.

A sly dog and purse-string controller, so no one said
anything. Aunt Millie smiled often but her mouth was

sewn up. Her reticence offering them few strands,
the women of the family enhanced them with embroidery

(washing lightly in vinegar to keep the colours fast). From
her straight nose and swarthy skin they plucked skeins

to compose the features of a Jewess, or herring-bone in
the outside daughter of a rich merchant or plantation owner.

Her mother was someone mysterious, whipped onto the
scene with a slanting backstitch. She once sang opera?

She was said to be of Panamanian or Columbian origin.
Something exotic enough — like a french knot — to mistrust

but work in. They reviled Aunt Millie's use of scent. From
the few words they extracted they thought they detected

a foreign accent. Sometimes they feathered in "Haitian,"
infilled with dark threads to signify the occult powers

of that nation – how else could she have snared such as
Uncle V? They thought she kept her distance because

she was all of the above and snobbish. *My dears, such airs!*
She and I were *What a pair!* Myself, orphaned with frayed

edges unravelling into their care. Everyone knowing my
pathetic history, I could wind myself up in Aunt Millie's

mysterious air, undulate in the sweet waves (artificially
induced) of her hair. She nurtured me on books and

reticence. The women of the family fed me cold banana
porridge (or so everything then seemed) told me tales

of girls who did and men who didn't marry them. Tried to
enmesh me in their schemes to undo Aunt Millie's disguise.

In the end they embroidered her an elaborate cover when
(I could have said) a plain winding sheet would have suited her.

For to me she gave her story, unadorned. The women of
the family willed me their uniform tension. Aunt Millie left

me her pearls. I sold them, became a blue foot traveller.
Kept no diary. Sewed up my mouth. Shunned embroidery.

Amazon Women

Gardening in the Tropics, sometimes
you come across these strong Amazon
women striding across our lands —
like Toeyza who founded the Wori-
shiana nation of female warriors
in the mountains of Parima — of whom
the missionary Brett and Sir Walter
Raleigh wrote. Though nobody believed
them, I myself could tell a tale or two
(though nothing as exotic as the story
of Toeyza and her lover Walyarima who
swam the river disguised as a black
jaguar whenever he visited her). Now
we've got that out of the way let me
hasten to say I'm not into sensationalism,
I merely wished to set the record
straight by averring that the story
of Amazon women might have begun
because when the warriors went away
— to war or voyages — it was the
women who kept the gardens going
and sometimes if the men were not
heard from again (as occasionally

happened) they banded together and
took up arms to defend the territory.
So somebody — like Cristobal Colón
or Sir Walter Raleigh — could have
come along and heard these (marvellous)
tales of (fabulous) lands full of
(pure) gold and fierce (untamed,
exotic) women (you know how men stay!)
And the rest (as they say) is history.
Mark you, the part about Toeyza's
husband sending her and the other
women to gather cassava for a feast
while he ambushed and killed her lover
is true (at least, my auntie says so
and her husband's uncle's grandfather
told him as a fact — and he got it
from someone who knew). I don't know
about you but the part I find
disgusting is that while they were
away, the husband (a chief at that)
skinned and hung the lover up
in the women's hut as a lesson
to faithless wives. (Though if men
go around in jaguar disguise, what
can they expect?) If you ask me,
that husband got what was coming
(poisoned with bitter cassava juice
mixed in with the beer) though
I can't see what the rest of the men
did to deserve equal treatment.
But that Toeyza (with liberated words)
led all the wives in flight and they
managed (despite pursuit) to fight
their way across the jungle to the
heights and freedom in their own
nation which ever since has been
justly celebrated as the Land of
the Amazon. The best part (I hear)

is that they allow men to visit them
once a year. Boy children they send
back to the land of their fathers,
girls they keep to rear (though
I'm not sure I would want my girl
raised by a band of women outlaws
keeping company with jaguars). But
you see my trial! I'm here gossiping
about things I never meant to air
for nobody could say I'm into
scandal. I wanted to tell of noble women
like Nanny the Maroon queen mother
or the fair Anacaona, Taino
chieftainess who was brutally
slain by the colonists, or of
the Carib women whom the said Colón
relied on for navigation
through the islands. I hadn't meant
to tell tall tale or repeat exotic
story for that's not my style.
But we all have to make a living
and there's no gain in telling stories
about ordinary men and women.
Then again, when gardening
in the Tropics, every time you lift
your eyes from the ground
you see sights that strain your
credulity — like those strong
Amazon women striding daily across
our lands carrying bundles of wood
on their heads and babies strapped
to their breasts and calabashes of
water in both hands.

Fishing in the Waters Where My Dreams Lie

I

The day my master sent me fishing for his
    dinner
is the best day up to now I can remember.

This sea I found was not the sea that bound
    and swallowed me
that brought me hither, delivered me as less
    than what I left behind.
Here no looming seaside barracoons nor
    tattered sails nor the waves
blue keening. What opened my eyes were
    the colours the sun
broke up on the water. Alone in my dugout
    shell, I dropped
my line and waited with baited breath,
    explored a vacancy
on my tongue. For here in this new world it is
    my master
who gives things names and here I am struck
    dumb, not knowing
how to summon them from the deep, what song
    to sing them
        so they'll leap.

O keepers of the deep release the catch or let
My master's vengeance fill this empty net.

By the powers of
Yemoja-Oboto
Agbe-Naete
Aizan-Velekete
Avrekete
Gede
Agoué
Olókun

II

I'm homing these waters
now I sing the joys of knowing
scales fall from my eyes hail
my brothers that swim from my
homeland to greet me here
clothed in the same bright dress
wearing new names

Each night I dream my net breaks up water
as water breaks up the shell-like image of the moon.

Praises I sing now to:

Agwé
Madre de Agua
Yemayá
Olókun

Sue Sinclair

Between Stations, October

The train stops abruptly
and a shiver runs through us like grass.
Local scenery becomes fine and sharp
as cats' claws.

We are waiting for a ghost, another train
to pass through us. We are audience,
the pianist paused in the middle of a bar,
needing someone to turn the page.

The fields lie still, expectant.
We listen like small animals, ready
to bolt down a hole. No one moves.

The Dorsals

Theirs the most domestic
of tasks:
       the shifting of weight.

They live under the harness,
get the job done; these

are the muscles
with which we bear
death, dirt, loss.

They seek no explanation.

No One Asks Leda to Dance

She stands on an island
in the goldfish pond, the tube poking
from her side as if she were a patient
escaped from hospital. If she just stands
still enough, no one will find her.

The jug she used to hold
is being cleaned or repaired;
we had no idea the water really poured
from her hip. But we were wrong
about her in all kinds of ways, a case
of mistaken identity. She is, after all,
only Leda's twin, and her destiny
is to be bronze, to continue to evade
the swan crouched at her feet,
who is no Zeus and for whom she feels sorry.

Without the jug in her up-turned hands,
she seems to be asking a question, curious
not about the swan but about the weather.
She's waiting for a change, waiting
for a season less empty. She wonders
when a leaf will fall. Soon someone will come
and lead her back where she belongs.

But what happens next is what always
happens next: nothing. The swan doesn't
fan his wings, doesn't show himself
to her, doesn't unwind his looped neck.
Time has been forgotten: the thicket
of seconds doesn't rustle behind
or ahead of her; she doesn't listen for it.
There is no about-to, no rush,
no end. The fish go on spinning invisible
webs in the pool.

Goldfish

As though just born,
   fins like the thin
membranes
that swaddled them.

They hang in the water
dreaming of imperial pools
they once graced,
     swishing their tails,
waiting to return to court,

and though they might want it
as badly as anyone,
we don't remember, they say,
pretend to be caught
by surprise
     though nothing
astounds them anymore:

throw in a penny and they will change
their minds again.

Dining Room, Morning after Mrs. Dalloway's Party

The vase of lilacs, the chairs
and table, salt and pepper shakers,
cream jug, and all the plates
a little drunk
and imitating one another,
silent jokes shared among themselves.
The maid is still asleep. Some gossip,
the pressure to shine in the right place at the right
time replaced by a kind of fluid
restlessness as their lives pour
from them like dreams before sleep.

The furniture hums to itself; the stillness
crackles. The room is full of light, invisible wasps
buzzing the left-over food (smears
of whipped cream). Some find their way up
to the maid's room, where she dreams of overcoats
helped on and off endless shoulders.
The half-ruined table floats
in the morning sun, dessert forks sprawled
every which way. Things turn inward
to sum up the evening. They sigh,
pensive. The lilacs droop further,
lean closer to their reflections
in the silver platter, wondering
what they should have done instead.
Perhaps there will be time tomorrow.
Always, for them, this question
of the proper moment.

Once Lost

A ring covered in powdered sugar
at the bottom of a box from the French bakery.
White gold, a wedding band, and we are both
so sad: it catches the light only
at certain moments. How little anyone knows of them,
the things we love and use most. We are cats
who look through their own reflections in mirrors, remote
as that. What the cats see is light, and they know there's no
use
in it, or in the rain, or in time itself. But we can't help
ourselves: we understand how unlikely it is,
where it came from, who wore it then. It's why you decide
to keep it: a kind of trust. Though you think about them less
now, they come to you at strange times of day:
notions of love and how,
sometimes, we can't find our way back.

Photograph of My Mother as a Child
or *Invitation to the Wedding*

You wouldn't have told it this way,
but this is the story: your aunt wearing her furs,
everyone else in double-breasted
wool coats. A ribbon perches in your hair,
but you won't smile, look into the lens as though
studying a strange animal. Your sister,
standing beside you, isn't even facing the camera,
has forgotten what she's supposed to do.
That's why you're holding her hand:
as the oldest, you remember everything,
and she is the sweet forgetful one
you long to be again.

It looks like it's snowing, soft flakes
in the thin air around you. Or it could be confetti.
Really the picture's just fading after so many years,
white flecks in the paper. And yours is the only
tiny face that knows what's happened.
If everyone else came to life, like a movie, like a dream,
they would look around in amazement, exclaiming,
"Where are we?" "How pretty the snow is!"
"Don't you look smart!" "The church seems so small!"
Like children, revolving, faces radiant
with lack of understanding, not yet realizing
they can't brush the white flakes
from their coats.

You don't move, look time in the eye
as you would a growling dog
on the way to school. They'll discover the truth
soon enough, and if not, so much the better.
That it snows in places you've never seen
and that time can't be harnessed
is not something everyone can understand.
And it *is* like the first snow as they laugh and smile,

though you will only go so far.
They thought this photograph
would tell them something. Still looking
into the camera, you wonder why
you should stop pretending now.

The Making of "Lawrence of Arabia"

Extra joints appear in the camels' ankles, and their long
   legs grow
longer, more supple:
            they wade like cranes or dusty flamingos
               through the ripples of heat.
The cameraman takes his eye from the lens, bewildered,
beaten at his own game, outwitted by light.

Dignity: how all things reach for themselves
beyond the stir of light and heat. The camels' hooves glisten,
   reflective
and changeable as the pupil of an eye. Beyond tents and cameras,
the mirage reveals the liquid surface of the world,
shimmering and dangerous.

Four Poems for Virginia Woolf

I   Portrait

Too much forehead. In photographs
she always looked sad. It should have been easy:
to sink to the bottom of oneself,
to be like sleep. But the thought of her own face
haunted her. She couldn't forget. The man staring
from under the dark cloth.

She couldn't sleep either: *good night, bad night, fairly good night:*
               Leonard's diary,
Sinhalese and Tamil characters
intricate as the bones
in the ear. A cryptic alphabet
from his days
in Ceylon, coiled letters winding
into themselves, a glimpse
of madness. What her thoughts
might have looked like.

From the camera: quizzical
brows, aquiline nose.
Her eyes, sometimes, and the weight of water
behind them.

II *A Sunday Drive*

      "*Of course you know the Goat is mad.*"
               — Vanessa Bell

the piece of her that kept
breaking down, breaking down
like an old car, the one you know is going
to sputter, backfire, and leave you stranded
in the country, again, but you drive it
because it's yours, and you know
the clutch, how it gives, gives out,
and retains a certain
fatalistic charm

Of course it was more serious
than that — more than a flat tire, someone
trudging off in the dust. You can't help
but be flippant between times. A kind
of forgetfulness that lets you make light,

make love, make the drive
into the country. To talk
as though it were nothing.
To picnic and look at the hills.

III Observation

she doesn't imagine it:
they stare when she passes,
can't help themselves, giggle
at the sight

there is something amphibious
about her: all eyes and faintly
ridiculous in cloche hat
and woolen coat, stepping out
to tea at Charleston
                    a caricature
the frog-lady shuffling
along, a lily-padded gait

who knew she noticed?
she never blushed, never looked up
but she doesn't know why
they nudge each other, dreams
she is naked and wakes up
sweating

she looks in the glass
and there it is, the trace
of her ancestors
half bone, half
                  cartilage
mutant limbs, transparent lids
and open, open eyes

IV The Pattles

Seven beautiful sisters, your mother's
great-aunts, a legacy
of bone structure. Arm in arm they step out
of the last century, turning heads
in every decade. They emerge
in your mother's face, the grace of her brow,
a perfect oval. A madonna, they said,
a saint. The angel in the house.

You are not your mother — they say this to you
when she is gone. But you knew it, you knew
because of the parties, how everyone
fell in love with her, revealed themselves —
not secrets but things they told
no one else. You did it too. No, you are
not your mother. No *boeuf en daube*.
You haven't got her knack for opening doors,
those lovely cheekbones, that skeleton key.

Whether or not to try it. To pull out the best
china, order the roast, and — then what?
You can't feel it as she did, seating them
around the table. Even the candles
won't light properly, cast the right shadows.
Their faces are dim; the room empty.

100 Love Sonnets
after a photograph of Pablo Neruda and Mathilde Urrutia

As though he were not bent slightly
over his sagging
belly to rest his chin
on her head, but were somewhere
closer to thought, weightless. His eyes
shut. She smells like earth and rain
and wood, all things he has shown

he's not afraid
to name.
      He's almost alone, but she
is the sliver of *almost* that interrupts
him, catches him
in his most private moments and causes
him to be always not done imagining
the socks and bread and fishermen,
the bones underground. He smiles to himself, glad
to have said what he meant. It comes so easily
when he slips his arm along the curve
of her back. He leaves his hand
in his pocket as if to show how effortlessly
he writes a hundred sonnets to her.

Her long, polished fingernails are tucked between
the shirt buttons he loves for their plainness.
Her hands, the showy jewel in her ring,
tease him. She waits for him to catch up with her,
mischievous. Her coiffed hair, the frivolous
poem he hasn't yet written, the one she promises
will come. Tomorrow, he says, his eyes still closed.
He wants to wait here forever. Yes, she says,
tomorrow.

Just a flyleaf photograph, but imagine it
his way for now:
                    their combined weight
and the ripening sun pulling them down
like pears hung
on a branch bent low enough to reach
the ground. A moment when they weigh
nothing, nothing at all,
barely touching the grass, this
is what he's been trying to explain.
That he remembers the look on her face
just seconds ago and
the expression before even that, before
they even met, what neither
of them knew, sonnets.

Karen Solie

Skid

Black ice squats hairless
on the single-lane, teeth
all knocked out.
Molecules still
as little hands in its lap,
it hums a tune called
faster.

You asked for this,
a moonless night and snow
for Christmas. You
and your gun control,
your precious profligate antelope,
each pair of eyes a swerve. You
and your cheap all-seasons.

Black ice lays low,
laughs off the social work
of salt and sand.
One more for the road,
it chuckles, spreading. *Come on,
you can pass this guy.*

Boyfriend's Car

Black Nova. Jacked up. Fast.
Rhetorical question. Naturally,
a girl would choose
the adult conspiracy
of smoked glass, darkened interiors.
Privacy. Its language

of moving parts, belts,
and unfamiliar fluids.

Hot. Mean. The words
he used for it.
She added a woman's touch.
The back seat shone
like a living skin. Oxblood.
Hair in the door handle,
white white arms
pretty against
the grain, the red.

She joined the club,
password muttered snidely
by tattletale skin.
Privacy. Bruises
smuggled like cigarettes
under her clothes.
A grown-up walk.
The responsibility not to speak
a certain silly thought.

When she asked
to go home he said
*Well now that depends
on you.*

Sturgeon

Jackfish and walleye circle like clouds as he strains
the silt floor of his pool, a lost lure in his lip,
Five of Diamonds, River Runt, Lazy Ike,
or a simple spoon, feeding
a slow disease of rust through his body's quiet armour.
Kin to caviar, he's an oily mudfish. Inedible.
Indelible. Ancient grunt of sea

in a warm prairie river, prehistory a third eye in his head.
He rests, and time passes as water and sand
through the long throat of him, in a hiss, as thoughts
of food. We take our guilts
to his valley and dump them in,
give him quicksilver to corrode his fins, weed killer,
gas oil mix, wrap him in poison arms.
Our bottom feeder,
sin-eater.

On an afternoon mean as a hook we hauled him
up to his nightmare of us and laughed
at his ugliness, soft sucker mouth opening,
closing on air that must have felt like ground glass,
left him to die with disdain
for what we could not consume.
And when he began to heave and thrash over yards of rock
to the water's edge and, unbelievably, in,
we couldn't hold him though we were teenaged
and bigger than everything. Could not contain
the old current he had for a mind, its pull,
and his body a muscle called river, called spawn.

Thanksgiving

On an afternoon so still it's possible to see
how the world can fill the holes we make
and complete itself again. Or how desperately
we want this to be so. Downstream,
Dad hauled an 18-pound pike into the boat
and we saw no change in the river.
Water closed as its tail left the surface,
continued to reflect for us what we needed
from clear sky, wild poplar, red maple,
from the last warm day of that year.

Near Bull's Head, mule deer wander the streets

of Estuary, a village abandoned when CN tore out
its only bridge for miles. That they feed
on wild onion and millet, from gardens flung
to seed, looked fine to us, if not holy,
though we knew people who had lived there,
who cried moving their beds from the valley.
Even Hutterite cattle blunting through wolf willow,
sweet sage ghosting around them,
seemed closer to the animal they once were.

We drove away at twilight, the fish curled
in a blue plastic basin, gills reaching for the place
that had so plainly surrendered it. Our heads
were full of how seldom we are together now,
and when my mother prepared the flesh
my father had provided, we took into ourselves
its longing to be home.

72 Miles

in memory of Ivor Solie

First week in November. A mild fall. Sandhill cranes have yet to rest in
stubble fields of the Wilde Hills on their way to wintering grounds in
California. The yard sleeps its ochre sleep. In his small house, a bulb
burning into the plain of noon attends all he has collected, the last
kindness a home offers to those who dwell alone, who broach the
question of their living in silence. Mute rush of crumbs, his work
clothes a husk on the floor. We think of him rising, washing, making
tea, and have only the sound of wind. A rural ambulance bore him
west past fragrant pastures, land at ease in fallow, crossed Alberta's
threshold in morning dark and hit asphalt a half-hour from Medicine
Hat, where we buy our guns and clothes. Our liquor. Our cures. The
Secondary 41 is more familiar than kin to us, how it winds around
ancient alkali sloughs, its fenceline climbing to the straightaway and
down to where the city lies in practical repose beside the river. To
where no one could stop his heart's return to itself as muscle.

When late July storms roll over the southern Sweetgrass ridge, birds turn quiet as plums. Thunder revs on electric air that drives the day's pressures before it, charging things with the animus shining behind the screen of the visible world, its mouth watering ozone breath and lightning forking from the black birthplace of funnels. Bone china rattles. There comes a time we must look away from the beauty of this gathering, this convergence of light and sound, time and space. The nothing that is everything at once. We remember strikes to the antennae on the roof, how as children we were sent to gather screws popped from the eaves and cooling in long grass as crickets crawled from under the foundation and began again to sing. Uncle. Brother. Brother-in-law. We are so few now the government has taken our doctors. It's 72 miles to town and half of these are gravel lined with sage and shotgunned signs. We pull together what we know, the contents of our own hearts' rooms so suddenly made strange to us.

The Bench

It's noon, hot, and you're wondering how you hoped
to find peace in a place that doesn't want you.
Decades ago, camping here with family, sweetgrass
and the book of stars seemed a gracious guide
to being in the world. Now you are merely something
for deer to avoid, and all you love
even less than that. Skulls of badger, red fox,
elk's long bones, bleach and settle in the way
things drained of instinct become a kind of stone. Land
neither remembers nor forgets. Battle Creek,
once red with blood, is clear again. Ice that carved
an ancient seabed north of Maple Creek
cracked on these granite hills, split east and west
to converge again southbound into Montana. This history
concerns you less than the accident of birth
that brought you here, local, to the borderland
between provincial parks. The girl you were found respite
from unending wheatfields in its meals of trout

and blessed shade, and you moved away imagining
a blue tent pitched forever by the lake. Mosquitoes
rise in tune from its muddy shore. Animals
light the evening lamps of their eyes and wait for you
to leave, for the city to reclaim you. Where
your new car fits the avenues precisely.

Nice

> *I think I'm kind of two-faced. I'm very ingratiating. It really kind
> of annoys me. I'm just sort of a little too nice. Everything is Oooo.*
> — Diane Arbus

Still dark, but just. The alarm
kicks on. A voice like a nice hairdo
squeaks *People, get ready
for another nice one. Low 20s,
soft breeze, ridge of high pressure
settling nicely.* Songbirds swallowing, ruffling,
starting in. Does anyone curse
the winter wren, calling in Christ's name
for just one bloody minute of silence?
Of course not. They sound nice.
I pull away and he asks why I can't
be nicer to him. Well,
I have to work, I say, and wouldn't it be nice
if someone made some money today?
Very nice, he quavers, rolling
his face to the wall. A nice face.
A nice wall. We agreed on the green
down to hue and shade straight away.
That was a very nice day.

Your Premiums Will Never Increase

Accidents can include permanent attributes of a thing; the technical meaning of the term is very broad.
— *Glossary*. Hellenistic Philosophy: Introductory Readings.

As if it couldn't wait. One would've kept driving
but for a wrecked air conditioner and record
high temperatures in the parkland. Who, cut off
at a blind approach and had it, cranked the wheel
toward a tourist trap to see a friend. The other,
in this company, was bold. They met by accident,

which is normal. That spring, a bear airlifted
miles from the townsite to a wilderness section
of the protected zone was back in four days. Warnings
were posted and generally ignored. Through
the summer they wrote each other on the loveliness
of this and that, in inevitable dialect, and surprised

themselves in bed. During a rare electrical storm
over Vancouver Island, a giant sequoia was split dead
centre. One half fell on a citizen's Saab, the other half
on his house. *What are the chances?* he laughed,
well-insured, to the press. Elsewhere, people won
prizes. Several more gave up. Others kept driving.

There are two kinds of motion, the straight
and the swerve. By winter, what passed between them
had done so, leaving evidence of the glitch winking
glib as a stripped screw. Sure, here was the trouble
all along. Some things don't turn out for the best,
and are not even interesting. Forget them. Because
this is about you, and what happens next.

Determinism

Someone's walking toward you, tree to tree, parting leaves
with the barrel of a rifle. There's a scope
on it. He's been watching awhile
through his good eye, you, washing dishes, scouring
what's burned with a handful of salt, so your shoulders shake
a little. Keep your back to him. It's sexier
under the bulb, light degraded,
like powder. The kitchen screens
are torn. You've worn something
nice. There's a breeze he's pressing through, boots
in the grass. There's a breeze and you smell him
blowing in on it. As if this has always
been happening and you've entered the coincidence of your life
with itself, the way a clock's ticks will hit the beat of a Hank Williams song,
the best one, on the radio, fridge hum tuned without a quaver
to the sustained notes of the bridge. As if
you've arrived at where the hinge
articulates. An animal
may be bleeding in the woods. He could be carrying a pair of grouse
by the feet. Only details are left, bruises of gesture, style's aspirin
grit. He shuts the door and leans the gun against the wall
like a guitar. You keep your back to him because
it's sexier. Because in turning
you will see the dinner in all its potential
as you speak, spring the catch, finish this, the weighted moment
buckling into consequence. The place
where you can face your history and see it coming.

Carmine Starnino

The Lesson

Anthony is standing outside his bedroom, calling for help.
For the last few minutes he has tried to turn his T-shirt around
after the initial error of slipping it on with the decal
behind him, and all he has been able to do is straightjacket
his left arm helplessly between his shoulderblades,
while his right hand hangs from the collar, twitching
like a snapped wing. He is breathing hard, a sweaty sheen
to his cheeks, but he tries again, turning and twisting
like an escape-artist struggling to unstrap himself from
a mismanaged trick, eyes closed like a saint overwhelmed
by a rapture that grips him by the body and won't let go.

First Kiss (Teresa)

Enrico stumbles out of the orchard, his right cheek burning.
There is a hiss, like rain on fire, as the field around me
turns up its underside in a sudden breeze. *Don't give it away*
Nonna once told me, *Make him pay a good price — that way
he'll want you more.* Sunlight was fluttering across the counter.
Nonna grabbed a fistful of feathers and tugged. *What about love?*
I asked her, *What if you love one another? Love is what
they tell you,* she said, *but once they get what they want
you're finished.* She cleared what remained from the wing
and tossed the chicken. If fell against the pile with a slap.

Navigation

The prettiest are hung, framed and flat under glass.
Others you draw down like a big window shade.
A quick tug, and they speed clatteringly upwards.

Of course, a forgotten packet of papers is always
mulling in some sea chest: a booty-print, soiled and salt-chewed,
with an X-marks-the-spot clue. Or this: in 1592,

a Portuguese, kerchief-sized navigational chart
two Dutch upstarts were clapped in irons for trying
to smuggle out. That, by the way, happened a lot.

Half-assed spy plots to unmurk the East Indies
in a tycoon scheme for trade. Portuguese galleons,
bunkers flush with spices, drugs, pearls and silk,

short-cut it home using state-secret Far East routes,
while Europe's direction-baffled merchant fleets
made do with chump-change goods. Those sham sketches,

jerrybuilt from rumour and the brags of adventurers,
reduced a few flag-proud sprints across the ocean
to epic ditherings on endless water, with the crew

scared stiff, adrift in that far-offness, that vast negligence
of hearsay, where each wave logged and ledgered
looked the same. (*No ifs-and-buts about it: we're lost,*

wrote one old salt. *And without the tiniest breeze to thumb a lift from,
though the hard-breathing sea's stirring up enough
of a draft to fuss with our spinnakers.*) But now with

our whereabouts debugged and the world's broad-
backed continents and sickle-shaped bays proofed against paraphrase,
now with bossy street guides telling us where to go

and the sea's cornerless distances feeling much too
fenced, and now that you even see yourself geographically —

a darkened spot experiencing a bout of low pressure

on a weather grid — you want to praise the exuberance
of those early cartographers, praise their whimsy
and wild bids. The guessed-at realms of Frisland, Drogeo,

and Icaria. And depictions which, in their heyday,
were steeped in weirdness: hooved man-monsters with eyes
epauletted on their shoulders, or rocs flying about

towing elephants in their talons, or a race of men
with a single foot the span of a parasol so that *In the hottest season
of Summer they lie along their backe and defend*

themselves with their foot against the Sunnes heat.
And what brought all this to mind wasn't the tale
of that lightfingered Dutch duo or the image of caravels

newly caulked and riding at anchor, clueless about
whatever coastline-connoitering plod they'll soon be
slowed to, but — of all things — your father and his

Columbus-confronting-the-flat-earthers frustration
when pressed with too many questions. "What the hell,"
he'd say, "Do you want me to draw you a *map*?"

Picking the Last Tomatoes with My Uncle

As if unearthed, they gave off the smell of damp loam;
a thick musk, like smoke, that made my eyes water
as we knelt together, our heads bent, and emptied
the plastic basins, crowding the tough, green fruit

on blankets along the cellar wall. *Devono tutti maturare*
he whispered to me while we worked — I stopped, drew one
back into my hand, and held it, its skin beginning
to flood with color, a lantern swelling with light.

On the Obsolescence of Caphone

Last heard — with lovely hiss on the "ph" —
August 1982 during an afternoon game of *scopa*
turned nasty. And now, missing alongside it,
are hundreds of slogans, shibboleths, small

depth charges of phrasing. Like an island-colony
of sea-birds screeching our own special cry,
I recall words all backwater squawk, recall
the curmudgeonly clunk and jump of their song,

a language dying out but always, someplace,
going on, surfacing in a shoe salesman's patter
or a grocer's chitchat, anywhere conversation's
an inventory of old expressions marked down

to near-nothing and preserved past all value,
spoken but never found on a page. Yesterday I listened
to some Italian roofers at work. Their hoots
guffaws and barkings-down to the truck. It was

buckaroo stuff, their dialect. Barisi, I think.
Eruptive, roguish, and hard-edged — a vigour
any poem would pestle to powder. But in the way
English can, by trumping up a term, pay out

something more interesting than you intended
— turn a smile into a smirk, make geese clack
overhead, or declare a birch's bole drubbed bare
by a storm — immigrant jabber can flush into

the open a new word that shivers in the surprise
and rush of its arrival, like that spurt of wine
my uncle, with a single suck on a plastic hose
threaded into a vat, would draw out, splashing,

into my glass. You *capish*? I say "immigrant"
but, really, what the hell do I know? A bunch
of banked-up bales I was never born to. Hey *stronzo*,
my uncle Louie would ring me early Saturday,

think you can take a little break from slapping
your dick around and help me? He dubbed it
'na giobba, said it'd be *'nu minuto*, but I knew
he'd be exasperated at my speed and call me

moosho-moosh and send me back to my book
— reading was making me too *stonato* for chores
he'd tell my father. Now I harvest my sounds
from men like these, key my jargon to the spontaneous,

try-it-on effects of their speech, diction gutsy
with curses, urge my poems to unschool themselves,
to roughen their step as they tramp and turn
to hoist and stack. No word too proud of its station.

No word dipped in oak-gall and soot. I want
a homemade vocabulary, tough-vowelled and fierce
for the sheetrock they shoveled, and the steel
they bolted with a ratatatatatat, and the bricks

they troweled with a one-on-two-bend-scoop-
spread-tap-settle; and the sledges they whanged! on iron.
For the meals they couldn't cook, but the rabbits
they'd gut after knocking their heads with a cut of wood.

For the plush boat-sized Chryslers they drove,
the two packs-a-day they puffed, and the grapes they grew
in gardens pegged-out with plums and pears,
apple trees grafted with five varieties of apple

and cherry trees spraying the ground with shade.
A word for their conviction that all you needed
was a wrench, a handshake, a little money down.
A word for the ends they never failed to meet

or the way they knew to drive a nail between
the haft's wood and head to rescue a hammer,
or the afternoons when, over espresso, they'd crack
that women need a slap or two, to feel wanted,

or the way they spoke, with mouths awakened,
mouths quickened by the volatile, unprissy,
impurifying syllables of *gabbadosta*, or *scimunito*
or *futtiti* — itself a good word for the situation

(No speak. *Stai zitto*. But me I was too much
Of a *chacciaron'* to stop and thus *scostumato*
is what I was called when I was rude enough
to talk back. *Le parole son femmine, e i fatti*

son maschi — words are female and actions male,
and they thought me *femminiello*, a bit faggoty
in my careful, English talk. So what's what?
My cousins ask when cornering me at weddings.

Well, you got gots is what you got. Go *zappa* —
go work in the fields. But I do, my friends, I do,
and I fear that when the Italian in me is done
scything his last square of grass he'll pick up

and go, and the speech I heard and, at times, spoke
will be the silence surrounding all my poems)
that might one day leave my poems illiterate.
I once dreamt of an eloquence like St. Ambrose's,

unblemished and discreet, lapidary and fluent,
augered by a swarm of bees hovering above
his infant mouth. Today, instead, I want my language
bashed to flinders and I will rummage among

its bits and scraps, its dwindlings and debris,
toting up the reusable versus the gone-for-good.
(And *futtiti*? It means ef-you-see-kay-e-dee).
I want to answer noise with noise, to hit upon

subtitles that fit the gist of what I hear. I always
thought of myself as an airborne assumption,
spored here from some other place, now I realize
I'm whatever comes across in the translation.

Song of the House Husband

Cherish it most when it steams —
"steam," though, fails to praise
its seethe of vapour, or, propped
upright, the suspirating hush as it catches
its breath. Flanks like the shins
of a ship or open halves of a mussel,
and, on its brow, the spirit-level's
impressionable bubble. Fructifying flatness,
it takes my trouser's frown, gives
back pleats. Takes my tired, tucked-in shirt,
makes it newly dapper. And really,
nothing's like the hiss of its hull
kissing a dampened dent (releasing
that rich, road-side scent of rain
on dust). Hope for the linens freckled
with folds. Hope for the crimped,
the crumpled, the crinkled, the crushed.
Hope for the rippled, the ruffled,
the rumpled, the rucked. O coffer
of creaselessness! I do not know
how to cut a straight furrow. I do not know
how to drive a batch of nails. But
grip your handle as I would a spade,
your heft the heft of a hammer.

The Last Days

And then there were birds inside our dryer duct.
Who'd have thought it fit for sparrows, two,
to be exact, I spied out days ago on the wire
and now, somehow, each brisked past the vent's

narrow neck (no bigger than my thumb) deep
into the tubing, a slimness through which, flattened,
they flowed, all chirrs and wing-whirrings,
as they flew off and returned, flew off and returned

to that fraction-of-a-fraction of a world, that squeeze-
yourself-small chamber. Amazing, that they'd
swap the ampler air for some daylight-snuffing aviary.
Amazing, that they'd trade their sky quiddity

to rattle around like moles in a seam of warm leaflessness,
a constant chirp and fidget I'd had enough of.
But you understood their bivouacking as cute, saw them
as some feathered truism of companionship

convening a valentine in our nook, and refused
to switch on the machine to blast them out, sensing an urgency
in their hurried departures and circlings-back
— carrying, what, twigs, leaves? — and you were right.

Soon there were chick-cheepings, six a.m. medleys.
Soon they were the one happiness in that house,
keeping us awake on separate sides of the bed,
each wondering if the other saw it as a good sign.

Good to Go

Small — a runt of a compass, really — with a tiny
bolt-hole hatch I lift on the needle cooped up inside.
The slightest toggle gives it a clock-ticking spin.
Useful for sailors and the sad at heart, all things

unanchored and adrift, all things bobbing in the blank
blue miles of strange southeasternmost quadrants,
new northwesterly latitudes. My marriage wasn't exactly
Here lieth monsters in wait, but more like I'd been

handed an old nautical map with whole countries
included on word of mouth and actual continents
casually left out. The compass was good, yet better
are those nineteenth century matrimonial charts

young grooms perused to avoid hazards like the Rocks
of Inconstancy above the Dead Lake of Duplicity,
and steer clear of — though if you must, make it short —
the Gulf of Self-Love near the Adulterer's Fort.

John Steffler

The Role of Calcium in Evolution

Sweet calcium we found we could live with,
stir into our cells' hubbub, tinker into
a trellis to carry our fierce red vine — its
eyeball blossoms, cunt orchids, cock orchids —
we could whittle it into stilts and paddles,
hooks, tongs, helmets, mallets, cleavers, awls,
rasps, rattles, tweezers, folding spokes,
but then, oh god the weight of all these
contraptions! Just throw them out and be
light! While the old bone hardware clatters
down like Victorian claw-foot settees
settling in scrap heaps — the ear trumpets,
the spurs compressed in archaeological
files — we float careless as fruit flies
in an armoury, all the weight lifted, trala!
But the dark rock candy of history dissolves
in the rain, leaking the diatom's binary
code, the lobster's molecular gospel into
the water we drink. Sleepless we pour over
Things You Can Make with Calcium in cellular
Braille. As soon as you throw something away
you need the damn thing! Hinged pincers
down here somewhere under the catapults and
greaves. Tell me how else to deal with the world!

Cape Norman

past the last house the gravel track widens to the horizon

and seeing better and better,
you negotiate the innumerable stones'
deepening textures — the wheel ruts' buttes and wadis
leading the eye down a long maze — until stopped
by the lighthouse

        the sea's plunge and assault, beyond
space, gannet-owned — the beacon's rolling blink,
the giant repeated groan like a conceptual monument
declaring our nation's response to the place:
a seizure
mechanically enacted for us all

at the mist-blown cliff you scramble down tumbled blocks
that were once bone —

        prehuman Egypt,
gods' jaws, twenty-ton lintels, upended stairs

blue shell ceramic flakes in thin drifts, salt-jewellery
fragments sharp on the palms

in a crevice, a tuft of white grass-hairs, bobbing —
pocked foreheads, worm script on the god's grey chins

daily for five hundred million years *The Palaezoic Times*
was delivered here — vast page laid upon page, accidents,

killings, jackpots, plagues, fused and fractured — you
crawl on the lost familiar text,
nylon hood flapping your ear

Book Rock

If all the used cooled blood gathered
in thick pools and became rock, organic
iron ore, and we mined it to forge steel,
    girders and rolled plate would
buzz with dense anecdote like limestone
walls — warm stone, bonestone — inside,
a humming saunter still carrying on

Barrens Willow

dumb giant, I have no words to fit what I find on Burnt
Cape: joints of a sprawled octopus-size tree — roots or
maybe branches meshed with a moss-clump shrub, alder?
bearberry? — its tiny various leaves

or this end tree, the other shrub?

what looks like a driftwood stick — white, gnarled: I reach
to touch — is hard as a porcelain handle bolted down, bone
beads stuccoed into the somehow live grain

leaf-puddle tree flush with the gravel it grows in — is
the willow something the great gull of winter shat
from the sky

unnatural snake twisting up from a cold cleft into sun,
opening a mouthful of leaves

it follows philosophy rather than habit, adopting any form
to suit its needs: trunk prone or upright, limbs fountaining
or burrowing

everything wants first of all something to hook to,
a seagull breast feather caught on a sedum stem, a father's
songs — a larch needle halts in the feather's lea — lichen
crumbs, moss dander sift in, a willow seed opens
a trunk of its mother's letters

Notes on Burnt Cape

frost causes rock to boil — wedging ice into cracks, it
splits stones, then slips its water blades deeper in,
levers them, spades the gravel up in rolling domes

on the scraped-bare cape each strewn boulder has a wind
shadow (pointing south-east) — a tapered green plant-woven
satchel stuffed with silt

trees, spilt like puzzle pieces, grow their branches
down among stones as though into air

you must lie down to distinguish the crowns of the willows
and birch

sky and sea vault away beyond reckoning — your car,
the road you followed, your house, you have to work
to recall

sometimes braided into the muscle of wind are clear
ocean sounds — waves leisurely sloshing, thumping, gulls'
reedy pleas or high slow staccato — rolled past the ear
in an intact bubble

Marie Uguay

Il existe pourtant des pommes et des oranges
Cézanne tenant d'une seule main
toute l'amplitude féconde de la terre
la belle vigueur des fruits
Je ne connais pas tous les fruits par cœur
ni la chaleur bienfaisante des fruits sur un drap blanc

Mais des hôpitaux n'en finissent plus
des usines n'en finissent plus
des files d'attente dans le gel n'en finissent plus
des plages tournées en marécages n'en finissent plus

J'en ai connu qui souffraient à perdre haleine
n'en finissent plus de mourir
en écoutant la voix d'un violon ou celle d'un corbeau
ou celle des érables en avril

N'en finissent plus d'atteindre des rivières en eux
qui défilent charriant des banquises de lumière
des lambeaux de saisons   ils ont tant de rêves

Mais les barrières   les antichambres n'en finissent plus
Les tortures   les cancers n'en finissent plus
les hommes qui luttent dans les mines
aux souches de leur peuple
que l'on fusille à bout portant   en sautillant de fureur
n'en finissent plus
de rêver couleur d'orange

Des femmes n'en finissent plus de coudre des hommes
et des hommes de se verser à boire

Pourtant malgré les rides multipliées du monde
malgré les exils multipliés

les blessures répétées
dans l'aveuglement des pierres
je piège encore le son des vagues
la paix des oranges

Doucement Cézanne se réclame de la souffrance du sol
                                        de sa construction
et tout l'été dynamique s'en vient m'éveiller
s'en vient doucement   éperdument me léguer ses fruits.

∽

maintenant nous sommes assis à la grande terrasse
où paraît le soir et les voix parlent un langage inconnu
de plus en plus s'efface la limite entre le ciel et la terre
et surgissent du miroir de vigoureuses étoiles
calmes et filantes

plus loin un long mur blanc
et sa corolle de fenêtres noires

ton visage a la douceur de qui pense à autre chose
ton front se pose sur mon front
des portes claquent des pas surgissent dans l'écho
un sable léger court sur l'asphalte
comme une légère fontaine suffocante

en cette heure tardive et gisante
les banlieues sont des braises d'orange

tu ne finis pas tes phrases
comme s'il fallait comprendre de l'œil
la solitude du verbe
tu es assis au bord du lit
et parfois un grand éclair de chaleur
découvre les toits et ton corps

∽

le cri d'une mouette crée la profondeur de l'air
divise les rues en espaces incertains
le vent est gris et sans effusion
et nous sommes assis à la table
où l'on a déposé des tasses de café des fruits
nous ne parlons plus
attirés par la fraîcheur de l'herbe et des nuages
et tout ce qui passe
projette ses ombres sur nos regards
la pièce sent le bois coupé et l'eau
dehors nous savons que tout se prépare
lentement à paraître

∼

il y a ce désert acharnement de couleurs
et puis l'incommode magnificence des désirs
il faut se restreindre à dormir à attendre à dormir encore
j'ai fermé la fenêtre et rentré les chaises
desservi la table et téléphoné il n'y avait personne
fait le lit et bu l'eau qui restait au fond du verre
toutes les saisons ont été froissées comme de mauvaises copies
nos ombres se sont tenues immobiles
c'était le commencement des destructions

∼

tout ce qui va suivre
maintenant t'appartient
des traces du rideau
et de la surface du sol
des plis du clair-obscur
à l'étang parfait de la nuit
et le mouvement très pur des respirations
le destin imaginaire des mains

c'est pour toi qu'il tremble
ce passage furtif et dérisoire
de clartés aux profondes strates
et l'ombre s'agrandit
au-dessus des montagnes
pour toi ce tremblement
qui complique l'espace
inaugure le déclin
de tant de splendeurs
toute la vacance
qui juge ses fleurs
et prépare ses fruits

∽

des fleurs sur la table d'une terrasse
des verres tintent
mais où est-elle donc cette ancienne histoire
de bonheur et de malheur cette pièce taillée dans le jour
où se tressent tant de propos et de songeries
et nous allions vers l'or la source et le rideau qui se lève
ou parfois une maison que l'on aurait connue en été
passant d'une chambre blanche à une chambre plus blanche encore
l'esprit s'ouvre
quand nous longions les vagues
l'air avait des lèvres

∽

il fallait bien parfois
que le soleil monte un peu de rougeur aux vitres
pour que nous nous sentions moins seuls
il y venait alors quelque souvenir factice de la beauté des choses
et puis tout s'installait dans la blancheur crue de réel
qui nous astreignait à baisser les paupières
pourtant nous étions aux aguets sous notre éblouissement
espérant une nuit humble et légère et sans limite
où nous nous enforcerions dans le rêve éveillé de nos corps

∽

Agnes Walsh

I Solemn

My mother scrubbed my face and braided my hair.
She told me to put on my dark blue corduroy dress,
the good thick one from Aunt Mary. She laid the crescent
of hat on her head and stuck a long white pin
with a pearled end into it. (And her head?) It
went in so deep but she didn't jump or cry out, or even wince.
What she did was pull the veil down from its fold until
it rested against her nose.

And gloves. Hers black and mine white.
"You must be very serious. And don't be scared, there's
nothing to be scared about. It's only death, and death can't
hurt you." She took me by the hand and closed the door
behind us and turned the key.

It was my first time for death. I was thought big enough.
So we walked down Swan's road to Mrs. Corrigan's.
The sun was all hallelujah and gave the grass that warm,
green smell. My friends were swinging in the playground,
singing "itsy bitsy teenee weenee yellow polka-dot bikini
that she wore for the first time today." "Look straight ahead,"
my mother said, "be solemn." And I was, although my shoes
pinched. I looked at the clouds moving

fast in the sky above and felt that shiver of life
when it holds you and shakes you between not knowing
and knowing *something*.
Men were outside the door smoking cigarettes
with tams pushed back, dressed up like Sunday.
One man moved himself off the door frame and said "Alice."
Mom said "Francis." Inside was like going into dark night.
The room was full of women and two nuns. Along the back

wall a long, black, shiny box, sleek as a trout. There were
rosary beads on laps and faces flattened with sorrow.

Up! I was swooped up and held above the box and
inside was the meringue of a lemon pie and a woman
lying in the meringue. Not really Mrs. Corrigan who used to
yell and chase us with the broom and tell us we should be
tied to the clothesline. She was far away, tired and cold.
"Kiss her on the hands," my mother whispered. My lips
felt pink, her hands felt white.

On the floor again I was given a triangle of ham sandwich
and a saucer of hot, sweet tea. "She's a grand good girl now
after going to a poor soul's wake." And all the women smiled
sorrowfully at me. And I solemn.

Solemn as could be.

Thomas

He wanted to be a body man in the car racket,
get his own cars and strip them down
then rebuild them like new.

I only encouraged him, started learning the year
of the cars and riddling them off.
As we'd turn the curve around Point Verde pond
and meet a 57 Chevy I'd call it out,
he'd purse a kiss at me and I'd edge in closer.
That was before seat belts.

Sometimes we'd stop the car below the downs
and devour each other whole.
That's the way it was.

I met him the other day in the parking lot
of the hardware store. His children were holding onto his legs,
their red heads aflame like his, still on fire in the evening sun.
He leaned onto the hood of his 62 Ford pickup and said,

you're still the same, girl, still the same.

Why don't you ask me what I'm driving, I said.
Well, all right then, what is it?
A horse and saddlebags, and in summer
a 650 Triumph opened up on Ship Cove Hill.

He threw his flaming head back and laughed.
It was an old joke about dreams.
I might have asked was he still a body man,
but I didn't. I wanted to imagine he still was.

Contacts

I never knew such a thing existed
I swear to God I never.

I was into Irving's and she came up to our table
and her blue eyes flooded me, I drowned in the blue.
I said, Oh my God, I never saw such blue eyes
before in my life, my God Almighty, I said,
you have the bluest eyes I ever saw. I was astounded.

She looked to the left and then to the right
to see who was listening, but I couldn't stop,
I had my head up almost in under her chin.
I mean, I said, I thought Elizabeth Taylor had blue eyes!
I thought Bob Dylan had blue eyes but. . .

She slapped the menu down on the table at us,
the heavy plastic thudding like a nun's strapper.
They're contact lenses, she hissed, they're goddamn
contact lenses. Do you want water with your meal?

When she gave us the bill she had her glasses on
and her eyes were grey or green or something.
I could hardly look at her. I thought she was lovelier but
I didn't dare tell her that then.

Frederick Ward

from **Riverlisp**
. . .

4. Fuss

a speckle thing —
just hardly wean
way from its mama

Fuss, the neighbor's (any neighbor's) kitten, walked in circles til she be exhausted   then lay down and half roll on her back pulling her body   end to end, in worm fashion; paws up whilest her head would stretch lean tween em, she to look at her roundness   and pink nipples which show'd thru the fur fuzz on her under side. She'd be murmurous   yowlin   — each a echo. Slower than the first. Then back up on her feets, circling her own circles, 'gin. Lord? Snap! As you please. In the middle of her circling, her back-half just fall to the ground — she not stopping but dragging — and quick silent "plup" out slides a baby kitten: FROM   HER   STOMACHS!   Little Etta let a yell, this happening right on the street in front of the Frolic Hotel. She and Skin, Etta's bald headed baby brother (six years he be) seen it all — "Skin?   look a that!"

Fuss, rise'd up on the ball of her paws. Hair, ears and tail all, rise'd up. She be spitting and snorting, hissing and gen'rally acting like she do when Jocko git at her. Skin, tried to STOMP! the baby cat but Etta reached grab'd him round the head from the back and pulled the boy way bout the time his foot would of got the thing   and 'stead of, made his whole body jerk stop in air, causing Etta to drop the child.

Skin were screaming and Etta apologising: "Shuddup Skin, you know'd I aint mean it" and trying to clamp her hand over his mouth — he bit her. Fuss be circling her baby kitten look like she gonna kill it her own selfs when "plup" nother baby — a spotted brown bread pudd'n looking one. Fuss jump! eyes wide and flaming a loud hiss spit; she started to gagging and shaking her head when "plup." That's right. This one all black. Skin swallow'd his crying and Etta Fry, just stood there silent. Lord, Fuss went on and laid out over by the door step to the Frolic, still hiss acting, her tail slicing the air and leaving her kitten babies "everything-less" at different stops long her circlings.

She aint want no part of them babies this being her first time being in a family way – she aint know'd what to do — til she calm down a while and begin acting she went round and sniff'd at them *hiss ready* then familiar like and lickin them. She picked one up by the head with her mouth Etta tensed. Fuss carried it some place.

• • •

6. Rufus

HE was laughing then cussing the last drop of wine filtered from the "good hole" missed his mouth, ran along the scar on his chin — mingled with his sweat down and hung around under his adam's apple. Mumbling to himself 'damn — if I could jest git this cat to shoot some craps.

"Listen hear man, I really believes the children aught to gits their education. I supotes the schools, you know?"

(which was true, every morning — like a truant officer — he'd be out shooin the children to school "git to school — damnit!")

'Yeah, hell. I pay tax on ever bottle of wine I buys and that moneys go to pay for schoolin, dont it? but I does think too, the children aught to be learnt to play the "numbers" cause in that way they'd know how to count and have some moneys besides hell them children up in new york does it! don't they — (shakin the words out of his mouth) — sure they do's."

In one motion: without asking he grabbed the man's hand pulling him down, he fell on one knee and came up with some craps in his hand   — rattlin   "that's the way we learnt, aint it, baby? Call it; what's it for?"   (the man did and won the next five.   "HOT DAMN!" m busted but that's all right baby no hard feelins. I'm go by us a bottle jest to show we's still friends."   (he did —)   "You drank first, buddy." As the man turned the bottle up   Rufus stabbed him in the neck and ran away laughing.

He got to his place still laughing   went in   dropped in a chair   and his hands fell between his legs. A minute passed   he became completely unnerved, his fingers discovering a hole in the seat of his pants   "damn only pair."

a sort of something happened to him:

Rufus thot on his life   the sightless child he saw himself to be   — hid his head in his arms and cried out: "O God, you could've changed all this. If you would've jest lead the way I would've gladly followed." He coughed   — more tears came —   his thots   "what the hell's the use?"

*"look at ME!
look at ME!
o Lord, what is I
got to do with this
world*

*what business
has you got to
conduct with me
that I cant
understand?"*

• • •

8. Blind Woman

"If you dont minds a blind woman, man you welcome to come with me; that is if you drives."

Juka done arranged it and the plan be made with such order and finesse that Juka be laughins so hard his eyes be watering and he be slobbering on himselfs: "Man, this is beautiful me and you, Micah man, we gonna give this woman a turn. Now, dig. She dont know and aint spose to know there be two of us, o buddy. So when we there dont you say a word. Did you wash off all that cologne stuff? Wash it! be sure dont want her smelling nothing and blowing our cool. Just acts natural and be quiet. She gots her own room at this Hotel Frolic we going to and so when we gits there, you go straight to the closet. AND CLOSE THE DOOR, MAN. Now when I . . . you knows . . . I'll excuse myselfs for to go to the toilet and then you come out and take YOUR PLACE" (they slap each other's palms) "the woman blind and wont know a thing."

Now gitting Micah into the hotel was another thing. But Juka figured out a plan: "Micah, you stay out here for one minute, then walk casually in and take th elevator up to th third floor. I'll meet you there."

Juka breath in hard and burst thru the front entrance of the Hotel Frolic, waving his hands and shout whispering: "Be cool, babies. The vice!" Now everybody in the lobby be caught off guard and went to doing something so the vice wont pay no tention to them not even talk to them. So when Micah walks in they dont see him much cause they dont want to see him and he is home free to the elevator and meets Juka and the rest happens just as planned, up to the time the blind woman feels a need to explore and reaching to Juka-Micah's head runs her fingers in thru a SCREAM'D LOUD all in one motion: "Who in the hell is YOU?"

Micah is suddenly thrown to the side of the bed, the woman scratching and kicking in space: "Juka! JUKKKKKA!"

Micah reached to pull his pants up but his "O NO"s! 'to realize he has no pants on and tipping off the woman as to his whereabouts.

Micah ketch stops the woman's hands fore they nails tore into his flesh: "Excuse me lady, my name is Koch? I aint here to hurt you. In fact, I sells books of the *good word* and I know you'll want to hear something that'll bring you peace. Just let me show you this wonderful book covered in white ivory with the master works of Leonardooooo . . . !"

The woman's foot connecting and Juka rushing into the room, pounding his palms together   eyes bulging: "Aw man, you done blew it!"

Micah and the woman roll fall to the floor   Juka grabbing Micah, they clothes — the blind woman still as afore and flip-floppin like a fish on sand: "JUKKKKA!"

Juka passing out whatever piece of clothing hits his hand to Micah: "This aint mine, Juka!"

"Hell with it, come on!"

No one payed tention to the running commotion and screaming at all. They just thot   *know'd*   the vice done caught somebody else and didnt want to git involved.

A Pattern of Escape

Mind you doesn't tramp
Out the sound of leaves

Nor let the mud suck
Escape from your ankles and

Bare your presence to the captor
Be the image of your Lord:

A thief in the night
Come'd collect your soul

Spirit yourselfs to the tip
Of the drinking gourd:

North to Canada — and when
The mother of the heavens:

THE MORNING STAR, smiles on you,
Rising in the east shortly before the sun

It's a warning.
Seek out a hiding place.

Dialogue # 3

Old Man (To the Squatter)

— Listen here, son. Did you think this were gonna work?
Were you fool enough to think this were gonna work?
They ain't gonna let us put nothing up like that and
leave it. They don't intend to let us git it back. You
ain't gonna git the land back with no shack on a mound.
That ain't why you put the shack out there. Africville
ain't a place. Africville is us. When we go to git a
job, what they ask us? Where we from . . . and if we say
we from Africville, *we are Africville*! And we don't git
no job. It ain't no place, son. It were their purpose to
git rid of us and you believed they done it — could do it!
You think they destroyed something. They ain't. They
took away the place. But it come'd round, though. Now that
culture come'd round. They don't just go out there and
find anybody to talk about Africville, they run find us,
show us off — them that'll still talk, cause we Africville.
NOT-NO-SHACK-ON-NO-KNOLL. That ain't the purpose . . . fer
whilst your edifice is foregone destroyed, its splinters
will cry out: *We still here*! Think on it, son. You effort
will infix hope in the heart of every peoples. Yet,
let's see this thing clearer. If our folk see you in the
suit, we may git the idea we can wear it. The suit might
fall apart, but son, it be of no notice. We need the
example. Now go back . . . and put your dwelling up again.

Najean

The missus was nice to me
'til she caught me dreaming one day

She soft-voiced herselfs
right into my gazings — asked of me:

> *"What you mooing in the
> fields about, Najean?"*

And I says it afore I thought who she be.
I blurts it right out:

> *"CANADA!"*

She slapped me so hard
I come'd erect

Stood dizzy with no movement,
the blow turning me round insides myselfs —

my apron come'd undone:
the straps fell to my sides

and tickled my arms...
I hiccuped.

From Who All Was There

Mary

Most I have were my fears and a hatchet when I
crossed over into Canada . . . I took my first night
in liberty high on a tree branch next of . . . all
as I could tell, a bird in shivers with its head
hid mongst a wing . . . I hummed to it to calm our
fears . . . give me confidence that the bird ain't
fly away during the night . . . be a sign to me,

owning up to my being human, that even not something shivering next to me I could consider with
a friendliness. Am I human. They never give me a
good characteristic to go on. Even my songs be
filled with the guilt grafted onto my soul. I
wanted to touch the bird but to do that I haves
to let go the branch and I'd lose my hold to it
cause my other hand grasped my hatchet.

The Lord do send us some tests, don't He? Breakfast be one of them. In the middle of my pity for
the bird . . . sunrise on my soul! I got hungry.
Since the bird's head were still neath its wing,
it had no head . . . I considered it cooked like the
fowl I served in bondage . . . and since it continued
to shiver, I thought what a mercy I'd bring to it.

But had not this been the lie what got me here:
were I not dead cause I possessed no tongue understood . . . were it even not a mercy, a right to beat
me cause I shivered with fear . . . have I not used it
gainst my own for proof? Am I mad? I am split
from my most confident self-assumption . . . yet the
Lord send a grace in some stranger's hand: a prayer
and a epistle . . . set my mind in *"the possibility"*
what changed the quality of my thought . . . kept it
safe whilst I seen them go crazy with their makings:
realized a spirit in me not noticeable as they checked
my teeth . . . snatched what be theirs from tween
my legs to beat on and chew on it . . .

The bird flown away . . . left its shiverings on the
branch and I climbed down into snow.

Yet Among-Us

She sometimes —
Goes off into rural thinking.

Says:
— It's the new music alright.
Playing to themselfs.

Moved out
And off from the woodshed and at best:

Like a pimple journeyed to the tip of the nose,
Ready to burst and spread all over the place.

I ain't looking into eyes
Listening for words.

I'm listening!
For the tone in every voice what died with all
Those who taught me everything.

Me Grandaunt

to Don Darlington

Her last days she sat at the kitchen table and done
nothing but stare at me. I'd mouse into the kitchen
and at the table I'd hide behind the cereal box with
me face so close to the cereal bowl it'd criss-cross
in me eyes and make two cereals. Sometimes I were the
cereal, in me eyelids, staring up at meselfs. I CAIN'T
TAKE IT would come in on me and I'd raise me eyes
— slit at a time — just slowly above the edge of the
cereal box. In the *"perceivable,"* her eyes were in
mine — even not squint quickly shut, and blind I'd slow-
sink back below the box into me cereal bowl — sometimes
up to as many times as what I could count, I'd done it.
Once the cereal tickled me nose:

— A knot of ancestors'll
ring you
keep your trouble tied to you
'til you surmounts it, son
Her voice raised in me as a sneeze.

On what were her last morning, she waited for me at the
table: no cereal box — and as I slid, head down, into me
chair, me grandaunt shoved towards me, one of the two
bowls of grits afore her. There were an old spoon in it.
Me head were bowed so, that breath sweat come'd on the
table top. Bird knuckles and fingers they were what
scooted it along . . . paused . . . made a fist: shook and jit-
tered up some more strength and courage, nudged it tilt
'til the bowl reached me — it were a winter getting to me.
  — Take this bowl of grits, son.
The pointing in her finger says it . . . in six waggles done it,
and in back of it, fuzzed through me eyebrows, were the
image of her breasts: swelling in some dignity and sinking
just below the edge of the table top. I quick-reached for
the bowl but missed: me hand come'd down on the end of the
spoon handle and flicked free some grits. The ancestors
raised me eyes up out of me heart: a little grits were on
the tip of her nose . . . her stare come'd of no change.

I slid from me seat . . . pushed it to the sink . . . climbed and
turned on the water tap. I wet a dishrag and retraced me
steps... went *"dutifully,"* me head still bowed, to wipe way the mess . . .
done it all the time in her stare whilst thinking on what
to do about her face. Then acting out her dignity, I
postured meselfs proud and allowed me decision to rise up
in me. I straightened me bowed head . . . into her stare: into
a frozen oval of lip: laughing, what have no sound . . .
Me grandaunt were gone.

Enos Watts

The Grandmothers of Argentina
Los Disaparecidos: the search for the grandchildren
for Golda

The women no longer walk
in the Plaza de Mayo
with placards
like icons raised
in religious processions —
the faces, names
of their lost sons and daughters

And the dark-eyed generals
have disappeared
from Casa Rosada

But in a land's healing season
wounds in the earth,
like the heart's wounds,
are open again; the women
must weep in the grief
of their knowing
as bones are lifted
into the sun

So cold an economy: one grave
for the family, bound
as they were
in their nakedness,
after the dark arrivals,
the boot to the door,
the last journey

Now under the light
the riddle of small empty boxes —

Can the bones of a child dissolve?

They were the young
who survived,
swallowed up
by their own cities,
vanishing into strange houses, stamped
with counterfeit names
There must be a thousand
in Buenos Aires alone,
no one knows

You discovered me, Grandmother,
like a new star
They call me Juanita
You tell me
my name is Maria Eugenia

Sometimes torture, even
the threat of death
will not rouse memory, will not
break a witness's silence
But there is one silent
eloquent witness:
a child's blood remembering
a grandmother's blood

The women no longer walk
in the Plaza de Mayo
They have placed their separate griefs
on private altars

A woman dreams the face of a child;
but there is no name
no familiar face
for her waking quest
She fears her own death
before the child is old enough
to ask who she is,
fears this even more
than the reach of the past,
more than the maze of a city.

Darren Wershler-Henry

from Ten Out of Ten, or, Why Poetry Criticism Sucks in 2003 (2003)

Ten Out of Ten: 3

Jeff Derksen — *Dwell*
(Talonbooks, 1993)

One of the cool things about Jeff Derksen is that it's hard to tell whether he's a genuine shit-kickin' redneck or actually the kind of good-for-nothing smartass punk that rednecks would sooner stomp all over than talk to. Regardless of bestseller status or deliberate lack thereof, along with Kevin Davies's *Comp.*, Dorothy Trujillo Lusk's *Redactive*, Lisa Robertson's *Debbie: An Epic* and Dan Farrell's *Last Instance* and *The Inkblot Record* duo, Derksen's *Dwell* ranks as one of the most consistently brilliant books produced by the Kootenay School of Writing. And of the bunch, it's definitely the most crazy from the heat, the near-unanimous fave Derksen text (his second after *Down Time*). We were damn near raised on this book and it still reads fresh today. Aside from the reflective "Temp Corp," the entire text sizzles with typewriter party action, proudly driving home kick-ass summer rockers like "Interface" and the long-striding, glorious "Hold On To Your Bag Betty"; plus chunky notebook monolith "Neighbourhood" and the book's biggest, most timeless classic, "If History Is the Memory of Time What Would Our Monument Be." Hot rockin' and brimming with confidence, *Dwell* is a non-stop road trip of southern-fried licks, the essential beer-stained 8-track soundtrack for your next Kelowna bender. Ride on . . .

(original text: review of Foghat, *Fool for the City*)

• • •

Ten Out of Ten: 5

Steve McCaffery — *The Black Debt*
(Nightwood Editions, 1989)

One of the most formidable artistic panoramas of all time, *The Black Debt* is the tour de force from a writer fraught with the demons of genius. One giant leap beyond a universe wholly self-created, into detailed worlds fully incomprehensible in mere language, Steve McCaffery traps then emanates an unwilling and vengeful muse into the deepest, fullest, and most colourful drama of psychoses ever ventured. Punishingly lead-poisoned or punishingly dulled by ether, *The Black Debt* is a frightening cascade of contrasting activities, all tied with a thread of verbal dementia from a writer bent on mutually pained destruction. Far beyond evil, this is an unearthly but man-made and administered programming, focused on a slow erosion of thought processes. From "Hegel's Eyes"-style noisefest "Lag," one envisions fearful glimpses of the apocalypse, which then descends to roost on the neck through riff monster "An Effect of Cellophane," a relentless tirade leading to an awful conclusion, Hell in a taxicab, redemption through pummelling. (And on the cover, "Monotony Test": a rodent better left unexamined.) The original coma of souls, *The Black Debt* refuses to move as if heard outside of time, essentially personified as one piece, one moment, one nightmare, yet schizophrenic, split, a ludicrously progressive, break-the-rules outpouring of ideas from the complexity of human brains blow skyward. Forget loving this book, as you may do with many other of your personality's black inky building blocks; for love, hate, anger and indeed pedestrian human processes of any kind have no seed here. View *The Black Debt* with only the cold, detached nerve ends of your intellect. All other approaches will meet certain death in collision with an unconceded, unrepentant, unimaginable collection of psychic machinery.

(original text: review of Black Sabbath, *Sabotage*)

Ten Out of Ten: 6

Ken Babstock — *Days into Flatspin*
(House of Anansi Press, 2001)

Days into Flatspin is Ken Babstock's most formidable masterpiece to date, quite possibly and paradoxically the most moving collection of rural Canadian lyrics of contemporary times, a book written by a downtown Toronto-dwelling Newfie raised in the Ottawa Valley that soundly crushes the aspiration of all poets with the hopes of someday being the first to create that elusive perfect, quintessentially georgic marriage of formalist and post-Black Mountain styles. Karen Solie has the heart, Doug Barbour has the finesse, and Dennis Cooley is the best at making us forget all our troubles, but it takes the mighty *Flatspin* to forge it all into one devastating weapon, adding a measured dose of futility to make it really cry the blues. *Days into Flatspin* is the soundtrack for genuine red-blooded recreation, for sitting on the porch, surrounded by weeds, in the middle of nowhere, with a rifle on your lap, smoking dope, waiting for something to move. It's got the most backwoods, fog-locked, no-influences resonance of any contemporary Canadian collection of lyrics to ever really let fly, even when riding the most agonised pedal-steel jams inked to page, as gloriously evidenced on the ferociously poignant "Public Space," "To Only Occasionally Ever Actually Look," "Carrying someone else's infant past a cow in a field near Marmora, Ont.," and classic highball "Drinker." Something just smokes entire bales of ditchweed about this fiercely lonesome collection from start to finish, despite some deep-seated mellow moments ("He Considers Nihilism from Inside a Culvert") and successful attempts at less adorned, light-hearted boogie ("The 7-Eleven Formerly Known as Rx"). All segues by sundown into a time-weary violence, making *Days into Flatspin* a major masterwerk of sonic earthtones. Best experienced in an alcoholic haze, utterly and ecstatically alone.

(original text: review of Status Quo, *Quo*)

• • •

Ten Out of Ten: 10

Kenneth Goldsmith — *No. 111 2.7.93 – 10.20.96*
(The Figures, 1997)

All balderdash and beauty, total trope and tremendousness, *No. 111* is the ultimate Warhol Factory full of infinitely-faceted rhymes in "er," maze-like alphabetical syllabic progressions and plagiarism unrestrained, a budding conceptual writer's dream, unlocking the treasure chest to cut-and-paste flights of fancy, and exercise in keyboard digitalis and syllable counting, wayward literary discipline and mystical wattage in the hear and now. I won't even get into the meaning of the title; suffice to say that this book is an obtuse textual explosion infuriating the writer's detractors with renewed vigour: direct resplendent descendant of the Oulipo and Douglas Huebler but with all the mechanics gone mad, a Sorcerer's Apprentice parable for the word-processing era. It kicks off with a manic monosyllabic abecedary — classic, hyperbolic, heavy, all hiccups and furtiveness as Goldsmith lays down the opening salvo. Next come the two-syllable rhymes, sandwiched together like plywood power chords, the progressive and the sublimely melodic. Finally, in a highly informative display that is the essence of totally unbridled verve (and nerve), all 7,228 syllables of "The Rocking-Horse Winner" caring nary an iota for the inevitable disbelief of a world briefly distorted by postmodernism. Hard to believe, perhaps, but I see a certain raw, intellectual anarchy, here let loose in the hands of a player rather than a bullshitter. Fact is, those who try to dis Goldsmith can't help but notice that *No. 111* stands up a heap taller than anything growing out in Iowa or haunting the chapel at St. Mark's. Hard work, no matter how misdirected, will always result in some sort of permanence.

(original text: review of Rush, *Hemispheres*)

• • •

Zoe Whittall

Stiff Little Fingers

Out of boredom, I was in love with the boy who sold drugs in the parkette across the street from my first apartment.

He worked at the graveyard on Mount Royal. Wore human bones around his neck. He smelled like I imagined a rock star would: gamey and gross but in a sexy way.

"You know, it's not like a final resting place. If your family doesn't pay up, you're outta there to make room for paying customers."

He sees bodies every day. No wonder he never calls his mother, has a heroin "situation," that look, that smell. At my telemarketing job I think about his long fingers
cupping my shoulders, his greying lips kissing mine.

After a month, he'd topped my earthy pile of loser ex-boyfriends. He called too much. Owed me money. Probably stole my bike, the cherry one with the skull-and-crossbones stickers.

People say he's in jail, rapping his knuckles against the iron bars, scraping skin. Thinking of me, maybe, wearing his old plaid shirts as I paint my new apartment. Looking for another guy who takes himself too seriously, or just takes too much.

I love the addicts, they'll never put me first. A piece of the pie — in the grand scheme of things, I will only be a piece. Always out of reach. My own fingers, out of his.

Six Thoughts on a Parkdale Porch

1.

Last fall I had a wisdom tooth pulled by a macho dentist whose nitrous machine didn't work. Through the window I watched a woman in cut-off sweatshorts throw her red pumps at a guy in plaid pants while the dentist sewed up my three stitches.

He called me tough.

My lover kept the tooth in a small tube meant for cocaine on a string around her neck. I mistook her action for devotion when it was simply the act of accessorizing.

2.

I like the first day of a bruise waking.

A June bug is making out with the porch light again.

S m a s hing up and burning, repeat: a giant ladybug with vertigo.

The dog barks at the ceramic bunny who was made to smile constantly. Porch ornaments.

I feel defeated pinching the bruise around its edge; my thumb and fingernail are making skinny hearts.

Starving is not holy.

3.

I'm nervous. Expecting sutures instead of flat skin.

I am waiting.

My eyebrows are giving me panic attacks.
Two perfect circle blisters.

4.

Toronto Welcomes the Pope. Suddenly even the guy who punches people outside the 7-11 is a believer.

Pilgrims are selling memorabilia on my way to work at the café on
Roncesvalles. Uniform-red shoulder bags walking in packs, singing
hymns.

Indignant invasions around my red streetcar seat.

Two giant blue cups of water for the pregnant woman at table #2.

The cops sweep up undesirables —
please step back and allow the holy visitors to enjoy
an unobstructed view.

I sweep up the café floor.

At 3 a.m. on Church street, red-shouldered boys with Jesus t-shirts
kiss each other on the steps outside Second Cup. Ecstasy jaws and
groping in the shadows, where the Lord was not invited.

5.

I almost died in a freight elevator on my way to get laid
by someone twice my age I couldn't even really talk to.

I chewed my nails until they bled, watered down prayers
when the box went black and the cables paused.
Ridiculous faith when fingers crossed.
I wish I may, I wish I might.

The click and whir of being saved

by invention.

6.

Today, I kicked the bank machine.

The mechanics of frustration; other people's receipts stuck to my
boot.

Patricia Young

The Fire

Suddenly this boy is too old
for plastic army men dressed in battle fatigues.
After dinner he hangs around the back steps,
bored and indignant and kicking up dust:
why can't he take the raft he's hammered together

into the middle of the bay? We're doing the dishes
when he slouches in. *Can I dig a pit, put rocks around it,
and build a fire?* It's been a wet summer
so we say yes to the fire and the great, green,
unignitable forest. For three days now

we've carried his meals out to where he's hunkered down
at the edge of a pit in a derelict lawn chair —
an old man chewing tobacco and staring
at nothing. Each morning he breathes
life into it and each night douses it with water.

He loves its insatiable appetite, feeds it crumpled
newspapers, broken branches, he cares for
this fire as though it were a lame rabbit
found in the woods. Tonight the indistinct figure
stabs at dying coals, waves

a glowing stick through the dark.
And what does he write across the sky, what blackboard
message after childhood but before girls
dive into his eyes? So much
has been forbidden —

slingshots, firecrackers, deep water.
But for now he is motherless, all crusty
hair and sooty face, a cave-boy
entrusted with something dangerous and
he will not leave it.

Grocery List

I don't want you meandering in the aisles.
You're not on a luxury cruise.
I know you, how you loiter

in the meat with finely dressed
women, gathering tips
on rare cuts and choice prices.

Bleach as you can see
is foremost on my mind.
The wonders of bleach fill my thoughts

like an invisible stain.
A thimbleful is all I'd need to disinfect
the words I've poured like germs

as in this crisp white page.
The items which follow should reveal
how I package my dreams:

oysters crammed into rectangular
tins. Head on the pillow, I settle
like a cornflake, years past expiry date,

stale and boxed in. But you'll miss all this.
I've always said you read too quickly.
Such subtlety will fly

over your head like the sound
of a cash register. When I tell you
I want the cheese sliced,

the bread soft, and the avocados ripe,
what I mean is, it's time we developed
new eating habits, what I mean is

we're ready for change. Am I being
too explicit, too painfully allegorical
when I tell you the cart you push past

the dried fruit is my heart and I want you to fill it?
When I write *salad makings*
am I being too obscure?

When I underline
tomatoes do you understand
how necessary they are? For colour, I mean,

although you have fallen for some salads,
good-looking and all green. (Think of it:
artichoke hearts bearing themselves

on lettuce leaves, proud without shame,
like women on centrefolds. To be
that camouflaged, to be so unseen!)

Jan Zwicky

Driving Northwest

Driving Northwest in July before
the long twilight that stretches into
the short summer dark, despite the sun
the temperature is dropping, air
slips by the truck, like diving,
diving,
       and you are almost blind
with light: on either side of you
it floats across the fields, young barley
picking up the gold, oats white,
the cloudy bruise of alfalfa
along the fencelines, the air itself
tawny with haydust, and the shadows of the willows
in the draw miles long, oh it is lovely
as a myth, the touch of a hand on your hair,
and you need, like sleep, to lie down now
and rest, but you are almost
blind with light, the highway
stretched across the continent
straight at the sun: visor,
dark glasses, useless against its gonging,
the cab drowns in it, shuddering, you cannot tell,
you might be bleeding or suffocating, shapes
fly out of it so fast there's no time to swerve:
but there is no other path, there is no other bed,
it is the only way home you know.

Prairie

And then I walked out into that hayfield west of Brandon,
evening, late July, a long day in the car from Nipissing
and long days in the car before that; the sun
was red, the field a glow of pink, and the smell of the grasses
and alfalfa and the sleek dark scent of water nearby. . .
I remember — now — chasing something underneath the farmhouse table as a child
and seeing the big hasp on the underside that locked the two main leaves: it seemed
rough and enormous, out of keeping with the polished surfaces
it held together, almost medieval, I was startled and a bit afraid; and later
as an adult, fumbling for it, blind, at the limits of my reach,
how finally it would let go with a sharp jerk and the leaves
would sigh apart: but it was there,
in that hayfield, that I felt some rusty weight in my chest stick
then give, a slow opening to sky —
                        it was that hasp, I know it now,
though at the time I did not recognize I was remembering,
nor, had you told me, would I then have known why.

Robinson's Crossing

        They say
the dog was crazy that whole evening:
whining at the door, tearing
around the yard in circles,
standing stock still in the cart track,
head cocked, whimpering.
They'd left him out and gone to bed, but he
kept barking until after midnight
when they finally heard him take off
down the railbed, east,
toward the river. Next morning
Ernest said he'd met him
a half-mile from the house. The train
had got in late but he'd
been eager to get home, so walked

the eight miles from the crossing
at the steel's end. They had finished
with the harvest down south, he had money
in his pocket. He was
two days early,
but the dog had known.

                My great-
grandmother slept
in a boxcar on the night
before she made the crossing. The steel
ended in Sangudo then, there was
no trestle on the Pembina, no siding
on the other side. They crossed
by ferry, and went on by cart through bush,
the same eight miles. Another
family legend has it that she stood there
in the open doorway of the shack
and said, "You told me, Ernest,
it had windows and a floor."

                The museum
has a picture of the Crocketts —
later first family of Mayerthorpe —
loading at the Narrows
on the trail through Lac Ste. Anne.
Much what you'd expect:
a wagon, crudely covered,
woman in a bonnet on the box seat,
man in shirt sleeves
by the horses' heads, a dog.
But what draws the eye, almost
a double-take, are the tipis
in the distance, three of them,
white, smudged — a view the lens
could not pull into focus.
And another photo,
taken in the '30s maybe,

of a summer camp down on the river flats
between our quarter and the town.
At least a dozen tipis; horses, smoke.
By the time I was a kid,
they'd put the town dump there;
but I remember we picked arrowheads
out of the west field every spring
when it was turned. And a memory
of my uncle, sharp, impatient with
my grandfather for lending out
his .22 to Indians:
last time, didn't he remember?,
he never got it back.

                 Robinson's Crossing
is how you come in to this country, still —
though it's not been on a map
since 1920, and the highway
takes a different route. You come in,
on the backs of slightly crazy Europeans, every time
you lift your eyes across a field of swath
and feel your throat catch
on the west horizon. It's the northern edge
of aspen parkland, here —
another ten miles down the track,
the muskeg's getting serious.
But my great-grandfather was right:
cleared, seeded, fenced,
trees left for windbreaks and along
the river's edge, it looks
a lot like England.
You could file
on a quarter section for ten dollars;
all you had to do to keep it
was break thirty acres in three years.
The homestead map shows
maybe two in three men

made it. Several of their wives
jumped from the bridge.

              There's no mention
in the local history book
of how the crossing got its name.
I found a picture of an Ernie
Robinson — part of a road gang
in the '20s — and of an old guy,
Ed, at some town function
later on. There's also
a photo of a sign, undated, shot
from an extreme low angle, as though
whoever took it had been standing
in the ditch beside the grade. I'll show you
where it was: just go out
the old road from the RV park, west,
about two miles. Nothing there now
but a farmer's crossing and a stretch
of old rail in the ditch. I'm guessing
that they closed it
when the steel moved on
after the war.

              A few years back
I was out behind the old house
picking twigs. (TransAlta
had come in and taken out
a poplar — it had left
enough junk in the grass
my mother couldn't mow.)
The rake had clawed
the grass out, more than
it had piled up twigs,
so I was squatting, sorting
dirt and grass by hand. The smell
was mesmerizing: musty, sweet,
dank, clay-ey; green —
and with a shock I realized

what it was: the same smell
as my family. Not because
our boots and gloves
were covered in it, nothing
you could shower off — it was
the body's scent, the one
that's on the inside
of your clothes, the one a dog
picks up. Our cells were
made of it: the garden, and the root
cellar, the oats
that fed the chickens, and the hay
the steers.
                    These days

the line north of the farmhouse
carries only freight,
infrequently; the highway's
being twinned; Monsanto
just released another herbicide-resistant
seed. Before the drought,
the river flooded every time it rained —
no trees upstream; this year
it's lower than it's been
since someone started
keeping records. The wooden
elevators, gone or going; ranks
of concrete silos that read
Agricore in flowing nineteenth-century
script — it's why

the story matters, why it
puzzles me. Here comes
my great-grandfather, he has made
Robinson's Crossing, he is walking
toward us, bone-tired
but whistling, it's a fine night, he has
money in his pocket,

and the dog, the family dog
is going out to meet him.

Another Version

Look, all I can tell you is
there was a car, big, dark blue,
a late-'40s Ford sedan; and rain,
and getting stuck, and rain and rain.
Forcing the back door wide enough
to struggle out, the ruts
shin-high, the gumbo
slick and shiny in the half-light,
gunmetal, the wet-iron
smell of it.
And how it packed itself
like pie dough in the wheelwells,
the scuffed burr of the spinning tires,
the men cursing and grunting as they rocked it,
exhaust thickening the drizzle
and the hubcap logo stopping upside
down, then right side up, then
upside down. And that we had to wait
until the tractor
came: the clank-whump
as the chain drew taut, the lunge,
the heave, the drunken
fishtail as we broke
the suck; and maybe also, thinking
even then that we'd misundersood,
had failed to grasp the meaning
of that monstrous union between
car and road, its refusal
of intent.
As though they knew, wanted
to save us. And we drove on.

Work

              On Tuesdays,
we would drive into the town.
Small town, long drive. Sometimes,
there might be something wrong,
a machine part broken or a twitchy
tooth. But mostly we just picked up
tea and flour and the mail. For the work
was on us then; we needed
next to nothing: work
like a spell of good weather
you know is going to hold, that mix
of surprise and deep contentment
in the morning when you draw the blinds:
of course. Something about
the arc of destination, its
updraft of light: work carries us
the way love can, but with
less sorrow. That whole summer
I wore mismatched laces in my boots,
one red, one white, because I knew
no order could improve upon
the one that gripped me: the world
unrolling like a field of daisies
in July, the truckbox full of tinned beans,
bread and beer, the road
tireless in its rise along the cutbank,
seared cries of the cicadas,
the dust, the heat.

Soup

O, lake of gardens
and with bread
one flesh,
you dwell
in roundnesses,
body of rain.
Not tea,
which throws
the towel
around our neck, says
get back out there,
keep your left
up.
You
say nothing,
make our toes
grow roots.
In stew
is brotherhood,
the warm mess
of connection and
the hide-hung
cave,
but soup,
you give us back
our earth-self
under
open sky.
O, Bolivar
of the sinuses,
Buddha
of the placemat:
you are
that letter
in the mother tongue
we wait for
all our lives.

Aspen in Wind

Little tree, tree of slopes and coulees
and wolf-willow scrub, tree of seven
months of winter and a two-week spring,
of childhood and the endless

sky of loss, I've come
for the light in your leaves,
those brief mosaics of starched silk, the rill
and sifting of the August air against

the speechless blue, for this light like light
off water gurgling past the snowbank in the first
real thaw, for shade, for the rest
of weightlessness, I've come

to close my eyes
under the bright wind of summer,
the light-in-water of the wind in your leaves,
the starched silk of their rushing, that quilt

of sorrow and of light.
What is the light for
but to lie down in? What is sorrow for
but to lie down in.

Bill Evans: "Here's That Rainy Day"

On a bad day, you come in from the weather
and lean your back against the door.
This time of year it's dark by five.
Your armchair, empty in its pool of light.

That arpeggio lifts, like warmth, from the fifth of B minor,
offers its hand — *let me
tell you a story* . . . But in the same breath,
semitones falling to the tonic:
you must believe and not believe;

that door you came in
you must go out again.

In the forest, the woodcutter's son
sets the stone down from his sack and speaks to it.
And from nothing, a spring wells
falling as it rises, spilling out
across the dark green moss.
There is sadness in the world, it says,
past telling. Learn stillness
if you would run clear.

Three Mysterious Songs

Lost Music

I was standing at the window,
maybe it was winter,
maybe it was raining. Anyway,
not pacing anymore.
I hadn't tried the door
in months.
          Who was it, then,
pausing on the other side
and looking in? That glance,
a firm sweet hand that pulled my gaze
to my own limb; the limb, where
dried, clean, open to the bone,
I saw that wound.

Music's Breath

Sorrow, I raise my hands to you.
So little we understand!
I was idling there
among the carved woods and the scented boxes,

and I know that it was love
saw me. But when it spoke,
it was your voice that said my name.

Forgotten Music

On the south and east
the house was open to the weather.
We moved inside it
sombrely, like ships,
and did not raise our eyes.
When death came, it came
as wild grass through melting snow,
the punk of spring
aloft in loose-limbed light.
What was it, on that evening,
ran chanting before the wind?
Though the sky was still sullen,
the night stiff with unseen stars.

Closing the Cabin

You can see how it will be:
the stillness in the light,
the vacant squares it makes on the kitchen floor

now the leaves are gone.
The way it gathers the room
into itself: the cups, the empty cuphooks,

the dent in the breadbox — an eloquence
we'll never manage, language
without tense.

Not ours: we speak
and then our lungs fill up with air again.
We're only passing through.

Glen Gould: Bach's "Italian" Concerto, BWV 971

North of Superior, November,
bad weather behind, more
coming in from the west, the car windows furred
with salt, the genius of his fingers
bright, incongruous, cresting a ridge
and without warning the sky
has been swept clear: the shaved face
of the granite, the unleafed aspens
gleaming in the low heraldic light, the friend
I had once who hoped he might die
listening to this music, the way
love finds us in our bodies
even when we're lost. I've known very little,
but what I have known
feels like this: compassion without mercy,
the distances still distances
but effortless, as though for just a moment
I'd stepped into my real life, the one
that's always here, right here,
but outside history: joy
precise and nameless as that river
scattering itself among
the frost and rocks.

Passing Sangudo

Sangudo, of the long hill and
the river flats; of the long shadows
in the river valley; Sangudo,
of the early evening, in the summertime,
on the way out Highway 43 after
a day in the city: how ugly
I used to think your name; and how,
unhappy in the car, unhappy

at the prospect of unwelcome dressed as welcome
that awaited us, I believed,
as we all believe, that growing up
meant never having to come back;
how, much though I deplored our town,
I was glad it wasn't you: that much smaller,
that much shabbier, the mud a little deeper,
the store fronts just that much more stark.
It must have rained most days that we drove past
because it rained most days then — or so it seems;
but of course plenty of times it must
have been winter, it being winter most of the year then
— or so it seems. And indeed the one recurring
nightmare of childhood, toboganning down the river bank
and falling through the ice, with my father for some reason,
as well as my sister, and all of us drowning, silently, the ice
growing rigid over us in jagged chunks — that winter dream
was set outside Sangudo, just where the highway
crosses the Pembina, twenty feet
downstream from the bridge.
So it is mildly surprising — like discovering, at 40,
your handwriting closely resembles your great-uncle's
though you've never met — surprising I should find
that what I remember now
is neither rain nor snow, but long shadows,
early summer twilight, the sweet forgiving
roll of the land, the car's movement through it
steady, a quiet humming, exactly as it should be,
coming from nowhere, destined nowhere, simply moving
driving past Sangudo, over the dark brown Pembina,
up the long hill, home.

Journey to a New Life
Winning Artwork by Louise Catinot

The Ireland Newfoundland Partnership (INP) is the Irish government body dedicated to advancing cooperation between Ireland and Newfoundland. In January 2005, the INP launched an art competition among school children in the South East of Ireland, entitled "Journey to a New Life" (The South East of Ireland is where the majority of the Irish who went to Newfoundland originated). Students were asked to illustrate what it must have been like for Irish families making the long journey by boat in difficult times to Newfoundland, two hundred years ago. The winner of the competition was Louise Catinot of Midleton, Co. Cork.

The Echoing Years
Poetry from Ireland

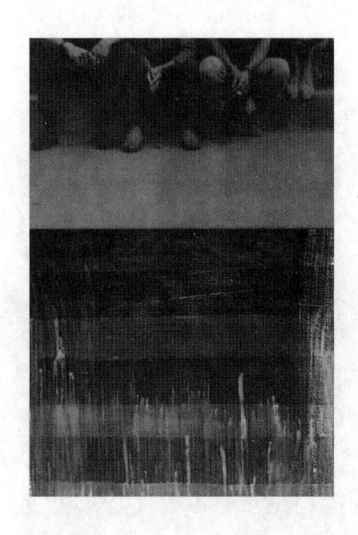

Leland Bardwell

Hard to Imagine Your Face Dead

Hard to imagine your face dead,
Not giving out, pontificating,
Just quiet, serene, the moustache resting
Over the broken tooth.

Those eyes — no longer
Like water brimming
Over a gutter caught with sun.

Your shoulders, no longer alert
In your cushion of death,
Their anger subsiding.

Better to imagine you lying
Alone and listless,
Like when the speed used to leave you
In the downbeat of your madness.

The Night's Empty Shells

I am always afraid
They will find me
Like the skinned arm of the child,

Break the joint between
The ulna and the radius,
Gouge out the mephitic matter,

Take the dance from my feet,
Splay the small bones,
Work the cement into the instep
Before I have settled the measure.

I am not here to ogle the sea,
Count the brent geese,
On the short strand below Ardtrasna,

I'm here to learn the light of Lislarry
Where shone the shebeen once:
A fisherman's star.

So sailed Praeger
After breakfast of poitín
And cold potatoes — a note

To the waves — a leaky boat,
A nod to the dawn
On the East of Innismurray.

For once on my gable
A beacon shone,
The end of the sea lane

To a safe hauling
Of the night's empty shells.

Innismurray

> Where there's a cow there's a woman and where there's a woman,
> there's mischief — St Colmcille who founded the monastery and banned
> all cows from the island.

Two thumb holes in the birthing stone
Beside the women's graveyard.

There she squats, prayers
Breaking from parched lips

To the great Man-God to deliver her
From the yearly gall of labour,

To beg for a man-child
To erase the guilt of her sex.

For being a woman
Has no pardon,

Skirts raised in the wind
On an island that floats

Like a bayleaf
In the unforgiving sea.

She crouches thus
Till the infant lies in the skutch

And she looks at the unmarked grave
Beneath whose soil her mother lies.

She ponders.

'No Road Beyond the Graveyard'
— *Chief Inspector Morse in a novel by Colin Dexter*

But the No Road beyond the graveyard
Is full of possibilities,
Eidetic visions, ghosts,
The valedictory sigh, perhaps.
But when I stand on this No Road,
I am thinking of an old woman
Who took the shoes of her son
And polished them, polished them,
Till you could see your face in them,
First the left then the right,
And placed them under the kitchen table
Before she died. And the son
Stands at the No Road
In the dulled shoes,
In a hopeless frame of mind.
There's no reason for this No Road.
No mention of falling stones,

Dangerous cliffs
Likely to flood.
Simply No Road,
No five-barred gate,
No "Dogs Keep Out,"
No "Danger Men at Work,"
No "Closed for Repair,"
Just, beyond the graveyard,
"No Road."
No cul de sac, no boreen
No bridle path.
The road doesn't go nowhere,
It simply isn't.
It's quiet too in the graveyard
No creature, no bird,
No field mouse. Quiet.
Rows upon rows of stones
Crosses, inscriptions, dates,
But quiet. In the end
One keeps one's ghosts
To oneself.

The Horse Protestant Joke Is Over

There's a small church
By the Big House
Outside of which
The notice reads
Everyone welcome.

Two grinning
Millionaires
Have bought the Big House

And they will have horses,
And they will have jeeps,

And maybe ride rough-shod
Over the parishioners
Of the little church
Which says
Everyone welcome.

Prison Poem III:
For a Friend Doing Life in Portlaoise

I walk the crazy paving, the path of lies,
The micro-chip of satisfaction,
And mingle with the funny-money men
Who gossip on the shoulders of the judges,
But I think of you between the intervals of pacing
Or silence as on the edge of circumstance.

And with twice and nothing of what they have,
The bastards.

I send you the white bird of attendance,
The swallow that left too soon, migrated South,
The simplicities of daisies under boots.

Remember Jean-Paul Sârtre and other soldiers of fortune
Who lived on the rim of existence and survived
The cinder that drops beneath the grate and stays alight,
The fish that lies beneath the shadow of the stone.

Sebastian Barry

The Wood-Pigeons
(aged 33, in Annaghmakerrig, 1988)

All day about here the wood-pigeons offered their ancient
rhythms to each other and to me, and grateful I remembered
as I always do under the spell of their structured call
my brother and myself when he was seven and myself twenty
away from here beside the lost pillars of Coollattin Wood.
In that time certainly I was happy with his peculiar
sweetness, willingness, trust, laughter, patience
though I had a journey ahead of me both dark and bright.
And now if I am ever forty-six and standing somewhere
by such trees and such a memory of such a brother
I will not be sorry that we are both ever a little older
but hold to the pigeons stalwartly echoing always
the same few metres, and all that is in them always the same:
Always, brother, and always, brother, and always, brother, all.

The Pinkening Boy

He is like a newly printed book, its spine not yet cracked open.
He is like a linen sheet, folded by the famous aunts
and then later unfolded onto the breathing bed.
He is like the first of things, the idea Plato had
of the ideal, the thing itself before the word.
Until I touched his hand no other watching creature
ever had, it bore the imprint of next to nothing
but his mother's making, the perfect guesswork
of her soul, a little printing press to make
the most indecipherable pattern on my fingertip.

He knows nothing or next to nothing and all he knows
is in his squinting eyes that hoard the blue of mackerel.
He is like the wood-pigeon with one perfect line

that keeps summing up the soft sums of summer.
He is like an arbiter of touch, of gentleness,
a judge of deftness, hold him just that bit too hard
and the kindly mew emerges, the criticism.
He is like the form you dream of, maybe every night
and wake forgetting, the page of all fresh marks,
the poem beyond comment or opinion, the pinkening boy.

The Owner

Where the cold wind breaks through the poor cover
of the whins, their meagre yellow the only garden
on this small hill in Mayo, and the birds of the bog
are as small as wrens and maybe are wrens,
Mike Igoe holds his acres. Sometimes at dusk
in the time between times, the light between lights
I can see Mike Igoe standing alone under
the particular branches of one of my trees,
heeled in slightly himself like a named cart
where the wall of one of my fields curves in.
And he'll be there just watching the plain below,
Meelick Tower, the lights of Swinford strengthening
at the moon's pace. And if I weren't on foot
by my remnant farm I would never see him,
and though I have talked with him now and then
and understood every word he said, nevertheless
I have no idea what is in his mind as he stands
without moving a whisker, every hair on his head
in its place with the Brylcreem, every light
in his eyes still and quick, as the plain darkens.
No wife, no children, twenty years in London,
and he loves the low grasses combed by the wind
and the little music of the stream where it jumps
the road. I own the road to the middle
by the solicitor's laws, and the sunken bird
that sings under the muddy twilight owns
the air, and Mike Igoe owns the next farm —
but his gaze by long history owns the curve

in my wall, and the under-air of the mothy trees
and the simple poetry of the unremarkable plain.
He has every right to be where he is.

The Man Monaghan

Never met the man Monaghan but you hear
about his deeds. He tried to get permission
for forty holiday chalets by the lake
and though foiled went to psychological war
with the objector on the upper ground.
Then he took the roof off the old cottage
and sold the planning permission he had for that
to another man, for a new house close by.
Then, he put the roof back on his own cottage
and new windows, and cleared the scrubby land
with a small dozer, aggressively, as if
hurting the whins and the reeds was as good
as his enemies. He murdered the lot of them,
so now that swathe of land beside the lake
is raw as a graze. The old house is embarrassed
and lonely, like an old man dragged into a fight
with people he knew as a child. It's strange,
the level of hate seething away there,
stories moiling around Monaghan like a storm.
The lake is peaceful, in the late summer
the swifts swoop down to the water
to take the flies, you have to be careful
when you cast. The land can take a lot
of hurt, it did in the past of course.
Maybe Monaghan's spirit belongs to former times,
the lost land of Cuillonaghtan when the tribes
feuded in the Field of Blood, as the story goes.
Maybe Monaghan would have had the praise
of the district in other days, as being
the enemy of the rich man, I don't know.
Perhaps his myth has ruined the real man.

Sara Berkeley

Strawberry Thief

You were a lot like planting a garden.
The seed, for example, buried deep in September,
the smell of raw lumber as we made the beds,
sun on my belly as though the sun could grow you,
and me on my knees in a heavy Spring,
labouring.

Bean seedling, starting with that soft, divided green,
already you are wild thyme, climbing rose, strawberry thief.
I cannot contain you, you send out shoots
beneath the wooden beds, coming up all daisy-eyed
among the raspberry canes, arms full of Douglas cones,
singing in your tiny cage of bird bones.

The last October sun is at our door,
the purple stars still cluster by the stairs;
any day the rain will come for our parade,
but I am gardening now, I am alone and on my knees,
the earth is warm and, if I can help you bloom,
you will be pollen for the bees;

you will shimmer in the lily beds,
shake out your petals in the breeze;
you will wear your fuchsia tutu and plié where you please
and you will leave me where I am
among the secrets of your growing.
My runner bean, with all the passion of your running
and the greenness of your going,
you lay me bare, you are my undoing.

How We Meet

That first day in the hills above Forest Knolls
we were burnt onto the yellow grass,
our silhouettes two kites in the vast blue surprise,
hearts in an updraft,
white hopes fluttering behind.

Yes, I said, I was married,
dressed in snapdragon innocence.
I dreamed, and that was me
sleepwalking, needing to be
slapped awake.

So, you said, making music
in the labyrinth of my inner ear,
there are innumerable possibilities here;
and on the bay shore of my peninsula
you strung six pearly beaches —
Chicken Ranch, Teacher's,
Shell, Shallow, Pebble, Heart's Desire.

When the days grew smoky and shorter
we met in a blue café.
If this happiness doesn't last,
you said, expect a deeper goodness.

In a Mexican mountain town
we lay in the still whirlpool of a whitewashed room,
the scarf of our siesta working loose.
Meet me at Santa Domingo, you said,
down by the church,
in the angelic peach and apricot of earliest sunset.
I knew of no better waiting.

If ever we meet in a glass house
with stones for hands
or crossed talk
I'd like it heard that I know how it feels

to be charmed, I'd like our love
to let us leave that place unharmed.

Still Life, Yellow Quilt

School's out; tables with their chairs on top,
blackboards black, playgrounds spinning ghosts,
the hot wind blows a dust-devil up,
the air's a sonnet.

Out at Chimney Point the water's beryl blue,
our house is drawn against the tides with pencil strokes,
our summer daughters stream into the sea,
down in the tide pools, fishing for stars,
our son's a roamer.

Somewhere between owl-light and lark,
before the first sounds of an August dawn,
Death comes in and sits down
and when she takes my hand she's warm.

I know I should be lying with the ones I love
on our yellow quilt in the seaside house,
temporary in sleep, unapproachable,
with the white waves washing music to our doors
and the gulls keening;

but I am drawn in spite of my concern
to welcome in my home this temperate guest
who counsels me to lay my burdens down
for it is not my time;

and it's not because my life is a script
that she has written out, line by line,
and laid upon the page for me to read,
but because I know I can't hold onto it
as I swim upriver to the place where I was caught;

and the weight of my life bears suddenly down
and its lightness bubbles up; my guest is gone
with the dawn broken loose from the night sky
on another languid, apricot August day.

So I lie down on the yellow quilt, my arms
loosely about their heads in the simple room;
Raphael should have painted us, golden and true,
with the white waves washing easily back and forth,
and the gulls crying.

Denise Blake

In Mourning

I blame Jackie Kennedy.
Her black suit, black gloves, nothing exposed.
Face covered by a black chiffon veil.
John-John saluting the star-spangled casket
as she stood, regal-still.

It was the only funeral I had ever seen.
We pored over the black and white *Life* photos.
I heard you admire her propriety.

I knew how to behave, Mum,
when the hearse suddenly died out
and your coffin had to be carried up Main Street.
It seemed right, in Kennedy terms,
to walk behind wearing a black lace mantilla.
Ladylike. First-ladylike.

But your young lady needed to cry.
Needed to mourn.
Needed to *caoin*.
Needed to kneel down in the mud
and howl like an orphaned cub.

Kaiyuglak — *Rippled Surface of Snow*

The Eskimos have so many words for snow.
On this Christmas Eve what word do we wish for?

It can't be our *apingaut*, first snowfall —
the boys bundled in padded suits, mittens, trailing scarves
and their red wellies, as they tried to catch the falling flakes.

But now, with all three in their different growings;
they won't worry if it's *kimaugruk* landing in a snowdrift,
blocking any hope of Santa's arrival.

They may hope for sugar snow — *pukak* — to add magic
on their planned dance-club nights.

I don't feel there is *mitailak* here, with fresh snow
covering an opening in the freezing floe,

and there isn't ice caked underneath,
or frost on a living surface,
or any sense of *sisuuk*, an avalanche, pending.

Midnight brings *nutagak*,
powder snow falling as in the snow-cone on our mantle.

Very soft *milik* coating the path that brought us here,
leaving a pure white canvas where tomorrow,
after all the trimmings, we will leave our mark.

Knowing the Wizard

I'm in An Grianán theatre as primary school girls
dance their way around Oz.
I knew every breath of the movie.

Our Ohio sidewalk became the yellow-brick road
when the summer fog rolled off Lake Erie.
The Tin Man was Uncle Charlie with his cast-iron look;
What's new? Did you see the Snoo?
The song "Lions and Tigers and Bears" made sense to me.
They crept around our house at night
waiting to pounce when I ran to the bathroom.

Once, we watched the movie in Rocky River hospital
after one of Auntie Gerrie's operations.
Dad let us up a concrete spiral of back stairs

— *no kids allowed* — just as Dorothy and the others
were creeping through the Wicked Witch's castle.

Lisa looked at her lying in a steel-framed bed
and said *Auntie Gerrie, are you tired*?
It became a family line, paraded out when we grew
too old to sing "Kumbaya" or "I'm a Sailor Home from Sea."

We used to live in a tornado belt. No one warned us
how fast the wind would rise up.
A twister carried me from Cleveland to Letterkenny.

The fog rising from Lake Erie,
and now the stage smoke from a four-foot
green-faced witch's castle, crimps my eyes.

It's not the huge "Somewhere Over the Rainbow"
moments, but the unexpected: the way Lion holds
her tail close as a teddy bear and a flying monkey
suddenly smiles down from the stage at her mum.

These girls won't stay in Munchkin land.
They will have to follow the yellow brick
quite a while before they find that out.

I've only just earned my ruby slippers.
Where the heart lies the feet will wander.
When I click the heels together, I'm home.

Early Lessons

Aunt Mary wanted to mould me into a lady,
little finger cocked when drinking from a china cup.
She soaked me in classical music,
brought me in her Cadillac through the ghetto
to the Greater Cleveland Art Gallery.
When I needed to visit the Ladies, she lined
the seat with log strips of paper tissue.

Years later, I return to the States.
Browse in a mall, queue to use the toilets.
The cubicle door opens. A tall woman steps out —
my age, my height, but not my colour.
I feel Aunt Mary near me, feel Aunt Mary in me,
as if the door had just swung into my face.
I realise why she reached for reams of white tissue.

And I'm back in her library room,
cocooned in a winged leather chair
reading *How Green Was My Valley*.
I hear a wash of conversation, the adults:
*property prices will fall if just one family
of them move in. We'd be overrun.*

I remember the bullet of shock
going through me, my school, my town,
when Bobby Kennedy was killed,
instead of the slight sting as if grazed
by a peashooter, for Martin Luther King.
What quagmire am I rooted in?

Letterkenny 567

The black phone didn't have a dial,
just a small side-handle to crank.
Number please?
Letterkenny 32.
The operator might say, *No point ringing there,
they are all away for the day.*
If you did get through there was a tick-tick
like a cricket in a night-forest.
Someone was listening.

Words came at me in swarms of locusts.
Chips were crisps. French fries were chips.
Jelly was jam. Jello was jelly.

No one knew what pizza was.
It wasn't only pizza we had left behind,
but clothes in psychedelic patterns.
There, I had worn the phone as an earring
while having endless talks full of baloney.

They didn't have baloney here, but Spam;
apple-pie sweets and gobstoppers.
I needed a lot of those.
Never asked the right questions:
Where does your Father work?
Never gave the right answers:
Yes. I do miss Cleveland.

You couldn't just ring Cleveland.
Calls were as sacred as Our Lady.
Neighbours came to our house
for urgent messages, left coins beside the phone.
And when I did make a local call;
Don't talk too long.
You're not in America now.

Vows

I, Donna Maria Rochester Hurley, take thee, Paddy Boyle
as my third husband. My love eternal. My final choice
so long as you accept:
my two daughters, Maria and Juanita, from my first marriage
to Juan Aquia Estibia and the regular visits of his two sons,
Jesus and Manolo to his first wife Antonia (who is not well),
but we won't be bothered by his son Rodrigo
by his second wife, (who was a bitch), Phillipa.
I share joint custody of my two sons, Tod and Jeff,
by my second husband, Joey Pastromi. I see them every
second Sunday in the winter months and the first two weeks
of each summer month. They spend one Christmas with me,

the next with their Father, and the third one with Joey's children
Becky and Beth in the winter home of his second wife
Kelly Anne (who was independently wealthy
and did not need any alimony from Joey).

For richer or poorer, in sickness and in health, till death do us part.

I, Paddy Boyle, take thee, Donna Maria Rochester Hurley
to be my wife, so long as you understand:
my aged mother, Margaret Magdeline will have to live with us.
She'll never be a bother, only give you a bit of advice since
you're a blow in. We'll have the occasional visit from my sister,
Maggie, and her four children but not from that useless
man she married (he never did a day's work). We'll help her
out the odd time; for school uniforms, Christmas, Birthdays,
Communions, Confirmations and the wee trip away for her nerves.
We'll see my brother John when he gets kicked out
of his home because his lazy wife doesn't understand
a man needs a few pints to get through a day.
And then there is our Jimmy. He is still looking for a lassie
who is a good housekeeper. Until he does, you'll just feed
him lunch and a decent dinner. Potatoes and meat.
None of your pasta nonsense. We'll probably have my uncles,
aunts and cousins drop in for a cuppa every Mart day, Dole day,
after evening mass, Stations and Graveyard Sunday.

For richer or poorer, in sickness and in health, till death do us part.

Eavan Boland

"Writing in a Time of Violence: A Sequence"
. . .

I: 5. The Dolls Museum in Dublin

The wounds are terrible. The paint is old.
The cracks along the lips and on the cheeks
cannot be fixed. The cotton lawn is soiled.
The arms are ivory dissolved to wax.

Recall the quadrille. Hum the waltz.
Promenade on the yacht-club terraces.
Put back the lamps in their copper holders,
the carriage wheels on the cobbled quays.

And recreate Easter in Dublin.
Booted officers. Their mistresses.
Sunlight criss-crossing College Green.
Steam hissing from the flanks of horses.

Here they are. Cradled and cleaned,
held close in the arms of their owners.
Their cold hands clasped by warm hands,
their faces memorised like perfect manners.

The altars are mannerly with linen.
The lilies are whiter than surplices.
The candles are burning and warning:
Rejoice, they whisper. After sacrifice.

Horse chestnuts hold up their candles.
The Green is vivid with parasols.
Sunlight is pastel and windless.
The bar of the Shelbourne is full.

Laughter and gossip on the terraces.
Rumour and alarm at the barracks.
The Empire is summoning its officers.
The carriages are turning: they are turning back.

Past children walking with governesses,
Looking down, cossetting their dolls,
then looking up as the carriage passes,
the shadow chilling them. Twilight falls.

It is twilight in the dolls museum. Shadows
remain on the parchment-coloured waists,
are bruises on the stitched cotton clothes,
are hidden in the dimples on the wrists.

The eyes are wide. They cannot address
the helplessness which has lingered in
the airless peace of each glass case:
to have survived. To have been stronger than

a moment. To be the hostages ignorance
takes from time and ornament from destiny. Both.
To be the present of the past. To infer the difference
with a terrible stare. But not feel it. And not know it.

• • •

I Marriage

1 In Which Hester Bateman, Eighteenth-Century English Silversmith, Takes an Irish Commission

Hester Bateman made a marriage spoon
And then subjected it to violence.
Chased, beat it. Scarred it and marked it.
All in the spirit of our darkest century:

Far away from grapeshot and tar caps
And the hedge schools and the music of sedition

She is oblivious to she pours out
And lets cool the sweet colonial metal.

Here in miniature a man and woman
Emerge beside each other from the earth,
From the deep mine, from the seams of rock
Which made inevitable her craft of hurt.

They stand side by side on the handle.
She writes their names in the smooth
Mimicry of a lake the ladle is making, in
A flowing script with a moon drowned in it.

Art and marriage: now a made match.
The silver bends and shines and in its own
Mineral curve an age-old tension
Inches towards the light. See how

Past and future and space between
The semblance of empire, the promise of nation,
Are vanishing in this mediation
Between oppression and love's remembrance

Until resistance is their only element. It is
What they embody, bound now and always.
History frowns on them, yet in its gaze
They join their injured hands and make their vows.

II Against Love Poetry

We were married in summer, thirty years ago. I have loved you deeply from that moment to this. I have loved other things as well. Among them the idea of women's freedom. Why do I put these words side by side? Because I am a woman. Because marriage is not freedom. Therefore, every word here is written against love poetry. Love poetry can do no justice to this. Here, instead, is a remembered story from a faraway history: A great king lost a war and was paraded in chains through the city of his enemy. They taunted him. They brought his wife and children to him — he showed no emotion. They brought his former courtiers, he showed no emotion. They brought his old servant — only then did he break down and weep. I did not find my womanhood in the servitudes of custom. But I saw my humanity look back at me there. It is to mark the contradictions of a daily love that I have written this. Against love poetry.

III The Pinhole Camera
solar eclipse, August 1999

This is the day
   and in preparation
      you punch a hole
in a piece of card.
      You hold it up against
a sheet of paper —
     the simplest form
of a pinhole camera —
      and put the sun
on your right shoulder.
      A bright disc
appears on your page.
   It loses half its diameter.
     And more than half
in another minute.
     You know
the reason for the red berries
darkening, and the road outside
     darkening, but did you know
      that the wedding
of light and gravity
     is forever?
The sun is in eclipse:
   if this were legend
the king of light would turn his face away.
     A single shadow

           would kill the salmon-rich
rivers and birdlife
       and lilac of this island.
          But this is real —
    how your page records
the alignment of planets,
       their governance.
          In other words,
the not-to-be-seen-again
            mystery of
a mutual influence.
           The motorways
       are flowing north.
The sycamores are a perfect green.
          The wild jasmine
is a speaking white.
    The sun is coming back. As
       it will. As it must.
           You track its progress.
I stand and watch.
          For you and I
such science holds no secrets:
    We are married thirty years,
       woman and man.
         Long enough
to know about power and nature.
         Long enough
    to know which is which.

IV Quarantine

In the worst hour of the worst season
    of the worst year of a whole people
a man set out from the workhouse with his wife.
He was walking — they were both walking — north.

She was sick with famine fever and could not keep up.

He lifted her and put her on his back.
He walked like that west and west and north.
Until at midnight under freezing stars they arrived.

In the morning they were both found dead.
    Of cold. Of hunger. Of the toxins of a whole history.
But her feet were held against his breastbone.
The last heat of his flesh was his last gift to her.

Let no love poem ever come to this threshold.
    There is no place here for the inexact
praise of the easy graces and sensuality of the body.
There is only time for this merciless inventory:

Their death together in the winter of 1847.
    Also what they suffered. How they lived.
And what there is between a man and woman.
And in which darkness it can best be proved.

V *Embers*

One night in winter when a bitter frost
made the whin-paths crack underfoot,
a wretched woman, eyes staring, hair in disarray,
came to the place where the Fianna had pitched camp.

Your face is made of shadow. You are reading.
There is heat from the fire still. I am reading:

She asked every one of them in turn
to take her to his bed, to shelter her with his body.
Each one looked at her — she was old beyond her years.
Each one refused her, each spurned her, except Diarmuid.

When he woke in the morning she was young and beautiful.
And she was his, forever, but on one condition.
He could not say that she had once been old and haggard.
He could not say that she had ever . . . here I look up.

You are turned away. You have no interest in this.

I made this fire from the first peat of winter.
Look at me in the last, burnished light of it.
Tell me that you feel the warmth still.
Tell me you will never speak about the ashes.

VI Then

>Where are the lives we lived
>when we were young?
>Our kisses, the heat of our skin, our bitter words?
>The first waking to the first child's cry?

VII First Year

>It was our first home —
>our damp, upstairs,
>one-year eyrie —
>above a tree-lined area
>nearer the city.
>
>My talkative, unsure,
>unsettled self
>was everywhere;
>but you
>were the clear spirit of somewhere.
>
>At night
>when we settled down
>in the big bed by the window,
>over the streetlight
>and the first crackle of spring
>
>eased the iron at
>the base of the railings,
>unpacking crocuses,
>it was

the awkward corners of your snowy town

which filled
the rooms we made
and stayed there all year with
the burnt-orange lampshade,
the wasps in the attic.

Where is the soul of a marriage?

Because I am writing this
not to recall our lives,
but to imagine them,
I will say it is
in the first gifts of place:

the steep inclines
and country silences
of your boyhood,
the orange-faced narcissi
and the whole length of the Blackwater

strengthening our embrace.

VIII *Once*

The lovers in an Irish story never had good fortune.
They fled the king's anger. They lay on the forest floor.
They kissed at the edge of death.

Did you know our suburb was a forest?
Our roof was a home for thrushes.
Our front door was a wild shadow of spruce.

Our faces edged in mountain freshness,
we took our milk in where the wide apart
prints of the wild and never-seen
creatures were set who have long since died out.

I do not want us to be immortal or unlucky.
To listen for our own death in the distance.

Take my hand. Stand by the window.

I want to show you what is hidden in
this ordinary, ageing human love is
there still and will be until

an inland coast so densely wooded
not even the ocean fog could enter it
appears in front of us and the chilled-
to-the-bone light clears and shows us

Irish wolves. A silvery man and wife.
Yellow-eyed. Edged in dateless moonlight.
They are mated for life. They are legendary. They are safe.

IX Thankëd be Fortune

Did we live a double life?
        I would have said
                we never envied
the epic glory of the star-crossed.
        I would have said
                we learned all by heart
the code marriage makes of passion —
                duty dailyness routine.
But after dark when we went to bed
under the bitter fire
                of constellations,
        orderly uninterested and cold —
                at least in our case —
in the bookshelves just above our heads,
        all through the hours of darkness,
                men and women
wept, cursed, kept and broke faith
        and killed themselves for love.
                Then it was dawn again.
Restored to ourselves,
        we woke early and lay together

listening to our child crying, as if to birdsong,
        with ice on the windowsills
                and the grass eking out
        the last crooked hour of starlight.

X A Marriage for the Millennium

Do you believe
that Progress is a woman?
A spirit seeking for its opposite?
For a true marriage to ease her quick heartbeat?

I asked you this
as you sat with your glass of red wine
and your newspaper of yesterday's events.
You were drinking and reading, and did not hear me.

Then I closed the door
and left the house behind me and began
driving the whole distance of our marriage,
away from the suburb towards the city.

One by one
the glowing windows went out.
Television screens cooled down more slowly.
Ceramic turned to glass, circuits to transistors.

Old rowans were saplings.
Roads were no longer wide.
Children disappeared from their beds.
Wives, without warning, suddenly became children.

Computer games became codes again.
The codes were folded
back into the futures of their makers.
Their makers woke from sleep, weeping for milk.

When I came to the street we once lived on
with its iron edges out of another century

I stayed there only a few minutes.
Then I was in the car, driving again.

I was ready to tell you when I got home
that high above that street in a room
above the laid-out hedges and wild lilac
nothing had changed

them, nothing ever would.
The man with his creased copy of the newspaper.
Or the young woman talking to him. Talking to him.
Her heart eased by this.

XI Lines for a Thirtieth Wedding Anniversary

Somewhere up in the eaves it began.
High in the roof — in a sort of vault
between the slates and gutter — a small leak.
Through it, rain which came from the east,
in from the lights and foghorns of the coast,
water with a ghost of ocean salt in it,
spilled down on the path below.
Over and over and over
years stone began to alter,
its grain searched out, worn in:
granite rounding down, giving way
taking into its own inertia that
information water brought — of ships,
wings, fog and phosphor in the harbour.
It happened under our lives, the rain,
the stone. We hardly noticed. Now
this is the day to think of it, to wonder.
All those years, all those years together —
the stars in a frozen arc overhead,
the quick noise of a thaw in the air,
the blue stare of the hills — through it all
this constancy: what wears, what endures.

Rosita Boland

The Astronaut's Wife

> Once you've been to the moon, I don't think there is 'normal'.
> — *Buzz Aldrin*

On our honeymoon
love made us weightless: we orbited
in each other's arms.
We lay in bed
and looked at the moon. We knew
it was illuminating our future.

The day they launched into space
I tracked with awed assurance
the moonlit path from our door to the road.
I thought it led straight to him.

But after they came miraculously back,
after the ticker-tape,
the handshakes, the pictures, the medals,
I slowly realised I had lost him.

Out in the depthless indigo
his mind was still floating
on the Sea of Tranquillity: flotsam
on a tide that never turns.

Now the moon haunts our home.
The blade of its light
slides in through closed shutters.
We wake at night
to see it shining on our skin,
and are afraid to move.

Diamonds

The Tsarina knew
that some darkness was seeping ever closer.
In the uneasy stillness of their palace
the Romanov women tried to prepare themselves
for whatever lay ahead.

Whispering together one silent dawn, their needles
moving like splinters of light, they ripped open
their silk and whalebone corsets
and secreted diamonds along those many seams.

That same day
Alexandra code-wrote in her diary
"Olga and I arranged our medicines."
They thought they were ready, prepared
for an uncertain future, their valuables
safely concealed against curve of breast
and hollow of heart.

The Tsarina did not know
they had created a bright filigree
of betrayal: grotesque armour.

Later that year, when the Bolsheviks
came for them at Ipatiev House,
their bullets ricocheted off diamonds.

Sightless

1

The child's first memory
was of standing in an open doorway
listening to her mother
singing a song about a bird flying.
She wondered what it was,
and what flight was.

Since then, she had held a bird
in the egg of her cupped hands,
its wings fluttering against
the membrane of her shocked fingers.

For her, flight now means
that sudden, astonishing absence,
conjured up when her hands broke open
and the bird disappeared
into the beyond.

2

She drew pictures
of what she thought her world looked like.
"This one has hills in it.
and my house."

Vertical lines marched across the page; her hills.
Among them, a small square box
drawn tight and snug as a safe.

In it, one dot of a door,
round as a keyhole to her world.

Gold — The Gleninsheen Gorget
for Martin Cowley

The glass case in the National Museum
can hardly contain the extravagance of it.
That handspan of gold around the neck,
a hammered perfection
of collar and decorated disc,
stitched together with twisted gold wire.
Gorget: a piece of armour for the throat.

It was found in 1932, glinting
in a fissure of the Burren, glimpsed there

by an astonished farmer going about his business.
The folded collar in the crevice
had been concealed
for a millennium and more:
secret fusion of stone and gold.

To look at this gorget is to realise
that discoveries are always possible,
that a life can be transmuted
by the alchemy of chance.
This has become my own armour.
It winks and gleams
somewhere within.

Teeth

Unlikely jewels,
the modern language of dentistry
hints at teeth's odd value, their strange history.
Porcelain. Pearl-white.
Crowns. Gold.

The first set falls out. Milk teeth,
the assigned colour of innocence,
left like a fable
at night under a child's pillow
in exchange for a coin.

Three hundred years ago
it was the practice to pay a small fee
for pulling teeth from the poor.
They were set in ivory gums for nobility;
the first false teeth.

Some eighteenth-century sets were ornamental,
made of silver, or mother-of-pearl.
Lord John Hervey of England commissioned a set
in Italian agate, and startled courtiers
with an eerie, translucent smile.

Later, teeth were extracted from the fallen
of the American Civil War and shipped
to Europe for re-use by the wealthy.
They chewed on meat and tobacco
with the aid of dead soldiers.

Later still, gold teeth
were plundered from the mouths of those
who died in the chambers
of Auschwitz and other camps,
and melted into jewellery.

There must have been men and women
who went on to wear those circles of tainted gold
on their wedding days:
the rings like open shining jaws
waiting for a chance to bite.

Tears

The Pharaohs
respected their tear-shedding eyes so much
they had a different doctor for each one.

The Greeks and Romans kept their tears.
Some ancient tear bottles survive;
slender, wide-lipped, with a rounded end
and made of iridescent glass.

Into these, mourners wept their sorrow
and their memories of the newly-dead.
The bottles were buried with the bodies:

little glimmers of grief and love
welling up underground;
prismatic compasses, ready for a reading
of whatever lay ahead.

Pat Boran

The Magic Roundabout

There was always something on his mind,
that Dougal. Such a curious dog,
his head like the head of little Florence
invariably cocked to one side or the other . . .

Each week something lost would have to be found.
Mystery would descend like a fog
on their simple, predictable world, but Dougal's innocence
if not stupidity would visit even more bother

on his friends, in truth strange folk themselves, inclined
to going round in circles, to monologue
and soliloquy, but showing complete indifference
to the voice that came from the sky. Plodder

that Dougal was, evidently blind
to the hallucinatory smog
the others passed their time in (hardly a fence
in all that countryside and, even odder,

mushrooms throughout the year, outlined
against the backdrop greens and greys); and slog
that adding two and two became, or telling the difference
between night and day, a rock and some small creature,

rather than take a break to let the plot unwind
in all its perfect nonsense, all its bog
logic or woodland magic, with the impotence
of a hero he'd persevere ever further

after a meaning he could never hope to find.
Not in a world like this. He should have played a log,
stretched out and waited for Zebedee's late appearance,
his "It's time for tea." The poor old tutter,

to use my family's word for a fool, could he not just find
a nice soft spot to lie back on and, like the mere cog
in the machine he was, seize the chance
to glimpse, even once, the hands of god the father?

Jupiter

It was the year I first saw Jupiter,
just an arm's length away down a telescope
someone had swiped from his brother's room
and hid in his coat. From a crater

in the old sandpit, the interference
of the sodium-yellow lights of the town
was wiped clean, wiped clear, the universe
no longer just a cloud of chalk dust

against the blackboard of sky. And there above us,
if trembling, coming in and out of focus,
Jupiter itself, the famous Red Spot
the only thing we talked about for weeks.

Until that night when the first young fellow
in Leaving Cert year — and, Christ, only now
do I see how well it was named for him,
for them — made his way out there alone,

his duffel coat over his arm concealing
what should have been someone's brother's telescope.

Tent

Maurice has lost his virginity
in a tent, or so he claims, out beyond
the new hotel with a foreign girl
who happened to be hitching through.

When the jeering has at last died down,
most of us grin, kick at the earth
or stare into the middle distance, shy
of being the first to give himself away.

That evening, like tourists on a trail
to some historic battleground, we troop
all the way out, the full mile or more
to the now famous field where the girl is

long since gone, though yes there does appear
to be a faint impression in the grass:
rectangular, for all the world like a door
and big enough for a man to pass through.

Katarzyna Borun-Jagodzinska
Translated by Gerry Murphy from the Polish

Theresa at the Laundry
(for Jan Sochon)

Those, for whom they smooth out
    for whom they smooth out
    for whom they straighten out.

Those, for whom they even out
    for whom they even out,
    for whom they erase
    the smallest stain,
    burn the mattresses,
    sweep the cells,
    sterilize with boiling water
    every physical trace,
    so that later
    they can retouch the eyelashes,
    renew the face-paint,
    because I did not seem
    quite dead enough.

Those, I will never forgive.

What's more, I intend to out-pray
that blue-rinsed sky
and those paper roses.

Photograph of Theresa Martin as Joan of Arc

Here, I am a small Joan,
well, obviously a little older.
In this ferocious tableau:
full armour, spear, sword, shield,

grin glinting like polished steel —
there is no inkling
that I am slowly climbing
the smouldering pyre of my own body.
The body in the context of martyrdom,
nothing else.
I'm still waiting
on a sign from Heaven,
although I have a good idea
about the mechanics of disintegration
and the indestructible lumps of ore
they will recover from my ashes.

Van Morrison Plays Mother Goose

How many miles to Babylon?
We will return before the fire dies out.
Babylon has smooth straight roads,
a tower in which a frantic glass elevator
races up and down,
lanterns that blaze out intermittently
for no discernible reason.
How many miles to Babylon?
I press a single cotton thread
into a small ball of wax.
How many miles to Babylon?
I light the candle at both ends
and apply a blow-torch to the middle.
We will return before the fire dies out.

Scarpia

"It won't do madam,
your voice is breaking
and today is the premiere."

She pretended not to hear.
She imagined the smear on the window
was an eye.
More like the blood stain
of a lover I had only finished interrogating.
He denied everything, as I knew he would.
I knew she would do anything
to save him, so I pretended she could.
Actually I detest shameless women,
even as she undid the first button,
she could see me placing the signed death warrant
in the drawer.

Mimi's Aria

I cook for myself,
still my hands are cold.
Once again the spoon rattles
in the empty pot.
The oven no longer heats,
the last chair has gone for kindling.
I sit on the floor.
When someone comes in
I pretend that I have lost the keys
to the recently stocked larder.
I have no illusions that anyone
would wish to paint my scrawny hips,
not to mention my gaunt face.
Neither will they describe me
in a poem.
The poets died out long ago,
too much fat around their stony hearts.
It's miserable here, sitting on the floor.
In the flat below,
the neighbour's children
are playing suicide bomber.

Aida

The last stroke of the trowel
and we are walled-up.
Very little air to breathe,
not to mind sing.
And yet we sing,
although what they expected
were loving whispers
and desperate notes
written in blood
on scraps of paper.
We sing.
Outside the army draws near,
bullets smash holes
in the plaster
spattering our faces.
Yet neither one of us squeals.

Scarpia's Aria

I also have a heart,
though you mightn't believe it.
A certain woman told me:
"Before dawn my daughter seduced the executioner,
it didn't work, he used her, then hurried off
to lather the noose."
"Later he sent me the soap, still marked by the rope,
so that I could clean my son's corpse."
"I thanked him, one must be grateful for any mercy."
I pity my inferiors, I pity everybody.

Colm Breathnach

Translated by Colm Breathnach

Bróga Nua

Báisteach ar fad
ab ea an lá.
Í chomh trom sin go bhféadfá
í a chasadh umat mar chlóca
nó snámh ar scoil tríthi
Sráid Phádraig síos.
Chuireas mo bhróga nua néata
ar seoladh ar locháin,
an t-uisce ag bordáil lem' stocaí bána,
Magellan ar a shlí chun na hÁise.

Nuair a thánag abhaile
ní rabhais i bhfeirg liom rómhór,
dúraís gur le haghaidh taistil
gurbh ea na bróga
is nárbh fholáir dom
agus mé fós im' stócach
bheith ag cleachtadh
faoi chomhair an bhóthair.

New Shoes

The day
was all rain.
So heavy you could fold
it around you like a cloak
or swim through it to school
down Patrick Street.
In the puddles by the kerb

I set my neat new shoes sailing,
the water lapping at my white socks
Magellan on his way to Asia.

You weren't too cross when I came home
you said the shoes were for travelling
and that as a youngster
I should be practising for the road.

Scarúint

Agus tháinig an lá
mar a thagann de ghnáth,
báisteach air
scairdfeadh ina tráth
lusanna an chromchinn
go náireach sna bánta.

An bheirt acu
in iarthar tíre,
glór an charr-raidió
ag lapadaíl dioscó i dtanálacht an locha
mar ar stadadar ar a dturas tráthnóna.

Ise ina gúna cadáis maighdeanúil
a bhfuil na gréasáin bhláthmhara air,
cíor ghorm phlaisteach ina folt fionn.

A léine siúd scaoilte faoina bhráid
na muinchillí craptha aníos ar a lámha
a chraiceann mar a bheadh adhmad stálaithe ann
a chuid gruaige ina gort fómhar-dhathach
na bróga air, an dá chloch reatha raonach'
nach dteagmhaíonn rófhada leis an gcaonach.

Tosaíonn an bháisteach
is tagann na focail imeachta
mar a chaitheadar teacht.

Parting

The day came as it usually does
threatening rain that would spill in its turn
the daffodils
embarrassed in the meadows.

The two of them out in the west,
the sound of the car radio
paddling to disco in the lake's shallows
where they stopped on their evening drive.

She in her cotton virginal dress
covered in flowery patterns,
in her blonde hair a comb of blue plastic.

His shirt open at the neck
the sleeves folded up on his arms
his skin like seasoned wood
his hair an autumn-coloured field
his two shoes, the two ranging rolling stones
that don't touch the moss too long.

The rain starts
and the words of parting come
as they must.

Forlámhas

D'fhógair sé forlámhas
gan fhreasúra
ar an oíche
agus fágadh faoi é
fearann na doircheachta a shiúl.

D'fhoilsigh sé aontacht aonraic
a chroí
is ní raibh aon duine lena thaobh.

Luaigh sé uaigneas uafar
a uathbheatha
is d'imigh a chuid focal uaidh . . .

Supremacy

He declared supremacy,
unopposed,
over the night and he was left
to walk the land of darkness.

He revealed the solitary unity
of his heart
and there was no one by his side.

He spoke of the dreadful loneliness
of his autonomous life
and his words left him . . .

An Fear Marbh

Tá Fear Marbh ages na héinne
ina luí ar a fhaid is ar a leathad
amuigh ar íor na spéire,

oileán ná tugtar turas air níosa mhó,
ball ná tráchtar thairis tríd an gceo,

ná siúltar na conairí air

sa tóir ar chuimhní gur dóichí

ná a mhalairt
go dtiteadar le faill fadó.

Tá oileán mara fada ard
ages na héinne
sínte ar iomall an chomhfheasa,

go dtagann a chumraíocht dhorcha
idir iad agus léas
le linn don ngréin dul fé.

Magh Meall mura bhfuil ann
ach aisling mheabhail
is Tír na nÓg
ina scailp cheoigh —
Í Bhreasail
mar fhís mhearathail —
tuigim go bhfuil oileán ann,
ar imeallbhord mo bheathasa,
ó thosnaigh arís an t-am
tar éis do bháis.

Ó cailleadh tú, a Fhir Mhairbh,
tá tú i d'oileán
sínte ar íor na mara.

Agus tá inneall á fheistiú i mbosca naomhóige
is an taoide ag gabháil bhun na cé i mbarróig
agus fear an bháid thíos ag fógairt
gur mithid domhsa teacht ar bord.

The Dead Man

Everyone has a Dead Man
lying on the flat of his back
out on the horizon,

an island not visited anymore
a place not touched on through the mist,

whose paths aren't walked

in search of memories

that more than likely
have fallen into the sea long ago.

Everyone
has a long high sea island
stretched on the edge of consciousness
whose dark form
comes between them and the light
as the sun goes down.

If Magh Meall
is only a false apparition
the Land of Youth
a fog bank
Hy Brasil
an optical delusion
I know there is an island
on the coastline of my life
since time began again
after your death.

Since you died, Dead Man,
you are an island
on the verge of the world.

And the engine is being put in a curragh
the tide is embracing the slip below
the boatman is summoning me
it is time I took my place on board.

Lorgaíodh mo Shúile tú

Lorgaíodh mo shúile tú
id chathaoir uilleann sa chúinne
nó gur thuigeadar ná rabhais ann níos mó.

Lorgaídís tú trén bhfuinneog
tuairim is a sé gach tráthnóna
nó gur chuimhníodar.

Bhí leathshúil ag mo shúilese
sa ghairdín cúil leat lá

nó gur chuimhníodar nach mbíteá
ann chomh minic sin riamh.

Lorg mo shúile cois cósta tú tráth
i gCóbh Chorcaí
agus fós lorgaíodar ar muir tú i mbá Chorcaí
mar b'aoibhinn leat báid is dugaí
is línéir is tugaí.

Lorgaíonn mo shúile
ar shráideanna deoranta anois tú.

Tá súil ag mo shúile fós
do shúile muinteartha a phiocadh amach
as measc shúile coimhthíocha an tslua.

My Eyes Would Look for You

My eyes would look for you
in your armchair in the corner
'til they realized you weren't there anymore.

They would seek you through the window
about six each day until they remembered.

My eyes had half a mind
they'd find you in the back garden one day
until they remembered you were never there much.

My eyes sought you by the coast once
in the Cove of Cork
and they even looked for you at sea in the bay
because you loved boats and docks and liners and tugs.

My eyes look for you now
on strange streets.

My eyes still expect
to pick out your familiar eyes
among the foreign eyes of the crowd.

Seana-ghnás

Mheasas a rá leo an lá san
gan cloí leis an tseana-ghnás

ach gabháilt ina áit sin
tuathal timpeall an tséipéil

le go gcuirfí mar sin an t-am
ag gluaiseacht ar an tslí chontrártha

is go ndéanfaí tú a bhreith arís as an gcomhrainn
in áit a adhlacadh i ndiaidh báis duit

ach tháinig sé ansan ina bháisteach
is tuigeadh dom ná féadfaí braonaíocha
a chur ag titim in airde
is ná féadfaí ach an oiread
cur i gcoinne an tseana-ghnáis.

The Old Ways

I wanted to say to them that day
not to follow the old ways

but to go widdershins
around the church instead

so as time would be made
to move in the contrary way

and you would be born again from the coffin
in place of being buried after death

but then the rain came
and I knew drops couldn't be made
to fall to the sky
and likewise there was no gain
in opposing the old ways.

Ar an Leaba Leathan

Ar an leaba leathan
cromaim os do chionn

mé an spéir, tú an talamh.

Doirtim póga ort
mé an néal, tú an fharraige.

Ar an leaba leathan

faoi ghile an tráthnóna
is an ghrian ag spaiteáil orainn
go dána trén bhfuinneoig,

is damh ar ard mé
beanna in airde
chun na bhFlaitheas.

Is bogha tarraigthe mé,
tú an lámh a theannann.

Is cláirseach ar tinneall mé,
tú an lámh a spreagann.

Tonn mé, tú a bhriseann,
a leathann ar an leaba.

On the Bed Spread

On the bed spread
I bend over you

I am the sky, you the land.

I pour kisses on you
I am the cloud, you the sea.

On the bed spread

in the brightness of afternoon

as the sun sneakily
watches through the window,

I am a stag on a height
antlers raised
to the skies.

I am a taut bow,
you the hand that draws.

I am a harp resounding,
you the hand that plucks.

I am a wave that you break
and spread on the bed.

An Ghéag Theasctha

Cad é an gá seo agam le filíocht a scríobh
i dteanga a chaith mo shin-seana-mhuintir i dtraipisí?

Cad é ach
tochas i ngéag a baineadh díom.

The Severed Limb

Why this need to write poems
in a language my great-grand-parents discarded?

What is it
but an itch in an amputated arm.

Deirdre Brennan

The Burning

*(Bridget Cleary was burned to death in her own cottage on
15th March 1895. She was murdered by her relatives in the belief
that the 'real' Bridget had been abducted by the fairies.)*

Given half a chance, I could sleep off
the wretched cold I've caught
but I daren't close my eyes
for they mark me at all times
like carrion crows, beaks at the ready
waiting to skewer me.

I can see deep into their hunger,
the way they slaver for my blood,
crowd in and gawp around my bed,
bent on flushing out the changeling
they'd like to think bedevils me.

Not one iota have I changed
and well they know it.
It is they who have become strange
claiming, all of a sudden
to see this spiteful otherness
that inhabits my skin,
watches them from my eyes.

The fairies have white blood
in their pale-skinned bodies.
Monthly, I can vouch that mine is red
though I've prayed God not to see it,
stormed heaven to fatten my belly with child.

My husband has persuaded
my own kith and kin to his side
swearing he has seen me

rub a shilling to my thigh,
that I sit on my secrets
with the smug look of a clocking hen,
don't open my prayer-book any more,
that I meet my egg-man-lover
in secret on the low road.

They put me to every test in the book,
hold me by the ears,
wave red-hot tongs in my face,
parade me back and forth to the hearth
dangling and smoking me
like a flitch of bacon over the fire.
They pour beestings warm from the cow
down my throat, prise open my teeth
to push in bitter herbs from a spoon
and the raging pain in my head
explodes like a star-burst.

Do they think to control me?
Judge me too big for my boots,
begrudge me my gold ear-rings,
the straw-hat made by my own hands,
my green stays, my striped petticoat?

The men circle me like marauding dogs
a sheep. No prayer of mine can shield me
from the lamp-oil pitched at me as surely
as they'd pitch slops into the yard,
no prayer can turn aside the tongs
and the flaming sod that sets me alight.

Will nobody help me?
Outside, I hear the clear bark
of the vixen from the rath.
She has fox-earth wherein to hide
and I have nowhere.

I see their frenzied faces,
smell my cooking flesh,

hear my own scorched screams
beseeching high Heaven for mercy.
Into thy hands, O Lord . . .
From the maw of Hell deliver me . . .

Their chanting roars like a gorse fire
tonguing the dark spaces
between my bones: *Away with you
come home, come home,
Bridget Cleary in the name of God.*

Swifter than snipe-flight
over the Ballyvadlea fields
I am thrown headlong
onto a storm of tangled manes
and thundering hoofs;
*my hair fuses with the night,
my eyes spark off every bog-hole.*

In the National Archives

Being dead before I was born
they became storied figures
elusive as veins of gold that sleep
in rocks, ancient flutes that after
centuries still hold a tune for me.

Turning reverently, one by one
each thick-leafed census table,
my eyes are torch-beams swaying
a zigzag path over the years
to where great-great-grandfather,
unable to read or write,
signs his witnessed X on the page.

I trace the light strokes up,
the heavy strokes down,

take some curious comfort
from the odd blob and erasure
that breaks the enumerator's
masterly penmanship.

Each name takes shape before me,
bodies not of flesh and bone
but formed by lamp-thrown shadows;
the great-great-grandmother, who could span
her waist with two hands when she came
a bride to this house with her dowry
from skivvying in New York,

her flamboyant husband, whose wit
drew the neighbours nightly to their hearth,
staggering home in the small hours
drunk from Keady fair;
their seven living children
and Henry, the dead baby, whose name
had got lost in the years, a small ghost
peeping through an erasure.

Another great grandfather, a cattle dealer,
summons his daughter home
from finishing school in Wigan Convent,
so he can afford to send his son
to the Holy Ghost's in Blackrock
and she married a man, handsome as Parnell,
bore him seven sons and two daughters
and dreamt of Wigan Convent.

I pick my way through their townland
hung about with damp cloud,
intrude on the earthen floors
of their friends and neighbours,
linger over scarcely remembered names —
McElvannas, Rafterys, Cassidys, McBeths,

but they give me no quarter,

steadfastly resist resurrection
and fade into their grudging fields
consigning me to a cold purgatory
where the eternity between me and them
becomes as empty as the space
between the stars.

About Being Human

It's knowing that we can match
bone for bone of ours with bone
of monkey, vole or seal.
It's opening our fin-like spread
of hands to the light; the need
to roost above stoat and fox,
walk among lions, close like oysters
around some pale seeds in us
that may take years to grow.

It's how we eat knowledge
in the way water swallows light;
look dreamily at acres of star-fields
where we've appliquéd whatever gods
we haven't abandoned to the murky fills
of ditch and bog. It's a hundred
tortoises in the Sultan's garden
candles strapped to their backs.
It's the death camps, the gulags, Hiroshima.

And to-day, as you drive away
to wherever it is you live, whatever
it is you do, it is your foetal cells
decades later still riding my blood.

'The Blue Dress'
(Henri Matisse)

He had to hate her to paint her
out of existence,
to cancel her out, imprison her
within great folds of cloth

voluminous sleeves
and rhapsody of frills
flouncing at the neck
elating the bodice
cascading in arabesques to hem.

Did he love her once
then froze her in this room
at some unclean time
lest at her touch
his world might fall to pieces?

And now he is master,
her nothingness complete.
The dress bubbles and flows
from compliant shoulders,
her hand a starfish in its depths.

Fallen Woman

He made visible the invisible,
coaxed her into being from molten glass,
raced against time to shape her space
until all the viscous honey of her
set rock-solid and translucent,
golden as amber drowned in Baltic seas.

If this be a fall, then she is all grace
her body propped on one radiant elbow;

head down, she might be studying red ants
or seedling heliotropes in the pink earth,
no Adam or God to witness that apple
clasped round and fat behind her back.

I shade my eyes before her incandescence,
try to interpret the scattered fronds
of an old language behind each refractive curve
and suddenly see, looped and coiled
in the belly of this unshamed Eve,
the serpent she has swallowed.

Repossession

In search of a place to rest your age,
(or should I say send you off to die?)
I start the engine, bear you down roads
alongside a watery sun low behind
winter shoots of willow and beech,
to corral your befuddlement
in a glumly-painted room
in an Old Folk's Home
in another town.

I desert you there in Indian territory,
Navajo to be precise, not that you'd know;
though your hands plane concentric patterns
of mudstone and shale, polish wings
of wheeling hawks and vultures on pages
of the *National Geographic* I've left you
while age, twisted, incontinent, miasmal,
watches you curiously from the door.

I find you seated alone today,
the dead-weight legs I couldn't budge
pyjama clad, your fingers tugging
at the catheter they have inserted

for the umpteenth time.
I read to you, show you family photos,
haul your spent brain after me.

It is useless. You've closed down. It is Sunday.
The matron just in from golf sits on your bed
teaspooning mush into your baffled mouth.
He was an educated man, she proclaims.
Who you are or were is lost to me these last months
but your eyes still turn in my direction.

The phone rings. Your face pale as a tussock moth
flies through the clearings and coppices
of my wakening. *If you hurry*, the voice says.
Ignoring your blue fingertips, pretending I don't hear
the scroop in your throat, your scantling breath,
I blow out the candle for the dying,
set out to repossess you, pleaching and bending
the years until I steal up on you
quite unprepared for you
to turn a formless face towards me,
bog-cotton hair a blur beneath your hat,
rag-doll legs flopping uncontrollably,
the sky primal and clouded with crows.

The Last Observance

Here where the land ends
in a scattering of islands,
small stone-walled fields
cowering away from the sea,
light trembling behind rain,
we vigil by drenched rocks
an eye on the turning tide,
waiting for you to decide
when it is time to move
in the last observance.

Gulls spill from the sky when
like a priestess, bare-footed,
in your black waxed jacket,
you step forward to prise open
what might be a lunch-box
except it holds the ashes
of your six-foot-tall father
borne by you to the Atlantic
all the way from the cattle farm
north of Brisbane.

I, who never saw the ashes
of the dead before, avert my eyes
not to intrude on your leave-taking,
study seaweed on the rock-line,
imagine to shape the man that was,
clavicle, femur, tibia and rib,
a tumult of bones I cannot name
and when I look again you are
already casting him on the tide
and it is whipping him to cream,
a galaxy of particles eddying,
whirling away from each other,
carried off before our eyes
beyond the shallows,
tugged by undercurrents
through channels between islands
to bed down with the bones of fish
and bird, niche between the eggs
of toadfish, lodge in a dog-whelk's shell.

This, his last wish fulfilled,
you say neither hymn nor
prayer for him but turn, face wet
with spray and tears, seeing
the long centuries of drowned stars
and moons like tabernacle lamps
hanging fathoms deep over him

and all of a sudden, you are longing
for home, the Pacific blue as a bird's egg,
the comfort of an opposite sun.

The Collector

Years later I can still recall
the sun-circle in the garden, the house,
how his old face beamed
when he pointed out his specimens
as though they were prize marrows
or a frippery of exhibition dahlias
acclaimed at the local show.

Not for him your neat rows of stamps,
pinioned butterflies or stuffed birds
frozen in flight under a glass sky
but the shrivelled body of a toad,
a dog's heart pierced with nine thorns,
a sparrow fastened in wax
wedged in the toe of a red high-heeled shoe.

I can still recoil from his real show stoppers,
tar covered foetuses romping from a wand,
the mummified corpse of Ursula Kemp
bumped off for witchcraft in 1582,
the skeleton of one Joan Wytte
the Fighting Fairy Woman of Bodmin.

All the long years of his delving,
knowledge scraped from the cauldrons of memory,
thumbnailed now on so many white cards
that conclude a world out of balance,
an ancient craft exorcised by new priests
muttering Latin and ringing bells.

Years later I can still remember

the half nude manikin splayed on an altar,
how she eyed me through a dark mist of hair,
how ribs of shadow danced on the sun-circle
shape changing to deviant shape
beckoning me. How I refused the dance.

Sníomh

Dá mbeadh deis agam arís,
Gan aon smaoineamh ionam,
Go raibh an tuar i gcónaí nite dom,
Ní bheinn lán tapóg san áit seo
Ag feitheamh ar na mallbhuillí cloig
A bhuailfeadh mo chinniúint
Is a d'fhágfadh i ribleoga mé,
Gioblach lasmuigh den damhsa.

Bhrodhróinn mo chluasa ar ghrág na bhfrog,
Ar rírá a n-impíocha
Go bpógfainn iad
Is chuirfinn mná abhrais faoi ghlas
I dtúiríní a gcaisleán
Sula mbeadh seans acu
Mé a mhealladh go dtí tuirní
Is snáthaidí a chuirfeadh codladh orm.

Is é mo chreach anois é
Nach rabhas ar m'airdeall
Nó ní bheinn anseo anocht
Ag éisteacht le taoisc bháistí
Is mé ag cur trí chéile i m'intinn
Cén fáth go bhfuilim sa seomra seo
Cochán tuí le m'ais
A chaithfidh mé sníomh
Go hórshnaithe roimh mhaidin.

Spinning

If I could do it over again
With no foreknowledge of what was in store
I wouldn't be sitting nervy, jumpy, in this place,
Listening to the slow ticking of the clock
That would strike the midnight of my fate
And leave me ragged and shoeless
Outside the dance.

I would revel in the croaking of frogs,
Take pity on their entreaty,
And kiss them. I'd lock old yarn-spinning
Women away in the turrets of the castle
Before they got any chance to trick me to their wheels
And jab me with sleep-bringing needles.

I am destroyed with the thought
I wasn't watching out
Or I wouldn't be here now, listening
To rain sluice down as my mind tries to deal
With being here in this room with a haystack
Which I must change to gold thread by morning.

Maighdeana Mara

Thug siad ansacht a gcléibh dóibh,
Ag cur na ndromanna dubha
Lena n-anamacha síoraí
Ar ghrá iascairí
Ar ghrá captaen mara,
Ar ghrá prionsaí
A tharrtháil siad ó bhá.

Ach d'éirigh siad caite
Ó bheith ag glanadh scadán
Traochta leis an bhfeitheamh

Ar mhairnéalaigh nach raibh dílis dóibh
Ceas orthu le prionsaí
Nach raibh tada á thaibhreamh dóibh
Ach torthaí an stocmhargaidh.

Ina luí dóibh ar ghaineamh na trá,
I gcolbha an uisce
Glúine trusáilte go smig acu,
Lírigh teangacha taoide
A súile, a gcluasa, a gcíocha,
Gur leádh go cúr bán iad
Is a leanaí ina leapacha ina gcodladh.

Mermaids

They gave them the love of their breasts,
Turning black backs to their souls
For the love of fishermen and sea captains
And princes they saved from drowning.

But they were spent from gutting herring
Exhausted waiting for the seamen who were never faithful
Their hearts broke for princes whose only interest
Was stock market reports.

They lay in the sand of the strand at the edge of the water
Their knees lashed to their chins,
Brine tongues washed their eyes
Their ears, their breasts until
They melted down to white surf
As the children slept in their beds.

Is 'Werewolf' mé anocht

Ní hionadh ar bith liom é
Nuair a chím m'anam
I riocht mic tíre léith
Ag sliodarnach as mo chorp.
Ní hionadh ar bith liom é
Nuair a bhraithim an sneachta
Faoi mo cheithre croibh
Is ceannsoilse na gcarr
Ag dalladh mo shúl
Ar mo bhealach chuig na cnoic.

Ach is ionadh liom
An folúntas im bholg,
A loime atá m'easnacha
Nuair a chíorann an ghaoth
An fionnadh ar ais orthu.
Is ionadh liom méid mo bhéil
Is na prislíní atá liom
Nuair a airím boladh caorach
Sa dorchadas
Nó nuair a chloisim feadaíl fhir
Ar fheirm i bhfad uaim.

Thuas i gCill Oisín
Ag faire dom ar imeall na coille,
Borrann cuimhne fann ionam,
Chomh fada siar im chloigeann
Gur doiligh dom
A tabhairt aniar,
Ar luaineacht na conairte
Oícheanta seaca,
Ar rithim ár reatha,
Ar seilg ár gcreiche
Go crespascal maidine.

Níl aon bhaol ann
Go mbéarfar gairid orm arís
Le binneas an cheoil
Lenar mealladh mé tráth
Chun scarúint lem chraiceann
Gur sheasas lomnocht
Mar mhnaoi gan chosaint
Ar aghaidh na sceirde
Is dream le geis acu romham
Ag crústach cloch orm.

Ní hionadh ar bith liom é
Nuair a airím riastradh im chorp
Is mé ag teannadh chun léimt
Fá mo bhéile,
Ach is ionadh liom
Mar a stadaim go hobann
Nuair a smaoiním ortsa sa leaba
Mar a d'fhágas thú
Clúdaithe faoid phluid leictreach,
Is iombháim an gleann le mo ghlamanna.

I Am a Werewolf Tonight

It is no surprise to me
When I see my soul
Slide out of my body
As a grey wolf,
When I feel the snow
Under my four feet
And lurch from blinding headlights
As I head out for the hills.

But I am surprised
By the emptiness in my belly
The gaunt ribcage

As the wind combs my sides,
I am surprised by the width of my mouth
And the saliva dripping
As I smell the sheep in the dark
Or hear a man whistle in a far farm.

Up in Cill Oisín, keeping watch at the edge of the forest
A memory stirs slow, deep down in my skull
So far back it's hard to dig it out
Of the speed of the pack, nights of frost
Of the rhythm of our run
Of the hunt for prey
Deep through night to dawn.

No danger I'll be caught easy
By sweet music, as I once was
Skinned, left standing like a defenceless woman
In front of that crowd of believers
Flinging rocks at me.

No surprise at all to me
That frenzy in my body
As I gather to leap
To my meal,
But then the shock
Of sudden thought of you in bed
Snug in the electric blanket.
I fill the valley with howling.

Translated by Gréagóir Ó Dúill

Vincent Buckley

Hunger-Strike

> **Warrior**: 1. One whose occupation is warfare; a fighting man; in eulogistic sense, a valiant or an experienced man of war. Now chiefly *poet.* and *rhet.*, exc. as applied to the fighting men and heroes of past ages and of uncivilized peoples.
> *Shorter O.E.D.*

To Redefine 'Warrior'

> Through this season
> of hot clouds, you have needed
> to redefine 'Warrior': One
> who makes war, with no weapons
> but the sticks of his forearms,
> the electric pain of his body
> in his cell, away from the air
> his family breathes, drenched with sweat
> of armed men, with machines,
> robots, automatics, clockbombs,
> hijacked milk-lorries,
> sprayguns and knapsacks of gas,
> plastic bullets, shields, visors:
> For the armed man is known by his tools,
> but a warrior by the death of his terrors
>
> and of their monstrous dream prototypes:
> tortured heads, with holes large as faces
> opened in them; a corpse hung at the ford;
> a serf enduring the thousand lashes;
> statues fighting; a masked man

beckoning between the armies;
a comrade lasting into his sixtieth day;
a lark, as he said to himself, at the window
but caught, crying, by the foot, in black wire.

Bobby Sands: One

Now he is laid on the sheepskin rug
so that his bones will not burn him,
pads are put on his heels
against the bedsores. He is blind
and deaf. The pain they told him of
jolts its thin current
into every movement. His teeth
protrude like the bones of a dead man.
He is dying for his word. *Geronimo*.

They would not let him alone.
Day and night they came and went
stirring his pallid shadow,
interpreters of his dying.
Day and night he hung on the wire,
his curled body outlasting them
till they fell silent; "he was the piper
walking in the front of battle."

Then, he died in a clean place,
crooked, on the waterbed, the Pope's
crucifix proudly beside him, his mind
open as a galaxy.
Le dur desir de durer
saw him buried as Geronimo.

Sands: Two

But, before that, he was lowered
into the deep trough
of others' wills, his wire thin bones
buzzing with speeches, lights

thick on his shrinking face,
died badgered with help,
not hearing
the faraway words his mother
spoke to the microphone.
For her the hard thing
must have been keeping her eyes down,
her lips steady, while blurting out
what they had said to each other: "We talked
about old times . . . when he was at school
. . . and in the youth club . . ."

This was the time when
everyone came to talk at him
and to come out and tell the world
what he wanted, and why
he should / should not want it
                [But he wanted not to give up,
                and not to die either. Geronimo.]

The sky was full of mouths: except the father,
who said nothing, the brother,
who was an arm to lean on
for the sister, who could not hide her eyes,
and the mother, all large
unweeping features, and going in,
and coming out, and going
only to come back next day
to the reporters husking like bees:
"How is he today?" "He's dyun."

Francis Hughes

    Colonel, press your cap down hard
    or keep your fingers in your belt,
    searchlights and men in every yard,
    the tree beside you red with haws,
    Saracens in the windgreen lanes,
    the day they bury Francis Hughes.

Is this the corpse you hate so much,
that awesome boy, going to Mass
on a weekday morning in Bellaghy,
loitering so the late dews pass
along his footstep to the door,
thinking the land's his own, perhaps?

Go to your tea, sergeant, trooper,
his shadow follows you with scorn
now that you've lowered his starved face
deep in the ground where he was born:
the long-eyed kinsman drumming on it
tunes you will never learn or bear.

Raymond McCreesh

Weeks later, it was his face
that loomed on the hourly news,
tilted back, fragile, laughing.
To whom someone said, on the 58th day,
do you want a drink of milk?
He was blind now. He said, I don't know.
Batlike his brain in and out
of his body-shape, the mind's landscape
entering and leaving sun and shade.
For days, on the wire services,
in press statements, they took his name:
Do you want a drink of milk? I don't know.

And they talked of his family
as if he were straining
to leave some mad priesthood, or to break
some taboo of the townland,
and the people he loved would not let him.
        Eloquent assassins,
        Oxbridge men, Sandhurst men,
        I am almost too ashamed
        To mention your shame.

Interlude for Exploration

>Standing at the microphone,
>he shot his cuffs and said, earnestly,
>"Good God, we're not barbarians,"
>while the other railed against all violence
>booming, "kill the killers."
>None of them is a barbarian
>they are all against violence
>which (let us be quite clear)
>they totally and unequivocally reject.
>What they *do* support
>is the police and the army
>and Saladins in the closed streets
>and plastic bullets at walking schoolgirls
>and blackened faces waiting in the darkness
>after the local dance; and the spacemen
>on each corner, with their guns cradled,
>and the knowledge that the Opposition is with them
>
>and that the Bishops, who hate violence,
>will ask no hard questions, and the columnists
>will be as full of similes as the poets,
>lightheaded (this way, that way)
>and Oxford will debate measure and process,
>and the *Tablet* moral or some other theology
>(all against, utterly against violence)
>and the sun will rise in the West
>if we want it, for we are dying
>as much, but not as fast, as
>their unarmed prisoners.

Interlude for Execution

>On the waste ground where they shot him
>two or three birds fly up
>flapping, as if the air's too heavy.
>The ground is drifting with lead.

Nothing grows. Vanished even
the permanent knuckles of the plane-trees,
and the people who heard him screaming
can grow nothing inside,
and can say or think nothing
while they wait for the suicide hour
flashing with law and order.

Patsy O'Hara

Fourth, Patsy O'Hara. We had seen his sister
moving from door to door
from taoiseach to taoiseach,*
with her unanswered face,
while all the time he sat, with hunched beard,
in his bugged, photographed cell,
waiting till they would make him
carry his body down the Creggan
moving in procession
slow and quiet as a milkman
while the young boys in their staring thousands
drummed their heels on Derry's walls.

Joe McDonnell

who said, and became famous for it,
"I've got too much to live for,"
and said later (or it may have been Kiernan Doherty),
"I don't want to die over a food parcel,"
died on my birthday. It was almost exact mid-summer.
The black flags at Walkinstown roundabout
were held up for hours by the waiting faces
and the midges at Phoenix Park
stung even the feckless Spanish students
in hot moist green that seemed to grow warmer
in the encroaching shadows
And Martin Hurson on Grania's birthday.
And Kevin Lynch and Kiernan Doherty
died shortly after the Commission
had failed to solve the English.

(That question of the ages:
How do you solve the English?)

And Thomas McElwee, the shy-looking cousin
countryman, a proper devil for cars;
whose eight sisters carried his coffin
into the silent crowded roadway,
then on, with other bearers, into
the roaring graveyard, where
the whole countryside swayed in late summer.

And another long-eyed northerner
enrolled in their love compact.

* *Taoiseach* is the Irish for the head of goverment.

Paddy Bushe
Translated by Paddy Bushe

Bolgam

I gcúilsheomra sa mhainistir a bhíodar,
Dealbha gleoite snoite as im yeac,
Na dathanna ag brú a chéile chun solais
Nuair a chuardaigh an ghrian an seomra.

Caomhnaithe le luibheanna is spíosraí,
Mhairfidís deich mbliain sa dorchadas
Go dtí go ngabhfaidís slí na fírinne
Mar sholáthar turais do oilithrigh.

Bhí dragúin ag lúbadh trína chéile
Le sceitimíní ag lútáil leis an mBúda
A bhí ina shuí croschosach ar an lótas,
Aoibh shíoraí air faoi ór a chaidhpe.

Ar spraoi i measc bláthanna rábacha,
Bhí bandia cíochnocht ag seinm siotáir
Faoi mar a bheadh sí á méarú féin
Chun aoibhnis a leáfadh an t-im.

Le boladh géar an ime sa timpeall,
Smaoiníos ar Imbolc, is ar bha draíochta
A thál bainne gan stad ar fhocal naoimh,
Is dheineas aon bholgam amháin den domhan.

Shamhlaíos fallaing mhíorúilteach Bhríd
Ag leathnú de shíor thar shléibhte soir,
Agus im míorúilteach sin an Oirthir
Ag brúchtaíl thar mhachairí uile Chill Dara.

Gulp

They were in a back room of the monastery,
Exquisite figures sculpted in yak butter,
Their colours pushing one another towards the light
As the sun searched through the dusty room.

Preserved with ritual herbs and spices,
They would live in darkness for ten years
Before undertaking a sacred journey
As food in the bags of pilgrims.

Dragons twisted and twined themselves
In fawning ecstasy around the Buddha
Who sat cross-legged on a lotus blossom
Smiling eternally below his golden hood.

Surrounded by a riot of flowers,
A bare-breasted goddess played a sitar
As though she were fingering herself
Towards a pleasure to make her melt.

With the tang of the butter in the air,
I thought of *Imbolc*, and of magic cows
That yielded endless milk on a saint's word.
And I swallowed the whole world at one gulp.

I imagined Saint Brigid's miraculous cloak
Spreading seamlessly eastward over the Himalaya,
And a sea of pungent, miraculous butter
Overflowing westward to the plains of Kildare.

Ag Aistriú Buddha in Der Glorie

In aghaidh mo thola, bhí sé caite uaim agam,
An smaoineamh go n-aistreoinn an dán sin le Rilke,
Cé go raibh sé fillte agus aithfhillte trím aigne
Mar a bheadh bratóg urnaithe ar chrann naofa.

Fuaireas róchoimhthíoch iad, na críocha úd
Ina raibh an dán agus an t-aistriúchán ag taisteal,
An ghramadach débhríoch, agus nósmhaireacht an táirsigh
Suite mar chonstaic ar mo chead isteach.

Ach nuair a bhaineas mo bhróga iartharacha díom
Roimh gabháil thar táirseach Teampall Phrah Singh,
Is nuair a shuíos croschosach ag análú tiúise,
Cloigíní ag bualadh i leoithne anseo is ansiúd,

D'aithníos Búda Rilke os mo chomhair in airde,
Ceannbhrat naoi gciseal go caithréimeach
Ar foluain os a chionn. I loinnir an íomhá,
Thuigeas go bhféadfaí go ndéanfaí teanga díom.

Translating Buddha in Der Glorie

Against my will, I had put to one side
The notion of translating that poem by Rilke,
Although it had wound itself around my mind
Like a prayer-flag around a holy tree.

They were too alien to me, those regions
Where poem and translation were travelling;
The grammar ambiguous, and the threshold customs
Squatting like guardians against my entering.

But when I took off my Western shoes
Before crossing the threshold of Wat Phrah Singh,
And when I sat, cross-legged, breathing incense,
Temple bells tinkling somewhere in the breeze,

I recognized Rilke's Buddha high up before me,
A nine-tiered canopy floating triumphantly
Above his head. In that resplendent image
Gleamed all the possibilities of all language.

Éin i gCliabháin

Ar fhalla íseal cois fuaráin
I measc na gcrann a chonac iad,
Stocaireacht na tráchta á dtimpeallú
Ar oileán in aigéan rachmais.

Thángadar ann le maidí siúil
Gach aon mhaidin, ag tarraingt na gcos,
Ag iompar leo a gcuid éiníní cheoil
I gcliabháin ornáideacha bambú.

Meigill mhandairíneacha orthu
Faoina gcuid caipíní Maoacha,
Toitín ag sileadh le gach aon bhéal,
Bhlaiseadar de chiúnas na seanaoise.

Agus lean an trácht leis á dtimpeallú,
Na héin i gcliabháin, na seanfhondúirí.

Caged Birds

They sat on a low stone wall
By a fountain among the trees,
The blare of traffic surrounding
That island in a sea of affluence.

They came with their sticks
Every morning, dragging their feet,
Carrying their songbirds
In ornate bamboo cages.

They had Mandarin goatees
Below their Mao caps.
Cigarettes drooping from their mouths,
They inhaled the silence of their age.

And the traffic surged non-stop around them,
The caged birds, the old brigade.

Catherine Byron

Coffin. Crypt. Consumption.

In 1397 the Aragonese knight Raymond de Perillios made the pilgrimage to St Patrick's Purgatory on Station Island in Lough Derg. He wrote his will, and the Mass for the Dead was said over his still-living body, laid in an open coffin, before he was walled into the cave of Purgatory for ten days and nights.

i Coffin

I was cloudwatching.
On my back.
The sides of the coffin a tight
fit for my shoulders, the
foot end of it just
out of reach of my feet.
I saw the bruise of rain
moments before its first
spit on my face.
My tongue was out for
anything it could get.

Then the thrown pall
shuttered it all away —
wet, wind and heaven.
Blackness tight as a lid.
The absolute dark of
Blue John caverns
a hundred metres under.

It was at that moment I felt
like death for the first time.
Queried my state.
I swallowed and went within me
down channels and bloodways

— was it sickness or damage? —
potholing duct and vessel
tracking the dumb in me
that had never uttered before.

My searching tongue
offered lungs a voice,
but alveoli
half-inclined to mutter
turned over again and slept.
I was down where nerves
ran clean and autonomic
the innocent of touch.
I brought within me
skin's receptors
poised for adrenalin
rushes. Alerted
the buds upon my tongue.

All that interior smoothness
merely bridled, the tissue
rucking up and then
subsiding in silence . . .

The taste of me iron and salt.

Peccavi. I have sinned.
The blood of others is
sticky on my hands.
I have no stomach for it.

ii *Crypt*
The first examination of conscience

There are bones
haunting the fridge
with mould on them like moss.
How many years now
since my carnivore days

when I picked the cage
of a chicken carcase clean?
Oh, and that pig's head
that I boiled for brawn
in a Scottish winter.
Remember how I needed
a brick to lid down the snout
when the boiling made the gristle
rear right up with the heat?
The brawn was clear and lovely
like a cache of garnet and pearls.
Never again, though. Never again.

The second examination of conscience

Eggs in a bucket
swimming in isinglass.
Whole eggs from the hens
the shells gone leathery as turtles',
whites gone all to water
yolk sacs slack and milky
so easily torn.
How I cashed in on their
mother-frenzy, my lovely
Rhode Island Red
Light Sussex cross
layers. From point of lay
to their moulting each Nov-
ember I forced them to be
egg-crazy, egg-a-day
wonders. I laid up
their overplus, stashed eggs
like oval ghosts in a pool
against their bald eclipse.
And all infertile: I'd
*coq-au-vin*ed long since
their solo cock of the coop.
Never again. I'll not

swallow any of that.
I have no stomach for it.

The third examiniation of conscience

When I bought the cleaver
at the butcher's suppliers
in the cold hinterland of East Kilbride
the man behind the counter
asked me quite straight
did I get on, like,
with my old man?
      Fine.
Oh, I knew then fine
what cleaving was:
to split with a blow
or to hold on tight.
A man and a woman
shall be one flesh.
Cleave thou only
unto him. One flesh.

iii *Consumption*

Come, Hades, lord of the inner channels
prince of peristalsis, potholer extraordinaire.
You alone know there is nothing at my core —
an extended nought, a hole from mouth to anus.

I have fasted for three days, and drunk no water
this last day — *light-headed, leaving home* —
I am pure pink for your pleasure. Thread me through.
This is the purest form of penetration.

This is the going up into the gaps.
This is the airy way of the hunger artist.
I beseech ye, o my bowels,
that I may not be mistaken.

Coco de Mer

I was a blow-in, passing through, until
I overheard you talking about Horace
and his Sabine farm, as though it was
in this very townland, and Horace was your neighbour.
I joined you, we drank like fish — the dark stuff —
and you swore then that never again would you
cross the Shannon River, drive east to Dublin,
never re-enter the Pale of your finished life.
And wouldn't it thrill you to swear, and keep to it,
that you'd never even leave Gorumna Island,
not cross the first sea causey to Lettermore
nor the second to Anna-a-hyaan and then the third
to Ballydangan on the mainland of Connemara!

But soon enough, off we sped
in your red diesel Toyota
by way of Ballydangan
to the quay at Carraroe.
It was there, at the fish-houses
you'd buy us both what we needed:
our fill of aphrodisiac *fruits-de-mer*.

Back on Gorumna as the late slow dusk
burnished the lough below your slated cabin
we swallowed fifty sweet, garlicky clams
and a hill of crawfish prawns — pure protein.

Though we stayed in our clothes to talk about Aeneas
leaving Dido on the shores of Carthage,
and murderers you had defended in the courts,
and the purchase of yeast, in bulk, your contribution
to the townland's *poitín* still, a syndicate —
it was the moon undressed us out by the lough,
hurried us withindoors, and laid us down
on the chill and grass-bleached linen of your bed.
Skin to skin, how pale our nakedness
below our windburnt faces, in the moon's glassed eye.

And how lilac-pale your cock, a shy mollusc
I sucked into the salt swim of my mouth
willing it muscle, the engorging beat of blood.
Oh, mine was the tide that was inching back from slack,
and you out of kilter, stuck at some sad ebb
in your dead wife's grip. I could not tongue you free
but moved alone in the rising and return,
sensing by sonar, now, the pulse of the English lover
I'd left, not lost to death, though I'd put a sea
and half an ocean to wash
between us, wash him away.

How I loved you then when I'd stilled you into sleep
written goodbye and godbless in salt on your table
and gathered my cast skin softly
by feel and phosphorescence.

It was after moonset. Only the prickle of stars
silvered my road up and away from you.
I drove without lights in my almond-green Morris Traveller
and across the three sea causeys:
Gorumna to Lettermore to Anna-a-hyaan.
I switched the headlights on when I reached the mainland
and kept them on till I braked at Carraroe.
I turned the car's engine to silence, and stepped out
past the shellfish houses, and down the dark slipway.
I was dark, too, black as if in a wetsuit
when I slithered back into North Atlantic brine.

Egyptians

i   Mummy to tombrobber

I have been stilled behind coursed ashlar
is it a hundred or three thousand years?
    Dry thorns score arcs on crusted sand outside.

The painter's rags are lying where they fell
when my flesh face was still a thing to paint.
    My bones are crumbling now like gingerbread.

The chink of chisel fiddles with my sleep
then you and light pour through a crack together.

Is it your eyes or light that moves my lips?
Is it your voice or air that wets my tongue?

By my articulate hand you lead me out
into the starlight like a lazarus.

You tell me that the room in which I lay
gave you a whiff of fresh delphinium.

    I would undo what you and I have done
    moving in starlight over shifting sands.
    I would retreat, and breathe again the air
    that's lost all savour but that errant blue.

ii Tombrobber to mummy

Now when moon lies hammocked over trees
now is the time for penetrating bone.

    Disc over disc we make a strange ellipse.

My mouth on your pelvis, tongue hunts sacral beads
follows the milky way into your ribs.

Tightness of bone. Its dryness drives me on
to scatter arcs of droplets on your dust.

    Starlight picks out their glisten, white on white

seedcorn of bloodflow and recurring tide:
here on the sandhills I put flesh on you.

iii Mummy's dream

My cordage slackens.
Gilt indicates
my nipples' wasting site
slipped bitumen
through linen.
There is opacity
between my thighs,
my belly's packed
with resin, mud.

I dream your coming
dream my dilapidation
shored by you.
Your spacing eye
sees lintels where collapse
had shut down shape.
My frescoes startle.
Cleared conduits
run their fluent ropes
through rock.

The shaly marrow
of my bones makes blood,
its ooze is slops
and leakage. See
it spits on
dust's pale tension.

Come to me quickly
through the riven hill.
Cup my flow in hands
that crave this sweet
viaticum.

The Getting of Vellum

Have you ever scribbled a telephone number, or a name
on the handy back of your hand?
Written something there on your own soft skin,
pressed and tickled across the grain of you
with the fine running point of a ballpoint pen?
It has the right ink that'll slide on
oily and easy, and stay there for hours.
Even a soapy scrub of your hand
won't shift it altogether.
It's perfect for jotting something down
in a hurry, something you need to hold onto
oh, for less than a day, maybe,
but vital for that day.
Paper is flighty, easy to lose,
and it isn't always to hand.
You'll not, after all, mislay
your own skin — will you?

Unlike the animal — lamb, or kid, or calf —
whose skin has been stripped off,
scraped clean of life's paraphernalia,
— flesh — fat — hair —
and transformed, even transfigured, into parchment
or — in the case of the calf — vellum
for the writing of the Word.

The monastery of Lindisfarne —
founded in the year of our Lord
six hundred and thirty five
on the island off the Northumbrian coast
known as Holy Island
that is cut off by the sea twice a day,
for several hours,
in the rhythm of the tides . . .

> We've found so little
> apart from cattlebone
> and a certain amount of shell . . .
>
> the bone is of early AngloSaxon,
> early seventh or eighth century date . . .
>
> and the calfbones are the most striking feature
> of the bones that we've got . . .

So many calves, on this tiny isle's
scant pasture, and wild sand dunes
and reedy shores . . . ?

> The island is a small place, and no way
> could the volume of calfskin be produced
> on herds that were actually
> born and bred on the island . . .
>
> there might have been a specialised
> centre on the island
> where calves could have been brought,
> and killed, and skinned,
> so the calfskin could then be turned into vellum
> for manuscript production . . .

A monastic abbatoir, then?
A vellum factory where the raw skins of
one hundred and twenty nine calves
were soaked and scraped and stretched,
their spine skin bound
into the spine
of the holy book they were made for:
the astonishing Lindisfarne Gospels?

Now the trimmed skin of their flanks
has been made into pale pages,
polished with pumice,
dusted with sandarac
against any trace of animal oiliness

that will halt the bite of ink.
And the pen?
A quill, a *penna*,
the flight feather of a goose
tempered and toughened
in a tray of heated sand,
then pared to a nib.
In the monastery *scriptorium*
Lindisfarne's Bishop Eadfrith
dips his goosewing quill
into vermilion ink
and inscribes the first words:
Incipit evangelium

That was thirteen centuries ago.
You can see the Gospels now, in the flesh,
in the British Library, under glass:
each illuminated folio undimmed,
the rawhide vellum white and stable still;
the calves' hides gathered
fleshside to fleshside,
hairside to hair,
but so transformed it's hard to say
which double page spread is which.

> *You know, the skins — I quite like,*
> *as a writing texture, just*
> *the little graininess*
> *of the roots of the follicles . . .*
>
> *Yeah, it makes like the*
> *surface when you haven't shaved . . .*

In the Vellum Works in Celbridge,
County Kildare,
in the last years of the twentieth century,
master calligrapher Denis Brown
is choosing skins from the fresh stock
of Joe Katz, Czech vellum maker extraordinaire.

Everyone has a different taste.
Some like them very white,
some people like to have
the yellowish old type finish,
then some of them, sometimes —
Denis takes the completely black one,
where there is pigmentation
still in them,
in other words, it was a calf
or a slunk
from a dark animal

A dark, yes . . . a dark animal
If you could sand that down . . .
This is one of the dark ones
I'd be interested in.

There's a body on them.
If I polish that —
that will become beautiful.

Beautiful vellum. Slunk vellum.
The most prized writing surface
for a calligrapher, even now.
This is the skin of a calf so young
it isn't even a veal calf,
hasn't drawn breath in this world:
a slunk, a slink,
a near-term foetus slung, or cast
by its mother — stillborn.
The getting of vellum starts these days
with the knacker's pick-up call at a farm,
the apparent waste of an aborted dairy calf.

The living calves
are already being weaned to the bucket.
The dairyman puts his fingers
into the warm milk
to teach them the hard lesson:

to suck from a metal bucket now,
not any longer from the warm flesh of a teat.
These liveborn calves
have been licked and glossed by their mothers
in the two days
before the dairyman parted them.

But miles away in the knacker's yard
there's no gloss on the coats
of the slunk calves
stacked on that mudded pallet.
Master knacker John Warman
lifts up the top one,
dirty black and white,
gangle of legs too long
for the scanty body.
He takes it, firmly, tenderly,
into the high workshed
and switches on the compressed air machine.

Born dead, a proper slink calf.
Never breathed. You get a lot like that.
Born dead —

This calf — I probably picked this up
Saturday afternoon. He still looks nice and fresh —

When they come out dead
they seem to keep better, y'know . . .

The knacker's blade is long and narrow
like a silver letter-opener.
John Warman punctures a hole
in the calf's oxter
where one foreleg starts from its chest.
He pokes the airline's nozzle into the hole.

The hide of the calf's belly
ripples and balloons free,

untethering all the membranes
that anchor skin to flesh,
to gristle, to bone.

>   *Now we don't touch that no more with the knife.*
>   *I'll tell you what we do now.*
>   *We get the skin down like that . . .*
>
>   *anchor the hide to the floor . . .*
>
>   *that's the hoist . . .*
>
>   *See now, that skin*
>   *by taking if off like that,*
>   *see — there's not a blemish on it . . .*
>
>   *Where you mark it out*
>   *with the knife, just to start it off,*
>   *you might just get a little bit of a*
>   *mark with the knife, which you can't help,*
>   *but the valuable part of the skin,*
>   *all the butt and back and that . . .*
>   *that's perfect skin, alright?*

Who would have thought it needed
a winch and a steel hawser
to slowly, steadily, undress a calf?
Sure I can skin a rabbit
with my bare hands,
take its soft vest of fur
up and over its head —
rather too like
undressing a baby.
But skinning a calf,
a three days dead calf,
is another thing altogether.
It's like watching a birth,
not a flaying,
seeing the calf being born
a second time,

this headfirst slow emergence
from its skin
as if from the birth canal.
So dainty and delicate
in its glassy, gleaming pinks
and whites, its untried
muscles and tendons,
its organs — lungs, gut, heart —
never used ex utero.
Uterine vellum. Slunk.

> *A lot of people just want it totally clear*
> *and white, they're looking for*
> *something very consistent,*
> *more or less like a paper*
> *or a parchment,*
> *so you don't get the individuality,*
> *you don't get the markings,*
> *the faults, the holes . . .*
>
> *For me as an artist*
> *I'm interested in all those*
> *inconsistencies*
> *as a starting point*
> *for the composition —*
> *like it may be even a hole,*
> *I'll start winding a line of writing,*
> *curl around it . . .*

In the last years of the twentieth century
artist calligrapher Denis Brown
has set his *scriptorium* up
in an ordinary new house
in an ordinary new estate
on Dublin's southern edge.
In a might-be bedroom,
his workroom,
his steel pen has been
moving across fresh vellum,

a piece the shape and size,
say, of a gospel page,
but a dark pigmented skin —

> *A good calligrapher*
> *will have his flow and his rhythm*
> *and he will be able to sense the spacing —*
> *it comes almost from your pulse, really.*

He inscribes the word 'VICTIM'
and while the ink is drying
into the skin's soft nap —
he is piecing shards of glass
into a spiky corona
to halo that single word
from the Latin: *victima* —
living creature offered in sacrifice.

He fixes shard upon shard
to a frame of burnt wood
that will hold
skin — word — glass
together
in a charred box.
A razor-edged dark hole
that might hold:
victima —
vitella — little calf —
flayed skin shading a lamp

illumination.

St Thomas Aquinas in MacNeice's House
September 23rd, 1957: South Belfast

This is our last autumn at Aquinas Hall, and today
Sister Dymphna is teaching us Geography on a world scale
so as we can hold our own when we move to Secondary.
She squeaks a great chalk circle on the board
to explain the poise of this day, the twenty-third of September,
before the sun moves on towards *Capricorn*
and December's chilly *Solstice*. Today is the *Equinox*
when day is as long as night and the sun stands
right above the *Equator*, though you wouldn't know it
   in Malone
for a gale is battering down from the Black Mountain
onto the rain-blurred panes of the high sash windows
of our classroom, that used to be the Cream Drawingroom
of the MacNeice family, before the Reverend was translated
to be Bishop in Carrickfergus. Would he ever have known
that Dominican nuns built their chapel in his rose garden,
their convent dwelling on the great back lawn?

Christ's kitchenette opens straight off the sacristy.
Sister Sacristan washes the dishes that have held
His Body, His Blood, here, in this ordinary sink!
And here, too, she scrubs and rinses the linen
that has been napkin under chalice and paten,
catcher of any stray crumbs and spills of Him,
drying cloth for the priest's fingers and lips,
wiper round of the chalice's fingerbowl:
corporal, purificator, words we girls only know
from the Catechism, the boys in our class
old hands at serving Mass. So Sister Thomas
takes us four at a time from Geography
for our Sacristy Lesson. All I can think of is crumbs
and smears and St Thomas Aquinas. Was he the one
who went on about all those angels on the head of a pin?

So what would he say about all the tiny bits

of Christ Our Lord being swilled down the drain in suds?
Each fragment His whole Body, like when the priest
snaps and snaps the Host when he's running short
at Communion, unto eighths, sixteenths, sixty-fourths,
and all of them Christ! Sister, Sister Sacristan,
what happens to all those Christs when you pull the plug?

*Child dear, it is Holy Water, though not as Holy
as the Water I put in the stoups, or Water from Lourdes,
and it goes straight down into earth. Never fear it would enter
the unworthy, ordinary drains. See, I'll fill it and show you.*

And we watch the water empty from Christ's own sink
with no spin to the left or the right, but in a perfect descent
just as, Sister Dymphna has told us, the water empties
from bath and sink when your ship *Crosses The Line*
and the sun's *Zenith* is exactly overhead,
and the contrary spins of the *South* and the *North
Hemispheres* are in balance, like *Night* and *Day*
today, at the *Autumn Equinox*.

                    And I know, without asking,
that Christ's Body and Blood descend in His Holy Water
to water the ghosts of the roses of Bishop MacNeice.

Minding You

You say you want to go home.
Shall I drive you there, one last time?
Across the water,
over the Bog of Allen
and the great Shannon divide —
home, to Ballinahistle?
To the field that has been in your head
from seventeen years old
to seventy seven,
the years you have been away?

This is the in-field, just over
the parkeen wall, and past
the ancient stand-alone thorn
and the line of damson trees.
Young Tony, your brother's son,
will show us again
the mounds and eskers of stones
he and his nephews have picked
like hard grey potatoes
from the field's ploughed lines.
Is it never done with,
the stone-picking in this field?

Seventy years ago,
your first grown-up work:
October potato-picking,
then the second
months-long harvest of stones
as winter's rains revealed them,
crop after crop.

I would take you now
and put cold stones in your hands
at the in-field's sodden edge,
lead you into December's
sticky furrows,
if touch, and step
could somehow bring you home,
here, in England,
to your own lost mind.

After the Nuptial Mass

i

I am closed to you.
I have been closed to myself
a sphincter tensed against all
introitus, my anatomy
rather like yours that I've
just glimpsed: no third opening,
all pleasure-points external.

That first wine we drank today
from the chalice, surely
that will loosen me?
Christ's blood will let you in?

Marriage is third-best
in life's vocations
but we have saved for it,
barring a once or twice
incontinent spill of your seed
unseen, contained below,
your face suddenly flushed
hot for Confession.

Tonight you press hard, harder
against what is this day
sanctioned for breaking, but
you cannot enter. Neither
blessing nor flesh, it seems,
will be enough to breach
my inconsiderate border.

So on our wedding night
I lie alone between our
brand new sheets while you,
a teetotaller, find
your own horizontal
elsewhere, in some pub.

ii
In the days that follow
I sketch your erections for hours,
standing male nudes in the
charcoal and deep red
of our first bed-sitting room.

How failure draws us close!
What friends we are! This
is our joy, we say, our victory
wrested in martyrdom.

iii
But after weeks on a list
I am brought at last to my real
marriage-bed: clinical,
under gas. The surgeon forces
a metal entry. Cuts and
constructs the woman I am
to be. How suitably I bleed
at this my defloration.

I wake wide-eyed to imprint
upon pain as my first lover.
For weeks it informs me of
each detail of my altered
inner geography,
that new-found bay of flame.

For months I cannot bear
to ease you to that interior.
And when at last you come
you are not any more
the explorer you might have been,
never venture far beyond
the mouth of the bay, never
make landfall in me.
Never disembark.

Mary Rose Callan

Clean as a Wish

i. Carbolic

Tonight she'll finger a welt
where she pressed too hard

against the white sink
watching the breeze lift a wing of

Mrs Mulligan's sheets over ivy next door
and a drift of smoke from the other side —

Mrs Quirke knitting a winter cardigan
before her daughter comes home

in fireside time; she sees
through her window the roofless wall

that might have become
a room with a glass ceiling, somewhere

to fold her hands and remember
girls' skin bleaching the hem of the sea

ii. Old Spice

The way he edges a finger
round the borrowed hardback
reminds her he is only
home on leave.

iii. Sunlight

When new, it is hard
as a slab of butter

wintering

on the uppermost shelf.
You stand on tip-toe
to reach it

though the edges
make your eyes water.
Now you spread your hands

in yellow wash
and read the parchment
flakes of your life.

    iv. Sandalwood

is the colour of her skin when she opens
the top button of her blouse on Christmas evening
after giving the whole day to her poor brother's children
still there in spite of hints to the mother.

I know this because she's rolled ovals of it
into the wooden box I find with my name
at the base of the tree. Flakes stick to my skin
when she lowers her head for a goodbye kiss.

    v. Pears

Her children fall into bed
like unwashed apples.

A magazine opens
on her lap, bruised at the seam

where she thumbed it last night.
The dream child's skin

transparent,
and clean as a wish.

Her Grief

I intrude on her beautiful face
cradled between hands on brow, under chin.
She could be asleep. If I look long enough

I see her as woman in childbirth
faint before that first cry. Spoonful
of water held to her lips. Trickle of cold

that cannot revive. His limbs,
running in dreamtime as once
she imagined them, spreadeagled by

gunshot on a road in Bethlehem.

Facts of Life

Now a common place
for revelations, that apple tree
where attitude is frozen,

my chin sky high,
eyes on Louise,
mine and my sister's eyes, glued

to her pronouncement
on blood that would come
and run for forty years.

Moreover, she said,
and her face was red as
Beauty of Bath, more —

over. Her store of wisdom
shrank to ground like the buckets of
windfalls in the shed

that always ran out

before Christmas. Spared,
we hung on branch and

branch, my sister's sandal
grazing mine, and, yes
it was dark in that tree,

and we were a thousand
miles removed
from the wooden bench

where her mother and ours
rolled down their stockings,
drunk on tea.

Moya Cannon

Murdering the Language

Why did I love
the neat examination of a noun under the pointer,
the analysis of a sentence lifted out of talk,
canal water halted in a lock?

> *Mood, tense, gender.*
> *What performs the action, what suffers the action?*
> *What governs what?*
> *What qualifies, modifies?*

When we whispered in our desks
we spoke our book of invasions —
an unruly wash of Victorian pedantry,
Cromwellian English, Scots,
the jetsam and the beached bones of Irish —
a grammarian's nightmare.

But we parsed a small rectangular sea
and never missed the flow
or wondered why victories won in blood are fastened in
    grammar
and in grammar's dream of order;
or why the dream of order draws us as surely as the dream
    of freedom
or why correct language is spoken only in the capital.

Our language was tidal;
it lipped the shale cliffs,
a long and tedious campaign,
and ran up the beaches, over sand, seaweed, stones.

Laws learned by heart in school are the hardest to unlearn,
but too much has been suffered since

in the name of who governs whom.
It is time to step outside the cold schools,
to find a new, less brutal grammar
which can allow what we know:
that this northern shore was wrought
not in one day, by one bright wave,
but by tholing the rush and tug of many tides.

Ellie Carr

from *Traveller Ways Traveller Words*

· · ·

What me husband done, ever he done is he med gallons an' he med buckets. He med pots out o' the galvanized. He sould them. He worked here for three shops in Longfort. He'd bring a cart load inta Longfort here an' sell them in the shops. He was a cushtomer, you know? To Drumm an' Connolly and . . . Connolly and Drumm an' Cosgro'e. Thee're all dead and gone thim people too, that he used ta dayle with. There's no one makin' tins now. He was th' only tradesman now for around Lanesborough. 'Cos we lived all our life there. We were jusht, he was local. They usen't ta put him down ta be a Traveller at all, though we were fond of the pint, d'ya see? We couldn't do 'ithout that!

· · ·

When the woman'd have a child (I know it was me anyways and it was a lot like me) an' you wouldn't tell your husband 'til the lasht month. There was no runnin' ta doctors. You'd keep it to yoursel' or you'd tell it to no person. Besht cumrade ya had you wouldn't tell it to them that you were expectin' a child. We use' to wear the white petticoats an' the check aprons and we wouldn't tell anyone we were goin' havin' a child. Never. We'd think it a shame. We never wanted to report what you'd be goin' havin'. I had a baby. God speed 'im, he's dead now an' me husband never knew 'til a fortnight before he was born. So what do you think o' that? An' now today after five weeks they're gone to the doctors having them pullin' the belly out o' them! Divil a doctor we'd go ta! The doctor knows more about them than their min. But divil a man doctor ever seen my belly!

· · ·

Well a May mornin', we'd all get out an' wash our faces in the dew. The May dew, the mornin' dew. You'd want to be out aroun' five o'clock though. An' we'd get the shout from me mother, God resht her. An' all th'ould people an May Day, we'd have the tints then covered with flowers for the Blessed, honourin' the Blessed Virgin. That's all ever I knew now. 'Tis lucky t'honour the Blessed Virgin an' you'd never get your skin peeled. Your skin wouldn't get peeled for the whole hot summer 'round about now. And do you know if you were out at four o'clock of a May mornin' you'd see the sun an' moon dancin'. And they said that never shall be. And ya would. I never saw it. I'd be runnin' for the grass! I might never get out at four o'clock you know for to see it. But 'twas the truth though. I knew people that did see it. They looked out an' their caravans in the winda, in the back winda, people that was wakened and they seen the sun and moon dance. But that's the only people ever I heard talk o' seein' it, so now.

• • •

Ciaran Carson

from The Inferno of Dante Alighieri

Canto XV

Now we march along the stony margin,
    clouds of water-vapour overhead
    shield bank and river from the fiery rain.

As, between Wissant and Bruges, in dread
    of inundation by the tide, the Flemings raise
    their dikes to keep the North Sea in its bed;

and as the Paduans, along the Brenta, likewise
    fortify their homes and stately halls
    against the annual melt-water rise:

of similar conception were these walls,
    except that the Unknown Engineer
    had not constructed them as wide, or tall.

By now, so far away had we been steered,
    that had I turned and looked astern, 'twould seem
    the wood we left behind had disappeared,

when here, along the promenade, a team
    of spirits cruised up towards us, like those guys
    who stare at others in the dusk, when gleams

the sickle of a new moon in the sky,
    from under puckered eyebrows squinting at us,
    as old tailors do the needle's eye.

And while that company was peering thus,
    one of their number recognized me, caught
    me by the hem, and cried: "How marvellous!"

And as he stretched his arm towards me, I sought
    to make out from his ravaged features who
    the fellow was — his face was very scorched —

and then I realized, this was one I knew;
   so I bent down and gently touched his face,
   and said: "O Ser Brunetto, is it you?"

And he: "O son, don't think it a disgrace
   if Brunetto Latini stroll a bit
   with you, and let his men troop on apace."

And I: "With all my heart I do beseech it;
   or if my companion over there
   agrees, we could, instead of walking, sit."

"My son," he said, "if any of us troopers
   stops a second, for a hundred years
   he'll lie, forbidden to brush off the fire.

So march on; I'll follow at your skirts from here.
   and later join my regiment, who shed
   for their eternal loss eternal tears."

I did not dare to step down from the high road
   to his level; but, like one who walks
   respectfully, I kept a down-bent head.

He then began: "What destiny or luck
   has brought you here below, before your time?
   And who's your man that leads you on the track?"

"Up there, in the tranquil sunny clime,"
   I answered, "in a valley did I stray,
   not too long after I had reached my prime.

I left its borders only yesterday
   at dawn; I almost entered it again,
   when he appeared, to guide me on my way."

"Follow your star," said he, "and you will gain
   a glorious harbour, if whatever judgement
   I acquired above still appertains;

And, had I lived, I might have lent
   some cheer to this great work of yours, for Heaven
   seems to smile on the experiment.

But the ungrateful tribe of bloody hellions,
   who formerly came down from Fiesole,
   mountainmen of stony disposition,

Will proclaim themselves your enemy
   for your good deeds, and rightly: bitter pears
   could never tolerate the sweet fig-tree.

Blind animals, as history declares:
   a people full of envy, pride and avarice;
   take care to cleanse yourself of ways like theirs.

Your future fame will come to such a pass,
   both sides will hunger for a piece of you;
   but far beyond the goat will be the grass.

Then let the beasts of Fiesole strew
   their litter all about, and not impede
   the plant (O hardy plant that rises through

their piles of bullshit!) in whose holy seed
   survives the Roman pride of those who stayed
   when that malicious mob came down to breed."

"Could any wish of mine come true," I said
   to him, "you still would walk the world of light,
   and not this dreary region of the dead;

for in my memory is etched the sight
   of you, as, sympathetic and paternal,
   hour by hour you taught this neophyte

the ways that man can make himself eternal;
   while I live, my tongue will demonstrate
   how for your guidance I am ever grateful.

Whatever episodes you now relate,
   I'll write, and keep with others in my text,
   for Her perusal, should I reach Her state.

About this much I'd have you unperplexed:
   so long as my own conscience is no foe,
   I'm ready for whatever happens next.

There's little new I haven't heard, you know;
   so let the Dame of Fortune spin her wheel
   of chance, and let the yokel wield his hoe."

My master then turned briefly on his heel
   and, glancing at me, spoke this caveat:
   "He hears the best who pays the closest heed."

Undaunted, I, continuing in my chat
   with Ser Brunetto, asked him if he'd name
   the more notorious of his fellow chaps.

"I'll mention some, to put you in the frame,"
   said he, "but won't enumerate the legion —
   time's too short for such a lengthy game.

Briefly, most of them are clergymen
   and literati, all of great renown;
   on earth they shared the same perverted yen.

Priscian saunters with that wicked crowd;
   beside him, Francis of Accorso slopes,
   and if your bent is for a scurvy clown,

you might have spotted him who by the Pope
   was transferred to a lesser diocese
   to fray his 'nerves' away like beat-out rope.

There's more; but now, I'll give the speech a miss,
   and leave with equal speed: for there I see,
   across the sands, smoke rising from the surface —

new troops approach, with whom I may not be.
   I recommend my *Treasure* to you; there,
   my spirit lives; no more I ask of thee."

With that, he turned about, and off he hared
   like one of those who at Verona run,
   to gain the mantle green; and he appeared

no loser, but like one who has already won.

Kyriakos Charalambides
Translated by Greg Delanty from the Greek

Of the People of Olympia

Day drowned in coolness. The mother from Olympia
goes to her daughter-in-law, Vassiliki, and says:
"Michalis, I'm sure, he won't come back;
marry, my girl, you're a flower at your age."
How do you know, mother, where did you learn this?"
"Premonition assures me, it's a year since he died."

The daughter sheds her black, gets into white,
walks to the church as if to a funeral.
She gives birth to a child, names him after the dead.

from "The Tyranny of Words"

To justify their actions they even changed the meaning of words.
                                    Thucydides
I have already said that there is too much tyranny of words on this island.
It depends, quite plainly, on the Turkish army's arrival in Cyprus.
Invasion means different things to different people.
                                    Sir Ian Gilmour

His snow-white palm
darkly catches the stubborn rain.
A hare pops out of the bushes and lets on
it's observing the lettuce.
Suddenly it steals our show and vanishes
into my heart clenched with tentacles of pain.
His breath reeks of tobacco.
This hare arrived in a helicopter.

At 1:15 p.m. he landed in Larnaka.
"He came to observe," smiling all round
while behind his head
nestled his royal pimp.

He came to see. Carnations pop open
with the beat of the music. He strolls the foundry
of words with hammers and tongs, the devil himself.
Drinks are served before the meal's even finished.
They shake hands.
Ianus washed his hands.
What mother gave birth to him, what iron lady
patched him up into a prince? He handed us over,
our dirty linen, our so-called friend.
He forgot the callous on his foot
as he strutted around, smugly smiling.
Six years earlier, on the 14th July,
I believed in that smile.
Another day made it to night.
It took five nights to enter the twentieth darkness.

Ships lowered their hold
and vomited.
Pirates who were about to turn gardeners
took Morfou, picked lemons from Lapithos.

• • •

Spoon Sweet

I paid a trip to my own place
to see who I am. I went and stood
at the bitter house, near the ditch.
A woman in a headscarf brought me water.
She offered me a sweet dessert. I thanked her.

She plucked fruits from the Garden
of the house of my desire, shining fruits

of all kinds bursting at the lip,
soaked in the sweet balm of grace,
in the communion of shared gifts.

I thanked her. I got up courage and requested
to see inside my house, if it was permitted.

"Certainly, it's permitted," she said;
"You can see the bedroom also."

I entered, seeing my framed mother look at me
from the wall. I abandoned
shame and begged to take
my mother, poor thing, from Troy.

"Hell, take her," she says, smiling nicely,
"What can I do now I know?
To be honest we thought she was an actress
with all those flowers surrounding her,
with the grace she holds that parasol,
and, oh, that braid."

Certainly, is was worth mentioning also
that dainty gloved hand
reclining on the sofa, but what can you expect?

How could she know how many centuries
flew past until we reached the syntax
of the spoon sweet? A big question.

That the woman permitted me to enter
my family home was good enough.
Let's not go further and get her narked.
The only thing I wish: to have permission
to see again from time to time
the sight of the house of my longing.

Death's Art

King Cambyses, that Persian hard as granite,
was mad to humble
the Pharaoh Psammetichus,
his prisoner from Egypt.

He ordered that his old enemy
be placed in a cage of burnished silver
and set high above the Avenue of Lions.

The Pharaoh's daughter was paraded before him
lugging a water pitcher and with her breasts exposed
to torture him even more.

But the Egyptian remained a silent monolith,
his eyes fixed to the ground.

Cambyses, obstinate as ever, ordered
that the son of the Pharaoh be bound
and savagely dragged before his father's black eyes
on the way to being executed.

Still Psammetichus gazed stubbornly
at the ground, his silence imprinted
with an ant's humility, a snake's wisdom.

A long procession of shackled slaves
was filed before him.
A sole servant
was the only Egyptian martyr.

The Pharaoh broke into tears seeing this man,
his daughter and son too much for grief, beyond tears.

See how the Pharaoh prisoner
was so schooled in the art of death.

Candaules' Wife

To Stavros Petsopoulos

Poor Candaules wanted to teach his friend, Gyges,
a lesson in aesthetics.
He asked Gyges to behold his divine wife
naked as she got ready for bed.

You can say the like of this is foul.
How does this differ from offering your wife over
for money to the first person that happens by?

Still, I don't think that's quite right.
Firstly, Gyges was the most loyal
friend and brother of Candaules, secondly
Candaules had a high sense of virtue
and restraint, worshipping
his heavenly wife,
seeing her as a star.

Gyges was his best friend simply,
his trustworthy confidante, his bodyguard.
He wanted Gyges to realize
the measure of his love for his queen.

"When I tell you that she is the most beautiful
woman nature ever gave birth to, I'm not convinced
you get the extent of beauty
with mere words.
If you wish, my friend, and your heart can bear it,
come and see her with your own naked eye,
she being naked too. You'll know what I mean then."
Gyges acquiesced, seeing
nothing would satisfy Candaules
except to behold her unearthly beauty.

Everything was to be on the sly.
Gyges would hide at the door that led
to the bedroom. From there he could watch her

remove her garments one by one
and happily lay them on the chair
with a delicate frolic.
You'd swear the gods were peering at her. She'd pour
her fancy garments off as if they were oil, intoxicating
                                          wine.

Candaules' nightwords were on the ball,
she lit up the whole place
with her marble body's grace — she dazzled
the surprised heavens.
Gyges closed his poor eyes.
His heart was shaken.

His mistake was that he didn't withdraw silently
just as he had entered, breaking the agreement.
She sensed he was there. She didn't turn away,
but lay down to sleep in the arms
of her husband Candaules. (She reckoned
she'd let on to be oblivious).

The next day she woke and summoned Gyges.
In front of the servants she addressed him
as if in some folk tale: "Make up your mind
to kill your superior and take me
as your wife along with all his riches,
or else be slain on the spot; choose.
I give you my body, my flesh. I give you
the kingdom of Candaules, or
I give you the choice to kill yourself. These
are your only options; you saw me naked
and there's nothing more obscene to me."

The unfortunate pair decided
on the execution of innocent Candaules.
Ever since Gyges first saw
the vision he was motivated.
He killed Candaules dreaming

of the perfumes of his wife,
the vials and sweet fragrance spilling
from the vial of his soul into the bedchamber
as Candaules beheld his wife naked
beside Gyges.

Nitocris, Queen of Babylon

She achieved much
for the good of the people.
After a great deal of ingenious consideration
she initiated bridges, fortifications, diversions
(we are speaking of river diversion).

Before she died she designed a clever place
for her tomb above
the central gate. Out of respect
nobody passed beneath her body.

She added one other safeguard
over her tomb.
It had the air of augery.
Over her grave was the engraving:
"When some king is short
of funding, let him open my tomb,
but only if necessary; otherwise
leave well enough alone."

For sure nobody raised a finger
to despoil a tomb.
Besides, doves nested there.
"Mylitta" was branded on their wings.
But the impetuous foreigner, Darius,
bade them open the tomb of Nitocris
(mostly, I figure, to gain access
to the forbidden gateway).

What did he see when the tomb was opened!
Not a penny – just bones
and a note that read:
"Money grubber, you wouldn't have opened this tomb
if you weren't such a character."
Being a cultured man
he shuddered,
interpreting it as a prophecy that read:
"You have opened your own tomb."
He ordered his guards to reseal it pronto
and to fetch back the birds.

Potiphar's Wife

> *And Joseph was a goodly person and well favored.*
> Genesis

Petefri, the chief chef and eunuch,
wanted to prove to himself
that he too could have a wife.

He said to the Pharaoh "If I can cook up
erotic dishes, by Horus, I have a right
to partake of the dainty titbits of life."

He was rewarded with the most desirable slave
of the palace. Now he too had a lovely dish.

Petrifi dressed her up in gold,
set a scarab at her neck.
He fastened a downy chastity belt
over her exquisite diaphanous belly.

He was overwhelmed with joy and power.
He went on cooking his master's ducks.

She withered, faceless and inviolate,
envying the mummies,

until one day Joseph came along.
He was handsome, twenty years younger than her,
forty years younger than her hubby.

He stood like a frigid Hebrew rock,
knowing duck-all about Phaedra and Euripides.
All he was concerned with was
his honor, and the cook's Egyptian corn,

the cook knew more about that
than the misfortune of his own wife.

If God could have intervened
he could have told the cook what to be careful of,
but as per usual God remained neutral
even though he sympathized with the woman.

She weeps and entreats him to stay
with her. "Take my heart, give me
your clothes, make me feel human again, Joseph."

But nope, Joseph was virtuous as ever,
bound to the strictures of his fathers
and to the key of trust.

Tears For Twenty-Five Years

> *For twenty-five years they mourned for another person because of a mistake of the authorities. The new tragedy came to the surface after the disinterment of the remains of the second lieutenant.*
>
> from a Cypriot newspaper, November 1999.

They wept for him for twenty-five years,
his pure innocent features. At least
that's what they thought, but then they learned
that the man they wept for was someone else —
he silently accepted their tears,
unable to tell them what he knew

(besides, their mourning suited him).

When the earth was dug up
and the broken note of the truth rose
to the surface, the people felt bitter;
for a quarter of a century
they lamented him, but
if they had only turned their heads a little to one side
they'd have seen him unshaven and unwept for
curled listening to them on his bed.

He walked alone for twenty-five years.
They didn't catch a whiff of him
(this accident of life suited him;
in heaven your external appearance doesn't matter
a great deal except
if you're a wizened crooked old person or deformed).

Now that his sweet face
emerges from the pallor of bone
they weep for their own all over again,
for the man who fell for the winged
birds and the heavenly garden.

Michael Coady

Interview on Main Street

— *So what kind of things do you write about?*

Here's one for starters coming down Main Street
though by the time he gets here you'll be gone.
From top of Bridge Street to Barrack Lane and back
is a five minute stroll for upright man.
For him it's a slow-motion marathon.

He's learned to stay the course upon two sticks,
and pace himself by window-sills and shops —
if you lived here you'd not need to be briefed
on how a vigorous, astute, hard-swearing man
could take up Zen and mime such passages.

How slow is slow before being in a state
of stopped? Is this what Einstein was on
about, the gist to the effect that stopped
is just another grade of going on?
(Such issues were aired near Slievenamon

one Field Day as the Prize was being passed
to the winner of the Slow Bicycle Race
when out of nowhere a stranger popped up his head
to claim that he'd just crossed the line, unmarked.
I'm first, he said, because I came in last.)

So far the question has been one of pace
and we have overlooked our old friend pain.
There's little here that's worth your while to tape:
try asking the two stick man how things are —
he'll peer at you and answer *not too bad*.

Instead, you could decide that it's a wrap
and head off to link up with the N7
before he's reached the sill of AllStar Travel.
You could evade rush hour, be home by the time
two stick man is back at starting point.

Low Winter Sun

Better to rot on the bare hillside
than be consigned
to that new graveyard
(the one with the *No Dumping* sign)

that they've opened beside the old —
a compound created
by some double-glazed official
devoted to tidiness and concrete.

Pity all those who'll end up there
laid out in well-drilled lines
unlike their kind nearby
in their disorderly domain

that's there because it happened
year on year in layers
of tumbled and tangled lives
composting, story on story,

into a deep meadow
of remembrance and forgetting
around tipsy stones inclined
sooner or later to fall

shamelessly
into the arms
of seeding grass
and illicit flowers.

That ground sings to me
of beautiful abandon,
where new arrivals were borne
and bedded in their time,

with muttering and panting
and unsteady steps
by the living
who had to feel their way

when they came in turn
to carry one another
over random humps and hollows
and hidden stones

that could wait for years
to trip you up,
like death,
at the right wrong time,

such as when
you were looking
the other way,
or stumbling

with wind and rain
in your face
or a low winter sun
in your eyes.

School Tour, Kilmainham Jail

These kids could scarce imagine
a lost dawn chorus greening on the air
above the Stonebreakers' Yard,

the swell of birdsong shattered
by an imperious voice
commanding thunder.

Yet the children's presence in the yard
is part of aftermath and story,
while far removed from Maytime

fusillade or instant aftershock
that triggered prayer and rage
and terror in the cells

against the muffled orders
for the tidying away
and brisk disposal of the parts

before the sluicing of the stones
in blushing water —
some forgotten

orderly of empire
baptising the beginning
of its end.

Enda Coyle-Greene

Another Moon

It could have been the beauty of the moon
that drew him in
towards the open window. Other insects pulled
against the seeping night, were pinned
against the glass: thinner-skinned,
the kitchen light dissected
them.

Perhaps the never bolted back door squealed
on unoiled hinges and alerted him.
My father, sleeping off
the television's squeezed white dot,
had the sound turned down. I never heard
the moon blow out
another moon

into a puddle in the field behind our house;
mud stopping where its round white *O*
sluiced stagnant water. I only saw
the mirror of the moon
move out from where it lay and leave
a loosened image floating
bald and white

as a man's bare head with a hand that clawed
against the high back wall. I could only hear
the hiss, the thump
thump thumping of her
cool reluctant iron: a dull
and far-away gun

going off, somewhere.

Grafton Street

For a while, the closed hours ticked
in the dark between the clothes rails,
waited, as the air stilled to tissue
paper folds, carefully
creased into place.

The shutter flickered as dreams turned
uneasily behind it: an eyelid,
a membrane, between what is real
and what can be bought
and carried off

or worn by the mannequins that hold
their aching poses by the escalator;
each raised arm like a cold stone
wing on a graveyard angel
dressed for flight.

But now, the day is opening again.
The light is a colour that runs and keeps
running — it has to be returned; it seeps
in as the metal stretches
and the door is unlocked

and the sound of the street slips past
the security man. It seems to him as if
the city never slept; he barely notices
that the gutters are coated
in dust the wind will lift

up, to send the way of blown skirts,
all over the curved slow hill of the street.
The sea can be felt then, its salt pressed
to air-shades, invisible
among the roof slates.

The shop assistant arriving for work
walks in as white fluorescence stutters, fits:
unpacked, unfolded, taken out,
her day ahead is a shirt,
still pinned.

Handed On

I consider the things I'll leave
after me: a ring, on my finger, last worn
by my godmother aunt
in her room at the Mater, its ruby eye alert
between two diamonds, only out of its box
for the glittering occasion
that dying must be.

Or the crown-stamped wedding band
that belonged to my mother-in-law's
mother-in law. I'm told she was tall
and bold and auburn-haired;
I have my own picture. I'm certain
she never saw me
wearing it.

There's my Claddagh, heart faced
to the right place, indicating that I'm all his —
that and the blue and white stones, chosen
by everyone that year
and the Celtic circle, real silver,
my daughter paid good money for
in Kilkee.

Between all of these there's my pen:
my lucky black, Amsterdam Hilton
very ordinary ballpoint.
I fool myself that it helps,
that by gently bearing down
on the page, I might leave something
there, as both of us age

and the ink runs out.

Opium

This is how it will be.

A large dog, yellow, I think,
will shake himself free
of a river, a sea.

Before he is dry
he will run to you, cloaked
in a river, a different sea.

Sometime, in winter perhaps,
you'll shift a screen of curtain,
sift the night

through an open window,
lean across your kitchen sink
to lift a cat in, black

I imagine. His fur will be
short, dense,
filled with fog.

You'll breathe him in, and in
your present tense
think only of your past.

Some day, somewhere
in a city I can't see,
a woman will pass

you in a crowd; drugged
by her perfume, the heady scent
she will leave after her,

you won't struggle as you fall
back to now:
and you will remember me

telling you this.

Vertigo
In memory of my father

It's not the only thing you left me,
this free-falling, light-headed lurch
towards nothing in particular.
Nor is it the best
you could have wished for me:
that I should be gripped
by the same plain fear
you couldn't even name
in the end.

In the end
I tried to sound it out for you,
looking down from my great height,
feeling two seasons shake
this tree,
this monstrous, bluey-green
undying obscenity,
my toes curled at the thought of flight
from these vertiginous branches.

No, it was never your intention
to leave me, to go like that, stepping off into air
the colour of your honest eyes,
quietly surprised at first, I imagine
by the ease with which you went
spinning down
as the ground came up:
while the wind sang the years
backwards
in your head.

The Rooms

*Who shall measure the heat and violence of the poet's heart
when caught and tangled in a woman's body?*
                    Virginia Woolf,
                    A Room of One's Own

This space is numbered. My eye counts the acres
reduced to this estate, the rows of roads, these blocks
on blocks of living place. I breathe. I shut down at night
but never dream of here. The walls are thin, sound travels
through them easier than air. The television burbles like a drunk
in my sitting room, while the radiators complain and heat goes
into corners I can't get to. Today

it's the first day of spring, St. Brigid's day, the patron saint
of poets, amongst other things. I would like to think
I'd never have to vacuum again, never drag that lumpen body
over floor-rugs by its tail until, smooth as a rule
never broken, all life sucked out of them,
they give in, lie in wait for skin and hair
to pare off someone else.

The stereo kicks in. Bass notes make the bricks wilt.
I ask myself, what else is there? There's the kitchen. I hear
poison is prepared there, that clothes endure the iron after
they've been pummelled, sluiced, then, guts removed, displayed
on the gibbet in a good stiff breeze
until they have atoned for any stains.
It's also where cats spin

their marble stares on mine, say, *We are here and you are here
to mind us.* They expect me to find their food. I would
if I could find myself. It is dark in the attic.
Of course, there are bedrooms: two to sleep in, one a box
I've been known to crawl into on occasion, barely
big enough for me to swing a word in,
stretch a pen.

Despite my best efforts, the rooms swell with creatures. I blink,
they are tall. I keep blinking. I shrink. They are fabulous

jewels worth stealing. They don't bother to whisper as they plot
their own lives, their beautiful futures. Stopped dead
on the landing, at the head of the stairs,
the bathroom accosts me, it shames me
into rubber gloves: I'm afraid

I'll leave my fingerprints somewhere.

So Many

We never noticed you,
although our placid moon-round faces
felt the furnace heat of yours
to be too close.

You invented lives for us: lies
of mythical additions and omissions,
where we became so many
heroines. We never knew
the meaning of the word; still,
you persisted in naming us
thus.

        But ask yourselves
where we are now. We didn't rot
beneath an unforgiving earth, no death
or birth attended us, or offered us
the chance to leg it
out of there, out of the blue front door,
away from you.

Click.

Our hard lids shuttered our dull eyes,
and so we never saw
your worn all summer cotton clothes,
your whitened over, scuffed Communion shoes,
or you, arrayed like us in rows:
like us, so many
dolls.

Anthony Cronin

On Seeing Lord Tennyson's Nightcap
at Westport House

And did he suddenly, while the little train clunked over the
    long stretch of brown bog outside Castlebar,
The farewell gaze of the younger Miss Browne still warming
    the impressionable cockles of his poet's heart,
The memory of her ladyship snoring through *Maud* last night
    becoming at last less painful,
Or while it clacked past the undrained fields between
    Claremorris and Ballyhaunis —
"They really are a feckless people, they never do anything
    except out of immediate need" —
Or perhaps as the Gothic spire of Roscommon topped a tangle
    of untended trees —
"They live in hovels but they spend thousands on churches" —
Did he suddenly remember
That he had not put in
The blasted nightcap?
And, seeing in his mind's eye the offending garment lying
    huddled on the bedside chair,
Hearing in his mind's ear how he had said to Lord Altamont's
    man,
"I'll pack the overnight bag myself,"
And remembering how he had reminded himself, I must put
    that in,
Did he wonder in panic,
Would they send out for one from the Shelbourne?
Or would he have to go shopping in Dublin?
— An appalling prospect, not to be entertained.
But he could not, he positively could not be without one on
    that draughty boat.
He would get his end.

And so, as the Byzantine mass of Athlone Cathedral swung
    into the frame of the window,
Did he sit in gloom,
Becoming aware,
Once again,
Of
The heartache
At the heart of
Things?

In Praise of Hestia, Goddess of the Hearth Fire

A goddess with no stories about her
Is obviously exceptional.
Though your average goddess may sometimes claim
She wants to be alone,
She hears the void hiss when she opens
A magazine which does not mention her name;
And nearly all are ready
To throw good men aside like sweetpapers
While risking everything except, they hope,
Their looks for a whirl with an oaf who will,
They secretly suspect,
Eventually sell the story to a tabloid newspaper.

How strange then that there should be one
Beautiful inhabitant of the divine village
Who is never involved
In a public brawl with another woman
Or in a law suit with a former lover,
Who will never stage a hysterical scene
For the benefit of the bystanders
Or the gawking barmen;
And who, though the sister of Zeus,
Is neither a snob nor a dissatisfied intriguer.

And little wonder too that we turn
With relief and joy to the worship of one
To whom no stories attach:
Hestia, goddess of the ever-burning hearth fire,
Of the suspended coal.
In her dealings with mortals
There are no dramatic entrances and exits,
No stand up, knock down, drag out ructions,
The goddess appearing as whirling sword wielder,
Screaming blue murder and bloody revenge,
Nothing except the ongoing,
Almost untellable tale
Of human content,
Of love's flame enriched by its shadows,
Of how walls have stood while the wind of malice
Moaned like a lost soul without.
She is the protector of all who,
However foolish their once lives,
Come to her as suppliants.
Who demands nothing except that when we come

It is as individuals,
Not as members of a crowd or caucus,
And as ourselves,
Not as heroes or saints or statesmen or sages,
More like ourselves
Than we have ever dared to be otherwise,
More like ourselves
Than we could ever hope to be but in her presence.

Meditation on a Clare Cliff-Top

A fine day after storm in County Clare.
The waves are snatching at King George's Head.
The short grass of the cliff fields being cropped
By bullocks with a placid eye, I walk
On dizzying heights above the thunderous caves;
Can look down on the gulls in spume-shot air,
America beneath me too, beyond
The curve of ocean covering the earth
And held like me by gravity. I lean,
Light blue opacity above, dark blue below,
My raincoat tented wide against the wind,
A balancer elate upon a height.

And soon the Atlantic sunset from the cliff.
I'm not one for description, but the rich
Red path to the horizon, the huge disk
Sinking it seems beyond an edge, the clouds
Flaring to crimson up above while dark
Waits to enshroud and curtain the whole show,
It makes me against reason feel a part
Of something of some huge significance,
Profound and fraught with meaning and for me.
Of course it's ludicrous it should induce
This feeling in me. Me, black dot on cliff,
The word is pantheist. The example Wordsworth.

Before he died astronomers had counted
Fifty thousand other suns out there.
Bessel discovered, using parallax,
That one, called Cygni, was some sixty million
Miles above his laurel-wreathed head.
He didn't let it phase him. Suns he said,
Using the plural, speaking as we know of
A presence that disturbed him with the joy
Of elevated thoughts, a sense sublime
Of something far more deeply interfused

That dwelt within the light of setting suns
And the round ocean and the living air.
And in, of course he said, the mind of man.

They've raised the ante since. It's not just suns
But galaxies, I think ten million million
Not to mind other bangs and universes
And universes too on top of that.
And since there are countless other solar systems
They tell us that there must be other planets
All with their sudden afterglows like this
— So beautiful that when you turn and look
It's like a gulp of wind to catch the breath.
And, they insist, there must be chaps like me
To walk on cliff-tops, even County Clares,
— Or if not chaps like me then legless beings
Far cleverer than us and on their way.

I somehow doubt it. Deep within the bone
I disbelieve that there is anywhere
Like this Clare cliff-top with its close-cropped grass,
Or any wind like this Atlantic wind
Or any beings like us, so blown about
With beauty, terror, mystery and wonder.
And if they haven't this, what do they have
That can transcend their doubtless mortal lot
And give them something they can call a soul
And make them interesting to you and me?

When I began to read first there was talk
Of life on other planets. Venus, Mars,
And even the poor old moon were said to have
Inhabitants who might one day arrive
In strange machines to trouble Wimbledon
And Surrey and such legendary places.
But now we know that we are quite alone
Within the solar rays. Jules Verne was wrong
And both the Well(e)s's, Orson and H. G.,

The men from Mars not there and no green men,
Venusians to give the Christians pause
With a strange message of another love,
Or Fabians cheer with factory laws undreamt.

We have zoomed through zeniths heretofore unknown
But now within our daring human fling,
Sending our best, the camera, the mike,
The bodiless, scooping, metal hands aloft,
Only to find there's no-one there at all.
Within the rays of our sun anyway
There's nothing "highly organised" but here,
Not even frog-spawn, lovely scum of life.
It's down now to bacteria lapping dust,
Dry work at best, mere anaerobes agasp,
And even these improbable, no
Sentience within the realms of ice
And in the gas clouds no great gas at all.

It may be even that we're quite alone
In this vast whistling gallery, a folly
On which we'll bounce our radio waves in vain
And vainly bounce our speculations too.
The odds against life anywhere are long:
A shimmering atmosphere like ours, a balance
Of breathable heat and cold, of wet and dry,
A sun a certain distance, neither more
Nor less, to fructify, not burn all life away,
Or fail to melt the envelope of ice.

I pick my steps going homeward in the dark
And keep as far as possible inland
In spite of restless bullocks on my flank.
Some of these fissures run in quite a way
And if you don't take care — say, thinking of
The mundane matters that afflict us all,
Or gazing at the star-pierced deep of sky
And musing on the planet Jupiter,

Whose air is pungent, poisonous ammonia,
Or Saturn, shrouded in storms of splintered ice,
You could easily wind up spiked on pointed rock
Or swept by swirling waves into a cave.

If we're alone, what then? Does that not make
This little earth of ours more precious still?
Our troubled human kind, inventive, lithe,
Ingenious, deceitful, precious also?
If there is no one else out there to talk to,
Argue with, fight and look to but ourselves.
We've company enough in all the beings
So various, so beautiful, so strange,
Who've been our victims and our friends so far.

Earth, water, fire and air Greek sages said.
It still seems that's the formula, a fine
Day your honour and the wave-torn cliffs of Clare,
Earth and its oceans home to myriads,
Whales, damselflies, jerboas, jumping mice,
Humped bison, hedgehogs, horses, yes, and bullocks,
Soft velvet clouds of migrant butterflies,
Grey polyps floating over churning sand,
And on the high brown veldt of Africa
The protozoa called Trypanosoma,
Which causes sleeping sickness, milling in
Together, where man toils, accommodates —
Man, gardener, builder, hunter, worshipper
Of buffalo and snake and kangaroo,
Who saw the stars, beneficent and pale,
As I see Venus now above the waves,
Low in the west, bright star of evening love.

Philip Crymble

Tomatoes

An unexpected letter in the mail today. Our names
    inscribed in fountain pen. The franking mark an inky
        Rorschach smudge. Inside the envelope: old clippings

from the local daily, a photograph enlarged on freckled
    paper, the sender's note of explanation folded sensibly
        and stapled to the rest. A little German lady owns

the house. Last year she saved our beef tomatoes —
    drove stakes into the soil, tied the leafy branches back
        with twine. Her father butchered rabbits raised

in cages here — used their droppings as a fertilizer.
    In shirtsleeves, trousers clasped with braces, he's dwarfed
        by plants that tower ten feet high. Old photographs are all

so public-minded. Behind our cellar door, the shadow
    of those vines. A wheel for sharpening. Dim electric
        light. The years of quiet violence. What that was like.

Rice Lake
for David, in memoriam

North at exit 464 to Bewdley on the 28, drive slowly
    out past highway 9, the lake will be there on your right.
        Keep going up to Balieboro, you just might find an old

dirt road that leads its way to places well beyond
    what's signed: places so far gone they're but a memory
        faint as gaslight from the mantle of a dying lamp.

Wood-smoke in our clothes and hair, your father's *Coleman*
    cooler stocked with long-necks, and the *Evenrude* still warm.
        We'd cast from shore a while, the slap and splash of water

on the dock, our talk of pan-fish, how to whet a knife. Closer
    then than blood between two brothers — close as life allows.
        Those summer nights burn stronger now you're not around.

Philip Cummings

Translated by Gréagóir Ó Dúill and Philip Cummings

Deochanna

Agus mé óg
ba ghnách liom fínéagar a ól
go díreach ón bhuidéal,
ach, ar theacht in aois dom,
thiontaigh mé chun an fhíona.
Anois,
agus mé leathshean,
blaisim arís den deoch searbh
mar gur tairgeadh dósan é
is go bhfuil mé réidh
lena dhiúltú.

Drinks

When I was young I used
drink vinegar by the neck.
As I grew older
I turned to wine.

Now, half old
I taste the tart and bitter once again
for it was offered to him
and I'm now big enough to
turn it down.

Uiscí Reatha

Ag amharc trí abhainn
ar an spéir,
mar nach fiú mé go n-amharcfainn go díreach
ar an spéir
nó gur chreid mé an tráthnóna sin
nárbh fhiú mé,
nochtadh dom gur ón spéir
a tháinig an abhainn
is gur chun na spéire
a rachaidh sí,
agus guím,
is mé ar bhruach na habhann
ag stánadh tríthi ar an spéir,
go mbeidh mé san abhainn
nuair a fhágfaidh sí an domhan seo,
nuair a fhillfidh sí
chun na spéire.

Running Water

Watching the sky
through the river
because I am not worthy to watch
the sky straight on
or because I believed that afternoon
I was not worthy
it was vouchsafed to me that it was from the sky
the river came
and to the sky
the river will go
and so I pray
standing here on the riverbank
staring through the river at the sky
I pray that I'll be in the river
when she leaves this earth
and returns to the sky.

Newton*

Chaith mé an oiread sin oícheanta
ag stánadh isteach san fharraige
gur tháinig cuid den fharraige isteach ionam:

gur fuaraíodh mo chuislí,
gur siocadh mo mheon,
gur briseadh mo chosanta,
gur líonadh mo thrá,
gur bádh mo dhúile uilig

ach amháin an dúil seo

de bheith de shíor ag siúl cois cladaigh
ag cruinniú méaróg daite ar dhóigheanna neamhghnácha
ag ealaíontóir na gcloch.

Newton

I spent so many nights staring into the sea
that some of it invaded me:

and froze my veins,
iced my mind,
broke down my dykes,
became my floodtide,
and drowned each one of my desires

except for this desire

to be always walking by the shore
collecting pebbles painted in an unusual way
by the artist of the rocks.

    * "I do not know what I may appear to the world, but to myself I seem to have been only like a boy playing on the sea-shore, and diverting myself in now and then finding a smoother pebble or a prettier shell than ordinary, whilst the great ocean of truth lay all undiscovered before me." LT Moore *Isaac Newton* (1934) lch.664

Anne

Lig mé duit imeacht inné,
dhá bhliain déag i ndiaidh imeacht duit.

Mhúch mé an choinneal sin
a choinnigh ó chodladh mé oiread sin oícheanta
nach léir anois dom am luí ná éirí.

Creidim anois
nach bhfillfidh do scáil
le mo mhealladh le cuimhní grá,
le mo chiapadh, le mo chrá.

I do dhiaidh
níl cumha orm,
ná brón, ná áthas,
ach fiacla ghaoth na farraige aduaidh,
friofac na sreinge deilgní,
fuacht oighear na maidne.

Tóg leat ar bhronn mé ort, a thaisce,
tá a bhfuil fágtha de thaisce s'agamsa
réidh anois
le titim arís.

Anne

I let you go yesterday,
twelve years after you left.

I extinguished that candle
that kept me from sleep so many nights
I can no longer distinguish dusk from dawn.

I believe now
that your shade will not return
to haunt me with memories of love,
to torment, to taunt me.

In your absence
I feel no nostalgia,
no sorrow, no joy,
but the bite of a seaborne north wind,
the spike of barbed wire,
the chill of morning ice.

Take with you all that I gave you, my treasure,
what is left of my own treasure is
ready now
to fall again.

Séamus

Col ceathar dom, *twice removed:*
ar dtús, chuaigh sé go dtí na Stáit Aontaithe;
ar fhilleadh dó, chuaigh sé isteach sna hÓglaigh.
Mar a dúirt mé, *twice removed.*

B'eisean a theagasc dom tarracóir a thiomáint, mar Séamus,
b'eisean a threoraigh mo lámha is mé ag bleán na mbó,
b'eisean a thug mé ag baint sméara leis
fadó, fadó ar maidin
nuair ba ghasúir muid
nuair nárbh ionann an bás ach sionnach ar thaobh an bhóthair
nár bhuairt aigne ach an dóigh ar shracamar an teanga de
ag súil leis an *vermin bounty* a fháil ó na póilíní.

Na póilíní,
a choinnigh a chorp i bpáirc iomlán lae
is iad ag cuardach bobghaistí, mar dhea, i smidiríní an tarracóra.

"Ó, Séamus, tá tú i mBéal Feirste?
Ag déanamh cúrsa innealtóireachta sa Tech?"

Is dócha gur theip air
mar a theip ar an bhuama a spréigh a chnámha
thart ar pháirceanna ár n-óige.

Seamus

A cousin of mine, twice removed:
first, he went to the US of A;
on his return, he joined the Provies.
As I said, twice removed.

He taught me to drive a tractor, the same boy,
his hands guided mine when I was milking the cows,
he took me berry-picking with him
once upon a time in the morning
when we were boys
and death was only a fox at the side of the road
and mental torment only the way to rip the tongue from it
hoping to collect the vermin bounty from the police.

The police,
who kept his remains lying in a field for a whole day
while they pretended to search for booby-traps in the wreckage of the tractor.

"Oh Seamus, you're in Belfast?
Doing an engineering course at the Tech?"

I suppose he failed it
just like the bomb which spread his bones
over the fields of our youth failed.

Reilig an Mhuine Ghlais

Ar ais i gceann de na háiteanna seo
an spéir ag glanadh i ndiaidh ceatha earraigh,
doirse agus dorchlaí ag oscailt sa bhrat dubhach os mo chionn
a ligeann anáil amach, a ligeann solas isteach
ar na seanleachta tríphointeacha,
cuid acu ar cromadh,
mar mhéara ag gobadh amach as an chré,
an chré as a dtáinig mé, an áit a bhfuil mo thriall.

Tá uaigh romham; tá uaigh i mo dhiaidh.

Ag ligint orm féin go bhfuil mé ag cuardach mhuintir mo mhná
siúlaim go fánach trí na huaigheanna
ag cruinniú bailte fearainn,
ag ríomh aoiseanna na marbhán.

Le fírinne, ní bhím ag cuardach rud ar bith i reilig:
faighim é.
Tagann néal suaimhnis orm sna háiteanna seo,
sásamh ciúin san éalú ón ghnáthshaol,
san eolas dearfach go bhfuil deireadh cinnte ann.

Fiú ar chuairteanna oíche,
níl iarracht d'eagla ghalrach
sa ghlacadh gur anseo a bheidh mé.

Tá uaigh i mo dhiaidh; tá uaigh romham.

Amanna, déanaim iarracht m'uaigheanna féin a aimsiú.
Le mearbhall a chur ar thurasóirí liteartha
roinnfear mo chorp faoi thrí:
cuirfear cuid de sa reilig faoin sliabh i *Sóller,*
grian ghoimhiúl na Spáinne agus an dreapadh doiligh
ina mbaic orthu nach bhfuil a gcroí istigh san oilithreacht;
cuid eile láimh le teach an phobail Thoraí,
áit a mblaisfidh mé an cúr is an sáile,
an fharraige niamhrach ag cur coisc ar fhiosracht;
tá an chuid is rúnda díom curtha sna focail seo.

Is cuma, mar tá mo luaithreach in achan phub in Éirinn cheana,
nó bhí roimh an chosc ar chaitheamh.

Níl sé molta sna treoirleabhair
— cé gur sábháilte reilig ná áit spraoi —
ach bhí tachrán liom an tráthnóna seo,
í ag rith go meidhreach idir ballaí ísle na n-uaigheanna.

Nuair a thug sí leapacha orthu
bhí mo dhán déanta.

Moneyglass Cemetery

Back in another of these places
the sky clearing after a spring shower,
doors and corridors opening in the dark clouds above me
letting life out, letting light in
on the old, three-pointed headstones,
some of them toppling,
like fingers poking out of the clay,
the clay from which I came, the clay which is my destination.

There is a grave in front of me; there is a grave behind me.

Pretending that I'm searching for my wife's people
I wander aimlessly among the graves
collecting townlands,
counting the ages of the dead.

In truth, I'm not searching for anything in graveyards:
I find it.
A cloud of peace descends on me in these places,
a quiet satisfaction in the escape from life,
in the positive knowledge that there is a definitive end.

Even on night-time visits,
there is no trace of morbid fear
in the acceptance that here is my mortal end.

There is a grave behind me; there is a grave in front of me.

Sometimes, I amuse myself trying to locate my own graves.
To confuse literary tourists
my body will be divided in three:
one part will be buried in the graveyard under the mountain in Sóller,
the punishing sun of Spain and the difficult climb
putting off those whose hearts are not really in the pilgrimage;
another part beside the chapel on Tory,
where I will taste the foam and the salty spray,
the shining sea blocking the merely inquisitive;
the most secret part of me is buried in these words.

It won't matter, as my ashes are in every pub in Ireland already,
or at least they were before the smoking ban.

It is not advised in the self-help books
— although a cemetery is safer than a playground —
but there was a toddler with me this afternoon,
running joyfully around the low walls of the graves.

When she called them beds
my poem was completed.

Celia de Fréine

Translated by Celia de Fréine

In Aois

Tar éis dom chara a ghortaigh a droim
pacaí teasa is tarraingthe a thriail
tá sí in ann í féin a chorraí
go mall ciotach.

Tugann sí cuireadh chun lóin dom.
Le cúnamh an chortasóin tá mise in ann
mé féin a fheistiú is a chorraí
go mall ciotach.

Le dua leagaim mo thóin ar shuíochán
paisinéara a cairr. Is ar éigean is féidir
le ceachtar againn éirí as is ár mbealach
a dhéanamh chuig an mbialann.

Ba sa rang céanna a d'fhoghlaim muid rince,
cispheil, is camógaíocht.
Mar chuid de chomórtas sraithe lá
shleamhnaigh mise an sliotar chuici.

Sháigh sise isteach sa chúl é.
Chaill muid an cluiche — a haon: a dó.

Getting On

My friend who hurt her back
and has been treated
with heat-packs and traction
can now move slowly and awkwardly.

She invites me out for lunch.
The cortisone has begun to work —
I can now get dressed
and move slowly and awkwardly.

With difficulty I ease myself
onto the passenger seat of her car.
The two of us barely manage to struggle out
and make our way to the restaurant.

We learnt Irish dancing together —
basketball and camogie.
Once during a league match
I slid the *sliotar* to her.

She rammed it into goal.
We lost the game — one: two.

Louis de Paor
Translated by Louis de Paor

Foghlaimeoirí

"*Kaykweeawillthoo?*" ar tú,
ag sleamhnú isteach lem ais,
cumhracht aibreoige leata
ar do chorp tar éis cheatha.

Ghlacas sceit
nuair a chuala an guth allúrach
ag labhairt liom
as do liopaí scartha.

"*Thorampogue ashtore,*" ar sise,
is thabharfainn an leabhar
gur tusa a labhair
nó gur bhalbhaigh a béal binn
trudaireacht bhriotach mo chroí,
lá breá is a theanga amuigh aige
le craos leabhair nótaí
ag alpadh focal sna Gorta Dubha:
— *clais, criathrach, díog* —
sa chistin ceann tuí,
— *clúid, gríosach, tlú* —
bolg le gréin ar Thráigh an Chloichir.

"*Gotcho,*" arsa an glór mínáireach im aice;
chuir a teanga lúfar isteach im chluais,
láimh shlim ar mo philibín cleite,
géaga láidre im thimpeall
nó gur éirigh de spreang orm
tonn focal teaspaigh
a bhain freang as mo dhrom righin,
a chlúdaigh mo chraiceann
ó rinn go sáil
le gramadach aclaí,
a mhúin dom ceacht ar Ghaorla gasta,
ar Bhéarlachas líofa na bpluid.

Homework

"*Kaykweeawillthoo?*" says you,
slipping in beside me
after your shower,
your body smelling of apricots.

I nearly jumped from my skin
when a stranger's voice
whispered to me suggestively
from your parted lips.

"*Thorampogue ashtore,*" she says,
and I could have sworn it was you
until her sweet talk silenced
the lisping stammer of my heart,
a *lá breá* with his tongue
hanging out, eager as a notebook,
guzzling words in the Black Fields
— *clais, criathrach, díog* —
in the thatched kitchen,
— *clúid, gríosach, tlú* —
belly-to-the-sun on Clochar Strand.

"*Gotcho,*" says the shameless voice
beside me, her quick tongue in my ear,
her soft hand on my *pilibín cleite,*
her arms wrapped around me
as a spurt of hot words
rises inside me,
straightening my spine,
covering my skin from head to toe
with flawless grammar,
teaching me a lesson
in fluent Sax-Gaelic,
in tongue-tied pillow-talk.

Dán Grá

Bímid ag bruíon
gan stad. Cloisim
focail mo bhéil
ag pléascadh ina
smidiríní gloine
is gréithre briste
ar t'aghaidh iata
aolta. Nuair a
scuabaim smionagar
goirt ár gcumainn
bhriosc den urlár
(ní ghortóinnse cuil),
braithim chomh glan
le manach cruabholgach
tréis a chaca.
Chomh sámh. Chomh
naofa. Foc na
comharsain. Bímis
ag bruíon gan stad.

Love Poem

We never stop
fighting. I hear words
hurled from my mouth
break in shards of glass
and smashed plates
on the shut door
of your whitewashed face.
When I sweep up
the shattered bits
and pieces of our brittle love
(I wouldn't hurt a fly),
I feel clean

as a constipated monk
after a glorious shit. So
unburdened. So serene.
Fuck the neighbours.
May we never stop fighting.

Ceartúcháin

I rang a ceathair sa scoil náisiúnta,
bhí fuarbholadh cailce is sceon
buachaillí beaga i mbrístí gearra
ina smúit ar fhuinneoga dúnta.

Ar bhord an mháistir,
mar a bheadh slaitín draíochta
i ngeamaireacht Nollag,
bhí bambú fillte i bpáipéar ruithneach
don ghramaisc nár fhoghlaim
a gceachtanna go beacht.

Im ainglín i gcúl an ranga,
chomh naofa le de Valera,
do labhair an Spiorad Naomh im chluais,
is litríomar in éineacht focail chrua
a thugann máistreacht na cruinne
do bhuachaillí maithe.

Do shiúil An Ceart
ar bhonnaibh leathair inár measc,
feairín piochta a raibh othras goile air
a mhúin dom uaillmhian agus dul chun cinn,
drochmheas don mhall, don amadán.

Dá gcífeá anois mé, a mháistir,
do bhuachaill bán,
cad déarfá liomsa mar amadán?

Corrections

In fourth class at National School
the musty smell of chalk,
of scared little boys in short pants,
left grimy streaks on shut windows.

On the teacher's desk,
like a magic wand
in a Christmas panto,
a bamboo, wrapped in tinsel,
for gurriers who never learned.

I was an angel in the back row,
saintly as de Valera;
the Holy Ghost whispered in my ear
and together we spelt correctly
hard words that gave the whole world
to good boys like me.

Justice walked amongst us on leather soles,
a fussy little man with a stomach ulcer
who taught me ambition,
how to get ahead,
contempt for the slow ones, the fools.

If you could see me again, sir,
your whiteheaded boy,
would you take me for a fool?

Gaeilgeoirí

Ócé, níor chuireamar Pinocchio,
ár dTaoiseach caincíneach, as oifig.

Níor bhain an saighdiúir
a mhéar thais den truicear aclaí
chun toitín a dheargadh
don sceimhlitheoir sceimhlithe.

Níor tháinig an Dr. Paisley ná Easpag Luimnigh
go dtí na ranganna éacúiméineacha
i gClub an Chonartha.

Níor chuireamar imchasadh na cruinne
oiread is leathorlach dá chúrsa docht
ná tír seo na dtrudairí geanúla
as a riocht
Gallda.

Cad leis go rabhamar ag súil?

Go mbeadh tincéirí chun lóin
in Áras an Uachtaráin?

Go n-éistfí linn?

Mhuise.

Tá gach focal mallaithe
den teanga bhalbh seo
ina mhianach caoch
faoi thalamah bhodhar,
ag pléascadh gan dochar
fénár gcosa nochtaithe.

Gaeilgeoirí

Okay, so we didn't impeach Pinocchio,
the Taoiseach with the remarkable nose.

The soldier didn't move
his itchy finger from the glib trigger
to light a cigarette
for the terrified terrorist.

Dr Paisley and the Bishop of Limerick
never showed up for their ecumenical classes

at the Conradh na Gaeilge Club.

We didn't tilt the world
one degree off its axis
or jolt this country
of genial stutterers
from its West British rut.

What did we expect?

That tinkers could drop in for lunch
at Áras an Uachtaráin?

That people would listen to us?

Wisha.

Every awful word
of this dumb language
is a blank landmine
under the careless earth,
exploding harmlessly
beneath our bare feet.

Searmanas

Tar éis na rásaí, thagadh sé ón dtobar
le dhá bhuidéal pórtair féna ascaill,
hata feircthe anuas ar a shúil ársa.

Ransaíodh sé cófraí, tarraiceáin is cupbhoird
nó go n-aimsíodh oscailteoir meirgeach
chomh breicneach lena leiceann
scólta ag grian is gaoth na mblian.

Shuíodh sé i gcathaoir uilleann
chomh socair le bó
nó coca féir i ngort istoíche,

ropadh tlú tríd an ngríosach chodlatach,
scaoileadh iallacha fada bhróg tairní.
Ansin, le caschleas gintlíochta dá láimh
a bhí oilte ar ghamhna fireanna a choilleadh
nó coileáin a bhá sa dip chaorach,
a cheansódh searrach sceiteach
nó leanbh contráilte,
le hasarlaíocht chaoin gan éigean,
bhaineadh sé ceann an bhuidéil.

Chloisimis osna faoisimh
an leanna dhuibh ag tarrac anála,
mar a bheadh seanduine
tar éis aistir fhada.

Níl iarsma dá scil rúnda im láimh shaonta,
im aigne bhruachbhailteach
gan chruáil, gan taise,
ach ar theacht ón tsochraid tar éis a bháis,
bhí foighne, féile is fíoch mo shinsir
ag borradh im dheasláimh inniúil
sa chistin tréigthe gan tine
mar a dh'ólas pórtar go maidin
in éineacht lem Dheaideo.

Rituals

After the races, he'd come from the well
with two bottles of stout under his oxter,
hat pulled low over ancient eyes.

He'd rummage in presses, drawers and cupboards
until he found an opener speckled with rust,
like his freckled face
burned by years of wind and sun.

Sitting in an armchair,

unperturbed as a cow
or a cock of hay in a field at night,
he'd poke the drowsy ashes,
undo the laces of his hobnailed boots.
Then, with a secret twist of his hand,
that didn't flinch from the business
of castrating bull calves
or drowning unwanted pups in the sheep dip,
a hand that could calm a frightened colt
or a contrary child,
with gentle sorcery,
he'd ease the top off the bottle.

You could hear a satisfied sigh
as the porter drew breath
like an old man
at the end of a long journey.

My clumsy fingers have none
of his secret skills;
my townie mind is neither kind nor cruel.
But when I came home after his funeral,
I felt the patience and generosity
and all the hardness of my people
welling in my hands
in that cold forsaken kitchen
where I drank porter until morning
with my Grandad.

Seanchas

D'fhág sí boladh fuinseoige
is móin ag dó ar theallach oscailte
le scéalta aniar as clúid teolaí a haigne:
oícheanta cuirfiú tar éis céilí,
chomh hairdeallach le giorria sínte sa chlaí,

tormán croí ag sárú ar thrudaireacht na gcarranna
nó go slogfaí solas brúidiúil na saighdiúirí
sa dorchacht ropánta:
reibiliúin gan mhúineadh ina dhiadh sin
a thug caint gharbh is salachar na mbán
ar a sála isteach sa chistin sciomraithe,
a chuir an tigh faoi dhaorsmacht
le drochbhéasa is focail mhóra go maidin.
Bhí sí neamhspleách rompu
agus ina ndiaidh
nó gur cheansaigh dochtúirí,
dlíodóirí, banaltraí is mná rialta
a hanam ceannairceach.

Chuir sí fiúise is buachallán buí
ag gobadh aníos tré stroighin
is tarra im chaint
is chloisfí stair a cine gan chlaonscríobh
im ghlór fuilteach i gclós na scoile:

I'll mobilize you, you bloody Blueshirt.

Old Stories

Her stories had the sting of mountain ash
and turf burning on an open hearth
in the corner of her mind:
curfew nights, after a céilí,
twitchy as a hare in the ditch,
her heartbeat louder than the stuttering engines
till the glare of the soldiers' lights
was ambushed by the dark.
Later on, loutish rebels
brought filthy language
and dirt on heavy boots
across her scrubbed floors,

occupying the house with bad manners
and big talk until morning.
She was independent before
and after them, until doctors,
lawyers, nurses and nuns
broke her stubborn heart.

She set fuchsia and ragwort
in the concrete and tar
of my talk, and you could hear
the unrevised history of her people
in my blood-spattered voice in the schoolyard:

I'll mobilize you, you bloody Blueshirt.

Didjeridu

Ní mheallfaidh an ceol seo
nathair nimhe aníos
as íochtar ciseáin do bhoilg
le brothall seanma
na mbruthfhonn teochreasach.

Ní chuirfidh sé do chois cheannairceach
ag steiprince ar leac
gan buíochas ded aigne cheartaiseach
le spreang tais na gcasphort ceathach.

Má sheasann tú gan chor
ar feadh soicind amháin
nó míle bliain,
cuirfidh sé ealta liréan
ag neadú i measc na gcuach
id chlaonfholt cam,
        gorma
pearóidí   glasa
     dearga

ar do ghuaillí loiscthe
is cucabora niogóideach
ag fonóid féd chosa geala.
Beidh treibheanna ársa an aeir
ag cleitearnach timpeall ort,
ag labhairt leat i mbéalrá
ná tuigeann do chroí
gallghaelach bán.

Má sheasann tú
dhá chéad bliain ag éisteacht,
cloisfir ceolstair a chine
ag sileadh as ionathar pollta,
géarghoba éan
ag cnagadh plaosc,
ag snapadh mionchnámh,
agus doirne geala
ár sinsear cneasta
ag bualadh chraiceann na talún
mar a bheadh bodhrán
ná mothaíonn
                    faic.

Didjeridoo

This music is not played
to lure a snake
from the woven basket of your distended belly
with a heatwave of torrid notes
and swooning melodies.

It won't set your rebel foot
tapping on stone
to taunt your straitjacketed intellect
with squalls of hornpipes and twisting slides.

If you stand and listen,

for a second or a thousand years,
lyrebirds will nest
in the devious loops
of your branching hair,
    green
blue   parrots
    red
will perch on your scalded shoulders
and a sarcastic kookaburra
make fun of your scorched white feet.
You'll hear parakeets and lorikeets
flutter round your head,
ancient tribes of the air
speaking a language
your wild colonial heart
can not comprehend.

If you can stand
for a minute
or two hundred years,
you'll hear the songs
of his people bleed
from a punctured lung,
sharp beaks
pecking skulls,
snapping small bones,
while the bright fists
of our gentle ancestors
beat the skin of the earth,
like a bodhrán
that feels
            nothing.

Inghean

Tá sí chomh lán de nádúr le crúiscín
a bheadh ag cur thar maoil le bainne,
nó le buicéad uisce
líonta thar a bhruach
ag stealladh farraige
ar ghaineamh spalptha.

Scairdeann sí áthas gan smál
is beireann chugam an farasbarr
curadhmhír an tsolais
i mbasa fíneálta
gan deoir a dhoirteadh.

Tá eagla orm breith uaithi
ar an dtaoide lán
i mbabhla scoilte mo lámh

nó go ritheann an sáile os mo chionn
is briseann ar mhéaracán mo chroí
ná toillfeadh seile cuaiche ann
                    murach í.

Daughter

She is full of love
as a milk jug, filled
to the lip and above
or a brimming bucket
spilling sea
on parched sand.

She pours pure joy
and brings me the best of it,
the champion's portion of light
in cupped hands,
never spilling a drop.

I am afraid to take hold
of the tide
in the cracked bowl of my fists,

but the sea rushes in over my head,
flooding the thimble of my heart
that couldn't, but for her,
                 catch a cuckoo spit.

Iarlais

Chuir sí a dhá láimh
in airde go humhal
gur bhaineas di
a geansaí róchúng
is d'imigh de chromrúid
ar a camchosa
ag sciorradh ar an urlár sleamhain
go dtí an folcadán.

I bhfaiteadh na súl,
ghaibh an iarlais uimpi
cló muirneach m'iníne
is rith isteach
sa tsíoraíocht uaim
ar bhóthar gan cheann
i Vítneam Theas,
chomh lomnocht
le súil gan fora,
gan luid uirthi
a cheilfeadh a cabhail thanaí
ar mo shúil mhillteach
nuair a chaoch an ceamara
leathshúil dhall uirthi, mar seo.

Nuair a nochtann tú chugam
ag scréachaíl le tinneas,
tá taise a cló buailte

ar do chraiceann fliuch,
loiscthe ag an uisce fiuchta,
ag allas scólta mo shúl.

Changeling

She did as she was told
and put her two arms
over her head
while I pulled off
her too-tight jumper.
Then she scuttled away,
slipping and sliding
on the greasy floor,
heading for the bath.

In the blink of an eye,
the changeling had taken on
my daughter's beloved form,
running away from me
into eternity
on an unending road
in South Vietnam,
bare as an unlidded eye,
without a stitch
to protect her nakedness
from my evil eye
when the camera winked
a blind eye at her, like this.

When you come back to me
screaming with pain,
the scars of the other one
are printed on your dripping skin,
burned by the boiling water
that sweats from my scalded eyes.

Timpbriste

Critheann an driosúr le sceon;
léimeann gréithre ar urlár coincréite.

Cromann bord stuama ag longadán ;
scairdeann brúiscín is citeal
imeagla ar chairpéidí olna.

Éiríonn an t-iasc órga as a chillín gloine
le gníomh raidiceach féinurlabhra,
neamhspleách ar uair a bháis.

Suíonn an sceimhlitheoir soineanta
in aice na teilifíse,
ag ithe calóg arbhair.

Accidentally

The kitchen dresser trembles with fright
as dishes hurl themselves on concrete floors.

A sensible teak table starts rocking;
jugs and kettles spill
their terror on woollen carpets.

The goldfish rises from his glass cell
in a radical gesture of self-expression,
free to die at last.

The terrorist, wide-eyed and innocent,
sits by the television
eating Corn Flakes.

Patrick Dillon

The Crododile

Cold, so cold, and when I passed before their eyes they knew me not
But muttered a strangeness and defiance, their hats tall, skin tallow
Eyes with all the meaning of a dollar.
Knew then I should have nursed that chill I took in Minnesota
But rode, rolled for days, wandered into the Cyclops sun.

Cold, so cold, that house dark and square against the dusk
Hollow cold in the hall and the candles guttering
You led me on into their gathering. They saw me not.
The men ruddy, chawing, talking as they totted up.
I saw their women, pinched and whispering in my eyes
Coming out with trays of beef and cheese and beer
Frayed by fear and bad religion, their menfolk's thumbs broad and hairy.
Fire rushing, sun failing, the flames mere trembling shades upon a wall
And cold, as if it never would be warm again.

These people put a value on honesty, pride and work
You said. I shivered, could not bear to see the body in its box.
We stood before a live one with a beard
Alone for a moment restless as a bear, could smell him
The big soft cheese and beer and nervous beef of him.
Hard not to do something with him
Talk of the fever to him, jump out and say Boo to him
Put some change into his gaseous eye
So . . . interrupted he looked.

These people lived quite hard upon themselves you said
But kept a crocodile about the place
To clear up any rotten growth or wildness.
And then you took me out to the yard where the crocodile ranged
A place of battered feeding troughs and remnant wire
The earth scuffed wide and bare
Dung and the river and the bright dark trees.

Then you told me how they had tried to clip the toes of the crocodile
To cut them at a beautiful angle
So as to have the beast pinioned and useful about the place.
We listened as the crocodile bashed about on the other side,
For it had leave to tear up laurels and fallen calves.
Then you told me what had happened to the baker's child.

Kristin Dimitrova

Translated by Gregory O'Donoghue from the Bulgarian

Auntie

Here comes my father's sister.
I can barely see her in her garden
among lush chrysanthemums,
hysterically wanton dahlias,
nodding yellow flower-clusters
too thin-necked to bear their beauty.

My aunt is a small woman
half-hidden under a scarf.
She walks slowly like a black bug.
Her noiseless shadow
follows among the flower stalks.

She has been twice married —
I can scarcely believe it.
The past has been devoured
by her tumbledown little house
& ivy widening the cracks.
Yet her faded face says nothing —
just exists among the chrysanthemums
& feeds them.

Those chrysanthemums look
as though grown in a slaughterhouse.

A Lament for the Saintly Mothers

I hate poets who go into raptures
because their mothers have turned
into worn-out madonnas.
Drudgery at home, drudgery in the fields,
& a rhyming son comes home,
drinks with friends,
gets a clean shirt
(in case, around the corner,
he meets death;
or possibly
someone better-looking)
& then he goes out again, heart full of pity
for his mother's sorry look.
People who have turned
their mothers into saints
have no excuse.

At least I do not see any.

Freight Depot

... it explains why
there are no quays in Sofia
or streets free
of bits of beer bottles.

A boy & girl are walking hand in hand
talking about an episode on TV.
She walks in her slippers
between the housing blocks;
he seems readier
for life — his sneakers
have started sneaking.
They look engaged — here people
get engaged first.

One day old folks will gather,
give them a couple
of blankets & new linen
& a chicken
will die in the pot
without having ever
stepped out of the cage.

First Blood

Mutilated doll by the garbage bin —
looked like practice
        for something
bigger.

Fused

First time I saw you
I kissed my inner man goodbye
& he just smiled
"Did you recognize him?"
he whispered in my ear.
Slowly he stepped out
& stood beside you
like something from an adventure novel.
Though his lion's mane
was lighter than your hair,
though he was smiling
like a kid who'd just shot the neighbour's cat,
someone focused the picture
& you fused with each other.
You swallowed him with the power
of truth that can be touched.

Yet sometimes
I see you toss your lion's head
& burst into laughter
like a kid who's just shot the neighbour's cat.
I throw a kiss at the rascal
who left me
on the day we met.

In the Train

In the train
an old Hungarian
woman without
front teeth
told me that two
of her three children
had died
& her oldest son

is now in America —
these are the photos,
there he is,
this is his family.
She smoked Bulgarian
cigarettes or rather
one very long
cigarette from Budapest

to Bucharest
& she said
"Now I have
nothing to live for."
Said it simply,
plainly, flatly,
with the dignity
of the toothless.

The Wall by the Swings

The children swing to unearthly music,
three pendulums measuring different times.
Somebody has scratched on the house wall

   I will be back for you

in needlessly deep letters.

The Local School

The first thing one can see over the heads
of the sturdy guys in sleeveless undershirts
chasing the neighbourhood football
are the portraits of big-time national writers
on the blind wall of the school.
Their eyes are painted so as to stare
into the future;
I suspect they secretly
watch the match;
their faces, somewhat reproachfully,
take the crooked passes as a chance
of limited participation.
THE HEADMASTER IS A NAZY
is written near the main entrance
& HOUSE OF PAIN
under the portraits —
no spelling mistakes this time.
Someone has taken
his literacy from here,
used it to express himself —
as far as he could,
as best he could,
as far as he has taken it,
far as he was given — an ink suit
for a wedding day, for a funeral,
or rather
a sleeveless undershirt.

A Visit to the Clockmaker

I crossed the street
to enter a secret shop
where hundreds of hands grind time.

Charted small faces leave aside their arguments
about missing moments & start
ticking reproachfully, peep
out of three walls of shelves.
Two alarm clocks
ponderously hurdle the minutes.
A grandfather clock with a pendulum necktie
shows me the way.
A sunbeam
inscribes on the counter
its own vision of accuracy.
Down there, the clockmaker
is tinkering with the open intestines
of a disbatteried body.

His door rang its bell.

"A new timepiece?"
I dislike giving false hope
so I said "A new chain, please."

Then thought *One who will manage to slice*
time into amazingly thin straps
& thus make good use of his life
will be the happiest of us all.

The clockmaker raised his gaze
& would not agree.

Seán Dunne

The Healing Island

My baggage rests on the quayside:
warm clothes for a week of winds,
notebooks for words that twitch
like a stick gripped above water.

*

A pyramid of turf in the grate.
Sparks spit and flutter in a chimney
wide enough to inhale my cares,
hoovering them with a fierce *whoosh*.

*

Mountains on the mainland fade
as rain clouds settle and swell.
Twelve summits disappear,
apostles assumed into skies and stars.

*

Silence in a children's burial ground.
I stop among souls that have not been
hearing on wires a message from Limbo.
Stones are scattered like broken toys.

*

I am missing you and long to tell
of fissures in cracked stone,
dragonflies on a well's skin,
filaments where prisms form.

*

To pass you with your red hair
would draw bad luck to a boat.
Sooner turn back than risk such loss
though mackerel teem in a sunlit sea.

*

There is news of a corncrake heard
among fields at the island's edge.
The story spreads in shops and lanes,
a hectic rumour of salvation.

*

Night is closing like a claw
on islands where monks prayed.
Across hillsides pocked with warrens
gusts gather the gist of psalms.

*

Woken by roosters, I reach
for my one book and find it dull.
No page seems equal to the deep
implosions of waves in coves.

*

Minnows dart across pools
quicker than thoughts in my head.
I crave the stillness of water:
depths clear and surface sure.

*

Striations on stones, the worn
force of centuries and the sea.
The thought of you as I work:
a glacier shifting earth's shape.

*

Smell of turfsmoke on island paths,
stink of crab claws in a ditch.
Reek of oil in a trawler's hold,
odour of wax in a Sunday chapel.

*

Flowers teem on ditch and wall.
Packed as mussels, firm petals part.
Frail stems teach the most:
thin as tissue, they outlast gales.

*

In a dream our hands meet,
fingers splayed starfish.
Your cries rise with the cries
of kittiwakes on sheer cliffs.

*

How to crack the cotton code
of sheets billowing on lines?
From the pier they seem a signal
inviting love to the far homes.

*

An empty school faces the sea,
models askew in windows:
plasticine huts in a chalk quiet,
a playground empty of cries.

*

I phone you from a call box,
windows misted and scratched.
Tones sound in an empty house,
a fact more bleak than gull's call.

*

Columns of geese straddle the road.
The erect leader turns left,
leading his squadron to rock pools
where they drink: sentries at ease.

*

Sheared sheep tremble in folds,
shreds of fleece catch in barbs.
Nets rot in an outhouse.
Hens lay in a rusted car.

*

Wisps of bog cotton on a hill,
wisps of wool near a saint's well,
wisps of smoke from a chimney:
wisps of words to weave new ways.

*

I remember being with you here:
red hair against white sand,
your black swimsuit among waves
striking as a glimpsed seal.

*

Neighbours' gifts: a creel of turf,
white eggs in a cardboard box,
a saucepan of cooked claws,
mackerel wet from the bay.

*

I gather shells from Duach beach.
Tiny as worries, they fill my palms.
The sea gives and neighbours give:
I open and yield to kindness.

*

Let me cradle your head with my arm
and whisper love poems, secrets.
Your hands in mine are loved.
Mine in yours are held in turn.

*

Before leaving I climb the mountain.
High among sheep and bladed winds,
I add my stone to the peak's cairn
and another for you: a summit reached.

Paul Durcan

Golden Island Shopping Centre

After tortellini in The Olive Grove on the quays
I drive over to the adjacent shopping centre,
Golden Island Shopping Centre,
Around whose acres of car park
I drive in circles for quarter of an hour
Before finding a slot in a space painted yellow:
GOLDEN ISLAND EXPECTANT MOTHERS

Two hours later I stumble from Tesco
With high-altitude sickness:
Dazed, exhausted, apprehensive, breathless;
In worse condition than
Many a climber on the South Col of Everest.
Such mobs of shoppers on a Sunday afternoon,
Such powerlessness.

Loading up the boot of my car
I see through a white mist
A small, bejowled, red-headed, middle-aged lady in black
Standing in front of my car
With a Jack Russell terrier in a muzzle.
She is writing down my registration number.

I inquire: "What are you doing?"
She snaps: "You can see perfectly well what I am doing."
I ask: "Why are you writing down my registration number?"
From under the visor of her black baseball cap
She barks: "You have no right
To park your car in the space reserved for
GOLDEN ISLAND EXPECTANT MOTHERS"

I rumble in an avalanche of offended dignity:
"How dare you!

I *am* a Golden Island Expectant Mother!
I am a fifty-eight-years old male of the species
And I have been expecting for nineteen years.
Only last week I had a scan.
Despite you and your terrier
Ireland remains my native land —
My Golden Island —
And I will park where I can.
So go soap your jowls in the jacuzzis of Malaga:
I AM A GOLDEN ISLAND EXPECTANT MOTHER!"

The Man with a Bit of Jizz in Him

My husband is a man —
With a bit of jizz in him.
On Monday night in Sligo I said to him:
"Let's go someplace for a week
Before the winter is on top of us."
He said: "Where would you like to go?"
I said: "Down south — West Cork or Kerry."
He said: "Too much hassle."
I said: "Where would you like to go?"
He said: "Dublin Airport early tomorrow morning.
I'll drive halfway, you drive halfway."
We caught the Aer Lingus Dublin-Nice direct flight:
180 Euro return.
Driving to Dublin he phoned his niece in Hertz.
He said: "I want a car in Nice."
Hertz gave us a brand-new Peugeot.
Only thirty miles on the clock.
(If you're over forty-five they give you a big car.
If you're a young fellow, they give you a small car
That you can go and crash.)
There's only two ways out of Nice Airport —
West or East: simple.
At the first filling station he stopped

And asked the way to St-Paul-de-Vence.
"St-Paul-de-Vence? Exit 48
And do not come on to the motorway again
Until you want to go back to Ireland."
An hour later I was lying on a duvet
In a three-star hotel in St-Paul-de-Vence.
It was spotless. Spotless!
I was that pleased with him I shook his hand
And pulled him in under the duvet with me.
An attractive middle-aged housewife I may be *but* —
There is nothing to beat a man with a bit of jizz in him.

A Robin in Autumn Chatting at Dawn

Late in the afternoon at the top of the lane
On my way back from a hop to the cliff
I came upon a human — a male — at the gable
Across the lane from the bridge over the mountain stream.
He was middle-aged, overweight, weary, anxious.
Quite like myself.

I uttered nothing and kept *my* head down,
He uttered nothing and kept *his* head down.
Rain clouds split open like rice-bags.
He stared at me as if I could shelter him,
As if I *should* shelter him. He dashed himself
Against the whitewashed, dry-stone wall under the sycamore
And stared at me as if the doomsday had arrived.
If I could have, I would have put a wing around him;
A forlorn, middle-aged man in his Day-Glo green anorak.

While he lurked there in the midnight of the tree
I poked about in the ruts of the lane
Amusing myself, which I do when I can.
The harder the rain teemed, the more revived I felt.
I turned up autumn leaves, gutting their undersides
Of their last midges.

The ony real dampener was the human
Feeling sorry for himself and glancing at me
As much as to say: "Poor robin!"
Why are humans so patronising of robins?
They don't mean to be, of course, but they are.
When the storm showed not a sign of abating
He began to slink back up the hill to the cottage.
I stood erect watching his plump rump,
His downcast neck. After he'd departed
I swooped into the nearest fuchsia, preened,
Had a quick perch, a good chirp.

Middle age for any creature is a problematic plummet
But why do humans have to be so crestfallen about it?
With my hands behind my back and my best breast out,
My telescope folded up in my wings, my tricorn gleaming,
I emerge on the bridge of my fuchsia, whistling:
All hands on deck! Hy Brasil, ho!

HEADLINES

At 8.40 a.m. on the morning of Sunday, 7 September 2003 on an island in Upper Lough Erne, County Fermanagh, Northern Ireland, an elderly couple, Mr and Mrs John James Reihill, stepped out of their farmhouse where the Reihill family have lived and farmed for generations and walked down the path through the fir trees and the hydrangeas to the shore in whose reeds their small rowing boat nestled, stepped in and set off across the waters of the lough to attend 9 a.m. Mass on the mainland in the Holy Cross Church in Lisnaskea. In Jerusalem the Israeli Prime Minister Ariel Sharon threatened to assassinate the Palestinian leader Yasser Arafat who the day before had compelled his own Prime Minister, Mahmoud Abbas, to resign. In Baghdad the US Defence Secretary Mr Donald Rumsfeld, who was due to address US troops in Tikrit, had to cancel his address for fear of being heckled by his troops. In Belfast, Mr

Gerry Adams reiterated his "firm view" that in the light of the discovery of the remains of Mrs Jean McConville in Shilling Beach and next week's excavation of a Monaghan bog for the remains of Mr Columba McVeigh, and in order that these excavations may bring "closure" to grieving families, it would be better for all concerned not to speak in public any further about the missing bodies of innocent people murdered thirty years ago by the IRA. In Dublin on radio, television and in the newspapers, serious discussions were held on the merits of rival TV chat shows. Mrs Reihill sat in the bow of the rowing boat in her brown Sunday dress, low black-heeled shoes, long green overcoat and white leather handbag with gold chain. Mr Reihill sat in the corner of the stern and switched on the ignition of the outboard engine. The small craft lifted its bow in the air and, as Mr Reihill sat low in the water, Mrs Reihill gazed down at her husband in his black corduroy cap, his black bespoke suit, his black-laced size eleven shoes and his ankle-length black-belted leather greatcoat. He seemed to smile through his bespectacled beard, but neither of them spoke. A sentinel heron watched from a stone and five swans sailed in procession past them. At Mass in Lisnaskea they heard the priest read from the Gospel of St Mark, 7: 31-37, where Jesus makes a deaf-and-dumb man hear and speak. Jesus said to the man: "Ephphatha," that is, "Be opened." After Mass and after chatting for three quarters of an hour with Mass-goers, Mr and Mrs John James Reihill visited the newsagents where, tomorrow being their wedding anniversary, each, without the other knowing, purchased a wedding anniversary card before making the return journey across the waters of the lough to their island home. Their sheepdog Bonny lay smiling on the wooden jetty. Pacing up behind his wife through the fir trees and the hydrangeas with his hands clasped behind his back Mr Reihill announced slowly and magniloquently to Mrs Reihill: "John James Reihill needs a cup of tea before he goes any further."

On Giving a Poetry Recital to an Empty Hall
to Theo Dorgan

The engagement was to recite for one hour
At the Ballyfree Community Arts Festival,
And I did, and I gave it my all
To the empty hall.

The empty chairs gazed up at me in awe.
I caught the eye of a chair in the third row
And it would not let go,
Toying with my plight.
A redheaded, dumpy chair on the edge that never
    once smiled,
And the more droll my poem, the more it pouted.

When I had done, the Chairman of the Committee
Before even the non-applause had died down
Scrambled up onto the podium.
He spoke with brusque authority
And at length
About the significance of poetry in the new
    millennium
And how it is always so much more congenial
To have a small audience or, better still,
No audience at all.
"It's more intimate," he sighed piously, "it's more
    intimate."
And he blew his nose and he shrieked:
Go raibh míle maith agaibh go léir —
To you all a thousand thank you's!
He turned to me and he winked and he muttered:
"That's the last poetry recital we'll have in this town."

The Annual Mass of the Knights of Columbanus

Although I am a bishop I think
I deserve, almost as much as the next man,
A degree of compassion and understanding.
There is nothing I would not do —
Or at least not *try* to do —
In the fulfilment of my obligations,
But I hesitate at having to say Mass
For the Knights of Columbanus.
I not only hesitate, I balk.
In fact, I sweat. I shiver.

To call a crosier a crosier
Or — where I come from — a wheelbarrow a wheelbarrow,
I cannot abide the Knights of Columbanus.
All those feathers and plumes and medallions
And starched wing collars and velveteen tailcoats
And chains and tricorn hats.
What a collection of high-faluting layabouts.
In this day and age of democracy and terror
There is no place in my mundane opinion
For such orgies of sanctimonious militarism;
Such pantomimes of piotiousness.
Yet here I am on the orders of the Cardinal
At half-past eleven on a Saturday morning
In the sacristy of the Cathedral in Galway
Preparing to celebrate the Holy Mass
For these effigies of pomposity,
These lechers of superfluous affluence.

Lord, help me to get through your Mass
Without having too many bad thoughts,
Especially at the Eucharist.
How I dread having to dispense Communion
To these whited sepulchres
Who insist on taking Communion on the tongue
Instead of in the hand.

Isn't it, O Lord, but yet another exhibition
Of ill-concealed conceit —
Taking Communion on the tongue?
They like sticking their tongues out
And putting their phlegmy, stalactite throats on parade
With their hands on their ceremonial swords,
Up to their hilts in wilful vanity,
Legal gobbledegook, real estate, indifference.

Dear God, when I have finished vesting and robing,
Please change me into a horse of a bishop
So that on the altar I can whinny
From time to time to let off steam.
Now — now am I ready?
To trot out onto the altar
And before beginning Mass
Give the Knights and their consorts
A neigh to remember.
That's it, a neigh to remember!

The Proud Cry of the Young Father

Standing in the middle of the kitchen of his new home,
Which he built with his own hands,
The young father throws his seven-month-old baby daughter
    high up into the air
Almost grazing the ceiling —
Beatrice (Bee for short) —
And her young mother, the bee-keeper, at the table smiles:
"Be sure and catch her on the way down."

"Oh I will!" he cries.
"Oh I'll be sure to catch her on the way down!"
He cries proudly from the Ontario of his soul;
He whose young man's voice was a Buffalo whisper
Has become all of Ontario, all wilderness and garden,
All hard work and all play;
A polar cry hopping up and down the cosmos.

The 12 O'Clock Mass, Roundstone, County Galway, 28 July 2002

On Sunday the 28th of July 2002 —
The summer it rained almost every day —
In rain we strolled down the road
To the church on the hill overlooking the sea.
I had been told to expect "a fast Mass."
Twenty minutes. A piece of information
Which disconcerted me.

Out onto the altar hurried
A short, plump priest in late middle age
With a horn of silver hair,
In green chasuble billowing
Like a poncho or a caftan over
White surplice and a pair
Of Reeboks — mammoth trainers.

He whizzed along,
Saying the readings himself as well as the Gospel;
Yet he spoke with conviction and with clarity;
His every action an action
Of what looked like effortless concentration;
Like Tiger Woods on top of his form.
His brief homily concluded with a solemn request.

To the congregation he gravely announced:
"I want each of you to pray for a special intention,
A very special intention.
I want each of you — in the sanctity of your own souls —
To pray that, in the All-Ireland
Championship hurling quarter-final this afternoon in Croke Park,
Clare will beat Galway."

The congregation splashed into laughter
And the church became a church of effortless prayer.

He whizzed through the Consecration
As if the Consecration was something
That occurs at every moment of the day and night;
As if betrayal and the overcoming of betrayal
Were an every-minute occurrence.

As if the Consecration was the "now"
In the "now" of the Hail Mary prayer:
"Pray for us *now* and at the hour of our death."
At the Sign of Peace he again went sombre
As he instructed the congregation:
"I want each of you to turn around and say to each other:
'You are beautiful'."

The congregation was flabbergasted, but everyone fluttered
And swung around and uttered that extraordinary phrase:
"You are beautiful."
I shook hands with at least five strangers,
Two men and three women, to each of them saying:
"You are beautiful." And they to me:
"You are beautiful."

At the end of Mass, exactly twenty-one minutes,
The priest advised: "Go now and enjoy yourselves
For that is what God made you to do —
To go out there and enjoy yourselves
And to pray that, in the All-Ireland
Championship hurling quarter-final between Clare and Galway
In Croke Park, Clare will win."

After Mass, the rain had drained away
Into a tide of sunlight on which we sailed out
To St Macdara's Island and dipped our sails —
Both of us smiling, radiant sinners.
In a game of pure delight, Clare beat Galway by one point:
Clare 1 goal and 17 points, Galway 19 points.
"Pray for us *now* and at the hour of our death."

Tarnowo Podgorne

6.30 a.m. in a roadhouse in Tarnowo Podgorne
About halfway between Warsaw and Berlin,
Lining up at the counter, a man and woman ask me
"Are you from Dublin? So are we.
What are you doing in Tarnowo Podgorne?
A poetry reading, is it?"
Marian is wearing a blue Dublin Fire Brigade shirt.
Rory is wearing a blue City of New York Fire Brigade shirt.
"We've got a transit van packed with stuff
For children in the Belorussian orphanages.
The sort of things we take for granted in Dublin —
Women's sanitaries, soap dispensers, Sudo cream —
Things you'd never think of —
And a transport incubator that we got from Holles Street.
Good luck with your poetry reading in Tarnowo Podgorne —
We're hoping to make it to Minsk tonight."

Andres Ehin

Translated by Patrick Cotter from the Estonian

I am

I'm a Moscow schoolboy
Sitting on the soft upholstery of a theatre stall
A Chechen aims his submachine gun at me
Two others are cutting a hole in the wall
To plant a mine there.
My eyes are on stalks
My piss is staining my pants

I'm a Chechen woman clothed in black, face masked.
They, infidel swine, killed my husband.
Now Allah will wreak his vengeance on them through me.

I am mankind
Surrounded by a black cloud of madness
I can see nothing anymore.

The colonels of several hostile armies
look aghast
as the big, tough toffee of war
begins to break apart by itself.
Before long it is completely in pieces
in the middle of the dining table
and out of it flows a mawkish-scented syrup of peace
which spoils completely
the military-patterned table-cloth

Afterwards the cleaning-lady of the casino
soaks the cloth in every possible
brand of washing-powder
to no avail,

because it is irredeemably
drenched with peace.

Dry colonels and their sweaty wives
wallow all night vying with each other.

They are unable to rise even in the morning
and continue their sleepless wallowing
even when the sun is high.

fish livers lie scattered on the ground
nuns chirp their hymns under the ice
night tugs day by its toes
in towers, clocks sprout like ears of wheat
the motley eggs of passion roll in the blue grass of sobriety

wind is heavy like radium
across good and evil
it flows like molten serum
cataracted forests
foam beneath us

to be sea
to embrace tender and ethereal islands
cats' eyes full of the motes of autumn mists
out of here now!
the satrap tried to place his heel on the last of primeval
                                                                      time
dogs kiss the night here

out of here now!
here silence has noodles up its nose
here punishment flares beyond the mountains
like a great woollen maze
here snow grows like the balance of payments
its suffering is exhibited on a golden plinth

your breasts expand

through the café window
like two pagodas

they are fondled by inexperienced evening
love is paring them
like a glinting knife

screeching trees
tell the boulevards
all they have heard
of the ignorance of humans
the disgusting behaviour of automobiles

lightening bolts hang
motionless in the sky
they gleam there even now
soon dust and soot will gild them
will do their work

the Lord's lightning fails to strike the earth
under the tree no one can
embrace the salamander
of heavenly fire

even without hearing we know the score
about the stagnation in paradise
about plots
about putsches
about the corruptibility of angels
alas

I'm a cripple with yellow, burning eyes
I sit in the town park next to the statue of Lenin
I have been sitting here since before spring came
Before the grass had yet started to sprout
I placed my slouch hat
Down at my feet

But by now the grass has grown over the edge of my slouch
hat
Trees sigh and motor traffic rumbles monotonously
I fall asleep.
As a matter of fact I fell asleep long before now
I wake up in the midst of a bleak, thick fog
My hair is sopping
Limbs are stiff
Nose is blue
And my slouch hat brims with slush.

Secret

at the storehouse they are exchanging potatoes for signatures
one potato one signature
just before spring the storehouse
is crammed with piles of soily signatures
in springtime the signatures grow soft
and white eyes sprout from them
women in white scarves
come to disbud them
some signatures are marked
by the gnawings of rats

in every signature is concealed
potato's immanent secret.

I am your Missing Car

I am your missing car, that sporty red Peugeot,
half the cops of Tallin spotted me on Parnu Street,
every day I'm driven to work by an ordinary decent criminal.

I'm your missing car, that great hulk, VW Passat.
A druggie with glassy eyes rips my upholstery

searching for the hit of speed that isn't there.

I'm your missing car, once a sleek and showy Jaguar,
now a smoking, tangled wreck, a dead girl's
luminous thigh, like Cicciolina's, visible amid the metal.

I am your missing car, your newly registered Merc,
inside which, a thief for cheap thrills texts you on your phone:
if you don't buy me back he'll torch your pad.

deep, below ground, breathe
                    birds
                    buried in dirt
if you dust one clean
                    her cornflower plumage
                    will luminously shine
such birds are
                    moose beetle swallows
                    ultramarine mole-eagles
with these birds
                    estonians play at being cherokees
                    cherokees play at being estonians
but these birds will allow
                    only the indigenous
                    to pluck their feathers so blue
we estonians and cherokees hail
                    from the land of tricoloured dogs
                    and underground birds
but where are we headed

Peter Fallon

from **The Georgics of Virgil**
(from book one)

• • •

471 How frequently we've watched eruptions of Mount Etna
and the expulsions from her furnaces spill on the one-
    eyed giants' lands
fireballs and molten lava.
The skies of Germany resounded with the din of war,
weird stirrings caused the Alps to tremble.
What's more, in quiet groves a voice was heard by many
    peoples,
a monstrous voice, and pallid spectres loomed
through the dead of night and — dare I say it? —
cattle spoke. The rivers ground to a halt, gaping holes
    appeared,
480 and in the sanctuary carved ivories began to weep the
    tears of mourning
and bronzes to perspire. The Po, king river, swept away
    in raging rushes
across the open plains whole plantations, cattle and their
    stalls,
swept all away. That was a time
when entrails, carefully scrutinized, showed nothing but
    the worst
and wellsprings spouted blood all day
and hilltowns howled all night with wolves.
And never was a time more streaks of lightning split
    a limpid sky —
nor dismal comets flared at such close intervals.
So was it any wonder that Phillippi observed for the
    second time
490 the clash of Roman forces in a civil war,
and gods above did not think it a shame that we, with
    our own blood,
would once again enrich wide-spreading Emathia and
    the plains below Haemus.

Nothing surer that the time will come when, in those
 fields,
a farmer plowing will unearth
rough and rusted javelins and hear his heavy hoe
echo on the sides of empty helmets and stare in open-
 eyed amazement
at the bones of heroes he's just happened on.
 O Romulus, god of our fathers, strength of our homes,
 our mother Vesta,
who watches over our Etruscan Tiber and the palaces
 of Rome,
500 stand back, don't block the way of this young one who
 comes to save
a world in ruins. More than enough, and long ago, we
 paid in blood
for the lies Laomedon told at Troy. Long, long ago
 since heaven's royal estate
begrudged you first your place among us, Caesar,
grumbling of your empathies with the cares of men and
 the victories they earn.
For right and wrong are mixed up here, there's so much
 warring everywhere,
evil has so many faces, and there's no regard for the
 labours
of the plow. Bereft of farmers, fields have run to a riot of
 weeds.
Scythes and sickles have been hammered into weapons
 of war.
Look here, the east is up in arms; look there, hostilities
 in Germany.
510 Neighbouring cities renege on what they pledged and
 launch attacks —
the whole world's at loggerheads, a blasphemous battle,
as when, right from the ready, steady, go, chariots
 quicken on a track
until the driver hasn't a hope of holding the reins
 and he's carried away
by a team that pays heed to nothing, wildly away and
 no control.

• • •

Janice Fitzpatrick Simmons

Cocoon

I love to walk on the long strand with my old,
good dog and my son on a warm day in September.
The pain of my husband's death is still present and
walks with us on the cooling sand. We walk far
and throw stones for our dog who is blind and deaf
and over protective. I thank God for what I have
and there is a sort of peace that comes with grief
after the cocoon falls away and you stand naked,
shaking before the future. Nothing will ever be the same.
You don't want it to be. Let change come. Let the changes
come, let all of them be good ones.

Blessings

You come home.
We are new to each other,
though our mouths meet blessing the other;
more passionate than the hospital allows, more tender.

You jokingly look down my jumper,
the way a baby looks greedily
at his mother's breast.
Do you remember our friend's son Jack;
Inga, he cried triumphantly.

During Jack's first year
we thought Inga was a Swedish girlfriend
from a past life, not the perfect name for breasts.
I smile at the baby's revelation, now seven years ago.
I wheel and sit with you
in the garden — transplanted for the new
accommodating room.

You say clearly, "a problem;
the words are broken." I stand and kiss you
until your tongue reaches for mine.
Today you have read Kavanagh's "Hospital";
your finger trembles, following the lines down the page.

I speak to you with my hands and eyes,
with broken words, with the poems of Patrick Kavanagh,
with tales of the garden and the hardiness of life.

Faith

Sometimes sitting alone here at night
I am you. I worry about bills and tomorrow,
my jaw clamps, I can feel my face setting
as yours did, my teeth grinding to find solution.

But I stuck to my words, father. I believed
in what you wanted me to; in these crazy words'
ability to lift me up enough to see the stars this lonely
August night; children away, husband in hospital.

And the beauty of it all, and the despair;
the world opening and my life part
of something else; the continuum — earthworms,
maggots, black holes, nebulae, worlds, microbes,

a whole line of history — human, mammalian,
ancient, bird-like, minutiae, changing and momentary.
Father, something else too, new and omniscient,
I know that I can speak with you, I know that you hear

under the clear black dome of an early autumn evening:
Orion pulsating in this Northern sky,
me taking in the pain of separation, the song
    of the seraphim,
your voice, the echo of golden eagles

released above Glenveagh bringing terror to the sheep;
angels whirring their own song of love and creation.

Making Room

I have painted the walls
something between mustard and sunshine.
Blue glass and wrought-iron lights
hang overhead. Your last paintings:
the one of Glasilaun at Renvyle,
the one of crows above a harvest field;
Kinnagoe's bright water blazing behind
the dark scimitars of wings hung there.
There are pictures of Anna and Ben,
our wedding, and that last Christmas
before the bleed. This, our last place; my bed
next to yours — the first separation. I reach
through cot bars to hold your hand.

Sex

Here is my head — a river full of stars.
The darkness of the river courses in my veins,
the fire of stars only chimera of desire
that is no more. I am caught between
what was and what is — my body connected
to the earth only by my love for our son, by a thread
of friendships. I cannot imagine a way to love
another man. My head is a river full of stars.
My eyes reflect a light of what was. I walk
where the wind blows through buttercup
and hemlock, the rain falls, it flows over me.

A Year On

This evening the summer sky is a profound blue,
high cirrus clouds going pink and grey
with a day off midsummer. A year has passed, beloved.
Fare you well oh honey, fare you well.

Your grave is again laden with stock and delphinium,
with roses you planted in our garden
in the place we sat to catch the last of the sun,
amid cherry and rose and hidden behind fuschia's
red ladies blowing in the summer wind
that bore the scent of the garden toward us —
sweet and fresh and living. There we are
holding hands and reading the same book together.
Fare you well oh honey, fare you well.

All I can do is to look back and try to give
our love a presence — roses I gathered on your grave,
roses I gathered on the mantelpiece,
above the fire I lit this evening, the fire I share
with our son, the dog and your circle around me —
your ghost-touch on my face, your ghost-weight
in our bed every night.
Fare you well oh honey, fare you well.

Alive, Alive, Alive

The heron rose from the drainage ditch in the field.
Its rusty legs, the wingspan greater than my height,
the grey-tipped feathers six feet from the car, taking
the air more gracefully than I have heard their flight

described by poets. What pressures their bodies take.
My child's favourite movie's hero says *life is pain*.
And we know how it is plagued by poverty and war.
But the simple physical ecstasy as the heron gained

height made me tremble the way I did when I first
kissed my lover. Taking in the feeling gratefully
of the first spring heat, the sun blazing on yellow
gorse and on the white strand, the black-backed gull

wings a dark shadow on palest marram grass;
I drove on, joy on wings, not expected, not past.

Roderick Ford

Giuseppe

My Uncle Giuseppe told me
that in Sicily in World War Two,
in the courtyard behind the aquarium,
where the bougainvillea grows so well,
the only captive mermaid in the world
was butchered on the dry and dusty ground
by a doctor, a fishmonger, and certain others.

She, it, had never learned to speak
because she was simple, or so they'd said,
but the priest who held one of her hands
while her throat was cut,
said she was only a fish, and fish can't speak,
but she screamed like a woman in terrible fear.

And when they took a ripe golden roe
from her side, the doctor said
this was proof she was just a fish
and anyway an egg is not a child,
but refused when some was offered to him.

Then they put her head and her hands
in a box for burial
and someone tried to take her wedding ring,
but the others stopped him,
and the ring stayed put.

The rest they cooked and fed to the troops.
They said a large fish had been found on the beach.

Starvation forgives men many things,
my uncle, the aquarium keeper, said,
but couldn't look me in the eye,
for which I thank God.

First Love

When I was a boy cycling home from school
on evenings in late summer when the drizzle fell,
I would stop and walk naked in an ancient wood I had to pass —
warm pools and sopping leaves beneath my feet,
scents of wet earth and early fungus on the air —
until I reached a certain tree-trunk lying on its side,
barkless and smooth as bone, luscious with dark slime.

Such excitements I had there, gripping the tree with my legs,
tight with blood, sliding slowly, my mind conjuring
the creature that dwelt within; her smiles and textures:
tangles of fine roots stinking of leaf-mould,
dark fruit heavy in the hands,
a sticky trumpet flower, its stamen a thick curl,
bright pollen crusting on my groin.

Later, my body washed in the soft rain, I dressed
and cycled furiously home to mum, for hot tea and brown eggs,
that I opened like the summer with my spoon.

Tom French

Touching the Bones

The wildlife documentary on elephants
showed four of them finding the bones
of a huge bull strayed from the herd,

lying by a dried-up watering hole, bones
bleached and half-submerged in dust,
his rib-cage like the rib-cage of a boat,

the feet chopped off for pots,
the huge tusks gone; and sunk beside him
the frailer skeleton of a calf that went off

after him, not knowing he was going off
to die, his frame picked clean of meat,
the fontanel still open like a bullet hole.

The others made a circle there and grieved
the great majestic grief of elephants,
throwing their heads back and blorting

through their trunks, like my mother and father
in the hallway when that news came through,
touching the indentations of the loved one's

skulls with the soft ends of their trunks,
snuffling at the holes, inhaling the last traces
of the lost lives. They rubbed their skin

against them and rolled the skulls in dust
as if to wash death from them, then turned
their backs on the bones and nudged them,

tenderly, in a circle with their huge heels.
We grieve because the dead forget us.
We bury their bodies in boxes underground

and when we chance on them in sleep
and reach to bring the skulls up to our lips
to slake our griefs in their crevices and curves,

to roll the shinbones and the thighbones
and the ribs in dust, to touch them with our flesh,
our dream hands reaching toward them make us wake.

Night Drive

The closest, Mother, we have been in years
was a night drive back from Achill on our own.
Our tyres pressed their smooth cheeks to the ice,
gripping nothing, squealing, barely holding on.

Something stepped into our beam and stood there,
dumbly, ready to confront its death.
I remember your right hand in the darkness —
a white bird frightened from its fastness

in your lap, bracing yourself for the impact,
hearing you whisper "*Jesus*" under your breath,
preparing your soul for the moment of death.
Then, just as suddenly, nothing happened —

the sheep stepped back into the verge
for no reason, attracted by a clump of grass.
For days I felt the pressure of your hand on mine.
You would've led me to the next world, Mother, like a child.

Asperger Child

'Our God is coming and will not keep silence.
Consuming fire runs before him
And wreathes him closely round.'
                        — Psalm 50:3

When he sits staring in at the flames in the range
my brother must see what the cat can see
because he sits there staring in at them like her,
his huge back hunched and turned to the television.

There seems to be some kind of plot in the fire-box
the two of them have been following all winter.
When the fresh wood cracks and spits out sap
he sits on the hands he'd abandoned in his lap

to stop them from zooming off above his head;
and like the cat we never named that pounced
from the high shelf once down onto the hot range
and spent the next day clopping around the house

with a Sudocrem pot attached to her burnt paw,
making my enormous brother helpless with laughter,
he seems to know that this dangerous orange flower
we stuff with blocks and sacks of turf can hurt

because it wants to make things as orange as itself;
but he leans above the range and risks the burn
because the other thing my brother seems to know
is that his not being able to see it will hurt him more.

The Post-Hole

In need of respite from the life of the mind
and divine contemplation, MacAemoc was digging
a post-hole when the farmers who'd left their work
to find him, because they were troubled and in need
of answers, came upon him in the bottom field

where the monks in the chapel told them he'd be,
in a hole so deep he could've been sinking a well.

The sight of the saint crouched down in it
stopped them in their tracks. He was grunting
under the shovelfuls of muck he was flinging up,
pumping sweat and cursing when he struck rock,
easing the welt in his palms with gobs of spit,
his cassock knotted at the knees to keep it clean,
his boxwood crucifix and beads lying in a heap

beside the hole because they were a hindrance
to the work. When the farmers sought to divine
the meaning of this sight and asked the saint,
he explained to them what they already knew —
that the post-hole for the corner post — the one
he was digging — needed to be that much deeper
for the post to take the strain and the fence to last.

So, when the hole was deep enough because
he could go no deeper, and his clear mind clearer
for the labour, the saint replaced his beads
over his head, undid the cassock knot, and went back
to his cell to practise the art of forgetting himself,
while the men returned to their work in the fields,
their questions answered, and their minds at ease.

Pity the Bastards
for Billy and Tadhg

who lived in the eternal bastard present all their lives,
knew bulldozed boundaries and ancient names
for fields and had no names themselves apart
from Christian names, who cycled miles to Mass
in market towns the livestock saw more often
than themselves, and swayed up boreens, pristine
in their Sunday best and pissed when the God of Churches
refused to let them do the hard work they were born to do.

Pity the bastards who clamped buck rabbits' heads
between their legs and funnelled *poitín* into them
until they bucked, the wide sky shrivelling in their
pissed eyes, who swore blind that spirits sweetened
the meat, bled them through their scraped-out holes
for eyes and tugged the fur off over skulls like tugging
crew-necked knitted jumpers over children's heads.

Pity the bastards who hunted free-range eggs in sheds
and bore them back in their flat caps like promises
or secrets, who worked for fags and died of lung complaints,
cows withholding milk for days because they missed
the rough, familiar touch, the singing in their flanks;
who tested suspect hay in sheds with bare arms slipped
between the haunches of the bales to feel, like a vet

buried to the armpit in a heifer, who grabbed at sops
like the wet heels of a runt calf and pulled and felt the crop
contract against the strain, clench against them,
scald them and relax; who did not need to be told twice
if a scum had built that the crop would light if it wasn't
dumped and torched that night, the way you dumped
the runt to save the heifer, who satisfied themselves

with saving sheds some summers instead of hay.
Pity the bastards who loved to leave their yard boots
on the loft stairs and stand to their ankles in the deep grain,
taking to turning it and falling into the rhythm
of the chore, the wheat trench dug and borne
across the boards to break against one gable end
and double back, *ad infinitum*, the glint and dust and brunt

of indoor work, when called for tea was to be called
back from the brink, the trance of being knee-deep
in it and rowing for their lives, of wheat waves
breaking on the upstairs walls, who turned
an ancient jumper inside out to break the trance
and went down for their tea, who put on boots
and felt like they had slipped off wings. *Pity the bastards*

who loved to stand out in a fine mist, to touch the damp
warmth stored on the undersides of stones; masters
of the punchline and the soundbite — "What would you do
with the jawbone of an ass?," the answer roared
to scandalize the woman of the house, "Kill thousands!";
who kept the billhook shone to keep the wound
it made from going septic, who hot-wired Zetors,

tampered with the diaphragms of chainsaws
and gave so long on all fours thinning mangolds
it often slipped their minds that they were men;
who owned no clothes except the clothes they wore,
were known for not being able to harm a fly and meant
no harm when they grabbed the hand of a married
brother's girl and rammed it down inside the waist-

band of a working pants where nature hardened
like a pickaxe handle. *Pity the bastards* and the
youngster sprinting from an outhouse in the dark,
her hand aloft like a torch to light the way,
whose nipples pinched by an uncle stung for days
under a blue school blouse, who knew to say
nothing. *Pity the bastards* landlocked all their

lives, who took a row boat out on a calm lake
once and felt brute power flow into the oars,
whose lungs ignited with a cold lake air, who,
once or twice, caught the drift of it and got it right,
whose bulk became all cut and thrust and heave,
on whom the dip and drip of blades conferred
a sense of having slipped into the stream of things,

who strained and stroked and rowed till
they were flat out, limbered up and numbed,
who came around and scrambled for the bank
and learned the farther inland they could see
the farther out from land they went, who abandoned
oars at the boathouse door, stowed the craft
on her stanchions and felt it as a kind of grace

when the hoisted shell assumed its given mass.
Pity the bastards who perfected the dead-butt
from the back wall, predicted the foul hop,
kept a clear eye on the dropping ball, a cool head
in defence, who swore by pesticides, believed in land,
supported Man United all their lives and suffered
Munich as a personal disaster, who took off

Elvis in the local after closing and cried like
children when he died, whose shit-caked boots
were as close as they ever came to blue suede shoes.
Pity the bastards who voted for Europe in the local
national schools where masters hammered
"seventeen different colours of shit" out of them
on a regular basis and, in the process, educated them,

who never got to grips with "quotas"
because they loved churns, who understood
instinctively that milk likes peace and curdles
if disturbed, to leave it in the draught between
two doors, who dipped fingers in it to the wrist
to coax an ailing weanling into drinking.
Pity the bastards whose winters made them

good at lighting fires, who kicked Moroccan
orange crates to bits for tinder, whose mothers
were their sisters and their fathers rogues,
who lived in dread of County Homes and dreamed
of dying in their own beds, who loved the epic
feat of memory and recollected all the Presidents
of the United States in order of incumbency,

the dates of the battles of Clontarf and Hastings,
who treated cows at milking time to every line
of "A bunch of the boys were whooping it up
at the Malamute saloon," emasculated cattle
with a steel Burdizzo and took malicious pleasure
in fingering the testicles expertly, like devotees
fingering shrivelled leather purses for their beads,

who remembered the headland of the field
they were working in precisely when Kennedy
got that high velocity bullet in the head
and fantasised about what they'd do to Oswald.
Pity the bastards who knew the knack with
landing a good punch was to time it right,
who karate-chopped rabbits to put them out

of their misery, who smeared Swarfega into
injured skins and loved the stink of it, who were
anti-Christ butchers when it came to roses
but thought a law protecting gentians sound.
Pity the bastards who were stuck to the ground
by a hard frost once like Gulliver, who spent
their lifetimes travelling sixteen acres extensively,

who spoke no language only English and thought
it lovely when the young ones picked up German.
Pity the bastards who cut crops from the centre
out to give the corncrakes time to make a break,
who dandled concertinas on their knees like babies
and loved the only note the wind could play
on the top of a gate because it had no fingers,

who loved to sing "Put another nickel in
the nickelodeon," and didn't know what
the words they were singing meant, and cared
less. *Pity the bastards* who slept in extra rooms
they helped build, in beds that smelled of fields
and sheds, who vividly recalled the automatic
Telecom exchange when it was Carey's forge,

who sacrificed one lung to TB or the God
of nicotine, who coughed until they coughed
blood, who thought themselves lucky. *Pity
the bastards* who bore the full weight of a bull
on their chests once and wore the gouged-out
hollows of its legs like negatives of breasts
and never claimed they'd got the better

of the beast but missed him when the sergeant
stopped out with a captive bolt in a cardboard box
to drop the old stud at his manger on the spot,
who prayed for the creature that had wanted them
dead because it knew no better, and only said
they'd smelled the breath of death that reeked
they said, of meadowsweet, wild flowers, ramsey,

half-digested grass. *Pity the bastards* whose Requiem
Masses were long, convoluted, concelebrated affairs
attended by kin who went into the Church
and wound up on the Missions in Brazil.
And pity them, because they left behind them
nothing, and took their names, and if they played
could imitate a hurt plover or a baby wailing

by pressing a rusty latch key against the strings,
who heard the waves at evening breaking in the key
of E, who went into the lakes, the earth, the sea,
holding stones inside their clothes like infants
to their chests, whistling into sheds with homemade ropes,
who took more jigs and reels and slow airs with them
than a human could play in a lifetime, to their graves.

Mending a Puncture

1

I loved the vulcanizing of a Dunlop patch,
its soft-star orange edges melding into black
(mysterious as dry white wafer turning fleshy
or haemoglobin showing up in wine),
my father out of uniform in working duds,
the injured tube against his upper lip,
and us hushed and listening in his shade
for pumped air escaping from an inner place.

2

When his lip or the sensitive skin of wrists
failed to detect the wound, the red basin,
filled at the sink and carried out, was used,
the tube held down and fed through, like drowning
a snake, hand's breadth by hand's breadth,
till bubbles burst the surface, streaming free.

Yellow pencil circled the afflicted spot
and a tiny shiny grater was there in the kit
to grate fine powder on the patch like angels' dust,
the excess blown away with one deep breath.

3

And then the loved bike righted, air pumped in,
him testing it and squeezing it and saying —
"Chance it. Cross your fingers and take her for a spin."
Father, I am following your ways of mending still
and keep the same faith in your method and my skill,
winding typewriter ribbon around the inside of the rim
to protect the mended rubber from the sharp spoke ends,
spitting in the dustcap, keeping an ear to the suspect wheel,
listening for the black patch holding, the new air staying in.

Striking Distance

I learned about love on a Templetouhy bog —
the light brown guttings of the first five spit were good
for nothing only footing, scraws held together by roots,
useless peat that burned too bright too quick.

When you hit the stone turf ten spit down
the long sods darkened. Then you knew for sure
here was where you wanted to be — all six feet four
of my father eye-level with the earth, stripped

naked from the waist up, dripping sweat, his feet
underwater, me primed to listen out for water seeping in,
and him, given to the rhythm of the swing, willing
to dig to the centre of creation for the good stuff

that burned all night and gave a gentle heat.
When the dammed-back water gushed I pounced
to haul him out, and on the one safe spot he'd saved
for himself to stand he was, for an instant, a father

met in hell, armed with a blade, inundated, stunned
by the groundswell under him, needing to be coaxed
before he'd take the hand held out and down to him,
holding me back like a ghost on the end of his *sleán*,

as though the right words needed to be spoken,
blood spilled on the earth to break death's spell;
and I was Narcissus reaching down for my reflection,
encountering something more substantial than a face,

the blade of the *sleán* flung up first, nicking my wrist,
facing Teiresias, blind to everything except to the neat wound
oozing, all my calling of his Christian name standing
for nothing until he put his lips to my skin and sucked.

Whatever it was that held him in that dug-out place of love
released him then — my hand reaching down met
his hand reaching up — and after I'd dragged him out, emptied
the kettle dregs out on the ground and packed away the *sleán*,

he sank back in the passenger seat and passed his keys to me,
and all the road home I wanted him to speak. And he said
   nothing.

Alan Garvey

Love

After the gentlest love-making
and ritual cigarette you whisper,
We've never seen a sunrise together.

There's more than an hour to go
and I know a lot can happen
between now and then.

What? You ask, as I murmur
a poem or two. Not much, except
for the pillows' dip, the inevitable tilt

as your eyelids are first to slip into sleep
and dreams of sunshine breaking the deep
where balls of twine unravel and bounce

between a kitten's claws and teeth
and the buds outside unfurl to leaf.

Judge These Books

In 1732 bookbinder Richard Smith had fallen into debt. He and his wife, Bridget, killed their two-year old daughter before hanging themselves.

Poverty's rags are pitiful as our table's fare
of stale bread and turnips, soup of water.
We have watched the flesh melt from our daughter.
Needles to bind vellum darn clothes while
this town's dirty looks judge these books by their covers.

There's nowhere to play in a one-roomed house —
just corners for a dog and cat, the mouse hole
we call a back door. Nothing falls on this floor but mud

from the soles of our boots. Nearby, merchants order lawsuits
whose stitches are gold; their needles' eyes

are run through and through by lies
yet I believe in the books I sew:
the sun's free gold, the smell of baking dough,
the rain's sweet music writ upon a fence.
The love of God is here,

a sense beyond our frail ken.
He knows how the wind blows and when.
Last night they hung three thieves on Gallows' Hill.
The cries of our child mix'd with sparrows'
shrieks as they fled trap and scaffold to the mill.

Mine ink runs short.
We have nothing left to sell.
If thee have charity, wish us well
as our souls heave in untimely flight
from this world to God's Grace and Light.

Poppy

I've been looking for you in places
like the door of a church
and all this time

you've been flirting your skirts,
free dancing dozens in hem
of hedge and field,

by the roadside for anyone
with his eyes off the wheel.
For us, though, Flanders has no appeal:

there's no heroic rush to the opposite line.
You're a spatter, a stain
on this land, the Queen's shilling

that paid for Tommy's new pants,
covered his knees, put meals in the stove;
the landlady's knock you appeased.

How can we forget poverty's sting
or wear you with pride?
We do our best — erase memory

with all manner of murder & herbicide
but each year you return
with a message, summer is here.

Post-box red with a deep recess
you appear as if waiting for a letter,
a postcard, *wish you were here.*

The Fields of Beaumont-Hamel

Lights go out and we embrace
the loved ones in our lockets;
uniformed we sleep with lice
and candles in our pockets;
dog-tags round our necks
like silver scapulars:
The Banks of Newfoundland's
our march for moonlit hours.

We did not slip nor walk
across the promised park
though wire remained unbroken
by shelling in the dark
as one by one the lights
went out, fading into swell:
Blue Puttees on the fields
in range of Beaumont-Hamel.

The Hun lay half a mile away —
sometimes he was more —
bunkers dug in deep ravines
emptied of their scores.
Better than the best we stood,
our bayonets were fixed:
Blue Puttees advanced by rank —
they cut us to the quick.

The wire unrolled its surf,
a shrapnel splash of shell;
bullets rained in hurricanes,
a hail of rain from Hell.
Our helmets washed ashore
like polished rocks and pebbles,
Blue Puttees put out to see
the fields of Beaumont-Hamel.

Half an hour was all it took —
half were dead or missin' —
names they loved are enveloped
in letters they have written:
Ryan, Dunne, Lind and Steele —
brave men, volunteers
whose numbered graves are crossed
and watered with our tears.

Harbour strewn with sunken boat,
sailor bone and relic;
lobster pot and broken gaff;
shattered fist of killick:
khaki leaves stain the ground
around The Danger Tree,
Blue Puttees lost at sea
on the fields of Beaumont-Hamel.

Alan Gillis

The Ulster Way

This is not about burns or hedges.
There will be no gorse. You will not
notice the ceaseless photosynthesis
or the dead tree's thousand fingers,
the trunk's inhumanity writhing with texture,
as you will not be passing into farmland.
Nor will you be set upon by cattle,

ingleberried, haunching, and haunting
with their eyes, their shocking opals,
graving you, hoovering and scooping you,
full of a whatness that sieves you through
the abattoir hillscape, the runnel's slabber
through darkgrass, sweating for the night
that will purple to a love-bitten bruise.

All this is in your head. If you walk
don't walk away, in silence, under the stars'
ice-fires of violence, to the water's darkened strand.
For this is not about horizons, or their curving
limitations. This is not about the rhythm
of a songline. There are other paths to follow.
Everything is about you. Now listen.

12th October, 1994

I enter the Twilight Zone,
    the one run
by Frankie "Ten Pints" Fraser, and slide the heptagon
    of my twenty
pence piece into its slot. The lights come on.

Sam the Sham
and the Pharaohs are playing *Wooly Bully*.

A virtual combat zone lights up the green
    of my eyes,
my hand clammy on the joystick, as Johnny "Book
    Keeper" McFeeter
saunters in and Smokey sings *The Tracks of My Tears*.
    He gives the nod
to Betty behind the bulletproof screen.

Love of my life, he says, and she says,
    ach Johnny,
when who do you know but Terry "The Blaster" McMaster
    levels in
and B Bumble and the Stingers start playing *Nut Rocker*.
    I shoot down
a sniper and enter a higher level.

Betty buzzes Frankie who has a shifty
    look around,
poking his nut around a big blue door, through which
    I spy
Billy "Warts" McBreeze drinking tea and tapping his toes
    to Randy
and The Rainbows' version of *Denise*.

On the screen I mutilate a double-agent
    Ninja and collect
a bonus drum of kerosene. *Game of Love* by Wayne
    Fontana pumps
out of the machine, when I have to catch my breath,
    realizing Ricky
"Rottweiler" Rice is on my left

saying watch for the nifty fucker
    with the cross-
bow on the right. Sweat-purls tease my spine, tensed ever
    more rigidly,

when Ricky's joined by Andy "No Knees" Tweed,
    both of them
whistling merrily to The Crystals' *Then He Kissed Me*.

What the fuck is going on
    here, asks
Victor "Steel Plate" Hogg, as he slides through the fire
    door. The kid's
on level 3, says Andy. At which point Frankie does his nut,
    especially since
The Cramps are playing *Can Your Pussy Do the Dog?*

Betty puts on Curtis and the Clichés'
    Brush Against Me
Barbarella instead, when the first helicopter shreds the air
    to the left
of the screen. Gathering my wits and artillery, I might eclipse
    the high score
of Markie "Life Sentence" Prentice, set on October 6th.

I hear Benny "Vindaloo" McVeigh say,
    right we're going
to do this fucking thing. By now the smoke is so thick
    the screen is almost grey.
The Shangri-Las are playing *Remember (Walkin' in the Sand)*.
    Frankie says
no, Victor, nobody's going to fucking disband.

Bob B Soxx and the Blue Jeans are playing
    Zip-A-Dee-Doo-Dah.
Through a napalm blur I set the interns free. They wear US
    marine khaki.
Jimmy "Twelve Inch" Lynch says, son, not bad for 20p.
    I leave the Zone and go
back to the fierce grey day. It looks like snow.

Cold Flow

Presley is singing *In the Ghetto*. The sky is almost blue.
Belfast, under blankets of snow, lies like a letter
not yet written. You aim a cigarette, as though it were a
  snooker cue,
at the red ball of her lips. Which never tasted better.
The hill path is glazed with rippled glass, and you gaze through
a frozen sea of trees, at the town's oyster-bedded pearl,
while smoke fudges the lough like a Cadbury's Twirl™.

While smoke fudges the lough like a Cadbury's Twirl™,
you see colour-fleck cars and butterfly people sprinkling
their hundreds and thousands across the soft icing roads,
  thinking
of singing to Elvis. But she turns away, as if to say how stinking
the snow will become. What a whizz. What a whirl. What a
  girl.
So clever. So bitter. You could have hit her. The sky-dome
  douses
whipped-cream snow, coating the strawberry brick of houses.

Whipped-cream snow coats the strawberry brick of houses,
while aeroplanes levitate like Aero Bars™ over the tip
edge of Belfast's fruit bowl. The sweet snow flies as the
  cloudless
sky cries, and you wipe your runny nose as the cold wind
  blows.
It was the cigarette that tasted good. Not her strawberry lips.
She is melting into the horizon's bones and, as an aeroplane
  drones,
desiccated coconut flakes fall on your face that turns toward
  home.

Desiccated coconut flakes fall on your face, turned toward
  home
laid out like a blanket, through trees that are ice-cream cones.
The melting path sparkles like a Genuine American Miller™

bottle. And 100,000 butterflies will die, jealous of caterpillars,
while flowers ignite themselves in protest, then surrender
to the infinite cold flow, icing the Milky Way through.
Presley is singing *In the Ghetto*. The sky is almost blue.

To Belfast

May your bulletproof knickers drop like rain
and your church-spires attain a higher state of grace.
My lily-of-the-valley, the time is at hand
to ring your bells and uproot your cellulose stem.
I bought hardware, software, and binoculars to trace
your ways of taking the eyes from my head.

And none of it worked. We've been coming to a head
for too long; aircraft prick the veins of your rain-
bow as they shoot you in soft focus to trace
the tramlines of your cellulite skin. But with the grace
of a diva on a crackling screen, you never stem
to their cameras, you're forever getting out of hand.

Once in school, on a greaseproof page, we had to trace
the busts and booms of your body, and I was ashamed to hand
mine in because it lacked what Da called grace.
And I wish I was the centre of a rain-
drop that's falling on your head, the key to your hand-
cuffs, the drug that could re-conjugate your head.

For Belfast, if you'd be a Hollywood film, then I'd be Grace
Kelly on my way to Monaco, to pluck the stem
of a maybell with its rows of empty shells, its head
of one hundred blinded eyes. I would finger your trace
in that other city's face, and bite its free hand
as it fed me, or tried to soothe the stinging of your rain.

Love Bites

His slacks slunk to his ankles in a whispering cascade,
revealing "I love you" on his buttocks' tattoed bouquet.
The tulips he sent her lurched like a fusillade
of fingers that she snipped and tied tightly, her heart's
    tourniquet,
until their bodies gelled together in a thick-set marmalade
like a bat and ball suspended in a dream-whip ricochet.
But soon his tattoo bled like an overfilled tortilla,
she took a bite but couldn't stop the streaming flotilla
of excuses: the tulips withered, her heart's waterfall
rained down. He drank like Bloody Mary from her castanet
coconut cups of breasts in a last bid to be enthralled,
to embalm the bouquet, on his arse, with this unguent.
Oddly, it worked, and he said "I'm your snuggleupphagus"
but she was gone. He rammed twelve pints down his
    oesophagus.

Casualty

Car like a comet, breaking all the lights, we speed
towards waiting rooms and vending machines.
The anaesthetic takes time to empty your head
so it becomes a stadium and the game postponed.
Through a window, dead white eyes are staring
upon the sterilized floors, as you lift high
into orbits where the stars have ceased to war:
The Lake Isle of Innisfree, The Forest Moon of Endor.
Then the doctor makes her first incision
with an amphetamine glint in her eye.

Niamh

As sure as fate, in she trickled
   like a long
drink of water, her red head aglow,
     the hieroglyphics
of her obscure face drawing the men's eyes
   through the smoke
as sure as piss-holes through the snow.

"That's why you'll never understand the,
   the immensity of Niamh —"
as broad as I was long, I said "dead on,"
    as if the spiralling
spews of his gabble gobbed me down, my
   rushing host, as if his
spittled chin-wag was a mystic Chiriguano.

I looked back on her, chattering as
   drinks slopped down.
With a draft, the cold still night
    got colder still,
the winds awakened to whirl around leaves
   as I went away
to where duracell disco-tans sweat bombastic

with unbound hair on fantastic
   breasts heaving
to the promise, the smell, of none-can-tell . . .
    "I like the one that goes
Come away" — as she noticed how her magnetic zip
   top drew my burning
eyes, I saw an old mate stick her tongue

through a fella's ear to soothe his brain
   as they played some House
of Pain. Just then, her arms were waving
   as they stretched her
hieroglyphics naked beneath the moon's cool
   beam. I guess her eyes
were agleam as someone gazed on the rush

of blood spurting from her nub of nose,
    and kicked her teeth
to shards, and her stomach. Meanwhile,
       my old mate asks
and "Yes, I went away," just like her fella,
    whose head was blown
by talking drums and fizzing forked tongues

leading him astray into the heart of Friday night.
    She said "fuckim!"
and went away, her flesh presented up from
    her high-heels
en brochette. Along the road to Damascus
    Street, I stopped in
for a curry stain and met Jane

who would later recall meeting Niamh
    stumbling,
stooping for her knickers, flung off outside
    the Vauxhall
with cuts all around her bleeding hair.
    Sirens blare
on the Dublin Road to Damascus, where discarded

diet-Virgin cups bleed into polyester
    slush piles,
as the MultiScreen Palace sweeps
    its Friday diffuse
clean into polyethylene units of ozone
    dust. Tonight's film
was *Eraser* and this town lacks form,

it's like malice through the looking glass
    bombarding past
and presently breaking down. I walk
    on and into
reveries of Niamh, Niamh's propensity
    to call:
Away, come away. Empty your heart.

Last Friday Night

So there wi were like, on the fuckin dance
floor an the skank was fuckin stormin like,
shite-posh, but we'd fuckin chance
it, great big fuckin ditties bouncin, shite,
an thighs, skirts wi fuckin arses man, tight,
that ye'd eat yer fuckin heart out fer. I
was fuckin weltered an Victor was ripe
aff his head cos we'd been round wi Johnny
like, downin the duty-free fuckin gargle, aye.

Anyway, wee Markie must've taken
a few a tha aul disco biscuits like,
loved up da fuck, goin like a mad yin
when some dicklicker came over like, for a fight.
Slabberin! So the fuckin lads go "right!"
an a huge fuckin mill-up started but
I fucked aff when this tit's head cracked aff a light.
Fuck sake like, my knuckles are still cut.
Shame ye wernie there, ya nut.

Progress

They say that for years Belfast was backwards
and it's great now to see some progress.
So I guess we can look forward to taking boxes
from the earth. I guess that ambulances
will leave the dying back amidst the rubble
to be explosively healed. Given time,
one hundred thousand particles of glass
will create impossible patterns in the air
before coalescing into the clarity
of a window. Through which, a reassembled head
will look out and admire the shy young man
taking his bomb from the building and driving home.

Eamon Grennan

from **The Quick of It**

* * *

because the body stops here you can only reach out so
     far because the pointed
blade of the headache maps the landscape inside the skull and
     the rising peaks with
their roots behind your eyes their summits among the wrinkles
     of your brow because
the sweat comes weeping from your hands and knotted
     nipples because your tears keep
kissing your cheek and your cheek feels the tip of another's
     tongue testing your tears
because the feel of a beard along the back of a neck is enough
     to melt the windows in a
little room because the toes the thighs the eyes the penis the
     vagina and the heart are
what they are and all they are (orphan, bride, pheasant or
     fox, freshwater glintfish of
simple touch) we have to be at home here no matter what no
     matter what the shivering
belly says or the dry-salted larynx no matter the frantic pulse
     no matter what happens

* * *

So this is what it comes down to? Earth and sand
skimmed, trimmed, filletted from rocky bone, leaving only
solid unshakeable bottom, which won't in the end give in

to the restless hammer, whoosh, and haul-away of tides,
but stands there saying, *Here I am and here I stay,*
     protestant

to the pin of its terminal collar, refusing to put off the sheen

of its sheer-scoured surface, no widow weeds in spite of loss
after loss, whole wedges of the continent, particles of the
   main
plummeting from one element to the other and no going
   back

to how things were once, but to go on ending and ending
   here.
• • •

When that great conflagration had finished with us, I sat in
   the silence of rocks
angled exactly against the gale that was still swallowing air
   from the southwest
and watched — on a cobbled stretch of sea bleached green
   and streaked by
stripes of navy blue — two big loons sitting calmly on the
   swell, unruffled
by the blast, out of range of that passionate self-immolation
   that was the surf
dashing itself against black rocks, a white mane riding its
   buckle-crown of green
and turning to a fleecy nothing, a salt collapse, then
   resurrection as grotted air
where scattershots of rainbow shards kept netting light, to
   which these
peaceful birds pay no attention, going at intervals under
   and staying there,
then breaking back to air again, glancing round to glimpse
   each other, settling.
• • •

Off the skin of water scumbled blue a ghostly steam-mist
   rises, as the frost-
chilled air kisses river surfaces and something changes.
   Something changes
when two outsides touch like that, each sensing the touch of
   that sudden other,

as something changes when our wrists and fingers settle and
   slowly stroke
each other, taking time to savour the way we feel what's
   happening here:
the cool of skin meeting the under-heat that blood is, and
   answering

its delicate imperative with this smoulder-burn, this
   element shift from
earth to air and what begins to feel like fire, as if a ghost of
   soul shimmered
above the skin we share, the way those wavering radiant
   exhalations now

curl their incessant ghost-shapes off the skin, air-kissed, of
   river water.
• • •

When I saw the deer's breath enter air and burn there — each
exhalation a puff of distant gunfire, the animal stopped
   foursquare
and surveying me, her ears upright and brindled like a hare's
and swivelling to any sound — I remembered what the
   plumber said

about the seven-point buck he'd been (with his hunter friend
who'd *taken it down* with bow and arrow) butchering.
   They'd opened

the soft white belly with knives, he said, and let the creature
bleed — *It's what you do* — and bleed. Of course he could
   only

stomach so much meat himself, he said, through he liked it for
breakfast sometimes, in sausages. *Spiced*, he said, *and fixed
   up nice.*
• • •

It must be a particular kind of grace, the way this wild
   morning a family of swallows
is harvesting the cloudy air: harnessed to its wheels and
   pulleys, they harness

the blast to their own advantage, or stop on it for a second
   before letting its breath
take them where it will, their small streamlined bodies abroad
   and at home

in its hugeness, their screams carried off so I can catch only
   the faintest trace
from where I stare out the kitchen window, wideawake to
   these tiny life bundles

in daily negotiation with the great unnameable force that
   lives in things, the way
they're beyond complaint, too busy living to be bogged or
   beaten down for long

by sudden swerves of weather; beyond even contentment;
   having only this instant
quick knowledge the moment gives them: and how to go
   on, making the most of it.
• • •

Although snow has wrapped the house in a quicklime bandage
six miniature daffodils in their earthen pot have begun to
　　blossom
and (if I lift my eye from the cloven signs of deer) the redbrick
　　wall
and the tall chimney of the Powerhouse are bright worldly
　　things
against the backdrop of weather turning its back on us.
　　Dark water

under a shelf of snow; stark sycamores a dozen crucifixions.
　　Stepped
up to its belly in snow, the cat watches some bird or famished
　　mouse
make its own cold life minutely happen.
　　　　　　　　　　　　　　But what are four
　　small oranges

peeled and placed on a starched tablecloth of snow a sign of?
　　Being
a gleam of something — not consolation exactly, but still
　　mattering.
　• • •

I'm trying to get one line or another right when a flock of
　　starlings startles —
mobbing a marsh hawk, staying up-sky of him, folding round
　　him their net
of black silk till he shrugs them off on a downdraft, the whole
　　flock closing
like a broken concertina into leaves where they become
　　invisible, only throats
crowding the air with clamour.
　　　　　　　　　　　　Meanwhile the hawk is

   elsewhere, hawk-brain
beating to another music: in the great blue hush of space, he
   pays attention
to the air itself — a live feather-tongued light-rush bearing
   him up, droll wingbeats
opening and closing it like breath.
                                     Invisible loonybells, the
   starlings go on
chattering their jangle-life in branches, telling me how my
   own head won't
let go its appetite, is an old knife on stone: bitten blade,
   handle bandaged.

• • •

Rained in all day like this, I keep towelling the windows dry,
trying to wipe the fog away that has me blind behind glass,
unable to see the world outside for what it is, how things

become shadows and blunted silhouettes of themselves, birds
only blurs where they shake a branch when they land or leave
or just dash past, a flash of cloud-particles snatching at crumbs

as I do myself each time I get the big window clear again and
   try
to take in all shapes and colours there, all those living bits
of matter that stand in their own ordinary uncanny light

until blearing begins again, and I see my own breathing does it.

• • •

Seamus Heaney

Anahorish 1944

"We were killing pigs when the Americans arrived.
A Tuesday morning, sunlight and gutter-blood
Outside the slaughterhouse. From the main road
They would have heard the squealing,
Then heard it stop and had a view of us
In our gloves and aprons coming down the hill.
Two lines of them, guns on their shoulders, marching.
Armoured cars and tanks and open jeeps.
Sunburnt hands and arms. Unknown, unnamed,
Hosting for Normandy.
      Not that we knew then
Where they were headed, standing there like
   youngsters
As they tossed us gum and tubes of coloured sweets."

Helmet

Bobby Breen's. His Boston fireman's gift
With BREEN in scarlet letters on its spread
Fantailing brim,

Tinctures of sweat and hair oil
In the withered sponge and shock-absorbing webs
Beneath the crown —

Or better say the crest, for crest it is —
Leather-trimmed, steel-ridged, hand-tooled,
   hand-sewn,
Tipped with a little bud of beaten copper . . .

Bobby Breen's badged helmet's on my shelf
These twenty years, "the headgear
Of the tribe," as O'Grady called it

In right heroic mood that afternoon
When the fireman-poet presented it to me
As "the visiting fireman" —

As if I were up to it, as if I had
Served time under it, his fire-thane's shield,
His shoulder-awning, while shattering glass

And rubble-bolts out of a burning roof
Hailed down on every hatchet man and hose man
    there
Till the hard-reared shield-wall broke.

The Nod

Saturday evenings we would stand in line
In Loudan's butcher shop. Red beef, white string,
Brown paper ripped straight off for parcelling
Along the counter edge. Rib roast and shin
Plonked down, wrapped up, and bow-tied neat and
    clean
But seeping blood. Like dead weight in a sling,
Heavier far than I had been expecting
While my father shelled out for it, coin by coin.

Saturday evenings too the local B-Men,
Unbuttoned but on duty, thronged the town,
Neighbours with guns, parading up and down,
Some nodding at my father almost past him
As if deliberately they'd aimed and missed him
Or couldn't seem to place him, not just then.

Out of This World
in memory of Czeslaw Milosz

1 "Like everybody else . . ."

"Like everybody else, I bowed my head
during the consecration of the bread and wine,
lifted my eyes to the raised host and raised chalice,
believed (whatever it means) that a change occurred.

I went to the altar rails and received the mystery
on my tongue, returned to my place, shut my eyes fast,
    made
an act of thanksgiving, opened my eyes and felt
time starting up again.
                    There was never a scene
when I had it out with myself or with another.
The loss occurred off-stage. And yet I cannot
disavow words like 'thanksgiving' or 'host'
or 'communion bread'. They have an undying
tremor and draw, like well water far down."

2 *Brancardier*

You're off, a pilgrim, in the age of steam:
Derry, Dun Laoghaire, Dover, Rue du Bac
(Prayers for the Blessed M. M. Alacoque,
That she be canonized). Then leisure time

That evening in Paris, whence to Lourdes,
Learning to trust your learning on the way:
"*Non, pas de vin, merci. Mais oui, du thé,*"
And the waiter's gone to take you at your word.

Hotel de quoi in *Rue de quoi?* All gone.
But not your designation, *brancardier*,
And your coloured bandolier, as you lift and lay
The sick on stretchers in precincts of the shrine

Or on bleak concrete to await their bath.
And always the word "cure" hangs in the air
Like crutches hung up near the grotto altar.
And always prayers out loud or under breath.

Belgian miners in blue dungarees
March in procession, carrying brass lamps.
Sodalities with sashes, poles and pennants
Move up the line. Mantillas, rosaries

And the *unam sanctam catholicam* acoustic
Of that underground basilica — maybe
Not gone but not what was meant to be,
The concrete reinforcement of the Mystic-

al Body, the Eleusis of its age.
I brought back one plastic canteen litre
On a shoulder-strap (*très chic*) of the Lourdes water.
One small glass dome that englobed an image

Of the Virgin above barefoot Bernadette —
Shake it and the clear liquid would snow
Flakes like white angel feathers on the grotto.
And (for stretcher-bearing work) a certificate.

Tate's Avenue

Not the brown and fawn car rug, that first one
Spread on sand by the sea but breathing land-breaths,
Its vestal folds unfolded, its comfort zone
Edged with a fringe of sepia-coloured wool tails.

Not the one scraggy with crusts and eggshells
And olive stones and cheese and salami rinds
Laid out by the torrents of the Guadalquivir
Where we got drunk before the corrida.

Instead, again, it's locked-park Sunday Belfast,
A walled back yard, the dust-bins high and silent

As a page is turned, a finger twirls warm hair
And nothing gives on the rug or the ground beneath it.

I lay at my length and felt the lumpy earth,
Keen-sensed more than ever through discomfort,
But never shifted off the plaid square once.
When we moved I had your measure and you had mine.

The Blackbird of Glanmore

On the grass when I arrive,
Filling the stillness with life,
But ready to scare off
At the very first wrong move.
In the ivy when I leave.

It's you, blackbird, I love.

I park, pause, take heed.
Breathe. Just breathe and sit
And lines I once translated
Come back: "I want away
To the house of death, to my father

Under the low clay roof."

And I think of one gone to him,
A little stillness dancer —
Haunter-son, lost brother —
Cavorting through the yard,
So glad to see me home,

My homesick first term over.

And think of a neighbour's words
Long after the accident:
"Yon bird on the shed roof,
Up on the ridge for weeks —

I said nothing at the time

But I never liked yon bird."

The automatic lock
Clunks shut, the blackbird's panic
Is shortlived, for a second
I've a bird's eye view of myself,
A shadow on raked gravel

In front of my house of life.

Hedge-hop, I am absolute
For you, your ready talkback,
Your each stand-offish comeback,
Your picky, nervy goldbeak —
On the grass when I arrive,

In the ivy when I leave.

Zbyněk Hejda
Translated by Bernard O'Donoghue from the Czech

from *A Stay in a Sanatorium*

A Poem
For my heart,
for my heart,
shall we already end it?

At first the sky was pink in the west,
then lightning chopped the dark thrones of Heaven
and we hid under a tree by a garden wall
somewhere in England
(that dark red building: surely it stands
by the banks of the Thames?),
and then it poured and, as when angels are in ecstasy,
the light of evening trembled and faded upwards.
In the street of St Apolinar
(the gas lamps already lighting)
there appeared a huge red umbrella,
protecting from the rain a couple
staggering beneath its weight.
"Fuck this, can you explain
what kind of umbrella you've brought?
That's no umbrella, it's a parachute."
And that gentle couple under their parasol
disappeared into the sunny night (strange!),
and it still rained, and the light drizzled softly
at eight o'clock in the evening in early June.

You are still within reach of a hand,
lying quietly on your stomach.
(That was a dream, somewhere in England,

a dream-skeleton, crouched in the mouth of desire.)
I can still feel you in my fingertips,
the thorn of your breast.
Your scent like a night ripped by rain
and lightning.
Why aren't you crying?
What is so funny?
Is it really that funny?
Or is there vast boredom everywhere,
infinite indifference?

The pianist in the café
is drinking like a fish.
That music!
And conversations as if poured.

A Stay in a Sanatorium

I was staying at the villa Albertinum
after a Viennese Professor Albert
There were four of us in the room
Mr Rohlena used to say
that his speech is rather slow
since that accidental Once
when he was stacking straw in the loft
snow was lying everywhere
he woke up in the hospital
and as he is waking up
first thing he sees
in the window
the cherry trees in full bloom
Mr Franc was a butcher
his illness was diagnosed
as a stupid
lung cancer
and metastases

whole nights he spent walking
to the toilet from the toilet
from the bathroom to the bathroom
when he wouldn't be back for ages
Mr Rohlena would get up quietly
and sneak out to look for him
Someone said to him
you don't get any sleep Mr Rohlena
But I am worried
he might trap himself somewhere
My third companion was a German from Lanskroun
I've forgotten his name
you didn't see him in the room much
he was hoping, the idiot, he didn't have TB
I don't have what you have, he'd say
and to avoid infection
before going to bed
he'd put a handkerchief over his gob
he spoke little
because speaking makes you breathless
you have to breathe deeply then
and so breathe in more germs
once he did get himself talking
he'd served at the Russian front
we were polishing off
the seriously wounded
what would you expect? he's lost his legs
and maybe his hands as well
plus he was possibly blind
they'd end up saddled with him
his parents or his unfortunate wife
stuck with him the rest of their lives
The revulsion this aroused
quite surprised him
It was humane
we gave them injections
In another villa there lived

a priest from Černilov
I'd have liked to have the odd word with him
but either he wasn't interested
in what I was interested in
or he didn't trust me
He liked talking to old farts and fogeys
about fishing and planting trees
where to put dung and what bait for what fish
it seemed he knew what he was talking about
the old fogeys listened to him
I wrote to Vladimír Holan
and he wrote back
a stimulating letter
Honza Lopatka sent me braces
(you couldn't get braces anywhere)
and a letter that cheered me up
but which I've mislaid or lost
I'd like to read it again today
a lot has changed
during that long period.

Sometimes through a hole in the fence
I entered the town
the way there went by the gardens
across a flower bed a woman stretched out her body
in a swimsuit but not over-revealing
I'm not even sure if she was beautiful
her stomach nice and rounded
over her slightly parted thighs
almost made me fall over
With the dizziness
my eyes went blank
Just below in a small garden
you'd often see lying about
a kind of dishevelled
Brigitte Bardot
we got used to seeing each other like that

in a café in the square
where I go for a coffee that time of day
I once turn round
she is standing behind me
smiling at me in such a way
that I have to address her
but I'm not saying anything
and I'm getting out of here
and she gives me a gesture
that says I'm an idiot
And our love was over
All
I'd have longed for
and not only with her
was not to have to speak
meet her with a touch, be inside her
but such luck I've probably
never in my life deserved
or women gifted with
such sheer lasciviousness
don't inhabit this world
Then once during his rounds
Dr Kroulík
turns to me
this is no way to do things oh no
walking round town like a healthy person
citizens are complaining
that you might infect
the whole of Zamberk
I enjoyed the morning
but even more the afternoon
rest on the terrace
You could see into the park
in front of my deckchair two high larches
on one of them
a strangely twisted twig
would catch my eye

and below the park
all this would remind me
of some forgotten place and event
on a jaunt with my parents long ago
how we entered a garden restaurant
where after long wandering in summer heat
a kind shade received us
on the table a white tablecloth
cool granadine
Later on
Mr Franc got up very little
finally he stayed in bed the whole time
his father would come to see him
a little old man
I wouldn't have thought
he was a butcher too
he was suffering from TB
in the pavilion next door
he'd come and sit by the bed
tell me son how are you feeling better already
then he'd place his walking-stick
between his knees
rest his chin on it
and stay silent
both silent
we'd fall silent too general silence
Once Jirka came to see me
he brought the Skvoreck's with him
all of them had just become
stars in a film of the new wave
The Report of the Feast and the Guests
Jan Zabrana came with them too
I don't know what we talked about
I no longer remember
Once Ivan Pelc came to see me
On behalf of the editors
Honza Nedved would send me news

it was when the Central Committee of Writers
was deciding to dissolve Tvar
Helena Wernischova would write
letters to me with pictures
what good letters she wrote
which immediately after reading them
you responded to filled with hope
and the next letter threw cold water
In the next letter again
two or three silken words
Alena had saved a fortnight of her holiday
she had come with Jitka
and rented an apartment in Zamberk
we went on one happy trip together
to Kamenicna
Towards evening on the way back
it was already misty autumn
in an old general stores
a gas lamp was burning
All of a sudden we found ourselves
in an idyllic century
Apart from a very few
bright moments
we were tormenting each other
with endless accusations
My mum came every Sunday morning
I'd wait for her always by the gate
watching for her figure in the distance
She would leave towards evening
She'd bring a bag full of
carefully prepared dishes
that she thought I liked
Each time we spent the whole of Sunday
walking around the district
A cock crowed
It reminded her of home

Towards the autumn I met Vera
wife of a local doctor
at the end of our first walk together
during our first fleeting kiss
she felt me hard with her hand
she agreed to another walk next day
and in return she graciously
invited me to spend a gracious
afternoon with her family
I wrote to Hanka every day
and twice a week phoned her in Prague
always at about 2 p.m.
And I imagined jealously
what was going on in Prague
when Hanka is under the sole surveillance
of her own husband
Mr Franc was taken to the clinic
Someone brought the news
that he was lying in a plaster crust
his bones breaking already
soon after
came the death notice
That garden restaurant
was at the very back
of a large park
people were sitting at small tables
and the place
was neither crowded nor empty
on the right side
on the way from the park to the restaurant
I become aware of a tall silver spruce or fir
a silver fir I think
dad pointed it out to me
and here and there mighty deciduous trees
beeches perhaps
  Prague 5 and 6 May 1987

Some Evening

Some evening we'll all sit down together
around thirty bottles,
me, you and Bob,
the two of you and me, the two of us and him,
someone is missing, but we'll only notice it
when we're already blind drunk,
sure, someone is missing here,
but I'm here, the missing one will say,
the one who is always with us,
the one always missing amongst us,
and on and on like that,
when we're completely drunk . . .

*

That night dawn is already breaking at 3 a.m. on your
                                 naked body,
Jarmila was asleep, I could hear her breathing
within reach of my hand, I'd have liked to stroke her
                                 hair,

the whole night I was fearing
that she'd wake up . . .
So again it came to nothing, alas! that dream
to have them both together: two is the dream. Me lying
in the middle, Jarmila asleep, me afraid
she'd wake up. Let her sleep . . . she's blind drunk.
It's a trick, what is sleeping to my right
is my bled-to-death pain, I am aware
of every murmur of its breath, but
I am turning to your stomach.
We're moving slowly in a smaller space
than the smallest cell: the meeting of bowels,
in the corridor a door slammed, water rumbling,
le jour se lève.
In my youth — later too — I wanted to write like Jiri
Kolár.

And what came of it?
Waste of words.
It's night again
and I'm playing endlessly
over and over the same record
as that night when we didn't get round to turning the player off
and during intercourse I was tempted
to match my movements to the music's rhythm
(I felt something funny was going on),
you kept gently restraining me
(the dance not right for the gravity of the moment),
but that light slowing down by you of the rhythm
was creating marvellous syncopes,
so marvellous I had to stop it
because I'd have had to start
laughing from sheer joy.

Don't you find, Alice,
that what I write is not written in poems?
(But is this really a poem?
Isn't it though, isn't it? I say,
self-destructive and unsure?)
For example Vladimir's pyjamas
and its buttoning system,
I couldn't undo it?
When my battle with the buttons
had exhausted my patience,
your fingers solved the problem
with a practised marital gesture
in a split second.
*

Where are the days
when I used to write beautiful verse!
I regret them desperately. But they are gone.
They are gone, departed,
and I am left stuck here.

All of a sudden I am old and surprised
it happened so unexpectedly.
    *

I had a dream
that I'm sitting in the garden.
I hadn't been there in my dreams for a long time.
I was looking down towards the road,
in a small oval hole before me was a fireplace,
another one, round, behind my back,
I am realizing
that my uncle always tidied the garden
at this time in the autumn,
and when we are here
he never leaves the house.
From the hearths a little smoke was rising still.
  1974 to 1982

Pearse Hutchinson

Translated by Gréagóir Ó Dúill

Fúinne

An bhfeiceann tú an fear sin thall, a bhfuil a chuid éadaigh
ar dhath na h-oíche is duibhe, agus a chroiceann ar dhath
an tsalainn is báine?
Deireann sé gur maith leis an ghrian.
Deireann sé go dtuigeann sé an ghrian níos fearr ná tusa
(ní deireann sé 'níos fearr ná an ghrian féin', ach ní lán-doiléir
go bhfuil fonn air a leithéid a rá).
Agus má fhiafraítear de cad is ainm dó, freagróidh sé:
Mac na Gréine.
Roinnt blianta eile, agus déarfaidh sé: Glaotar an Ghrian
orm, ach níl siad ach ag magadh fúinne.
Roinnt bheag eile, agus déarfaidh:
Athair na Gréine.

About Us

Do you see that man there, he whose clothes are coloured as dark as darkest night, whose skin is as white as the whitest salt?
He says he likes the sun.
He says he understands the sun better than you do (he doesn't say "better than the sun itself" but it is not absolutely unclear that he wants to say something like that).
And if he is asked what his name is, he says "Sunson."
In a few more years he will say: "I am called the Sun, but they merely mock us."
In a few more years he will say
Father of the Sun.

Oritsegbemi Emmanuel Jakpa

Harmattan

1

Outside my window the digger, digging
plunges the spade, with target perfection,
in gravelly ground
hissing needle-edge-sharp sound
into palpable rhythm as
green buds crack in the dry harmattan
throw dust around.

At each succeeding stroke
this hard land trenches longer and deeper
by the bitter glint
of the spade.

During our aerial suspension
the digger pauses, stares into blue haze:
that mirage over on the noon highway,
these primal years that run from us
useless as free paper in a printing press
or the jocund lovers who deep in the night
disappear like methylated spirit.
Insults of the proud
stick in the digger's memory like a tattoo.
When he tries to wash it off, it will not rub off.
Of his father's tutelage, — firewood
is only for those who can take heart.
That is why not all can gather it.

He shakes his head.
Grip grip, grip hard
and downright down
strikes the vengeful spade.

2

In our airtight dragnet, roadblocks everywhere.
Borders tight as steel ziplocks
checkmate every hope.
Yet many people of lesser talent
slip out, unabated, with ease.

The logic of existence
replants us in alien soils.
We tear round the hairpin
corners of the word
divided to the vein:
to stay put or to go.

So, the periodic spade strikes, each stroke
the rasped desolation and anger of the soul.
Tribulations of a black-gold age.
The excavations and makings
of our blood and drainage.

Before the harmattan and the digger
unmoving I sit;
before his intimate vengeance
a watcher,
I write.

His spade, my spade.
I'll hold my own.
Crack with it.
Dig with it.

Eden

1

No serpents are found in Ireland
lots of potatoes, barley, wheat and oats
no snakes though?

North and south, east and west
high tides dash against your coasts,
the castle that pierces
a blue capital sky
poseur of eight centuries
(Moher and its cliffs
Rathlin, the Giant's Causeway)
could not earth you in ice and time
all those colonial years.
Today on the slopes of MacGillicuddy's Reeks
sheep graze all day regardless
of fireworks and cool festivals that burst
upon Dublin's palate
along drizzly boulevards.

2

Sharpen the world's memory with your songs
of how you weathered flog and wrong.

Sing of Yeats, the king of the cats, and those who try
to make this earth a better place to live and die.

3

When wind tears at the thatched eaves again
in Africa,
my Africa,

sends the mothers running again
in search of their children,
we see Ireland pluck the talon of a falcon.
When we make good rafter after rafter
for the approaching monsoon
Ireland soars for us in the Tai-chi of its storms.

4

In the end
fire makes stronger
the sequoia tree.
Difficulty makes good.

Biddy Jenkinson

Translated by Juliette Saumande

Tuireamh Marie Antoinette

Les Épouses (eorpacha, baineann)
ar thuras oideachasúil ag taispeántas eisceachtúil
de cuid Chumann Seandachtaí Nua-Eabhrac Inc.

. . . ar thóir "coupe" seaimpín ón Château de Rambouillet
cuach de phoirceallán bán luisneach Sèvres
a múnlaíodh, lá a glóire
ar chíoch chlé Marie Antoinette

Mé á adharcáil sa scuaine
ag borrchíocha na hIodáile
cliabhrach *soignée* na Fraince
péarlaí comhchruinne Shasana
— broinnfhairsinge Lucsamburg fiú —
Táim caol ard cláruchtach
ach choinníos cnámh chléithín na hÉireann
in airde is tonnchíocha na hEorpa dom chomáint
i dtreo chíoch-chuach Mharie
an t-aon cheann a mhaireann slán
d'fhoireann ceathrair

> *Siopa milseán Bhabs*
> *mise in aois a cúig*
> *ag déanamh breith na seachtaine*

> *"Winedrops!"*
> *Bhog Babs a hucht den chuntar.*
> *Cleatar winedrops cródhearga sa mheá*

> *Shonraíos go raibh*
> *mar a bheadh dhá mhála milseán*
> *faoi chabhail ghúna Bhabs*
> *tóin-chun-tosaigh gránna*
> *a loit a gúna*

*D'fhliuch mo shúile le trua di
mar d'fhliuchadh ag an am
don phiast a ndeachaigh spáid tríd
don turcaí a ramhrú sa ghairdín don Nollaig*

"D'habitudes les verres viennent par six de huit!"
"Peut-être que le modèle s'est fatiguée
après quatre moulages!"

*Ó mhionfhógraí an "Evening Mail" d'fhoghlaimíos
go ndíoltaí bindealáin ar leith
le cnapáin mhíchumtha mar iad a cheangal siar
nárbh í Babs amháin, dá réir, a d'fhulaing a leithéid*

Moill ar an ardaitheoir
argóint faoin mórchathair Eorpach ab fhearr le
bustenhalter, porte-nichons, reggiseno
a cheannach ann

*sa "Monument Creamery," Sráid Camden
bhíodh cnoc ime ar chuntar marmair
Béithe óga á sleaiseáil le céaslaí ime
Na paiteoga á bpleancadh, á gcaitheamh san aer
iad ag tuirlingt go dronuilleogach néata
Súile gorma, cuacha fionna, cótaí bána ar na béithe
Ach máchaillí Bhabs orthu uilig!
An gcacaidís siar nó aniar?
Nó, Dia dhár sábháil
siar aniar i dteannta?*

*Chráigh a gcás mé
go bhfaca i bhfuinneog siopa Gorevans
uchtanna gloine agus cíochbhearta orthu
Ní raibh ar Bhabs mar sin
ach lúireach gloine ceangailte le strapaí bándearga
cosaint ar ghadaí a mbeadh scian aige
Agus chaitheadh cailíní an ime scabaill ghloine
ar fhaitíos go rachadh bean díobh ar mire
is go gcrústálfadh sí a compánaigh
le goblaigh chrua*

"Mais qui a fait les moulages, mes enfants?"
"Le roy, bien sûr, chérie!"
"Mais non!"
"Mais oui!"

> *Tigh Gorevans ghearrtaí gloine*
> *Thagadh mná an cheantair ag casaoid*
> *buachaillí dána lena liathróidí peile*
> *Chuireadh fear an tsiopa rialóir ar phlána*
> *Slais!*
> *Cliotram an fharrasbairr sa ghabhdán*

> *Mo shuaimhneas ina smidirchíste*
> *'Bé nár thuig Babs agus iad siúd*
> *leochailleacht gloine?*

Ucht aontaithe na hEorpa
ag tonnadh ón ardaitheoir faoi mhórtas
is ag briseadh thart ar an gcás gloine
mar ar lonraigh
leathchíoch néamhanda na banríona
in uathadh

"Il y a loin maintenant
de la coupe aux lèvres!"

> *Seaimpín sa chuach*
> *Bean domhnaigh*
> *ag bisiú boilgíní*
> *le biscuit de Rheims*
> *í ag scairteadh go gealgháireach*
> *"Ithidís cístí!"*

> *Cleatar winedrops sa mheá*
> *Cliotram gloine sa ghabhdán*

Tost.

"Les seines sont tellement délicats!"
arsa an Fhrainc

agus muid ag trá.

La chute de Marie-Antoinette

Les Épouses (toutes Européennes) lors de la visite instructive d'une exposition exceptionnelle sous les auspices de la Société new-yorkaise des Antiquaires

. . . en quête de la coupe à Champagne du Château de Rambouillet
une coupe en porcelaine de Sèvres, resplendissante,
moulée jadis, son jour de gloire,
sur le sein gauche de Marie-Antoinette.

Et moi, votre humble servante, tamponnée dans la file
par le giron généreux de l'Italie
l'élégant buste de la France
les joyaux jumeaux — des vrais ! — de la Grande-Bretagne
— et même par le vaste périmètre du Luxembourg —
Bien que grande, fine, la gorge plate,
je maintins le sternum d'Irlande dressé
contre la marée des corsages gonflés à blocs de la belle Europe
qui m'emporte vers
le sein Graal de Marie
seul survivant
d'un service de quatre

    La confiserie Chez Babs
    J'ai cinq ans
    et je prends la décision importante de la semaine

    « Des boules de gomme ! »
    Babs hissa son vaste coffre et le dégagea du comptoir.
    Le tintement des boules rouge sang sur le plateau de la balance.
    Je crois remarquer deux sachets de bonbons cachés dans le corset de Babs,
    un affreux derrière devant
    qui gâchait sa jolie robe.
    Mes yeux s'embuent de pitié
    comme ils le faisaient à cette époque
    pour le ver sectionné par la pelle
    ou la dinde de Noël
    engraissant dans la cour

« D'habitude, les verres viennent par six ou huit ! »
« Peut-être que le modèle s'est fatigué
après quatre moulages ! »

> Dans les réclames de l'Evening Mail
> j'ai vu qu'il existait des bandages spéciaux
> pour comprimer les vilaines bosses comme celle de Babs,
> elle ne devait donc pas être la seule à souffrir de ce mal

L'ascenseur prenait son temps.
Débat : dans quelle ville d'Europe
acheter le meilleur
« bustenhalter », « porte-nichons », « reggiseno » ?

> Chez Monument Creamery à Camden Street :
> une motte de beurre sur une plaque de marbre.
> Des jouvencelles à l'ouvrage l'attaquent à la palette en bois,
> battant des morceaux de beurre, les projetant dans les airs
> jusqu'à ce qu'ils en redescendent en rectangles parfaits.
> Yeux bleux, ravissantes bouclettes blondes, blouses blanches
> mais toutes, sans exception, avaient la même difformité que Babs.
> Cagaient-elles par l'avant ou par l'arrière
> ou encore, seigneur !
> par les deux ?

> Je m'inquiétais de leur cruel destin
> jusqu'au jour où je vis dans la vitrine de Gorevan's
> des bustes de verre parés de harnais roses.
> Ainsi, Babs portait un plastron en verre
> pour se protéger des couteaux des bandits.
> Et les filles de la laiterie étaient carapaçonnées dans des cottes de verre
> au cas où l'une d'entre elles, emportée par son élan,
> mitraillerait ses compagnes
> d'une salve de beurre dur.

« Mais qui a fait les moulages, mes enfants ? »
« Le Roy, bien sûr, chérie ! »
« Mais non ! »
« Mais oui ! »

> *Il y avait un vitrier derrière chez Gorevan's.*
> *Les femmes du quartier y venaient,*
> *pestant contre les gosses et leurs ballons de foot.*
> *L'homme aposait sa règle contre un pan de verre.*
> *Slash !*
> *Les chutes pulvérisées dans la corbeille.*
>
> *Pulvérisé aussi mon soulagement. Retour à l'inquiétude.*
> *Babs et les crémières,*
> *comprenaient-elles comme le verre est fragile ?*

Le front uni de l'Europe
deferla de l'ascenseur, majestueux,
et se brisa pour mieux se disperser autour de la vitrine
dans laquelle un sein royal aux reflets irisés
luisait, solitaire.

« Il y a loin maintenant
de la coupe aux lèvres ! »

> *Champagne dans la coupe,*
> *une fille étourdie*
> *remue les bulles*
> *avec un biscuit de Reims,*
> *hilare,*
> *« Et si l'on mangeait du gâteau ! »*
>
> *Des boules de gomme tintent dans la balance*
> *Le verre pulvérisé dans la corbeille.*

Silence.

« Les seins sont tellement délicats ! »
dit la France

tandis que nous refluions.

Rita Kelly

Translated by Rita Kelly

Beir Beannacht

D'éalaigh tú thar chiumhais na maidine,
ní nach ionadh
bhí an t-éalú ionchollaithe i do theacht.
Fanaim
ag comhaireamh na mbáisteachaí thar an fhuinneog,
sileann an t-am.

Ritheann sé liom go bhfuil duine éigin
ag an doras, téim:
asclán bláthanna, aghaidh choitianta, fear
in éadaí dubha —
sea, is mise, domsa, duitse —
spréann na feileastraim ina gclaimhte,
lasracha gorma ina bhaclainn aige.
Nach rídheas an mhaise dhuit
an lá a chur trí thine.

Iris — teachtaire na nDéithe
cuireadh go Dido í san anallód
leis an aon fhuascailt amháin
d'éinne ag lúbarnaíl ar an mbreocharn
agus Aeneas imithe leis chun a dhán
a líonadh.

Anois
níl fágtha ach leid an mhiotais:
na feileastraim sínte ar an mbord
agus faoin mbord sínte
faic.

Tá do chailleadh gan chorp.
Ní féidir an fhoilmhe a chur faoin bhfód.

Fare Well

You crept away over the edge of morning,
no great wonder really,
the going was embodied in your coming.
I remain
counting the rains which fall across the window,
time spills.

It occurs to me that
there is somebody at the door, I go:
a bouquet of flowers, a common face,
a man in dark clothes —
yes, that's me, for me? For you.
Irises, spread, spears,
blue flames across his arms.
How lovely of you
to set my day ablaze.

Iris — messenger of the gods,
she was sent to *Dido* long ago
with death, the only relief
for a body writhing on a pyre
and *Aeneas* gone off with himself
to fulfil his fate and keep word.

Now
there is only left a hint of myth:
irises stretched on a bare table
and stretched under the table
nothing.

Your loss is without a corpse.
There is no burying an emptiness.

Brendan Kennelly

from *Cromwell*

. . .

Our Place

The murders are increasingly common
In our place which certain of the old songs
Celebrate as a changeless pastoral heaven.
Due, however, to some folk's sense of wrong
Nothing is right nowadays. I must confess
I've become a bit of a callous bastard
Myself. Sipping the latest atrocities
From our one good paper shows how little I care.

Consider, for example, this morning's gem:
Two youths, both about sixteen, and said
To be savagely bored and out of work
Battered an old man to death in his bed.
Making his sister lie in a style of some shame
They pinned her through the neck with a garden-fork.

. . .

In Oliver's Army

No man shall depart a mile out of the Army, upon pain of death
No man shall draw his sword without order, upon pain of death
No man shall hurt a man bringing food, upon pain of death
A sentinel asleep or drunk or forsaking his place shall die without mercy
No man shall give a false Alarum, upon pain of death
He that makes known the Watchword without Order shall die for it
If a Pike-man throw away his pike, he shall die for that
No man shall abandon his colours, upon pain of death
None shall kill an Enemy who yields and throws down his Armes
Rape, Ravishments, Unnatural Abuses shall meet with death

Let God be served, Religion be frequented
Let sellers of meat avoid the unsound, the unwholesome
Let Heaven be praised with sermon and prayer
Let all faults be punished by the Laws of War.
. . .

A Bad Time

Having butchered everyone in the church
The soldiers explore the vaults underneath
Where the choicest ladies are hidden
Hoping to cheat the general death.
One of these, a most handsome virgin,
Kneels down to a Thomas à Wood, with prayers
And tears, that he may spare her life.
Sudden pity; he takes her in his arms
Out of the church, intending her escape.
A soldier sees this and pikes her through.
À Wood, seeing her gasping, takes her money
And jewels, flings her down over the works.
Massacre flows for five days in succession.
A bad time for virgins, local people say.

The Soldiers

The soldiers cut the head, hands and feet off the crucifix
They load themselves with citizens' goods
They excavate the crypts, break open the marble
Tombs in hope of plunder, they fill the church
With corpses, they dress in the precious vestments,
They invite a few trampled souls to Mass
They dash the holy images against the walls
And bear a headless statue of the Virgin in procession.
"How now, Mary of Ireland, how now? Eat some peas"
A soldier calls but a stone falls on his head.
He is not pretty.

Blood continues to run in the streets
Warmer now than ever it ran in human veins
Because the soldiers have set fire to the city.
• • •

Reading Aloud

Oliver Cromwell is a cultured man
Though he's not fond of the drama.
"Buffún" he said "I once read all *The Faerie Queene*
Or, to be more precise, I tried to.
Spenser had a little estate down in Cork
And he found peace there, deep, unending,
Like his poem. But think of all the work
He put for years into these singing
Stanzas. That poem is one of England's glories.
Few Englishmen bother to read it now
Though much of it is still fresh as a berry
On a hedge in the middle of the Maharees.
I plan to spend next winter reading it aloud
To myself in my little estate down in Kerry."
• • •

A Running Battle

What are they doing now? I imagine Oliver
Buying a Dodge, setting up as a taxi-driver
Shunting three dozen farmers to Listowel Races.
I see Ed Spenser, father of all our graces
In verse, enshrined as a knife-minded auctioneer
Addicted to Woodbines and Kilkenny beer,
Selling Parish Priests' shiny furniture
To fox-eyed housewives and van-driving tinkers.
William of Orange is polishing pianos

In convents and other delicate territories,
His nose purple from sipping turpentine.
Little island is Big, Big Island is little.
I never knew a love that wasn't a running battle
Most of the time. I'm a friend of these ghosts. They're mine.

Thomas Kinsella

Tao and Unfitness at Inistiogue on the River Nore

Noon

The black flies kept nagging in the heat.
Swarms of them, at every step, snarled
off pats of cow dung spattered in the grass.

Move, if you move, like water.

The punts were knocking by the boathouse, at full tide.
Volumes of water turned the river curve
hushed under an insect haze.

                Slips of white,
trout bellies, flicked in the corner of the eye
and dropped back onto the deep mirror.

Respond. Do not interfere. Echo.

Thick green woods along the opposite bank
climbed up from a root-dark recess
eaved with mud-whitened leaves.

        *

In a matter of hours all that water is gone,
except for a channel near the far side.
Muck and shingle and pools where the children
wade, stabbing flatfish.

Afternoon

Inistiogue itself is perfectly lovely,
like a typical English village, but a bit sullen.
Our voices echoed in sunny corners
among the old houses; we admired

the stonework and gateways, the interplay
of roofs and angled streets.

The square, with its "village green," lay empty.
The little shops had hardly anything.
The Protestant church was guarded by a woman
of about forty, a retainer, spastic
and indistinct, who drove us out.

An obelisk to the Brownsfords and a Victorian
Celto-Gothic drinking fountain, erected
by a Tighe widow for the villagers,
"erected" in the centre. An astronomical-looking
sundial stood sentry on a platform
on the corner where High Street went up out of the square.

We drove up, past a long-handled water pump
placed at the turn, with an eye to the effect,
then out of the town for a quarter of a mile
above the valley, and came to the dead gate
of Woodstock, once home of the Tighes.

*

The great ruin presented its flat front
at us, sunstruck. The children disappeared.
Eleanor picked her way around a big fallen branch
and away along the face toward the outbuildings.
I took the grassy front steps and was gathered up
in a brick-red stillness. A rook clattered out of the dining room.

A sapling, hooked thirty feet up
in a cracked corner, held out a ghost-green
cirrus of leaves. Cavities
of collapsed fireplaces connected silently
about the walls. Deserted spaces, complicated
by door-openings everywhere.

There was a path up among bushes and nettles
over the beaten debris, then a drop, where bricks

and plaster and rafters had fallen into the kitchens.
A line of small choked arches . . . The pantries, possibly.

Be still, as though pure.

A brick, and its dust, fell.

Wedding Service

We approached the College chapel
along a gravel path by the old Library,
and across a wide private square in the heart of the City.

There was no trouble, parking the car.
Once the scrutiny is over at the back gate
you are at ease, in a protected world.

The car door shut: and the sound, softened,
died along an avenue of old trees
by the high dark wall, topped with a fence of spears.

Past a park, and playing fields,
                              a quiet walk.
And across the front square to the chapel porch,
where the bridegroom received us, kindly and tall.

Full of care for her guests — those of us
liable to be unfamiliar — he showed us in
all the way to our places
in an enclosed pew, on a low seat.

                *

I looked about me. At the plain walls
panelled in ancient wood. The aisle windows
rising up to the timbered ceiling, with clear glass.

The pulpit, out in the middle of the floor.
Three coloured windows at the far end
above an empty platform.

                        With a tang in the air.
Asiatic. Familiar and out of place.

The other ill-fitting particulars
our own presences, settling ourselves,
over-aware, where we sat. Looking across
at a number of other guests.
Looking at us, not at the altar.

Soon, the families and more immediate guests
had assembled, and walked between us in procession
to their various places. And sat waiting.

                    *

Somewhere out of sight a small bell rang

and a priest entered, with a single server,
carrying between them
everything needed for the Mass

— a censer, tossing and exhaling;
the bell; the Book;
and the chalice and tabernacle.

In this place purged of sacrifice
and the manipulation — and any recognition —
of our dark side. No muttering over body and blood.

Direct access.
With regard for property,
in the proper hands.

And Mass was said, diffident and determined.
With a brief address, after the Communion,

for the special occasion. Spiced
with a few remarks for its happening here.

After which the celebrant stepped forward
to the waiting couple, and raised his right hand
in the coloured light to bear witness.

All their hands primal.
The Bride comely.
The Groom steadfast.

The ring fixed on her thin finger
in loving kindness
and firm succession of the flesh.

Chrysalides

Our last free summer we mooned about at odd hours
Pedalling slowly through country towns, stopping to eat
Chocolate and fruit, tracing our vagaries on the map.

At night we watched in the barn, to the lurch of melodeon music,
The crunching boots of country men — huge and weightless
As their shadows — twirling and leaping over the yellow concrete.

Sleeping too little or too much, we awoke at noon
And were received with womanly mockery into the kitchen,
Like calves poking our faces in with enormous hunger.

Daily we strapped our saddlebags and went to experience
A tolerance we shall never know again, confusing
For the last time, for example, the licit and the familiar.

Our instincts blurred with change; a strange wakefulness
Sapped our energies and dulled our slow-beating hearts
To the extremes of feeling — insensitive alike

To the unique succession of our youthful midnights,

When by a window ablaze softly with the virgin moon
Dry scones and jugs of milk awaited us in the dark,

Or to lasting horror, a wedding flight of ants
Spawning to its death, a mute perspiration
Glistening like drops of copper, agonised, in our path.

King John's Castle

Not an epic, being not loosely architectured,
    But with epic force, setting the head spinning
With the taut flight earthward of its bulk, King John's
    Castle rams fast down the county of Meath.
This in its heavy ruin. New, a brute bright plateau,
    It held speechless under its cold a whole province of Meath.

Now the man-rot of passages and broken window-casements,
    Vertical drops chuting through three storeys of masonry,
Draughty spiral stairways decaying in the depths,
    Are a labyrinth in the medieval dark. Intriguers
Who prowled here once, into the waiting arms
    Of their own monster, revisit the blowing dust.

Life, a vestigial chill, sighs along the tunnels
    Through the stone face. The great collapsed rooms, the mind
Of the huge head, are dead. Views open inward
    On empty silence; a chapel-shelf, moss-grown, unreachable.
King John directs at the river a grey stare, who once
    Viewed the land in a spirit of moderation and massacre.

Contemplatives, tiny as mice moving over the green
    Mounds below, might take pleasure in the well
Of quiet there, the dark foundations near at hand.
    Up here where the wind weeps bleakly, as though in
        remembrance
Against our own tombstones, the brave and great might gather.
    For the rest, this is not their fortress.

Pause en Route

Death, when I am ready, I
Shall come; drifting where I drown,
Falling, or by burning, or by
Sickness, or by striking down.

Nothing you can do can put
My coming aside, nor what I choose
To come like — holy, broken or but
An anonymity — refuse.

But when I am ready be
What figure you will, bloodily dressed
Or with arms held gauzily
In at my door from the tempest.

And, if your task allow it, let
The ceaseless waters take us as
One soul conversing and, if it
Deny, let that civility pass.

Little, now as then, we know
How I shall address you or
You me. Embarrassment could go
Queerly with us, scavenger.

Nothing sure but that the brave
And proud you stopped I will not sing,
Knowing nothing of you save
A final servant functioning.

from **Readings in Poetry**

29

1   When in disgrace with Fortune and mens eyes,
    I all alone beweepe my out-cast state,
    And trouble deafe heaven with my bootlesse cries,
    And looke upon my selfe and curse my fate,
5   Wishing me like to one more rich in hope,
    Featur'd like him, like him with friends possest,
    Desiring this mans art, and that mans skope,
    With what I most enjoy contented least,
    Yet in these thoughts my selfe almost despising,
10 Haplye I think on thee, and then my state,
    (Like to the Larke at breake of daye arising)
    From sullen earth sings hymns at Heavens gate,
        For thy sweet love remembered such wealth brings,
14   That then I skorne to change my state with Kings.

30

1   When to the Sessions of sweet silent thought,
    I summon up remembrance of things past,
    I sigh the lacke of many a thing I sought,
    And with old woes new waile my dear times waste:
5   Then can I drowne an eye unused to flow
    For precious friends hid in deaths dateles night,
    And weepe afresh love's long since canceld woe,
    And mone th'expence of many a vannisht sight.
    Then can I greeve at greevances fore-gon,
10 And heavily from woe to woe tell ore
    The sad account of fore-bemoaned mone,
    Which I new pay as if not payd before.
        But if the while I thinke on thee (deare friend)
14   All losses are restored, and sorrowes end.

Shakespeare: Sonnet 29

First quatrain

Lines 1 and 2   Noting that the syntax is suspended with the first word; and registering the opening scene :

A condition of isolation and shame, rejected by circumstance and by mankind. Regarded with ignominy in the eyes of men; his own eyes pouring tears.

Line 3   The rejection equated with the expulsion from Eden. The private weeping now an outcry, complaining — and looking — toward Heaven; Heaven deaf; the cries unavailing.

Line 4   The cries — and the regard of the eyes — turned back with curses upon the self.

A first quatrain of emotional and sensual extremes. Intense in imagery, so that the word "disgrace" reads as the actual deprivation of grace, and the word "outcast" as the act of casting out; the eye imagery strong in line 4 so that the outcast — disgraced in men's eyes in line 1 — is disgraced in his own eyes also.

Second quatrain

Lines 5-8   The syntax still suspended. The basis given for the emotions of the first quatrain; the standards against which the complaints are measured: others more gifted by circumstance — one more gifted with looks, another with ease of friendship; one colleague with a particular technical skill, another with a range of theme, so that even in his chosen calling he is unsatisfied.

The second quatrain, without imagery, empties the sonnet of the extremes of the first.

Third quatrain

The extremes of the first quatrain, and their removal in the second, prepare for a third quatrain of dramatic effect.

Line 9   The solutions begin: of syntax ("Yet"); and of the emotional crisis ("almost").

Line 10   The happy accident ("Haplye") occurs on a memory of the beloved,* initiating a change in the outcast state. This is the second use of "state" in a rhyming position, readying it for a change of meaning.

Line 11   His state, rising like a lark — from nowhere, out of the dark into the light — with tiny explosive effect (a small richness of dentals and three small 'k's in a setting of open vowels) . . .

Line 12   . . . gives voice to the outcast world. The voice is tiny, and Heaven's gate remains shut, but the voice is singing hymns and no longer complaining. The imagery of the first quatrain restored, transfigured.

Lines 13 and 14 Ending with a couplet of lowered intensity: the problem solved; the argument proven. And the third use of "state," the meaning enhanced by "Kings," and the introduction of the idea of wealth.

The concept of wealth is treated in the next sonnet.

* The two previous sonnets having dealt with the pain of the beloved's absence

An Anthology of Poetry from Canada and Ireland 855

Shakespeare: Sonnet 30

First quatrain

Lines 1 and 2   The image of a judicial assembly established, in an atmosphere of pleasant nostalgia. Memories called up from the past for silent scrutiny.

Line 3   Nostalgia turning to melancholy, quiet — but sighing, no longer silent, with the memory of things sought in the past, and not achieved.

Line 4   The memory sharpening, the sigh increaseing to a wail, with the renewed painful awareness of things once possible and let pass, or achieved and squandered; key words "waile" and "waste." The judicial assembly reduced, now, to the one.

Second quatrain

Line 5   With the solitary, sharpened memory — and accompanying the wail — tears that had flowed once for the loss, and ceased, flow again as though for the first time . . .

Line 6   . . . for the loss of precious friends lost in death's timeless dark;

Line 7 and 8   weeping once again for the grief that had healed in a past love, and lamenting again the cost, or loss, of past experience. Beginning with "dear" and "waste" in line 4; and developing through "precious," "dateles," "canceld" and "expence"; the idea of loving friendship has combined with that of accountancy and wealth. The woe for lost friendship is a debt due, and presented again for payment — dateless, that was thought cancelled. Key words are "woe" and "mone."

Third quatrain

Lines 9-12   The full account presented for payment. The uncancelled woes lamented and counted over heavily, as by an accountant or clerk, and paid again as if for the first time, with the repeated excessive open vowel sounds of "woe" from line 7 and "mone" from line 8.

Lines 13 and 14   Tensions of sense and sound solved in a simple couplet. All losses, and sorrows, made good by the thought of the dear friend. After the excessively articulated mourning of lines 10 and 12 it is difficult to articulate line 13 without exercising the muscles of a smile.

Barbara Korun

Translated by Theo Dorgan from the Slovene

Stag

I wake to a warm stag's tongue between my legs,
the evening light comes horizontal in through open doors.
Gently he nuzzles my breasts, this stag, and licks me,
his coarse tongue warm on my vulva, my breasts, my face.
His scent intoxicates me — earth, moss, fear and decay —
the raw odour of instinct.
He lies down beside me against my smooth belly,
I run my hands over his matted hair.
He holds his head proud, he gazes away from me into the
                                                    woods.
His bare penis is reddening in the shadows of dusk.

Time thickens. I reach out into the dark, I touch a man's
                          body.
Desire flares in me, I am suddenly all heat.
He makes love to me simply, directly; he holds me close.
In his hands are the north wind and the south wind.
Rivers and oceans run through his body.
His mouth is warm and full of summer rain.
The room fills with songs of earth, of beyond our earth.
Sometimes a flash of moonlight reveals his face.

He does not look me in the eye, he protects me from
                                                  himself.
Sometimes when he is with me I no longer feel the ground.
Sometimes lust pools in his navel like a clear spring.
Sometimes he fountains, spewing lava.
He never hurts me.
With infinite care he turns me belly down on to the earth,
when he bites my neck and I smell his hot breath I know
I am to be spared.

With the coming of dawn I feel horns in his hair.
Fur sprouts from his head to his back, his rump.
On his belly are sudden tufts of bestial grass.
He has a stag's head at daybreak, his eyes on me barely
                                                human.
Eyes from the other side of the frontier.
Absent-minded, his hands of horn caress me.
I watch his antlers burgeon and spread.

The scent of morning flushes the hut, he stands to go.
One brief glance at me as I stand in the door
and I am split in two, I fall to the ground in flame.
I listen to the pock of sharp hooves going away,
I feel how my burnt halves are putting out flowers.

Wolf

. . . and he is strange to me, strange, he who is all wolf and eats into my body from underneath, he shoves his snout into all my orifices and licks, licks, it is strange, so strange, I want to hide away, shrink into myself, escape into my head, be away, be off . . . I am afraid to feel this, afraid of my body, afraid to feel his body. He eats into me more, his mouth a maw, his teeth so sharp, devouring me, he is devouring me like a soft, juicy meal, tearing me open, pushing between my legs with his tongue, nose, jaw, pelt, paws, pestle . . . he rams it deep, in to the root, over and over and over again, into this body no longer mine, a pure violence I permit, I allow, I do not defend myself but I will not be washed away . . . I am soft and pliant, he tosses me like a rag doll, I think to myself that this is how it is, he is a man, I am a woman, this is how it should be, this is how it happens, he makes me thinner and thinner, only a thin membrane left, thin skin, thin . . . and then paradise flowers in my head, heaven in my body, heaven, no, not the heaven of the body . . . and still he is deep in me, shoving me, tearing me, pushing deep into me, searching, searching . . . but I am replete, full and fulfilled, bright and calm, so full to the brim that I do not care what it is with me now, I would not care if there was

blood running, I am beyond all pain and pleasure and I know,
I know that everything is going to be all right, I cannot trust
this wolf but everything is going to be all right, the power that
is in me now is stronger than he is, this power that is changing
him, healing him, healing me, healing the wound . . .

White Bulls

I open the window
and out of the night
white bulls leap into the room.
A dark figure
turns in her sleep.

Her skin is cold.
Dutch linen,
light of the moon
in each crease and fold.
Her skin is silken
when it melts,
her underparts velvet
as she yields to me,
the forest mass of her sex.

A mouth accepts me,
a pool of rose water.
With my tongue
I draw damp lace
across her buds.

A blazing white landscape,
a lost traveller,
the rustling and crackling
blackness of her hair.

Tip of my tongue
on the taut skin of unhearing,
a string of gabbled syllables,
a high note plucked.

Nick Laird

Cuttings

Methodical dust shades the combs and pomade
while the wielded goodwill of the sunlight picks out
a patch of paisley wallpaper to expand leisurely on it.

The cape comes off with a matador's flourish
and the scalp's washed to get rid of the chaff.
This is the closeness casual once in the trenches

and is deft as remembering when not to mention
the troubles or women or prison.
They talk of the parking or calving or missing.

A beige lino, a red barber's chair, one ceramic brown sink
and a scenic wall-calendar of the glories of Ulster
sponsored by JB Crane Hire or some crowd flogging animal feed.

About, say, every second month or so
he will stroll and cross the widest street in Ireland
and step beneath the bandaged pole.

Eelmen, gunmen, the long dead, the police.
And my angry and beautiful father:
tilted, expectant and open as in a deckchair

outside on the drive, persuaded to wait
for a meteor shower, but with his eyes budded shut,
his head full of lather and unusual thoughts.

Remaindermen

Because what I liked about them best
was their ability to thole,
that weathered silence and reluctance,
fornenst the whole damn lot.

They've lived alone for years of course,
and watched their cemeteries filling up
like car parks on a Saturday,
their young grow fat for export.

There are others who know what it is
to lose, to hold ideas of north
so singularly brutal that the world
might be ice-bound for good.

Someone has almost transcribed
the last fifty years of our speech,
and has not once had the chance
to employ the word *sorry*

or press the shift to make the mark
that indicates the putting of a question.
The arch was put up wrong this Spring
outside my father's office.

When you enter it states
Safe Home Brethren,
and upon leaving the place
Welcome Here.

The Signpost

Knee-capped on the second Tuesday of the month
by two of the stringy cunts
he'd last bought a round for at Christmas

put paid to the plans for ascending Everest,
and playing for Rangers, even in goal
(though it left open Glentoran, as his father'd suggested).

*

The pistol jammed and they kicked him over.
They could break his legs, they offered,
but he waited, and another gun was brought,

and the barrel held against his calf
(friends, see, so they spared his knees),
and the trigger pulled and the bullet shot.

*

Opening fire: slitting the skin of the side of the flame.
He'd held a bomb the same weight as he'd been when born.
Pan back. Agree with that, the thought he had until he blacked,

what with one arm splayed under, and the other
swung over the blade of his shoulder,
he must, from above, make sense as a signpost.

*

From the Royal's window he got a clear view.
An air vent on a roof lent a heat haze to Belfast,
and two cranes swung their arms low over the city,

as if giving a blessing. Incredible to stay upright
with all that gathered weight. He spied his father's house,
but all the lights, strange that, were out.

To the Wife

After this iceblink and sudden death of the mammals —
that wolfhound our youngest will poison with gravy on sponges,
the calf whose back leg you fatally shatter, driving home fast,
too sad, from the clinic — and after neither of us have a mother
or father and we've washed up our miniscule five o'clock dinners,

having pottered around the stores all afternoon, mumbling,
buttonholing assistants to complain about prices or rain,
and change over our eyewear to examine the papers
with that contemptuous squint we'll both have adopted,
and decide how we've read all the books that we will,
and think even those in the end offered hassle and pain,

do you think we could find a way back to an evening
when holding each other will not be about balance
and all of the tunes are inside us and wordless?

The Evening Forecast for the Region

The weatherman for Boston ponders whether, *I'd bet not,*
the snowstorm coming north will come to town tonight.

I swim around in bed. My head's attempting to begin
its routine shift down through the old transmission

to let me make the slope and slip the gearstick into neutral at
    the crown
before freewheeling down the ocean-road descent into the ghost
    town,

there, the coastal one, with a stone pier bare as skin, familiar
seafront houses hunched and boarded-over for the winter,

and beside the tattered nets a rowing boat lies upturned on the
    beach.
Aside from a mongrel, inside, asleep at someone's slippered feet,

everything faces the sea. But the plumbing's sighs are almost
    human.

Airlocks collect and slide from duct to duct so the radiators whine.

The hiding places grow further hidden. A priesthole's given over
to a spider's architecture. A well tries on a grassy manhole cover,

threaded, dangerous as fingers. An ivied sycamore in the forest
   at Drum Manor,
resonant and upright and empty as an organ pipe, where for a
   panicked hour

a boy will not be found. I arch one foot to scratch the other.
I would shed myself to segue into sleep. I would enter

but the opening is of a new off-Broadway *Hamlet*. The gulf is war.
This hiatus, my father's hernia. The cleft's a treble on the score

of Scott Joplin's "Entertainer." This respite is a care home,
the recess a playground. This division I slither into is a
   complicated sum:

thirteen over seven. I give in. I turn the television on.
The weatherman for Boston is discussing how, *Thank Heaven*,

the snowstorm missed, and turned, and headed out to sea.
Is it particularly human, this, to lie awake? To touch the papery

encircling bark but watch through a knot, and wait?
Everyone on earth is sleeping. I am the keel-scrape

beneath their tidal breathing which is shifting down through
   tempo
to the waveform of the sea. The gathered even draw and lift of air.

Further east a blizzard of homogenous decisions breathes above
the folding and unfolding pane and counterpane of waves

as if the white so loves the world it tries to make a map of it,
exact and blank to start again, but the sea will not stay under it.

The ricepaper wafers are melting. Millions of babynails cling
to the wind lifting hoarsely off the Atlantic. The whole thing

is mesmeric. For hours the snow will fall like rhythm.
                                                               Listen.

Ann Leahy

A Good Rogeting

I keep to myself on one side of a bed
whose other half is occupied by books
meant to match my moods, catch the thread
of all my thoughts, from hard-angled works
of reference, to magazines, loose-leaf pads.
A collection of love-lorn verse
hugs an impenetrable masterpiece
while Judith Hearne's eclipsed by glamour ads.

When I bring a new one back
over dinner with a glass of wine
I imagine removing its paper bag
running my fingers down its spine
how I'll fan the pages to inhale
its pristine smell, then make it my own:
easing back the sleeve and going down
on the biographical detail.

Sometimes that's the best bit
on evenings when I'm not in form
to get stuck in or to commit
not even to paper. One volume
alone then seems able to interject:
Chambers Twentieth Century Dictionary —
something new every read
and no long-term effects.

I can fall asleep over a phrase whose
meaning remains a stranger and wake
in the morning with *Roget's Thesaurus*
poking me urgently in the back.

Mince Customer

Pinned to the door
was a diagram of a heifer
with sections straight-lined

across her side: sirloin
jigsawed between rib
and rump, shank slotting

into round. And the people
who came in, we sorted them
by the cuts they bought:

mince customers wanted cosseting,
all the work done for them;
a fillet woman wanted only lean,

leaving all the fat
and gristle on our hands;
but a brisket man

was a prince, who'd take
his lean where he could get it
between the bone and thews.

Inside too a series of lines
ran through the house like skewers.
As a child you couldn't see them,

but bit by bit you'd puzzle out
the no-nonsense pattern they laid down,
plot yourself a course in which

your silverside was out
with your flank protected
your tenderloin concealed

or else you'd feel the chill
from the refrigeration unit
as sure as any mince customer.

Cold Storage

There was a cold room
at the back of our house.

Our father propped the door open,
and the butcher shouldered sides of beef,
and sheep slit down their spines.

Speared on hooks they hung,
flanked by ox-tongues, long and thick
as a healthy man's thigh.

On the floor lay fleshy chickens
packed in boxes, their hearts and sweating
entrails bagged within their breasts.

Upstairs, you and I peered at the silver
fleck on a fish's eye in the kitchen
foreground of a painting by Velasquez,

or turned the page to trace the head
of John the Baptist through strips of greaseproof
meant to parcel out rack chops and T-bone steaks.

Later, after you and I had gone, our mother
scrubbed splatters of blood from the concrete,
hoovered up the last flakes of sawdust.

The room — windowless and airless
but no longer cold — stood empty but for
wool coats and leather jackets

that assembled there and hung
side-by-side like distant cousins
of the earlier occupants.

Now it's my turn to stand with my back
against the door, as the removal
men deliver boxes crammed

with kitchen knives, a fold-up barbecue,
your College thesis, Labour Party card,
out-sized atlas, home-made chess pieces.

Still wrapped in tissue, they lie on the floor,
in the dark, waiting . . . to be sectioned up
portioned out, bartered with siblings

each one trying to piece the present
back together bit by bit; each one after
the thing that seems to have your heart in it.

Michael Longley

Swallow

When the swallow detoured into the kitchen
Kissing corners, highlighting the dusty shelves
With its underside, those exhausted feathers
That never quite made it through the open door,
We too were on the verge of moving house:

In the fridge a neglected rainbow trout,
A mouse mummifying underneath the piano,
Dead friends, draughts from the rafters, artisans
From the Land of Promise or thereabouts
Thatching with the wings of birds our house.

Northern Lights

When you woke me up and showed me through the window
Curtains of silk, luminous smoke, ghost fires,
A convergence of rays above the Black Mountain,
The northern lights became our own magnetic field —
Your hand on my shoulder, your tobacco-y breath
And the solar wind that ruffled your thinning hair.

Björn Olinder's Pictures

I have learned about dying by looking at two pictures
Björn Olinder needed to look at when he was dying:
A girl whose features are obscured by the fall of her hair
Planting a flower,
                and a seascape: beyond the headland
A glimpse of immaculate sand that awaits our footprints.

A Norwegian Wedding

Because the Leprosy Museum is still closed
We find ourselves in St Olaf's, eavesdropping
On a Norwegian wedding. The Lutheran light
Picks us out from among the small congregation.
How few friends anyone has. I'm glad we came.
Christ holds his hands up high above the lovers
And fits his death into the narrow window. Oh,
His sore hands. How many friends does a leper have?
Bride and bridegroom walk past us and into the rain.
It is mid-May. All of the roads out of Bergen
Are bordered with lady's smock and wood anemones.

Broken Dishes

Sydney our mutual friend is kneeling by your bed
Hour after hour on the carpetless hospital floor.
He repeats the same kind words and they become
An invocation to you and you start to die.

You love your body. So does Sydney. So do I.
Communion is blankets and eiderdown and sheets.
All I can think of is a quilt called *Broken Dishes*
And spreading it out on the floor beneath his knees.

The Mustard Tin

You are dying and not sleeping soundly because
Your eyes stay open and it doesn't seem to hurt.
We want you to blink and find three of us standing
For a few seconds between you and the darkness.

Your mouth has opened so wide you appear to scream.
We will need something to close your terrible yawn.

I hoke around in my childhood for objects without
Sharp edges and recover the oval mustard tin.

A daughter strokes your forehead and says: "There. There."
A daughter holds your hand and says: "I'm sorry."
I focus on the mustard tin propping your jaw,
On the total absence of the oval mustard tin.

The Daffodils

Your daughter is reading to you over and over again
Wordsworth's "The Daffodils," her lips at your ear.
She wants you to know what a good girl you have been.
You are so good at joined-up writing the page you
Have filled with your knowledge is completely black.
Your hand presses her hand in response to rhyme words.
She wants you to turn away from the wooden desk
Before you die, and look out of the classroom window
Where all the available space is filled with daffodils.

A Sprig of Bay
in memory of Seán Dunne, 1956 — 95

I

Stepping among recent windfalls and couch grass
Like wet raffia unravelling and beech seedlings,
I glimpse this rundown orchard's original plan
In the lofty bay tree and the well it canopies,

And drink spring water to your memory and pick
Leaves for the dried beans in your Cork bedsit
As you appear out of those long-haired bearded days
To accept, Seán, cook and poet, a sprig of bay.

II
I wish I could introduce you to this friend of mine
Who is rebuilding a ruined flax mill as a ruin
— If it is a flax mill, or a mill for grinding wheat
(A millstone leans against the wall) — no matter what,

You walk away from the rainy fields into a rainy
Room, windows that let the winds come in, a chimney
That opens up to a square of sky and ivy. Sean,
Wear like a gigantic bangle the cracked millstone.

III
In the abandoned schoolhouse I shelter from the rain
With hundreds of pupils and look beyond boreen
And hollow bog (the "spother" in these parts) to where
The last turf was stacked for Old Head and the hookers,

And I imagine you, Sean, as in a game of hide
And seek covering, uncovering the eyes of childhood,
Or else, absent because you laboured through the night,
You are the boy who snoozes on the last turf-cart.

A Poppy

When millions march into the mincing machine
An image in Homer picks out the individual
Tommy and the doughboy in his doughboy helmet:
"Lolling to one side like a poppy in a garden
Weighed down by its seed capsule and rainwater,
His head drooped under the heavy, crestfallen
Helmet" (an image Virgil steals — *lasso papavera
Collo* — and so do I), and so Gorgythion dies,
And the poppy that sheds its flower-heads in a day
Grows in one summer four hundred more, which means
Two thousand petals overlapping as though to make
A cape for the corn goddess or a soldier's soul.

The War Graves

The exhausted cathedral reaches nowhere near the sky
As though behind its buttresses wounded angels
Snooze in a halfway house of gargoyles, rainwater
By the mouthful, broken wings among pigeons' wings.

There will be no end to clearing up after the war
And only an imaginary harvest-home where once
The Germans drilled holes for dynamite, for fieldmice
To smuggle seeds and sow them inside these columns.

The headstones wipe out the horizon like a blizzard
And we can see no farther than the day they died,
As though all of them died together on the same day
And the war was that single momentous explosion.

Mothers and widows pruned these roses yesterday,
It seems, planted sweet william and mowed the lawn
After consultations with the dead, heads meeting
Over this year's seed catalogues and packets of seeds.

Around the shell holes not one poppy has appeared,
No symbolic flora, only the tiny whitish flowers
No one remembers the names of in time, brookweed
And fairy flax, say, lamb's lettuce and penny-cress.

In mine craters so vast they are called after cities
Violets thrive, as though strewn by each cataclysm
To sweeten the atmosphere and conceal death's smell
With a perfume that vanishes as soon as it is found.

At the Canadian front line permanent sandbags
And duckboards admit us to the underworld, and then
With the beavers we surface for long enough to hear
The huge lamentations of the wounded caribou.

Old pals in the visitors' book at Railway Hollow
Have scribbled "The severest spot. The lads did well"
"We came to remember," and the woodpigeons too

Call from the wood and all the way from Accrington.

I don't know how Riflemen Parfitt, Corporal Vance,
Private Costello of the Duke of Wellingtons,
Driver Chapman, Topping, Atkinson, Duckworth,
Dorrell, Wood come to be written in my diary.

For as high as we can reach we touch-read the names
Of the disappeared, and shut our eyes and listen to
Finches' chitters and a blackbird's apprehensive cry
Accompanying Charles Sorley's monumental sonnet.

We describe the comet at Edward Thomas's grave
And, because he was a fisherman, that headlong
Motionless deflection looks like a fisherman's fly,
Two or three white after-feathers overlapping.

Geese on sentry duty, lambs, a clattering freight train
And a village graveyard encompass Wilfred Owen's
Allotment, and there we pick from a nettle bed
One celandine each, the flower that outwits winter.

A Prayer

In our country they are desecrating churches.
May the rain that pours in pour into the font.
Because no snowflake ever falls in the wrong place,
May snow lie on the altar like an altar cloth.

The Horses

For all of the horses butchered on the battlefield,
Shell-shocked, tripping up over their own intestines,
Drowning in the mud, the best war memorial
Is in Homer: two horses that refuse to budge
Despite threats and sweet-talk and the whistling whip,

Immovable as a tombstone, their heads drooping
In front of the streamlined motionless chariot,
Hot tears spilling from their eyelids onto the ground
Because they are still in mourning for Patroclus
Their charioteer, their shiny manes bedraggled
Under the yoke pads on either side of the yoke.

Scrap Metal

I

Helen Denerley made this raven out of old iron,
Belly and back the brake shoes from a lorry, nuts
And bolts for legs and feet, the wings ploughshares
("Ridgers," she elaborates, "for tatties and neeps,")
The eyeballs cogs from a Morris Minor gearbox.

The bird poses on the circular brass tray my mother
(And now I) polished, swipes of creamy Brasso,
Then those actions, melting a frosty window pane,
Clearing leaves from a neglected well, her breath
Meeting her reflection in the ultimate burnish.

The beak I identified first as a harrow tooth
Is the finger from an old-fashioned finger-bar
Mower for dividing and cutting down the grass,
And, as he bends his head to drink, the raven points
To where the surface gives back my mother's features.

II

The head I pat is made out of brake calipers
With engine mountings from a Toyota for ears,
The spine a baler chain, the ruff and muscular neck
Sprockets, plough points, clutch plate, mower blades,

The legs a Morris Minor kingpin or swingle tree.
Snow in Aberdeenshire and Helen's garden. A wolf
At the forest's edge where scrap metal multiplies
Waits on claw-hammer feet for the rest of the pack.

Laertes

When he found Laertes alone on the tidy terrace, hoeing
Around a vine, disreputable in his gardening duds,
Patched and grubby, leather gaiters protecting his shins
Against brambles, gloves as well, and, to cap it all,
Sure sign of his deep depression, a goatskin duncher,
Odysseus sobbed in the shade of a pear-tree for his father
So old and pathetic that all he wanted then and there
Was to kiss him and hug him and blurt out the whole story,
But the whole story is one catalogue and then another,
So he waited for images from that formal garden,
Evidence of a childhood spent traipsing after his father
And asking for everything he saw, the thirteen pear-trees,
Ten apple-trees, forty fig-trees, the fifty rows of vines
Ripening at different times for a continuous supply,
Until Laertes recognised his son and, weak at the knees,
Dizzy, flung his arms around the neck of great Odysseus
Who drew the old man fainting to his breast and held him there
And cradled like driftwood the bones of his dwindling father.

Ceasefire

I
Put in mind of his own father and moved to tears
Achilles took him by the hand and pushed the old king
Gently away, but Priam curled up at his feet and
Wept with him until their sadness filled the building.

II
Taking Hector's corpse into his own hands Achilles
Made sure it was washed and, for the old king's sake,
Laid out in uniform, ready for Priam to carry
Wrapped like a present home to Troy at daybreak.

III
When they had eaten together, it pleased them both
To stare at each other's beauty as lovers might,
Achilles built like a god, Priam good-looking still
And full of conversation, who earlier had sighed:

IV
"I get down on my knees and do what must be done
And kiss Achilles' hand, the killer of my son."

All of These People

Who was it who suggested that the opposite of war
Is not so much peace as civilisation? He knew
Our assassinated Catholic greengrocer who died
At Christmas in the arms of our Methodist minister,
And our ice-cream man whose continuing requiem
Is the twenty-one flavours children have by heart.
Our cobbler mends shoes for everybody; our butcher
Blends into his best sausages leeks, garlic, honey;
Our cornershop sells everything from bread to kindling.
Who can bring peace to people who are not civilised?
All of these people, alive or dead, are civilised.

Dave Lordan

In the Model Village

We're not being smart
Tom Thumb *is* our blacksmith
We've a dozen Spinning Jennys here on loan from Lilliput
The Sly Fella's calling to arms from the back of a lorry
the length of a shoebox
The Big Fella and his penny farthing
would fit in your pocket

There's a rosy six inch Irish maiden for you
collecting plastic apples in our knee-high forest
mind don't step on Molly Malone's first cousin
and she hawking a basket of plasticine salmon

We're not supposed to use the church spire for leaning
but its handy for an elbow-rest when you're smoking
and the nave is just the right height and angle
for comfortable sitting

and believe me
if we needed to
or were ever asked
we could easily dismantle the brewery
stamp on the charnel house
kick in the workhouses' walls
flatten the schools and the barracks
trample the cotton mills into the ground

We'd go down on all fours
and like the big bad wolves
we'd huff and we'd puff
till the whole of Pearse Street
and Emmett Square were just whirling smithereens

but we're not that dangerous or threatening
and we never were truly
one good sweep of a yard brush
would clear away our part in the rising
and we're at least fifteen score miles
and three generations away
from the slightest need
for TNT

Instead, when we're suspended
in the long dying
of an August afternoon
between a busload of Spanish artillerymen
and a troop of Korean nuns
we pore over *Lonely Planets*
and *Rough Guides*
and Philip's maps of the universe
plotting our autumn's escapes
to the never-ending highs
in Shane McGowan's Siam

when the gulf stream is flowing royally in
to occupy Inchydoney Bay
and the cavalier breeze with its muskets of sand
its acids and powders of citrus and flesh
is blasting the stink of ancient shite away
then us summer guides can count
on making it through
to our various starlit elopements
to the rainbows of the moon

While we're waiting
we're here and at your service
we'll give you the essence of four hundred years
in fifteen learned off paragraphs
and recite the short story of how
our settlement grew on a stone in the wood
tripped over a long time ago
by a very minor Tudor

That's our miniature town in a nutshell
That's our model village for you
Do come and visit sir and don't forget
to bring along your friends
You know very well Clonakilty's future depends
on the kindness of giants like you

so God be with you sir
and God's blessings on your wife and family
and God help us.

TEA

All night long
I've been listening to his racket,
Now Uncle Georgie's making tea again,
Same craic every night of his week old visit,
Home alone from lonely London.

First loose slip-ons slapping the lino
Then the handle rattling on the kitchen door,
rusty scraping of a lock, hinges slowly creaking open,

Again
again I hear a switch being flicked,
sugar crunch, tea leaves shaken,
the kettle spout its whistling hiss,
teaspoon and cup
ring out like a bell.

The Longest Queue

This a story I heard from a friend
who heard it from an Iraqi engineer
who fled away to Ireland

from bomb clouds and anthrax
in the rain and queues for food.
He rings home once a month
to speak to his dying mother
and to hear news of his family and neighbours.
That night he told the story he
had asked after a friend of his,
a doctor with two beautiful daughters
and a young boy.
His mother went silent, darkly silent,
fifty pence gobbling silent.
A couple of months ago this doctor
lost his job and was left to
live on government rations,
not a lot to go on by all accounts
and anyway he owed some money
to a smuggler for getting
his mother over the border to Jordan.
Faced with starvation he improvised
and sent his two beautiful daughters
one eighteen, the other fifteen
out to sell their bodies,
and his ten year old son to shine shoes and beg.
Financially it worked out,
they'd even set some money aside.
But the man was broken hearted,
not to speak of how his children must have felt.
So the man decides to cook a chicken for his family.
He goes to queue in the marketplace.
It's a short queue since chickens
cost six weeks average wages.
Then the slightly longer line for vegetables
and the four hours waiting for bread.
Maybe he thinks to himself
that the only thing longer than this bread queue
is the waiting list at the coffin-makers.
Next day is some kind of religious feast

so he tells his kids to be at the dinner table at seven.
He's got a surprise for them.
While preparing the chicken
he searches through his leftover medicines
for a suitable poison
to inject into the breast and leg meat.
The daughters and the son arrive in time
and they sit around the table chatting,
faking good humour for the good of their father,
like they always do.
The doctor divides the meat among them,
a breast and leg for himself,
a breast for the eldest daughter,
a leg for the younger,
a leg and two wings for the son.
He gestures to his son to share out the vegetables.
They say their prayers quickly, mouths watering.
Since none of them has eaten meat for
months and months they take
their time, chewing each mouthful
with the relish reserved for a luxury,
rolling it round with their tongues,
squeezing the taste out with their teeth.
The boy asks for more and gets it.
They do not talk while they are eating.
They concentrate on the taste and the smell.
The doctor is a subtle and a skilful cook,
his children notice nothing unusual,
he gives nothing away with sighs or tears.
They do not even notice themselves dying.
In a few minutes they are all dead.
They have joined the longest queue of all.
I hope this isn't a true story
but I'd say it probably is.

from "Reflections on Shannon"
. . .

Fuck the la-dee-da
fuck the you and fuck the me and fuck the I
Fuck the spirit
Fuck the allegory
Fuck elective affinity
Fuck the subject
Fuck the object
Fuck neutrality
Fuck Buddha
Fuck the shamrock
Fuck the leafy love-banks
Fuck the holy trinity
Fuck the oaks and the yew trees
Fuck the visionary sheep
Fuck County Meath
Fuck Homer
Fuck the canon
Fuck Judges
Fuck competitions
Fuck the bursary
Fuck the cheese and wine reception
Fuck poetry
Fuck the higher power
Let me make this situation clear
There is a mass murder ongoing in Iraq
invasion occupation expropriation
The country we live in is
aiding and abetting
aiding and abetting mass murder
by allowing our airport to be used to transport
the cluster bombers
machine gunners
rocket launchers

torturers
child killers
rapists
shoot on sighters
hit and runners
who are committing this mass murder
Do I think I can heckle you into doing something about it?
Do I think just by telling you what you already know
it will shame you into doing something about it?
Does all this shouting and flag waving make me feel any better?
What am I going to do about it?
• • •

Holding Chirac's Hand in Temple Bar

They are of neon
They are of strobelight
They are of ink and dye
They are of rubber and plastic and fur
Or they are simply here
Walking the cobbles
In Temple Bar
Drunk and stoned
On a Friday night
With gel and stilettos,
Tattoos and thigh-boots,
Belly-tops and wonderbras,
Wigs and masks.
Some have stuck-on tails
Some bunny ears
Some leprechaun hats
Some plastic arses
But their mouths have no faces
Their singing is senseless
And the cobbles absorb and forget
Their laughter and sighs

Their urine and vomit,
While ould orators' ghosts
Are beaten down and bleed
Into the cracks of the street.

Around the corner
On Dame Street
Near the Green
I saw three Muslim girls
Wearing the hijab.
More power to them.

Alice Lyons

Thank God It's Dry

Disregarding Mary in the post office
the Mary with the permanent hairnet:
It's promised bad. She headed off
any brazen praise of bold good
weather. Six years coming this
heat wave over Ireland. Mesmeric
the buzzing bees, checking stalks
of self-heal the way you'd check for mail

in the "pigeon hole" before e-mail.
The lost year. How real life stalks
the meat of you. Mesmeric
the cabbage white-bouncing dot in this
karaoke meadow. It sings a song of good
death. You lifted his coffin and headed off
for Mass behind a cousin in sleazy fishnets
the weight on four shoulders and off his.

The Polish Language
For Barbara Falkowska and her family

If language could shrug shoulders
lift eyebrows and turn palms up
you might have a tiny idea.

To make an effigy, you'd need
a lot of concrete, more than you'd think
a stork, some amber
honey from bees that live near rape
a quantity of shirts freely removed
from the backs of anyone you meet

big lumps of lead and coal
and a great deal of wood from a primeval forest.

A poultice of sliced onions on the throat
may help you speak it.

Cats are known to rub up against its sibilance.

Crush a cherry and a beet
in your fingers to arrive at its colour —
czerwony.
If that fails to convince, make a soup.

When you are fed up with the world
say *sprzykrzy*
or phone information in Zakopane
and just listen.

As a matter of fact
in this sonorous, consonant tongue
my art was revivified.

My Polish brothers and sisters
in art (the ones who survived)
robbed of flint you made fire
out of evil you wrote *live.*

Gearailt Mac Eoin
Translated by Gréagóir Ó Dúill

Deireadh Caithréime

Castar orm riamh iad,
na daoine croíbhriste
'bhíos ag ceasacht an aoibhnis
a bhí le bheith ann.

Rinne seo smaointe,
bhí siúd eile 'na scríbhneoir,
ba thaoisigh iad ar dhaoine
i bhfad ó shin ann.

Iad eile níor ní leo
cúltroid na hoíche
ná duairceas na bpríosún
i bhfearann na nGall.

B'ardaigeanta croíúil,
ba spleodrach a ndílseacht
in óige na haoise
a bhí le bheith ann.

Anois bíonn olc orm
leis an daoine croíbhriste
is mé ag ceasacht na saoirse
a bhí le bheith ann.

The End of Triumph

I still meet them
the broken hearted
who lament the happiness
we were to have.

This one a thinker
that one a writer
they were leaders of men
in the long long ago.

Another did not shirk
night firefight, retreat
or dark prison cell
in the other island.

High-minded, laughing
with a bubbling loyalty
in the early days of that century
that was to occur.

And now they annoy me
these broken hearted ones
as I lament that freedom
we were to have.

Agus an Samhradh Thart

Níor bhaineas blátha Earraigh dhuit,
níor mharaíos breac duit ná bradán
gidh tú mo dhiongbháil, nár aithníos.
Och, d'imigh tráth na súchraobh tharam.

Ach cúb i leith do ladhairicín.
Bíodh cuireadh ciúin id' mhallrosc glas
is tiocfad leat a baint na sméar
go líonfaimid do cheaintín stáin.

Agus céadshioc bán na Samhna romhainn,
siúlfad leat an coinleach briosc,
's le h-éirí gealaí bainfead fómhar
dubh-airní dhuit ón droighneán donn,

go ndéanfam driopás, lámh ar láimh,
coiséadrom suairc go ros na gcoll
is bronnfad lán do chiseáin tuí
de chnónna ramhra, in ómós, ort;

agus idir Nollaig agus bliain
cruinneód meall sceachóirí rós,
agus réitigh muislín, uisce, mil
is crúba lao, go ndéanfam glóthach.

Now Summer's Over

I didn't cut you flowers in springtime
I caught you no trout, no salmon,
raspberry season slipped by, and though
you were my only match, I could not see.

But call me with your index finger,
invite me with your quiet eye
and I shall come to you, berrying —
we'll go berrying together.

I'll walk with you the brittle stubble
as the white November frost first forms
as the moon rises we'll make a harvest
of dark sloes from the blackthorn trees.

We'll hurry to the hazel grove,
hand in hand, lightfooting it
and I'll fill your straw basket
with fatfleshed nuts to overflowing.

Between Christmas and the new year
I shall gather in the red rose hip
with muslin, water, honey, gelatine
and we'll lay up such store!

Tomás Mac Síomóin
Translated by Gréagóir Ó Dúill

1845

Lá a raibh
each dubh gan mharcach
ar cosa in airde
ag toirniú
ar chrúba
ciúine

Lá a raibh
fallaing ag leathadh
a dorchacht'
thar learga na gcnoc
lá a dtáinig
spealadóirí
gan súile

Lá a bhfaca
naomhóga anaithnid'
gan dola ar an bpoll
céaslaí i lámha
marbhán

Lá a ndeachaigh
spealadóir
gan súil ina cheann
ar mhuin eich dhuibh
gur ghluais curacháin
go tamhanda righin
i dtreo na tíre

1845

One day
a black horse, riderless
thundered a gallop
on hooves
of silence.

One day
a cloak of darkness
spread over the hillsides —
that day scythesmen came
blind, eyeless

That day, too,
strange curraghs came,
no tholepins on the thwarts
their oars in the clasp
of dead men.

That day
a scythesman
with no eye in his head
came on the black back of a horse,
a curragh came torpid stiff
landward.

Ilena Mălăncioiu

Translated by Eiléan Ní Chuilleanáin from the Romanian

The Headless Bird

According to custom, the old people have shut me away
Not to scare me stupid when they killed the bird,
And I am listening by the bolted door
To the trampling and the stuggle.

I twist the lock time has worn thin
To forget what I have heard, to get away
From this struggle where
The body races after the head.

And I jump when the eyes, thick with fear
Turn backwards, turn white,
They look like grains of maize,
The others come and peck at them.

I take the head in one hand, the rest in the other,
And when the weight grows too much I switch them
                                                around
Until they are dead, so they are still connected
At least in this way, through my body.

But the head dies sooner,
As if the cut had not been properly done,
And so that the body does not struggle alone
I wait for death to reach it passing through me.

The Bear

In the high mountain grass, my body curled like the
                                    snakes
Crept out to warm themselves in the sun and stiff with
                                    pain
I wait for the bear to arrive, to stoop beside me,
To stay there awhile, sniffing me in silence, again.

Seeing that I am alive and that I want him to heal
                                    me
To begin the soft trampling from shoulder to feet
So I feel him gliding over my ribs and kneeling without
                                    wanting to
And getting down on the grass when he knows it's
                                    hurting me,

Climbing up again gently along the spine as far as the
                                    neck
Hearing my vertebrae crackling under his wild right paw
And I can't cry out in fear since while he's passing over
                                    me
To heal me, if I screamed he might put out his claws,

Let me rid myself of this female husk of a snake curled
                                    in the sun,
Let the bear find the earth shifting as he makes me
                                    straight,
Gently, under his weight, trembling as he bends,
Let me coil myself again groaning quietly and wait.

Then let the cure come, let me go through the trampled
                                    grass
And feel for once my body hot from his heavy tread
While the bear moves off slowly as if he were still
Stepping not on the earth, but on a woman's shoulders
                                    instead.

A Dog

thin air colder and colder
a dog stretched stiff and frozen alone
with one white ear stuck to the ground
and open to the sky the other one

the shepherd left ages ago
the herds too went off
in this silence the one sound
the voice of the lamb up above

makes the mountains wrap up in white mist
then raises the mist to scatter on the wind
revealing still a dog abandoned
lying with one ear stuck to the ground

Song of Joy

Paired with my guardian angel
we were only couples boarding the ark
and we lived through the curse and we came ashore
in that ancient country
where the people place their wishes
in the entrails of birds
and in the land as seeds.

There you brought me secretly sparrows' eggs
for my meal in the morning
and cuckoo's milk in the evening
and joy for all my life
and one intense grief
because it could not last
until old age.

All passed in a great secret
we woke and the quince had flowered overnight
the sparrows never knew when you stole their eggs

we did not know the hawks had hatched their brood
on our own roof, we rejoiced
in the land where we had come ashore
and the sky under which we waited.

You Gave Me a Long Look

You looked at me long and distrustfully,
why haven't you done your eyes today, you said
once, and said it a second time
and the woman in the next bed said
go on, Miss, make-up your eyes.

So I went shaking to the mirror
where your bed, reflected, looked
a trifle sloping, as if
you and it were sliding down
and I began

to do my eyes up, slowly, slowly,
as if I was doing a sum
so as not to cry out in pain
and calmly you said to me
you're much better like that.

The Doctor on Duty

Go away quickly, she said to me, I'm afraid,
you see that Dr X is on duty
he surely knows what to give me to help me to breathe,
he told me nobody dies while he's on the ward.

And indeed, that very young doctor
who was not as famous as his heart was good
came in the middle of the night and gave her
something that kept her breathing until the next day.

Afterwards she understood
that his shift was finished and we had started
that terrible day about which already
she had begun to say it would never be over.

The one who was on duty looked down
on us without interfering:
I never said that nobody dies
while I am on duty, I am not at fault.

Let the Grass Grow Over Her

Let the grass grow over her,
don't root it out and do not plant flowers,
she would not have wanted to see them any more,
she would have wanted to make it into Spring
into the orchard

on her own feet,
she would have preferred not to know
even then when she could no longer breathe
she would have wanted not to be alone
but the whole world was going away.

She saw as in a dream how it passed,
she saw as through the water that bore her off
she saw it no more and terrified
she saw the world again through a bed of flowers
that was laid over her.

Take off the flowers stuck in the sockets of her eyes
let her see clearly as before;
maybe even now she would prefer
to go out a while in the green field.
Let the grass grow over her.

Laid Beside You

Lying beside you
in the grandparents' burial plot
where you can see right into the church
as far as the altar
I waited for the priest to come out with Holy
                              Communion.

The people were dressed as in the old days,
they knelt with their backs to us,
nobody knew I was buried,
if they had called to me I would have answered
from under the flat stone

which I had pulled slowly over me
without realising it
as I would draw a rug
where we were sleeping together
leaving you half bare.

I looked fearfully at the altar,
not knowing why the Communion was not brought out
and I fretted when nobody came,
then by good luck you felt the bitter cold
and pulled away the stone slab covering me.

It Snowed on the Body

snow fell fine in the mountains towards the peaks
we seemed the first to walk through the harsh season
when we found a trail of blood in the snow
and then the body where it was leading

lost almost we had believed nothing there
lost too the trace that brought us to the spot
only the blood thickening sharp on snow

pressed quickly through the thin dazzling white

we stared astonished how the trace reappeared
constantly from somewhere among the mountains
                                        below
the snow fell on the body before our eyes
it fell slow on the crows stripping the bones

Thomas McCarthy

He Meets His Future Sister-in-Law, Miss Teresette O'Neill, 1811

My sister-in-law, late of Napoleonic Provence,
Carries six packets from her father's Italian days.
My brother is ill with joy. His bride so young,
His ageing fingers can hardly un-parcel gifts
Carried so deftly from the depths of France.
She is beautiful as the miniatures her father sent

And answers all the prayers a merchant ever sent
Heavenward. All the lavender of Provence
In her deep blue eyes, she is like France
After Revolution; bringing the red excitement of days
Into our grey offices. No merchant-ship ever held gifts
As beautiful. I barely remember love as young

As Miss O'Neill. Once, when I was under oath, young
And vulnerable in the church at Rome, misfortune sent
Me a passionate Trastevere girl. Her native gifts,
Her wifely love, drenched me like perfumes of Provence.
Seeing Teresette, so young, reminds me of those days,
As far away now as deep, blockaded France.

How fortunate of my brother, our agent long in France,
Certifier of old claret casks, to have found so young
A treasure. What spectacular luck in his tedious day
Of bargaining on the Bordeaux *quai*. Heaven-sent
Is Miss O'Neill; an unexpected treasure of Provence
Disembarking now at Passage with her parcelled gifts.

It is youth like hers, distilled in Europe, that has the gifts
Our troubled country needs. Wandering through France
One sees the uprooted and well-loved. Even in Provence

An exquisite Miss O'Neill, so vital and young,
Can hardly find a merchant house to nest. War has sent
Her into my brother's arms; war has filled his days

With her fragrance now. His autumnal, merchant days
Will be filled by her. I don't envy him these gifts
Suddenly arrived from France. War has often sent
Unexpected treasures to the rocks of Roche's Point. What
    France
Has made of Teresette is a miracle. She is so young
That all the merchants of Castle Street dream of Provence.

Days of Napoleonic colour draw to a close in France,
Yet gifts forever grow there. A land still young
With Revolution sent her here, fragrant as lost Provence.

He Turns to His Wife, 1797

You turn away from me in the fragrant heat
Of this Montenotte summer —
You are besieged with the bustle of parenthood,
More fatally besieged than I could ever be.

I watch the children cling to your waking hours,
Clinging as if their lives depended on you
For clean air, apples, for Olympian favours.
I am neither nurse or mother, but distant

With the precise tables of a marine clerk;
I am the scrivener, merely, of their triumphs —
Miss Callanan, I kiss the laurels on your shoulder
As you drowse beside me; you grown warm

With the radiant sandstone of August.
Your whippet lies lazy beside us, his black
Muzzle moist with dreams, your worn trug
Full of redcurrants overturned.

The heat of the city rises to our land
To sit upon your head like a crown.
Peace in our land, a peaceable Kingdom,
An English century seems peaceably to wind down

After the storms of regicide.
Ships out of France begin to trade once more,
The New World prospers.
A Murphy coaster skims the tide.

Ships like children attend to you,
Forever seeking you on the far shore —
Minerva in the summer's medallion,
Perfectly at ease after Mercury's wars.

He Watches His Wife Create a Silhouette Portrait, 1812

Sunday afternoon light falls on the still pools
Of rejected paper. A flotilla
Of shapes assembles about her feet:

All concentration in her perfect fingers,
My own beloved Miss Callanan
Cuts from memory the coal-black card.
I watch the anchor-chains of paper unfold
To lie upon the surface of her shoes.

It is a convict's head, one bound for Van Diemen's Land,
That we saw for less than three minutes
When our carriage turned into the Lower Quay.

Voilà! The image becomes itself
When she raises her arms to the window:
One convict that dares not leave
The native earth
Of her loose-bound silhouette-book.

He Contemplates a Stolen Bozzetto *of Canova's* Cupid and Psyche, *1811*

I place my hands on this abstract clay,
A reluctant *bozzetto*
That I bought for you, Miss Callanan,
On a rainswept Gironde quay.

Who knows which officer of the Empire,
Which prelate of the Gallican Church,
Placed it upon a north-bound cart,
Ill and creaking like a kidnapped Pope.

Out of Città Vecchia, once,
The frigates of Europe fled with art.
I found it on sale near the Barton wines:
All business done, thinking of you.

My hands grew warm upon its abstract
And unfinished form.
I thought of your love, the warmth
Of sacraments, harmonies pressed open

By the art of our marriage:
Fifteen years this piece has graced our room
As certain-faithful as the morning sun
Rises behind our Montenotte wall.

I prefer its unfinished clay
To Canova's more perfect *Cupid and Psyche*.
There is, beloved Miss Callanan,
A contrapuntal harmony we recognize

As vulnerable as unfinished art —
I would not claim a perfect unity
For us, mere humans that we are,
Any more than kingdoms far apart:

Slim, adolescent limbs that promise much
In an unbroken marital sense
Are like idyllic, mystical unions embodied here,
Born of Italian clay, Canova-like, yet deeper.

He Witnesses a Military Execution, 1804

I think of the great griefs of all our Regiments,
The kneeling and the frightened of the enfilade
Who shall be nameless in each History painting.

A roguish young Private of Hompesoh's Dragoons
Faces the Mardyke at his final hour.
He says that more than his companions' volleys
He fears the desolation of Caribbean exile —

And in the manner of all the unconnected,
A poor common soldier, his wish is granted.

He Witnesses Another Hanging, 1813

Today we witnessed the adroit hanging
Of Margaret O'Malley, thief and countrywoman.
Last year her half-brother was shot at Mardyke fields
For the swearing of illegal oaths —
But wretched Mrs O'Malley, at Gallows Green,
Mother of five young souls,
Would this day be wholly alive
Had she not fallen in love
With a cupboard of her master's Belgian linen —

Though it was not her corpse, borne aloft
By a wailing crowd of Buttevant cousins,
That my friend, Homan Jephson, remarked upon
As we rested in the Nile St coffee-house:
No, not that —
But the fact that Homan had, at last,
Won the valued civil contract
To supply four years of hardened scaffold wood.

While we spoke he wiped his untroubled brow
With a crimson kerchief of imported cloth.

He Buries His Father, 1809

The two old priests out of St Brendan's Parish,
One wearing his *bran-new* vestments,
The other a true friend of poor Henry Sheares,
Intone your name at the burial Mass:
You were the best father a merchant could have.

In all truth, it is as simple as that.
When I was a boy you established my right
To fish. You gave the Earl of Orrery hell.
You gave his friends, Deane and Bastable, hell.
A lover of life, you said a boy *must* catch salmon.

It was because of you I began to trade on water.
Our company's ships I see below Montenotte;
Their cargoes of iron rising from the polished decks
Remind me of the last salmon you gave my wife.
She cried when she saw your hands tremble

As your only son cries today. With trembling hand
You caught a fish, dear father. You stayed in my house
All evening, the three of us sharing the knowledge,
Like priests making the thurible charcoal blister
Or like blacksmiths upsetting iron at the anvil.

He Goes Through His Father's Belongings, 1809

Here are the seven letters from your wife when young.
She had just left the novitiate in France
Where she'd struggled to pray away her love for you.
Gentle, yet she was no respecter of language:
"Wasn't I the *amadán* not to see our *fíor-amour?*"
She needed to get home before the words came apart:
The worst part of exile was the broken tongue

Though French life was deep in her Callanan heart.
Her own father was with Chevalier Dillon at Fontenoy,
Avenging his death at the Siege of Maastricht.

What is heroic about France gets lost in translation,
Except for this, her love-bond with the Dillon Brigade,
That, and the nervous memory of my father
When he waved goodbye on the road to Cove.

Her writing, now, is heavy and possessive,
Generous with all the ink of an exiled Sisterhood.
Lucky you, father: God couldn't hold her back.
Now the both of you are in the realm of archives
Where you can make peace with Kings and Prelates.

Her crisp stationery is frail in my hands, the edges
Roughly guillotined, the ink still Ursuline blue.

He Writes to His Estranged Sister, 1803

Beloved Letitia in Boston, forgive this trespass.
I met your own Pol's brother at the Mallow Spa.
He says you paint the birds of the New World

And that a son is born to you named Nathaniel Pat.
Though he be not the first Corkman born in exile,
I celebrate his birth. This September day

I have made cash deposits in his name —
Your Nathaniel Shea is now a capital Boy.
Though his fair mother gave her heart to birds,

Her New England son is now well-banked
In his ancestral harbour. May he come back,
With you, into his plumaged kingdom!

As for us, we prosper like pigs
In our city of silver-smiths and bacon.
European tyranny has been defeated for ever:

Unhappy politics is a scandal that's settled.
Now our lives are lifted by the prosperous din
Of priests at work, legal prayer, church repair.

He Recalls a Letter from Home, 1771

Now there's nowhere cool to hide,
This late August in Rome.
A letter that has come to me
By kindness of
A Protestant landlord —
Owner of a Kildare estate,
Purchaser of Chevalier Piranesi's
Latest folio of stones —

A letter that sets my heart on fire
Provokes me to seek the shade
Of a wayward bergamot:
My Austrian Catholic cousin, John,
Has bled the family books
To death. A useless card-skill
Learned in an Austrian regiment
Has lost us to a Mallow rake.

One thousand guineas lost
At the Mallow spa
Has ruined four uncles
And my father too. Twice
Four hundred firkins
Bound for the Carolinas,
All auctioned off to save face,
To keep me in this, my Roman furnace.

He Spends Christmas at Clonakilty, 1809

Chilled to the bone at Ballinascarty, we took a glass of
    malt,
Headed westward then to my wife's dear town:
Snow as sharp as needles, an eastern wind,
Christmas in the promise of a blazing turf fire.

A doctor's child, my wife thinks of poor *spailpíns*
At this time of year, their unlit cabins at the roadside,
Hunger of the unwanted labourers we can see
From our quick-trotting four-and-sixpence day coach.

This Christmastide we have salted loins of beef,
Bacon and pullets, a roasted snipe,
And bread-stuffing bursting from the roasted goose;
Each garnish like a trace of small-pox on the skin.

He Considers the Rev. Dill-Wallace, 1817

This day my mind is full of the unhappiness
Of others.
In the heavy rain of afternoon
I receive a messenger
From that small home near Trinity Church.

I worry about Doctor Dill-Wallace,
My devoted friend and companion;
Sweet itinerant father of the Home Mission,
Unhappy now, like one disannexed and disgraced.

Though of the Romish faith myself
And friend of the four Capuchins in the Marsh,
I admire the Doctor's Bible-work
In the barbarous regions beyond Cork.

His winters in Corkaguiny
Among the aboriginals of Dingle and Ventry
Have yielded nought in the sight of God:
Each new light that made appearance
Seemed not to lift his Munster Presbytery.

This rain-drenched Eastertide
His Dingle flock has stoned him;
Sending him into undignified flight
Like Mr Knox who got a call from Alt.

In his letter he says he hears them still,
Crying *"Deontas! Deontas!"* —
The name of a strange Gaelic God.
This word has drained my weak friend
Who has lost quarter guineas in hundreds.

Their *Deontas* God has a hunger without end.

He Sees a Warehouse Burning, August, 1798

Drawn by smoke and spills of burning cloth,
I run to Isaac Hewett's Distillery house.
A sheet of flame illuminates the summer night,
The crackle of fires like torn tackle and sail,

The screams of labourers and water carriers
And bringers of scarlet buckets of sand
Pierce the quayside and the blaze:
The intoxicated blaze, that *fou incensé*,

Leaping from windows and reddened beams.
I see Isaac with an empty bucket in his grasp,
Isaac at the point of giving in, of running away,
Flanked by his eldest boy, Isaac George.

I place my hand on his dear Protestant head
And he turns to face me, worn and devastated.
Sparks shower above us like a new Liberty Tree.
Without speech, we share the grief of friends.

Medbh McGuckian

Mappa Mundi

My tongue, coated red,
loses itself in the Englishness
of water, and their sense
of weather, a kind of water
in the form of feeling.

I fold nature into
my gently bewildered body
as a girl leaves her hair
open to be enjoyed
by the moon's fine touch.

Rain returns to its rightful
place, and trees,
sparingly branched, become
their own justification,
cleaned like a vessel by ashes.

A voice collects
fire and air
within the throats of old women,
playing with the darker eye
on a silver horse's skull,

believing in the merry war
as they would have believed
in a new poet.
But what had happened
on the street, or fallen

in the dark
at the foot
of a window,
would not
have astonished a forest.

If the eye consists
of a million worlds, to show how the earth
is a house
exchanged for three tulips bulbs,
first define the eye,

this perforation,
that wells up as spring melt,
or celandine, the red stone
growing in the stomach
of the swallow.

House without Eyebrows

I will remember, with my entire body,
how you were torn. It was wind-still.
A room of idols. You were light blue
on the inside, drowning in darkness;
the sun also spread a despairing
light for me. Great sheaves of lightning
stroked your neckless face, your straight
throat, your small, smooth head,
your yawning eyes, wide open hands.

They brought a blue-green aura to your upper body
though you were brown-violet on the outside,
with a darkened alertness, without blue,
not an atom of blue, the blue well taken out,
the blue fog of your dress a muffled creeping
in the breathed yellow of your blouse.

But your arm, made up of all whiteness,
underfed, warmed its sleeve,
your hair, unwound, touched the ground
like a track in snow or a coin's embossment.
A dance comes to mind
though the blood-red words of your skin
stand in the worn grass and have no wings.

My Sister's Way to Make Mead

No inner swirl. I apply myself
to tend my crazy health.
I take the king's drops and drink
chocolate.
After seeing in the rice a crooked pear
I run and play with the children.

Often I have prayed a softly pace
and almost read my eyes out,
secretly turning the hour glass
in my pocket for its gruesome,
sweet infinity.

I dead-coloured his picture
since he is not out of the four seas,
nor can he die of moonlight
or the pairing of the light and shade.

If I were an avowed impure,
a demi-rep, my key to the fields
would be to call another woman husband.

But a vessel of rare wine from *thee*
gave me a greater compliment
than if I had it full of pearl
some other way:

and so
this creamware dish's
lilac monologue
wanders from those mouldy bonds
to such a charitable body as yourself.

The Gorgon as Mistress of the Animals

We are not without our she-saints —
Cecily of the Branch, Julia the Giddy,
Bridget's bowl, Eostre, saints that wield
charms amongst poultry, Patrick's Shelia.

Shelia's Pulse, or Blush, or Brush,
Shelia's Batch, or Breeze, or Wedding,
or Gown, is when Shelia uses the bough
of a tree to slip-jig snow our way:

just when we have gone two spades deep
into the soil for the feel of fields,
pregnant with snow, a lifeless resurrection
coats the horizon where shrines come from.

So that she may seem to lean and bow
rather than to lie she is inscribed
above the corpse door, sacred in her nakedness,
like an afterbirth on top of a tall tree,

or the shape of the Greek symbol, Chi-Rho.
Women that are slippery, with half-an-ell
of silk on the hem of their blue Sunday clothing,
measure a coldblood cord from her

the length of Christ's body, and tie it
three fingers above the knee. Let no one
hang amber about her neck, or trust
St Olan's Cap or Columcille's Pillow

but, womb-bound in the straw,
swallow three grains of coriander
one after the other without their touching
the teeth, along with the 51st Psalm

written in ink, three words arranged
in three rows, then rinsed off in a porridge:
the number of words come dividing the number gone,
which good folk used to call Holy Marys.

Woman Forming the Handle of a Cane

During that beacon year
it was no banal head but my model's head,
the busy textures of her milky way,
junction of greys in the whitescape,

that hardly allowed me in.
It was conquerable country,
her caretaker's body,
very particularly touching the arm

of the chair, the wallpaper
seeming to reach like an arm
around her shoulders.
Now the ungiving street

has become a little missal-
sized landscape from which
I am never parted.
The gallows across the estuary

is no corrosive stranger, not an illness
I would willingly give up,
but Sunday on the Island, the cushion
on which Jesus slept on the boat.

Nigel McLoughlin

High Water

Day and daily, I have come to this ford
loaded down with rag and ronian,
have pitched them down and dowsed them,
and hopped them off the stones.
My fingers are flint and my palms
sandpapered, cracked and hacked
from the constant hard water.

Day in and day out, I bring them,
other people's clothes, as my mother did,
as my young child will when I'm too old.
This is a family business.
I've cried, now and then, when the ache
in my hands gets too much or when
a hack cracks open and stains
some new-washed garment red.

That's what happened yesterday —
as if I hadn't enough to do
without washing simmets twice —
I was in tears, scrubbing and rinsing,
and working myself into a temper.
As I lifted the clothing to the light
to check the stains had gone,
they caught me by surprise.

The leader gave me the strangest look,
I caught it out of the corner of my eye —
he turned sour-faced and pale.
I thought it better to be off —
those men were trouble — I knew
them from their South Armagh brogue.

I heard their leader died a short time later
lashed to a pole with a crow on his shoulder,
and now the Ulstermen are saying I'm bad luck.
Come hell or high water, I'll be back again
tomorrow, for there's another bundle ready
and you'll find me here, sousing
and dousing, wringing out the blood.

Bomb

They're washing away the blood today
and tomorrow the funerals will start.
The rumour mongers have fallen into
an enumeration of bits and body parts:
all that was found of so-and-so,
what him up the road was missing,
the difficulties in trying to identify
and separate what belonged to who.

I sing dumb and tut and shake my head
or try and change the subject. I know
the process you have to go through,
looking at scraps of clothes or a shoe
for some form of final proof, but I can't
tell them. Sometimes it's better not to know,
that in the end you bury nothing, or next to.

A Hill Farmer Speaks

No-one envies me my spire of fields
when the sun barely creeps above the maam
in the bowl of winter, the whirlpool of early spring
and I'm out pounding the land in all weathers
climbing up the sheer face after sheep
or up to my oxters at lambing time.

Not even the hill walkers want
to cross my bare quarter, under
the brooding bulk over Doire Uí Fhríl
where the wind sheers in from Toraigh.
It's no wonder I took the second job
to see the animals foddered over winter.

No-one understands why I stay,
why, day in and day out I hob-nail
my barren acres, where I know every stone
and own each knuckle of ground,
the dark mass of the hill
is mine to the bone.

Paula Meehan

My Father Perceived as a Vision of St. Francis
for Brendan Kennelly

It was a piebald horse in next door's garden
frightened me out of a dream
with her dawn whinny. I was back
in the boxroom of the house,
my brother's room now,
full of ties and sweaters and secrets.
Bottles chinked on the doorstep,
the first bus pulled up to the stop.
The rest of the house slept

except for my father. I heard
him rake the ash from the grate,
plug in the kettle, hum a snatch of a tune.
Then he unlocked the back door
and stepped out into the garden.

Autumn was nearly done, the first frost
whitened the slates of the estate.
He was older than I had reckoned,
his hair completely silver,
and for the first time I saw the stoop
of his shoulder, saw that
his leg was stiff. What's he at?
So early and still stars in the west?

They came then: birds
of every size, shape, colour; they came
from the hedges and shrubs,
from eaves and garden sheds,
from the industrial estate, outlying fields,
from Dubber Cross they came
and the ditches of the North Road.

The garden was a pandemonium
when my father threw up his hands
and tossed the crumbs to the air. The sun

cleared O'Reilly's chimney
and he was suddenly radiant,
a perfect vision of St Francis,
made whole, made young again,
in a Finglas garden.

Not Your Muse

I'm not your muse, not that creature
in the painting, with the beautiful body,
Venus on the half-shell. Can
you not see I'm an ordinary woman
tied to the moon's phases, bloody
six days in twenty-eight? Sure

I'd like to leave you in love's blindness,
cherish the comfort of your art, the way
it makes me whole and shining,
smooths the kinks of my habitual distress,
never mentions how I stumble into the day,
fucked up, penniless, on the verge of whining

at my lot. You'd have got away with it
once. In my twenties I often traded a bit
of sex for immortality. That's a joke.
Another line I swallowed, hook
and sinker. Look at you —
rapt, besotted. Not a gesture that's true

on the canvas, not a droopy breast,
wrinkle or stretchmark in sight.
But if it keeps you happy who am I
to charge in battledressed to force you test
your painted doll against the harsh light
I live by, against a brutal merciless sky.

'Not alone the rue in my herb garden . . .'

Not alone the rue in my herb garden
passes judgement, but the eight foot
high white foxgloves among the greys
of wormwood, santolina, lavender,
the crimson rose at our cottage door,
the peas holding for dear life to their sticks
and the smaller drowning salad stuff.
The weeds grow lush and lovely
at midsummer, honeysuckle roving
through the hawthorn: my garden
at Eslin ferociously passing judgement.

We built this soil together, husband;
barrow after barrow load of peat
sieved through an old chip strainer
and the heaps of rotted manure
pushed over frosty paths on still
midwinter days, or when an east wind
chewed at our knuckles. Cranky
of a morning when the range acted up,
we still saved wood ash and dug it in,
by Christmas laid a mulch of hay
and tucked it all up safe in beds,
turned off the light and spent the most
of January and February, the bitterest days,
at chess, or poem and story making.

You were beautiful in my father's
ravelled jumper, staring at the rain,
or painting revelations of the hag
that scared the living daylights out of me.
One canvas was blacker than
the lower pits of hell after an eternity
when even the scourging fire has gone out
and the tortured souls are silenced.

O heart of my husband, I thought,
how little have I fathomed thee,
when you went and overpainted it
on a St Brigid's Day of snow and crocuses,
with a green-eyed young fiddler,
named it *Mystery Dame with Red Hair.*

We built this garden together, husband;
germinated seeds in early spring,
gambling with a crystal dice,
moon calendars and almanacs,
risked seedlings to a late black frost,
wept at loss — but some survived
to thrive a summer of aching backs.
A festive air when the poles went up
and scarlet runners coiled along the twine.
Mornings I walked out after a shower

had tamped the dust and turned
the volume way up on birdsong,
on scent, on colour, I counted myself
the luckiest woman born, to gain such
an inland kingdom, three wild
rushy acres, edged by the Eslin
trickily looping us below the hill,
our bass line to the Shannon
and the fatal rhythm of the Atlantic swell.

I did not cast it off lightly,
the yoke of work, the years of healing,
of burying my troubled dead
with every seed committed to the earth,
judging their singular, particular needs,
nurturing them with sweat and prayer
to let the ghosts go finally from me
with every basket of harvest
I garnered in golden light for our table,
something singing in me all the while,

a song fate, of fortune, of a journey,
a twisty road that led away from you,
my husband of the sea-scarred eyes.

Now that I return to visit you,
abandoned gardens, abandoned husband,
abandoned cat and dog and chickens,
abandoned quilts and embroideries,
high piled books, my dusty drafts,
a life I stitched together out of love,
and we sit together by the window
in the summer light, the sculptural
clouds of June, their whimsical shadows
oblivious of the grief on our faces,
in sorrow at what we built and lost
and never will rebuild, O my friend,
do not turn on me in hatred,
do not curse the day we met.

from *"Berlin Diary, 1991"*

• • •

5 *Folktale*

A young man falls in love with Truth and searches the wide world for her. He finds her in a small house, in a clearing, in a forest. She is old and stooped. He swears himself to her service — to chop wood, to carry water, to collect the root, the stem, the leaf, the flowering top, the seed of each plant she needs for her work.

Years go by. One day the young man wakes up longing for a child. He goes to the old woman and asks to be released from his oath so that he may return to the world. *Certainly,* she says, *but on one condition: you must tell them that I am young and that I am beautiful.*

• • •

7 At Pankow S-Bahn

I remember this episode. A German friend, a native of Berlin, has come to visit me on Papa Stour, a small island in the Shetland Islands. The first time he needs a shit, I give him a shovel and tell him to walk to the wild side of the island. From then on he calls the place *The Shitlands*. Close to the end of his stay we are sitting by the range after a long day gathering fuel. It's been hard work; mostly retrieving pine poles from a deep cove — no path down, straight over the cliff on a rope — but a good haul to be traded for coal or burnt itself. A fortnight's heat, a fortnight's writing and hot water worth of pine. It's two in the morning. There's the dusky light of this far northern midsummer, the *simmer dim* as the people around call it. He's picking out a tune on my Epiphone, humming. It's a Dylan song — *when you got nothing, you got nothing to lose*. I'm working through a basket of mending. I'm pleased with a patch on my jeans, the tricky way I have found to set it in, following the contours of my own ass. Neat. I embroider a small *Om* in white silk for luck on the crotch, though any man now would reach a *vagina dentata* rather than *The Gates of Awe*. He asks me to mend his waistcoat, a tear, *a couple of stitches would do it, it was my grandfather's*. I estimate. Two hours work. A darning job on the heavy worsted; and a finicky delicate stitching needed for the lining. Silk? A button gone. Have I a match? What's this? In the candlelight I make out the raised pattern on the remaining buttons. *Swastikas? Was your grandfather a Nazi?* Blurted out into what becomes a moment's terror — a look of pure hatred. I cannot unpick those words.

   I fix the waistcoat carefully. You would have to look hard to find the mending. I strengthen some seams and sponge away the shiny grime at the neck, drape it above the range. If I hold anything of that day forever it will be his face staring down at me over the cliff's edge as he feeds out the rope with great care and concentration, my life in his hands.

from **Suburb**

* * *

Stood Up

Leaning against the tree for over an hour,
young man waiting — for his girl, I assume.
All Souls' Day and the leaves falling dreamily.
I've seen the girl he's waiting for, a flirt,

up at the pub with the shiny gang, a short time
ago. Skulling pints. She's having a baby.
At least that's the word out there on the street.
They say it's not his. The first day of winter

is sweet and mild and gold and blue. He looks
beyond the aspen's tremulous leaf
to where small children fan the embers

of last's night's bonfire. They coax a flame. It sucks
the air vigorously, then hesitates, then takes like grief
that's easier borne now than it will be to remember.

* * *

Stink Bomb

The smell of which still hangs about the house
despite the scented candles, the essential oils
I've burned and censered through the rooms
like a priestess in a diabolic rite.

Of course the row we had could have roused
the undead and the dead alike. It left me coiled
in a foetal crouch behind the couch, some womb
I was trying to get back to. And shite

if we didn't wake next door's dog; the Hound from Hell
Himself, right on cue. You'd have to laugh. Or die
trying. Between your irrefutable logic

and my inarticulate sobs, we missed the door bell
ringing, we missed the children singing *trick
or treat, trick or treat, the ghost afloat, the witch afly.*

* * *

Sudden Rain

I'm no Buddhist: too attached to the world
of my six senses. So, in this unexpected shower,
I lift my face to its restorative tattoo,
the exultation of its anvil chime on leaf.

On my tongue I taste the bitter city furled
in each raindrop; and through the sheeted fall of grief
the glittery estate doth like a garment wear
the beauty of the morning; the sweet reek of miso

leached from composting leaves. Last night's dream
of a small man who floated in the branches of an oak
harvesting mistletoe with a golden sickle

I intuit as meaning you'll be tender and never fickle
this winter, though this may be synaesthetic
nonsense; I've little left to go on, it would seem.

The Tantric Master

For I shall consider his beautiful navel firstly
— an altar! — whereat I've often offered flowers,
the yellow buttercup especially, a monstrance I can elevate
to the memory of his mother who surely taught him to pet.
And honeysuckle and meadowsweet and the wild dog rose:
one for its scent, one for its sound, and one for the tone of his skin
that is all petal to me.

            For I shall consider
secondly each individuated pore of his entire body
and consider each at length having nothing better
to do with my time, and each being a universe unto itself.
This I call rapture.
            And thirdly, to make no bones
about it, being the crux, the hardest part of the matter,

I shall consider his noble and magical wand. He do good
business throughout the night with it. He enchant,
and spellbind and wind me round his little finger;
or, on a moony night in April, even his little toe.

Which brings me to his nails: he keepeth that trim and smooth
the better to pleasure me. So subtle his touch I can feel
the very whorls of his fingerprints and could reconstruct from
                                              memory
his mark on my breast. Each ridge the high mountain,
each trough the deep canyon, unfathomable;
but, I having buckets of time, do fathom, do fathom.

For I shall consider the mesmeric draw of his nipples,
like standing stone circles on the broad plain of his chest,
megalithic power spots when I lay my hot cheek
on the coal of his belly and sight through the meadows
and the distant forests the trajectory of sun and other stars.

His mouth, I won't go into, being all cliché in the face of it,
except to say the dip of his lip is most suited to suction and friction,
and other words ending in tion, tion, tion, which come to think of it
when I'm in the grip of it, is exactly how I make sweet moan.
                        For I shall consider
him whizzbang dynamo and hellbent on improving my spiritual
                                                    status.
You can keep your third eyes and your orbs sanctimonious
the opening of which my master believes *is* the point.
He says I'm a natural and ultimate enlightenment a mere question
                                                      of time.
But in patient devotion I'll admit to deficiency. The theory of being
not a patch on just being is. Yap I distrust! Show me.
Don't tell me the way. The right place for talk of this ilk
is not during, not after, and foretalk will get you nowhere at all.
The best that I hope for in our daily instructions
is the lull between breaths, spent and near pacified.

Máire Mhac an tSaoi
Translated by Gréagóir Ó Dúill

Mutterrecht

Tá barraíocha mo mhéar
Lán de ghága, de ghearbacha;
Ní réitíonn an sobal leo.

Idir bhail agus bhinib
Cuimhním ar mo mháthair
Agus ar mo sheanamháthair;
Shaothraíodar araon lena ré . . .

D'fhonn ná teanntófaí
Sa chistin mise
Os chionn an dabhaigh ag níochán.

Mutterrecht

The tips of my fingers
Are full of scabs and fissures,
Broken by the detergent.

My condition and reaction
Makes me think of my mother
And my grandmother;
They spent their lives working

So I should not be enclosed
In the narrow kitchen
Above the sink, washing.

Immanuel Mifsud

Translated by Maurice Riordan from the Maltese

Confidential Reports — in the Form of a Public-Private Confession

He says he used to watch the Devil masturbate.
He says he'd tell him while he was praying
to go down and lick the evil off the world.
He says he enjoyed it. He started to have faith.
He would cut himself to see the black blood
sprinkle its mysterious blessing on the night.
And at the full moon he'd shout out the Mass
up in the hills where no-one could hear it.
He'd fallen for a woman who'd choked to death,
who smiled at him from a grave, left slightly ajar.
That way, she could see the moon swell up in the evenings.
He says he tried to give her the son she craved.
He tried twice but he failed on both occasions.

He used to worship the dark. Then the dark abducted him.

*

Her brother was putting her to sleep.
And he touched her swelling body
where the rust-brown blood seeped out.
They heard their father pant in the night,
their mother hushing him with her hand.
For even the sins of marriage must be hidden.
She was aroused by her brother's fingers,
by her father's noise, her mother's raw silence.
It was as if it rained inside her body, or the ice
turned to water and mixed with the water
of her brother moving on top of her.

Then out of the blue a boy was born
with a moon-face and a voice that frightened her.
He cried for six days before he stopped.
They buried him in the corner of a field.

She loved in the dark. And the dark loved her mind.

*

She vowed in front of her three children
she would never again sleep beside her husband —
not after the filthy beds of the men
he went to every day behind her back.
She'd found him out in broad daylight,
her husband, the father of her children.

*

That quiet bisexual man
is always hovering near the front door,
leaning out when the sun comes up,
in the hope she'll give him a face to look at,
in the hope he might know at last the shape
his own dark look should take.
Every night he says he dreams his face has died
and in the dream it becomes a belladonna lily.
His nails grow sharp and turn bright red,
the colour of his handsome rosebud mouth.
He's out on the open sea, his broad hips
stirring the waves, his chest full with milk.

In the morning he finds he hasn't shaved that week.

Geraldine Mills

Blighted

Your name came to you seaward
upon a ship returning home from Boston
where your mother never settled.
All those brownstone houses starving out the sky,
streets paved with streets, no gold
of whin, or corn at saving, celandine.
Against the tide she bought a passage
on a ship still marked with famine, typhus
back to places that she hungered for,
kept hidden in her shawl your dead sister
until they docked in Cobh and buried her.

Before the year was out
her name was put to use again.
You carried the weight of that ship on your back,
the cold backwash of her eyes,
the way the streets of Holyhoke
seeped into your tight mouth
the sea streeled out from your hair.
You heard the cry of her along the lazy beds
as you barrowed swill to the pigs
caught her on the wing of salt air, your body listing.

Kept hidden in your shawl
a woman longing
to fall upon the wither of that name,
each letter blighted one by one
the sea to open up and swallow them,
to stand at its edge and howl.

What We Understood

It was enough for her to say *smell that*,
the hazel that one of us was sent to pick
brandished before us, threatening
as she lined us up against the kitchen wall,
moving the stick under nose after nose *smell that*.

All summer our teeth sank into its unripe nut
not given time to harden against us,
we dug our nails in and under the hazel embryo,
scooped it out, ate it like crumbs of shop bread
white and soft. Hadn't she told us every year,
hives we'd be full of them, glutting on kernels still raw,
scratching all night till she was worn out
painting us with calamine.

That morning when she told me to run
to the neighours with the message and not forget,
I ran past the tinkers' camp in the hazel trees,
their dog's breath curling white in the cold air;
past the haunted house, the clear of the spring well,
repeating over and over again,
*tell Mrs Topping your father's dead
remember tell her.*

Out of Old Stories

The Shadow and the Heart

These days the skies hurt with blue,
the flames of earth are lifted and carried
across the stone terraces that reminded you
of fields around Leam, Recess, Gortacarnaun.
*We have never known such heat, the locals say
and look how the snails sit tightly packed
as corncobs on the tops of fence posts.*

The mulberries have injured us with their juice
like the last time we picked them together;
it bled the length of our arms, down legs,
mixed with the sweat of our bellies.

When out of nowhere but somewhere the rain came
we trapped it in the waiting bowls of our hands
and you told me that if a shower of rain came
while the sun shone, a fox's wedding was taking place.

Touching my face you turned me to where you said
you saw them coming through the olive trees,
the vixen's blazing tail covered in Queen Anne's lace,
her cheeks rouged with mulberry,
a canny look in the groom's eye

and you slipped away, followed the bridal party
out along the lemon trees, through the chicken run,
strewing them with caper flowers.
Out along the camino, a wilderness of dust,
slipped with them down the mountainside
your basket of fruit spilled on the ground.

About Lifelines

Aunt Una had difficulty with ageing.
She watched hands, counted
the creeping of liverspots
the wrinkle of skin, its weathering.
Hands were a dead give-away as were necks
she was heard to say, and measured
a person's years by the way skin lived.

Aunt Una drank white wine
as if it were part of her past,
the silver boa that girdled her wrist
eyed me with its ruby glint,
her nails gaudy and false.

"So easy to forget," my mother sniffed,
coats thrown on the bed for warmth,
frogs that hopped in under the door in the wet
and landed in the tin basin with the bread.

Aunt Una would hold my hand up against hers,
measure its import, its mortality and say
"see what the years will do to you"
flicking the snake of ash from her ivory holder
into my father's cap.

I didn't like her talking like that,
my hands were my own business,
and anyway she was old,
old and scrawny as the chicken
my mother plucked in the back kitchen,
her head covered in a pink head scarf,
the smell of singeing feathers about to choke the air.

Cutaway Philosophers

Turfed out of Dublin for the summer
we came running to our grandfather
and the bogs of Galway; townies
un-learned in the way of how a sleán
in the hands of the wise slices into mystery.

What they talked of while he footed,
clamped the wet sods with his neighbour
we took no notice; dull as the monotony
that they shaped while we shook
birds from their hiding places,
scratched the shine from our shoes
in the squelch of bog bitter.

Fired by other elements, we never asked
how the wind curled round the asphodel

or the world spun in the cutting into history;
how time put a skin on axe-heads, bog butter, bones
or how it was that given earth, air and water
we would be bringing home fire.

Boy at the Window Waiting

If he remembers it will be ordinary things:
paint peeling, the old bakelite switch,
her tweed coat the colour of shearwaters,
its sleeve curved to the underwing of her elbow.
It hangs alone in under the stairs where he hid
from her sad eyes and her step that paced the floor
above him, knowing that her body held the muscles to soar.

Walking along the green road to the cliff
where white feathers of foam broke the bread of land,
seabirds gliding she lifted up her arms;
stretched them. There was the whisper of upstroke,
the whole of their flapping that captured the up draught
and let her feet leave. Away up over the Atlantic;
past scree sliding down the hill, rabbit holes,
walls built in defence of wind until there was only sky.

She cried "I the mother of Icarus brought up in this land
of mean sun, will fly." Letting go of everyday myth
steamed up in a pot of potatoes, bread sliced like waves;
wallpaper coming down, a coat frayed at the cuffs.

Poet as Magpie

She flies in on the sniff of a line
to thieve it from the gaping mouth
of the storyteller — hard lived —

then sits in the trees, grackles,
pecking at it piecemeal
wondering how to put fat on it.

Adds to it a grain of untruth
that she steals from the cat's bowl,
nothing is black and white after all.

She pretends it's hers to swallow
the lore of the fox or a mother's venial past,
one for sorrow, six for gold.

She brings each pilfered piece back to her store,
sits on it while the farmer turns his gun on her,
then spits it back at him — a secret not to be told.

Wednesday Women

This is where we women meet,
the third Wednesday of every month,
sitting in our padded chairs
deciding to have tea or coffee,
brought to us on lap trays
painted with blue cornflowers.

Outside the rain pours down
on cars queuing for parking space,
on a world wondering by;
while in here we are sheltered
by sunbursts on the curtains,
a music station playing Arvo Pärt.

We ask each other how we've been
since we last met, how well we look
the colour in our hair
so good so real, a perfect match
you could hardly tell the difference.

They come in their purple masks
to plug us in, search out veins now paper thin
so that these Wednesdays
they have to dig them out like lugworms
and send the pain shooting to the stars.

John Montague

Border Sick Call

for Seamus Montague, MD, my brother,
in memory of a journey in winter
along the Fermanagh-Donegal border.

> *Looks like I'm breaking the ice!*
> — Fats Waller

> *Weary, God!*
> *of starfall and snowfall,*
> *weary of north winter, and weary*
> *of myself like this, so cold and thoughtful.*
> — Hayden Carruth

1

Hereabouts, signs are obliterated,
but habit holds.

We wave a friendly goodbye
to a Customs Post that has twice
leaped into the air
to come to earth again
as a makeshift, a battered trailer
hastily daubed green: *An Stad.*

The personnel still smile
and wave back,
their limbs still intact.

Fragments of reinforced concrete,
of zinc, timber, sag and glint in the hedge
above them, the roof and walls
of their old working place:

> *Long years in France,*
> *I have seen little like this,*
> *même dans le guerre Algerienne,*

the impossible as normal,
lunacy made local,
surrealism made risk.

Along the glistening main road
snow plough-scraped, salt-sprinkled,
we sail, chains clanking,
the surface bright, hard, treacherous
with only one slow, sideways skid
before we reach the side road.

Along ruts ridged with ice
the car now rocks, until we reach
a gap walled with snow where
silent folk wait and watch
for our, for your, arrival.

The high body of a tractor
rides us a few extra yards
on its caterpillar wheels
till it also slips and slopes
into a hidden ditch
to tilt helpless, one large
welted tyre spinning.

2

Shanks' mare now, it seems,
for the middle-aged,
marching between hedges
burdened with snow,
low bending branches
which sigh to the ground
as we pass, to spring back.

And the figures fall back
with soft murmurs of
"on the way home, doctor?"

shades that disappear
to merge into the fields,
their separate holdings.

Only you seem to know
where you are going
as we march side by side,
following the hillslope
whose small crest shines
like a pillar of salt,
only the so solid scrunch
and creak of snow crystals
thick-packed underneath
your fur boots, my high
farmer's wellingtons.

Briefly we follow
the chuckling rush
of a well-fed stream
that swallows, and swells
with the still-melting snow
until it loses itself
in a lough, a mountain tarn
filmed with crisp ice
which now flashes sunlight,
a mirror of brightness,
reflecting, refracting
a memory, a mystery:

> *Misty afternoons in winter*
> *we climb to a bog pool;*
> *rushes fossilised in ice.*
> *A run up, and a slide —*
> *boots score a glittering*
> *path, until a heel slips*
> *and a body measures its length*
> *slowly on ice, starred with*
> *cracks like an old plate.*

Into this wide, white world
we climb slowly higher,
no tree, or standing stone,
only cold sun and moorland,
where a stray animal,
huddled, is a dramatic event,
a gate a silvered statement,
its bars burred with frost,
tracks to a drinking trough,
rutted hard as cement:
a silent, islanded cottage,
its thatch slumped in,
windows cracked, through which,
instead of Christians, cattle
peer out, in dumb desolation.

> *And I remember how, in Fintona,*
> *you devoured Dante by the fireside,*
> *a small black* World's *Classic.*
> *But no purgatorial journey*
> *reads stranger than this,*
> *our Ulster border pilgrimage*
> *where demarcations disappear,*
> *landmarks, forms, and farms vanish*
> *into the ultimate coldness of an ice age,*
> *as we march towards Lettercran,*
> *in steelblue, shadowless light,*
> *The Ridge of the Tree, the heart of whiteness.*

3

We might be astronauts creak-
ing over the cold curve
of the moon's surface, as our boots
sink, rasp over crusted snow,
sluggish, thick, dreamlike,

until, for the first time
in half-an-hour, we see
a human figure, shrunken
but agile, an old, old man
bending over something, poking
at it furiously with a stick:
carcass of fox or badger?

"Hello," we hallo, like strangers
on an Antarctic or arctic ice floe —
Amundsen greeting a penguin! —
each detail in cold relief.

Hearing us, the small figure halts,
turns an unbelieving face, then
takes off, like a rabbit or hare
with a wounded leg, the stick its pivot,
as it hirples along, vigorously
in the wrong, the opposite
direction, away from us,
the stricken gait of the aged
transformed into a hobble,
intent as a lamplighter.

We watch as our pathfinder,
our potential guide, dwindles
down in the valley, steadily
diminishing until
he burrows,
bolts under,
disappears into,
a grove of trees.

"And who might that be,
would you say?" I ask my brother
as we plod after him
at half his pace. "Surely
one of my most urgent patients,"
he says, with a wry smile,

"the sick husband gone to get
his sicker wife back to bed
before I arrive." And he smiles
again, resignedly.

"And besides, he wants to tidy
the place up, before the Doctor
comes. Things will be grand
when we finally get there:
he just wasn't expecting anyone
to brave the storm.

"But there'll be a good welcome
when we come."

And sure enough all is waiting,
shining, inside the small cottage.
The fire laughs on the hearth,
bellows flared, whilst the dog rises
to growl, slink, then wag its tail.

4

My brother is led into the bedroom.
Then himself, a large-eared, blue-eyed gnome,
still pert with the weight of his eighty years,
discourses with me before his hearth,
considerately, like a true host.

"Border, did you say,
how many miles to the border?
Sure we don't know where it starts
or ends up here, except we're lost
unless the doctor or postman finds us.

"But we didn't always complain.
Great hills for smuggling they were,
I made a packet in the old days,

when the big wars were rumbling on,
before this auld religious thing came in.

"You could run a whole herd through
between night and morning, and no one
the wiser, bar the B-Specials,
and we knew every mother's son
well enough to grease the palm,
quietlike, if you know what I mean.
Border be damned, it was a godsend.
Have you ever noticed, cows have no religion?"

> *Surefooted, in darkness,*
> *stick-guiding his animals,*
> *in defiance of human frontiers,*
> *the oldest of Irish traditions,*
> *the* creach *or cattle raid,*
> *as old as the* Táin.

Now, delighted with an audience,
my host rambles warmly on;
holding forth on his own hearth:

"Time was, there'd be a drop
of the good stuff in the house,"
the head cocked sideways
before he chances a smile,
"but not all is gone.
Put your hand in the thatch
there, left of the door,
and see what you find."

Snug as an egg under a hen,
a small prescription bottle of colourless poteen.
"Take that medicine with you for the road home.
You were brave men to come."

5

Downhill, indeed, is easier,
while there is still strong light,
an eerie late afternoon glow
boosted by the sullen weight
of snow on the hedges,
still or bowing to the ground
again, as we pass, an iceblue
whiteness beneath our steady tread;
a snow flurry, brief, diamond-hard,
under a frieze of horsetail cloud.

The same details of field, farm
unravelling once again, as the doctor
plods on, incongruous in his fur boots
(but goodness often looks out of place),
downhill, with the same persistence
in a setting as desolate as if
a glacier had just pushed off:

> *Thick and vertical*
> *the glacier slowly*
> *a green white wall*
> *grinding mountains*
> *scooping hollows*
> *a gross carapace*
> *sliding down the*
> *face of Europe*
> *to seep, to sink*
> *its melting weight*
> *into chilly seas;*
> *bequeathing us*
> *ridges of stone,*
> *rubble of gravel,*
> *eskers of hardness:*
> *always within us —*
> *a memory of coldness.*

Only one detail glints different.
On that lough, where the sun burns
above the silver ice, like a calcined stone,
a chilling fire, orange red,
a rowboat rests, chained in ice,
ice at gunwhale, prow and stern,
ice jagged on the anchor ropes;
still, frozen, "the small bark of my wit,"
la navicella del mio ingegno.
Why could I not see it on the way
up, only on the journey home,

I wonder as my brother briefly disappears
across the half-door of another house,
leaving me to wait, as glimmers gather
into the metallic blues of twilight,
and watch, as if an inward eye were opening,
details expand in stereoscopic brightness,
a buck hare, not trembling, unabashed,
before he bounds through the frozen grass,
a quick scatter of rabbits, while
a crow clatters to the lower wood,
above the incessant cries of the sheep herd.

6

When my brother returns, breath pluming,
although he risks only a swallow,
the fiery drink unleashes his tongue:
from taciturn to near-vision,

"I heard you chatting to old MacGurren,
but the real border is not between
countries, but between life and death,
that's where the doctor comes in.

"I have sat beside old and young
on their death beds, and have seen

the whole house waiting, as for birth,
everything scoured, spick-and-span,
footsteps tiptoeing around?

"But the pain is endless,
you'd think no one could endure it,
but still they resist, taste the respite,
until the rack tightens again
on the soiled, exhausted victim."

> But the poem is endless,
> the poem is strong as our weakness,
> strong in its weakness,
> it will never cease until it has said
> what cannot be said.
>
> The sighs and crying of someone
> who is leaving this world
> in all its solid, homely detail
> for another they have only heard tell of,
> in the hearsay called religion,
> or glimpsed uneasily in dream.

"People don't speak of it,
lacking a language for this terrible thing,
a forbidden subject, a daily happening,
pushed aside until it comes in.

"I remember the first time I saw it
on my first post as a *locum*."

(That smell in the sickroom —
stale urine and *faeces* —
the old man on the grey bed,
his wife crouched in darkness.

Many generations of family
lined up along the stairs
and out into the farmyard:
the youngest barely aware

of the drama happening inside
that unblinking frame of light;
but horseplaying, out loud.
Three generations, and the tree shaking.

He has lain still for months
but now his muscles tighten,
he lifts himself into a last
bout of prayers and imprecations.

The old woman also starts up
but there is no recognition,
only that ultimate effort, before
he falls back, broken,

The rosary lacing stiff fingers.
"I did not expect to witness
the process in such a rush:
it still happens in these lost places.")

7

Just as we think we are finally clear,
another shade steps out from the shadows
(out of the darkness, they gather to your goodness),
with its ritual murmured demand:
"Doctor, would you be so good to come in?
The wife is taken bad again."

All the clichés of rural comedy
(which might be a rural tragedy),
as he leads us along a tangled path,
our clabbery *via smaritta*.

Briars tug at us, thorn and whin
jag us, we trudge along a squelching drain;
my brother and I land ankle-deep in slush,
a gap guttery as a boghole,

and he has to haul us out by hand,
abjectly, "Sorry we've no back lane."

In his house, where an Aladdin burns,
we step out of our boots, socks,
before the warm bulk of the Rayburn,
and my brother pads, barefooted,
into the back room, where a woman moans.

Nursing a mug of tea in the kitchen
I confer anxiously with her cowed man.
"She's never been right since the last wain,
God knows, it's hard on the women."

Three ragged little ones in wellingtons
stare at the man from Mars,
suck their thumbs and say nothing.
There is a tinny radio but no television.
A slight steam rises where our socks hang.
At last my brother beckons him in.

We leave, no more conversation;
the labourer stumbling before us,
his hand shielding a candle
which throws a guttering flame:
a sheltering darkness of firs, then,
spiked with icicles, a leafless thorn,
where the gate scringes on its stone.

When we stride again on the road,
there is a bright crop of stars,
the high, clear stars of winter,
the studded belt of Orion,
and a silent, frost-bright moon
upon snow crisp as linen
spread on death or bridal bed;
blue tinged as a spill of new
milk from the crock's lip.

8

Another mile, our journey is done.
The main road again. The snow-laden car
gleams strange as a space machine.

We thrust snow from the roof;
sit cocooned as the engine warms,
and the wipers work their crescents clean

With a beat steady as a metronome.
Brother, how little we know of each other!
Driving from one slaughter to another

Once, you turned on the car radio
to hear the gorgeous pounding rhythms
of your first symphony: Beethoven.

The hair on your nape crawled.
Startled by the joy, the energy,
the answering surge in your own body.

In the face of suffering, unexpected affirmation.
For hours we've been adrift from humankind,
navigating our bark in a white landlocked ocean.

Will a stubborn devotion suffice,
sustained by an ideal of service?
Will dogged goodwill solve anything?

Headlights carve a path through darkness
back through Pettigo, towards Enniskillen.
The customs officials wave us past again.

But in what country have we been?

Sinéad Morrissey

Pilots

It was black as the slick-stunned coast of Kuwait
over Belfast Lough when the whales came up
(bar the eyelights of aeroplanes, angling in into the airport
out of the east, like Venus on a kitestring being reeled
to earth). All night they surfaced and swam
among the detritus of Sellafield and the panic
of godwits and redshanks.

                    By morning
we'd counted fifty (species *Globicephala melaena*)
and Radio Ulster was construing a history. They'd left a sister
rotting on a Cornish beach, and then come here, to this dim
smoke-throated cistern, where the emptying tide leaves a scum
of musselshell and the smell of landfill and drains.
To mourn? Or to warn? Day drummed its thumbs
on their globular foreheads.

                     Neither due,
nor quarry, nor necessary, nor asked for, nor understood
upon arrival — what did we reckon to dress them in?
Nothing would fit. Not the man in oilskin working in the warehouse
of a whale, from the film of Sir Shackleton's blasted *Endeavour*,
as though a hill had opened onto fairytale measures
of blubber and baleen, and this was the money —
god's recompense;

                     not the huge Blue
seen from the sky, its own floating eco-system, furred
at the edges with surf; nor the unbridgeable flick
of its three-storey tail, bidding goodbye to this angular world
before barrelling under. We remembered a kind of singing,
or rather our take on it: some dismal chorus of want and wistfulness

resounding around the planet, alarmed and prophetic,
with all the foresight we lack —

                     though not one of us
heard it from where we stood on the beaches and car-parks
and cycle-tracks skirting the water. What had they come for?
From Carrickfergus to Helen's Bay, birdwatchers with binoculars
held sway while the city sat empty. The whales grew frenzied.
Children sighed when they dived, then clapped as they rose
again, Christ-like and shining, from the sea, though they could have been
dying out there,

                     smack bang
in the middle of the ferries' trajectory, for all we knew.
Or attempting to die. These were Newfoundland whales,
radically adrift from their feeding grounds, but we took them
as a gift: as if our own lost magnificent ship
had re-entered the Lough, transformed and triumphant,
to visit us. As if those runaway fires on the spines of the hills
had been somehow extinguished . . .

                     For now,
they were here. And there was nothing whatsoever to be said.
New islands in the water between Eden and Holywood.

Little House in the Big Woods

Some things we shared.
Like the *Little House
in the Big Woods*, which for me
occurred prophetically

in the voice of Mrs Ledley
inside the free-milk sickish smell
of primary six. I remember
the enormity

of living in a hill;
leeches in the creek
and the slither of blood
they left in their wake

as a mark of trespass.
Our classroom windows
would be crying, as usual,
and out on the rim

of the playground,
crows' heads in rows
would be cocked to one
side, like policemen's.

But we were afloat
on an unstoppable continent:
each hand-built house
giving way to the next
                as fast

as you could toss a hot potato
into glittering space
on a sleigh ride
after a syrup party . . .

For you it read differently —
the overdue library book
you couldn't give up.
As summer rolled on its back

and the driveway evaporated,
you would carry it out
past the sun-blistered gate
to your cubby-hole under the carport.

An apron of eggs.
Where your love for
the soon-to-be blinded sister
bloomed like a cold sore.
             We swap

reminiscences we don't understand.
Squash (a word which was never
explained) in the rafters.
Pa's toleration of Indians.

Juist

They thought me too thin. I'd vomited all morning on the ship from Norddeich
and felt more fragile than I looked. At noon the sun cleared over the island —
clean as a coin where water ended it, and held, whole, in the centre of vision
until proximity halved, then quartered it. Farms to the left without crops.
To the right, a sky of kites, kissing aggressively.

Nineteen. My first job. Time. And my life unavoidably occurring in stages
predictable from birth and regular as menstruation. The next station,
a landscape to change in. A resort in the North Sea for Germans
no one I knew had heard of, where one white side of the island was beach
and the other side, mud. Nine weeks to be stepped onto, crossed over, stepped off of.

The family fed me soup and a schnitzel and seemed disappointed.
Regular islandmen downed schnapps at the bar — pink, clear, frozen, on fire —
while the lies in my letter rose into the atmosphere and hung there:
the eight brothers and sisters I'd somehow invented to prove housework flair
and a willingness to share; German; French; Italian; Spanish.

When my first customer requested tap water, somewhere an executioner
cocked his gun and grinned. A word I'd never heard of. My notebook shook.
New tables terrified me with their limitless stores of unencountered vocabulary.

My face, rigid in panic as though the wind had changed, followed my body,
dislodged and desolate, for a week. To some I was merely bait;

others discovered a kindness in themselves they never knew existed
and enthused so warmly over unordered dishes I secretly wept.
The Captain (my own appellation) flung me like a tennis ball from table to table
and I bounced and skidded till closing time. He thought me a thief,
and at bedtime demanded a reckoning of coins as a pseudo-sadistic ritual.

I was exhausted, and then my body broke itself in.
A customer photographed me (*du als Kellnerin*) and I pinned the image
above my bed as a witness to the unthinkable. I became streamlined —
two plaits, soft shoes, trousers with pockets, a calculator, and across my heart
every salad, every stew, every fish, every meat dish on the menu, and every note and
    coin.

A kitchen help came from the East. A year since the GDR
had so spectacularly effaced itself, and he was here, saving money for six people.
One night he loomed over my bed, smashing imaginary plates against the wall.
Then he asked me to dance. By the time they gave me a door key my wages were
    missing.
He spent his last night alone in the dune before vanishing.

The North Sea current was strong. Bathing times changed with the tides.
On afternoons off, I swam as far as the flags. Whatever way my shift fell,
I worked twelve hours, but I still always stole to the sea, even at midnight.
Once, after thunder, lightning was swimming in sea water, and waves, peeling
apart from themselves, hurled phosphorescent plankton into visual ecstasy . . .

And all this for me. I'd cycle three miles to the harbour —
no cars on the island, deliveries came by pony — and sit glued
as full moons bounced up over the water, glad to be lonely, and greedy
for the island skies unbroken by buildings and the island stars no streetlight
diminished or dimmed. Night skies on Juist were miraculous. *My aurora borealis.*

And stories of course. The semi-professional corpse-hunter who trawled
fifteen miles of beach every morning scouring for a reward:
the over-confident, the victims of heart-attack, the drowned washed back
to where they started. A birth on the restaurant floor.
The year the sea between Juist and Norddeich froze.

I bought every newspaper the morning the Gorbachev coup broke on the world.
Once, in the middle of a do-able dinner shift, I started to cry, the first time
the Captain had seen me. He gave me a strawberry schnapps and patted my head.
Grown men have cried here, we thought you'd cry sooner.
I washed all my own clothes in the sink till my knuckles bled.

I discovered a derelict hotel. The Nazis built it to match
their enormous year of 1936: a challenge to the horizon. Now gone to ruin
and seabird colonies. Only the basement stayed open as a bar.
I slammed vodka bananas on my second last night there
and lost reason on the dance floor. My one night off of the summer.

And then leaving threatened. My self grown raw and tremulous and impressionable
in the space between changing shape, and then to be torn from the source
of everything painful, everything valuable. I cycled the island,
willing the skies and sands to monopolise vision —
not to let me leave without them. The morning the ship sailed

breakfast was Christmas, with cards and gifts and forgiveness,
and Juist grew initially wider, my back to the sea.
I carried my grief on my knees, spread out like a hanky. The island was emptying.
Islanders were shutting up shop, banking the profits of summer, imagining darkness —
long nights in which no work would be necessary — and
the coming of frost.

Reading the Greats

Is it for their failures that I love them?
Ignoring the regulation of *Selected Poems,*
with everything in that should be in —
all belted & buttoned & shining —
I opt instead for omnivorous *Completes.*
For their froth. Their spite. For avoidable mistakes:
Larkin on Empire, say, or Plath on Aunts.

The thrill of when they dip, trip up, run out
of things to write about before they start,
is the consolation of watching
a seascape suddenly drained and stinking
of flies & fishheads & bladderwrack.
And the tide impossibly distant. And no way back.
Yes, I love them for that.

In Praise of Salt

I'm salting an egg in the morning.
It's one year on. The radio is documenting
the threats we face . . . The cut and lash
Of voices pitched to shatter glass.

For a second I don't hear the kettle boil
and wonder: if Iraq mined salt instead of oil?
At Leonardo's table, salvation spilled
as Judas scattered salt. And we're still poised to kill.

In India they made salt and shook an Empire.
Salt makes us what we are, and takes us there.

from "The State of the Prisons"
A History of John Howard, Prison Reformer, 1726 – 1790

As for me, I will behold thy face in righteousness:
I shall be satisfied when I awake, with thy likeness.

Psalm 17:15

• • •

4

They say I rode like a horseman of the Apocalypse.
My circuit broadened: to Scotland, to Ireland, to the Continent.
It intensified: I saw schools, workhouses, hospitals for the indigent,
Asylums for the insane. I saw those confined by quarantine
As well as by crime. In truth, each journey was slow and treacherous:
60,000 miles of stony road, potholes, ditches and slime

Stretch between Dublin and Constantinople. And I remember them all.
I was travelling now obsessively.
The boy spent school holidays at Cardington without me.
My servant sent reports. *There are problems, Sir,*
Wrote Thomasson, warily, almost daring to be vocal,
Problems of a certain delicate nature —. Ignorance was my error.

Fame was busy, ever preceding me. I was never alone
For long in a new city. Popes and princesses asked me to dine.
When Catherine the Great demanded my company, I declined
On account of her lax morality. I thought her a glorified courtesan.
Joseph of Austria was a true compatriot: not a month on the throne
And he'd visited every prison and hospital, sometimes with only a footman.

I was summoned by the Roman Fisherman. He was non-commital.
I know you Englishmen do not value these things,
But the blessing of an old man can do you no harm. I kissed his rings.
Then ignoring decorum, inspired by the Lord,
I mentioned my time with the Inquisitor General
Of Valladolid of Spain. He was gravely discomforted.

Shall my tongue be tied from speaking the truth
By any earthly king? To term that court, by an ingenious ruse,
the HOLY Inquisition, was a monstrous abuse.
I saw its instruments: Scavenger's Daughter, Little Ease.
I took tea in a room with a garrulous oil painting, smooth
As sin, of 97 heretics on fire in a procession. Even the breeze

Was painted as a victory. And this was what had to stop.
This table wrapped in black cloth with a bible on it
Used to draw blood. This braying intolerance.
Power in the clotting of candle wax and confessions at midnight.
The Osnabrück Torture. The Terror of insignias. Pomp.
This being ünderground. We had to let in the light.

5

A lone voice in the wilderness? Perhaps.
But I wasn't a desert prophet. I didn't spin a vision out of nothing,
Not attempt the Celestial City without researching everything.
I looked where long centuries had averted their gaze.
I made the commonest filth — the swarming of dungeon rats —
A suppurate state malaise.

My plan was simple, practical, and above all, cheap.
Salary the turnkeys. No profits to be made from pimping,
Turning barman, extortion, or doctoring
In ignorance and at extravagant expense. No fees
For removing leg irons, access to the fireplace, or supplying of cheese and meat.
No garnish to be sought off new arrivals. No hierarchies.

If idleness breeds vice, industry brings a smiling account balance
And the promise of self-sufficiency. Attach a factory,
A cloth works or a smelting house, to every penitentiary.
Let every inmate be supervised there. Out of such labour,
An income for provisions, heating, clothing and medicine, in accordance
With daily needs. Allow extra for good behaviour.

I came home famous. *The State of the Prisons* such a manifest success
It engendered an Act of Parliament. Yet all along,
Sickness was festering in my only son like sedition in a nation
With a missing king. The French Revolution unfurled across the Channel
As the desperate hints of scandalised servants converged into flesh
And betrayal. The boy was irrecoverable.

What example had I inculcated by wallowing in evil?
My absence gave licence to the deviant Thomasson,
Who defiled himself with numberless men, at dockside brothels in London,
Taking his charge along with him.
The boy contracted venereal disease, ravaged by the Devil
In a butler's turncoat. Syphilis had already attacked my son's facial skin

By the time I finally encountered him, flailing and spitting in my hallway.
Demented with hatred. Pretence was useless, sophistry over,
As he raved he had known neither father nor mother,
That I had twisted him with neglect. I wept. He was destined for an asylum.
Must reform cost exponentially? My conscience sears me, as with David I say:
O my son Absalom, my son, my son.

• • •

Richard Murphy

Kassapa

Perhaps the king, whose name evoked the sun,
Riding his elephant, under a pearl umbrella,
Through parched rice-fields on the dry zone plain,

Had seen this rock aspiring from the earth
To penetrate the clouds loafing in heaven:
And put five hundred of his virgin brides,

Dressed in cascades of jewellery, to make
A splash on the summit, and entice the gods
To cast their semen on the ground as rain:

Then shone here, as the god of wealth, supreme
In rice and gems, going about on three legs,
Devising arts to give the gods sublime

Erections that would last: broad galleries
Of golden girls the rock itself embraced
Inside a wall whose mirror caught their souls:

And sheathed the rock-head in a lion mask
To father a strong race, out of whose mouth
At festivals he made great fountains pour.

*

>You who remain
>fresh on the rock
>may think:
>
>"In our endless youth
>surviving here
>we've never met
>
>a man we could love
>who did not die
>when slain."

*

Beyond looking brilliant
Have they nothing in mind?
You men call them faithless.
Didn't your gold brushwork
Make them what they are?

A woman wrote this for women
Sealed in the rockface
As gems on show to the crowd.
Their star sapphire eyes
Look far too bright to be touched.

*

From Hunagiri Temple
I've come with all I possess:
Needle, fan, begging bowl
And my robe as a novice.

A person much talked about
Lives up in that cave, whoring.
Be wakeful in thought:
Guard the door of hearing!

She spreads a broad grin
Round a soul she's devouring.
Terrible thing to have seen.
I can't stop shuddering.

*

The wet monsoon
   came to us in a thunderstorm
      bursting with relief.

Clay pots and brass bowls
   overflowed with drips
      from leaks in broken roofs.

Hundreds and thousands
>of trees like birthday cake candles
>>were lit in a flash and blown out.

Tuna and seer-fish
>got whirled into the sky
>>and landed among spice gardens.

A curlew felt cheated
>and left the country
>>filing a wretched complaint.

From the summit of parched hills
>waterfalls roared
>>like tom-toms beaten in temples.

In our cots at night we crowed
>when firefly swarms kept bringing
>>miniscule buds of light.

You, with your eyes half closed
>as a nymph on the Lion Rock
>>stirred up these airs.

If we'd known the secret
>of sapu flowers at your fingertips
>>would it have helped?

>>*

As a woman I'll gladly
>sing for these women
>who are unable to speak.

You bulls come to Sigiri
>and toss off little lovesongs
>making a big hullabaloo.

Not one has given us
>a heart-warming sip
>>of rum and molasses.

Maybe none of you thought
    we women could have lives
    of our own to get through.

Sigiriya, 11 January 1987

Early this morning
    I walked on the ramparts
    and came across lotuses,

A playful flotilla
    becalmed on the moat
        hauling white sails down,

As warm rain was falling:
    each leaf collecting in the palm
    of my hand as a child

Drops that scatter and split
    like mercury: held very still
    they pool and unite.

        *

We were lightly fanned
    by a friendly wind
        with a scent of jasmine

Around an octagonal pond
    where the king could recline
        in his pleasure ground

Backed by a huge rock lingam
    watering a lotus bed
        whenever it rained:

We could see our reflections
    Blossoming from the mud
        in fragrant, flamboyant air.

*

The freshness we found
    near the cobra hood cave
        on white marble steps

Going up to the clouds
    came as kindness from someone
        who usually makes our blood boil:

All the better when we stood
    above the gallery walkway
        between rock and mirror wall,

And watched a transparent
    drop-curtain of rain
        coming down from the gods

By drip-channels grooved
    in the overhanging cliff:
        and saw the violent green

Jungle of the country
    from this high point of love
        diffused through a purifying screen.

*

They came here, looked around, and went,
With this karmic picture
Etched upon their minds.

But they couldn't stop their hands
Wanting to touch
As they climbed and stumbled down.

You salacious people,
Keep your hands off the images!
Don't go giving each breast a rub.

Kate Newmann

Put to Loss Because of the Snow
for Shay O'Byrne

Tom Crean, Antarctic explorer, 1877–1938, is buried in Annascaul, County Kerry.

At the funeral, no one spoke
of how the man who survived
such longitude and latitude,
could be defeated by the road
from Tralee to Cork hospital
— his stomach lurching,
his appendix burst.

And there was no talk here
of the mysterious fall
that finished him with the Royal Navy,
left his vision damaged.
Closing continents behind his unsmiling lips,
silence coming down like thick Dingle mist.

In 1901, Crean was part of Scott's expedition to the Antarctic.

From the day he let the cattle
into the potatoes
— his father's anger like a blizzard;
him walking out into the night —
fifteen years old, youngest of ten,
until he found himself
feet sinking in Antarctic white
to the depth of a furrow,
pulling the sledge like a plough,
listing like a farmer.

Their dreams were ice-bound.
Crean's skin held the foot-prints
of Joyce's frost-bitten feet,
that night when each man held them
to their breathing hearts 'til blood flowed.

Hearing that Shackleton had got within ninety-seven miles of the Pole, in 1910 Scott, accompanied by Crean, set out again.

He stood by Scott for years.
Stood, as the train smoke left the platform
and they read Shackleton's name in the smudged headline.

Back to the bloody business
of killing seals, skua gulls and penguins,
guts slucking onto snow,
the Emperor Penguin heavier than a child.
Snow-blind: too much white light entering the eyes.

Sitting with Evans, sewing
through tough winter, stitching
the hours of endless dark,
knowing, when you're walking,
how sweat can form against you
an extra pelt of solid ice.

Crean stayed among the final eight
struggling to the Pole,
shared Christmas dinner of horse-meat,
onion, curry powder, caramels,
ginger, plum pudding, cocoa.

Until the day sundered into a huge crevasse
with Scott's half-muttered reason
for sending him back:
That's a bad cold you've got, Crean.

That's a bad cold you've got, Crean.

*Crean, Lashley and Evans returned to base camp
as Scott and his party proceeded towards the Pole.*

Against the magnetic pull of their disappointment,
Crean, his eyes on fire
— a poultice of old tea-leaves —
tobogganed with Lashley and Evans
down two thousand feet — casting
off into a drop whiter than death
to land unharmed. Crean singing
The Mountains of Mourne as they pitched the tent,
the tune freezing as it left his throat.

As though he'd never stopped walking
since that day with his father and the cattle
Crean saved them all,
the last biscuit eaten with ice,
a four day walk in eighteen hours,
feet drawn on to the rough prayer of his breath.

*Scott reached the Pole to discover that Amundsen had been
there before him. All five men in his party died on the return.*

A winter later,
breath heavy with daily onion
given against scurvy,
Crean found a theodolite, a snow boot
slit to fit a swollen foot;
the tent, half-buried in time and cold,
tea-leaves, tobacco, the final letters,
Scott's skin yellow and glossy
that came to Crean in sleep
again and again, like a song half-sung;
sank in him like the fated Titanic,
all aching loss and unanswered question.

*In 1914 Crean accompanied Shackleton on an expedition
to cross Antarctica on foot from coast to coast.*

There were no bands playing,
no strains of a violin
as the ice, shrieking like a braking train,
closed in on the Endurance,
crushed it, thrust it skywards.

Sensing where the ice would shatter —
a game of chess,
of moving men and dogs,
their days like photographic plates
exposed on snow.

Their bowels seized
with nothing but Adelie penguin;
the only fresh fish
from the belly of a snow-leopard —
undigested in its gut.

Crean's spirit froze as all sixty dogs
that he had reared, who heeded
every cadence of his warm Kerry accent,
were led by him to be shot.

A hopeless launch into the boats
caulked with seal's blood,
diarrhoea from the uncooked dogmeat,
the only light, from Crean's pipe,
reindeer hairs in everything,
the putrid smell of reindeer sleeping-bags
beginning to rot.
It was a long helpless drift
into history, swallowed
with the last cup of tea.

The boats arrived on Elephant Island on 15th April, 1916, and Crean, Shackleton and Worsley sailed to South Georgia to seek help. Years later they admitted to each other that they had all felt the presence of a fourth person.

Far from the gasp of shell, the deadened sound
of bullet stopping in flesh, the muddied muffle
of a bloody end in trenches,
twenty-two men were left on Elephant Island
to battle their bodies' reluctance to ice,
surviving on limpets, sugar, seaweed and meths,
snow snatching its colour from their unguarded eyes.

On the day of the Easter Rising,
Crean, Shackleton, Worsley
embarked to trek the unbroken promise
of South Georgia's ice-scape.
A five minute sleep
in thirty-six hours, struggling
against the welcome blanket of absence,
the dread melt away from living.

Aware that pain has a gravity all its own,
they sat on coiled ropes and skidded
down a glacier into civilization,
hair to their waists, clothes they had worn for a year.
Counting frost-bite from the circles on their skins,
less real than the unseen presence
who ghosted their mutual silence.

Crean returned to Britain, and eventually to Ireland.

Nothing in the frigid truth of snow
had terrified Crean like the prospect
of an exam to get promotion,
reduced at the age of forty
to the gangly child at a too-small desk
learning little, except to wish for elsewhere.

When the horses were shot,
when the dogs were shot,
when Evans was dying,
when Scott excluded him,
Crean had cried. And now,
too late for tears,

his country's surface
treacherous and sundering,
half-submerged,
all the songs half sung,
too much white light entering the eyes.

Nuala Ní Dhomhnaill
Translated by Paul Muldoon

Na Murúcha a Thriomaigh

Ar an gcarraig lom seo ar a gcuireann siad isteach
an t-am de ló is a ngainní á dtriomú acu
tagann galair cnis mar oighear is gríosach orthu
is codladh grifín ón mbríos gaoithe is fiú ón leoithne,
rud nár thaithíodar as a n-óige is nár chleachtadar riamh
ar na bánta íochtaracha, iad ag iomrascáil is ag déanamh
gleacaíochta leis na leanaí ríoga. Dar leo tá goin na ré
gach pioc chomh holc leis an ngréin á mbualadh;
gorm a bhíonn siad i ndiaidh goin na gealaí
is buí i ndiaidh an ghrian á leagadh.

Nuair a thagann an rua orthu is go méadaíonn an braon
ins na harasaipil níl luibh ná leigheas a thabharfaidh
aon chabhair mura bpiocfá cúpla rúta de mheacan
an táthabha. Caitear é seo a bhaint i gcónaí
i dtaobh thall den abhainn is é a ullmhú
de dhroim uisce, chun ná geobhaidh an phiast bhaineann
a bholadh is ná neadóidh níos doimhne istigh
idir coirt is craiceann, idir feoil is leathar.
Deintear céirín ansan dó a thairrigíonn an nimh.

Caitheann na mná muincí troma thart faoina muineál
is na fearaibh ceirteacha dearga
nó rud ar bith a chlúdódh rian na sceolbhach.
Deireann an dochtúir liom go bhfuil an sine siain
ar lár ina lán acu. Caitear an ribe tuathail
i mbarr a gceann a stoitheadh nó é a chuimilt go maith
le céir sara gcnagfaidh sí seo thar n-ais iontu.
"An gcualaís an cnag?" a fhiafraíonn sé dóibh
nuair a tharlaíonn an leigheas. Tá dearmhad glan déanta acu
faoin am seo ar shuathadh mearathail na gcaisí doimhne

is a chlaisceadal na míol mór sa duibheagán.
Uair má seach airíonn said fós é ag sioscadh
ar an ngaoith is tugann said Port na bPúcaí air.
Cuireann said fíor na croise idir iad agus é.

Sánn siad an fonn a ghabhann leis i gcúl an choicís
nó i bhfolach i bpoll sa chlaí i dteannta
lomadh na gruaige is bearradh na hingne,
an ionga úd a fuaireadar ón lia súl
is na spéaclaí nár chuireadar ariamh orthu.
Tá sé ag lobhadh ansan i gcónaí i dteannta
ceirteacha na gcneathacha, an fhuil mhíosúil
is náireach leo, a meabhraíonn dóibh is a chuireann
in iúl an slabar is an glóthach tiubh
dár díobh iad. Ní fhreagraíonn siad d'éinne
a ghlaonn as a n-ainm is as a sloinne orthu
ó théann an ghrian ina luí. Tá sé suite meáite
is go daingean i gceann gach uile dhuine acu
gurb ionann freagairt do ghlaoch shaolta
nó do ghlaoch síoraí.

Ní shínfeadh fear ná bean acu ar shúisín
ná ar leaba go mbeadh a gcosa sínte i dtreo na tine.
Dar leo gur cóiriú an duine mhairbh é sin.
Ní maith leo cloch a thabhairt isteach
'on tigh Dé Luain. Dá dtabharfadh leanbh
leis isteach i dteach í do chuirfí iachall air
í a chaitheamh amach arís. Tá cur ina coinne acu.
Fágann na rabhartaí earraigh a rianta fós
ar chlathacha cosanta a n-aigne; gach tonnchosc díobh
ina ghlib ag bruth farraige is ag brúscar raice —
focail a scuabtar isteach mar a bheadh carabháin charraige
ar líne bharra taoide nuair a bhuaileann an ré roithleacáin
aimsir ré an tSathairn, focail a thugann scáil
na seanré fós leo, focail ar nós
"más reamhar, com seang, meanmain uallaigh."

The Assimilated Merfolk

Barely have they put in on this bare rock
than their scales start drying out
and they suffer such skin complaints as windgall and blotching
and get pins-and-needles from the breezes, never mind the zephyrs,
unaccustomed as they were to either
on the underwater plains where they used to wrestle and besport
themselves with the princelings. As far as they're concerned, moonstroke
is every bit as serious as too much sun:
they turn blue after moonstroke
and yellow after the sun has laid them low.

If they happen to get shingles, or when a boil
comes to a head, there's no herb or native remedy that will offer
any respite except maybe a couple of roots of hellebore
from the opposite bank of the river, the hellebore itself prepared
somewhere over water, thereby ensuring that the she-grub won't get wind of it
and burrow deeper
between the outer and inner subcutaneous layers, between flesh and hide.
A poultice is made from this which draws out the poison.

The women wear heavy neck-ornaments
while the men favour kerchiefs,
anything at all that hides the signs of their gills.
The doctor reports that the uvula
is displaced in the vast majority of them. The topmost hair
of their heads must either be torn out by the roots or thoroughly stiffened
with wax before the uvula snaps back.
"Did you hear the snap?" the doctor enquires of them
when the cure takes effect. By now they've clean forgotten
the dizzying churning of the deep currents
and, from the abyss, the whales' antiphonal singing.
From time to time they hear a snatch of it
on the wind and call it "The Fairy Tune."
They make a sign of the cross between themselves and it.

They fling the air of the tune into the heap of leftovers
or hide it away in the same hole in the ditch where they dispose

of hair-clippings and nail-parings,
the ointment they got that time from the eye-doctor,
those eye-glasses they never wore.
The air of that tune is forever breaking down
along with the menstrual rags, the menstrual blood
they shy away from, reminiscent as it is
of the ooze and muck
from which they sprang. They never answer anyone
who calls them by their name or surname
once the sun's set. For they've determined,
and hold it now as an article of faith,
that to answer such a mortal call
is to answer an eternal one.

Not one of them, man or woman, would stretch out on a sofa
or a settle-bed if their legs were to be turned toward the fire.
They associate this with the laying out of the dead.
They don't like it if a stone is brought
inside the house on a Monday. If a child
were to bring one in he'd be compelled
to bring it out again. They really take against that.
The high spring tides leave their mark
on the sea-walls of their minds, the edge of every breaking wave
ragged with flotsam and jetsam and other wreckage,
words carried ashore like the shells of sea-urchins
and left at the high-water mark when they get the head-staggers
at the time of the Saturday moon, words that are still imbued
with the old order of things, phrases like
"wide-thighs, narrow-waist, hare-brain."

Collette Ní Ghallchóir
Translated by Gréagóir Ó Dúill

Antain

Uaigneach
Uaigneach
thú anocht, a Antain
i bhfad ó bhaile

Do chnámha a bhí aclaí tráth
Sínte fuar anocht
Ar mharmar i mBristol

Cuirfear thall é
Dúirt an Raidió
Ar fhód a bháis.

Ní fheicfear a chónair
Ag sníomh siar
ar bhealach chúng na locha
Ná muintir a mhuintire
á chaoineadh
Sa reilig úd cois cuain.

Sáifear síos é
'gcréafóg fhuar na gcoimhthíoch

Maith dó, a Dhia, a chionta
agus maithfidh seisean duitse
a phearsanacht agus a nádúr.

Antain

Lonely, lonely, you are
Antain
so far from home.

Once so agile, now your limbs
Lie on marble in Bristol.

He will be buried there
The radio announced.

His coffin will not be seen
Winding the narrow road beside the lake.
Nor his people be heard
keening him in the graveyard
above the harbour.

He'll be stuck down
in alien soil.

Forgive him, Lord, his trespasses
as he forgives you the hand you gave him.

An tAmharc Deireanach

Bhéarfaidh mé an t-amharc deireanach thart,
a dúirt sí
Ar pháirc an droma
ag titim anuas ón Screig
Ar an Abhainn Fhia
's í ag cogarnaigh le Cruach an Airgid
Luífinn anseo go suan
a dúirt sí
Ach caithfidh mé a bheith curtha leisean
i mbéal na trá.

The Last Look

I'll take the last look around
she said
at ridge field
as it drops from the rocky hillside.
At Deer River
as it whispers to the Silver Mountain.
I'd lie here peaceful for eternity
she said.
But I'll have to be buried beside himself
at the edge of the strand.

Máire Áine Nic Gearailt
Translated by Gréagóir Ó Dúill

Teicheadh

Níl le déanamh ach géilleadh
Do shruth na farraige seo
Gabháil go réidh le rabharta na mblian —
Le suaitheadh is tarraingt na haoise
I dtreo caoinché ónar seoladh fadó riamh
I ngleoiteog an dóchais.

Ó ceileadh an Bhreasaíl i mbroinn na mara
Níor bádh de thaisme criú an aonair
I bhfad ó bhaile buaileadh talamh
I mball strainséartha.

I gcathair an láithrigh, cuirtear glas ar dhóirse
Mall san oíche
Is i gcónaí i suan, cloistear cnead na taoide
Faoi bhun na bhfaill isteach
Ar thonn tuile na fáistine suíonn fidléir —
Idir chodladh is dhúiseacht
Cloistear a phort ar an ngaoith . . .

Ar líonra na haimsire
Beirtear isteach
I mbarróg an tsáile sínte amach
Aghaidh ar ché na macallaí.

Fleeing

Nothing to do but yield
To this ocean current
Be ready to go with the flow of the years —
With the boiling and draw of the century
Toward quiet harbour from where, long ago
You sailed on a canoe of hope.

Since the Land of Youth was lost in the bowels of the sea
The one-man crew survived by chance
To make landfall far from home
In a strange place.

In the city of the present, people lock their doors
Late in the night
And in perpetual sleep, the tide sighs
Around the base of the cliffs.
On the flood tide of the future a fiddler sits.
Those half asleep, half waking,
Hear his tune on the wind.

On the web of the weather
A brine embrace brings it longdrawn out
To the harbour of echoes.

Áine Ní Ghlinn

Translated by Gréagóir Ó Dúill

Teangmháil

Tháinig tú chugam
ag an am san den oíche
a dtagann borradh faoin tost.

Tháinig chugam d'uaigneas
is theangmhaigh sé le m'uaigneas.
Fuaireadar faoiseamh i bpóg

nár mhair ach tamaillín
sular imigh tú leat arís
ar bhealach príobháideach

d'uaignis féin
ach sheas an phóg san aer
is dhein scamall di

a thuirlingíonn uaireanta
ag an am san den oíche
a dtagann borradh faoin tost
chun an t-uaigneas a dhíbirt.

Contact

You came to me
at that time of night
when silence swells.

Your loneliness came to me
and made contact with my loneliness.
Both gained relief from a kiss

that lasted only a moment
before you went away again
on the private road

of your loneliness
but the kiss stayed in the air
and was made cloud

which descends sometimes
at that time of night
when silence swells
to chase loneliness away.

Iomrascáil Oíche leis na Mairbh

D'éalaigh mo mhéara leo dod lorg san oíche
Níor aimsíos ach piliúr a bhí scallta ag na deora
agus a méara cnámhacha ag cíoradh do chuid gruaige.

Measaim uaireanta go mbíodh aithne agam uirthi
go bhfeicim a cnámharlach sínte led thaobh
a beola fuara ag diúl do bhrionglóide.

Brionglóid ina mbraithim fuacht lá Samhna
an bháisteach ag lascadh anuas ar do charbhat dubh
do shúile stáirseáilte os cionn bháine do bhóna.

Casann tú chun síoda a gruaige a shlíocadh.
Dúisíonn tú le foilmhe na teangmhála.
Sileann do mhéara tríd an aer.

Braithim anois iad ag díriú ormsa
ach tá mo shúile dúnta.
Níl uaimse iomrascáil a dhéanamh leis na mairbh.

Night Wrestling with the Dead

My fingers wandered to find you in the night
found nothing but a pillow scalded by tears
and her bony fingers combing through your hair.

I sometimes think I used to know her,
that I see her skeleton stretched out by your side
her cold lips sucking out your dream.

A dream when I feel the cold of a November day
rain lashing down on your black tie,
on your starched eyes above your collar's white.

You turn to sleek her silken hair
you waken with the vacuum of the contact
your fingers fall through air.

I see now your eyes turning to me
but close my eyes.
I do not wish to wrestle with the dead.

Yilmaz Odabaşi

Translated by Patrick Galvin & Robert O'Donoghue from the Turkish

from "Feride"

Name Feride
nationality the world
no religion one voice
and I know the rest

we sheltered running from
the same rains
night came
a broken branch where we stood
recklessly I took her to me
our skins met first
and our sweat

she was my woman night and day
the rest I know the rest

rain fell threadlike
into the night
birds flapped their wings
as our world grew colder
clouded in sorrow the stars
lost their way

Feride moved in battledress
as waters raced to flow

waters devoured waters
days devoured days
life devoured us both
like a beast
like a curse
like a barrel

then Feride slept for nights
a forgotten god gorged himself
when Feride was silent
the earth drowned
but the earth of my heart
would dry

I stole her from speechless and shapeless shadows
I shall not leave her to anyone anyone

I shall wrap her in kisses
I shall not leave her to anyone

Feride smells like grain like a honeyspike
shyly she turns her eyes away
the rest I know the rest

days were sluggish
we sang songs in the evening breeze
a broken tipped carnation stood on our table
we dressed our wounds asked after those
returning from revolutions
we counted executions

women and men laboured on
brides at stream mouths drivers at
driving wheels guerrillas at guns

but the fucking wars of the hair-brained generals did not
                                                                               stop

whores leaked from the slit of the night
curses filled the skin of slits
curses filled the newspapers
nights smelled of alchohol and sperm
as days laid bare their grieving
on darkly bloodied cloths

blood clotted the days with tortures fired in fascism

a long distance driver recalled his roads
like I remembered Feride
patrols filled the nights

what's up

no I.D.

Feride is on strike
in the overcrowded markets
better to cast her to mountains
add her to clouds
than leave her to anyone

I stole her from fires
in burnt out nights
I held her to me
calming her dove's pain
with wings of light

I revived her
I shall not leave her to
anyone
anyone

I arrested her skin with my palms
sealed her lips in red fire
I devoured her
she became

Feride is the daughter of April
her skin the scent of April sun
the smell of grass and swallows

mountains sleep in her breasts
when she becomes love
she is woman coming to me

love has no watches
shirts calendars

it is like a desolate wind

wherever she turns
I turn my face
to that horizon
the rest I know the rest

Feride smokes tobacco dipped in ballads
her heart sings echoes of a typhoon
she comes from death
she comes from singing
and she lies in my arms

I shall not leave her to
anyone
anyone

Jean O'Brien

Severed

No dreams are given her, just drug
induced deep; no place to nurture her,
she rolls out on a tumbrel of fear.
She smells the faggot smoulder

can at times see their spark
light the skies and graze the stars.
The moon is simply
out of the question.

Our lives are laid out at her feet,
tender plants inconsolable
in our greed. We pluck and pluck
her, our hands turn green —

tossed sheaves, a swathe of corn
rises to arch nearer the sun,
cracked like the corncrake,
the feet cut from under us.

Veronica's Epiphany

If she had been on Mount Ararat
she would have been a spore
that fastened to the inside of the Ark,
a low relief carving, holding the outline
in the dark of something indistinct
but beatified. She moved in different times,
sea level had dropped, the Mount was far
away. Golgotha was a small hill seen
from her mother's window.

Still his face swam before her as she slept,
etched itself on her, fixed in her mind
a growing thing waiting out its time.
When she saw his face in flesh,
with sweat and dirt and blood,
she imprinted it on her apron to keep
sight of him as he rose above it all,
a bright dove rising
the olive branch trailing from its beak.

She passed the hawthorn tree,
its blossoms white periwinkles
in a sea of sand. It drew blood
from hands that pulled at it
to make a crown for the crucified.
The road to Golgotha is little more
than a rabble of dust; brushing death
aside she reached home
just as the storm broke.

Her young daughter's nervous cry,
almost like laughter reached her ears
as the room and sky lit up —
fire sparking from hawthorn sticks
the child had found and brought home,
her special gift. *I gave her life
and now, this child has brought me
death, opened me up to it like an oyster
letting in the sea.*

Veronica

With one eye on the horizon, Veronica
steps boldly from the crowd, apron at the ready.
It is only March, but already the sun is high,
baking the dirt road to Golgotha.

With all the people milling round the dust
cannot settle. Soldiers are everywhere, pushing
to part the crowd threatening to engulf the man.
Over their shouts, a cry goes up, derisive, *King of the Jews.*

On up the track he stumbles. What his crime is
Veronica does not know, but no matter.
As he shuffles forward she holds her apron
to his face and steps away again.

She told her mother afterwards that his eyes
brightened for a moment and when she
pulled the stained apron from her pocket
found his face outlined on it, she took it to the river

with the other soiled clothes, but no matter how
she rubbed and scrubbed could not shift that look.
Now it hangs high on her wall looking towards heaven.

Yes, I can bake a cake.
"But can she bake a cake?" asked a newspaper after
Amelia Earhart had flown solo across the Atlantic.

And sometimes in the aching loneliness
of taut unforgiving sky, she wished she'd stayed
and baked some more. Time bent and blended
into nothing. The engine a soothing sound,
she watched the Vega's instruments and dials
as if their numbered faces would reveal
her soul's dominion. She became a two-winged

seraphim flying in heaven's slipstream, that
radar operators logged as angel, mistaking
her for geese blown off course and heading east.

Instead she chose to fly from Harbour Grace
to some unknown place in Ireland.
First landfall after all that blue air and sea,
the pasture beckoned green and grounded.
A few startled cows felt wind rush past
their ears, heard the sound of wings and saw
a red Mayfly go past, touch down. A farmer
stood his ground and greeted her,
said she was in Gallagher's field
and worried would she sour the milk.

Mícheál Ó Cuaig
Translated by Gréagóir Ó Dúill

Uchtóga

Sa bhfómhar a chuaigh muid
Triúr i gcriathrach
Ag baint deasú tí is sciobóil den fhiontarnach.

Le stracaí glan na taithí
Chruthaigh m'athair carnáin,
Is bhailigh mise is mo mháthair le barainn,

Dá fháisceadh in' uchtóga —
Cúig cinn a rinne ualach —
Gur chóirigh iad ar bruach cois Átha Íochtair.

Bhí briotaíl aisteach sa gcomhrá
An lá úd mar b'eol dúinn triúr
An ghile ag éag is an ghrian

Ag cailleadh an chatha;
Bhraith muid críoch is scarúint
Is mise ar thob eang eile' chur sa gcinniúint.

Ní mé céard a mheall mé
Siar trí rosamh mblian
Don chriathrach cúlráideach sa ngleann,

Ach tá na huchtóga
Ag éamh le tamall —
An fhead ón speal, an fuadar ciúin, is an crapadh.

Armfuls

We three went to the pitted bog
To cut the withered mountain grasses
As mending for the house-roof and the barn.

Experience gave my father long clean movement
As he shaped heaps,
And my mother and I gathered all in, thrifty,

Taking armfuls, pulling the grass in, compact,
Five armfuls to the load, placed
With care down by the lower ford.

Talk was clumsy that day
And we knew the brightness of the day was dying
The sun, too

Losing its battle.
We felt an ending, a separation
As I was making ready to strike a track in fate.

I can't say what it is that drew me, now
Back through the haze of time
To that secluded mountain bog, to the glens

But the gathered armfuls now
Embrace no longer,
The scythe is whistling, the paced ingathering too quiet, all
Draws in . . .

Toibreacha

Ní caitear le toibreacha mar ba chóir
Ó thriomaigh an t-éileamh orthu.

Bhíodar naofa — an chuid díobh
Nár luadh míorúilt leo ach fíoruisce.

Tugadh urraim dóibh an uair úd,
Sciúrtaí iad go grinneall.

Is ceann a choinníodh braon
Ar thriomach mór ba mháithreach chruthanta é.

Ceann fánach nach bhfuil anois ó aithne,
Ná cosáin go dtí iad amhlaidh

Leac is cloch le fada as áit
Caonach ramhar ar an uisce . . .

Ach ní caoineadh a fheileann tobar
Ní hamhlaidh a bhásaigh mar síltear.

Tá an fíor ag brúchtadh fós
Mar a bhíonn dínit i seandaoine.

Wells

Wells aren't treated now as they should be
Since the need for them dried up.

They were holy, even those of them
Which had no miracles attached to them but that of water.

They were given respect those times
And were scoured right down to the bedrock.

That which flowed even in the time of drought
Was true motherfount.

All but the odd one now is lost and hidden to us
Even the footpaths to them overgrown, forgotten.

The stone wall, the coverstone now dislodged,
Thick scum on the water . . .

But a well is no cause for crying,
It doesn't die as is thought.

No, the fresh spring still flows
As dignity does in old people.

Aodh Ó Domhnaill

Translated by Gréagóir Ó Dúill

Oifigiúil

Tá
Deasc i ndiaidh boird
I ndiaidh boird
I ndiaidh deisce
Ag stánadh ar aghaidheanna
Cromtha.

Tá na fallaí bán
Agus an t-urlár
Nach mór.

Trasna an bhóthair
Tá oifig acu
Faoi fhallaí buí.

Nach breá dóibh.

I Meiriceá
Léimeann daoine
Ón seachtú hurlár déag
Ach níl siad siúd
Ina gCaitlicigh.

Official

There they are, desk on desk, table after table, staring at the lowered faces.
The walls are white, and the floor is, nearly.
Across the street they have an office with walls of yellow.
        Isn't it well for them.
        In America, people jump
        From the seventeenth storey
        But they aren't Catholics.

Bernard O'Donoghue

from Sir Gawain and the Green Knight

. . .

497   Though people are cheerful when they've all been
          drinking,
     a year passes quickly and changes its moods;
     the end rarely matches the spirit it starts in.
500   Yuletide is past and the New Year is too,
     and each season follows the other in sequence.
     After Christmas comes shrivelling Lent
     that tries the body with fish and dry bread.
     Then the earth's weather weakens the winter:
     the cold shrinks underground, the clouds draw up
          higher.
     The bright rain falls in warming showers,
     straight on to the ground so that flowers appear.
     Both meadows and fields are covered in green;
     birds hurry to build and sing with excitement
510   out of joy at the summer that follows so sweetly
          all over the hills.
          Blossoms swell and bloom
          In dense, reckless array,
          and rich notes, unpausing,
          are heard throughout the wood.
     After the soft breeze of the summer season
     and the west wind that fans seeds and grasses,
     the growth is abundant that issues all round,
     when the soaking dew drops off the leaves
520   with the touch of heaven that the warm sun brings.
     But then comes autumn to harden the grain,
     to warn it to ripen ahead of the winter.
     Its dryness makes the dust swirl around
     and fling up high off the face of the earth.
     The rough wind in the sky wrestles with the sun;

the lime-tree leaves loosen and fall to the ground,
and the grass turns grey that had just been so green.
All ripens, then rots, that sprang in such hope.
So the year passes on through its series of yesterdays,
530   and winter comes round again, as nature demands,
       ever the same.
    The moon around Michaelmas
    has a touch of winter to it,
    and Gawain thinks again
    about his fearful quest.

Yet until All Saints' Day he stayed on with Arthur,
who held a feast on that festival in honour of Gawain,
with great celebration by all the Round Table.
Fine knights and beautiful ladies
540   were filled with despair for the sake of this man,
but yet they displayed nothing but gaiety:
many who grieved for him were still making jokes.
After dinner he spoke seriously to Arthur
and talked of his journey, openly saying,
"Now, lord of my life, I ask leave to depart.
You know how grave this adventure will be;
to speak more of its pains would be wasted breath.
But tomorrow I must set off to receive that blow,
to seek out that creature in green, God help me!"
550   Then the best of the company crowded together:
Iwain and Erec and many another,
Sir Dodinel the Wild, the Duke of Clarence,
Lancelot and Lionel, the noble Lucan,
Sir Bors and Sir Bedivere, both big men,
and other famous knights, such as Mador de la Port.
All this great company drew near to the king
to advise Gawain with heavy hearts.
Much deep sorrow was felt in the hall,
that one as valued as him should go on this quest,
560   to suffer a dire blow, unable to hit back
       with his sword.
    The knight still kept cheerful

and said, "Why should I despair?
With destiny, good or bad,
you can only take your chance."

• • •

590 When he was fully dressed, his armour was lordly,
the least link or knot shining with gold.
Thus, armed as he was, he went to hear Mass,
celebrated solemnly at the high altar.
Then he went to the king and his court companions,
and took fond farewells of the lords and the ladies,
who escorted him with a kiss, praying for him to Christ.
Then Gryngolet was prepared, fitted with a saddle
that gleamed brightly with a line of gold fringes,
newly harnessed all over, ready for the road.
600 The bridle was plaited with the brightest gold,
and the ornate side-skirts and rich chest-trappings,
crupper and horse-cloth matched the saddle-bows.
It was all fastened with light red-gold nails
that shone and sparkled like the beams of the sun.
Then Gawain fervently kissed his helmet,
which was strongly forged and padded inside.
It stood high on his head, clasped at the back,
with a light silk band across the neck-guard,
picked out and encircled with the finest gems
610 on its broad silk edges, with birds such as parrots
embroidered on the seams amid periwinkles
and turtle-doves and love-knots, set there so thickly
it must have taken years for ladies to stitch them
    back in their chambers.

• • •

640 First he was faultless in all his five senses;
next, he never failed in his five fingers,
and all his trust was in the five wounds

of Christ on the cross, as the Bible describes.
And whenever this knight was hard pressed in battle,
his firm belief, above all else,
was that his strength came from the five joys
that the noble queen of heaven took in her child.
It was fitting then that Gawain had
her image depicted inside his shield,
650   so when he looked at it his heart would not falter.
The fifth five virtues that Gawain maintained
were generosity and sympathy first of all,
chastity and courtesy which he never failed in,
and above all compassion. These five things
were fixed more firmly in him than anyone else.
And all five were rooted in this knight,
each locked to the next so that there was no end
or beginning to any: fixed and unwavering,
neither overlaying nor divided on any side,
660   without end at a corner to be found anywhere,
no matter at which point you started to test them.
On his shield this device was marked out
With red gold on a red background.
"The pure pentangle," the people called it
   traditionally.
      Now fine Gawain is ready
   he takes his lance at once
   and bids them all farewell —
   as he thought, for evermore.

• • •

740   One morning he rode in good heart by a hillside
into a deep forest, endlessly wide,
high hills on both sides and below him dense woods
of huge ancient oaks, massed in their hundreds.
Hazel and hawthorn were tangled together,
covered all over by rough, ragged moss,
with desolate birds on the bare branches,

all piping pitifully from the pain of the cold.
The man on Gryngolet passed beneath them
through swamps and through boglands, all on his
   own,
750   concerned for his obligations in case he should fail
to honour the Lord who, that very night,
was born of a maiden to soften our sorrows.
And so, sighing, he said, "I beg you, Lord,
and Mary the dearest and mildest of mothers,
for some shelter where I may devoutly hear Mass
and Matins tomorrow. Most humbly I ask
and say my 'Our Father', 'Hail Mary'
   and Creed."
He prayed as he rode
760   and wept for all his sins.
Many times he blessed himself,
Saying "Christ's Cross be my help!"

He had hardly blessed himself three times
before he saw, in the wood, a moated dwelling
on a mound above the plain, closed in by the branches
of huge tree trunks all round its ramparts:
the finest castle a knight ever owned,
pitched on a meadow with a park all around it
and a spiked palisade, densely constructed,
770   surrounded by trees for two miles and more.

• • •

807   He called, and there soon appeared
a watchman overhead,
who courteously asked
what the wandering knight desired.

"Good Sir," said Gawain, "would you please bear my
   message
to the lord of this castle, my appeal for shelter."

"By Saint Peter, I will," said the porter, "and I am sure
you will be welcome to stay here as long as you like."
He went away quickly and soon he was back
817 with fine company, who welcomed Gawain.

• • •

824 Knights and squires came thronging down
to lead him with ceremony into the hall.
When he lifted his helmet, they all rushed forward
to help this guest by taking if from his hands,
and to take too his sword and his shield.
Then he warmly greeted each of those courtiers,
830 and many proud men competed to honour him.
They clothed him richly and led him to the hall,
where a fine fire blazed in the hearth.
Then the lord of the company came from his chamber
to greet him in the hall with every due honour.
He said, "You are welcome to use as you wish
everything here. All is yours to have and to hold
    to your heart's content."
"Thank you," said Gawain,
"and may Christ repay you for it."
As men of similar manners
841 they embraced each other.

• • •

928 By the time dinner was over and the prince had stood
    up,
it had nearly come to the fall of night.
930 The chaplains made their way to the chapel
and rang the bells loudly, as they had to
for the high evensong of that great feast day.
The lord responded and the lady also;
she gracefully entered a beautiful pew,

and Gawain happily made his way there as well.
The lord took his sleeve and led him to his seat,
greeted him by name in the friendliest way,
and declared him the most welcome person alive.
Gawain thanked him heartily, and after embracing,
940   they sat together quietly throughout the service.
The lady wanted a look at the knight
as she came from her pew with all her fine ladies.
She was the most beautiful, both in body and face,
of figure and manners, of all of them there;
more beautiful than Guinevere, Gawain reflected,
as she came through the chapel to greet her guest.
Another woman led her by the left hand,
older than she was — a venerable lady,
much reverenced by those noble people.
950   These ladies were very unalike in appearance,
for the younger was fresh, while the other was withered.
Bright red adorned the first lady all over;
rough wrinkled cheeks hung slack on the other.
The young one wore scarves and many bright pearls;
her breast and white throat exposed to view
shone brighter than new-fallen snow on the hillside.
The old lady's neck was covered by a wimple,
pulled over her sallow chin with chalk-white veils.
Her forehead was masked in silk, muffled all over,
covered and screened with jewellery all round,
960   so nothing could be seen but her grey eyebrows,
her eyes and nose and her bare lips,
which were ghastly to look at and horribly chapped.
Hardly to be thought a worldly beauty,
      the Lord save us!
      Her body was short and fat,
      her buttocks spreading wide.
      Nicer to look upon
968   was her companion for sure!

• • •

          At the first sound of the hunt the wild creatures
1150   panicked.
          Deer plunged through the valleys, crazy with fear.
          They raced to the heights but were quickly forced back
          by the circle of beaters with their deafening shouts.
          They let the stags go, with their towering heads,
          their muscular backs and their high antlers,
          for the lord had strictly forbidden disturbance
          of the deer in the close season.
          The hinds were rounded up with "How!" and "Hup!,"
          and the does driven in uproar to the lower ground.
1160   You could watch as they rained their slanting arrows.
          At each point of the wood a shower of them flew,
          and their broad heads brutally bit into brown flesh.
          They screamed and they bled and they died on the
                  hills,
          and the careering dogs pursued them with a frenzy.
          Hunters with loud horns chased in pursuit
          with ringing calls nearly cracking the cliffs.
          Such creatures as escaped the vigilant marksmen
          were pulled down and ripped apart at the hides,
          once they'd been driven down to the river.
1170   The men were skilled at those lower stations,
          and their massive greyhounds fell on those beasts
                  quickly
          and hauled them to the ground straightaway
              in the blink of an eye.
            The lord, delirious with delight,
            rode, dismounted again,
            and spent the day in excitement
            right to the fall of night.

          While the lord was busy by the borders of the wood
          the bold Gawain kept to his soft bed.
1180   He lay there till daylight shone on the walls,
          beneath his bright bedspread, screened all around.
          As he dozed there in peace, he warily heard

a little noise at the door as it stealthily opened.
He raised his head up out of his clothes
and slightly lifted the edge of the curtain;
peeping out cautiously to see what it was.
It was the lady, most lovely to look at,
who shut the door after her, in secret and privately,
and stole towards the bed. The hero, embarrassed,
1190   lay hurriedly back down, pretending to sleep.
She stepped forward silently and stole to his bedside,
lifted the curtain and crept inside,
sitting down softly on the edge of the bed.
And there she stayed, to see if he'd wake up.
The hero lay low some considerable time,
pondering inwardly what all this might mean
or amount to. It seemed pretty strange,
but still he said to himself, "It would be more fitting
1199   to ask her openly what she is after."

• • •

Dennis O'Driscoll

Missing God

His grace is no longer called for
before meals: farmed fish multiply
without His intercession.
Bread production rises through
disease-resistant grains devised
scientifically to mitigate His faults.

Yet, though we rebelled against Him
like adolescents, uplifted to see
an oppressive father banished —
a bearded hermit — to the desert,
we confess to missing Him at times.

Miss Him during the civil wedding
when, at the blossomy altar
of the registrar's desk, we wait in vain
to be fed a line containing words
like "everlasting" and "divine."

Miss Him when the TV scientist
explains the cosmos through equations,
leaving our planet to revolve on its axis
aimlessly, a wheel skidding in snow.

Miss Him when the radio catches a snatch
of plainchant from some echoey priory;
when the gospel choir raises its collective voice
to ask *Shall We Gather at the River?*
or the forces of the oratorio converge
on *I Know That My Redeemer Liveth*
and our contracted hearts lose a beat.

Miss Him when a choked voice at

the crematorium recites the poem
about fearing no more the heat of the sun.

Miss Him when we stand in judgement
on a lank Crucifixion in an art museum,
its stripe-like ribs testifying to rank.

Miss Him when the gamma-rays
recorded on the satellite graph
seem arranged into a celestial score,
the music of the spheres,
the *Ave Verum Corpus* of the observatory lab.

Miss Him when we stumble on the breast lump
for the first time and an involuntary prayer
escapes our lips; when a shadow crosses
our bodies on an x-ray screen; when we receive
a transfusion of foaming blood
sacrificed anonymously to save life.

Miss Him when we exclaim His name
spontaneously in awe or anger
as a woman in a birth ward
calls to her long-dead mother.

Miss Him when the linen-covered
dining table holds warm bread rolls,
shiny glasses of red wine.

Miss Him when a dove swoops
from the orange grove in a tourist village
just as the monastery bell begins to take its toll.

Miss Him when our journey leads us
under leaves of Gothic tracery, an arch
of overlapping branches that meet
like hands in Michelangelo's *Creation*.

Miss Him when, trudging past a church,
we catch a residual blast of incense,

a perfume on par with the fresh-baked loaf
which Milosz compared to happiness.

Miss Him when our newly-fitted kitchen
comes in Shaker-style and we order
a matching set of Mother Ann Lee chairs.

Miss Him when we listen to the prophecy
of astronomers that the visible galaxies
will recede as the universe expands.

Miss Him when the sunset makes
its presence felt in the stained glass
window of the fake antique lounge bar.

Miss Him the way an uncoupled glider
riding the evening thermals misses its tug.

Miss Him, as the lovers shrugging
shoulders outside the cheap hotel
ponder what their next move should be.

Even feel nostalgic, odd days,
for His Second Coming,
like standing in the brick
dome of a dovecote
after the birds have flown.

England

> *Without nostalgia who could love England?*
> — Anne Stevenson

Somewhere out there, England lingers
under the bushy brow of thatch that juts
above half-timbered houses in Home Counties.
A mill village survives where a raft
of flag irises rises near the grain loft
and the vicarage garden party is tastefully

announced on a hand-painted sign.
A family pile in Queen Anne style,
available at a knock-down price,
catches the needle-sharp eye
of a Lloyd's "name" in the auction pages
of *The Field* or *Country Life*.
The hand-crafted. The home-made. The family-run.
Pink briar roses sink their claws
— like painted nails — into the gable walls
of listed cottages at Winchelsea and Rye.
Jersey cream dissolves in steaming scones
at the Salvation Army cake sale.
A smell of new-mown hay, of boiling jam,
of hops vented through an oast house cowl.

England is still out there somewhere,
an owl roosting in a cobwebbed barn.
You can overhear a pub argument about
the best brew of beer, best-ever shepherd's pie
Alistair Cooke is delivering his four millionth
"Letter from America"; so many record-breaking
West End performances of "The Moustrap" or "Cats";
the ten thousandth revival of "An Inspector Calls."
Tin-plate, ration-coupon laughter from the audience
of a radio panel show; Lilliburlero marching
on the BBC World Service, Big Ben chiming
to the second with the tea-time news,
the sig tune for "Coronation Street" a national anthem.
Johnners greets listeners from Lords
as sunlight is rolled out along striped grass.
The tabloids have murder in their hearts.
That and exclusive photos of the latest
female tennis sensation at wet Wimbledon.
Scoreless draws in the Premier League.
Soft going at Newbury and Kempton Park.
Rain stopping play at a county cricket fixture.

Pastel-painted timber seaside chalets.

Miles of white clifftop caravans like dumped fridges.
A day-trip across ridged Channel waves:
cheap pints of bitter in the car ferry bar,
chips with everything in the cafeteria.
English Breakfast Served All Day in Calais.
Vera Lynn. VE celebrations. Our finest hour.
Poppy wreaths, brittle as old majors'
bones, wilt beneath the stony-faced
gaze of the Great War memorial.
Shakespeare settings by Roger Quilter
and Gerald Finzi in aid of the church tower
restoration fund, the vicar's wife doing
the page-turning needful for the accompanist.
A few tremble-lipped parishioners, feeling
their age, clear throats as the harmonium
is tuned and lend their bronchial best
to "The Day Thou Gavest, Lord, is Ended"
while watery light through leaded glass
lands, like a housefly, on the brass plate
commemorating the valiant dead of Ladysmith.
Elgar's "Pomp and Circumstance" arranged
for the Queen's visit by the colliery band.
Ralph Vaughan Williams's "The Lark Ascending"
in rehearsal at the Free Trade Hall.
Gurney's Severn mists, Houseman's blue
remembered hills, Hardy's wind and rain.
A Wilfred Owen troop train falling silent
at an unscheduled stop; or Edward Thomas's
halting express at Adlestrop taking on board
a consignment of pre-war blackbird song.
A brawny chestnut shields the clover-fattened
cattle in a hedgerowed field from searing noon.
Water-colour enthusiasts choose the ideal
viewing point to capture the flamboyant sunset.

The quiet courtesies. The moderation.
The pained smiles. Things left unsaid;

passed over in silence, an unwritten constitution.
Miles of graffitied tower blocks, near treeless
motorways wide as triumphal boulevards.
Race riots in Brixton and the North.
The peal of street-pleasing steel bands at Notting Hill.
Allotment cabbages with gaping caterpillar wounds.
Words like *tavern* and *shires* and *lea.*
Blazered Henley. Top-hatted Ascot.
Black herringbone for the Royal enclosure.
The wine-jacketed coach driver pointing
his blue-rinse passengers to the loos.
A single-room supplement for Christmas
at a refurbished Grand Hotel in some down-at-heel,
sea-eroded, once-genteel Edwardian town.

Romantic England is neither dead nor gone,
nor with Olivier in the grave.
It is out there somewhere still; plain-speaking
Stanley Baldwin's "corncrake on a dewy morning,
the sound of the scythe against the whetstone . . .
a plough team coming over the brow of a hill."
Homely John Major's England still holds its own
somewhere: "long shadows on county grounds,
warm beer, invincible green suburbs, dog lovers."
Goodly, portly Sir John Betjeman envisions his England:
"oil-lit churches, Women's Institutes, modest
village inns . . . mowing machines on Saturday afternoons."

It is somewhere at the back of the mind,
like the back of a newsagent's where plug
tobacco is sold; shining like the polished
skin of a Ribston Pippin or Worcester Pearmain.
It preys on imagination, like pleated ladies
sporting on bowling lawns; like jowelled men
of substance nursing claret in oak-panelled
smoking rooms of jovial private clubs.
See it all for yourself — the quadrangled choir school,
the parterred garden with the honesty box,

the fox-hunting colonel on his high horse,
the Gothic Revival haunt leading through
a topiary arch to gazebo, yew maze,
pet cemetery — on your jaunts about
cobbled market towns, treks down lanes
rutted with what surely must be haywain wheels.

Listen to England as it thunders from Pennine becks
like a loud speech heckled by a Hyde Park crowd.
Listen to its screaming day traders, its bingo callers,
its Speaker demanding "Order!" in the lower chamber.
Listen to the big band music to which couples
relax at the Conservative Club dinner dance.
Listen to the wax of silence harden
round the red leatherette upholstery
after closing time at the Crown and Rose;
steel shutters come down hard on the Punjab Balti;
grease congeals on the mobile kebab stall.
Listen to the tick of its Town Hall clocks,
like a Marks and Spencer shirt
drip-drying above a chipped enamel bath.
Listen to the silence in which England finds its voice.
It declaims this sceptered isle, this earth of majesty.
It claims some corner of a foreign field.
It chants while the chaffinch sings on the orchard bough.
It chants history is now and England.
It pleads green and pleasant land.
It pleads for all its many faults.

At the Seminar

I

An electronic blip from house-martins as they pass
an open window at the conference centre; frantic birds,
on errands of mercy, transporting relief supplies to tricorn beaks.
We sneak a glance at our mobiles for text messages.

Crawling across the hotel lawn, sun puts mist in the shade:
a transparent morning now, our vision unhindered for miles.
A golfing party, armed with a quiver of clubs, aims
for the bull's-eye of the first hole; others, near a pool
blue as our EU flag with its water sparkle of stars, dry off:
shrink-wrapped in towels, they sink back into resort chairs.

II

For serious objective reasons, we are informed, our keynote
speaker is delayed; the Chairman's interpreted words
are relayed simultaneously through headphones:
In order to proceed to a profitable guidance for our work
which will be carried out with a feature of continuity and priority . . .

I see the lake basking in its own reflected glory, self-absorbed,
imagine turquoise dragonflies, wings wide as wedding hats,
fish with scarlet fins, water-walking insects.

I intervene. I associate myself with the previous speaker's views.
Discussions go on in all our languages as I unscrew
still mineral water, bottled at some local beauty spot.
Certain administrations suffered cuts as they weren't entrusted
with new attributions likely to fill in the logistical gap
resulting from the inference of the frontierless economic area . . .

In two hours (less, if — with luck — that stupid clock has stopped)
our final workshops will convene in the break-out rooms.
Then it will be time to draw conclusions at the plenary,
score evaluation forms, return to our respective floors
to dress down for the bus tour of the Old Town.

III

Now the rapporteurs start synopsising
the workshop findings on felt-tip flip-charts.
The Chairman is summing up: *New challenges*
overlook the world scenery in our global stance . . .

Lily pads strut across the lake like stepping stones;
fish risk an upward plunge; martins — plucking
sustenance from thick air — lunge at their mud nests.
Hold the world right there. Don't move a single thing.

Lord Mayo

You have come to a bad end, Lord Mayo,
to find yourself lodged in digs next to mine.
Yours is the grave my house looks down on.
Or would if your tomb could protrude
like a well-fed belly through your waist-band
of nettles and ground elder and brambles.

Fancy not having a lackey who can make
the railings stand to respectful attention,
keep you sealed off from mere mortals,
lend the rusted bars a bit of class with a dab
or two of paint, lop off that ridiculous
top hat of ragwort and silk poppies.

It's a strange reversal of the old order
that you should be mucked about
without frieze coat or gaiters, while we —
fast-forwarded a century and a bit later —
are double-glazed, centrally heated,
en suite'd, dry-lined, living it up.

What a state you are lying in,
for a man of your stature, having
shrunk to this rectangle smaller
than a billiard-room, your name the mud
of a poor Irish county, a bogged-down
empire on which the sun never rises.

Or — to be impertinent and frivolous at once —
it connotes the mayonnaise option at the sandwich

counter. And such chop-licking wraps,
such goat's cheese and aubergine melts,
such sushi specials and antipasto misto
are now served in our lunchtime delis.

You'll observe how uppity the peasants
have become: hurtling off-road 4 by 4s
(the new coach and four) from crèche
or ironing service, ordering carry-out
meals — Indian, Thai, Chinese — no less exotic
than florid shrubs uprooted from the colonies.

One thing, I'll say, Lord Mayo, in your favour:
song thrushes love to bits the berries
that sprout from your personal yew tree
(a yew that responds eerily to gales),
unbuttoning them lustily like a scullery maid
undone in some stately basement kitchen.

As for the elderberry bushes, clustered
at your feet like a pleated curtain
on a four-poster bed, how appropriate
in your lordly context is Heaney's image
elevating those ball-bearing berries to "swart caviar."
Use your silver coffin-plate for daintiness

when you scoop them up to taste: a dish fit for a king.

The Light of Other Days

I freely admit to having always
detested John McCormack's voice:
the quivering tenor pitch,
the goody-good way he articulates
every in-dee-vid-you-al syllable,
prissily enunciating words
like an elocution-class nun.

And — though clearly not his fault —
the hiss on old 78s is oppressive
as if he had a fog (*sic*) lodged in his throat,
as if a coal fire in the parlour where
those songs supposedly belong
were leaking methane
through the gramophone horn.

Or perhaps that surface hiss
is the dust coating mahogany cabinets,
their Sunday-best hush
of wedding-gift china,
tarnished silver trophies,
inscribed retirement salvers,
cut-glass decanters
that have lost their shine;
the locked parlour gone musty
as the cover of Moore's *Melodies*
(shamrocks, harps and wolfhounds
wriggling their way out
from an undergrowth of Celtic squiggles).

McCormack's mawkish rendering
of *I Hear You Calling Me* nauseates
so much the gramophone could be
winding me up, deliberately needling me,
applying surface scratches to my body,
tattooing my skin with indelible images
from the Eucharistic Congress of 1932
when, for the mass congregation,
he sang *Panis Angelicus* in that
ingratiating way of his, sucking up to God.

Why do I bother my head tolerating
this travesty? Why don't I force him
to pipe down, snap out of my misery
like an "Off" switch, send the record
spinning against the wall at 78 revolutions

per minute, rolling it like his
rebarbative 'r's before I throw?

Am I compelled to let it run its course,
an infection, wait until the stylus
lifts its leg to finish, because, well,
this sickly song calls back to mind
a father whose tolerance for such
maudlin warbling knew no bounds?
Could he, by some remote chance,
be the special guest expected indefinitely
in the stale, unaired parlour
laid with deep-pile carpets of grime?
Does McCormack's loathsome
voice succeed in restoring
that father figure, at least momentarily,
remastering him from dust?

Seán Ó Leocháin
Translated by Gréagóir Ó Dúill

999

Dhiailigh mé na huimhreacha ar fad —
gach cód sa leabhar, gach uimhir ar an liosta —
is cé gur lean mé go dílis gach treoir dár thug
eolaí an teileafóin is an fógra sa bhosca,

i bhfad ná i ngearr ní raibh freagra le fáil
agus méara i gcluasa ar uair na práinne.
Is cé go bhfuil súile ruaimneacha ag stánadh isteach
agus béil ag imeacht lasmuigh den bhosca

leanfaidh mé orm go ndéanfaidh mé an glaoch
is mé ag tosú as an nua ó bharr mo liosta
cé go bhfuil an slua lasmuigh mar shochraid, ag síneadh
siar ó mo bhosca atá chomh cúng le cónra.

999

I dialled all the numbers —
every code in the book, every number on the list —
and although I followed closely every instruction
in the telephone directory and on the notice in the kiosk

nobody answered, quick or slow, fingers
stuffed in ears this time of urgency, emergency.
And although rheumy eyes stare in
and mouths are moving outside the box

I'll go on, start all over 'til the call gets through,
I'll start again on the list from the beginning
although the crowd outside are like a funeral wake,
stretching out from my box that is enclosed and lidded tight.

Traidisiún

Nuair a thóg sé amach an casúr
a bhí sa teach leis na cianta cairbreacha
níor rith sé leis a insint dóibh
mar a chuir sé ceann úrnua air
bliain nó dhá bhliain roimhe sin
ná mar a chuir sé cos úrnua ann
is mar sin de siar go dtí a shin-seanathair
a bhuail an chéad tairne riamh leis —
ar scáth a raibh le ceilt aige
ó ba é an casúr céanna i gcónaí é.

Tradition

When he took out the hammer
that was in the house for generations
it did not cross his mind to mention
that he gave it a new head
a year or two before
nor that he replaced the shaft
and that it had always been like that
back to his great-grandfather
who hit the first nail with it —
for he had nothing to hide —
it remained the same hammer throughout.

Tóraíocht

Leanamar do chomhairle ina hiomláine
is ba mhaith an chomhairle í —
áit a maróimis ár gcuid, gan í a bhruith ann;
áit a mbruithfimis ár gcuid, gan í a ithe ann;

áit a n-íosfaimis ár gcuid, gan dul a luí ann;
áit a rachaimis a luí, gan éirí ann.
Ní dheachamar i gcrann aon choise
ní dheachamar in uaimh thalún,

ní dheachamar in oileán mara
is cé go ndearnamar rud go huile
is go hiomlán ort, thángthas orainn faoi dheireadh
agus olc ná maith níl aon dul as againn.

Pursuit

We followed your advice in every detail
and it was good advice:
where we killed our food, not to cook there;
where we cooked our food, not to eat there;

where we ate our food, not to lie there;
where we lay down, not to rise up there.
We never climbed a tree with just one trunk,
we never went deep down into a cave in the ground,

we did not flee into an island in the sea
and though we did it all, the whole thing
that you advised, they reached us in the end
and good nor bad we now have no escape.

Michael O'Loughlin

Latin as a Foreign Language

I suppose I should feel somehow vindicated
   To see our declensions bite deeper
      Than our legionaries' swords —
      But somehow I don't.
   We're a mixed lot here, devils
   To drink; old senatorial types and
Discarded favourites, poets without patrons etc.

When asked why they're here they might answer
   About duty to the empire, missionary zeal
      Or simply the spirit of adventure —
      All rot, of course.
   No one leaves Rome unless
   He has to, or not exactly because he has to
Like a vulgar soldier in a conscripted legion.

But things somehow conspire to force him out.
   Not all poets find patrons, not all
      Fits smoothly into public life —
      You know how it is.
      One wrong word in the wrong ear.
   One fateful opportunity fluffed, and
You may as well forget it. Who understands these things?

Some say they lie in the lap of the gods but either way
   We end up here in the backwaters of empire
      Drumming our illustrious tongue
         Into barbarian skulls
      And polishing up the phrases
   Of the oafs who govern in Rome's name.
Like I said, a mixed lot, refugees all from obscure failures.

Some marry local girls, and sprout blond beards
   And curls overnight. Poor bastards!
      How can they take seriously
         Those bovine bodies
         Those gaudy faces lisping bad breath.
   Who could write poetry for such as these?
I think about these things a lot, but come to no conclusion

During the freezing winter nights sitting round the wine
   And olives, telling tales of sunnier days
      Sucking ancient bits of gossip
         Down to the dry pit
      Cato elaborates his pet theory;
   How Rome will someday crumble to dust
Beneath the barbarian heel, and only our precious language

Will survive, a frail silken line flung across the years
   But I don't know. Who among these barbarians
      Would give a fart in his bearskin
         For Horace or Virgil
      Or any of us? All they want is enough
   To haggle with a Sicilian merchant, or cheat
The Roman tax collector out of his rightful due.

But late at night, when I stumble out into
   The sleet and cold I was not born to
      And feel the threatening hug
         Of those massive forests
         Stuffed with nameless beasts
      And the great godless northern sky
Threatening me with its emptiness and indifference

To me and all that are like me — then, sometimes,
   I think he may be right; that
      We are the galley slaves
         Sweating below
         Bearing the beautiful
      Princess who sits in the prow
Across the ocean to her unknown lover.

Boxer

The days lurch towards me like a punch-drunk boxer
Swinging away with their horrible hammy fists
Pummelling away, unable to hurt me
— But I can't bring myself to avoid them,
With their battered Ernest Borgnine faces
And their cauliflower ears
And their stupid swollen horse's eyes
Begging me to let them win.

I can't bring myself to look at you
My head squats down on my chest
Like an old bag full of sawdust
And we continue, and the heart endures,
The heart in its red tent
A crushed head with a boxer's face
Its eyes clogged with blood
Blood streaming out of its ears

Three Fragments on the Theme of Moving Around in Cities

I. Epitaph for Matt Talbot

"Skua!" "Skua!", the gulls shriek
Skiting above the stinking Liffey
Where your name flaps
Like a plastic sack
Along the deserted quays
In the minds of old women
Carrying their shopping
From chapel to chapel.

II. Little Suburban Ode

In our cold, gloomy Napoli
Pasolini's Nordic children
Cruise the icy pot-holed streets
In stolen diplomatic limos

Rocketing round the broken corners
Like steel balls in a pinball game
Before they fly right off the board
— Or slot home safely in the suburbs.

III. Berlin

Under a bruised sky the empires meet
And freeze. I don't like that I like it here,
The cold stench of flesh become stone
The palled appalling innocence of the heart
A giddy dog loping through ruins
A god on the morning of creation
His mouth full of juicy bones.

To a Child in the Womb

Little Brendan, snug in your coracle
you are right to be sailing west
to surrender your tonsured head
to the wave's harsh lick.

Your clerks have copied our manuscripts
in every one of your cells
decorated with birds and beasts
such as you'll see in the New World.

Here in the old country
the Dark Ages are always beginning
and the light that was in Troy
falls on empty motorways.

We are standing on the shore
our feet sinking into the earth.
We raise our hands to bid farewell
to catch you when you fall

over the world's edge.

Yellow

I stamped through the pastures
booting the heads off buttercups
I stormed in out of the wheatfield
into a country kitchen
and let out my gurrier roar:
"Yellah! Yellah! Yellah!"
But she took me on her knee
and said: no, it's yellow
but that was a colour
I had never seen
till I saw her stretched on a hospital bed
the yellow of cancer and nicotine

Mary O'Malley

Anniversary

Somewhere between the tight silences, the hard
screaming rows, we have dodged words,
blades aimed to go in deep and wound

and sometimes they have hit, as they say, home,
have gone in and found bone
or worse, poison-tipped, a lobe of lung

or liver. Amazing how with all that going on we
have found time to build a house we like,
rear two children we love but do not always see

and look bewildered when we realise
our almost grown-up son could soon be moving out
with our prayers, but not without our hurts,

as each wonders what damage we have done
and will love ever be enough to make it up to them
and one another. We are still together — amazing

that skiving off from adult duties this afternoon
I find myself astride your hips, our laughter ringing
along the beechwood in our ochre bedroom.

My Mac

I was in Dun Eochaill when lightning struck
my Apple Mac and roasted its little modem.
I stepped outside the prehistoric fort
summoned on the mobile phone
to watch the thunder heading towards me
— a pathetic fallacy, I know but one I'm fond of.
"It's happened again," he said.

We bought a PC. It sits in the nook, gaudy and vulgar
like a trophy wife. Fit for soccer and
turning tricks, trying to get us interactive.
I hate it like poison. I don't want to interact
with my dictionary, nor yet a thesaurus.

Now when I go into my room and turn on my modest
long-suffering machine, an electronic pen, nay quill,
I sit thinking how like a blank white page
the screen is, how still and unassuming the little icon.
The apple in the top left hand corner will become
the first decorated letter on a saint's vellum if this goes on
much longer. Why can't the people who made
the atom bomb fix this? Why do I have to sit looking
at burnt offerings, asking what attracts lightning. Twice.

Angry Arthur
For Maeve

He sat on his bed in a rage that grew
like a thundercloud and ripped its electrical
discharges across the sky and into the earth
where it caused such tectonic havoc —
a subterranean clatter of dishes —
that the house shook, the planet tore apart
and Arthur was left on a raft of rock out in space
lamenting his temper.
         For years
it was your favorite book and when
every door in the house banged, the walls shook,
and we said "Forget the damned dishes so"
and you stomped upstairs, leaving the dog
covering his eyes in relief, the air shivering
in your wake and the proper parenting guide
in flitters at our feet
         you always lay

on your duvet covered raft, way beyond us.
"I'm not sorry," you'd shout and I screamed back
"See if I care," because at those times
I was only your own age and afraid
you would stay out there
in your lonely orbit and leave us forever
because we had been bad.

The Poet's Fancy

The moment the long stride
is heard across the countryside
the bush telegraph of otter,
badger, thrush flashes the message.
"Quick lads, run, scatter, dive.
It's the poet." They're afraid of their lives
where they'll end up —
in a trap, at the end of a hook
or dead on some godforsaken road
in the west of Ireland,
their little paws raised for all to pity.

Either that or having sex
in trees, pools, nests, anywhere but beds
with the entire cast of the Faber Book of Beasts
looking on — poets have no sense of decency.
They could even lose their pelts,
skins, feathers.
By the time his shadow falls across the river
the only thing to greet the poet's eager look
is the swirl of a disappearing tail
and the hush of a thousand thrushes
holding their breath. The badger,
knowing what he knows, has long gone.

Liam Ó Muirthile

When Will I Get to Be Called a Man
i.m. Rory Gallagher

Cloisim an Delta ag feadaíl aníos ón seanriasc
i riff na blues, mar a bheadh glao cuirliúin.
Phrioc na soilse flioscaí bána amach ar mo chulaith
fé na dioscaí stróib oíche a bhí an seoltóir
leictreach ag floscadh na blues ina rac 'n ról. Phlugáil
sé isteach is sheol a phabhar sa chiorcad a las
na sruthanna aeir os cionn na habhann, is ba léir
ár slí isteach in aimpéir na bhfear ar domhan.
"Olann san éadach," a liúigh bean ar an urlár rince
ar bogadh nuair a dheineas iarracht sailchnis
a scuabadh díom, is chroith cith cáithníní fearmón
ar mo ghuala ag spineáil gan aon dul siar.
An gob fada, folt den fheamainn dhubh, cromadh
droma, na truslóga ag lapadaíl i láib na Laoi,
leanas cuid den slí é ag seachaint na poill nárbh eol
d'éinne ach dó féin, fear na habhann ar mhinicíoch
na blues fó-thoinn. Cloisim an Delta ag glaoch aníos ón
sean-riasc i riff an chuirliúin, an fhead chaol
ón nead ag cuilitheáil ina fead leictrithe i dtiúin.

Basáin Mhara
do John Keogh

Seolaimid an cuan amach
ag leanúint samhlacha éisc
ag sondáil ar scáileán,
ach ag brath ar do ghrinneas
caol ar an domhain

is tú ar an stiúir anois, atáim.

Bhí góstaí riamh ag éamh
os cionn an chuain;
na faoileáin gan anam
ar lánboilg ag guairdeall
thart ar an tigh solais,
scréachairí ina dtost go fóill.

Tá caoineadh cine crochta
ar aer na mara, an uaill ghoirt
a scuab sruth na muintire
san Atlantach, is sinne
leis an suaill béal amach
ag dul ag iascach basán mara.

Glanaimid linn go dtí an cuaisín,
áit ar mharaís breac go minic
cheana; faill ard ag titim le talamh
isteach ón gceann tíre, na slata
feistithe, inneall múchta, ag imeacht
le sruth, réidh don chéad chaitheamh.

Leis an díthrá ar an éadomhain,
is mó an seans iad a fháil;
crochann na línte ar barr uisce,
na clocha grinnill ag caitheamh
a scáil aníos agus sinn ag druidim
le talamh, is na duáin gan aon bhasán.

Maolaíonn ár seanchas ár dtnúthán,
is músclaíonn do spéis i ngach gné
bheo den iascach mo dhúil féin
gan ainéistéis sa bheatha, is an tonn
a bhraithim fém bhonn ar thóin
an bháid ag luascadh le sruth reatha.

Cuirimid dínn gan oiread is breac
a mharú. Beirimid ar na doruithe
is le cúpla tarrac tá lán buicéid
maircréal againn ar bord; cé méid
bíoga sa soicind sara mbíonn an dé
deiridh múchta ina gcuid putóg?

Fágann tú an stiúir fúm ag filleadh,
is le sracfhéachaint amháin siar
tugaim fé ndeara do lámha
liachta i mbun aclaíochta scine
ag sciobadh na bputóg as an mbreac
mara, mar a glanadh mo dhlúth
féin chun siúil le bás mo dhlúthchara.

Baile an Tae

Cuireann siad an tae amach dúinn le féile chroíúil
   i mbuaile an tí i mBaile an tSléibhe
is táim thar n-ais i dtigh feirme m'uncail tráthnóna
   Domhnaigh agus sceitimíní orainn tar éis
achrann an bhóthair ón gcathair. Táimid tagtha ó
   Hangzhou is deinim gáire an athuair ag
cuimhneamh ar mo mháthair á rá: "Ólfaimid an
   tae as na sásair inár seasamh is ná bac
aon dua a chaitheamh le cupaí a ní," nuair is
   gloiní a chuirtear chugainn de scoth tae
Longjing. Cuireann na gloiní ag siollaireacht tur
   te sinn chomh cluthar ag an mbord leis
na leapacha tor tae neadaithe sa sliabh fé
   cheobhrán an lae, is bainim gáire as
muintir an tí ar eachtraí dóibh gur beathaíodh
   muca le tae an chéad uair a tháinig
boscaí raice de i dtír ar oileán ar chósta Atlantach
   na hÉireann. Tá cuireadh againn chun
suipéir is ní fada go mbíonn scrogall á ghearradh

fén sconna, cleití á stoitheadh is á ní in uisce
bog i mbuicéad, is deir an feirmeoir tae gurb é an lá
is fearr chun an barr a bhaint lá ómós
a thabhairt do na mairbh. Tá oiread is a bheathódh
   muc sa bhéile ar an gcnoc — feoil, glasraí fiaine,
bambú, yamanna, seilire spíosraithe is cumhracht mhilis
   an tae ó na goirt ar an aer tríothu. Deir ár n-aoi
Síneach gurb é a nós riamh an fhlúirse is blúire de gach mias
   mar a thagann a bhlaiseadh, gurb é an fuíoll a fhágtar
seachas pláta a ghlanadh comhartha brothall boilg duine is é
   sásta ina aigne. "Sú coiligh óig," a deirim leo a deir
muintir sa bhaile an sú is fearr ar fad is tugann sé léim as a
   chraiceann á rá gur coileach sé mhí a mharaíodar
dúinn féin, na heachtrannaigh a thaistil chucu i bhfad ó bhaile.
"Tá íocshláinte sa tae agus ardú meanman," ar sé,
"Tá, nuair a dháiltear le croí mór é tá baile anseo i gcéin
   i mbaile an tae," a deirim, agus cóngas an bhia
eadrainn. "Dhá dhuilleog le chéile, dédhuilleach ar an gcraobh
   an uair is ceart stoitheadh lá ómóis an earraigh,"
ar sé, ag ardú a ghloine Domhnaigh dá shinsear féin, is ardaím
   mo ghloine áiméin dom mháthair féin, gloine tae
   seaimpéin dá suáilce ionamsa.

Li Am ar Fhalla Mór na Síne

Pé tocht a bhuail mé ar an slí anuas na céimeanna
   ar Fhalla Mór na Síne, chaitheas stopadh
chun mo cheann a chur amach tríd an mbearna
   lámhaigh agus ligint do na deora teacht
le súil nach gcífeadh mo pháirtithe iad. Ba mhó de
   ghliondar a bhí ann ná náire go raibh an
mianach fós im gháire agus im chorp mé a thabhairt
   suas is anuas stráice amháin d'éachtaí móra an
domhain, is a rá gur ceann d'éachtaí móra an duine
   é céim a chur le céim chun an turas iomlán
a dhéanamh go laethúil go ceann scríbe; abair é sin

os ard leis an mbean ag *pedal*áil ualaigh ar an
trírothach fé mar a bheadh an tigh á thabhairt léi aici
ar a cúl is cloisfidh tú "Gread leat a *bendan*"
nó pé focal eile atá acu ar stumpa amadáin i nGaeilge
na Síne. Fós féin éacht de chuid na bhFlaitheas
ab ea é mo dhá chois a bheith ar talamh a chreideas féin
ag ligean lem thocht buíochais is don diabhal —
a fhuip ina ghlaic agus a cheannaithe chomh dubh leis
an daol sa teampall Dao-ach — le gach mioscais.
"Grá Li Am" a sheolas go dtí mo mhac gan buille ceart
a dhéanamh ar litreacha na haibítre,
ag téacsáil ar an bhfón póca, is ba shaighdiúir mé ag
máirseáil san am cianda ar an *Chángchéng*
ag cuimhneamh ar an mbaile i gcéin, is gurbh é an t-am
a bhí an uair sin ann an t-am a bhí anois ann
agus an fón póca im dhorn mar phíce chun sáite
ag cnagadh *ping-ping* do chur "Grá Li Am"
abhaile ina íce ráite os cionn Beijing.

Ringabella

Tearmann suain
ón taobh eile den chuan
chun éaló ó phlód an Domhnaigh.
Trá bheag chloch, crainn chun scátha,
tráchtaireacht iomána ag teacht
is ag imeacht ar chuma na mbád
ar múráil ag casadh a ngob
sna siotaí gaoithe.

Shamhlaínn clog ag bualadh fó-thoinn,
is chaithfí éisteacht chomh cruinn
leis an dtaoide chun é a chlos
is a chuirfí bior ar chluais
chun breith ar phointe boise
scóir díreach is tráchtaire an chluiche
ag dul as sa tuile ag líonadh.

Chaithfeá scaoileadh leis,
fé mar a ligeas Rinn an Bhile
isteach im líon is gur bhraitheas
ná féadfainn an chling a bhí,
a bhaint go deo as an dá ainm
i gcomhcheol seanma.

Cloisim anois an ceol céanna
iontu araon is bainim cling eile
as ringabellabile, rinnabhilebella,
á scaoileadh amach le gáire
mar a bhíonn an poc amach
á thógaint fó-thoinn ag mo chúl báire.

Eitseáil Bheo

Bíonn rud éigin de shíor ag teacht
idir an dán atá le déanamh
agus an ceann a deintear.
Cág ag grágaíl Gotcha!
ó cheannlíne gháifeach na gcrann.
Cló trom na bpréachán
ag sileadh dúigh sa bháisteach.
Aigéad an lae mhiotalaigh
ag ithe faonsolais.
Wow áil aláraim ag cur
ceoltéama an chillscannáin as tiúin,
nuair is ceisteanna
bunúsacha is gá a fhiosrú;
ábhar orgánach a ocsaiginiú
trí fhótaisintéis focal;
forógra fornocht an tséasúir
a dhréachtadh ar thréigean duilliúir;
conas sonas a eitseáil
trí línte a ghreanadh ar ghloine,
conas sonas a chur

ag análú,
nuair a dhúnann an doras
de phlab sa díle.
Osclaíonn míle.

Suantraí Sarah is Asmahane

*cailín a fuair bás lena máthair Asmahane i mbuamáil Bhéiriút,
Lúnasa 2006*

Ó, cé hí seo atá ina luí
chomh támh
ag doras beag mo chroí,
lena folt donnrua
is éadan na fola
is an dá choisín
ina ruainní feola?
Seó sín seó, hó-ó-ó
Lú lú ló, ú-ó.

Ó, cé hí seo atá ina luí
chomh támh
fé smionagar an tí,
gan dídean fé dhíon
dom leanbhaín sámh,
ach seomraín mo chroí
is mo chual cnámh?
Seó sín seó, hó-ó-ó
Lú lú ló, ú-ó.

Ó, cé hí seo atá ina luí
chomh támh
is chomh ciúin ó,
ní i gcófra na marbh
a chuirfinn tú a chodladh
ach i gcliabhán óir
is mo lámh á bhogadh.

Seó sín seó, hó-ó-ó
Lú lú ló, ú-ó.

Ó, sí Sarah atá anseo ina luí
chomh támh
ag doras beag mo chroí,
m'iníon is mo ghreann
mo chailín deas donn,
is óró bog liom í
an cailín deas donn.
Seó sín seó, hó-ó-ó
Lú lú ló, ú-ó.

San Aonad Alzheimer

"An bhfeiceann tú an fráma sin thall?"
"Crochta san aer? Cad tá ar siúl ann?"
"Ó . . ."
"Sníomh is dócha."
"Sea, sníomh."
"An bhfuil mórán daoine ag obair ann?"
"Céad caoga duine ag sníomh."
"Agus cén gnó atá agat féin?"
"An áit a rith."
"An bhfuil ag éirí go maith leat?"
"An-mhaith."
"Ag obair ó mhaidin go hoíche."
"Ó mhaidin go hoíche. Ach tá cuid acu . . . seo . . . antrioblóideach."

Luíonn sé siar ina chathaoir, lúbtha ar chuma crúca ar
a chliathán, as láthair uaidh féin sa seomra lae
istoíche. Glúine ar chuma dhá ubh ag gobadh
trín bpluid. Mílí ar a chneas páipéir ón teilifís ag
caochadh sa chúinne. Ligeann fear liú allta. Greadann
fear tráidire lena bhosa. Pléascann buama san Iaráic
i súile fir. Scaipeann lúidíní leanaí, matáin

máithreacha, polláirí póilíní, ionathair aithreacha, ar
fud an bhabhla torthaí agus ar na fallaí. Titeann
cloigeann teasctha anuas ón síleáil agus rabhlálann
ó thaobh taobh ar an urlár. Straois ait ar a chlab
basctha.

"Tá tart an bháis orm."
"Ól braon uisce as seo tríd an dtuí."
"Seo, breá réidh anois, ní theastaíonn uaim tú
a thachtadh."

An Seanduine

do Iarla Ó Lionaird

An garsún ag canadh
Aisling Gheal
is é chomh hiomlán
laistigh den amhrán,
bhí a oiread den aisling
á chanadh súd

is a bhí de féin
ag gabháil amhráin.
Sheol an aisling tríd,
is d'ardaigh ár gcoiscéimne
go buan oiread na fríde
os cionn talún.

Ba dheacair riamh
ó shin dhá chois a leagadh
ar chlár an domhain
gan cuimhneamh go rabhamar
bonn ar bhonn ag siúl
in *Aisling Gheal Gharsúin*.

An oíche cheana
sheasaimh an t-amhránaí fir

i suantraí an tseanduine
is shníomh lúba fada gutha
a chuir codladh thar n-ais
ina chodladh.

Nocht an seanduine
i gcúinne na hadharta
ag titim chun suain
ina shiúl aislingiúil,
is an suantraí á bhogadh
siúd go buan le guth garsúin.

Derry O'Sullivan

Translated by Gréagóir Ó Dúill

Finit

níor tógadh amach an phlocóid
go dtí deireadh na féile:
an chraic,
bairillí gáire caite an fhuinneog amach
ar mheisceoirí déanacha, ar oibrithe mocha,
súil aníos ainchreidmheach acu
ar ár n-árasán lasta,
rud anaithnid ag eitilt
ó thráthnóna go maidin
lastuas, níos gealtaí
ná carbad ceangailte
de stair na gaoithe,
piachán ceoil ar
scornach ár gcarad,
guth ar ghuth á
mhúchadh idir mhéara,
tuirse gur fágadh sinn
beirt, an "Slán" deiridh ráite,
ag amharc ar chuisíní scaipthe
(timpeall a trí phléasc orainn
fiús sa seomra suite
ach fágadh an chistin)
gan focal
shíneamar ar na leacacha
i dteannta gréithre is sáspan,
ár gcoirp aon chorp
gan tionlacan
ach fuaim bhán
ar raidió lasta,
an clár deiridh thart.
Nuair a thosnaigh céadnuacht
an lae
thógais amach an phlocóid.

Finit

The plug wasn't taken out
till the end of the party
the craic,
barrels of laughter hurled out of the windows
down onto the late night drunks, the early morning shiftworkers,
with their unbelievers' eyes
turned to our brightlit apartment,
to the unknown that flew down from evening to morning
madder than a chariot harnessed
to the edge of the wind,
as the throats grew hoarse
as mouths fell to fingers, to tiredness
until we were left alone, we two,
the last "goodbye" said,
and we looked around at the scattered cushions
(the fuse went in the sitting room, about three o'clock
but we had power in the kitchen)
without a word we lay down on the flagged floor
among the dishes and the saucepans
our bodies one body
and with no sound but the white noise
of the turned-on radio,
the last programme over.
And when it started over, the first
news of the day
it was then you pulled out the plug.

Paul Perry

The Gate to Mulcahy's Farm

The gate to Mulcahy's farm is crooked,
sinking into infirm soil like a ship
from the Spanish Armada if you like,
forged and felled in some dark cave

to find itself jaded with flaking eroded gilt
leaving the striations, prison-like,
shaded a coppery green. A gate without
a handle and unlike all others in any

neighbouring field without the dull sanguine
frame that swing to and fro like a hinge,
or a door itself to some other world.
No, this is no ordinary gate and there is

something majestic in its stolid refusal
to swing, something absurd even.
Perhaps this is another version of heaven,
imagine the bedroom it might once have graced,

this brass headboard, this discarded,
transported remnant of love's playground,
and look, two golden and intact globes
rest on either end, both transcendental transmitters,

receivers maybe of rough magic,
piebald love, communicating not sleep,
sleep no more, but wake, wake here
to the earth and imagine if you want

the journey of such an armature
of fecund passion, what hands gripped
these bars, what prayers were murmured
through the grate of this ribald cagery?

Imagine too the man who must have
hurled and pitched and stabbed
this frame into the ground, in a dark rain of course
after his wife had died, her passing to us unknown

though you know this
that there must have been some act
of violence within this frame-work,
some awful, regrettable pattern caught

in the form of what, wind rushing through a brass
headboard, an exclamation point to the querulous
division of fields, could we be talking border-country,
and the broken, airy, moss-eaten stone walls.

Think about when the farmer died and the farm
was sold, think about what happened the field, empty
of its cows, still with its stones and grey soil,
maybe this is Monaghan,

maybe some day it, the brass headboard
you are looking at now, will be sold
to an antiquarian in a Dublin shop,
brought there on a traveller's horse and cart,

not smelted down or disassembled, but sold
to a shop where some lady with a wallet
will buy the thing, the elegant shabbery before you
that is the gate to Mulcahy's farm. As for the bed

itself, we can speculate, let it have sunken
into the earth, or better still let the earth be the bed,
the cot, mattress and berth to this sinking headboard,
this beautiful incongruous reliquary of misplaced passion.

Dana Podracká

Translated by Robert Welch from the Slovak

A Parcel from Prison

I, a political prisoner, confirm
by the signature below, that I have consigned
to the state all my personal and civic possessions
and that I have no formal requests to make
to the authorities. I also declare that,
while under escort I lost one handkerchief,
possibly at the time of my arrest.
I agree to the following items being struck from the list:

> a pair of broken spectacles in a case
> an old hand brush
> a neckerchief
> a pair of mittens
> a chessboard with pieces
> another 4 handkerchiefs
> 12 books
> application forms for a retrial
> a Ziak fountain pen

Leave me just enough strength
to fight free of the snares of misgiving
when the sun falls before sunset
on the grey concrete floor summoning
the shadows that wait to greet me.

A White Bedsheet

I could only write it with the white
graphite pencil of the blind, white
on a white sheet that is a blank
mouth to swallow every word so that
I can recall only the essential part,
the skull of it:

Belbo: I hope you do not think that when
       Rabbis speak of the Torah
       they mean just the scroll,
       the words inscribed thereon.
       The Torah is really us, those who
       use the language so as to change
       the nature of the body. Change
       what is written in the Book
       and you modify the world and when
       you modify the world you will change
       the nature of your body.

Belbo, please, don't leave. Say
if change is only possible alone,
or can it be accomplished with someone
else, a partner, the two roped
together like a pair of mountaineers?
Like Rembrandt to his paintings,
or Nietzsche to his Christ.

Or like the starving little girls,
Anna and Maria, who with two hands clasped
each other, and with the other two prayed
that their bodies might be changed to bread
to improve the world; which they would wrap
in a white sheet in a double cross
which needs to be bleached in the sun.

The Place of Execution of the First President

Thank you, Lord, for the gift of sadness
that brought me even past the metal door
into the cell where they hanged our president
and where now they kennel dogs in cages.

I can hear them barking and then their howling
fades to a quiet that succeeds in which
a silver chalice is lifted up, the final Mass
is being said behind the metal door,
and there is a last breaking and sharing of bread.

Thank you, Lord, for the gift of shame
in which the dog-handler told us of the lime-pit,
a place in the yard where you could see
the sunrise, as he tried to hide, in the pocket
of his uniform, his ten o'clock snack.

Billy Ramsell

Breath

These are the fragile hours, the bird-dominated silent hours
that dawn is too simple a word for.

For this Sunday morning light is pearl-pale and fragile
as it reveals the almost empty quay,
gulls that spire from the river to feast on Saturday night's debris,

a drowsy street sweeper and you and me
standing almost still on a foot bridge
as we stare into the mussicating, stout black Lee.

Because keeping schtum was never my strong point
I can't resist staining the silence
with some remarks about how special you are.

But as I draw breath to speak,
as I inhale one waft of this sweet dirty morning,
I remember Flaubert's lament
that language is a broken inadequate thing,
a toddler's tune played on pots and pans,

that every poet's words of love
tell us only of the poet himself,
for the lover resists description
as cliffs the devouring tide.

Because you are the mirror in which I see myself
without failure or defect
you reflect my words back at me
and whatever lines I shape with this breath
will scramble in air
like these greedy, hunting gulls
and circle your beauty
but never alight on you perfectly.

With this breath I could sketch some things for you:
children gathering stones on a beach in September,
plucking only smooth, round ones
from the infinitely varied layer
that conceals the sand like a second skin,
like beautiful, damp scales.

I could say your hair is honey
and your skin a sweeter, more translucent honey
and all this might even be true
but it is passé, just a cliché,
and says more about me than it does about you.

Or I could say: *"Lady take my hand
and walk me through this sleeping world.
And we might risk it all, take one chance
on each other before morning has unfurled
its curtain on the litter, the river, everything"*

But now the poem is sounding like a song
and as you know, too well, I cannot sing.

Or with this breath I could launch into a list again
mention the wooden room in which you live,
all the things you give to me without even meaning to
but sometimes intentionally,
that your every second thought is for somebody else
(in this, however, you have no choice)
how you dance, when you dance,
with rhythm with excellent poise,
that I have been woken by your heart's easy rhythm
or that the healthy part of you outweighs my own unhealthy part . . .

But that's just talking about me again.
It's all I can do.

Before this weary, new, hungover world
tilts another few degrees
I will unleash this breath into the morning I snatched it from,
not as praise or recollection

or in the form of some desperate plea,
but into your own mouth
and I will taste the air
that has made your lungs bulge,
flooding their intricate networks
down to the endless forested alveoli,
that has sampled the capillaried intimate dark
no-one will ever know,
that tastes like your kisses tasted
when you kissed me dozens of times before,
like millet, alfalfa, rosemary, and yarrow
of bread and lemon,
of salt or banana or the night before.

Middle Distance

Strange Intimacies
and *Love's Treadmill: Romance in the Post-Human Epoch*
are the titles of two books I will never write
about the hours we spent jogging by the river.

When the factories sparkled on the estuary's far-side,
showering the water
with the glitter of night-shifts and sleepless machines

we huffed and puffed through the melting twilight,
trundled through bushes, as the gravel whispered
and the chalk dust flew, in the August air
with steady acceleration, we moved through those laneways,
tangled with brambles, heavy with scent and temptation.

"This is so much nicer that the gym," you panted,
"that mucid air, the endless treadmill and MTV,
all that staring into the middle-distance of the mirror."
At some moist, heaving version of yourself
straining against the glass, sprinting for the world,
to be spat, drenched and uncertain, into existence.

I picked up the pace as the evening wilted
but you stayed on my shoulder only inches behind.

This, jogging together, is the strangest intimacy
when our breathing harmonises
and our rhythms mingle
in a fugue of breath and heartbeat,
and in the sweat sprays
from out bodies heaving in tandem.

But it can't last, and, after our sprint finish,
when you leaned on me
and I was breathing sea-salt from your beach-brown skin
and from your hair some clammy tang

I realised you would always be somewhere in the middle-distance,
that I could no more reach you than I could my own reflection in the gym's mirror,
that I could repeat these steps forever and never come to you.

"That was brilliant . . . Savage cardio . . . Let's do it again"

If I could breach you behind the glass of yourself . . .
If I could touch with a remembered touch . . .

I looked out at the nitrified river,
at the bubbles popping gently on its agitated surface
until my breath came back.

Complicated Pleasures

We were in bed together listening to Lyric,
to a special about the Russians,
when the tanks rolled into Babylon.

For a second I could feel their engines,
and the desert floor vibrating,
in the radio's bass rattling your bedroom
as the drums expanded at the centre of the *Leningrad*,
as those sinister cellos invaded the melody.

We'd been trying, for the hell of it,
to speak our own tongue
and I was banging on about Iberia when your eyelids closed:
"*Tá do lámh i mo lámh*" I whispered "*ar nós cathair bán
sna sléibhte lárnach, d'anáil ar nós suantraí na mara i mBarcelona.
Codladh sámh.*"

But as I murmured "sleep, my darling, sleep" into your sleeping ear
I found myself thinking of magnets
of what I'd learned in school about the attraction of opposites,
that the two of us, so similar,
could only ever repel each other.

For the closer I clutched your compact body
the further apart we grew.

You have eleven laughs
and seven scents
and I know them like a language.
But what will it matter when the bombs start falling
that you could never love me?

So I just looked at the night sky through your attic window
and thought that the planets, like us, are slaves to magnetism,
gravity's prisoners, as they dance the same circles again and again.
And even the stars ramble mathematically,
their glitter preordained to the last flash.

Then you turned in my arms
and it was midnight again on the beach at Ardmore,
when the starlight collected in some rock pool or rain pool
among the ragged crags at the water's edge
and the two of us sat there
and we didn't even breathe
determined not to disturb that puddle's flux,
the tiny light-show in its rippling shallows,
the miniature star-charts that for a moment inhabited it.

Which made me think of the satellites

gliding and swivelling in their infinite silence,
as they gaze down on humanity's fumbling,
on you and me, as you sniffled against my neck
and the drumming, drumming flooded your bedroom,
on powerful men in offices pressing buttons
that push buttons in powerful men,
on the tanks, like ants, advancing through the wilderness.

Those pitiless satellites, knowing for certain in their whispering circuits
that, like our island's fragile language,
like Gaudi's pinnacles and the *Leningrad* symphony,
— even worse — like your teeth and our four hands,
the very stars through which they wander would be gone,

those brittle constellations with the billion sinners that orbit them,
extinguished in a heartbeat, absolved instantly,
as if your hand had brushed the water slowly once.

Still Life with Frozen Pizza
to Ger Gleeson

I unwrapped the plastic and slid the icy disc
onto the oven shelf. 15 minutes later, as the TV rippled

into wakefulness, the tray made a presentable still life:
the pizza's cracked lunar surface, its pepperoni nipples,

the burnt ridge round its edge, the remote
that liked to sit in my hand, snug as a gun

in its futuristic sleekness,
a phaser permanently set to stun.

I navigated *Countdown*, sitcoms, pantomime wrestling,
rolling news. Somewhere bombs were falling:

the crosshairs at the centre of the grainy video.
A building dissolved in dust, its crater spoiling

the streetscape's geometric perfection. *Sky sports*,
I thought, *the next one will probably be pay-per-view.*

Full, I balked at the pizza's final quarter,
then pierced its plasticky skin with a spurt of goo.

A girl bawled at the camera, weary, untranslated,
a film of dirt on her denim, her face.

I popped the last cheese-string into my mouth, sat back
with a quiet burp of contentment, and flicked over to *Will & Grace*.

Ireland

This is the box I wake up in. My neighbours' noises drift
through its walls, their plumbing, curses and alarms

as I inhale your L'Oreal scent from the pillow.
You hit snooze and I lie in your arms.

As that malevolent box counts down to its whinny
I monitor the progress of the people upstairs. Each inhabits

a box like this one, a 120 foot flimsy box.
Boxes, it seems, are never single and breed like rabbits.

For these boxes we live in are formed from an older more solid box
and thousands of boxes process through the morning

at a funeral's pace; polished, plush and angular.
In a box like this, in the crystalline dawn, besuited and yawning,

I travel to manicured fields, where herds of grey, enormous boxes
swallow us. My own little box has a picture of you

in your autumn sweater, snapped by some Swede at the foot
of the Matterhorn, tacked above the beige box I stare into

at nested Window-boxes, at the endless tundra of empty boxes
beyond my cornered encampment of numbers, those figures in cells

on which so much depends. I wait for my Coke to drop from the box
on the mezzanine as I look down on a spreadsheet of cubicles.

Then I lunch on a frozen box. It rotates, in a box, for 5-7 minutes.
Ping! After which we repair to the Beckett suite

for the marketing quarterly, where we try, as per instruction,
to think outside the box. Then I'm ticking boxes in triplicate,

back in my box, or triplicating information in a white whirring box.
Till the boxes travel again, filling the twilight with snarls, whispers and exhaust,

and return me to our box, to our walls that can't shut out
upstairs' television, canned laughter and talk show host,

or the hoovering downstairs. Blushing with headlights and streetlights,
pulsing with sirens, violence and alarms, the night leans against this little box.

I want the News, *The Simpsons*, sizzling steak, But before
I turn on the box I get down on my knees and kiss your gentle, scented box.

Southern Shores

To your tiny ears my words make no more sense
than static, or management-babble,
or out-of-tune Chinese,
as you waddle down the beach beside me
your fragile hand in mine
over the sand that is almost hot enough to scald us.

There's an old couple stretched out on a picnic blanket
(licking sand-coated ice cream
as their crackling transistor
holds forth on a hurling match),
and two bikini'd teenagers playing netless tennis

that we step gingerly past
toward the ocean that offers us

a winking cerulean invite.

But up close, despite the sun,
it's freezing of course, and oddly grit grey,
and seaweed bobs suspended here and there
in colourful clumps

and I leap back, despite myself,
from its stinging opacity.

But it dowses our toes
and logs us into the ancient systems of water,
the falls, flows and evaporations that cocoon the earth,

> that join this ice-water lapping our ankles
> with the rain that greases the tenements in Moyross and Knocknaheeny

> that connect these shallows we jink and high-step through
> with the haze rising from the silos rusting in Kazakhstan

> that bind this tide now so suddenly up to my knees
> with the perspiration in the inner jungle that forms in beads
> on the fur of the sable monkey with the yellow fang and the filthy blood

> that link each weedy wave darkening my shorts
> with the Evian chilling at the marketing quarterly.

So what does it matter on this half-deserted strand
if I tell you the monsters are not real?

To your ears my words make no more sense
than radio interference
and besides these riders will not pass by
but will do things to the world and you.

And there is no queue
of wand-waving matriarchs to gird you with wishes,
only worriers like me.

Eve, this world will botch and bungle you,

just as it did the rest of us, despite anything I might say.

But on the off-chance let me wish you privacy.
I want to give you silence and darkness
not the city's glare and clang,
some fantastic leafy place
far from its night sky stained pink from the streetlights
that stain the back of the eyelids pink,
from its non-stop concerto
of road works and car alarms.

As a suckered frond,
of brown, textured flesh,
organic, alien,
attaches
itself
to my ankle

I want these stanzas to be a cove of words,
a storm-wall to see off the syrupy tide
of slogans, copy and strap-lines
that will daily wash over you,
each calibrated phrase refined
to your precise demographic,
moulded by moguls
to sell you
and sell you things
to shape you like shoreline.

But to your ears these words
make no more sense
than the shushings of the ocean

as you cling to me
and I trudge out further against
its weight of water,
past reptilian lengths and punk hair-dos
that slowly bob by us
and black things that are like webs.

And what does it matter,
as I plod out from that half-deserted strand
through massed, vast flotillas of seaweed,
that you can't understand me?

For these erosions, these alterations
the world has visited upon you,
and the alterations that will yet be visited,
can be reversed or limited by speech
no more than this tide now so clotted
with browns and magentas
it could push seaweed up the beach forever
in damp mounds that consume the holiday homes
and choke the motorways
with mountainous wedges of stinking life
and make a streaming garden of the village.

Gabriel Rosenstock

Translated by Gabriel Rosenstock

As gach póir Díot

As gach póir Díot scallann an ghrian
Ar Do dhamhsa gan chríoch
Taobh dorcha na gealaí is geal
Má osclaíonn Tú Do bhéal
Éalóidh réaltaí, canfaidh iomainn Duit
Is Tusa iadsan
Ealaí ag eitilt go gasta ar gcúl
Conas a shamhlóinn barróg Uait
Mura bpléascfainn Id réaltbhuíon?

From each and every pore

From each and every pore look how the sun beams
On Your eternal dance
The dark side of the moon is bright
If You open Your mouth
Stars will escape and chant their hymns for You
You are they
Swiftly swans fly backwards
How can I imagine Your embrace
Without exploding in Your galaxy?

Seanfhalla

Féach an seanfhalla coincréite seo
Á théamh ag an ngrian.
Is gearr go mbeidh na seangáin amuigh

Chun damhsa Duit

Cé acu ab fhearr Leat é?
Gasta nó mall?
Nó iad a bheith ina stad?

Old Wall

Look at this old concrete w**all**
Wa**rmed** by the sun.
Soon the ants will **com**e out
To dance for You

What would You like?
Something rapid or languorous
Or that they be perfectly still?

Sneachta na mBunchnoc

Nuair a leánn sneachta na mbunchnoc
Fanann Do ghile linn
Ní istigh ná lasmuigh Duit
Ach i ngach cearn den chruinne
Is i mbólaí nár aimsíodh fós

Snow on the foothills

When the **snow** of the foothills vanishes
Your brightness stays
Neither inside nor outside are You
But in all the uni**verse**
And expanses not yet known

Do nochtacht

Chomh geal sin
Nach gcorraíonn suáilce ná duáilce ionam

Sea, Taoi nocht os mo chomhair
Ach nach bhfuil an féar nocht?
Tá an ghealach nocht
Nocht atá an drúcht
Is ní siocair pheaca dom iad.
Tusa nár pheacaigh riamh! A ghile!
Conas a pheacóinnse?

Your nakedness

So bright
Neither virtue nor vice stirs in me

Yes, You stand naked before me
But is the grass not naked?
The moon is naked
Naked the dew
They are not occasions of sin.
You who never sinned! Bright being!
How could I?

Gustaí mhí Aibreáin

Beireann Tú orm.
Mothallaíonn Tú mé.
Análaíonn Tú tríom.

April Gusts

You catch me.
You tousle me.
Breathe through me.

Samhradh

Ní sheasfad é
Ní sheasfad do shamhradhsa
Dófar m'inchinn
Ina gualach dubh
Chun portráid Díot a bhreacadh

Summer

I won't be able for it
I won't be able for Your summer
My brains will fry
Will turn to charcoal
To sketch Your portrait

Colúr Marbh

Dhein duine éigin
Tú a chlúdach le páipéar donn
Is Tú i Do luí ar an gcosán
Ach ní mór dúinn Do bhás laethúil a fheiscint
Is Tú ag filleadh ar neamhní

Dead Pigeon

Someone covered You
With brown paper
As You lay on the footpath
But we must see Your daily death
As You return to nothingness

Yugapat-srishti

Ní raibh puth ann roimhe seo
Ní raibh cloch
Ná abhainn
Ná pláinéad
Anois díreach a dheonaigh Tú dúinn iad

An neomat beannaithe so

Yugapat-srishti*

Not a puff of breeze existed
Not a stone
River
Or planet
This instance You bring them all into being

This sacred moment

instantaneous creation

Coillteán

Ligeas d**om** féin bheith im choillteán
Ar maos i mbainne is i gcodlaidín, gearradh mé
D'fhonn na nótaí is airde, is binne a chanadh Dhuit
Is bhíos i m'ain**geal** ainnis os **com**hair an tsaoil
Chanas gur chailleas mo ghuth
Is mo chiall
Tá mo smig maol
Triailfead cleas eile amárach
Im ghréasaí br**óg**
Sea, tosnód as an nua ag Do dhá throigh

Castrato

I allowed myself be**com**e a castrato
Steeped in milk, in opium, I was cut,
To sing the highest, the sweetest notes for You
What a miserable angel I was in the sight of the world
I sang until I lost my voice
And my senses
My chin is bare
I will try new tactics t**om**orrow
Be a shoe**mak**er
Yes, begin all over again at **Your** feet

Deirid gur daonnaí mé

Deirid gur d'fhuil is d'fhe**oil** mé
Ní he**ol** dóibh faic
D'ólais gach braon dí**om**, shlogais gach orlach,
Límse an smior atá ag glio**scar**nach t**im**peall do bhéil

They say I am human

They say I am flesh and blood
Little do they know
You drank each drop of me, **swallowed** every inch
I lick the **marrow** that **glistens** around **Your** mouth

Tóg Chun do Dhraenacha Mé

Ní chloisim an bháisteach os cionn an tráchta
Ach chím Do chuilithíní á síorleathnú
Tóg chun do dhraenacha mé
Síos faoin gcathair linn
Áit a nglanann na francaigh a bhféasóga
In ómós Duit
Do dhorchacht i réim

Take Me to Your Drains

I cannot hear the rain above traffic
But I see Your ripples everexpanding
Take me to Your **drains**
Let's go beneath the city
Where rats clean their whiskers
In **hom**age to You
Your darkness reigns

John W. Sexton

Vortex

My ten-year-old son is standing in the bath,
his body surrounded by an aura of steam;
bathwater runs down the spiked stalagtites of hair
that crown his head. His blue eyes are incredibly bright,
but communicate no more than the water at his feet.

    He is speaking a giggling song of invented words,
and I realize that he is mimicking the water,
for he has loosened the plug with his toe,
and the bath is turning in the vortex of its own substance,
sucking itself down into the foul sump beneath the house.

    And now he is braying like a donkey,
for a dissolving lump of soap has caught in the plughole,
and the tune played by the bath
has changed to this raw screech.

    I lift out the soap, and am surprised
that it seems alive with light, and for some reason
I am reminded of the soap created by Joseph Mengele
in the factories of Auschwitz. It was, from the accounts
of those who used it, a beautiful translucent soap,
made from the boiled remains of the murdered Jews.

    I lift my son from the bath and stand him on a towel.
He is quiet, no longer talking to the bath, for the bath is dry.
I rub his hair vigorously with a small towel;
he doesn't like it, but I persevere because it must be done.
I dry his body gently and am intrigued
that his skin has taken on some of the qualities
of the soap. Perversely, I am reminded once more
of Dr. Mengele. I remember a photograph I have seen
of him sitting in his office at Auschwitz-Birkenau.

On his desk is a lampshade, the twin of one
that he presented to the Feuhrer. It is made from human skin,
and I think,
    O Doctor Mengele, if my son was in your hands,
    what fine lampshade would you make of him?
    What cure would yours be
    for the light that is smothered inside him?

    As I dry his arms and thighs
I see that the imprinted pattern of teethmarks,
where he has bitten himself over and over again,
has begun to fade.
Being double-jointed, no part of his body is immune
from his teeth. His toes are raw,
where he has bitten the nail to the quick.

    As I clean the bath I send him into the hall
to put on his pyjamas. When I go out to him
he is lying on his back on the floor,
clapping the soles of his feet together,
applauding himself with his feet.
    O my silly son
    where is it that you came from?
    Wherever it is,
    you brought yourself whole, as you are.

    In the kitchen
I finish his hair with the dryer.
He takes hold of my waist and squeezes as tight as he can,
his fingers pinching my flesh.
"Squeeze," he says, "Squeeze."
Putting the dryer aside I loosen his fingers.
I lean down and kiss his head,
his wonderful clean hair,
but he is oblivious to my affection.

    Later I check on my son in his bed.
He is fast asleep, his arms folded loosely over his head.
    Mengele is standing at the far side of the room.

The hallway light from the crack in the door
slices through his body, swirls of dust are his only organs.
By his side, and along the sides of the bed,
I can see a half-circle of children, emaciated, their faces miserable.
Some are visibly retarded, some invisibly so,
but I can see what they are, know what they are,
have the space inside me that they fit.
        Mengele gazes at my sleeping son, but he says nothing,
his face betrays nothing.
        Only the children are talking, to themselves,
muttering incoherent mantras,
their voices like a vortex
drawing waters into unknown depths.

Frogspawn

I pulled them, dull, insensate, from the pond,
their black yolks a blind many-eyed mass. Light
shone through the jar, charged the transparent womb
of trembling jelly, but failed to penetrate
those dark eggs.
        Left on top of the wardrobe
by next morning they had sprouted like beans.
Three more days and they had tails and whiskers
and congregated on the jar's glass floor.
I put the jar to my ear, imagined
their urgent gossip.
        A breath could disturb
the surface of their world, and I would watch
as they scattered to nowhere, their esses
of tails waving them forwards through water
that contained no possibilities.
        That
day I poured them into a fishbowl, placed
it on top of the bookcase and waited.

Waited as I wait now for them to grow
large enough to pour back into the pond.
After that I know they will be taken
into the mouths of fish and birds.
                         Although,
no doubt, some will become frogs, get eaten,
again by birds, or sported to death by cats,
or scissored by the teeth of lawnmowers.

Or lay eggs of their own, that come to this.

Roland Gets It

Martin Marky had traded a headbutt
in the schoolyard, just 'cause Roland was smart.
Roland's head began to grow a turnip,
swelling its way over his skull through Maths
and even into History. "I don't
like the look of that," said his mother. "That's
what you get for fighting. Sit down and rest.
And don't fall asleep. Are you dizzy? Is
there a headache with it?"
                         "Yes, mum. I know,
mum. I will, mum. I won't mum. No, mum. Yes,
mum," said Roland. In the livingroom, plonked
down on the sofa, he began to die.
On the telly they were doing King Lear.
Roland watched through pain, felt the telly suck
him into itself. An old man croaked out
a song. And the song became real. Became
Roland. The turnip exploded into
pulp. Roland was everywhere at once. Coal
was shovelled into his mouth. The factories
of England smothered the countryside thick
with smoke. Winston Churchill gave the order
to bomb Berlin with anthrax. But first they

had to make the bomb; then he changed his mind.
Roland was astride an ebony horse,
dressed in armour oiled in blood. He rode through
a forest. Everything was totally
fucking mad. The ebony horse took him
fast as a breath up to the wooden gates
of a tower. Roland put a trumpet to his lips
and began to blow. The tower fell down
and squashed Roland flat. Fuckit anyway
didden ee blod id ollup an is ed
filled yup wiv th'yoll ov imman istree
ental ee fond imselv
                    awakening
against the hillside grass. He rose, naked,
sloughing off sleep. A white horse, taking leave
of its chomping, clipped up hoof-fulls of earth
as it came to him. And he took himself
up on its back, and rode the steepening
slope, down towards the beginning of is

Eileen Sheehan

Lady in White

Out of contrariness,
out of blackguarding,
out of need
for a small rebellion,
myself and my daughter
built a snow-woman.

Outside of the house
out of clumped snow
we fashioned her —
a sexy dame with a jaunty hat,
big bellied and laughing.

Then we were laughing too
and pleased to meet her
and she not at all surprised
that we'd conjured her to appear,
for one night only,
in our small town-garden.

Meanwhile word had spread
and women from the neighbourhood
were gathering, leading
small girls by the hand. The child
from up the street squirmed
through the laughter to present
her own string of shiny beads.

The man from next-door
couldn't help but give a sideways grin
at the sight of madam in her finery.

And as for herself she just stood there,
coquettishly tilting her head
and taking it all as her due.

But later, as myself and my daughter
held our aching hands to the fire,
she remained, looking
in through the window,
splitting her sides, growing thinner.

By morning she had disappeared
like we knew she would:
snow being the wrong medium;
too slight, too cold to hold her.

Until all around us from
the grass, the garden wall, the roof tops,
the bare trees, the very air,
there exhaled a kind of glistening.

Peter Sirr

The Names of the Houses

The village licks its fingers, belches, sighs, invites the yarn,
the childhood folly dragged up again and again
and as funny as ever. You know the pie has succeeded
in *Rustic Delight*, while over in *Well-Satisfied*
the prospective son-in-law has them eating out of his hand.
Architecture of contents, profit all year round,
and the houses full of mirrors. And all looked down upon
by the bloated in heaven, the sated
belt-loosening forebears telling it like it was,
joy without end, flagrant happiness
with, maybe, in the off-limits backstreet, the smelling–to–
    high-heaven
shithole hovel of the village weirdo —
look at him now, the witless fool, slopping out
in *The Place of Violence, The Maiden's Ruin, The Life as
    Normal*.

from "Here And There: A Notebook"

Here is a tight terrace
through whose thin walls
lives leak continually,
laughter and rows,
howl of petulant dogs,
my neighbour's piano
spilling daily into my head.
The street is narrow, the houses
so close, to glance out the window
is always to be met by eyes
glancing back. Humane horizons . . .

A Turkish family
lives opposite, the men serious
and dark-suited, the women in their
flowered dresses and headscarves.
How many generations?
How many children are there?
What is she thinking about,
the woman whose eye I catch,
smoking a cigarette by the window,
her elbow resting on the sill?
The men sit in bars so bare, so ugly
the natives hurry past, wondering at
that plantless brightness,
kitchen chairs on a wooden floor, a din
of maleness — strange islands
in a sea
of *gezelligheid*.
What do I know?
I've lived here a year
hermetically sealed
from the life of the street,
worrying about connections.
Yesterday, a week to Christmas,
a man I've never seen before
called with branches of catkin,
told me to put them in water,
then disappeared.
Last year, on New Year's Eve, at midnight
I stepped outside to watch
the fireworks. A door opened
across the street, the house
whose curtains are always drawn,
and a man came out, unshaven,
wearing an old string vest.
In his hand he held a revolver
which he fired twice into the air,
then he came and shook my hand

and went back in, smoke trailing
from the gun barrel.
His son keeps his Alfa Romeo
outside my window, sleek and black,
on the bonnet a huge transfer
of a wolf snarling. The man himself's
tattooed, forearms aglow
with sex and power.
I prick my skin
to let the pigment in
but little holds.
Again and again
the eye migrates, complains,
wherever it goes
is a city like this
undiscoverable,
in the dim suburbs of perception
a surfeit of detail.

Housesitting

This is a life, and I move
towards it, the aisles
crammed with pet food
the cliffs with substantial houses
angled to receive
the narcotic sweep of bay
A painted sailor looks seaward from a lawn
in an attitude of readiness
A hand reaches from the dreamlife of the town
to pat him on the head
In the new economy
a man leans to me in the hill-top park
to tell me the price of a house below
and abruptly goes
Who, ever, is at home in a life?
The dog claws the wall and strains over

I stare for hours at water
an infinitely concentrated carelessness
begins there
in which I may be learning
to lend myself to myself
to lodge and withdraw like the sea
or be the beach ignorant of its own account
On my sleeve
a labrador's heart
See how fiercely she has laboured this large stick
all the way home, so that I can hardly walk beside her
Joy, fear, hunger
grip, then leave
I sleep
on a landing close to myself and wake
to my own breath, listen, stirring
beyond the door

from "A Journal"

• • •

In the beginning I went back to the rain
that had hung in the air for hours and finally came down
on the long road to the waterfall: it was a day of water
first the teasing sting of drizzle on our faces, the thickening
texture of our hair, then the gathering frown
and the accelerating shower swelling the ditches and the
    stream —
We could distinguish several kinds of watery sound
we almost wrote them down
in a book of rain, a journal of water
an almanac of matted curls and glazed hands
Rain on the roofs, rain on machines, the fury of drains
and the muffled resignation of piled wood
My anorak loud, your softening coat

and at the growing thunder of the fall . . .
At the entrance we bought our tickets
watched the man return to his snug lodge and continued on
passed by a solitary car. It rained and rained
and the wetter we were the deeper we fell
Your hair shone to a gold I'd never seen before
your teeth glittered and your damp skin burned me to the
    bone
We found a kiosk and stopped
for coffee, sandwiches, cake, all we could eat
as if the food might melt before us, the shop recede, leaving
    only
the desolation of the picnic benches, the clattering rubbish
    cans
the weeping *Fir* and the sad *Mná* listening all day
to the water roar. We followed the noise till we came to it
walking across the grass to the shining din
half its hundred feet obscured by its own spray
the driving rain and the crouched sky:
it fell in three great strands like fingers splayed
across the rocks and we leaned as close as we dared
past the danger sign, the No Climbing notice
You asked if we had a religion of water, if the site was sacred
and I saw the silent crowd, the water-priest shouting from
    his rock
the children led to angry life or death. Houdini on his wire
honeymooners, desperate divers making sure . . .
The sky darkened, we walked slowly away
two days later you were gone again, the heaped engines
pouring: you climbed into the morning
and I went back to the rain-soaked bed, I leaned
like a maniac into the rocks until there was nothing left
but the ruinous crash
of water entering water, the madness of falling water
    • • •

The Writer's Studio

(after the Francis Bacon Studio in the Municipal Gallery, Dublin)

They've been worrying for ages
how best to show your chaos.
Two days from the opening
a curator rearranges papers,
spills ink on the floor, half-eats an apple
and throws it in a corner, but still
the disorder comes to order;
the flung pipe, the forgotten shirt
sculpted and composed, with the notebooks,
the scrawled-on walls and mildewed postcards.
It's all there, through the peephole,
this reconstruction of your mind
from which you are entirely absent.
You're in heaven cursing the dullness of angels,
throwing your clothes around like clouds,
prowling the fragrant avenues
for a fight, a drink, someone to talk to
or sleep with, and if some freak wind
planted you here among your own things,
you'd sweep the lot from under your eyes,
tear it all down; rip the postcards, the T-shirts,
rob the till and drink it dry and float
back up to your high bed and wake up
having forgotten everything. We
who so loved your life we made a fetish of it
will stand in the air, hoping to catch
whatever falls: broken crockery, a smashed cloud,
we'll see your hand in the wind and rain,
hear your voice in the roaring streets,
follow you from porn shop to pub
and back again. And then a tree will fall,
or a leaf, someone lean out a window,
a cat slope
down a laneway
and
at last
we will understand you.

Dolores Stewart

American Wake
for Peter Ward, Coolough, Galway & Boston, Mass.

He's walking the land again, maybe for the last time, marking off
The mearing walls by heart, the language no different from the Gaelic
Spoken in a Boston pub when the chairs were pitched out of the way
To nail the map back home to the floor, for fear of missing a trick
In the swivel of the index finger.
                        Or the fist.
What he's driving before him are the livestock of his memory,
Their swishing tails playing him to a padlocked barn and unscoured
Milk churns waiting to be filled.
                        By and by.
Why he goes to the trouble of fixing a new lock onto the farmyard gate,
Or hiding the antique plough beneath a tangle of blackthorn
After he'd taken it out to size it up as he'd done when it was new
To the earth and shy of furrows is a riddle to mind old bones, the likes
Of tenant and landlord both —

Sir Valentine the Sunday man
On the run from summonses and writs
Six days a week,

Or the last of the Clanricardes
Eating his dinner out of creased newspaper
In Regent's Park,

Lost for want of the rent.

Like seldom told ghost stories herded into meadows of night, and
Sidestepped now, he shrouds the holding and goes, making himself
Scarce, flying out from Shannon, maybe for the last time. For keeps.

Maryville, Winter, 2001

Through those Alzheimer's eyes
your old worn walking stick becomes an object
of wonder, a page written in an old script
or a bead on your rosary —
signposts to a meaning staring you in the face.

Photographs surround you, immune images
from the world you've let go of, your memory
a rusty valve that unexpectedly opens —

and you remember, you remember an uncle
on your mother's side, the American judge
who came down hard on a word, insisting

on emphasis on the train to Galway
in the days before Wall St. wiped him out.
And you remember, you remember as if

it were yesterday, the day the Black & Tans
came to Oughterard and you hid
with your sister behind a breathless hedge.

*I admit the space between us, the train
waiting at Platform Five,*

*the muffled sounds of those out and about
and heading home,*

the world beyond you . . .

as, finally, you decipher that old script and grip
the walking stick, humming an old music hall tune
while keeping time on the way to an immaterial world.

And you smile, you smile.

Death of Socrates

Even though he made a name for himself
With the corner boys, always asking
The same question and in such a roundabout way
That they couldn't make head nor tail
Of what he was getting at, he hadn't the sense
Of a child when it came to the real world, nor
The sense to know that there are people who like
Questions.
     And people who don't.
And even when they handed him the cup
With enough poison in it to wipe out all the rats
In Athens, he spent all the time he had left talking,
Talking, drawing them out into the heartbeat
Of the question and demanding to know
Whether they thought it was better to die
In the right than in the wrong. Like they cared.

Dóchas

Ar nós fréamhacha
faoi chlúdach i bpáipéar nuachtáin
i gcónaí ag súil leis an earrach
agus le breith,

tagann mearbhall orm
faoi ghleacaíocht an tsolais
agus an racht cainte
atá i ndán dom.

Hope

Same as roots
wrapped in newspaper
and always waiting for springtime
and for birth,

I become confused
at the gymnastics of light
and the urgent talking
is in store for me.

Idir Scylla agus Charybdis

Ag crosbhóthar Holyhead, Oileán Ellis
an domhain thoir, thug mé faoi ndeara
scuaine thaibhsiúil ag éisiúint
as chomhfhiosacht na hÉireann,
cuma strainséirí orthu,
faoi bhrú chlár ama
's iad ag déanamh ar stáisiún na traenach
thar thithe tostbhéalach, dubhchlúdaithe,

ag triall ar ghealchathracha Shasana.

Stopann siad nóiméad
ar an seanbhealach geimhriúil —

>   fad atá muid ag fanacht
>   le am seolta an bháid,
>   an clog dearg digiteach
>   ag tarraingt ar bhreacadh an lae,
>   lorraithe na hoíche ar tí an tír a thrasnú,
>   an domhan tostach tititheas a chodladh —

stopann siad nóiméad sula n-imíonn siad as,
as radharc cúng na súl,
as criathar na cuimhne, ag tarraingt siar
ó leithscéalta na staire.

Between Scylla and Charybdis

At the crossroads of Holyhead, the Ellis Island
of the old world, I noticed
a showy crowd showing clear
an Irish consciousness,
looking like strangers
obedient to the urgency of timetables
making for the train station
and the closemouthed blackvisaged houses

making for the bright cities of England.

They hesitate a moment
on the wintry roadside —

> while we wait for the boat's
> departure time,
> as dawn nears
> as the lorries rev ready to cross the whole country
> as this silent world wakens from its sleep —

they wait a moment before they go
before they leave our narrow sightline
before they drop through the riddle of memory, backing out
of the excuses made by history.

Ar Iarraidh

D'fhág an fíon deora dearga
ar imeall na gloine,

d'fhág na géanna fiáine
clingireacht san aer,

d'fhág an ghealach
an t-aon dul as ón dorchadas,

d'fhág do ghlór
macalla álainn i mo chuimhne,

ach níor fhág an Nollaig úd coiscéim ar bith
sa sneachta taobh amuigh den teach.

As an áireamh freisin,
an fáinne, sean-órga, ar iarraidh.

Paidrín ar strae sna réalta,
agus poll in mo phóca fós.

Lost

The wine left red drops
on the lip of the glass,

the wild geese left
a susurration in the air,

the moon left
the only way out of the dark

your voice left
a beautiful echo in my memory,

but that Christmas left no footstep
in the snow deep around the house.

Out of the reckoning too,
the ring of old gold I'm missing.

The stars are lacking a rosary of beads
fell through the hole in my pocket.

Ceol Johnny Phádraig Pheter

Dhearc mé siar,
chun fuascailt a fháil
ó bhagairt na farraige
agus achainí na ndaoine
i ngéibheann sa mbád.

Ar tí bheith tinn
('s is olc an tinneas é)
tháinig ceol chugam ar an ngaoith
os cionn chleataráil na mbád
agus achrann na taoide
agus an dream ag déanamh imní faoi.

Lá samhraidh doininne,
idir Inis Bó Finne
agus an Cloigeann,
bhain muid aicearra amach
ar dhroim cheol coisricthe an bhoscadóra.

Johnny Phádraig Pheter's Music

I looked back
for relief from the sea's threat
and the plea of the people
caught in the boat.

Just as I got sick
(and it's a bad sickness)
music came to me on the wind
above the clatter of the boat
and the warring of the tide
and the noise of the people in fear.

One stormy summer's day
between Inishbofin and the mainland
we reached safety
on the back of a concertina's blessed music.

Translations by Gréagóir Ó Dúill

Samantha Thomas

Late August, Donegal

Four in one, a rose, the sun, a single
entry. Below
layered stone a measured hand
stacks dusk as sun-raped hills wave a violent
beckoning to the moon.
And the wind flays you out evenly,
and soon you don't see yourself at all.

Vanities eroded you walk slowly on
towards the bridge.
A poisoned king lies shrouded in
his glen, red berries for weapons. Summer
velvet pressed overhead,
his daughter stock-still, one forefoot punched through
the muddy bank, breathless, gloveless, unattended.

Beside her the river Raye's moon flood ices over
steelshod with salmon, all
parts of fortune shifting back and in and up
to the Stone of Forgetting.
A moment of darkness
holds the horizon as you cross the bridge
palms high for measure and oval and bloodless,
the sun lifts again.

Man O' War

An average of 3,000 oaks were
needed to build one Man O'War.

"Cad a dhéanfaimid feasta gan adhmad?"*
from ***Cill Chais***

Mistress:
Hell, give me a mirror,
let me look upon you.
You've suffered yourself well.
No prayers left here
only the mutter of bellicose depths
answered in waves of sleep.

Maidservant:
Her own worst enemy
the suicide of crème pots
and powder. Lace and silks.
The attacker is unseen,
dwells well nested
hiding in full view.
There in her head.

Rapparee:
Here away from the others
I can hear my own breath,
need no one, keep no one.
I find my way and do not
burn my eyes or sting my feet.

Trees:
Nearly 3,000 form this body
yet there is no creature more empty.
Airtight, seaworthy,
arriving every second.
Pulling forward
too fast too fast too fast too fast.

You say you didn't see?
— Ma'am, it was only a dream.
But I saw him there. It was a man in only a red vest and black breeches.
— Yes?
Well, it was his countenance, it was vile.
He was dirty and scratched.
— I've never seen this man here.
But you were talking to him, by the trees.
— Trees ma'am?
Yes!
— It was not me ma'am, and there are no longer any trees here.

* "What now that the forests are gone?"
   (translated by John Ennis)

Man-Eating Leopard of Rudrapraya

The always shirtless, bibbed in nicotine
"*old goat,*" my mother snorted.
Exported from Anglia, repatriated
from India then mystifyingly locked like a tick
on to the volcanic haunch of Soufriere's coast.

His small dry beach house was our home
once he was gone. *He* would tell the story.
My father's still hairless face jealously
relishing each hyperbole suspecting maybe
he would never become so long in the tooth.

. . . It was the influenza gave Her a taste for it . . .
bodies in the ravines after the war
. . . even snuk in windows in the night.
Killed one hundred and twenty-six . . .

The lizards slid right down into
the house then and sat up on the chairs
so dad stacked the rocks in tiers half way
up the dry mountain behind us and the
lizards stayed in the lime trees.

Then with the rest he stacked a jetty
straight out into the black green bay that he
and Ashille could launch from with their tanks
and spears each day, floating lucidly over
the urchins sniggering between the rocks below.

Before Soufriere he couldn't even swim.
But with the almost witchy Midwestern fear
of sea reformed he began to hunt alone
usually returning with whatever we wanted
from its blue brave wilderness.

Once even finding a small breathing
space in a cave twenty feet below
with glowing yellow patches on the
black walls. *That's too far,* mom said
when she heard, *that's just too far.*

Sick with flu for a fortnight, I had days to watch
him from my top bunk slip into the water
and scout out from the broken jaw of beach
before submerging. If I saw him bob up again
I'd call out to my mother bowed at the bright sink,

stars streaming from her head
a patience preparing, she never looked
and I could never catch a glimpse of him emerging,
only hearing the soft tink of gear against
the rocks and sandy padding of feet
once he was already in the house.

Morne Grande

Before long she was finding her way easily
no one need walk with her. And the wrath came
more quickly and thoroughly as she was alone.
Now, she was not the thin lost child everyone
had fussed over and what she had become,
so doll-like and painted so flagrantly healthy,

was something the men would stop aiming
their blows to watch walking by. And that day
thru the cane fields swinging hot with blades
it was what they said that sliced her as she made
her way and they taunted, *"Not such a long way
now, eh dou-dou?"* The women's eyes flickering

in a different, sharper way from the men's own.
Like her they'd be in *douillete* by that evening
for harvest mass. She was going for madras to finish
her jupe and get the red ribbons for threading
through lace in the sleeves and neck of her chemise.
It would be the first *grande robe* she had sewn

for her own. Watching herself in the mirror
at the shop she couldn't help but superimpose
the *graise d'or* on her neck or in her thick hair
the *zepingues temblants* with her aunt's *tete-en-l'air*
pinning it up. And to top (she paid her bill) the splendid clothes
a saffron tinted mouchoir and *zanneau chenille* (a matador's
guile), swinging heavy and sweet as dove's eggs
                    from her skillful ears.

Verlaine

Come on let's play a game I lose. I'm left lying here alone
And beauty does not play. The version of this I'm thinking
Of: You delete the mending needle and booze it up over
My sensible shoes. You gave it all over to some benediction,
Some pope of the after hours and now I'm the foolish virgin
Bride who waits to see her midnight robber beau come home and
Defile her. When you finally stop for nothing I'll make you eggs Cro-Magnon.

Your escape is starry-eyed but I'll never let you get too far beyond the
Bastards at the gate. And you'd never even know you made it if
You did. How many times did we say this would never happen.

Oh, where I want to live! And how I want to envelope each sigh to you.
I fold them in my sheets. My sheets are full with them already.
If you knew the scent I could arouse in you, you may have come in like a lotus.

Instead I lie beside myself. Beside herself. I'll write to you from now
On. Because it's the wailing I'm trying to stop from happening. If I
Bestow it to the sea your ships will enter each gale in fours with their
Torn elder masts and planks of beseech. I couldn't watch. I prefer to feel you,
I feel you like a hundred empty shells in me. My belly fills with your
Tide and each one chokes contentedly. You leave and they bake in the heat
Of madness. I'll care for them and believe them. My beach is as
Wide as your storm.

Áine Uí Fhoghlú
Translated by Áine Uí Fhoghlú

What's that in English?

M'ainm, a d'iarr sí. D'fhreagair mé.
What's that in English?
Mhínigh mé
go réidh, mar is umhal lucht
ainm Gaeilge,
go mbeadh sé mar a chéile
i bpé teanga
ba mhian léi. Ó sea, ar sí
go cneasta, ach do cháipéisí
is teastais, an t-ainm Béarla
a bhaistear anso
is nach saonta dall
a bhí mise a shíl
go mbreacfadh peann pé rud
a dhéarfaí leis a scríobh —
ó, ní hea,
ar sí, an ríomhaire! Ná tuigeann tú
ná tuigeann an ríomhaire
na hainmneacha Gaeilge?
Agus bhí a chruthú aici,
taobh léi, thaispeáin
dom — go mórálach mar a bheadh
bonn óir buaite
i bhfeis aici —
an trófaí:
liosta fada ríomh-ráiméise
i dteanga éigint
nár tháinig lucht a labhartha
ar an saol fós.

Anois, mar sin, *let's get down to business please,*
an é *Murphy* nó *McMurrough*

mar bhí Murchadha aici anuraidh
ba chuimhin léi, *I'm getting good at these!*
Bhí san go breá gur tháinig lá
gur tharla éigeandáil is
gur theastaigh cabhair ó chloigeann
cnagtha. Sheas an bháirseach
ós mo chomhair: *name?* bhí's agam gur
dhócha go mb'fhearr seans
snáth agus snáthaid
a fháil uaithi
chun go ndeiseoinn mé féin,
ach seo linn arís . . .
no, no — in English, **please** *is* thosnaigh
radharc a cúig chéad is a trí
de ghníomh a míle is a naoi
den scig-dhráma searbh.
Chrom mé ar litriú is mhéadaigh
ar a fearg: *I'll send for the police!*
aici mar bhagairt
is sa deireadh ghéill mé
gurbh fhearra dhom bheith
fé ghlas i ngéibhinn is
bhí an fhuil
ag sileadh
as mo phlaosc Gaelach.
Tháiníodar
name? a d'fhiafraigh an Garda
go mí-shásta
ní rabhas fhéin ró-chinnte fé'n
dtráth so
is thugadar an biorán suain dom
gur dhúisíos i seaicéad srianta
i gcillín bog bán,
mé fhéin is m'ainm cadránta
is mhúin sé seachtainí dóite ansan dom
gan a bheith ag lorg trioblóide
is ag cur donas is stró ar
státseirbhís Fódhla.

Dheineadar *labota*-maí is stoitheadar
as an slí mo bhéasa aite díchéillí
bhaineadar amach na seana-chuimhní
ar m'ainm is mo shloinne
chun ná beinn go deo arís ag crá
lucht na n-oifig stáit.

Anois tá mé measartha, múinte, umhal, béasach,
dealraithiúil, comhoibritheach, neamh-éilitheach,
réasúnta
is tuisceannach
— im'ghnáthdhuine

is nuair a fhiafraíonn cléireach
what's that in English?
géillim gan aon cheist don Bhéarla:

my name in English? Of course adeirim.
It's Beauty, Daughter of the Sea-warrior,
sometimes mis-spelt the Sea-hound
married to Grandson of the Sea-pirate —
and wasn't that some alliance!

Níl sí cinnte an gol nó gáire a bheadh
tráthúil agus an dúshlánach atá mé
nó fós glan-chraiceáilte.

As cúinne mo shúile,
leath-chliathánach
chím a cara ag comhrá
go sásta le beirt fhear
óg ón iasacht ar cuairt anso
le mí anuas
no, no need to spell, I know that
one well
B-o-g-u-m-i-l, Bogumil Bartodzieski,
I love the Polish names ar sí

'tis just the Irish gets me!

What's that in English?

My name, she asked. I answered.
What's that in English?
I explained, respectfully
because you're meek when your
name's in Irish,
that it would be the same
in whatever language she liked.
Oh yes, she said kindly,
but went on to remind me
for certs or documentation
it is the English translation we use here
and wasn't I the innocent one
to think that a pen would write whatever
it was instructed to!
Oh no, she said, *it's the computer —
don't you understand that the computer doesn't
understand Irish?* And she had proof
(as if it were a gold medal
she had won at a feis)
proudly produced the trophy:
a printout of computerised nonsense
in some strange language
whose people had not arrived yet.

*Now so, let's be thorough, please
is it Murphy or McMurrough* because she
had a "Murchadha" last year she remembered
I'm getting good at these!

That was okay until the fatal day
a crisis came and help was needed
for a fractured skull. The scary lady
towered over me: *name?* I knew I might as well
get needle and thread and sew myself up
but, here goes again . . .
No, no — in English **please** and thus began
act five hundred and three, scene

one thousand and thirteen
of this sour satire.
I began to spell but her anger just increased:
I'll send for the police her threat
and finally I agreed that I'd be better off locked up
blood still trickling
from my Gaelic skull.

They arrived: *name?* the Guard asked me
grumpily

I wasn't quite sure myself anymore
so they gave me a sedative
and I woke up in a straightjacket
in a soft white cell
myself and my contrary name
and six withering weeks at that game
taught me well
not to be making trouble and causing
stress and bother in civic offices.

Now I am well-behaved moderate,
humble, respectful, obedient, undemanding,
reasonable
and understanding
— an ordinary person

and when a secretary asks me
what's that in English?
I give in immediately to the request:
my name in English? Of course, I say
*It's Beauty, Daughter of the Sea-Warrior,
sometimes mis-spelt Sea-Hound
married to Grandson of the Sea-pirate —
and wasn't that some alliance!*

She's not quite sure whether to laugh or cry
and whether I'm being defiant or just
stark raving.

From the corner of my eye,
sideways I glance,
I see her friend chatting up
two young men who've been here
a while now
*no, no need to spell, I know
that one well
B-o-g-u-m-i-l, Bogumil Bartodzieski,
I love the Polish names says she,*

'tis just the Irish gets me!

Sa tír

Sa tír atá breac le
crainn tógála, dréimirí
is leoraithe ag sceitheadh a gcuid *Readymix*
mar bhualtrach bó fan na mbóithre
itheann na coileáin Cheilteacha
bia Sri Lancach is ólann fíon Francach
ar dheiceanna de chéadras Cheanada
tá comharthaí na gceantálaithe mar mhaisiúchán
ar gach cuaille aibhléise
an tír ina holltoghchán
ollmhór ollshiamsach
mar a gceannaíonn an euro an vóta
sa tír ina bhfuil gach rud anois ar díol
deirtear go bhfuil lucht na mbailte slachtmhara
chun marcanna breise a dháileadh
ar shlacht na bhfógraí
FOR SALE atá á dtáirgeadh is
lipéidí dearthóra ceangailte leo
tá oifig an cheantálaí ar maos le
eurónna agus guíonn sé, cairpéad bog
faoina ghlúine,
ná tráfaidh an tuile

a snámhann sé ann choíche
i dtír na dtranglam tráchta
i dtír na n-órdóg ataithe le
teicst beaic, tác sún, sí-iú l8r . . .
sa tír ina snastar gluaisteáin
chomh mór le heitleáin
le tiomáint céad slat go siopa
sa tír ina bhfuil an chraic ina púdar bán
mar a gceannaíonn an euro an vóta
suíonn ógánach tanaí fionn
lena sheaicéad is a chlogad buí
ar fhalla trí stór leath-thógtha
ag ithe a cheapairí
as mála plaisteach *LIDL*
féachann soir uaidh is cuimhníonn
ar bhotháinín bídeach
sna sléibhte
i bhfad i gcéin.

In the land . . .

In the land that is speckled with
cranes, ladders
and lorries spattering their *Readymix*
like cow dung along the roads
Celtic pups
eat Sri Lankan food and drink
French wine on decks
of Canadian cedar
the estate agents' signs are like
decorations on every lamp post
the country is one huge election carnival
where the euro buys the vote
in the land where everything is now for sale
they say that the Tidy Towns Committees
are thinking of giving extra marks

for the tidiness of the FOR SALE signs
being produced with designer labels
the auctioneer's office is awash with euros
and he prays, a soft carpet under his knees
that this tide he swims in
will never ebb
in the land of gridlocked roads
in the land of thumbs swollen from
text back, talk soon, c u l8r
in the land where cars big as
'planes are polished
to drive a hundred yards to the shop
in the land where the "craic" is made
of white powder
where the euro buys the vote
a fair haired skinny young man
with his visi-vest and hard yellow hat
sits on a half built three storey wall
eating sandwiches from a LIDL's plastic bag,
looks to the east
and thinks of a tiny mountain cottage
way off, in the distance.

Íota

Stánaim ar an bhfonsa óir
glinnbhuí niamhrach
ar do mhéar
sheang
ar do shúil chomh lonrach
le réiltín fíoruisce
glioscar-ghearrtha, chomh foirfe
i gcló go santaím é d'ól,
molaim thú.

Feicim dath an fhíona
id fholt

ólaim cumhracht an aitinn
is tú go grástúil ag gluaiseacht
tharam,
móraim thú.

Is nuair a sheolann tú chugam
ar an leoithne mara
is do chrot draíochta
leathnocht i mbrothall trá
meileann an mearthall m'anam
leanaim rian éadrom do choise
go héidreorach sa ghainimh
coipeadh na habhann
é mo phaidir
i gcillín dubh seo na mianta
cuireann an marbhtheas
íota tarta orm,
adhraim thú.

Scuabann na tonnta
chun siúil ár lorg
sa ghainimh réidh . . .

ach tá do mhéin chomh dílis mín
leis an bhfuarán sléibhe,

gáireann tú liom
dubh dall
ar mo shaint
chugat.

Desire

Bright yellow shining
that gold hoop on your slim finger
your eye as bright as a star
of springwater

sparklingly cut, so perfectly
formed that I desire to drink it,
I praise you.

I see the colour of wine
in your hair
I inhale the scent of the furze
as you go gracefully by,
I adore you.

And when the sea breeze
sends you towards me
your magical shape half bare
on the sun-soaked beach
confusion grinds my heart
I follow your light footsteps
aimlessly in the sand
my prayer
a melting dream
in this black prison of desires
the sultry heat
parches my mouth,
I worship you.

Waves rush
to wipe away the traces
in the smooth sand . . .

but your soul is as true and precious
as a mountain stream,

you smile at me

completely blind
to how I crave
you.

An Tine Bheo
(i.m. Frances Newton dying by lethal injection, Texas, 14th September 2005)

A craiceann mar éabann le hais
éadach geal cadáis
ar an leaba shingil ghlan
tá creasa sábhála
sa seomra sciúrtha
níl ponc as ord

tá gach rud chomh bán

díbríonn smeachadh méire boilgín
chíonn sí loinnir an tsolais
i mbior na snáthaide agus
i spéaclaí glé snasta
mar a millfeadh smidín dubh amháin
an ócáid.

Airíonn sí guth cianársa
á glaoch abhaile ar chosán
uaigneach an athmhuintiris
ach tá a cosa gearrtha, fuilteach
a béal tíortha ag an ithir rua
amuigh i ngort an chadáis
ní shéideann siolla ina treo
seinneann ceoltóir na gormacha
ar chaoláin
is féitheoga a hionathair.

Dúnann sí a súile mar áirní
is a beola mar shú talún méithe

braitheann luisne teasa ina gnúis
ó chaor thine Mississippi
atá fós gan múchadh.

The Burning Fire

Skin like ebony against
bright cotton cloth
on the clean single bed
there are safety belts
in the scrubbed room
nothing's out of order

everything is so white

flick of a finger
banishes a bubble
she sees the reflection of light
in the point of the needle
and in clear polished glasses
where one black speck
would spoil the occasion.

She hears an ancient voice
calling her home
on the lonely path of
reconciliation
but her feet are cut and bleeding,
her mouth parched by the red earth
out there in the cotton field
no puff blows her way
a musician plays the blues
on the sinews and strings
of her tightened guts.

She closes her eyes like sloes
and her lips like juicy strawberries

feels the burning glow in her cheeks
from the roaring Mississippi fire
still raging.

I Seomra Feithimh an Dochtúra, 1974
(do Shiobhán)

Níorbh aon stró turas le fána ar dhá rothar
ón scoil,
éalú.

Suite ar fhuarma, drom le falla
fuar titeann mo shúil díomhaoin
ar iris *Time*, áirnéis gan éileamh:
sa phairlimint seo mar a gcíortar
ceisteanna páistí easlán
atá sa mbaile ag ól *7up* beirithe
ní cás aicídí Nixon.

Foghlaimím tuairimí téarnaimh
gach máthar acu
sula dtéann siad ina nduine
agus ina nduine
suas dhá chéim arda cloiche,
taobh thiar den doras gorm
a nochtar gach rún
don bhean feasa
i bhfaoistiní na Máirte.

Faighimid oiliúint mhaith mar
is leor nod dúinne atá leath-eolach
dírímid ár súile ar an urlár soiminte
agus ar na rúitíní thall, ar an
tinteán folamh, ar bhreodheirge
an téiteora leictreach, ar an doras gorm
éistímid go géar le
cogar-mogar is scigireacht
ar chúrsaí collaí
ó choirpigh neamh-fheimineacha
a bhriseann gach dlí
gach maidin lena nguí agus a ngníomh
in aghaidh na torthúlachta
tuigimid milseacht

a gcuid *Smarties*.

Níl ar iarraidh
ón dtionól ach bean amháin —
níl sí
ar fónamh inniu,
is dócha.

In the Doctor's Waiting Room, 1974

The spin downhill from school on two bikes
was no bother,
an escape.

Sitting on a form, back to the cold wall
my idle eye falls on a copy of *Time* magazine,
an unwanted utility:
in this parliament where debates concern
unwell children at home drinking boiled *7up*
Nixon's ailments are not priority.

I learn the curative opinions
of each mother there
before they proceed one by one
up two stone steps,

behind the blue door
all secrets are revealed
to the wise woman
in Tuesday confessions.

We get a good education here
because a nod is as good as a wink
to us, already half wise
we fix our gaze on the cement floor
and the ankles beyond, on the
empty fireplace, on the glow of the
electric fire, on the blue door

we listen sharply to whisperings
and skittering about carnal matters
from these non-feminist criminals
who break every law every morning
with their prayers and deeds against
fertility
we understand the sweetness
of their *Smarties*.

There's only one woman missing
from the gathering —
she's not feeling too well today,
I suppose.

Fiailí

Tá ár dteach fáiscthe
i mbaclainn na ndriseacha
aol ag titim ina chalóga ar na
feochadáin is na cupóga a d'eascair
trí scoilteacha,
neantóga ag luascadh ar
dhíon dreoite is níl le feiscint
sa ghairdín ach an cúpla cineál
a fuair togha na haire.
Cuireadh leasú leo
is tá duaiseanna
buaite acu ag mór-thaispeántaisí
boird na n-uaisle
maisithe acu.

Mhol an lucht féachana
an binsín a bhláthaigh
is níor thug éinne faoi ndeara
na buinneáin a leag
an sean-sheiceamar uaidh go glic
phréamhaíodar
agus scoilt
an fúinniméad.

Tagann ógánaigh gach
deireadh seachtaine is ólann
ceirtlís ó channaí
scrábann graifítí ar na fallaí
satlaíonn mar a raibh an scoth faoi bhláth
ar imigh a lá
tá bunanna toitíní ina n-easair
ar an urlár smionagrach
is feadann an ghaoth aduaidh
trí phánaí briste.

Táimid suite i dtigín
soghluaiste i Muineachán sa gheimhreadh
1983 an bhliain; thugamar
chugat síolta a caitheadh a choimeád
in áit dhorcha
agus is ar fhiailí
atáimid at trácht
deir tusa liom nach n-éireoidh leo
greim a fháil go deo
agus cad is fiú mo thuairimse
seachas tuairim sean-gharraíodóra?

Is minic a chuimhním ar ár gcomhrá
ar fhiailí.

Weeds

Briar-arms hug our house now
and flaking limewash falls
on the thistles and docks
emerged through splits,
nettles sway on the sagging
thatch, the garden
shows only the few
well-pruned species.
Fed on flower food

they've won prizes at the best
shows and graced tables
in posh places.

While all eyes praised
the few that flourished
no one noticed the saplings
cleverly dropped by the giant
sycamore
they took root
and fractured the foundations.

Youths come at weekends,
drink cider from cans and scrawl
illegible graffiti on the walls
they tread where once the finest
bloomed whose day has gone
cigarette butts litter the shattered floor
and the north wind whistles
through broken panes.

Sitting in a mobile home in Monaghan
it's winter 1983; we've brought you seeds
that had to be kept in a dark place
and our conversation
is about weeds
you tell me they'll never get a hold
and who am I to argue with
a gardener of your experience?

I often think of our conversation
about weeds.

An tUllmhúchán

Anonn leis go seilf na gcruaearraí
an ciseáinín miotail ar crochadh
go ciotach dá leathláimh
shín uaidh suas is roghnaigh
giomhán de théad níocháin —
chuimhnigh ar
a mháthair, a géaga sínte
ina threo is a mhéaranna beaga
ag tochras an cheirtlín
olna, á chasadh, á chasadh, á chasadh
agus é ag ídiú óna lámha
dheireadh sí leis: "nuair a stadann
an snáth, stadann an chniotáil"
mar mhíniú ar dhíth —
óráiste a dhath, ar nós an ghliomaigh
bheirithe
bheir go héadrom ar a cheann is
go díomhaoin scaoil
tuathal, dhaingnigh deiseal arís: taithí
ag a mhéaranna iascaire ar
spladhsáil
na téada
ag oscailt is ag dúnadh a mbéal leis
mar a bheadh balbhán ar díth focal.

Ar a shlí go seilf na gcosmáidí
bheannaigh sé
do bhean comharsan,
ag an gcúntar
scréach an gléas scannála
is é ag léamh an bharrchóid
ar an mbuilín beag,
an dá shlis liamháis, an *éclair* seacláide
an rásúr, an galúnach, an slaod fiacal,
is an line níocháin
"beidh tiormacht maith inniu ann"

arsa an cailín freastail go gealgháirach
agus í ag néatú
a chuid earraí isteach
sa *Bag for Life*.

Ní bheadh aon ghá
aige le hadhaint na tine
nár mhaolaigh riamh fuacht
a chnámha préachta
ná le lasadh lampaí
a choimeádadh an dorchadas
tamall ó dhoras
go n-ídeodh an ola,
bhí an bród is an sceimhle
ag coraíocht ina éadan
gan phúicín
ag feacadh a ghlúine dó,
is gan aon chois leis i dtaca
nuair a sciorr an screallach.

Minic
a chuimhnigh mé ó shoin,
n'fheadar ar tháinig
aon chreathán ina lámh
nuair a bhain sé an cadhnra
beag as an gclog

sé nóiméad déag
is seacht soicind
tar éis a trí
is é ag cur a bhalcaisí
ar tuar?

Getting Ready

He went over to the hardware shelf
the wire basket hanging awkwardly
off one arm
stretched up and chose a hank
of light rope —
he remembered his mother, her arms
outstretched towards him and his little fingers
winding the ball
of yarn, winding, winding, winding
as it disappeared from her hands
she would say to him: "when the yarn ends,
the knitting stops,"
by way of explaining want —
orange it was, like a boiled
lobster
carefully he caught its end
between his fingers and playfully
loosened it, tightened it again:
fisherman's fingers were deft at
splicing
the cords
opened and closed their mouth
to him just like a mute wanting
for words.

On his way to the cosmetics shelf
he made smalltalk
with one of the neighbours, at the counter
the scanner shrieked
as it read the barcode
on the small loaf, the two slices of ham,
the chocolate éclair, the razor,
the soap, the toothpaste
and the clothesline
"there will be good drying today"
the checkout girl said cheerfully

as she neatly packed his shopping
into the *Bag for Life*.

There would be no need
to light the fire that
never warmed his perished bones
or the lighting of lamps
that would keep the darkness out a while
'till the oil would run out,
pride and terror
wrestled in his unhooded face
as he genuflected
without a foothold
in the crumbling rock.

I often wondered since
did his hand shake
at all
when he removed the
small battery
from the clock

sixteen minutes and
seven seconds
after three
as he put his clothes
out to dry?

Grace Wells

Aşure

Aşure is the Turkish name given to the last dessert Mrs Noah made before boarding tthe ark. Because she was emptying her shelves one final time, it contains an amount of everything.

Let me grate almond for you this night.
While gulls wheel their floodlit vigil above the Blue Mosque
let me shred pistachio green as limes from the Bazaar. Let me
rub coconut to powder. I will take raisins crated in Tarsos,
yellow sultana by the handful.
Grant me the İznik bowl I refused you buy,
for it alone could hold this night, this Aşure.

Let me empty these cupboards the way Mrs Noah
emptied hers that last night before the rains came.
Baking powder, bicarbonate of soda, cream of tartar.
Clove against toothache, mint for digestion,
thimble of brandy to ease our grief.
The light is low in this room. Soft brown
sugar. Nutmeg. Scent of cinnamon on my skin.

I will rasp orange rind, stir a syrup
thick with corn flour, arrowroot, gelatine;
cut an apple sideways to reveal its star.
Mrs Noah took chick peas, the last rice, last
scrape of pearl barley, so who would notice
the salt from these tears? Let them fall
as I beat egg white, whip cream, fold in flour.

Jet bead of currant, maroon glacés, crystal ginger,
nothing too good for this night, this Aşure,
so if there is a wail, a keen in the mouth
tart as lemon, let it be the morning call to prayer,
for they are laying you in the best sheets my love,
your boat is leaving, everything ship shape
and ready, every last thing prepared.

The Only Medicine

What's left,
when the father of your children
has thrown a basket at you hard,
upturned the kitchen table, breaking
all the china you possess,
driven off into the night. His absence
clothing the house and the children
as they struggle with the buttons on pyjamas
and your thoughts are of leaving
but you don't leave.
You don't go anywhere,
they love him, want the two of you
to be together,
and that
seems more important than anything else.

The air buzzes with returning landrovers,
but still he does not come.
And this has all happened because
you are both under pressure.
You hate that landrover
and can't bear the poverty,
nor the stress of the unpaid bills,
how everything could fall apart
about your ears, even if you do
own you own home and four acres,
though the house has no bathroom and the land
so badly fenced the stock keep escaping
and Mrs Lawless rings to say your
mule and donkey
are breakfasting on her lawn.

The only medicine is words,
to write it all down, to say
how that desperate blue bottle
lands so accurately

between the eyes, to record
the butterfly that flaps trapped
in the lampshade, the way
you share this house with nature
or she shares it with you,
as if grass would start growing
between the floorboards.
And the world is in chaos
and their father is a violent man
and tomorrow, tomorrow, tomorrow
your daughter is two years old.

Horse Fair

Their child and marriage barely a year,
she pushes the buggy amidst horseflank and sinew
a waltz of colt and foal, piebald and skewbald, roan
and bay, hooves skittish, laden with threat.

The lens of her Practika too narrow
to capture the full scene, not swift enough
for the bargains sealed; palms pressed
together over flesh changed hands. Her focus

returning always to the one man
who'll grin for her and pose. He walks
the fair green at her back, setting the pace
until she becomes the herded; driven.

Later the town streets, amongst stalls
of cheap trinkets, always an elbow
from the fingers of vendors, the shadow
of touts and hawkers. Slowly

she'll understand he belongs,
a man who'd sell his grandmother. Sell his wife.

The Funeral Director's Wife

Often I have watched his hands about a corpse,
the closing of the mouth like the closing of a tin can
gaping and wide; the jagged edge of memory
prevents a smoothing over.
He will conquer death, make of it a business;
dressed in ceremony his chiselled face
sets more stone-like with the years.

He doesn't know I sit with them.

The talk in whispers is of first kisses,
the way a loved one's lips turned sour in argument.
We share trinkets, baby hair kept tied in ribbon, flowers pressed
between the leaves of faint-ink letters
from sisters gone over the Atlantic at seventeen.
There is the telling of waking alone to the dark night
and of the shamings, teachers and fathers,
and I hold them, hold their passing, hold the dearest of things

while in the scrubbed yard he reverses the hearse.

The Muezzin's Call

Crossing the Suir at Ferryhouse,
passing the frosted orchards,
a sound in the throat rises,
resonating voice of the land.

Passing the red acacia, this ullulation
sweetens to a note. Passing the holly
red with berries, passing the hotel entrance,
aware they hear me, the health-club visitors,

the chambermaids, the waking sleepers,
past the last yellow leaves of the fingered
birches, past the woman

whose face has caved in with sadness,

beneath the only mistletoe for thirty miles,
over the Gashouse Bridge, through
the November morning I go, that one note
rising up and out of me, over the town

calling, calling the world to prayer.

The Lone Parent Does Not Write

Between a bad back
and a deadweight hoover
it's been a month or more.
Let's not talk about the duvet cover
walking out of the bedroom
in search of a good home.
At the sink I'm breeding botulism,
— a resistance experiment,
results are good,
besides my kids have more brains
than to get sick; if their mother
stopped this frantic whirl
to tend a fevered brow,
she'd keel over, squeeze them from the bed.

This morning allows
I find our rooms again,
hoover the top of rugs at least,
nothing too fancy,
nothing extreme.
This way I'm left with an hour,
a tiny sacred hour,
to climb the laundry mountain
to part the sea of toys
and walk through
with the Egyptians at my back,

to stand,
just for one hour, here
in the Holy land.

The Hostage Place

Invisible the insect held within the amber of our father's boat.
Hull he built himself, condensing his finest fibres into boards
that bore the lick of sun and wave until their taut wood sung.

Evening light could strike its umber sail to flame, light a vision
that denied the bite of rope, of salt, the angry sting, for though
the rudder steered, our father drove with a lashing tongue. And

I never wanted to feel the look upon my mother's face upon my own.
That horizon gaze which stared beyond and saw nothing
left each of us unable to find a course out from his dark hold.

Each of us still able to inhabit the place we'd crawl; the prow locker,
cupboard for pump and bailer, anchor, and metal chain that clinked
into each wave, where to the kind sound of water receiving wood

we learned to sleep, cheeks pressed into the sweating,
yellow flesh of a life vest.

Enda Wyley

Going Home

It was always hard
to enter the house
without you
appearing at the creaking
top of the stairs,
one arm arched in time-keeping
the other lowered to an itching testicle
fallen drowsy from your pyjama stripes —
all my late night boldness questioned.

It was always hard
quickly to smooth
a crumpled lipstick smile,
pulled at hair,
party clothes stained beyond glamour,
hard to push still smoking ashtrays
and half-empty beer bottles under the sofa,
rush boyfriends out the dining room window,
venetian blinds cracking resistance,
before you shadowed the doorway —
you have turned my home into a brothel —
all my late night boldness revealed.

And yet it is harder now
to enter the house with you gone.
I let Mahler's fourth fill the place —
think I am nine again,
my ear pressed to your upstairs room,
the record player within
pushing the door to a close,
my parents inside
crying, it seemed to me,

to a classical beat on a Saturday afternoon.

And I wonder
what noise can be left now?
Only the sound of my own footsteps
in empty rooms,
then the click of lights turned down.

Love Bruise

Afterwards she found it by accident,
shaped like a huge cougar prowling below
the jungle basin of her pelvic bone —
a tawny bruise that rode
her outer thigh's skin folds.

> *— I banged into a table edge,*
> *a car door bit into my side,*
> *where a knee-high daughter pinched*
> *greedy for my attention, I bruised.*

Days later it is fading —
becomes only a flash of pebble,
now purple, thumb-print size
under the waterfall roll
of dirt and suds from her morning shower.

> *— I grazed myself on the trellis nails,*
> *rusty diamonds on the garden wall,*
> *was hit by snowballs pelted at me*
> *one school-closed January day.*

She tells herself all these things,
over and over — even in her sleep.
They are easier than the truth:
the pain of your pull within her —
then away from her when you go.

Marlborough Road

On Marlborough Road
the houses have names —
Aclare, Larcana, Ardeevin,
Shalamar, Woodstock, Hazelhurst
and St Elmo on the way to the station
where the ghost creaked the gate long ago
one early winter morning
and became a wide-eyed Red Setter before me,
as frightened of a girl as I was of him,
our still worlds interrupted.

Going home up Marlborough Road,
I see the garden boats covered in canvas,
the spiked green railings
darker than the hedges
and the copper beech and monkey trees.
The old black Morris Minor is still there
and the domes of the many glass houses.
I hear the shunting of an approaching train
bringing more people home
to this sage, quiet suburb.

And just for this fifteen minute stretch
of house-lined road and hill,
there is peace on Marlborough Road to remember.
I am five years old again, opening our front door,
shocked to see your handkerchief
wave like a flag of blood on your forehead,
and to hear you call my mother's name for help,
your footprints large red accident marks
stronger than the trails left behind you
by birds on our snow-filled drive.

You were my father who growled at nurses — *God almighty,*
how can a child be expected to eat that on her own? —
when, sick in my second year of life, nurses left me

jam sandwiches and a mug of hospital tea.
You were my father who appeared at the top
of Keem Bay, unexpected to us as the thunder storm,
with coats and hats, umbrellas and warm rugs
pulling us safely up the cliff edge and home to holiday beds,
wind and the gulls crying out in joy
Abba, Abba, Abba.

You were our father
my mother watched the kitchen clock for,
climbing up the stairs at five thirty
to make her lips redder, her bright face brighter
just before we shouted *He's home, he's home!*
leaving behind our laundry-bin lid and kitchen-pot toys
racing each other to open the door to you
and tell of our day's hard work —
of our tree house creations and go-cart inventions,
of the apples and pears we'd stolen from next door's garden.

I have never seen you fall since
but that day your head fell
in tiredness against the train window
just before the flash of Sandymount Strand outside,
then later fell harder onto concrete
halfway along that snowy January road.
And coming home again now, I remember how
you must have slipped, then bled, unfairly vulnerable —
and in my head I want to help you up, brush you clean.
But Marlborough Road's icy beauty keeps pulling my father down.

Two Women in Kosovo

"I'm going to jump," her sister whispers,
holding out her hand.
And so they jump together — so naturally
they might be young girls again

leaping at waves on their holidays, jumping
across rivers on their way to school,
pulling each other over the road
to grown-up things.
From the side of the truck
out onto the rolling dust and scrub they jump,
tea and bread they've just eaten with the others
a thump in their stomachs when they fall.
Holding hands tight, they jump —
two women in Kosovo leaving behind
their children, their mother, their husbands
gunned down by soldiers
in a roadside café minutes before
and now a mountain of grief
being driven to a mass grave
somewhere these sisters will never find.

One looks back for a second,
feels her whole life piled ugly there,
feels it was beautiful once —
the pull of her man reaching for her
in the middle of the night,
the bitter pain she knew when her four year old
left her for his first day at school,
her mother calling her back home
on a cold winter's night.
Luck chooses where we are born,
passes us through life
unscathed by violence.
Luck is this brave woman now
defying the brutal guards,
rising alive
from her pretend death
and the horror of corpses, the people she's loved —
a frightened survivor pulling
her frightened sister forward,
a sister whispering "jump!"

Diary of a Fat Man

I am so fat now
that the woman I love
will not lie down with me —
so I make her shape in the mountains
of potatoes I boil and mash,
feel her breasts in the dough I knead and prick,
her bread nipples rising erect at 200 degrees Celcius,
hear her noises gurgling with the bubbling
of tomato, ginger, cinnamon,
her kisses extra sweetness oozing.

Skin, heaped spoons of crème fraîche,
eyes, sharp kiwi green,
arms, the curve of bananas, melons, fresh bread rolls,
mouth, a dazzling lemon split apart —
I am so fat now
she is all of this to me and more.
I make my bed in the sitting room,
unable to climb the stairs.
I sleep with my heavy boots on,
unable to pull them off.
Sometimes she passes by my door —
the dart of a thin shadow,
her breasts suddenly shrivelled
as an avacado's outer layer,
her skin rough like uncooked rice,
her eyes two empty plates pleading,
*I look at you
and can never eat again.*

Her voice has the rancid stench
of food left over for weeks.
She is becoming nothing —
ice-cream melted on a hot kitchen floor,
boiled water evaporating in a room.
But I make her again — my woman.

Her love among the carrots, onions,
broccoli, steak and garlic
is so heated in my thick, tasty stew
that I do not notice
her open the front door
then leave the house for good —
the smell of food
a jaded world forever clinging
to her hair, her skin and clothes.
Not hearing, I scoop, scoop,
scoop from my pot
into the biggest
bowl I can find.

Master Chef

In a little while, will you come and cook the chicken —
climb down our stairs under Vermeer's blue-gowned muse,
pass the four glass squares of our green front door and walk
to the kitchen through the white-washed rooms?

Will you leave the things you love — Robert Bly, Francis Ponge,
Wagner's screeching sirens, and come to look at our chicken?
I want you to pepper and lemon it, thyme it with your fingers,
fatten it with butter, press succulent rhymes under its skin

so that it is a roast of rhythms, metaphors and garlic, clever puns,
limes and lyrics, throbbing oven songs between our sky blue presses.
The cat on the yard wall licks its lips, t-shirts on the washing line
are a stirring armless, headless screen protecting your great work.

Oh master cook, oh my fine poet, my much loved chef, even the man
dangling from the shamrock-green crane that swings over Patrick St.
pauses to inhale your culinary odours rising sweeter than the weed
he inhales before jumping to his death, the crowd below well teased.

We push the kitchen window open, poetry rushing into the skies
a plough, a Venus, a firmament of ideas! —
your hair a scribble of lines, your kiss sweet as a haiku on my cheek,
and this chicken startling the darkness into a well fed dawn.

Mint Gatherers

While you are off gathering mint,
we stain our fingers
with a fresher smell
in the long, narrow room —
its tiny window making
four perfect purple squares
out of the far away mountain —
that room with the yellow blanketed bed
that holds us wrapped in heat and love
over the kitchen, below the Alpine spider,
our own spindly guard and his soft cylindrical web
in the angle of the latticed door.
The house is ours for that brief time

while you are off gathering mint
in your neighbour's field high on the hill.
You raise your hand in the afternoon heat,
rub water across your cheek, can lick already
the green coolness on the roof of your mouth —
while we back there, taste each other.
There are no words. The lizards lie still
in the cool of the old barn. The lime tree shades
the balcony where we rise at last to stand,
now waiting for you to come back,
certain you'll hang from hooks
in the old kitchen ceiling
a bunch of fresh mint leaves to dry,
just below where we had lain.

Emperor

While others might relax after love,
he is up and about in his boxer shorts,
watering flowers on the balcony —
not caring that it's overlooked
by a hundred city windows opposite.

Back inside, he pads barefoot
their apartment's wooden floors,
blasts Wagner's *Ride of the Valkyries*,
sucks dates, climbs up a fold-out chair
to check on the highest shelf

Commodus's exact background
in his encyclopaedia,
before the wood beneath his feet
flips back, his toes are caught red sore
and he shouts his pain to the waking walls.

Then he is that ancient emperor —
everybody, everything against him
and hearing the mob's gleeful roars
in the theatre where his anger rules,
he feeds her to the lions.

Table 2.

PPSNs Issued to EU Accession State Workers, May 2004 – May 2006	
Accession State	PPSNs Registered
Poland	116,206
Lithuania	35,497
Latvia	17,998
Slovakia	16,951
Czech Republic	8,885
Hungary	6,061
Estonia	4,045
Malta	295
Slovenia	165
Cyprus	52
Total	206,145

Source: Irish Times 11th May 2006

The issue of large numbers of work-permit holders entering the Irish labour market has become an issue for public concern, with fears of Irish workers being displaced by "cheaper" foreign labour. This debate is hardly unique to Ireland, however, and with job-creation figures continuing to be favourable in the Irish economy generally, there have been limited demands for more exclusionary practices, in absolute contrast to the Asylum Seeker / Refugee category which this essay turns to next. Indeed, such was the furore surrounding asylum seekers that consideration of a far larger group, labour migrants, was rarely debated until quite recently (Culleton, 2007).

An asylum seeker can be defined as one striving to secure the protection of this State and as one recognised by the state as a refugee. As Cullen notes (2000), an asylum seeker is "in effect making an application to become a refugee." From just thirty-nine applicants in 1992, the numbers seeking asylum grew to 11,634 in 2002. These numbers lead to considerable unease within political and media circles, reflecting a growing sense of Irish society being "swamped" with foreigners keen to "exploit the Irish Welfare system." Several legislative measures were enacted in the 1995–2006 period, with a largely exclusionary intention, including the Refugee Act (as amended) 1996, the Illegal Immigrants (Trafficking) Act 2000, and the Immigration Act 2004, to highlight some of the larger pieces of legislation. Because of a combination of the above measures, and a Europe-wide general decline in asylum applicants, the number of applicants in Ireland has since dropped steadily. 2003 figures show a decline to 7,900, and this trend continued through 2004 and 2005 with 4,766 and 4,304 applications, respectively (Breen et al, 2006). As of the end of 2006, there are approximately 23,000 people legally resident in Ireland who arrived originally as asylum seekers (Crowley, 2006).

While the above has been a necessarily brief overview of the dramatic shifts in Irish demographic trends, it should be clear that, since 1995, Ireland has been presented with a series of difficulties in constructing immigration policies within the context of what MacEinri notes is "a rapidly changing picture, limited experience, an often less than positive attitude towards difference, and a largely mono-cultural tradition" (2007). Undoubtedly, Irish society has become visibly different in a little over a decade. In particular, for people living in urban areas in Ireland, the sense of palpable change cannot be denied. Where once a dark-skinned face would have been a novelty, it is now unremarkable (O'Connell, 2003). One could certainly construct an argument outlining how Ireland's immigration policies are discriminatory regarding countries of origin, skills and a general unwillingness to accept the "other" into Irish society (see for example, Lentin 2004, Lentin and McVeigh 2006). However, while there is little doubt that high-skill migrants appear to receive a greater degree of attention, the current regime could hardly be seen to be motivated by the "ethno-economic" hierarchy historically prevalent in Irish immigration policy which has traditionally favoured "Western" whites and, later, EU citizens (see Culleton, 2003). In the final analysis, what is apparent, from even such a brief assessment as this, is that Ireland can no longer be regarded as a country of short-term or transient immigration patterns (MacEinri, 2007). Ethnically diverse communities will form a growing section of the Irish population in the foreseeable future. While similar experiences in other European nations have witnessed difficulties for both immigrants and host societies, they have also created opportunities to interact, learn from each other and foster innovation and creativity within and between various ethnic communities as is argued for Canadian best practice, a civic ideal President McAleese espoused in her address to the British Council in London to mark St. Patrick's Day (2007), "The Changing Faces of Ireland — Migration and Multiculturalism" (Mac Cormaic, 2007 and Millar, 2007). What is clear from the multitude of voices and from a multitude of places given voice within this anthology is that notions of "belonging" and "identity" are questioned in fascinating ways.

Sources

Breen, M. Devereux, E. Haynes, A. *Media and Migration* University of Antwerp (UCSIA) Dialogue Series Special Issue Antwerp 2006

Crowley, N. *An Ambition for Equality* Irish Academic Press Dublin 2006

Cullen, P. *Refugees and Asylum Seekers* Cork University Press Cork 2000

Culleton, J. A Vast Lost Chance ERGA: *The Academic Journal of WIT* vol 1 pp53-63 Waterford 2003

Culleton, J. *Ireland, Immigration and Ethnic Minorities,* Curam (Irish Association of Social Care Workers) Dublin 2004

Culleton, J. *"Ireland's Immigrant Children" Child Care in Practice* vol 10: 3 pp 265- 270) July 2004

Culleton, J. *"Institutional Racism in Ireland: Ethnic and Religious Minorities in Criminal Justice and Social Care Provision Systems" European Journal of Social Education* no 12/13 pp51-63 2007

Fanning, B. *Racism and Social Change in the Republic of Ireland* Manchester University Press 2002

Fanning, B. *"Immigration, Racism and Social Exclusion"* in Fanning and Rush (Eds) *Care and Social Change in the Irish Welfare Economy* University College Dublin Press Dublin 2006

Feldman, A "Social Research and Immigration" in Fanning and Rush (Eds) *Care and Social Change in the Irish Welfare Economy* University College Dublin Press Dublin 2006

Lentin, R *From Racial State to Racist State: Ireland on the Eve of the Citizenship Referendum* Varient, 2 (20): 7-8, 2004

Lentin, R and McVeigh, R., *After Optimism? Ireland, Racism and Globalisation,* Metro Eireann Publications, Dublin 2006

Mac Cormaic, R., "Canada could be vision of future, happy to be defined by its diversity . . . Multiculturalism is a core value but new immigrants find the career path steep . . . There is nothing accidental about Canada's ethno-cultural mosaic. Though it falls short of its own target to admit 1% (310,000) of its population in immigrants each year, Canada is more open than anywhere else." *The Irish Times,* 20 June 2007

MacEinri, P. "Immigration: Labour, Migrants, Asylum Seekers and Refugees" in Bartley and Kitchin (Eds) *Understanding Contemporary Ireland* Pluto Press London 2007

Millar, F. "What is perhaps unique to the Irish situation now is the speed and scale of change for we have absorbed in one decade what many other so-called 'countries of immigration' absorbed over many decades if not centuries" (Millar, quoting from the President's Address, *The Irish Times,* 15 March 2007. The transcript of the address can be found at www.ireland.com/focus/mcaleese/index.html).

O'Brien, C. "Former EU Accession state workers exceed 200,000," *The Irish Times,* 11 May 2006

Punch, A. Ireland's Growing Population: an Emerging Challenge in Reynolds and Healy (Eds) *Securing Fairness and Wellbeing in a Land of Plenty* Dublin CORI Justice Commission 2005

Watt and McGaughey (Eds) "Improving Government Service Delivery to Minority Ethnic Groups,' Office of First and Deputy First Minister, Northern Ireland and NCCRI Dublin 2006

Notes on Contributors (Canada)

Kateri Akiwenzie-Damm was born in 1965 in Scarborough, Ontario. A Band Member of the Chippewas of Nawash First Nation, she received an MA in English literature from the University of Ottawa in 1996. Akiwenzie-Damm is a strong Indigenous arts activist, performance poet, and writer. She is the owner and Managing Editor of Kegedonce Press in Canada. Her poetry collection, *my heart is a stray bullet*, was published in April 1993. Her chapbook, *bloodriver woman*, was published in 1998. Her CD, *standing ground*, was released in 2004. She edited *Without Reservation: Indigenous Erotica* (Kegedonce Press/Huia Books, 2003) and co-edited *Skins: Contemporary Indigenous Writing* (Kegedonce Press/Jukurrpa Books, 2000). She currently lives on her traditional homeland at Neyaashiinigmiing, the Cape Croker Reserve. Akiwenzie-Damm credits much of her love of writing to her maternal grandmother, O. Irene Akiwenzie, a respected public speaker, writer and descendant of the Kegedonce line of orators and hereditary chiefs.

Jeannette Armstrong is an Okanagan Indian who was born in 1948 on the Penticton Indian Reserve in British Columbia and is the granddaughter of Thomas James Armstrong, who immigrated from Ireland in the mid-1800s, and Okanagan Indian Christine Joseph. Jeannette Armstrong is a writer, teacher, artist, sculptor and activist. She speaks both Okanagan and English and received a traditional education from Okanagan elders and her family. Her publications include two children's books, two novels, *Whispering in Shadows* (2000) and the seminal work *Slash* (1987), and a collection of poems, *Breath Tracks* (1991). She is also editor of *Looking at the Words of Our People: First Nations Analysis of Literature* (1993). In 1978, she obtained a BFA from the University of Victoria. In 1986, Armstrong became the director of the En'owkin International School of Writing in Penticton, a creative-writing school organized by and for Native people which grants diplomas through the University of Victoria. She has been invited to speak to numerous international audiences on native issues including native education and indigenous rights. In 2000, she received an Honarary Doctorate of Letters from St. Thomas University. In 2003, Jeannette won the Buffet Award for Indigenous Leadership from Eco-Trust, a $25,000 US fellowship, and other awards include the 2005 Angel Award, from the Westside Arts Council, for her contribution and Leadership in the Arts in the Okanagan. That same year, she was named the Poet of the Week by the Canadian Parliamentary Poet Laureate, George Bowering. Armstrong currently serves as the Executive Director of the En'owkin Centre, an indigenous cultural, educational, ecological and creative arts post-secondary institution. In addition, she is also currently completing her PhD from the University of Griefswald-Interdiscipline North American Literature and Environmental Ethics, Germany.

Tammy Armstrong lives currently in Fredericton, New Brunswick. Holder of a BFA and MFA in Creative Writing from UBC, she has had three collections of poetry published: *Take Us Quietly* (Goose Lane Editions 2006), *Bogman's Music* (Anvil Press 2001), which won the Alfred G. Bailey Award – and was shortlisted for the Governor General's Award – and *Unravel* (Anvil Press 2004). Her work has been included in anthologies in Canada, including *Breathing Fire 2: Canada's New Poets* (2004), the US and in the UK. Armstrong also published a novel, *Translations: Aistreann*, in 2002 with Coteau Books.

Martine Audet (Montréal, 1961-) Martine Audet a publié sept recueils de poésie, dont *Les murs clairs* (1996), *Doublures* (1998) et *Orbites* (2000), aux Éditions du Noroît, et *Les tables* (2001), *Les mélancolies* (2003) et *Les manivelles* (2006) à L'Hexagone. Elle participe régulièrement à des événements littéraires, notamment les Marchés de la poésie de Montréal et de Paris, la Biennale internationale des poètes de Val-de-Marne, en France, et ses poèmes paraissent dans des revues (*Action poétique, Arcade, Aube, Entrelacs, Estuaire, Le Sabord, Liberté, Mœbius et Trois*), ainsi que dans des ouvrages collectifs, des anthologies du Québec et d'ailleurs. Entre autres distinctions, elle a reçu le Prix Estuaire des Terrasses St-Sulpice (2000) et le Prix Alain-Grandbois de l'Académie des lettres du Québec (2001).

Martine Audet (Montreal, 1961-) Martine Audet has published seven books of poetry, of which *Les murs clairs* (1996), *Doublures* (1998) and *Orbites* (2000) were published with the Éditions du Noroît, and *Les tables* (2001), *Les mélancolies* (2003) and *Les manivelles* (2006) with L'Hexagone. She takes part on a regular basis in different literary events, particularly the Marchés de la poésie, in Montreal and Paris, and the Biennale internationale des poètes de Val-de-Marne, in France. Her poems are published in reviews such as *Action poétique, Arcade, Aube, Entrelacs, Estuaire, Le Sabord, Liberté, Mœbius and Trois*, as well as in collective works and anthologies in Quebec and abroad. Amongst others distinctions, she was awarded in 2000 the Prix Estuaire des Terrasses St-Sulpice and, in 2001, the Prix Alain-Grandbois by Quebec's Académie des lettres.

One of Canada's most respected poets, **Margaret Avison** was born in Galt, Ontario, lived in Western Canada in her childhood, and lived many years in Toronto. In a productive career that stretches back to the 1940s, she produced seven books of poems, including her first collection, *Winter Sun* (1960), which she selected in Chicago when she was there on a Guggenheim Fellowship, and which won the Governor General's Award. In a work that continued to focus on her interest in spiritual discovery and moral and religious values, *No Time* (Lancelot Press) also won the Governor General's Award in 1989. Avison's published poetry up to 2003 has been gathered into *Always Now: the Collected Poems* (Porcupine's Quill, 2003), including *Concrete and Wild Carrot*, which won the 2003 Griffin Prize. Her most recent book, *Momentary Dark*, was published in 2006 by McClelland & Stewart. Margaret Avison is the recipient of many awards, including the Order of Canada and three honorary doctorates. Avison passed away July 31, 2007.

Born in Newfoundland, **Ken Babstock** grew up in the Ottawa Valley and now makes his home in Toronto. He is an editor of poetry as well as a poet, having worked in the past at the Banff Centre for the Arts, and, presently, as poetry editor for House of Anansi. He has published three collections of poems, *Mean* (Anansi, 1999), which won the Milton Acorn Award and the Atlantic Poetry Prize, *Days into Flatspin* (2001), and *Airstream Land Yacht* (2006), which was shortlisted for the 2006 Governor General's Award and the 2007 Griffin Poetry Prize. In 2002, he took part in Poetry International Rotterdam.

Born in Ottawa, **Anurima Banerji** (graduate of McGill University in Canada) is currently based in New York where she is a doctoral candidate in the Department of Performance Studies, Tisch School of the Arts/NYU. She is also an accomplished performer, having appeared on stage at Buddies in Bad Times, The Box, Bluestockings, Clit Lit, Dixon Place, Divers/Cite, Harbourfront, Luna Sea, North by Northeast, Writer's Block, WOW Cafe Theatre, and YAWP! For the Asian Heritage Festival, she and percussion artist Ganesh Anandan created an original dialogue of music and poetry. *Cities on Fire, But Only at Night*, a collaboration with poet Faizal Deen, was first presented at Desh Pardesh, a South Asian diasporic arts festival. Banerji's poetic work has been shaped by the diverse experiences of living in Montreal, Delhi, Calcutta, Toronto, and San

Francisco over the past years. Her first book was *Night Artillery* (Tsar 2000), and she is currently completing her second poetry manuscript, *A Dark Atlas of the Body*.

Born in Minnesota, **Mike Barnes** has lived most of his life in Canada. At present, he lives in Toronto where he writes poetry and fiction. He has published two books of poetry, *Calm Jazz Sea* (Brick, 1996), which was shortlisted for the 1997 Gerald Lampert Award, and a more recent collection, *A Thaw Foretold* (2006). As well, he has published two collections of short stories and two novels. A memoir, *The Lily Pond*, will be brought out by Biblioasis in 2008.

Born and raised in Burnaby, B.C., **Stephanie Bolster** teaches creative writing at Montreal's Concordia University. One of the poets included in the 1995 *Breathing Fire*, she has since published *Two Bowls of Milk* (McClelland & Stewart, 1999) and *White Stone: The Alice Poems* (Véhicule Press, 1998), which focuses on the lives of Alice Liddell and Lewis Carroll and which won the Governor General's Award in 1998. Her most recent collection, *Pavilion* (McClelland & Stewart, 2002), contains a section which deals with the poetry and death of Diana Brebner, who worked with her on *White Stone*, and with the death of Brebner's daughter, struck by lightning two months after the passing of her mother. Bolster also edited a book of Brebner's work, *The Ishtar Gate: Last and Selected Poems*.

Toronto-based **Roo Borson** was born in California in 1952. Borson has published ten books of poems, most recently *Short Journey Upriver Toward Ōishida* (2004), winner of the Griffin Poetry Prize and the Governor General's Award for Poetry. Borson's *Selected Poems* was nominated for the Governor General's Award for poetry in 1994. Often anthologized, Borson has gained popularity not only in Canada but also South of the border in the United States. With Kim Maltman and Andy Patton, she is a member of the collaborative poetry group Pain Not Bread. She lives in Toronto.

Born in Vancouver and raised in Ladner, **Tim Bowling** worked for many years as a deckhand on a salmon fishing boat. He now lives and writes full time in Edmonton. His poetry appeared in *Breathing Fire: Canada's New Poets* (1995) and in his seven collections since, including *Darkness and Silence* (Nightwood, 2001), which won the Canadian Authors Association Award, and *The Witness Ghost* (Nightwood, 2003) and *The Memory Orchard* (Brick, 2004), both of which were shortlisted for the Governor General's Award. His most recent collection is *Fathom*, from Gaspereau (2006). He has also written three novels, the most recent being *The Bone Sharps* (Gaspereau 2007). A non-fiction work, *The Lost Coast: Salmon, Memory and the Death of Wild Culture*, will appear with Nightwood Editions in Fall 2007.

Dionne Brand is a poet and novelist living in Toronto. Her eight previous volumes of poetry include *Land to Light On*, which won the Governor General's Award for Poetry and the Trillium Book Award in 1997, and her last volume, *thirsty*, which was a finalist for the Trillium Book Award and the Griffin Prize and which won the Pat Lowther Memorial Award for Poetry. Dionne Brand's most recent novel, *What We All Long For*, was published to great acclaim in Canada and Italy in 2005.

Jacques Brault (Montréal, 1933 -) Poète, romancier et essayiste, Jacques Brault a enseigné à l'Institut des sciences médiévales et au département d'Études françaises de l'Université de Montréal, de 1960 à 1996. Depuis 1970, il collabore à de nombreuses émissions littéraires pour Radio-Canada FM et sur les ondes de la Communauté radiophonique de langue française. Traduite en plusieurs langues, l'œuvre de Jacques Brault a été récompensée par de nombreuses distinctions : le Prix Québec-Paris pour *Mémoire* en 1968; le Prix Duvernay en 1978; le Prix Athanase-David en 1986;

le Prix du Gouverneur général du Canada 1970 pour sa pièce de théâtre *Quand nous serons heureux* publiée dans *Trois Partitions*, et en 1985, pour son roman *Agonie*. En 1991, il a reçu le Prix Alain-Grandbois pour *Il n'y a plus de chemin*, et le prix Gilles-Corbeil en 1996. En 1999, sa traduction de l'œuvre de E. D. Blodgett (*Transfiguration*) lui a valu le Prix du Gouverneur général.

Jacques Brault (Montreal, 1933 -) Poet, novelist and essayist, Jacques Brault taught in the Institut des sciences médiévales and in the Études françaises Department of the Université de Montréal from 1960 to 1996. Since the 1970s, he has been a contributor to several literary programs — CBC's French FM radio network and the airwaves of the Communauté radiophonique de langue française. His works have been translated into many languages and awarded several distinctions: the Prix Québec-Paris, for *Mémoire* in 1968; the Prix Duvernay in 1978; the Prix Athanase-David in 1986; the Governor General's Award in 1970, for his play *Quand nous serons heureux*, which was published in *Trois Partitions,* and, then, again in 1985 for his novel *Agonie*. In 1991, he won the Prix Alain-Grandbois for *Il n'y a plus de chemin* and the Prix Gilles-Corbeil in 1996. In 1999, he won the Governor General's once again for his translation of E.D. Blodgett's work *Transfiguration*.

Diana Brebner's three volumes of poetry published in her lifetime — *Radiant Life Forms, The Golden Lotus and Flora & Fauna* — won major Canadian literary awards: the League of Canadian Poets' National Poetry Competition, the Gerald Lampert Award, the Pat Lowther Memorial Award, the Archibald Lampman Award and the CBC Literary Competition. She died of cancer in 2001. Brebner's *The Ishtar Gate: Last and Selected Poems* (2005) was edited by poet Stephanie Bolster, who also provided the introduction to the posthumous volume.

Poète, romancière et essayiste, **Nicole Brossard** est née à Montréal en 1943. Depuis la parution de son premier recueil, en 1965, elle a publié une trentaine de livres dont *Le Centre blanc, La lettre aérienne, Le désert mauve, Hier* et *Cahier de roses et de civilisation*. Deux fois récipiendaire du Prix du Gouverneur général (1974, 1984) pour sa poésie, elle compte parmi les chefs de file d'une génération qui a renouvelé la poésie québécoise dans les années 70. Elle a cofondé en 1965 la revue littéraire *La Barre du Jour* et, en 1976, le journal féministe *Les Têtes de Pioche*. Elle a aussi coréalisé le film *Some American Feminists* (1976). En 1991, elle a publié avec Lisette Girouard, une *Anthologie de la poésie des femmes au Québec* (*Des origines à nos jours*) et en 2002 *Poèmes à dire la francophonie*. En 1991, le prix Athanase-David, la plus haute distinction littéraire au Québec, lui était attribué et, en 1994, elle était reçue à l'Académie des Lettres du Québec. En 1999, elle reçoit pour une deuxième fois Le Grand Prix du Festival international de la Poésie de Trois-Rivières pour ses recueils *Musée de l'os et de l'eau* et *Au présent des veines*. En 2003, le Prix W.O. Mitchell lui est attribué. En 2006, elle reçoit le Prix Molson du Conseil des Arts du Canada. Ses plus récents livres sont *La capture du sombre* (2007) et *Après les mots* (2007). Ses livres sont traduits en plusieurs langues et lui valent aujourd'hui une réputation internationale. Elle vit à Montréal.

Nicole Brossard was born in Montréal in 1943. Poet, novelist and essayist, twice Governor General winner for her poetry, Brossard has published more than thirty books since 1965. Many among those books have been translated into English: *Mauve Desert, The Aerial Letter, Picture Theory, Lovhers, Baroque at Dawn, The Blue Books, Installations, Museum of Bone and Water* and, more recently, *Intimate Journal, Fluid Arguments* and *Notebook of Roses and Civilization*. She has co-founded and co-directed the literary magazine *La Barre du Jour* (1965-1975), has co-directed the film *Some American Feminists* (1976) and co-edited the well-acclaimed *Anthologie de la poésie des femmes au Québec*, first published in 1991 and in 2003. She has also won le Grand Prix de Poésie du Festival international de Trois-Rivières in 1989 and in 1999. In 1991, she was attributed le Prix

An Anthology of Poetry from Canada and Ireland 1133

Athanase-David (the highest literary recognition in Québec). She is a member of l'Académie des lettres du Québec. She won the W.O. Mitchell 2003 Prize and, in 2006, she received the Molson Prize of the Canada Council of Arts. Her work has been widely translated into English and Spanish and is also available in German, Italian, Japanese, Slovenian, Romanian, Catalan and other languages. Nicole Brossard writes and lives in Montréal.

Mark Callanan was born and raised in St. John's, Newfoundland. After graduating with a BA in English Literature from Memorial University of Newfoundland, he lived and worked in Leeds, West Yorkshire, for nearly two years. His first poetry collection, *Scarecrow* (2003), was published by Killick Press. Callanan's work has appeared in Canadian and English journals and in two anthologies: *Breathing Fire 2: Canada's New Poets* (2004) and *The Backyards of Heaven: An Anthology of Contemporary Poetry from Ireland and Newfoundland & Labrador* (2003). Callanan is the book reviewer for the St. John's-based *Independent* newspaper and a regular contributor of reviews and essays to *Books in Canada* and *Canadian Notes & Queries*. He lives in St. John's.

Anne Carson was born in Toronto and grew up in several small Ontario towns. A poet, literary critic, essayist and translator, she earned graduate degrees in Classics from the University of Toronto and a diploma from the University of St. Andrews. She has published ten books of poetry, including *Men in the Off Hours* (Knopf, 2001) and *The Beauty of the Husband* (Knopf, 2002). In addition to the Griffin Prize, which she won in 2001 for *Men in the Off Hours*, she has been awarded a Guggenheim Fellowship (1998), a MacArthur Fellowship (2000) and the T. S. Eliot Poetry Prize in 2001. She lived for many years in Montreal and taught Classics at McGill University. Presently, she is a Professor of Classics and Comparative Literature at the University of Michigan. In 2005, she was made a Member of the Order of Canada.

Francis Catalano (Montréal, 1961 -) Poète et traducteur, Francis Catalano a publié dès 1980 des poèmes et des textes (critiques, traductions) dans des revues : *Nouvelle Barre du Jour, l'Écritoire, Mœbius, Exit, Estuaire, Entrelacs, Liberté, Spirale, Arsenal* (France), *Ritmica, Action poétique, Estuaire* (Luxembourg), *Annali academici canadese* et *Il Veltro*. Il a traduit quelques poètes et romanciers italiens contemporains. Il participe également à plusieurs événements littéraires au Québec et en Italie où il a donné des conférences sur la poésie québécoise. De plus, il est à l'origine d'événements multimédias dont *Le crache-cœur* en 1995, *Index* en 1997 et *Ikoïskow* en 1999. Son premier recueil, *Romamor*, paraît en 1999 aux Écrits des Forges et marque le début d'un cycle qu'il poursuit avec *Index* en 2001 et *M'atterres* en 2002 (publiés chez Trait d'Union). Il a aussi publié *Panoptikon* chez Triptyque en 2005. Il a remporté le Prix John-Glassco 2006 pour sa traduction de *Instructions pour la lecture d'un journal/Didascalie per la lettura di un giornale* (Écrits des Forges, italien-français) de Valerio Magrelli.

Francis Catalano (Montreal, 1961 -) Poet and translator, Francis Catalano started publishing (in the beginning of the 1980s) poems and writings (criticism and translations) in different reviews: *La Nouvelle Barre du Jour, l'Écritoire, Mœbius, Exit, Estuaire, Entrelacs, Liberté, Spirale, Arsenal* (France), *Ritmica, Action poétique, Estuaire* (Luxemburg), *Annali academici canadese* and *Il Veltro*. He has translated a certain number of contemporary Italian poets and novelists. He has taken part in several literary happenings in Quebec and in Italy (where he has also given lectures on Quebec poetry). Furthermore, Catalano is the originator of different multimedia performances, such as *Le crache-cœur* (1995), *Index* (1997), and *Ikoïskow* (1999). His first book of poetry, *Romamor*, published in 1999 with the Écrits des Forges, marked the beginning of a cycle followed by *Index* in 2001 and *M'atterres* in 2002, both of which were published by Trait d'Union. His latest book, *Panoptikon*, was published by Triptyque in 2005. He was awarded the

2006 John-Glassco Prize for his translation of Valerio Magrelli's book *Instructions pour la lecture d'un journal/Didascalie per la lettura di un giornale* (Écrits des Forges, Italian-French).

Herménégilde Chiasson (Saint-Simon, Nouveau-Brunswick, 1946 -) Reconnu sur le plan international, considéré comme l'un des plus grands poètes du Canada français, celui que l'on considère comme le père de la modernité acadienne, Herménégilde Chiasson est d'abord poète, mais aussi cinéaste, artiste visuel et dramaturge. À ce jour, il a à son actif une quinzaine de titres de poésie et une vingtaine pièces de théâtre pour la plupart inédites. Il a réalisé une quinzaine de films et a exposé ses œuvres dans de nombreuses galeries. Herménégilde Chiasson a reçu le Prix France-Acadie pour *Vous* en 1991 et le Prix du Gouverneur général du Canada pour *Conversations* en 1999. En 1990, il était nommé Chevalier des Arts et des Lettres par le gouvernement français et, en 1993, il a reçu l'Ordre des francophones d'Amérique. Il est maintenant lieutenant-gouverneur du Nouveau-Brunswick.

Herménégilde Chiasson (Saint-Simon, New-Brunswick, 1946 -) Internationally renowned, Herménégilde Chiasson is considered as one of the greatest poets of French-speaking Canada and the founder of modern writing in Acadia. First and foremost a poet, he is also involved in film making, the visual arts and playwriting. To this day, he has written about fifteen books of poetry and twenty plays, most of which remain unpublished. He has directed fifteen films or so and shown his visual artwork in several galleries. In 1991, he was awarded the Prix France-Acadie for *Vous* and the Governor General's Award for *Conversations* in 1999. In the same year, he was proclaimed Chevalier des Arts et des Lettres by the French Government, and, in 1993, he was given the Ordre des francophones d'Amérique. He is presently Lieutenant Governor of New Brunswick.

A seventh-generation Canadian of African-American and Cherokee heritage, **George Elliott Clarke** was born in 1960 in Windsor, Nova Scotia. Primarily a poet, he has also auuthored plays, opera libretti, screenplays, a novel, and literary and social criticism. His poetic works include *Black* (2006), *Blue* (2001), both from Raincoast / Polestar Books, *Whylah Falls* (1990), from Polestar, which won the 1991 Archibald Lampman Award, and *Execution Poems* (2000), from Gaspareau Press, which won the 2001 Governor-General's Award. *Whylah Falls* is now in Chinese translation (2006). Another set of Clarke's poems appears in Romanian as *Poeme Incendiare* (2006). His study *Odysseys Home: Mapping African-Canadian Literature* (2002), from University of Toronto Press, served to establish that field. A professor at the University of Toronto, his honours include the Pierre Elliott Trudeau Fellowship Prize (2005).

Leonard Cohen's first poetry collection, *Let Us Compare Mythologies*, was published in 1956. *Book of Longing* (2006) is Cohen's first book since the 1993 collection *Stranger Music: Selected Poems and Songs* and his first book of new material since *Book of Mercy* (1984). Cohen is also well known as a singer and performer: he has made seventeen albums, the latest of which is *Dear Heather* (2004). He also appeared in the 2005 feature-length documentary *Leonard Cohen: I'm Your Man*.

Born in Woodstock, Ont., **Don Coles** was educated at the University of Toronto and Cambridge University. He lived for more than a decade in Sweden and in various other European countries before he returned home to take a position at York University in Toronto. A teacher and a skilled editor of poetry, in particular, he has had a major influence on a large number of Canadian writers in his work at York and as the senior poetry editor for many years at the Banff School of Fine Arts. He is the author of ten books of poetry, including two published by The Porcupine's

An Anthology of Poetry from Canada and Ireland 1135

Quill, *Kurgan*, which won the Trillium Prize in 2000, and *Forests of the Medieval World*, which won the Governor General's Award in 1993. *How We All Swiftly*, published by Véhicule, brings together a selection from six of his earlier collections of poetry. A novel, *Dr. Bloom's Story* (Knopf, 2004), was nominated for the Toronto Book Award. A new work of non-fiction, *A Dropped Glove in Regent Street*, will soon appear from Véhicule Press.

Born in Nova Scotia, **Judith Cowan** grew up in Toronto and was educated at the University of Toronto and L'Université de Strasbourg, France. She has lived in Trois-Rivieres for many years and has translated the work of a wide range of Quebec poets, including Gerald Godin, Yves Préfontaine and Yves Boisvert. She has won various awards for her writing and is a successful writer of original fiction, as well as a translator. Her story collection *More Than Life Itself* (1997) was shortlisted for the Quebec Writers' federation First Book Award.

Lorna Crozier is one of Canada's best-known poets. Born in Swift Current, Saskatchewan, she now lives in British Columbia, where she is a Distinguished Professor at the University of Victoria and Chair of its Department of Writing. She has authored more than a dozen books of poetry, including *The Garden Going On Without Us* (1983), *Angels of Flesh, Angels of Silence* (1988), *Inventing the Hawk* (1992), *A Saving Grace: The Collected Poems of Mrs. Bentley* (1996), and *The Blue Hour of the Day: Selected Poems* (2007). Her work has won many awards, including the Governor General's Award, the Pat Lowther (twice), and the National CBC Literary Competition. Because of her contribution to Canadian poetry, she has been chosen to represent both her home province and her country at important literary and political events. She has also edited several anthologies, including two volumes of *Breathing Fire: Canada's New Poets*.

Beth Cuthand is Cree and was born and grew up in La Ronge, Saskatchewan. She has published three books, *Horse Dance to Emerald Mountain* (1987), *Voices in the Waterfall* (1989), and an IPPY Awards Bronze Medal winner, *The Little Duck* (1999, Reprinted 2003 & 2006); in addition, she has edited a number of other works, and her poems have been published in numerous anthologies. Beth currently lives in Merritt, BC with her husband, Gerry William.

Mary Dalton is the author of four books of poetry, the most recent of which are *Merrybegot* (2003) and *Red Ledger* (2006), both published byVéhicule Press. *Merrybegot*, also available in audiobook form, won the 2005 E. J. Pratt Poetry Award and was shortlisted for several other honours, including the Pat Lowther Award. *Red Ledger*, named one of the top books of the year in *The Globe and Mail*, was shortlisted in 2007 for the Atlantic Poetry Award and the E. J. Pratt Poetry Award. *Between You and the Weather*, a riddling chapbook, is being released by letterpress publisher Running the Goat Books and Broadsides in 2007. Mary Dalton teaches in the Department of English at Memorial University of Newfoundland.

Jean-Paul Daoust (Valleyfield, Québec, 1946 -) Poète et romancier, Jean-Paul Daoust est diplômé de l'Université de Montréal et a enseigné au Cégep. Il a collaboré à plusieurs revues, dont *Hobo-Québec, APLF, Jeu, Spirale, Lèvres urbaines, Jungle* (France), *SCRAP et Rampike* (Toronto), ainsi qu'à *Estuaire*, dont il a été le directeur. Il a publié plus de vingt-cinq recueils de poésie, dont *Taxi pour Babylone* (1996) en coédition Écrits des Forges / Orange Bleue, *Les versets amoureux* (2001), Écrits des Forges / Éditions PHI, et *Cobra et Colibri* (2006) aux Éditions du Noroît. Jean-Paul Daoust a participé à de nombreux festivals au Québec, à Toronto, à Moncton et en France. Il a de plus collaboré à l'organisation de plusieurs événements poétiques. Jean-Paul Daoust a obtenu, en 1990, le Prix du Gouverneur général du Canada pour *Les Cendres bleues*, qui a été traduit en anglais et en espagnol.

Jean-Paul Daoust (Valleyfield, Quebec, 1946 -) Poet and novelist, Jean-Paul Daoust has a degree from the Université de Montréal and has taught in a junior college (Cégep). He has been a contributor to many reviews, such as *Hobo-Québec, APLF, Jeu, Spirale, Lèvres urbaines, Jungle* (France), *SCRAP and Rampike* (Toronto), as well as the editor of *Estuaire*. He has published more than twenty books of poetry, including *Taxi pour Babylone* (1996), co-published by the Écrits des Forges & Orange Bleue (France); *Les versets amoureux* (2001), the Écrits des Forges / Éditions PHI (Luxemburg); and *Cobra et Colibri* (2006) with the Éditions du Noroît. Jean-Paul Daoust has taken part in a number of festivals in Quebec, Toronto, Moncton and France. Moreover, he has been instrumental in organizing many poetry performances and happenings. In 1990, he won the Governor General's Award for *Les cendres bleues*, translated afterwards into English (*Blue Ashes*) and Spanish (*Cenizas Azules*).

Degan Davis's poetry and non-fiction has appeared in a number of literary magazines, including *The Fiddlehead, The New Quarterly* and *Grain*. The poem appearing in this anthology was a winning entry in the Newfoundland & Labrador Arts and Letters competition. He was also awarded the Percy Janes First Novel Award for his manuscript *The Forgetting Room*.

Monique Deland (Montréal, 1958 -) Formée en art visuel et en littérature à l'Université Concordia et à l'Université du Québec à Montréal (UQÀM), Monique Deland a enseigné les arts plastiques à des étudiants du secondaire. Elle a publié trois recueils de poésie, *Géants dans l'île* (Éditions Trois, 1994), *L'intuition du rivage* et *Le nord est derrière moi* (Noroît, 2000 et 2004), et elle collabore à de nombreuses revues telles : *Arcade, Art Le Sabord, Brèves littéraires, Estuaire, Exit, Les Écrits* et *Trois*. Lauréate du Prix Émile-Nelligan 1995 (pour *Géants dans l'île*) et du Grand Prix de Poésie Le Noroît 1993 pour *Ta présence à peine*, elle reçoit également le Prix Québec-Amérique 1997 pour *Rivages, Pour une esthétique de l'ambivalence*. Membre du comité de rédaction de la revue de poésie *Estuaire* depuis 1999 et critique de poésie depuis 1995. À paraître en 2007 au Noroît : *Miniatures, balles perdues et autres désordres*.

Monique Deland (Montreal, 1958 -) With a degree in Visual Arts and Literature from Concordia University and the Université du Québec à Montréal (UQÀM), Monique Deland has taught fine arts at the high-school level. She has published three books of poetry: *Géants dans l'île* (Éditions Trois, 1994), *L'intuition du rivage* and *Le nord est derrière moi* (Noroît, 2000 et 2004). Contributor to many reviews, such as *Arcade, Art Le Sabord, Brèves littéraires, Estuaire, Exit, Les Écrits* and *Trois*, she was awarded the Prix Émile-Nelligan in 1995 for *Géants dans l'île* and the Grand Prix de Poésie Le Noroît in 1993 for *Ta présence à peine*. She also won the Prix Québec-Amérique in 1997 for *Rivages, Pour une esthétique de l'ambivalence*. Member of the editorial committee of *Estuaire* since 1999 and poetry critic since 1995, she is working on a book to be published in 2007 at Le Noroît : *Miniatures, balles perdues et autres désordres*.

Jean-Marc Desgent (Montréal, 1951-) Poète, nouvelliste et critique, Jean-Marc Desgent est diplômé en littérature et en anthropologie de l'Université de Montréal. Il travaille comme imprimeur avant de devenir, en 1976, professeur au Cégep. Membre du comité de rédaction des Éditions Cul-Q de 1975 à 1977 et collaborateur régulier de *Hobo-Québec*, il a fait paraître certains de ses textes dans les revues *Ovo, Jungle* (France), *Mensuel 25* (Belgique), *Vagabondages, La Nouvelle Barre du jour, Travers, Lèvres urbaines et Nos livres*. Jean-Marc Desgent a été deux fois lauréat du Grand Prix du Festival International de Poésie, en 1994, pour son recueil *Ce que je suis devant personne* et en 2005, avec *Vingtièmes siècles*, pour lequel il se méritera aussi le Prix de poésie du Gouverneur général et le Prix Estuaire des Terrasses Saint-Sulpice. En 2000, il a reçu le prix Rina-Lasnier pour son recueil de poèmes *Les Paysages de l'extase* et, en 2002, il a remporté le Prix Félix-Antoine-Savard pour une suite poétique publiée dans la revue *Mœbius*. En 2006, il remporte le Prix Jaime

An Anthology of Poetry from Canada and Ireland 1137

Sabinès/Gatien Lapointe pour l'ensemble de son oeuvre traduite en espagnol. Il a été le poète invité d'honneur au septième Marché francophone de la poésie de Montréal.

Jean-Marc Desgent (Montreal, 1951-) Poet, short-story writer and critic, Jean-Marc Desgent has a degree in Literature and Anthropology from the Université de Montréal. He started working as a printer before he became a professor in a junior college (Cégep) in 1976. Member of the Éditions Cul-Q's editorial committee from 1975 to 1977 and a regular contributor to *Hobo-Québec*, he has published writings in reviews such as *Ovo, Jungle* (France), *Mensuel 25* (Belgium), *Vagabondages, La Nouvelle Barre du Jour, Travers, Lèvres urbaines* and *Nos livres* (Quebec). Jean-Marc Desgent won the Grand Prix du Festival International de Poésie in 1994 for his book *Ce que je suis devant personne* and, once again, in 2005 for *Vingtièmes siècles*, a book which earned him the Governor General's Award and the Prix Estuaire des Terrasses Saint-Sulpice. In 2000, he was given the Prix Rina-Lasnier for his book of poems *Les Paysages de l'extase* and, in 2002, the Prix Félix-Antoine-Savard for a series of poems published in the review *Mœbius*. In 2006, he won the Prix Jaime Sabinès / Gatien Lapointe for his works translated into Spanish. He was the honorary poet of Montreal's seventh Marché francophone de la poésie.

Joël Des Rosiers (Cayes, Haïti, 1951-) Descendant direct de Nicolas Malet, signataire de l'Acte d'indépendance d'Haïti, grand voyageur, médecin psychiatre, poète et essayiste, Joël Des Rosiers vit au Québec depuis la fin de son enfance. Étudiant à Strasbourg, il a hébergé clandestinement nombre de réfugiés et de sans-papiers. Il a publié au Québec plusieurs recueils de poésie remarqués: *Métropolis Opéra* (1987); *Tribu* (1990); *Savanes* (1993), pour lequel il a obtenu le Prix d'excellence de Laval; et *Théories caraïbes* (1996), pour lequel il a obtenu le Prix de la Société des écrivains canadiens. *Vétiver* a paru en 1999 aux Éditions Triptyque et a été traduit en anglais par Hugh Hazelton ainsi que publié au Manitoba (Signature Editions, 2005).

Joël Des Rosiers (Cayes, Haiti, 1951-) A direct descendent of Nicolas Malet, the revolutionary colonist and signatory of the Act of Independence, Joël Des Rosiers is a poet, essayist, a medical doctor and a psychiatrist who has travelled widely. He moved to Canada during his adolescence when his family was granted exile. While a student in Strasbourg, he provided clandestine accommodation for refugees and sans-papiers in Alsace. He has published books of poetry that have garnered significant attention, such as *Métropolis Opéra* (1987); *Tribu* (1990), finalist for the Governor General's Award; *Savanes* (1993), winner of the Prix d'excellence de Laval; and *Théories caraïbes* (1996), winner of the Prix de la Société des écrivains canadiens. *Vétiver*, his latest book, won the 1999 Grand Prix de Montréal and the 2000 Grand Prix du Festival de la poésie in Trois-Rivières. All of his books have been published by Éditions Triptyque. *Vetiver* translated from the French by Hugh Hazelton was published in Manitoba (Signature Editions, 2005).

Adam Dickinson was born in Bracebridge, Ontario, where he grew up around the Muskoka Lakes. His poems, articles, and reviews have appeared in a number of literary journals and in anthologies such as *Breathing Fire 2: Canada's New Poets* and *Post Prairie*. His first book of poetry, *Cartography and Walking*, was published by Brick Books in 2002 and was shortlisted for an Alberta Book Award. The collection that became this book won the 1999 Alfred G. Bailey Prize from the Writer's Federation of New Brunswick for the best unpublished poetry manuscript. His second book of poetry, *Kingdom, Phylum*, was published by Brick Books in 2006 and was a finalist for the 2007 Trillium Book Award for Poetry. Adam received an MA in creative writing from the University of New Brunswick before moving on to Edmonton where he completed his PhD in English at the University of Alberta. He is currently professor of poetics at Brock University in St. Catharines, Ontario, where he teaches poetry, creative writing, and literary theory.

Née à Québec, **Hélène Dorion** a publié plus d'une vingtaine de livres, parmi lesquels *Ravir : les lieux* (2005) qui lui a valu le prix de poésie de l'Académie Mallarmé et le prix du Gouverneur général du Canada, un essai, *Sous l'arche du temps* (2003), et Jours de sable (2002), roman pour lequel elle a reçu le prix Anne-Hébert. En 2006, les Éditions de l'Hexagone ont publié une rétrospective de son œuvre poétique intitulée *Mondes fragiles, choses frêles*. Elle est aussi l'auteure de nombreux livres d'artistes. Elle collabore régulièrement à des ouvrages collectifs et ses textes figurent dans de nombreuses anthologies de poésie francophone. Son œuvre, traduite et publiée dans une quinzaine de pays, lui a valu plusieurs prix littéraires décernés au Québec et à l'étranger. Elle fait partie du jury des prix internationaux de poésie de langue française Léopold Senghor et Louise Labé. En 2006, Hélène Dorion a été reçue à l'Académie des lettres du Québec et, en 2007, elle a été nommée Chevalier de l'Ordre national du Québec.

Hélène Dorion (Quebec, 1958 -) From 1991 to 1999, Hélène Dorion was the literary editor for the Éditions du Noroît and played an important role in the making of a series of audiocassettes promoting poetry and music. She also takes part on a regular basis in meetings, readings and symposiums in Quebec, Europe, the United States and South America. Hélène Dorion is a jury member of the Prix francophone de poésie Louise-Labé and is part of the Académie Mondiale de Poésie. She has published since 1983 over twenty books of poems and prose in Quebec, France and Belgium, such as *Jours de sable*, prize-winner of the Prix Anne-Hébert, as well as an essay *Sous l'arche du temps*. In 2002, an anthology of her poems by Pierre Nepveu, *D'argile et de souffle*, was published in a pocket book collection (TYPO). For her works, translated in a dozen countries, she has been awarded many prizes in Quebec and abroad, such as the Prix Alain-Grandbois of the province's Académie des lettres, the Prix de la Société des écrivains canadiens, the Prix Aliénor, the Prix International de Poésie Wallonie-Bruxelles and the Prize of the International Poetry Festival in Rumania. She was awarded in 2005 the Prix de l'Académie Mallarmé and the 2006 Governor General's Award for her latest book, *Ravir: les lieux*.

Marilyn Dumont. Her first collection, *A Really Good Brown Girl*, won the 1997 Gerald Lampert Memorial Award presented by the League of Canadian Poets. This collection is now in its eleventh printing, and selections from it are widely anthologized in secondary and post-secondary literature texts. Her second collection, *green girl dreams Mountains*, won the 2001 Stephan G. Stephansson Award from the Writer's Guild of Alberta. Marilyn has been the Writer-in-Residence at the universities of Alberta and Windsor, Grant MacEwan Community College in Edmonton, and Massey College, University of Toronto. She teaches Creative Writing through Athabasca University and was a mentor for the 2006 Wired Writing Program at the Banff Centre for the Arts. Marilyn continues to work on a fourth manuscript in which she explores Métis history, politics and identity through her ancestral figure Gabriel Dumont.

Louise Dupré (Sherbrooke, Québec, 1949 -) Poète, dramaturge et romancière, Louise Dupré détient un doctorat en lettres sur la poésie québécoise au féminin. Elle est actuellement professeure de littérature et directrice du Département d'études littéraires à l'Université du Québec à Montréal. Louise Dupré a fait paraître une quinzaine de titres, qui lui ont valu de nombreux prix et distinctions. Elle a signé huit recueils de poésie, dont *Noir déjà* (1993), Grand Prix de poésie de la Fondation des Forges, *Tout près* (1998) et *Une écharde sous ton ongle* (2004) aux Éditions du Noroît; les romans *La memoria* (1996 ; Prix Ringuet de la Fondation Jean-H-Picard 1997) et *La Voie lactée* (2001) chez XYZ éditeur, ainsi que le texte dramatique *Tout comme elle* (2006) chez Québec Amérique. Les romans *Memoria* (1999) et *The Milky Way* (2002) ont été publiés en anglais chez Dundurn Group (Toronto) dans des traductions de Liedewy Hawke et *The Blueness of Light : Selected Poems 1988-2002* a paru en 2005 chez Guernica (Toronto) dans une traduction d'Antonio D'Alfonso. En 1999, elle était reçue dans les rangs de l'Académie des lettres du Québec.

Louise Dupré (Sherbrooke, Quebec, 1949 -) Poet, playwright and novelist, Louise Dupré has a doctorate in women's writing in Quebec poetry. She is presently a professor of Literature and head of the Literary Studies Department in the Université du Québec à Montréal (UQÀM). She has published fifteen books, for which she has been awarded several prizes and distinctions. Among these are eight collections of poems, such as *Noir déjà* (1993; Grand Prix de poésie de la Fondation des Forges); *Tout près* (1998) and *Une écharde sous ton ongle* (2004) with the Éditions du Noroît; two novels : *La memoria* (1996 ; Prix Ringuet de la Fondation Jean-H-Picard in 1997) and *La Voie lactée* (2001), with XYZ éditeur, as well as a play *Tout comme elle* (2006) with Québec Amérique. Both novels, *Memoria* (1999) and *The Milky Way* (2002), were translated into English by Liedewy Hawke and published by the Dundurn Group (Toronto). *The Blueness of Light : Selected Poems 1988-2002* was translated by Antonio D'Alfonso and published in 2005 by Guernica Editions (Toronto). Since 1999, Louise Dupré has been a member of Quebec's Académie des lettres.

Paul Dutton is a poet, novelist, essayist, and oral sound artist, whose principal artistic focus has for many years been the fusion of the literary and musical impulses. He has taken his art to festivals, clubs, concert halls, and classrooms throughout Canada, the United States, and Europe, appearing solo and in ensemble (The Four Horsemen, CCMC, Five Men Singing). The most recent of his six books is the novel *Several Women Dancing*, and the most recent of his five solo recordings is the CD *Oralizations*.

Gary Geddes is a wide-ranging man of letters and has published many books of poetry, as well as fiction, drama, creative non-fiction, criticism and translation. His poems have been translated into Chinese, Dutch, French and Spanish. His Canadian distinctions include the E.J. Pratt Medal and Prize and the Canadian Authors' Association National Poetry Prize. He is the editor of *20th-Century Poetry & Poetics* and *The Art of Short Fiction* and *15 Canadian Poets X 3*. His *Active Trading: Selected Poems* (1975 – 1995) was a Poetry Book Society Recommendation.

Susan Gillis's work has been anthologized most recently in *The New Canon* and *Reading Writers Reading*. Her second book, *Volta*, won the 2003 AM Klein Award. She has lived on the Atlantic and Pacific coasts of Canada and now makes her home in Montréal.

Goh, Poh Seng was born in Kuala Lumpur. He is the author of four novels published in Asia: *If We Dream Too Long, The Immolation, Dance of Moths,* and *Dance with White Clouds*. He has also published five books of poetry: *Eyewitness, Lines from Batu Ferringhi,* and *Bird With One Wing* (also published in Asia); *The Girl from Ermita & Selected Poems* and *As Though the Gods Love Us* were published in Canada. He has just completed a recollection based on his student days in Ireland called *Tall Tales & Misadventures of a Young W.O.G. (Westernized Oriental Gentleman)*.

Born in Jamaica, **Lorna Goodison's** work has appeared in such prestigious publications as the *Norton Anthology of World Masterpieces* and in major international anthologies of contemporary poetry, including the *HarperCollins World Reader* and the *Vintage Book of Contemporary World Poetry*. Among the best-known poets of the Caribbean region, Lorna Goodison's eight volumes of poetry include *To Us, All Flowers Are Roses,* which was awarded a Gold Star by *Booklist* magazine, *Travelling Mercies, Controlling the Silver,* and *Goldengrove: New and Selected Poems*. She is also the author of two collections of short stories and a memoir, *From Harvey River: A Memoir of My Mother and Her People* (2007).The recipient of the 1986 Commonwealth Poetry Prize, Americas Region, Goodison teaches creative writing at the University of Michigan. She divides her time between Ann Arbor and Toronto.

Susan Goyette lives in Halifax, Nova Scotia with her two teenagers. Her first Brick book, *The True Names of Birds* (1998), was shortlisted for the Gerald Lampert, Pat Lowther and Governor General's Awards for poetry. Her novel *Lures* was shortlisted for The Thomas Raddall Award for Fiction. Her second poetry collection, *Undone* (2004), was nominated for the Atlantic Book Prize for Poetry and for the Dartmouth Book Award. She has been a member of the faculty at The Maritime Writers' Workshop, The Banff Wired Studio and Sage Hill. She is currently finishing her second novel.

Catherine Greenwood lives on Vancouver Island. Her first book of poetry, *The Pearl King and Other Poems*, was a 2006 Kiriyama Prize Notable Book.

Louise Bernice Halfe, also known as SKYDANCER, was born in Two Hills, Alberta. She was raised on the Saddle Lake Indian Reserve and attended Blue Quills Residential School. Halfe earned her bachelor of Social Work from the University of Regina and a certificate in Drugs and Alcohol Counselling from Nechi Institute. Her first book of poetry, *Bear Bones & Feathers* (Coteau Books), was awarded the Milton Acorn People's Poet Award and was shortlisted for the Gerald Lambert national poetry award and the Spirit of Saskatchewan Award. Halfe's second book, *Blue Marrow*, a mixture of prose, poetry and journal writing from voices of the past, was a finalist for the Governor General's Award for Poetry in 1998. Originally published by McClelland & Stewart, it, too, is now available from Coteau Books. Her third book, *The Crooked Good*, is being published by Coteau in the fall of 2007.

Richard Harrison is the author of six books of poetry, a nominee for the Governor General's Award, and a winner of the City of Calgary Book Prize and a Milton Acorn People's Poet Award. He was born in Toronto in 1957 and has lived also in Peterborough, Montréal and Calgary where he has taught English and Creative Writing at Mount Royal College for the past twelve years. Richard's poems have been translated into French, Spanish, Portuguese and Arabic. The poems in this book are from *Hero of the Play: 10th Anniversary Edition* (Wolsak & Wynn, 2004) which was launched at the Hockey Hall of Fame to introduce him as the 1995 University of Calgary Markin-Flanagan Writer-in-Residence at the Saddledome, home rink of the NHL Calgary Flames.

Hugh Hazelton is a translator, poet and the publisher of White Dwarf Editions, a press specialising in poetry and short stories in English, French and Spanish. A special interest for him is the comparison between the literatures of the Americas and the diffusion of Canadian writing in the Spanish-speaking world. A graduate of Yale, Concordia and Sherbrooke, he teaches Spanish and Spanish translation at Concordia. He was active as an editor and translator in *Rupturas: la revue des Trois Amériques*.

Ray Hsu is the author of a book of poems, *Anthropy*, which won the 2005 Gerald Lampert Award and was shortlisted for the Trillium Book Award for Poetry. He has published poems in literary journals, including *The Fiddlehead, New American Writing, Fence* (US), and *nthposition* (UK). He is completing his PhD at the University of Wisconsin-Madison.

Catherine Hunter is a poet and novelist who lectures in English at the University of Winnipeg. Cyclops Press published her spoken word CD *Rush Hour* (2000). Her collections of poetry include *Necessary Crimes* (Blizzard Publishing, 1988), *Lunar Wake* (Turnstone Press, 1994) and *Latent Heat* (Nuage Editions, 1997), for which she won the Manitoba Book of the Year Award. Her most recent book is the crime novel *Queen of Diamonds* (Turnstone Press, 2006).

Born in Nelson, British Columbia, **Patrick Lane** has travelled widely in Canada and worked in its woods and fields as well as its universities. He has published twenty-one books of poetry, including *Poems, New and Selected*, which won the Governor General's Award in 1978, and *Selected Poems: 1977-97*, which won the Canadian Authors' Association Award for Poetry. Other important collections are *Old Mother* (Oxford, 1982), *Winter* (Coteau Books, 1989) and *Mortal Remains* (Exile Editions, 1991). Lane has read extensively around the world, and his poetry has been translated into more than a dozen languages. A writer of prose fiction and non-fiction as well, he has written a very successful memoir, *There Is a Season* (McClelland & Stewart, 2005). With Lorna Crozier, he edited *Breathing Fire* (1995) and *Breathing Fire 2* (2004) which showcase the work of young Canadian poets. His latest work, *Last Water Song*, is to be published by Harbour Publishing. Also, in 2007, he was awarded the BC Book Prizes' Lieutenant Governor's Award for Literary Excellence.

Tania Langlais (Montréal, 1979 -) a publié en 2000 aux Herbes rouges un premier recueil remarqué, *Douze bêtes aux chemises de l'homme*, pour lequel elle a remporté le Prix Émile-Nelligan. Elle a fait paraître ensuite chez le même éditeur, en 2004, *La clarté s'installe comme un chat*.

Tania Langlais (Montreal, 1979 -) published in 2000 a first book that drew attention, *Douze bêtes aux chemises de l'homme* (Les Herbes rouges) and for which she was awarded the Prix Émile-Nelligan. Her second book, *La clarté s'installe comme un chat* (2004), was brought out by the same publishing house.

Irving Layton (1912 – 2006) was born Israel Pincu Lazarovitch in the Romanian town of Tirgul Neamt. Less than a year old when his family immigrated to Canada, he grew up in the poor and tough St. Urbain Street district of Montreal, which undoubtedly contributed to shaping his art and nature. His politics were left wing and his manner confrontational. His career as a poet, editor, publisher, and teacher lasted more than four decades and has had an enormous influence on the development of a distinctive modern poetry in Canada. He published more than forty books, including a memoir, *Waiting for the Messiah* (1985), and one of the most important collections of poetry published in this country, *A Red Carpet for the Sun* (1959), which earned him the Governor General's Award. In 1976 he was made an Officer of the Order of Canada. He was twice nominated for the Nobel Prize for Literature. Layton died in Montréal in January 2006.

Nadine Ltaif (Liban, 1961-) a passé son enfance dans un Liban ensanglanté par la guerre ; elle vient s'installer au Québec en 1980 et obtient une majeure en Études cinématographiques et une maîtrise en Études françaises à l'Université de Montréal en 1986. Elle a publié, depuis 1987, cinq recueils de poèmes : *Les Métamorphoses d'Ishtar* (Guernica, 1987), *Entre les fleuves*, (Guernica, 1991; finaliste au Prix Émile-Nelligan), *Le livre des dunes* (1999) et *Le rire de l'eau* (2004), aux Éditions du Noroît. Elle a également participé, en tant que poète, à un livre d'art : *Vestige d'un jardin* (1993). Elle a publié notamment dans les revues *Brèves Littéraires*, *Rupture* et *Arcade* et elle collabore à des documentaires et des films d'auteur indépendants.

Nadine Ltaif (Lebanon, 1961-) had a childhood in Lebanon marked by war. She emigrated to Quebec in 1980 where she majored in Cinema and obtained a Masters degree in French Studies at the Université de Montréal in 1986. She has published since 1987 five books of poems: *Les Métamorphoses d'Ishtar* (Guernica, 1987), *Entre les fleuves*, (Guernica, 1991; finalist for the Prix Émile-Nelligan), *Le livre des dunes* (1999) and *Le rire de l'eau* (2004; Éditions du Noroît). She has also worked on an art book, *Vestige d'un jardin* (1993). Her poetry can also be read in reviews, such as *Brèves littéraires* and *Rupture* and *Arcade*. She works on documentaries and with independent film makers.

Born in Ontario, **Laura Lush** lives in Toronto and teaches English as a Second Language at the University of Toronto. She has travelled extensively and lived for four influential years in Japan teaching English. As well as being a short-fiction writer, she has authored three collections of poetry, her latest being *The First Day of Winter* (Ronsdale, 2002). Her first book, *Hometown* (Véhicule, 1991), was shortlisted for the Governor General's Award for poetry, and her work has won other prizes, including the Bliss Carman Award for poetry at Banff.

Living in Quebec, **Robert Majzels** is a Montreal-born prose writer, playwright, translator and teacher. His play *This Night the Kapo* won first prize in the Dorothy Silver Competition and the Canadian Jewish Playwriting Competition. He has translated several novels by France Daigle, short stories by Anne Dandurand and, with Erín Moure, two books of poetry by Nicole Brossard. He is the author of *Apikoros Sleuth* and *City of Forgetting* (Mercury).

Don McKay is the author of eleven books of poetry. Among his numerous awards and honours are two Governor General's Awards, for *Night Field* (1991) and for *Another Gravity* (2000), and the Griffin Poetry Prize in 2007 for *Strike / Slip*. He was also previously shortlisted twice for the Griffin, for *Another Gravity* and *Camber: Selected Poems* (2004). His deep interest in natural history and the Canadian wilderness infuses most of his work and is the subject of his two books of essays, *Vis á Vis* (2001) and *Deactivating West* (2005). McKay is also widely respected in Canada as a poetry editor and publisher. He edited *The Fiddlehead* for seven years and is presently the associate director for poetry at the Banff Centre. In 1975, he and Stan Dragland founded Brick Books, which continues to be one of Canada's important publishers of Canadian poetry. McKay has lived and taught literature and writing at universities across Canada.

Robert Melançon (Verdun, Québec, 1947 -) Poète et critique littéraire, Robert Melançon a étudié à l'Université de Montréal et à l'Université de Tours, en France, et enseigne au Département d'études françaises de l'Université de Montréal. Il collabore à plusieurs périodiques, dont *Liberté, Ellipse, Renaissance et Réforme, La Revue des sciences humaines, Études françaises, Voix et Images, Estuaire, Écrits du Canada français, Livres et Auteurs québécois* et au quotidien *Le Devoir*. Robert Melançon a reçu le Prix du Gouverneur général du Canada à deux reprises : pour son recueil de poésie *Peinture aveugle* en 1979 et pour sa traduction, en collaboration avec Charlotte Melançon, du *Second Rouleau*, de E.M.Klein en 1990. En 2003, le Prix Victor-Barbeau de l'essai lui est décerné pour *Exercices de désœuvrement*. En 2005, il obtient le Prix Alain-Grandbois pour *Le Paradis des apparences*.

Robert Melançon (Verdun, Quebec, 1947 -) Poet and literary critic, Robert Melançon studied in the Université de Montréal and the Université de Tours in France and teaches in the French Studies Department (UdeM). He is a contributor to many reviews and periodicals, such as *Liberté, Ellipse, Renaissance et Réforme, La Revue des sciences humaines, Études françaises, Voix et Images, Estuaire, Écrits du Canada français, Livres et Auteurs québécois* and *Le Devoir*. Robert Melançon was twice the prize-winner of the Governor General's Award for his book of poetry *Peinture aveugle* (1979) and for his translation in collaboration with Charlotte Melançon of E.M. Klein's novel *The Second Scroll (Le second rouleau;* 1990). In 2003, he was awarded the Prix Victor-Barbeau for his essay *Exercices de désœuvrement*. In 2005, he won the Prix Alain-Grandbois for *Le Paradis des apparences*.

Anne Michaels is the author of three poetry collections: *The Weight of Oranges* (1986), winner of the Commonwealth Prize for the Americas; *Miner's Pond* (1991), winner of the Canadian Authors' Association Award; and *Skin Divers* (1999). Her internationally celebrated first novel, *Fugitive*

An Anthology of Poetry from Canada and Ireland 1143

Pieces (1996), won major awards in four countries, including the Orange Prize for Fiction, the Trillium Book Award, the Chapters/Books in Canada First Novel Award, the Guardian Fiction Award, the Giuseppe Acerbi Prize, and a Lannan Literary Award.

Roy Miki was born in 1942 on a Manitoba sugar beet farm. His parents had been uprooted from their home in British Columbia and relocated there during the Second World War. A poet, writer and editor who teaches at Simon Fraser University in Vancouver, he has been an important figure in the Japanese-Canadian redress movement and was a member of the Strategy Committee when a settlement was reached. Aside from many other writings, he has four important books of poetry: a selected, *Saving Face* (Turnstone, 1991); *Random Access File* (Red Deer College Press, 1995); *Surrender* (Mercury Press, 2001), which won the Governor General's Award; and *There* (New Star Books 2006). In 2006, he was made a Member of the Order of Canada for his contribution to the community and the arts. He was also the recipient of the 20th annual Gandhi Peace Award.

Hélène Monette (Saint-Philippe-de-Laprairie, Québec, 1960 -) Poète et romancière, interprète et lectrice sur scène, Hélène Monette a étudié en arts plastiques et en littérature à l'Université du Québec à Montréal et à l'Université Concordia. Elle a participé à de nombreuses lectures publiques; elle est souvent accompagnée de musiciens, dont Bob Olivier, Pierre St-Jak et Nicolas Letarte. Elle a pris part à des tournées et à des festivals au Québec et à l'étranger (France, Mexique, Portugal), et a collaboré à des émissions de radio et à des films. Hélène Monette a publié dans plusieurs revues dont *Moebius*, *Arcade* et *Le Sabord*. Après avoir publié trois recueils de poésie aux Écrits des Forges, dont *Lettres insolites* en 1991, Hélène Monette a publié chez XYZ Éditeur un recueil de récits, *Crimes et chatouillements* et un roman, *Le goudron et les plumes*. *Plaisirs et paysages* kitsch (contes et poèmes, 1997) a été en nomination au Prix du Gouverneur général. Aux Éditions du Boréal : *Unless* (1995), *Le Blanc des yeux* (1999) et *Un jardin dans la nuit* (2001).

Hélène Monette (Saint-Philippe-de-Laprairie, Quebec, 1960 -) Poet, novelist and performer, Hélène Monette has studied Art and Literature in the Université du Québec à Montréal and in Concordia University. She has taken part in several readings with musicians, such as Bob Olivier, Pierre St-Jak and Nicolas Letarte, in festivals in Quebec and abroad (France, Mexico, Portugal), and contributed to radio programs and films. Hélène Monette has published writings in reviews such as *Mœbius*, *Arcade* and *Le Sabord*. After three books of poetry with the Écrits des Forges, including *Lettres insolites* in 1991, she published a book, *Crimes et chatouillements*, as well as a novel, *Le goudron et les plumes*, with XYZ Éditeur. *Plaisirs et paysages kitsch* (tales and poems; 1997), published by the Éditions du Boréal, was nominated for the Governor General's Award. Her other narratives — *Unless* (1995), *Le Blanc des yeux* (1999) and *Un jardin dans la nuit* (2001) — were also brought out by the same publisher. One of her earlier books, *Montréal brûle-t-elle?* (Les Herbes rouges), was translated into Spanish in Mexico.

Pamela Mordecai was born and grew up in Jamaica. A former language arts teacher with a PhD in English, she was for fourteen years editor of the *Caribbean Journal of Education*. The author of over thirty books, including textbooks, children's books, four collections of poetry and a reference work on Jamaica, her poetry appears in journals worldwide and in major anthologies of Caribbean and African-Canadian literature. Her writing for children is represented in anthologies and textbooks on both sides of the Atlantic. She has a strong interest in promoting the writing of women and has edited ground-breaking anthologies of their writing. She has also written short stories, plays and articles on Caribbean literature and publishing. Her family came to Canada in 1994. She lives in Toronto.

Pierre Morency (Lauzon, Québec, 1942 -) Poète et dramaturge, Pierre Morency fait des études en lettres à l'Université de Laval. En 1967, après quelques années d'enseignement et d'activités théâtrales, il décide de vivre de sa plume et devient auteur et chroniqueur radiophonique à Radio-Canada. Il y écrira plus de deux cents textes radiophoniques, de même qu'une série de soixante émissions portant sur les oiseaux. Il donne également de nombreux récitals de poésie au Québec et à l'étranger, et publie dans les revues *Liberté, Hobo-Québec* et *Odradeq* (Liège). En 1976, il participe à la création de la revue *Estuaire*. En 1989, il a amorcé, avec *L'Oeil américain*, la publication d'une série d'ouvrages sur ses expériences de naturaliste. Pierre Morency a remporté de nombreux prix : le Prix du Maurier pour ses *Poèmes de la froide merveille de vivre* en 1968; le Prix Claude-Sernet (Rodez, France) pour l'ensemble de son oeuvre en 1975; le Prix de l'Institut canadien de Québec pour l'ensemble de son oeuvre en 1979; le Prix Alain-Grandbois et le Grand Prix de poésie de la Fondation des Forges; le Prix Québec-Paris en 1988; le Prix Ludger-Duvernay en 1991; le Prix France-Québec en 1992 et le Prix littéraire des abonnés de la Bibliothèque de Québec pour *Lumière des oiseaux*, prix qu'il reçoit à nouveau en 1995 pour *Les Paroles qui marchent dans la nuit*. En mars 1993, il est reçu Chevalier de l'Ordre des Arts et des Lettres de la République française. Il a également reçu le Prix Athanase-David 2000 qui couronne l'ensemble de la carrière et de l'œuvre d'un écrivain.

Pierre Morency (Lauzon, Quebec, 1942 -) Poet and playwright, Pierre Morency studied Literature in the Université de Laval in Quebec City. In 1967, after a few years of work in the fields of teaching and theatre, he decided to live as a full-time writer and started working for CBC's French-speaking radio network. He has written over two hundred texts for this particular medium, as well as a series of about sixty episodes on North American birds. He has given several poetry readings in Quebec and abroad and has published in reviews such as *Liberté, Hobo-Québec* and *Odradeq* (Liège, Belgium). In 1976, he played a role in creating the review *Estuaire*. In 1989, he started publishing a series of books, *L'Oeil américain*, inspired by his experiences as a keen observer of wildlife in the North American context. Pierre Morency has won many prizes: the Prix du Maurier, for his *Poèmes de la froide merveille de vivre* in 1968; the Prix Claude-Sernet (Rodez, France), for his works in 1975; Quebec City's Prix de l'Institut Canadien in 1979; the Prix Alain-Grandbois and the Grand Prix de poésie de la Fondation des Forges; the Prix Québec-Paris in 1988; the Prix Ludger-Duvernay in 1991; the Prix France-Québec in 1992; the subscribers' Prix littéraire de la Bibliothèque de Québec for *Lumière des oiseaux*, a prize he would once again be awarded in 1995 for *Les Paroles qui marchent dans la nuit*. In March 1993, France honored him with the Chevalier de l'Ordre des Arts et des Lettres. Furthermore, he won the Prix Athanase-David in 2000, which the Government of Quebec awards on a yearly basis to recognize one's career in writing.

Award-winning poet and playwright, **Daniel David Moses** is a Delaware from the Six Nations lands on the Grand River in Southern Ontario. He holds an Honours B.A. from York University and an M.F.A. from the University of British Columbia. He writes full-time and works with the Native and cross-cultural arts communities in Toronto. Amongst his publications are *The Indian Medicine Shows: two one-act plays* (Toronto: Exile Editions Limited 1995), poetry collection *Delicate Bodies* (Nightwood Editions, 1992), and *Coyote City: A Play in Two Acts* for which he was nominated for the Governor General's Award in 1991. With Terry Goldie, he is also editor of *An Anthology of Canadian Native Literature in English* (Don Mills, Ontario: Oxford University Press, 1992, 1998 and 2005).

Born in Calgary, **Erín Moure** is a poet and translator who has lived for many years in Montreal. She has a dozen books of poetry to her credit, many of which have won major awards. These include *Domestic Fuel* (Anansi, 1985), which won the Pat Lowther Memorial Award, and *Furious*

(Anansi, 1988), which won the Governor General's Award. Two of her books, *Sheep's Vigil by a Fervent Person* and *Little Theatres*, have earned nominations for the Canadian Griffin Prize. Also nominated for the Governor General's Award, *Little Theatres* won the A. M. Klein Prize for Poetry. Moure's most recent work is *O Cadoiro*. She has also translated French, Galician, and Spanish works of poetry.

Born in Huntsville, Ontario, and living now in Toronto, **Alayna Munce** is a young writer of fiction, a poet and an editor of poetry. Her first novel, *When I Was Young and in My Prime*, was published in 2005 by Nightwood Editions and nominated for a Trillium Award. Munce has also won prizes three times in *Grain* magazine's annual Short Grain Contest. Her work has been published in a range of Canadian literary journals, including the anthology *Breathing Fire 2: Canada's New Poets* (2004). Earlier, in 2003, she won a CBC Literary Award. An attendee at the Banff Centre's writing studio for poetry and fiction, she variously writes and works both in bars and as assistant production manager for Brick Books.

One of **Susan Musgrave's** ancestors, Sir Richard Musgrave (of Cappoquin, County Waterford), was knighted for his *Memoirs of The Irish Rebellion of 1798*. While Susan Musgrave's recent *You're in Canada Now, Motherfucker . . . A Memoir of Sorts*, has not yet entitled her to a peerage, Douglas Coupland (author of Generation X) wrote, "This is the best book I've read in a long time." She teaches in the University of British Columbia's Optional-Residency MFA in Creative Writing Programme and lives on the Queen Charlotte Islands / Haida Gwaii.

Pierre Nepveu (Montréal, 1946 -) Pierre Nepveu est poète, essayiste et romancier et enseigne la littérature à l'Université de Montréal. Boursier du gouvernement français, il a poursuivi des études de maîtrise à l'Université Paul Valéry de Montpellier avant de terminer un doctorat à Montréal en 1977. Entre 1969 et 1978, il enseigne la littérature québécoise et française dans plusieurs universités canadiennes : McMaster (Hamilton), Sherbrooke, Colombie-Britannique (Vancouver) et Ottawa. Depuis 1978, il est professeur au Département d'études françaises de l'Université de Montréal. Pierre Nepveu est codirecteur de la revue *Ellipse* de 1972 à 1975, critique de poésie dans la revue *Lettres québécoises* de 1975 à 1982, et dans la revue *Spirale* depuis 1985 dont il a été codirecteur et membre. Il fait également paraître des textes dans *Liberté, Études françaises, Voix et images, La Nouvelle Barre du Jour, Estuaire* et *Le Devoir*. Il dirige actuellement la revue *Études françaises* à l'Université de Montréal. Auteur de six recueils de poèmes dont *Lignes aériennes* (2002), pour lequel il obtenait le Prix du Gouverneur général et, en 2003, *le Grand Prix du Festival international de la Poésie*. Il a aussi consacré de nombreux travaux critiques à la poésie québécoise contemporaine. Le Prix du Gouverneur Général du Canada lui a été attribué à deux autres reprises pour son recueil de poésie *Romans-fleuves* en 1997 et pour son essai *Intérieurs du Nouveau Monde : Essai sur les littératures du Québec et des Amériques* en 1998. Enfin, il a remporté, en 1999, le Prix de critique littéraire Jean-Éthier Blais pour *Lignes aériennes*. Une rétrospective de son œuvre poétique, *Le sens du soleil*, a paru à Montréal aux Éditions de l'Hexagone et, en 2005, il a obtenu du Gouvernement du Québec le prix Athanase-David pour l'ensemble de son œuvre. Pierre Nepveu a également participé à plusieurs Rencontres québécoises internationales des écrivains, ainsi qu'à des conférences aux États-Unis et en Europe. Il est membre de l'Académie des lettres du Québec.

Pierre Nepveu (Montreal, 1946 -) Pierre Nepveu is a poet, essayist, and novelist and teaches literature in the Université de Montréal. With a bursary from the French Government, he undertook a Master's degree in Montpellier's Université Paul Valéry, then finalized a doctorate in Montreal in 1977. From 1969 to 1978, he taught Quebec and French literature in several universities across Canada: McMaster (Hamilton), Sherbrooke, British Columbia (Vancouver), and Ottawa. Since

1978, he has been a professor in the French Studies Department (UdeM). Pierre Nepveu was co-director for the review *Ellipse* from 1972 to 1975, poetry critic for *Lettres québécoises* from 1975 to 1982, and for *Spirale* since 1985. He also publishes texts in *Liberté*, *Études françaises*, *Voix et images*, *La Nouvelle Barre du Jour*, *Estuaire* and *Le Devoir*. He has written six books of poetry, including *Lignes aériennes* (2002), for which he won the Governor General's Award and, in 2003, the Grand Prix du Festival international de la poésie. Previously, he was twice awarded the Governor General's for his book of poetry, *Romans-fleuves* (1997), and for his essay *Intérieurs du Nouveau Monde : Essai sur les littératures du Québec et des Amériques* (1998). A collection of his poetry, *Le sens du soleil*, a retrospective, was published in 2005 in Montreal by the Éditions de l'Hexagone, for which he was awarded Quebec's Prix Athanase-David. Pierre Nepveu has taken part as well in different international events, such as writers' meetings and lectures in Quebec, the United States and Europe. He is a member of Quebec's Académie des lettres.

bpNichol (1944–1988) was a major literary innovator who remains one of Canada's most important and original poets, his influence extending throughout the country and beyond. His body of work constitutes a holistic expression of all the dimensions of language and vocal expression—sonic, visual, intellectual, emotional. He worked in a multitude of forms: lyric, sound, visual (manual, typewriter, type, and computer), and conceptual poetry; fiction, theory, criticism, children's literature and TV, comics, song, and music theatre. Among his works are *The Martyrology* (nine books in six volumes), *Zygal*, *Truth*, and *Art Facts*.

David O'Meara was born and raised in Pembroke in the Ottawa Valley. He has worked as a bartender in various Eastern and Western Canadian cities and taught English in South Korea. His first collection of poems, *Storm still* (McGill / Queens, 1999), was shortlisted for the Gerald Lampert prize. His second collection, *The Vicinity* (Brick Books, 2003), won Ottawa's Archibald Lampman Award and was shortlisted for The Trillium Book Award for Poetry. His latest collection will be brought out by Brick in 2008.

Michael Ondaatje was born in Sri Lanka and has lived in Canada since 1963. His works include *The Conversations: Walter Murch and the Art of Editing Film*, *Anil's Ghost*, *The English Patient*, *In the Skin of a Lion*, *Coming Through Slaughter*, *The Collected Works of Billy the Kid*, and his memoir, *Running in the Family*. His collections of poetry include *Secular Love*, *The Cinnamon Peeler* and *Handwriting*. He has made two documentary films: *Sons of Captain Poetry* (on the poet bpNichol) and *The Clinton Special* (about Theatre Passe Muraille's *The Farm Show*), available from Mongrel Media September 2003 (Films by Michael Ondaatje). His new novel (spring 2007) is *Divisadero*.

Elise Partridge grew up in the Eastern U. S. and was educated at Harvard and Boston University. She lives now in Vancouver working as an editor and tutor. Her poems have been published in journals in various countries, including *The Fiddlehead*, *Poetry* and *Poetry Ireland Review*. She won a Special Commendation in the 1987 Arvon International Poetry Contest judged by Seamus Heaney and Ted Hughes, and received an honourable mention from Paul Muldoon in the 2000 New York Yeats Society Contest. She is one of Canada's strongest new voices, as her first collection, *Fielder's Choice* (Véhicule, 2002), makes abundantly clear. Her second book, *Chameleon Hours*, will be published in 2008 in Canada by Anansi and in the U.S. by the University of Chicago.

Sunshine-Coast resident who lives near Sakinaw Lake with his wife and three kids, **John Pass** has been working for nearly twenty years on a quartet of books (under the umbrella title *At Large): The Hour's Acropolis* (Harbour, 1991), shortlisted for the Dorothy Livesay Poetry Prize; *Radical Innocence* (Harbour, 1994); *Water Stair* (Oolichan, 2000), shortlisted for both the

An Anthology of Poetry from Canada and Ireland 1147

Dorothy Livesay Prize and the Governor General's Award; and *Stumbling in the Bloom* (Oolichan, 2005), winner of the 2006 Governor General's Award. Pass teaches English in the Adult Basic Education program at Capilano College.

Alison Pick was the winner of the 2005 CBC Literary Award for Poetry, the 2003 National Magazine Award for Poetry, and the 2002 Bronwen Wallace Award for most promising Canadian poet under the age of 35. Her collection *Question & Answer* was shortlisted for the Gerald Lampert Award and for a Newfoundland and Labrador Book Award. Alison's first novel, *The Sweet Edge*, was a *Globe and Mail* Top 100 Book of 2005 and has recently been optioned for film. Her new collection of poetry, *The Dream World*, is due out from McClleland & Stewart in Spring 2008.

Kyran Pittman is a poet and essayist living in the American south since 1966. Her poetry has appeared in numerous American, Canadian and Irish anthologies, including *New Century North American Poets*, as well as in the *Globe and Mail* and *TickleAce*. Her essays have been published in major North American newspapers and magazines. Raised in Corner Brook, her grandmother was Mary Pittman who published poems and short stories under the pseudonym Len Margaret. Her father, Al Pittman, was a poet, playwright and author of short fiction and books for children. She describes herself as a Newfoundlander with a Canadian passport and an American green card, but belonging to no country. She journals online at www.notestoself.us

Yves Préfontaine (Montréal, 1937 -) À 18 ans, il commence une carrière d'auteur-animateur à Radio-Canada. En 1959, il participe à la fondation des revues *Situations* et *Le Québec libre*, se joint au comité de direction de la revue *Liberté*, dont il devient par la suite le rédacteur en chef. En 1959-60, il sera membre-fondateur du Rassemblement pour l'indépendance nationale (RIN). Étudiant au doctorat à Paris de 1966 à 1970, il concevra et animera plusieurs émissions consacrées aux différents aspects, politiques et culturels, de la société québécoise à l'invitation de l'ORTF (aujourd'hui Radio-France). De retour au Québec, il enseignera à l'Université McGill et à l'Université du Québec à Montréal, et occupera de différents postes au Gouvernement du Québec, aux Affaires publiques de Radio-Canada (Québec) et à Radio-Canada International. Il est également directeur de cabinet du ministre d'État au développement culturel, Camille Laurin. Yves Préfontaine publie ses deux premiers recueils, *Boréal* et *Les temples effondrés*, à vingt ans. *L'antre du poème, aphorismes et fragments*, paraît en 1960 aux Éditions du Bien public. Il obtient, en 1968, le premier prix des Concours littéraires et scientifiques du Québec et le Prix France-Québec pour *Pays sans parole* (l'Hexagone 1967); et, en 1990, le Prix Québec-Paris pour sa rétrospective *Parole tenue* (poèmes 1954-1985, l'Hexagone 1990). En 1994, il obtient le prix Pey-de-Garros (France) pour l'ensemble de son travail littéraire. Suivront en 2000, le Prix Félix-Antoine-Savard de poésie et en 2002, le Prix Estuaire-Terrasses-Saint-Sulpice pour *Être — Aimer — Tuer* (l'Hexagone 2001). Ses poèmes sont traduits en anglais, en espagnol, en italien, en hongrois, en roumain et en croate.

Yves Préfontaine (Montreal, 1937 -) At the age of eighteen, he started a career as a writer and broadcaster for French CBC and also worked later on as an editor and communications consultant. In 1959, he was one of the founders of the reviews *Situations* and *Le Québec libre*; he also became a member and editor of the still well-known review *Liberté*. In 1959-60, he played an important part as a member and founder of the Rassemblement pour l'indépendance nationale (RIN). From 1966 to 1970, and while studying in Paris at a doctoral level, he conceived and hosted several programs on different political and cultural aspects of Quebec society for the ORTF (Radio-France). Back home, he taught at McGill University and the Université du Québec à Montréal (UQÀM), worked for the Government of Quebec, CBC's Public Affairs Department and CBC International. In addition to this, he worked as the principal private secretary of the State Minister to Cultural

Development, Camille Laurin. At the age of twenty, Yves Préfontaine published his two first books of poetry, *Boréal* and *Les temples effondrés*. *L'antre du poème*, a book of aphorisms, was brought out in 1960 by the Éditions du Bien Public. In 1968, he was the prize-winner of Quebec's Concours littéraires et scientifiques and the Prix France-Québec for *Pays sans parole* (l'Hexagone,1967); in 1990, he was awarded the Prix Québec-Paris for his collected poems, *Parole tenue* (1954-1985, l'Hexagone). In 1994, he was awarded the Prix Pey-de-Garros (France), in 2000, the Prix Félix-Antoine-Savard and, in 2002, the Prix Estuaire-Terrasses-Saint-Sulpice for *Être — Aimer — Tuer* (l'Hexagone 2001). Several of his poems have been translated into English, Spanish, Italian, Hungarian, Rumanian and Croatian. His book *This Desert Now (Le désert maintenant)* was translated from the French by Judith Cowan, a long-time translator of Quebec poets, and published in 1993 by Guernica Editions.

Steven Price was born and raised in Colwood, BC. *Anatomy of Keys* (Brick Books, 2006), his first collection of poetry, won the 2007 Gerald Lampert Award and was named a Best Book of the Year by the *Globe and Mail*. A graduate of the University of Virginia Writing Program, he teaches poetry and writing at the University of Victoria.

Perhaps Canada's most popular poet, **Al Purdy** (1918-2000) was born in Wooler, Ontario and raised in Trenton. He hit the road early in his life because of the difficult economic conditions of the time, working at various jobs in Vancouver and Montreal and other Canadian cities and towns. As well, he spent six years in the R.C.A.F. Later, he was to settle in Ameliasburg and build an A-frame home and write about rural Ontario and his Loyalist ancestors. In his long life, he travelled extensively throughout the country and wrote more about the land and people than any other Canadian poet. He also travelled widely outside his country writing about places like Greece and Russia and Mexico. In sixty years of writing, he produced thirty-three books of poetry and nine collections of essays and correspondence. He earned many awards, including two Governor General's — in 1965 for *The Cariboo Horses* and in 1986 for *The Collected Poems of Al Purdy*. In 1982, he was appointed to the Order of Canada.

Matt Rader is a grad student at the University of Oregon, as well as being a literary chapbook publisher and co-founder of *Crash: Vancouver's Indie Writers' Fest*. His poetry and chapbooks have won plaudits from various quarters: *sub-TERRAIN, Broken Pencil, Geist* and *This Magazine*. His work was published in *Breathing Fire 2: Canada's New Poets*. His first collection, *Miraculous Hours,* was published by Nightwood Editions (2005) and was shortlisted for the 2006 Gerald Lampert Award.

Born in Baltimore, **Michael Redhill** has lived in Toronto most of his life. He is a poet, short-fiction writer, novelist, playwright and editor. He has published five collections of poetry, including *Lake Nora Arms* (Coach House Press, 1993; House of Anansi Press, 2001), *Asphodel* (McClelland & Stewart, 1997) and his most recent, *Light-crossing* (Anansi, 2001). His fiction includes *Fidelity* (Doubleday, 2003), a collection of short fiction, and *Martin Sloane* (Doubleday, 2001), a first novel that was nominated for the Giller Prize, the Trillium Award, and the City of Toronto Book Award and won the Commonwealth Writers' Prize for Best First Novel. A new novel, *Consolation*, came out in 2006 and made the long list of twelve for the Man Booker Prize. His play, *Goodness* (Coach House, 2005), was named Best of Edinburgh in 2006. Redhill is also the publisher and editor in chief of Brick.

Armand Garnet Ruffo's work is strongly influenced by his Ojibway heritage. He is the author of three books of poetry, *At Geronimo's Grave* (Coteau Books, 2001), *Grey Owl: the Mystery of Archie*

Belaney (Coteau Books, 1996), and *Opening in the Sky* (Theytus Books, 1994). In 2002, he was awarded the Archibald Lampman Award for Poetry and, in 2000, the Canadian Authors' Association Prize for Poetry. In 2006, his work appeared in the National Gallery of Canada's retrospective catalogue on the Ojibway painter Norval Morrisseau, founder of the woodland school of painting. Ruffo currently lives in Ottawa and teaches at Carleton University.

Gregory Scofield is a Métis poet, writer, activist and community worker whose maternal ancestry can be traced back five generations to the Red River Settlement and to Kinesota, Manitoba. He has published five award-winning books of poetry, as well as a memoir, *Thunder in My Veins: Memories of a Métis Childhood*. *Singing Home the Bones* (2005) is Scofield's first book in five years; it reclaims, through poetry and storytelling, the untold history of the Métis people and Scofield's own biological family.

Since the early 1990s, Jamaican-born **Olive Senior** has lived in Canada. Although she returns to Jamaica frequently, her permanent residence is in Toronto. Senior has published poetry, short stories, and scholarly works related to Jamaican heritage and culture. Her poetry collections include *Talking of Trees* (1985), *Gardening in the Tropics* (1994), *Over the Roofs of the World* (2005), which was nominated for the Governor General's Award, and *Shell* (forthcoming 2007). In acknowledgement of her cultural work and contributions to literature, in 2005 she was awarded the prestigious Musgrave Gold Medal by the Institute of Jamaica.

Sue Sinclair is one of Canada's most promising young writers. She grew up in Newfoundland and lives and works now in Toronto. She has three collections, *The Secrets of Weather and Hope* (Brick, 2001), *Mortal Arguments* (Brick, 2003), and *The Drunken, Lovely Bird* (Goose Lane Editions, 2004). A fourth book will be published by Brick Books in 2008. Sue Sinclair was one of the poets whose work was chosen for *Breathing Fire 2*.

Daniel Sloate was born in Windsor, Ontario. He majored in French at the University of Western Ontario and subsequently spent fifteen years in France where he obtained a doctorate in French literature and where he began to publish his first books of poetry. While in France, he began his translation career which he continued on his return to Canada. He has translated Rimbaud's *Illuminations* as well as several Quebec poets: Jean-Paul Daoust, André Roy, Hélène Dorion, Claude Beausoleil and Denise Desautels, among others. He taught translation at the Université de Montréal and McGill University. He is now retired.

One of the country's strongest new writers, **Karen Solie** was born in Moose Jaw, Saskatchewan, and raised on the family farm in the south-western part of the province. Her first collection, *Short Haul Engine* (Brick, 2001), won the 2002 Dorothy Livesay Poetry Prize and was shortlisted for the Canadian Griffin Poetry Prize. Her second book, *Modern and Normal* (Brick, 2005), was shortlisted for the Trillium Award. She has travelled back and forth across the country frequently in the last few years, giving readings and working as a resource person and writer-in-residence at the University of Alberta and the University of New Brunswick. Her work has appeared in *Open Field: 30 Contemporary Canadian Poets* (Persea, 2005) and *The New Canon: An Anthology of Canadian Poetry* (Vehicule, 2006).

Carmine Starnino is a Montreal poet, essayist, editor, and critic. He has published three acclaimed books of poetry, *The New World* (Véhicule, 1997), *Credo* (McGill-Queen's University Press, 2000), which won the 2001 Canadian Authors' Association Prize, and *With English Subtitles* (Gaspereau, 2004), which won the 2004 QWF A.M. Klein Prize for Poetry. Starnino is as well-known for his unapologetically clear and strong views about Canadian poetry, expressed in his literary criticism, as he is for his poetry. His reviews and essays have appeared in *Books in Canada, Arc, Canadian Poetry, CNQ National Post,* and *The Globe and Mail* and have been brought together in *A Lover's Quarrel* (Porcupine's Quill, 2004). As well, he works as associate editor for Maisonneuve magazine and is poetry editor of Signal Editions, an imprint of Véhicule Press.

John Steffler was born in Toronto in 1947 and grew up in a rural area near Thornhill, Ontario. He studied at the University of Toronto and the University of Guelph. In 1975, he moved to Newfoundland and began teaching at Memorial University's Sir Wilfred Grenfell College in Corner Brook, from where he just recently retired. He is both a fiction writer (former finalist for the Governor General's Award) and a poet, whose poetry collections include *An Explanation of Yellow* (1980), *The Grey Islands* (1985), *Flights of Magic* (1987), *The Wreckage of Play* (1988) and *That Night We Were Ravenous* (1998). On December 4, 2006, John Steffler was named as the Parliamentary Poet Laureate of Canada, the third poet to be given that honour since the position was established in 2002. He is currently writer-in-residence at Concordia University.

Cole Swensen is the author of eleven books of poetry and translates French poetry, prose, and art criticism. Her translation of Jean Fremon's novel *The Island of the Dead* won the 2004 PEN USA Award in Literary Criticism. She also edits La Presse Books, a small press dedicated to contemporary French poetry.

Marie Uguay (1955-1981) a publié des poèmes dans les revues *Vie des arts, Estuaire* et *Possibles* ainsi que trois recueils de poésie aux Éditions du Noroît, dont *Signe et rumeur* (en 1976) et *L'outre-vie* (en 1979). Elle apparaît dans *La Nuit de la poésie 1980*, de Jean-Claude Labrecque, qui réalisa aussi un film sur elle avec l'aide de Jean Royer. Elle reçoit le prix littéraire Radio-Canada en 1981, peu de temps avant de mourir du cancer, à 26 ans, et la médaille de la Fondation Émile-Nelligan, à titre posthume, au moment de la parution de son troisième recueil, *Autoportraits*, en 1982. L'ensemble de son oeuvre est regroupé dans *Poèmes*, aux Éditions du Noroît (1994). Ses poèmes ont été traduits en anglais en 1983 dans la revue montréalaise *Ellipse*, puis en 1990 par Daniel Sloate, dans *Selected Poems*, aux Éditions Guernica.

Marie Uguay (1955-1981) has published poems in reviews, such as *Vie des arts, Estuaire* and *Possibles*, as well as three books of poetry with the Éditions du Noroît: *Autoportraits* in 1982, *Signe et rumeur* in 1976 and *L'outre-vie* in 1979. She appears in *La Nuit de la poésie* 1980, a film by Jean-Claude Labrecque, who also directed with the help of Jean Royer a documentery on Marie Uguay. She was awarded the Prix littéraire Radio-Canada in 1981 just before she died of cancer-illness at the age of twenty-six. Posthumously, she was given a medal by the Fondation Émile-Nelligan in 1982, while her third book, *Autoportraits*, was being published. Her collected poems, *Poèmes*, were published by the Éditions du Noroît in 1994. Her writings have been translated into English in 1983 by the Montreal-based review *Ellipse* and, then, in 1990 by Daniel Sloate (*Selected Poems*, Guernica Editions).

A native of the Placentia Bay area, **Agnes Walsh** is a poet, playwright, storyteller and translator. Her first collection of poems, *In the Old Country of My Heart*, was published by Killick Press (St John's) in 1996 and released as an audiobook by Rattling Books in 2004. Her latest collection, *Going Around With Bachelors*, was published by Brick Books in 2007. Walsh is also the founder of the Tramore Theatre Troupe on the Cape Shore of Placentia Bay which was where many Irish from the Waterford area settled. With Stan Dragland, she has adapted an Icelandic novel by Nobel Prize-winner Haldor Laxness for the theatre. Her work has been translated into French, Portuguese and Icelandic. In 2006, she was named the first poet laureate for St. John's.

An Anthology of Poetry from Canada and Ireland 1151

Born in Kansas City, Missouri, **Frederick Ward** studied music at the Conservatory there and at The School of Contemporary Music in Toronto (the creation of Mr. Oscar Peterson and company, which does not exist any longer). His compositions have been played by several recognized groups in the United States, and he has worked with the National Film Board in the Maritimes. Ward has edited two anthologies: *Anthology of Nine Baha'i Poets* and *Present Tense*. His books include *Poems* (Duende, 1964); *Riverlisp: Black Memories* (Tundra, 1974); *Nobody Called Me Mine: Black Memories* (Tundra, 1977); *Fields of Endless Day* (film script, O.E.T., 1977); *Riverlisp* (Theatre Centaur, 1975); *Jno: A Play in 12/8 Gospel Time, A Room Full of Balloons* (Tundra, 1981); and *The Curing Berry* (Williams-Wallace, 1983). He now divides his time between Montreal and Nova Scotia.

Born in Long Pond, Manuels in Conception Bay, **Enos Watts** is one of Newfoundland's most respected poets. He has published three collections of poetry, *After the Locusts* (Breakwater 1974), *Autumn Vengeance* (Breakwater 1986) and *Spaces Between the Trees* (Pennywell 2005), which was shortlisted for the Winterset Award and longlisted for the ReLit Award.

Born in Winnipeg, **Darren Wershler-Henry** is Assistant Professor of Communication Studies at Wilfrid Laurier University and is a writer, critic and the former senior editor of Coach House Books. Darren is the author of three books of poetry, *NICHOLODEON: a book of lowerglyphs; the tapeworm foundry* (shortlisted for the Trillium Prize); and *apostrophe* (with Bill Kennedy, shortlisted for the ReLit Award). His most recent book is *The Iron Whim: A Fragmented History of Typewriting*.

Zoe Whittall is the author of the novel *Bottle Rocket Hearts* (Cormorant, 07) and two volumes of poetry, *The Emily Valentine Poems* (Snare, 06) and *The Best Ten Minutes of Your Life* (McGilligan, 01). Her work has been anthologized widely in books like *Baby Remember My Name: Queer Girls Writing in their 20s* (edited by Michelle Tea) and *Breathing Fire 2: Canada's New Poets*, edited by Lorna Crozier and Patrick Lane. *The Globe and Mail* recently called her "the cockiest brashest, funniest, toughest, most life-affirming, elegant, scruffy, no-holds-barred writer to emerge from Montreal since Mordecai Richler." Originally from Quebec, she's lived in Toronto since 1997.

Born in Victoria, **Patricia Young** has published eight books of poetry, including *All I Ever Needed Was a Beautiful Room* (Oolichan, 1987), which won the 1988 Dorothy Livesay / B. C. Poetry Prize, and *The Mad and Beautiful Mothers*, (Ragweed, 1989), which won the 1990 Pat Lowther Memorial Prize. Two later collections, *More Watery Still* (Anansi,1993), and *Ruin and Beauty*, (2000),were shortlisted for the Governor General's Award for poetry. Her first book of short fiction, *Airstream* (Biblioasis, 2006), won the inaugural Metcalf-Rooke Award. She is the 2007/08 writer in residence at the University of New Brunswick.

Born and brought up on the prairies, **Jan Zwicky** now lives on Vancouver Island where she teaches philosophy at the University of Victoria. In addition to six collections of poetry, she has written two philosophical works, the second receiving a Governor General's Award nomination in the same year that *Robinson's Crossing* (Brick, 2004) was nominated for poetry. Her earlier collection of poems, *Songs for Relinquishing the Earth* (Brick, 1998), won the 1999 Governor General's Award. *Thirty-Seven Small Songs & Thirteen Silences* (Gaspereau, 2005) is her most recent book. As well, Zwicky is an editor and musician.

Notes on Editors and Consultants

Born in Vancouver, **Randall Maggs** teaches Canadian Literature and Creative Writing at Sir Wilfred Grenfell College in Corner Brook, Newfoundland. With John Ennis and Stephanie McKenzie, he is an editor of *However Blow the Winds*, a companion work to *The Echoing Years*. His new book of poetry, *Night Work: The Sawchuk Poems*, will be published by Brick Books in February 2008 and launched at the Canadian Hockey Hall of Fame and the March Hare. A participant in Newfoundland's March Hare festival of words and music from the beginning, he has been its Artistic Director since 2002. He is also a craftsman and visual artist and took part in the 2001 Ireland and Newfoundland collaborative exhibition, *Wood: A Sculptual Investigation*. In 2007, he was awarded a Coracle Fellowship funded by Memorial University to promote exchanges between Ireland and Newfoundland.

Stephanie McKenzie holds a PhD in literature from the University of Toronto and is Assistant Professor in English at Sir Wilfred Grenfell College (Memorial University of Newfoundland). She is the author of a book of literary criticism, *Before the Country: Native Renaissance, Canadian Mythology* (forthcoming with University of Toronto Press 2007) and a collection of poetry, *Cutting My Mother's Hair* (Cliffs of Moher: Salmon Poetry 2006). In 2002, she founded a publishing house on the West coast of Newfoundland, Scop Productions Inc., and co-edited and co-published (with WIT, School of Humanities) *However Blow the Winds: An Anthology of Poetry and Song from Newfoundland & Labrador and Ireland* (2004) and *The Backyards of Heaven: An Anthology of Contemporary Poetry from Ireland and Newfoundland & Labrador* (2003). She also published (and co-edited with Marc Thackray) *Humber Mouths: Young Voices from the West Coast of Newfoundland & Labrador*. With Martin Ware, McKenzie also co-edited *An Island in the Sky: Selected Poetry of Al Pittman* (Breakwater Books, St. John's 2003).

Born in the Irish midlands, **John Ennis** is the author of thirteen books of poetry: from The Gallery Press, *Night on Hibernia*, 1976 (winner of the Patrick Kavanagh Award 1975); *Dolmen Hill* (which features "Orpheus," called by Robert Hogan "the most amazing long poem any Irish poet has written since Kavanagh's *The Great Hunger*");* *A Drink of Spring* (1979); *The Burren Days* (1985); from The Dedalus Press: *Arboretum* (1990); *In A Green Shade* (1991); *Down in the Deeper Helicon* (1994); *Telling the Bees* (1995); *Selected Poems* (1996); *Tráithnínt* (2000); *Near St. Mullins* (2002); from Scop: *Goldcrest Falling* (2006); from WIT / AIT: *Oisíns Journey Home* (2006), a long heroic poem on the now defunct Newfoundland Railway. Educationalist, beekeeper, editor, chair of the Centre for Newfoundland and Labrador Studies at Waterford Institute of Technology, where he is Head of the School of Humanities, he received the Irish American Cultural Institute Award in 1996.

Dominique Gaucher est née en 1955 à Montréal. Sociologue, elle travaille depuis plus de vingt-cinq ans dans la Fonction publique québécoise; elle est l'auteure de plusieurs publications scientifiques. En 1995, elle recevait le Premier prix de prose de la Société littéraire de Laval et, en poésie, le Prix Piché-Le Sortilège du Festival international de poésie de Trois-Rivières. Elle a publié poèmes et nouvelles dans diverses revues et un recueil de poésie intitulé *Solos* (Écrits de Forges, 1999). Un autre recueil est en préparation. Elle dirige la revue *Brèves littéraires* depuis l'automne 2006.

* *Dictionary of Irish Literature*, Gill and Macmillan (1980)

Jean-Pierre Pelletier. Né à Montréal. Il a étudié la littérature et la philosophie. Poète, traducteur, enseignant. Cofondateur de *Ruptures, la revue des trois Amériques* (1992-1998) et membre de l'équipe éditoriale de la revue *Brèves littéraires* (2006-2007). Il a fait paraître en 2006 un livre de poèmes, *L'Amnésique* et une traduction de poèmes de Dorotea Sanchez, *La Comedia rouge sang* (Adage, 2006). Paraîtra aussi une édition bilingue de la poète colombienne, Yvonne-América Truque (Adage et la Naine blanche, 2007). Deux autres livres sont en préparation : *Baraques et baraka*, et *Alluvions*. Collabore à des revues du Québec, des USA et de Colombie à titre de poète et de traducteur.

Permissions / Acknowledgements (Canada)

Akiwenzie-Damm, Kateri: "stray bullets (oka re/vision)" and "sturgeon" are reprinted by permission of Kateri Akiwenzie-Damm and Kegedonce Press. "partridge song" and "rainstorm in volcano: eight poems for rain," are reprinted by permission of Kateri Akiwenzie-Damm.

Armstrong, Jeannette C.: "History Lesson," "Threads of Old Memory," and "Rocks," from *Breath Tracks* (Williams-Wallace 1991). Reprinted by permission of Jeannette C. Armstrong and Theytus Books.

Armstrong, Tammy: "Hockey," from *Bogman's Music* (Anvil Press 2001). Reprinted by permission of Anvil Press. "No One Goes with the Exhibition Boys" was originally published in *Take Us Quietly* copyright © 2006 by Tammy Armstrong. Reprinted by permission of Goose Lane Editions.

Audet, Martine: "Les labours blancs . . . ," "De certains rêves . . . ," et "Il nous semblait parfois . . . ," de *Les manivelles* (Éditions de l'Hexagone 2006). Reproduits avec l'autorisation de l'auteur et de l'éditeur.

Avison, Margaret: "Balancing Out," "Ramsden," "Ambivalence," "He Was There / He Was Here," "Remembering Gordon G. Nanos," "On a Maundy Thursday Walk," and "Lament for Byways" (originally published in *Concrete and Wild Carrot*, Brick 2002). Reprinted from *Always Now: The Collected Poems / Margaret Avison* (in three volumes) (Porcupine's Quill 2003) copyright © Margaret Avison, 2003. Reprinted by permission of Porcupine's Quill and the author.

Babstock, Ken: "Marram Grass," "Essentialist," "Windspeed," "Late Drive Toward Innisfil," and "A Birth in the Stern," from *Airstream Land Yacht* (Anansi 2006). Reprinted by permission of House of Anansi Press and the author.

Banerji, Anurima: "Summer, or I Want the Rage of Poets to Bleed Guns Speechless with Words," from *Night Artillery* (Tsar 2000). Reprinted by permission of Tsar Publications.

Barnes, Mike: "Stirring a Can of Soup on the Stove," from *Calm Jazz Sea* (Brick 1996). Reprinted by permission of Mike Barnes and Brick Books.

Bolster, Stephanie: "Aperture, 1856," "Whose Eyes," from "In Which Alice Poses for Julia Margaret Cameron, 1872," "Two Deaths in January, 1898," "Close Your Eyes and Think of England," and "Portrait of Alice with Christopher Robin," from *White Stone: The Alice Poems* (Véhicule Press 1998). Reprinted by permission of Véhicule Press.

Borson, Roo: From "Summer Grass" ("River" and "Rivers to the Sea") in *Short Journey Upriver Toward Ōishida* by Roo Borson © 2004. Published by McClelland & Stewart. Used with permission of the publisher. From "Autumn Record" in *Short Journey Upriver Toward Ōishida* by Roo Borson © 2004. Published by McClelland & Stewart. Used with permission of the publisher.

Bowling, Tim: "Grade One" and "Watching the Academy Awards in the Bar of the Patricia Hotel," from *The Memory Orchard* (Brick 2004). Reprinted by permission of Tim Bowling and Brick Books.

Brand, Dionne: From *thirsty* by Dionne Brand © 2002. Published by McClelland & Stewart. Used with permission of the publisher. From *Land to Light On* by Dionne Brand © 1997. Published by McClelland & Stewart. Used with permission of the publisher.

Brault, Jacques: "c'est un soir pas . . . ," de *"Trois fois passera* (Éditions du Noroît 1981) p. 40; *"Neige d'un soir* . . . ," de *Moments Fragiles* (Éditions du Noroît / Le Dé Bleu 1984) p.36; "Ce n'est plus le moment . . . ," de *Il n'y a plus de chemin* (Éditions du Noroît 1990) p.65; "Bucolique," de *Au bras des ombres* (Arfuyen / Éditions du Noroît, 1997), p.11. Reproduits avec l'autorisation de Les Éditions du Noroît.

Brebner, Diana: "The Blue Light of the Neutron Pool," "The Green Canoe," section 3 of "At the Schwarzschild Radius," "Morning on the Guitar," and "Port," from *The Ishtar Gate: Last and Selected Poems* (McGill-Queen's UP 2005). Reprinted by permission of McGill-Queen's University Press.

Brossard, Nicole: "Typhon dru," de *Musée de l'os et de l'eau* (Noroît, 1999). Reproduit avec l'autorisation de Les Éditions du Noroît.

Brossard, Nicole: "Typhoon Thrum" (English). Trans. Robert Majzels and Erín Moure. From *Museum of Bone and Water* (Anansi 2003). Reprinted by permission of House of Anansi Press.

Callanan, Mark: "The Delicate Touch Required for China," from *Scarecrow* (Killick Press 2003). Reprinted by permission of the author.

Carson, Anne: "New Rule," "Shadowboxer," "Father's Old Blue Cardigan," from "TV Men:" — from "Akhmatova (Treatment for a Script)," "Antigone (Scripts 1 and 2)," and Thucydides in Conversation with Virginia Woolf . . ." — from *Men in the Off Hours* (Random House of Canada 2001); "But a Dedication is only Felicitous . . . ," "Here is My Propaganda . . . ," and "To Clean Your Hooves . . . ," from *The Beauty of the Husband* (Random House of Canada 2002). Reprinted by permission of The Knopf Publishing Group.

Catalano, Francis: "Vus d'en bas . . . ," de *Romamor* (Écrits des Forges 1999), p.17. Reproduit avec l'autorisation de l'auteur et Les Écrits des Forges Inc. "néo-libéralisme à clavier . . . ," de *Panoptikon* . . . (Les éditions Triptyque 2005). Reproduit avec l'autorisation de l'auteur et Les éditions Triptyque. "Les idées fondent comme du beurre . . . ," de *M'atterres* (Les éditions Trait d'union 2002). Reproduit avec l'autorisation de l'auteur et Les éditions Triptyque. "Amérique terre archaïque . . ." et *"Homo lupus est* . . . , " de *Index* (Les éditions Trait d'union 2001). Reproduits avec l'autorisation de l'auteur et Les éditions Triptyque.

Chiasson, Herménégilde: de *Répertoire* (Écrits des Forges et le Dé bleu 1993), nos. 1-8 (pp. 9-10); nos. 101-108 (pp. 34-35); nos. 201-208 (pp. 59-60); nos. 301-308 (pp. 84-85); nos. 401-408 (pp. 109-110). Reproduit avec l'autorisation de l'auteur et Les Écrits des Forges Inc.

Clarke, George Elliott: "Identity I," "Child Hood I," "Reading *Titus Andronicus* in Three Mile Plains, N.S.," "Duet," "Hard Nails," "Spree," and "Trial II," from *Execution Poems* (Gaspereau Press 2001). Reprinted by permission of Gaspereau Press and the author. "Look Homeward, Exile," "Four Guitars," "Night Train," "Blues for X," "Rev. F. R. Langford's Miracle," "A Sermon to the Undecided," and "The Sermon of Liana," from *Whylah Falls* © 1990, 2000 by George Elliott Clarke. First published in 1990 by Polestar Book Publishers. Reprinted by permission of Raincoast Books, 9050 Shaughnessy Street, Vancouver B.C., V6P 6E5.

Cohen, Leonard: "Paris again . . .," "Too Old," "Layton's Question," "Robert Appears Again," "Pardon Me," "The Party Was Over Then Too," "Butter Dish," "The Collapse of Zen," "Oh and one more thing . . . ," and "A Note to the Chinese Reader." From *Book of Longing* by Leonard Cohen © 2006. Published by McClelland & Stewart. Used with permission of the publisher.

Coles, Don: "Forests of the Medieval World," "Night Game," and selections from "The Edvard Munch Poems," from *Forests of the Medieval World* (Porcupine's Quill 1993); "Kingdom," "Reading a Biography of Samuel Beckett," "'There are no words to remember, but I do have that gaze,'" "Sampling from a Dialogue," and "Romance," from *Kurgan* (Porcupine's Quill 2000). Reprinted by permission of Porcupine's Quill and the author.

Cowan, Judith, trans.: translation of Yves Préfontaine's "Non-lieu" ("Non-lieu"), from *This Desert Now* (Guernica 1993). Reprinted by permission of Guernica. Translation of Pierre Nepveu's "On promet d'excaver le sol . . . " ("They're promising to excavate the ground . . ."), "Je pressens cette terre sans arbres . . ." ("Already, I see this land stripped of trees . . . "), "Nouveau Monde" ("New World"), "L'homme des plans" ("The Plans Man"), and "Bilan" ("Summing Up"), from *Mirabel* (Véhicule 2004). Reprinted by permission of Véhicule Press.

Crozier, Lorna: "You're So Covered with Scars" and "South Dakota Refuge," from *The Garden Going On Without Us* by Lorna Crozier © 1985. Published by McClelland & Stewart. Used with permission of the publisher. "Dictionary of Symbols," "Variation on the Origin of Flight," "Home Care," "The Memorial Wall," and "Skunks," from *Inventing the Hawk* by Lorna Crozier © 1992. Published by McClelland & Stewart. Used with permission of the publisher. "Dust," "Not the Music," and "Mrs. Bentley," from *A Saving Grace: The Collected Poems of Mrs. Bentley* by Lorna Crozier © 1996. Published by McClelland & Stewart. Used with permission of the publisher. "Small Gesture" and "Hoping to Fix Up, a Little, This World," from *Whetstone* by Lorna Crozier © 2005. Published by McClelland & Stewart. Used with permission of the publisher.

Cuthand, Beth. "For All the Settlers Who Secretly Sing." Published by permission of the author. "Post-Oka Kinda Woman" (originally published in *Gatherings: the En'owkin Journal of First North American Peoples*, vol. V, 1994, Theytus). Published by permission of the author. "Zen Indian," from *Voices in the Waterfall* (Theytus 1992). Reprinted by permission of Theytus Books.

Dalton, Mary: "To Be Sold" and "I'm Bursting to Tell: Riddles for Conception Bay," from *Red Ledger* (Véhicule Press, 2006). Reprinted by permission of Véhicule Press.

Daoust, Jean-Paul: de *Les cendres bleues*, pp. 53-55 (Les Écrits des Forges 1990). Reproduit avec l'autorisation de l'auteur et Les Écrits des Forges Inc.

Davis, Degan: "Hockey," first published in *The New Quarterly*, no. 94, Spring 2005. Reprinted by permission of the author.

Deland, Monique: "la question toujours la même . . ." (p.38), "certains lendemains . . ." (p.41), "mes mains frileuses . . ." (p.51), "La nuit a rejoint la ligne . . . " (p. 59), "J'accumule des retailles . . ." (p.77), "Une voix sans corps annonce . . ." (p.79), et "la joue sur l'oreiller . . ." (p.86), de *Le nord est derrière moi* (Éditions du Noroît 2004). Reproduit avec l'autorisation de Les Éditions du Noroît.

Desgent, Jean-Marc: "65," de *On croit trop que rien ne meurt* (Écrits des Forges 1992), p.41; "Le monde de monstres est banal . . . ," pp.42-43, et "Je vois l'intelligent théâtre . . . ," p.64 de *Vingtième siècles* (Les Écrits des Forges 2005). Reproduits avec l'autorisation de l'auteur et Les

An Anthology of Poetry from Canada and Ireland 1157

Écrits des Forges Inc. "Les premiers paysages," de *Les paysages de l'extase* (Les Herbes rouges / poésie 1997). Reproduits avec l'autorisation de l'auteur et de Les Herbes rouges.

Des Rosiers, Joël: "le 26 octobre 1951 . . . ," "mon père assembla . . . ," "l'enfance est d'immortalité . . . ," "pour *Guillane* . . . ," et "il fut difficile de quitter . . . ," de *Vétiver* (Les éditions Tryptique 1999). Reproduit avec l'autorisation de l'auteur et Les éditions Triptyque.

Dickinson, Adam: "When We Become Desirable," "Believing the First Words You Hear," and "Fort Smith Fire Brigade," from *Cartography and Walking* (Brick, 2002). Reprinted by permission of Brick Books and the author.

Dorion, Hélène: "*En ce temps-là* . . . ," "Une maison brûle . . . , " "Recommence devant moi . . . ," et "Tu refais le voyage . . . ," de *D'argile et de souffle* (Montréal, Éditions Typo, 2002). Reproduits avec l'autorisation de l'auteur. "Le monde dévore nos paupières . . .," de *Ravir : les lieux* (Clepsydre / La Différence 2005). Reproduits avec l'autorisation de l'auteur et de l'éditeur.

Dumont, Marilyn: "Circle the Wagons," "The White Judges," "Letter to Sir John A. Macdonald," "Leather and Naughahyde," "Let the Ponies Out," and "The Sky is Promising," from *A Really Good Brown Girl* (Brick 1996). Reprinted by permission of Brick Books and the author.

Dupré, Louise: "Là, voilà ta demeure . . . ," "Tout est possible à l'ombre des jardins . . . ," "Tu peux encore lever la main . . . ," "Rien ne suffit à ton regard . . . ," "Cela arrive toujours sans prévenir . . . ," et "Tu relèves ta robe . . . ," "Tes morts, tu en es venue . . . " de *Tout près* (Éditions du Noroît 1998). Reproduits avec l'autorisation de Les Éditions du Noroît.

Dutton, Paul: "One Plus," "Lost Way Lost," "Kit-Talk," "Strata," "Thinking," "Dreaming," "Jazzstory," "Succession," "Obscure," "Truck," "Content," "Night," "Several Times Table," "Shy Thought," and "Words." Reprinted by permission of Paul Dutton.

Geddes, Gary: "Subsidies" and "Junk Food Pastoral" in *Active Trading: Selected Poems 1970-1995* (Peterloo Poets and Goose Lane Editions, 1996). Reprinted by permission of the author.

Gillis, Susan: "Distant Islands (But of course they were further apart)," "Habitat (South elevation)," "Habitat (We stand here looking)," and "River (Dear X.)." By permission of the author.

Goh, Poh Seng: "The Girl from Ermita," from *The Girl from Ermita and Selected Poems* 1961-1998 (Nightwood 1998). Reprinted by permission of the author.

Goodison, Lorna: "from Dante's *Inferno*, Canto XV Brunetto Latini," "Questions for Marcus Mosiah Garvey," "Crossover Griot," and "Poor Mrs. Lot," from *Travelling Mercies* by Lorna Goodison © 2001. Published by McClelland & Stewart. Used with permission of the publisher.

Goyette, Susan: "This Contradiction of Passion," "Sisters," "More Widow Than Queen Victoria," "Sinking," and "A Chinese Lantern for Audrey," from *The True Names of Birds* (Brick 1998). Reprinted by permission of Brick Books and the author.

Greenwood, Catherine: "The Diving Girls' Prayer," "In Service to a Dream," "Pearl Farmer's Wife," and "Dream Thief," from *The Pearl King and Other Poems* (Brick Books 2004). Reprinted by permission of Brick Books and the author.

Halfe, Louise: "Der Poop," "In Da Name of Da Fadder," "Pāhkahkos," "Nōhkom, Medicine Bear," "You've Got to Teach White Women Everything," from *Bear Bones and Feathers* (Coteau Books 1994), and excerpt ("*Father, these robes I wear confuse me . . .*"), from *Blue Marrow* (Coteau 1998). Reprinted by permission of Coteau Books.

Harrison, Richard: "Coach's Corner" (originally published in *Hero of the Play*, Toronto: Wolsak and Wynn Publishers Ltd., 1994) and "Elegy for the Rocket," from *Hero of the Play: 10th Anniversary Edition* (Toronto: Wolsak and Wynn Publishers Ltd., 2004). Reprinted by permission of the author.

Hazelton, Hugh, trans.: translation of Joël Desrosier's "le 26 octobre 1951 . . ." ("on October 26 1951 . . ."), "mon père assembla . . ." ("my father assembled . . ."), "l'enfance est d'immortalité . . ." ("childhood is immortality . . ."), "pour *Guillane* . . ." ("for *Guillane* . . ."), and "il fut difficile de quitter . . ." ("it was hard to leave . . ."), from *Vetiver* (Signature Editions 2005). Reprinted by permission of the author.

Hsu, Ray: "Early Work: An Eclogue," from *Inferno* XXXII-XXXIII ("Our bread-famished mouths . . ."), and "Dora (Confession, 0.93 Seconds)," from *Anthropy* (Nightwood Editions 2004). Reprinted by permission of Nightwood.

Hunter, Catherine: "Two Thousand and Two," published in *Post-Prairie: An Anthology of New Poetry* (Talonbooks 2005). Reprinted by permission of the author.

Lane, Patrick: "Drought 1980," "Weasel," "Monarch I," and "The Dream of the Red Chamber," from *Old Mother* (Oxford 1982). "The Happy Little Towns," from *Selected Poems: Patrick Lane* (Oxford 1987). Reprinted by permission of the author.

Langlais, Tania: "sa façon, la sienne. . . ," "quand elle retire sa petite robe . . . ," "s'il fallait que tu meures . . . ," "rien ne se raconte plus . . . ," "tu lisais l'autre nuit . . . ," "et "je suppose que ça va finir . . .," de *Douze bêtes aux chemises de l'homme* (Les Herbes rouges / poésie 2000). "n'en pouvant plus je l'ai écrit . . . ," "je ne soigne personne . . . ," et "le désordre ça prend combien de boîtes . . . ," de *La clarté s'installe comme un chat* (Les Herbes rouges / poésie 2000). Reproduits avec l'autorisation de Les Herbes rouges.

Layton, Irving: "Fishermen" and "Aran Islands," from *The Collected Poems of Irving Layton* by Irving Layton © 1971. Published by McClelland & Stewart. Used with permission of the author's estate. "The Swimmer," "On Seeing the Statuettes of Ezekiel and Jeremiah in the Church of Notre Dame," "The Fertile Muck," "Berry Picking," "An Old Niçoise Whore," "To the Girls of My Graduating Class," "Song for Naomi," and "The Predator," from *A Wild Peculiar Joy* by Irving Layton © 1982, 2004. Published by McClelland & Stewart. Used with permission of the author's estate.

Ltaif, Nadine: "La Simûrghiade" from *Entre les fleuves* (Guernica 1991); Reproduit avec l'autorisation de Guernica. "Reconnaissance" et "Si j'étais un homme . . .," de *Élégies du Levant* (Éditions du Noroît 1995); "Début mai . . . ," "Un arbre dans sa solitude . . . ," "Les arbres nus du printemps . . . ," et "Quand je pourrai écrire un chant . . . ," de *Le livre des dunes* (Éditions du Noroît 1999); "Je suis de retour dans les contrées sauvages . . . ," de *Le rire de l'eau* (Éditions du Noroît 2004). Reproduits avec l'autorisation de Les Éditions du Noroît.

Lush, Laura: "157 Islington," "Home," and "Mr. Ishigami," from *Hometown* (Véhicule Press 1991); "Children," "The Last of Us," "Darkening In," "Strays," "Border," "Gavey H.," "Kelly,"

"Riverside Heights," "The Session," "Komachu's," and "Mama-san," from *Faultline* (Véhicule Press 1997). Reprinted by permission of Véhicule Press. "The Wellesdale" and "The Year My Sister Came to Live with Me," from *The First Day of Winter* (Ronsdale Press 2002). Reprinted by permission of Ronsdale Press.

McKay, Don: "Softball:" from *Sanding Down This Rocking Chair on a Windy Night* © 1987. Published by McClelland & Stewart. Used with permission of the publisher. "Meditation on Shovels," from *Night Field* by Don McKay © 1991. Published by McClelland & Stewart. Used with permission of the publisher. "Chickadee Encounter," "Meditation on Antique Glass," "Setting Up the Drums," and "Matériel," from *Apparatus* by Don McKay © 1997. Published by McClelland & Stewart. Used with permission of the publisher. "Hover" and "Sometimes a Voice (1)," from *Another Gravity* by Don McKay © 2000. Published by McClelland & Stewart. Used with permission of the publisher. "Song of the Saxifrage to the Rock," "Precambrian Shield," and "Song for the Songs of the Common Raven," from *Strike / Slip* by Don McKay © 2006. Published by McClelland & Stewart. Used with permission of the publisher.

Mélançon, Robert: "Peinture aveugle" et "l'été" de *Peinture aveugle* (VLB éditeur 1979); "Les dieux en décembre" de *L'avant-printemps à Montréal* (VLB éditeur 1994). Reproduits avec l'autorisation de l'auteur et de VLB éditeur. "Description d'un après-midi" de *Le dessinateur* (Éditions du Noroît 2001). "36" de *Le paradis des apparences* (Éditions du Noroît 2004). Reproduits avec l'autorisation de l'auteur et Les Éditions du Noroît.)

Michaels, Anne: "Three Weeks" and "Ice House" from *Skin Divers* © 1999. Published by McClelland & Stewart. Used with permission of the publisher.

Miki, Roy: "fool's scold, 1.4.97," from *Surrender* (Mercury Press 2001). Reprinted by permission of the author.

Monette, Hélène: "Un coin du jardin sans soleil . . ." de *Plaisirs et paysages kitsch. Contes et poèmes* (Les éditions du Boréal 1997). Reproduit avec l'autorisation de Les éditions du Boréal. "160 secondes," et "Il n'y a personne qui crie . . . ," de *Estuaire* no. 119 (2004). Reproduits avec l'autorisation de Estuaire.

Mordecai, Pamela: Selections from de *Man: a performance poem* — "Jesus Is Condemned to Death," "Jesus Meets His Mother," "The Women of Jerusalem Mourn for Jesus," "Jesus Is Nailed to the Cross," and "Jesus Is Taken Down from the Cross" — (Sister Vision Press 1995) and excerpts from the glossary. Reprinted by permission of the author and Sister Vision Press.

Morency, Pierre: "Le monde dans la peau" et "Je t'écris," de *Poèmes 1966-1986* (Les Éditions du Boréal 2004). Reproduits avec l'autorisation de l'auteur et de l'éditeur.

Moses, Daniel David: "Song in the Light of Dawn," "Rooms Under Rain," and "Falling Song," from *Delicate Bodies* (Nightwood Editions 1992). Reprinted by permission of Nightwood. "The Line" and "The Persistence of Songs," from *The White Line* (Fifth House Publishers 1990). Reprinted by permission of Fifth House Publishers.

Moure, Erín: Excerpts from "Seven Rail Poems" ("VIA Tourism" and "We Are a Trade") from *Wanted Alive* (Anansi 1983). "Shock Troop," from *Domestic Fuel* (Anansi 1985). "A History of Vietnam . . . ," "Goodbye to Beef," "Fifteen Years," "Thirteen Years," "West to West," "In These (Tough) Times," "Miss Chatelaine," and "Meeting," from *Furious* (Anansi 1988). Reprinted by permission of House of Anansi. "Homage," from *Empire, York Street* (1979). Reprinted by permission of the author.

Munce, Alayna: "To Train and Keep a Peregrine You Cannot Miss a Day." Printed by permission of the author.

Musgrave, Susan: "Magnolia," "Understanding the Sky," No Hablo Ingles," and The Room Where They Found You" (first published in *The March Hare Anthology 2007*). Published by permission of the author.

Nepveu, Pierre: "Étendue" et "Belvédère," de *Romans-fleuves* (Éditions du Noroît 1997); "On promet d'excaver le sol . . . , "Je pressens cette terre sans arbres . . . ," "Nouveau monde," "L'homme des plans," et "Bilan," de *Lignes aériennes* (Éditions du Noroît 2002). Reproduits avec l'autorisation de Les Éditions du Noroît.

bpNichol: "St. Anzas VIII," "early morning variation," and "Moth," from *Gifts: The Martyrology Book(s) 7 &* (Coach House Press 1990); "Blues," from *Selected Writing: As Elected* (Talonbooks 1980); untitled poem ("Sometimes as other sums . . ."), "for steve," and "probable systems 13," from *Zygal: A Book of Mysteries and Translations* (Coach House Press 1985); Chain 1 excerpt ("i m / u r / n g i c so clearly . . .") and Chain 10 from *The Martyrology: Book 5* (Coach House Press 1982). "Hour 25," from *The Martyrology: Book 6* (Coach House Press 1987). "The Frog Variations" and "Prayer," from *Art Facts: A Book of Contexts* (Tuscon: Chax Press, 1990) Reprinted by permission of the estate of bpNichol.

O'Meara, David: Selections from "Desert Sonnets" from *Storm still* (Carleton University Press 1999). Reprinted by permission of McGill-Queen's University Press. "Rough Directions," "Fun," "At the Aching-Heart Diner," "Poise," and "The Unhappy Condition," from *The Vicinity* (Brick Books 2003). Published by permission of Brick Books and the author. "Boswell by the Fire" and "Something Akin to Worship Now" (unpublished poems). Reprinted with the permission of the author.

Ondaatje, Michael: "Blurred a waist high river . . . " and "She leans against the door . . . ," from *The Collected Works of Billy the Kid* (Anansi 1970); "Sally Chisum / Last Words on Billy the Kid 4 a.m.," from "Rock Bottom," "The Cinnamon Peeler," "Women like You," and "Birch Bark," from *Secular Love* (Coach House Press 1984); "An hour later he could have stopped . . . ," from *Running in the Family* (McClelland & Stewart 1982); "The Siyabaslakara" from *Handwriting* (Random House of Canada 2000). All works reprinted by permission of the author.

Partridge, Elise: "One Calvinist's God," "On the Road to Emmaus," "Four Lectures by Robert Lowell, 1977," "Rural Route," and "Two Scenes from Philadelphia," from *Fielder's Choice* (Véhicule Press 2002). Reprinted by permission of Véhicule Press.

Pass, John: "Sundeck in Houselight," "Nestbox," "Browse," "Underberries," "Wind Chime," "To the Branch from Which the Robin Flew," and "These Are the Days," from *Stumbling in the Bloom* (Oolichan Books 2005). Reprinted by permission of the author.

Pick, Alison: "'Tell me, what is it you plan to do with your one wild and precious life?'" from *Question & Answer* © 2003 by Alison Pick. First published in 2003 by Polestar Book Publishers. Reprinted by permission of Raincoast Books, 9050 Shaughnessy Street, Vancouver B.C., V6P 6E5.

Pittman, Kyran: "Launch" by kind permission of the author. The poem appeared in *The March Hare Anthology* (2007).

Préfontaine, Yves: "Peuple inhabité," "Pays Ô soudain éclaté," et "Pays sans parole," de *Pays sans*

Parole (L'Hexagone 1967). Reproduits avec l'autorisation de l'Hexagone. "Non-Lieu" de *Le désert maintenant* (Écrits des Forges 1987), pp. 92-93. Reproduit avec l'autorisation de l'auteur et Les Écrits des Forges Inc.

Price, Steven: Selections from *Anatomy of Keys* — VII "Such newsreels flicker still . . . ," VIII "Then guy-ropes creaked, plashed and I sank . . . ," and XX "The torn rope is twice useful . . ." — (Brick 2006). Reprinted by permission of Steven Price and Brick Books.

Purdy, Al: "Roblin's Mills" and "The Cariboo Horses," from *Cariboo Horses* (McClelland & Stewart 1965); "The Country of the Young," from *North of Summer; Poems from Baffin Island* (McClelland & Stewart 1967); "Dream of Havana," from *Wild Grape Wine* (McClelland & Stewart 1968); "Rodeo," from *Sundance at Dusk* (McClelland & Stewart 1976); "The Blue City," "Double Focus," "Story," and "Dog Song 2," from *Piling Blood* (McClelland & Stewart 1984); and "The Buddhist Bell" from *Being Alive: The Selected Poems of Al Purdy* (McClelland & Stewart 1978). Reprinted by permission of Harbour Publishing.

Rader, Matt: "Cruelty," "Faith," "Clearing Out," "Paradise Meadows," "Wolf Lake," and "Preparations," from *Miraculous Hours* (Nightwood Editions 2005). Reprinted by permission of Nightwood Editions.

Redhill, Michael: "One Year," "Happy Hour," "True Story," and "Casson," from *Lake Nora Arms* © 1993, 2001 Michael Redhill. Reprinted by permission of Anansi Press. "VIA, Outside Quebec City," "Murder," and from "Coming to Earth (Alzheimer Elegy)," from *Asphodel* by Michael Redhill ©1997. Published by McClelland & Stewart. Used with permission of the publisher.

Ruffo, Armand Garnet: "At Geronimo's Grave" from *At Geronimo's Grave* (Coteau 2001). "Grey Owl, 1937," "Alex Espaniel, 1920," "Influences," "An Imagined Country," "Archie Belaney, 1915-1916," "Archie Belaney, 1930-31," "Joe Hasrak" and "Later," from *Grey Owl: The Mystery of Archie Belaney* (Coteau 1996). Reprinted by permission of Coteau Books. "Poem for Duncan Campbell Scott" and "Poetry" from *Opening in the Sky* (Theytus 1994). Reprinted by permission of Armand Garnet Ruffo and Theytus Books.

Scofield, Gregory: "Pawâcakinâsîs-pîsim / December—The Frost Exploding Room" and "Pêyak-Nikamowin—One Song," from *Love Medicine and One Song: SÂKIHTOWIN-MASKIHKIY ÊKWA PÊYAK-NIKAMOWIN* (Polestar 1997), and "T. For," "Not All Halfbreed Mothers," and "Ode to the Greats (Northern Tribute)," from *I Knew Two Metis Women* (Polestar 1999). Reprinted by permission of the author.

Senior, Olive: "Peacock Tale, I," "Emperor Penguin," "Thirteen Ways of Looking at Blackbird," "Embroidery," from *Over the Roofs of the World* (Insomniac Press 2005). "Amazon Women" from *Gardening in the Tropics* (Insomniac Press 2005), "Fishing in the Waters Where My Dreams Lie" from *Shell* (Insomniac Press 2007). Reprinted with permission of Insomniac Press.

Sinclair, Sue: "The Dorsals" and "Four Poems for Virginia Woolf," from *Secrets of Weather and Hope* (Brick Books 2001). Reprinted by permission of Brick Books and the author. "Between Stations, October," "No One Asks Leda to Dance," "Goldfish," "Dining Room, Morning after Mrs. Dalloway's Party," "Once Lost," "Photograph of My Mother as a Child or Invitation to the Wedding," "The Making of 'Lawrence of Arabia'" and "100 Love Sonnets" were originally published in *The Drunken Lovely Bird* © 2004 by Sue Sinclair. Reprinted by permission of Goose Lane Editions.

Sloate, Daniel, trans.: from translation of Jean-Paul Daoust's *Les cendres bleues (Blue Ashes:*

Selected Poems, 1982-1998; Guernica 1999). Reprinted by permission of Guernica.

Solie, Karen: "Skid," "Boyfriend's Car," "Sturgeon," and "72 Miles," from *Short Haul Engine* (Brick Books 2001); "Thanksgiving," "The Bench," "Nice," "Your Premiums Will Never Increase," and "Determinism," from *Modern and Normal* (Brick 2005). Reprinted by permission of Brick Books and the author.

Starnino, Carmine: "The Lesson," "First Kiss (Teresa)," and "Picking the Last Tomatoes with My Uncle," from *The New World* (Véhicule Press 1997). Reprinted by permission of Véhicule Press. "Navigation," "On the Obsolescence of *CAPHONE*," "Song of the House Husband," "The Last Days," and "Good to Go," from *With English Subtitles* (Gaspereau Press 2004). Reprinted by permission of Gaspereau Press and the author.

Steffler, John: "The Role of Calcium in Evolution," "Cape Norman," "Book Rock," "Barrens Willow," and "Notes on Burnt Cape" (first printed by *The Malahat Review* No. 154, Spring 2006). By permission of the author.

Swensen, Cole, trans.: translation of Hélène Monette's "160 secondes" ("160 Seconds") and "Il n'y a personne qui crie . . . " ("No one is crying . . . "), from *The New Review of Literature* vol. 2. 2, April 2005 (Graduate Writing program of Otis College of Art & Design). Reprinted by permission of Cole Swensen.

Tipper, Christine: translation of Nadine Ltaif's "Simûrghiade" — Simurghiade — (from *Changing Shores*, forthcoming by Guernica, 2008). Printed by permission of Guernica.

Uguay, Marie: "Il existe pourtant des pommes . . . ," "maintenant nous sommes assis . . . ," "le cri d'une mouette . . . ," et "il y a ce désert acharnement . . . ," de *Poèmes* (© Les Editions du Boréal et Stéphan Kovacs, 2005). Reproduits avec l'autorisation du Boréal et Stéphan Kovacs. "Tout ce qui va suivre . . ." de *Latitudes: 9 poètes du Québec*. Traduction et sélection by Álvaro Faleiros (Éditions du Noroît, 2002). "des fleurs sur la table . . ." et "il fallait bien parfois . . . ," de *Autoportraits* (Noroît 1982). Reproduits avec l'autorisation de Stéphan Kovacs.

Walsh, Agnes: "I Solemn," "Thomas," and "Contacts," from *Going Around With Bachelors* (Brick Books 2007). Reprinted by permission of Brick Books and the author.

Ward, Frederick: Selections from *Riverlisp* — "Fuss," "Rufus," and "Blind Woman" — (Tundra Books of Northern New York and Tundra Books of Montréal 1974) and "A Pattern of Escape," "Dialogue # 3," "Najean," "From Who All Was There," "Yet Among-Us," and "Me Grandaunt," from *The Curing Berry* (Williams-Wallace 1983). Reprinted by permission of Frederick Ward.

Watts, Enos: "The Grandmothers of Argentina," from *Spaces Between the Trees* (Pennywell Books 2005). Reprinted by permission of Flanker Press.

Wershler-Henry, Darren: Selections from *Ten Out of Ten, or Why Poetry Criticism Sucks in 2003* (2003) — "Jeff Derksen — *Dwell*," "Steve McCaffery — *The Black Debt*," "Ken Babstock — *Days into Flatspin*," and "Kenneth Goldsmith — No. 111 2.7.93-10.20.96" — (Calgary: housepress 2003). Reprinted by permission of the author.

Whittall, Zoe: "Stiff Little Fingers," from *The Best 10 Minutes of Your Life* (McGilligan Books 2001). Reprinted by permission of McGilligan Books. "Six Thoughts on a Parkdale Porch" by permission of the author.

Young, Patricia: "Grocery List" and "The Fire," from *Ruin and Beauty* (Anansi 2000). Reprinted by permission of House of Anansi.

Zwicky, Jan: "Driving Northwest," "Bill Evans: 'Here's That Rainy Day,'" and "Passing Sangudo," in *Songs for Relinquishing the Earth* (Brick 1998). "Prairie," "Robinson's Crossing," "Another Version ('Look, all I can tell you is . . .')," "Work, "Soup," "Aspen in Wind," Three Mysterious Songs," "Closing the Cabin," and "Glenn Gould: Bach's 'Italian' Concerto, BMW 971," from *Robinson's Crossing* (Brick 2004). Reprinted by permission of Brick Books and the author.

Notes on Contributors (Ireland)

Leland Bardwell's five collections of poems to date commenced with *The Mad Cyclist* (1970). As a fiction writer, she has published five novels as well as a volume of short stories. As a playwright, she has worked with RTE and BBC. Her stage credits include *No Regrets: The Life of Edith Piaf* (1984) and *Jocasta* (2001). She is co-editor of *Cyphers* and is a member of Aosdána. *The Noise of Masonry Settling* (2006) is published by The Dedalus Press. Leland Bardwell lives in County Sligo.

Sebastian Barry was born in Dublin in 1955. His poetry collections include *The Water-Colourist* (Dolmen Press, 1983), *Fanny Hawke Goes to the Mainland Forever* (Raven Arts Press, 1989) and *The Pinkening Boy* (New Island, 2004). He has also written plays, among them *Boss Grady's Boys*, *The Steward of Christendom* and *Our Lady of Sligo*, and has won the BBC Stewart Parker Prize, The Irish-American Fund Literary Award, and the London Critics' Circle Award, among others. His novels include *The Whereabouts of Eneas McNulty* and *A Long Long Way*, which was shortlisted for the Booker Prize in 2005 and the 2007 Dublin Impac Prize and won the 2006 Kerry Group Irish Novel Award. He lives in Wicklow with his wife, Alison, and three children, Merlin, Coral and Tobias. His new play, *The Pride of Parnell Street*, was premiered in London in September 2007.

Sara Berkeley was born in Dublin and now lives in California. Four collections of her poetry have been published in Ireland, the UK and Canada: *Penn* (1986), *Home-Movie Nights* (1989), *Facts About Water* (1994) and *Strawberry Thief* (2005). In 1992, a collection of her short stories, *The Swimmer in the Deep Blue Dream,* was published and, in 1999, her novel *Shadowing Hannah*.

Denise Blake was born in Ohio, USA, in 1958 but moved to Ireland in 1969 where she grew up in County Donegal. Her poems have been widely published in a variety of journals, as have her translations from the Irish of Cathal Ó Searcaigh's poetry. Her first poetry collection, *Take a Deep Breath,* was published by Summer Palace Press in 2004. Some of her translations have been included in *By the Hearth in Mín a Léa,* published by ARC Publications. She has read at many festivals around Ireland, and her work has been regularly broadcast on RTE Radio's *Sunday Miscellany.*

Eavan Boland is Melvin and Bill Lane Professor in the Humanities at Stanford University, California. Her collections include *The Journey* (Poetry Book Society Choice, 1987), *Selected Poems* (PBS Choice, 1990), *Collected Poems* (1995), *The Lost Land* (1995), a book of prose — *Object Lessons* (1995) — and *Code* (2001). She publishes with Carcanet Press and has been shortlisted for the 2007 Forward Prize for Best Collection for her recent book of poems *Domestic Violence* (2007).

Rosita Boland was born in County Clare in 1965. She has published two collections of poems: *Muscle Creek* (Raven Arts, 1991) and *Dissecting the Heart* (The Gallery Press, 2003). She is also the author of *Sea Legs: Hitch-hiking the Coast of Ireland Alone* (New Island, 1992). She won a Hennessy Award for Fiction in 1997. She works as a journalist with *The Irish Times* and has travelled extensively, particularly in south-east Asia.

Pat Boran was born in Portlaoise, Ireland, in 1963 and currently lives in Dublin where he is Programme Director of the Dublin Writers' Festival. In recent years, he has been Dublin City Writer-in-Residence and has held residencies at Dublin City University and with Dublin City

An Anthology of Poetry from Canada and Ireland 1165

Libraries. A frequent contributor to books and arts programmes on RTE Radio 1, he presents the RTE Radio 1 poetry programme *The Enchanted Way*. He has conducted writing workshops throughout Ireland, and a revised and expanded edition of his popular writers' handbook, *The Portable Creative Writing Workshop*, originally published in 1999, will be reissued in 2007.

Katarzyna Borun-Jagodzinska's collections include *Wyciszemia (Quietenings*, 1997), *Moly Happening (A Minor Happening*, 1999) and *Wiecef — Wiersze o Zmroku (More — Poems at Twilight*, 1991). Living in Warsaw, Borun-Jagodzinska became an editor with the monthly *Temperance and Hard Work*. Her poems, well peppered with the absurd, are translated in this volume by Cork poet Gerry Murphy and taken from the collection *Pocket Apocalypse* (Southword Editions, Cork 2005).

Colm Breathnach: Sé cinn de chnuasaigh filíochta atá foilsithe aige, *Cantaic an Bhalbháin* (1991), *An Fearann Breac* (1992), *Scáthach* (1994), *Croí agus Carraig* (1995), *An Fear Marbh* (1998) agus *Chiaroscuro* (2006). Bhuaigh sé an phríomhdhuais filíochta trí huaire i gcomórtais liteartha an Oireachtais ag Conradh na Gaeilge. I 1999 bhronn an Foras Cultúrtha Gael-Mheiriceánach "Duais an Bhuitléirigh" air mar aitheantas ar a shaothar filíochta. Dhein sé aistriúchán i gcomhar leis an Dr. Andrea Nic Thaidhg ar an úrscéal *Katz und Maus* le Günter Grass faoin teideal *Cat agus Luch*. Tá sé ag obair mar aistritheoir i Rannóg an Aistriúcháin.

Colm Breathnach has published six collections of poetry, *Cantaic an Bhalbháin, An Fearann Breac, Scáthach, Croí agus Carraig, An Fear Marbh* and *Chiaroscuro*. He has won the principal poetry prize at the annual Conradh na Gaeilge Oireachtas literary competitions three times. In 1999, the Irish American Cultural Institute awarded Colm the "Butler Prize" in recognition of his work. With Dr. Andrea Nic Thaidhg, he has translated the Günter Grass novel *Katz und Maus* into Irish under the title *Cat agus Luch*. Colm works as a translator in Oireachtas Éireann, the National Parliament of Ireland. He publishes with Coiscéim and Cló-Iarchonnachta.

Rugadh **Deirdre Brennan** i mBaile Átha Cliath, tógadh í lár tíre, chuaigh le muinteoireacht. *I Reilg na mBan Rialta* (Coiscéim, 1984), *Scothanna Geala*, (Coiscéim, 1989) agus *Thar Colbha na Mara* (Coiscéim, 1993).

Deirdre Brennan is a bilingual writer of poetry, short stories and drama. Her work has appeared extensively in poetry anthologies. She is a founder member of Éigse Carlow Arts Festival. Her collections include *I Reilg na mBan Rialta* (Coiscéim, 1984) and *The Hen Party* (Lapwing, 2001). Her new book, *Swimming with Pelicans / Ag Eitilt fara Condair*, was published by Arlen House in September 2007.

Vincent Buckley, who took his MA from the University of Melbourne, also studied at Cambridge. He was appointed Lockie Fellow in the Department of English at Melbourne in 1958 and was awarded a personal Chair in 1967. Vincent Buckley's seven volumes of poetry range from the intensely personal and intimate to rumination on the past and present of Ireland and Irish politics (two of his poetry collections were published by Dolmen Press in Ireland). He lived in Ireland for a time. He also lived in Edmonton, Alberta (Canada) writing and publishing. His critical writings include volumes on poetry, the novelist Henry Handel Richardson and the Campion paintings by Leonard French. His essays on Slessor, Fitzgerald, Hope, Wright and McAuley remain influential. His autobiography, *Cutting Green Hay: Friendships, Movements and Cultural Conflicts in Australia's Great Decades,* was published in 1983. He was awarded the Dublin prize, the University of Melbourne's award for an outstanding contribution to art, music, literature or science in 1977 and the Christopher Brennan Award from the Fellowship of Australian Writers in 1982. His *Last Poems* was published by McPhee Gribble, Penguin Books Australia, in 1991.

Paddy Bushe has published seven collections of poetry, including the more recent *Gile na Gile* (Coiscéim) and *The Nitpicking of Cranes* (The Dedalus Press). He has twice been awarded an Arts Council bursary. His awards include The Strokestown International Prize and The Michael Hartnett Award. Rugadh Paddy Bushe i mBaile Átha Cliath sa bhliain 1948; tá cónaí air anois in Uíbh Ráthach i gCiarraí.

Catherine Byron's poetry collection *Settlements* (1985) was hailed as a "classic of Irish exile." *The Getting of Vellum* was inspired by her creative collaboration with Dublin-based artist and calligrapher Denis Brown. They also collaborated on Catherine Byron's *The Fat-Hen Field Hospital* (1993), new work being created on vellum, glass and printed page. Catherine Byron grew up in Belfast, raised daughters and goats in the West of Scotland and presently lives in the English midlands. Author of *Out of Step: Pursuing Seamus Heaney to Purgatory* (Loxwood Stoneleigh, 1992), she teaches writing and Medieval Literature at Nottingham Trent University. She also created the first web-specific poem for the Poetry Society's website, "Renderers." She also published *Samhain* (Taxus / Aril, 1987).

Mary Rose Callan's collection *Footfalls of Snow* is published by Bradshaw Books, Cork. Her first collection was entitled *The Mermaid's Head*. Her poem "Seawife" won the Edgeworth Poetry Prize 2003. "Ilford, 1922" won the Boyle Poetry Prize, 2001.

Moya Cannon was born in Dunfanaghy, County Donegal in 1956 and now lives in Galway. She studied history and politics at University College, Dublin, and international relations at Corpus Christi College, Cambridge. She has published two collections of poems, *Oar* (Salmon Press, Galway, 1990) and *The Parchment Boat* (The Gallery Press, 1997). A "New and Selected," entitled *Carrying the Songs*, will be published by Carcanet Press in September, 2007. She has been an editor of *Poetry Ireland Review* and has been writer-in-residence at Trent University, Ontario, and at the *Centre Culturel Irlandais*, Paris. A recipient of the Brendan Behan Award and of the Lawrence O'Shaughnessy Award, she was elected to Aosdána, the affiliation of Irish writers and visual artists, in 2004.

Ellie Carr was a member of the traveller community in Ireland. Her recorded reminiscences of traveller life and culture were originally published in *Traveller Ways Traveller Words* (Pavee Point, 1992) as well as in the *Field Day Anthology of Irish Women Writers*, vols IV and V (Cork University Press, 2002). Ellie Carr died in a caravan fire. Her travels were centred on the midlands of Ireland.

Ciaran Carson lives in Belfast and has won many awards for his poetry, including the T.S. Eliot Prize for *First Language*. He has also published five books of prose, including the novel *Shamrock Tea*, which was shortlisted for the Booker Prize. His translation of *The Inferno of Dante Alighieri* was published by Granta in 2002. He also publishes with The Gallery Press.

Kyriakos Charalambides is a Greek Cypriot poet and has published nine books of poetry. Three of them were awarded the First State prize for Poetry (Cyprus). A translator of Romanos the Melodist's *Three Hymns*, he is also the recipient of the 1998 Cavafy Prize (Egypt). His *Selected Poems* were translated by the Irish poet Greg Delanty for the Cork 2005 European Capital of Culture series of translations.

Michael Coady lives in the town of his birth, Carrick-on-Suir, County Tipperary and was elected to Aosdána in 1998. His most recent publications by The Gallery Press are *All Souls* and *One Another,* each integrating poetry, prose and photographs. "A lapsed trombone player," he has been involved in music of various kinds and published a personal memoir of the Clare traditional musicians Pakie and Micho Russell and an illustrated miscellany of short prose work (*Full Tide*, Relay Books, 1999). Coady's work in poetry and prose includes a critically-admired memoir of family migration and displacement in America. Literary awards include the Patrick Kavanagh and the O'Shaughnessy prizes for poetry. In Spring 2005, Coady held the Heimbold Chair in Irish Studies at Villanova University, Pennsylvania. He is currently working towards a further collection incorporating poetry, short prose forms and photographs.

Patrick Cotter works as a publisher and festival organizer for the Munster Literature Centre. He has published a number of chapbooks, including *The Mysogynist's Blue Nightmare* (Raven Arts Press), *A Socialist's Dozen* (Three Spires Press) and *The True Story of Aoife and Lir's Children & Other Poems* (Three Spires Press). His work features widely in anthologies. He is currently working on a translation of love poems by Paul Celan. His play *Beauty and the Stalker* was produced at the Granary Theatre in Cork in 2000. His own poetry has been translated into Estonian, Italian, Spanish and Swedish. In this book, he translates the poems of Andres Ehin from Estonia.

Enda Coyle-Greene lives in County Dublin. Widely published in journals and anthologies, her work has also been broadcast on RTE Radio 1 and Lyric FM. Her first collection, *Snow Negatives*, received the Patrick Kavanagh Award in 2006 and is forthcoming in 2007 from The Dedalus Press.

As well as ten collections of poetry, **Anthony Cronin** has written a number of admired prose works, including biographies of Flann O'Brien and Samuel Beckett, the classic memoir of Dublin in the fifties, *Dead as Doornails*, novels and collections of essays. He is married to the writer Anne Haverty and lives in Dublin. He was recently elected a Saoi of Aosdána, a distinction conferred for exceptional artistic achievement.

Born in Belfast, **Phillip Crymble** emigrated to Canada with his family as an adolescent. In 2002, he was awarded an MFA from the University of Michigan, receiving both the Hopwood Award and a Cowden fellowship. The recipient of a Canada Council for the Arts Professional Writers' grant and a recent finalist in both The Poetry Business (UK) and South Tipperary Arts Centre's annual chapbook competitions, his work has appeared, or is forthcoming in, a wide range of international publications. His first collection (*Wide Boy*, 2007) is published by Lapwing Press.

As Béal Feirste dó; saothar leis ar *An Chead Chló*. Oibríonn sé in Ollscoil Uladh: **Philip Cummings** is the arts editor of *Lá*. He recently won an inaugural Glen Dimplex Award for Irish-language poetry. *Néalta* appeared in 2005. He publishes with Coiscéim.

Celia de Fréine is a poet and playwright. She has published three collections of poetry: *Faoi Chabáistí is Ríonacha* (2001) and *Fiacha Fola* (2004), both published by Cló Iar-Chonnachta, and *Scarecrows at Newtownards* (2005), published by Scotus Press. Her poetry has won several awards, including the Patrick Kavanagh Award and *Gradam Litríochta Chló Iar-Chonnachta*; she has three times won the *Oireachtas na Gaeilge* award for best play, most recently for her new play *Tearmann*, which also won *Duais Fhoras na Gaeilge* at Listowel Writers' Week in 2006. She was awarded Arts Council Bursaries in 1997 and in 2000.

Greg Delanty, who translates the work of Kyriakos Charalambides in this volume, has also translated Aristophanes and Euripides. With Nuala Ní Dhomhnaill, he edited *Jumping Off Shadows: Selected Contemporary Irish Poetry* (1995). In the U.S., where he teaches in Vermont, he has been politically active in anti-war demonstrations. His poetry collections include *The Ship of Birth*, *The Blind Stitch* and *The Hellbox*. He publishes with Carcanet Press.

Born in Cork in 1961, **Louis de Paor** has been involved with the contemporary rennaissance of poetry in Irish since 1980 when he was first published in the poetry journal *Innti* which he subsequently edited for a time. A four times winner of the Seán Ó Ríordáin / Oireachtas Award, the premier award for a new collection of poems in Irish, he lived in Australia from 1987 to 1996. His first bilingual collection, *Aimsir Bhreicneach / Freckled Weather*, was shortlisted for the Victorian Premier's Award for Literary Translation. He was also granted a Writer's Fellowship by the Australia Council in 1995. He is the recipient of the Lawrence O'Shaughnessy Award 2000, the first poet in Irish to achieve that distinction. His most recent collection, *agus rud eile de*, published by Coiscéim (2002), was awarded the Oireachtas prize for the best collection of poems in Irish in 2003. A bilingual collection *Ag Greadadh Bas sa Reilig / Clapping in the Cemetery* was published by Cló Iar-Chonnachta in November 2005 and reprinted in March 2006. *The Gaelic Hit Factory*, a collection of songs and poems in Irish composed and recorded with longtime collaborator John Spillane, was released in October 2006. His latest collection is *Cúpla Siamach an Ama / The Siamese Twins of Time*, published by Coiscéim (2006).

Patrick Dillon grew up in Termonfeckin in County Louth. In 1997, he was awarded a scholarship to participate in The Poets' House Summer Poetry Workshop in Donegal. In 2002, he was selected by Poetry Ireland for their Introduction Series. He has completed a novel called *The Cup*. His poetry has appeared in various journals of poetry. In 2006, his translation of the novel *Happiness Apartments*, by Yu Zhiguan, won a Trafford Prize.

Kristin Dimitrova, who lives in Sofia, Bulgaria, is one of the defining poets of her generation. A winner of multiple awards for her poetry, her collections include *Jacob's Thirteenth Child* (1992), *A Face Under the Ice* (1997), *Closed Figures* (1998), *Faces with Twisted Tongues* (1998), *Talisman Repair* (2001) and *The People with the Lanterns* (2003). *A Visit to the Clockmaker* (2005) was translated from the Bulgarian by Cork poet Gregory O'Donoghue as part of the Cork City of Culture series of translations (2005).

Poet, broadcaster, translator, editor and documentary scriptwriter, whose poetry has been translated into several languages, **Theo Dorgan** is also the editor of *Irish Poetry Since Kavanagh* (Four Courts Press, 1996). His widely-acclaimed prose memoir of an Atlantic crossing under sail, *Sailing for Home*, was published in 2004. He is a member of Aosdána and of The Arts Council.

Seán Dunne moved between his native Waterford and Cork where he worked as a literary editor with *The Cork Examiner*. His books include *Against the Storm* (1985) and *The Sheltered Nest* (1992). His portrait-of-the-artist as young Waterford boy and teenager appeared in his best-seller *In My Father's House* (1991). The Seán Dunne Literary Festival (which is twinned with The March Hare Festival in Newfoundland) honours him yearly in Waterford. The Gallery Press published his posthumous *Collected Poems* in 2006.

Paul Durcan, who lives in Dublin, has published eighteen books of poetry including *Daddy, Daddy* (Winner of the Whitbread Award for Poetry, 1990), *A Snail in My Prime: New and Selected Poems* (1993), *Christmas Day* (1996) and *Greetings to Our Friends in Brazil* (1999). In 2001, he received the Cholmondeley Award for poetry. *Paul Durcan's diary*, which was on the Irish best-seller list, was published in 2003 and contains two chapters on his reading tour of Newfoundland as guest of The March Hare Festival. In 2004, he published *The Art of Life* and, in October, 2007, Harvill Secker are publishing his new book *The Laughter of Mothers*.

Andres Ehin was born in Tallinn in 1940. Poet, translator, novelist, editor, short-story writer, radio play author, journalist and essayist, he studied at the University of Tartu at the same time as

An Anthology of Poetry from Canada and Ireland   1169

Jaan Kaplinski. Ehin subsequently found work as a free-lance writer, editor and journalist, working from 1965 to 1974. As a poet, Ehin has published many collections, including *Spiritual Nostrils* (1978), *I Sip the Darkness* (1988), *Full-Moon Midday* (1990), *Consciousness is Snakeskin* (1996) and *Subconsciousness Is Always Jolly* (2000). He has won a plethora of awards and prizes, including the Looming Prize for best novel of the year and The Estonian Culture Capital Foundation Award. He lives in Rapla with his wife, the poet Ly Seppel. Patrick Cotter translates the poems of Ehin in this anthology.

Peter Fallon lives with his family in Loughcrew in County Meath in the midlands of Ireland. At the age of eighteen, he founded The Gallery Press which is widely regarded as Ireland's pre-eminent literary poetry publishing house. He has been Writer Fellow at Trinity College, Dublin, his *alma mater*, and poet-in-residence at Deerfield Academy in Massachusetts. In 2000, he was inaugural Heimbold Professor of Irish Studies at Villanova University. He is a member of Aosdána. Peter Fallon's collections of poems include *News of the World: Selected and New Poems* (1998) and *The Company of Horses* (September 2007). *The Georgics of Virgil*, a Poetry Book Society Recommended Translation, has been reissued by Oxford University Press in its World's Classics Series.

Janice Fitzpatrick Simmons comes from Boston, Massachusetts. She was co-founder and director of The Poets' House in Donegal. She is currently in charge of the MA Programme by Research in Creative Writing in the School of Humanities at Waterford Institute of Technology. She has an MA in Literature from the University of New Hampshire. She has five volumes of poetry published, including *Leaving America* (Lagan, 1993), *Settler* (Salmon, 1995), *Starting at Purgatory* (Salmon, 1999), *Ghost Whiskey* and *Bowsprit* (Lagan, 2005). She was married to Ulster poet James Simmons who died in 2001.

Roderick Ford's *The Shoreline of Falling* won the Listowel Poetry Collection Prize in 2004. He also won the Listowel Single Poem Prize in 2005. *The Shoreline of Falling* (2005) is published by Bradshaw Books, Cork.

Tom French has worked in Spain, France and the US. He currently lives in Dublin and works for the County Wicklow library service. In 1999, he received an Arts Council Bursary in Literature. He also won the inaugural Ted McNulty Prize. His work was nominated for The Pushcart Prize: Best of the Small Presses (2002). *Touching the Bones* is his first collection and is published by The Gallery Press.

Patrick Galvin has published six collections of poems, including *New and Selected Poems* (Cork University Press, 1996). He has had seven stage plays produced. *Song for a Raggy Boy*, the second volume of his memoirs, was adapted by him and released internationally on film in 2003. Described by Thomas McCarthy as "the living maestro of Cork," Patrick Galvin, also an RAF bomber during the war, a member of Aosdána and winner of the Irish-American Cultural Institute Award for Poetry, recently celebrated his eightieth birthday in his native city. His poem "The Madwoman of Cork" remains one of the most quoted in the Irish canon. With Robert O'Donoghue, he has translated the poems of Yilmaz Odabaşi in this volume.

Alan Garvey has worked as an arts administrator, part-time lecturer and community arts facilitator. He lives in Carlow with his partner, Tara, and son Keir. He has published three chapbooks of poetry. He has featured in poetry readings in Newfoundland and in Toronto. *Herself in Air* (Lapwing) appeared in 2006. He is presently working on a new volume as part of his MA in Creative Writing at Waterford Institute of Technology.

Alan Gillis was born in Belfast in 1973. He lives in Edinburgh with his wife and son and teaches at Edinburgh University. He is the author of *Irish Poetry of the 1930s* (OUP, 2005) and co-editor, with Aaron Kelly, of *Critical Ireland: New Essays on Literature and Culture* (Four Courts Press, 2001). His first collection, *Somebody, Somewhere* (The Gallery Press, 2004), was shortlisted for the Irish Times Poetry Now Award and received the Rupert and Eithne Strong Award for best first collection. His second collection, *Hawks and Doves* (The Gallery Press, 2007), was a Poetry Book Society Recommendation.

Eamon Grennan teaches at Vassar College and divides his time between the US and the West of Ireland. He has published seven collections of poetry, among them *Selected and New Poems* (2000) and *Still Life with Waterfall* (2001), which won the Lenore Marshall Prize for Poetry in 2003. His *Leopardi: Selected Poems* won the PEN Award for Poetry in Translation. His *Facing the Music* is a collection of essays on modern Irish poetry. The Gallery Press published *The Quick of It* in 2004.

Seamus Heaney, awarded the Nobel Prize for Literature in 1995, is regarded as one of the foremost poets worldwide of this generation. Eminent critic, essayist, editor and translator, he has twice won the Whitbread Book of the Year Award — for *The Spirit Level* (1996) and *Beowulf* (1999). Recent poetry collections include *Electric Light* (2001) and *District and Circle* (2006). He lives in Dublin and publishes with Faber.

Zbyněk Hejda divides his time between Prague and the Village of Horni Ves. His first volume of poetry was published in Prague in 1963. When he joined Charter 77, he was dismissed from his job in publishing and survived as janitor. During the 1980s, he published with Samizdat presses. He has translated the poetry of Emily Dickinson, Georg Trakl and Gottfried Benn into Czech. The poems chosen for this anthology are taken from *A Stay in a Sanatorium & Other Poems,* translated from the Czech by Bernard O'Donoghue from versions by Šimon Daníeček.

Rugadh i nGlaschú; cónaí air i mBaile Átha Cliath ó bhí sé beag óg, seachas tréimshí a chaith sé san Eilbhéis, sa Spáinn agus i Sasana. *Faoistin Bhacach* a chéad chnuasach Gaeilge, 1968. *Le Cead na Greine* (1989). Is file Béarla é fosta agus comheagarthóir ar an iris filíochta *Cyphers*: **Pearse Hutchinson**, poet and translator, is the author of many acclaimed collections, including *The Soul that Kissed the Body,* selected poems in Irish with translations into English (1990) and *Barnsley Main Seam* (1995). A broadsheet in honour of his eightieth birthday, 16 February 2007, featured poems in eight languages from seven countries reflecting the spectrum of Pearse's interests and affiliations. He publishes with The Gallery Press.

Oritsegbemi Emmanuel Jakpa is a Nigerian poet with a number of publications in poetry and awards achieved. His poems have featured in anthologies. He has been accepted on the MA Programme in Creative Writing offered by the School of Humanities at Waterford Institute of Technology. He has been workshopping his poems by email with John Ennis.

Ainm cleite an fhile a scríobh *Baisteadh Gintlí,* 1987; *Uiscí Beatha,* 1988 agus *Dán na hUidhre,* 1991. Drámadóir freisin í: **Biddy Jenkinson** is a pseudonym. She writes poetry, drama and short stories. Her first collection was *Baisteadh Gintlí* in 1987. She publishes with Coiscéim. Her work is much anthologised, and other collections include: *Uiscí beatha* (BÁC: Coiscéim, 1988); *Dán na hUidhre* (BÁC: Coiscéim, 1991); *Amhras neimhe* (BÁC: Coiscéim, 1997); *An grá riabhach* (BÁC: Coiscéim, 1999); and *Mis* (BÁC: Coiscéim, 2001).

An Anthology of Poetry from Canada and Ireland 1171

Born in Galway 1953, **Rita Kelly** writes in English and Irish — poetry, fiction, drama, and criticism. Four collections of poetry have been published since 1981: two new collections are due in 2008. She has won various awards for her work, including a Seán Ó Riordáin Memorial Award, an *Irish Times / Merriman Award*, and the Listowel Award. Bhuaigh a leabhar *Kelly reads Bewick* duais na mbliana dár foilsiú é. She has worked as Writer-in-Residence for Co Laois & Co Cavan. Her work has been included in most of the major anthologies from Ireland in the last twenty-five years. Her work has featured on courses at Yale and has been translated into Italian, French, German & Dutch. Déartear go bhfuil sí mar chuid bheag de na scríbhneoirí dhátheangacha atá ag saothrú leo in Éirinn faoi láthair. Ní dhéanann sí fhéin mórán deighilt idir na teangacha ina saothar féin. She has just completed an MA in Creative Writing at Waterford Institute of Technology. She is about to start on a PhD.

Brendan Kennelly served as Professor of Modern Literature at Trinity College, Dublin, from 1973 until recently. He is the author of twenty books of poetry, including six volumes of *Selected Poems*. Recent books include *The Man Made of Rain* (Bloodaxe, 1998), written after he survived major heart surgery, and *Begin* (Bloodaxe, 1999). He has written three epics, including *Cromwell* and *The Book of Judas*. Author of *Poetry My Arse* (Bloodaxe, 1995), he is also a dramatist and translator from the Greek and the Irish.

Thomas Kinsella has been Professor of Poetry in Southern Illinois University and Temple University, Philadelphia, as well as founder and director of the Temple University Irish Tradition Programme in Dublin. He retired in 1990 and lives in Wicklow and in Philadelphia. He is a major translator from old and modern Irish; his translations are widely represented in *However Blow the Winds* (2004). As poet, he has published with Dolmen Press, Oxford University Press and Carcanet Press. He is the founder and originator of Peppercanister. Recent volumes in 2006 included his *Marginal Economy* and *Readings in Poetry*: Peppercanister 24 and 25, respectively. He was awarded the Freedom of the City of Dublin in 2007, an honour rarely bestowed.

Barbara Korun is a leading figure in a generation of radical young Slovene women poets. Her work has been published in many anthologies and reviews and has been translated into twelve languages. She works on the editorial boards of the literary journals *Apokalipsa* and *Nova Revija*. Her collections of poetry and prose poems include *Zapiski Iz Podmizja (Notes from under the Table*, Apokalipsa, 2003) and *Razpoke (Fissures*, Nova Revija 2004). Theo Dorgan translated her work in the volume *Songs of Earth and Light* for Southword Editions, Cork 2005 European Capital of Culture series of translations.

Nick Laird works as lawyer, poet, novelist and critic. His essays, reviews and poems have appeared in various journals in England and America, including *The London Review of Books, The Times Literary Supplement, The Guardian, The Times, The Daily Telegraph, New Writing 11* and *New Writing 13*. His first collection of poetry, *To A Fault*, and his first novel, *Utterly Monkey*, were published in 2005. *To A Fault* was shortlisted for the 2005 Forward Poetry prize for Best First Collection, and *Utterly Monkey* for a 2006 Commonwealth Writers' Prize. He lives in Northern Ireland and publishes with Faber.

Ann Leahy lives in Dublin. Her poems from *Teasing Roots from the Stem of a Geranium* won the Patrick Kavanagh Award. She was commended in the British National Poetry Awards of 1999. She has also been runner-up in other UK competitions, including that of *Stand Magazine*. In 2000, she was successful in the UK New Writer Award, the Gerard Manley Hopkins Award and the Maria Edgeworth Award. Her poems, some of which have been translated into Russian and Dutch, have also been broadcast on radio and published in various journals in Ireland, England and Germany.

Michael Longley was born in Belfast (where he still lives) and educated at Royal Belfast Academical Institution and TCD where he read Classics: the classics, especially Homer, exercise an important influence on his work. His collection *The Weather in Japan* (2000) won *The Irish Times* prize for poetry, the Hawthorndon Prize and the T. S. Eliot Prize. He worked for The Arts Council of Northern Ireland from 1970 until 1991. He was awarded the Queen's Medal for Poetry in 2001. His widely-acclaimed *Collected Poems* was launched by Cape Poetry in November 2006. He was announced the fourth Ireland Chair of Poetry at a ceremony in Belfast in September 2007.

Dave Lordan was born in Derby, England, in 1975. He grew up in Clonakilty in West Cork. He took an MA in English Literature in University College Cork in 1998 and an MPhil in Creative Writing in Trinity College Dublin in 2001. In 2004, he was awarded an Arts Council bursary. In 2005, he won the Patrick Kavanagh Award for poetry. His work has been published widely in journals and anthologies, and he is a regular and popular performer of his own work. *The Boy in The Ring* was published by Salmon Poetry in 2007. He is an experienced creative writing teacher and workshop leader.

Alice Lyons is the author of *Staircase Poems*, a book that documents her poetry and installation project at The Dock, Carrick-on-Shannon, County Leitrim in 2005-2006. She is the recipient of the Patrick Kavanagh Award for Poetry, the Ireland Chair of Poetry Award and a recent bursary in Literature from the Arts Council. She is currently directing an animated film of her poem entitled *The Polish Language*. Born in Paterson, New Jersey, she has lived in Cootehall, County Roscommon since 1998.

As Co. Bhaile Átha Cliath dó; ina bhainisteoir árachais sa chathair. *Labhraí Loingseach*, 1988, *Sneachta Cásca*, 1991, *Néalta Taistil*, 1994: from County Dublin, **Gearailt Mac Eoin** works in insurance. He has published a number of collections of poetry in the Irish language with Coiscéim.

As Baile Átha Cliath dó agus ina léachtóir ansin. Eagarthóir *Comhar* ar feadh i bhfad. *Damha agus Dánta Eile*, 1974, a chéad chnuasach, dhá cheann eile in diaidh sin (*Codarsnaí* agus *Cré agus Cláirseach*) agus mórchnuasach, *Scian*, 1990: **Tomás Mac Síomóin** is longtime lecturer in Dublin Institute of Technology. Influential editor and critic, he has specialised in poetry and fiction. He has published with Sairséal & Dill.

Ilena Mălăncioiu is a Romanian poet, who lives in Bucharest. Her poetry was translated by Eiléan Ní Chuilleanáin as part of the Cork City of Culture series of translations. Ilena Mălăncioiu has worked in Romanian television, in films and literary journals. She has also published critical and autobiographical works. Her poetry was heavily censored in communist times. In 2004, she received the prestigious Romanian Writers' Union prize for her *Opera Omnia* (*Complete Works*).

Thomas McCarthy was born in Cappoquin, West Waterford, 1954, and was educated locally and at UCC. He was the winner of the Patrick Kavanagh Award for 1977 for *The First Convention* (Dolmen Press, 1978) and winner of the Alice Hunt Bartlett Prize, 1981, for *The Sorrow Garden* (Anvil Press, London). Other publications with Anvil Press include *The Non-Aligned Storyteller* (1984), *The Lost Province* (1998), *Mr. Dineen's Careful Parade* (2001) and *Merchant Prince* (2005). He has been a librarian in Cork since 1978, apart from a year as Visiting Professor of English, Macalester College, Minnesota, 1994-1995. A member of Aosdána and a fellow of the Royal Society of Arts, London, he is married with two children, two dogs and three cats.

Medbh McGuckian was the first Belfast woman to attain full recognition in the Ulster Renaissance. She published initially with Oxford and, since the nineties, with The Gallery Press, County Meath. Her last collection, *The Book of the Angel* (2004), was shortlisted with Seamus Heaney and Paul Muldoon for *The Irish Times* Poetry Now Award. She is currently working on a new collection, *My Love Has Fared Inland*. She is a tutor in poetry at Queen's University Belfast.

Nigel McLoughlin's poetry collections include *At The Waters' Clearing* (Flambard / Black Mountain, 2001), *Songs for No Voices* (Lagan, 2004) and *Blood* (Bluechrome, 2005). His poetry and translations from Irish and German have been published widely in journals and anthologies in Ireland, Britain, USA, Canada, Australia, Japan, Nepal and Malaysia. He has been guest poetry editor for *The New Writer* and *The Black Mountain Review*. He is Field Chair in Creative Writing at the University of Gloucestershire.

Paula Meehan was born in and still lives in Dublin. She has published five acclaimed collections of poetry, the most recent being DHARMAKAYA (Carcanet Press / Wake Forest University Press, 2000). She has also written for the theatre, for contemporary dance companies and in collaboration with visual artists and musicians. With Theo Dorgan, she acts as adjudicator for the yearly Patrick Kavanagh Award.

As Baile Átha Cliath dí agus baint ariamh aici le Dún Chaoin. Seal ina státseirbhíseach, ina scoláire, ina foclóirí, ina bean tí–pósta le Conchúr Crús Ó Briain. *Margadh na Saoire*, 1956, *Codladh an Ghaiscigh*, 1973 agus *An Galar Dubhach*, 1980; mórchnuasach, *An Cion go dtí Seo*, 1987: **Máire Mhac an tSaoi** has been a diplomat and lexicographer. She is one of the first of a line of illustrious women poets in modern Ireland. She is also critic and scholar and has written an historical novella. Her autobiography, *The Same Age as the State* (The O'Brien Press, 2006), has been widely acclaimed.

Immanuel Mifsud's *Confidential Reports* (2005) has been translated into English as part of the Cork City of Culture 2005 series of translations. He is the leading Maltese writer of his generation and has published fiction as well as two collections of poems. Most of his published work has been in theatre, which he often directs. He teaches at the University of Malta.

Geraldine Mills was the Millennium winner of the Hennessy / Tribune New Irish Writer Award. Her first book of poetry, *Unearthing Your Own*, was published in Cork by Bradshaw Books in 2001. *Toil the Dark Harvest* followed from Bradshaw in 2004. She lives in Galway. She is a short-story writer also.

John Montague was born in Brooklyn, NY, in 1929, but he returned to Ireland at the age of four and grew up on his aunts' farm in County Tyrone. He was educated at St Patrick's College, Armagh, UCD and Yale. Perhaps Montague is best known for his Ulster epic *The Rough Field*, but he is also a highly acclaimed love poet and a poet of international as well as Irish scope. He has taught in Ireland, the United States and France, and has translated French poetry. His *Collected Poems,* from The Gallery Press, appeared in 1995. He became first Ireland Professor of Poetry in 1998. He continues to publish volumes of poetry and prose; his second memoir, *The Pear is Ripe,* will appear in September, 2007.

Sinéad Morrissey was born in Portadown and educated in Belfast and Dublin. She received the Patrick Kavanagh Award for Poetry in 1990, an Eric Gregory Award in 1996, and the Rupert and Eithne Strong Award in 2002. In the same year, she was awarded a MacCauley Fellowship from the Irish Arts Council, was Writer-in-Residence at the Royal Festival Hall for the Poetry International

Festival, and was shortlisted for the T.S. Eliot Prize for her second collection, *Between Here and There*. She was Writer-in-Residence at the Seamus Heaney Centre for Poetry, Queen's University, Belfast, in 2002. She publishes with Carcanet Press.

Howard G. B Clark '21 Professor in the Humanities presently at Princeton University, **Paul Muldoon** was also Professor of Poetry at the University of Oxford (1999 to 2004). He won the 2003 Pulitzer prize for *Moy Sand and Gravel* (2002). His latest collection is *Horse Latitudes* (2006). He is the recipient of many prestigious international awards for his poetry. *The Times Literary Supplement* ranks him as "the most significant English-language poet born since the second World War." In *The New York Times,* he recently castigated contemporary motor-way Ireland for its desecration of Tara of the Kings. He publishes with Faber and Faber and Farrar, Straus and Giroux. In this book, he translates from the Irish of Nuala Ní Domhnaill.

Gerry Murphy's poetry collections include *A Small Fat Boy Walking Backwards* (1985, 1992) and *Rio de la Plata and All That* (1993). He has also published a number of pamphlets. His work has appeared in a range of anthologies. His *End of Part One: New and Selected Poems* (with a preface by John Montague) was published by The Dedalus Press in 2006. He translates the poetry of the Polish poet Katarzyna Borun-Jagodzinska featured in this anthology.

Richard Murphy was born in the West of Ireland in 1927 and now lives in South Africa. Major works as a poet include *The Battle of Aughrim* (1968), *High Island* (1974) and *The Price of Stone* (1985). The Gallery Press published his *Collected Poems* in 2000. Richard Murphy published a memoir, *The Kick* (Granta, 2002). *The Mirror Wall*, turned down by Faber, was simultaneously published by Bloodaxe Books, Newcastle-upon-Tyne, Wolfhound Press, Dublin, and Wake Forest University Press; it won the Poetry Book Society Translation Award in England.

Kate Newmann has worked as festival Officer for The Verbal Arts Centre in Derry. *The Blind Woman in the Blue House* (Summer Palace, 2001) was her first collection. Winner of various awards for her poetry, in 2006 she launched a CD with poems set to music by Irish composers Deirdre McKay, Elaine Agnew and Bill Campbell. She compiled *The Dictionary of Ulster Biography* (QUB, 1994). Her new collection of poetry, *Ratamataz Polka,* with Arlen Press, is scheduled to appear in autumn 2007.

Eiléan Ní Chuilleanáin is Dean of Faculty of Arts (Letters) in Trinity College, Dublin. Her latest book, *The Girl who Married the Reindeer,* was published by The Gallery Press in 2001 and Wake Forest in 2002. Her poetry has been translated into Italian. She has translated Ilena Mălăncioiu's *After the Raising of Lazarus,* excerpts from which appear in this volume. She has also translated from the Irish of Nuala Ní Dhomhnaill and from the Italian of Michele Ranchetti. A recent special issue of *The Irish University Review* was devoted of her work (vol.37 No.I, Spring-Summer 2007).

Rugadh i Sasana, tógadh i dTiobraid Árann í, chaith cuid mhaith ama i nDún Chaoin. Rinne cónaí sa Tuirc agus san Isiltír; cónaí anois uirthi gar do Bhaile Átha Cliath. Is iad na cnuasaigh filíochta is mó léi *An Dealg Droighnin*, 1981, *Féar Suaithinseach*, 1984, *Pharaoh's Daughter,* 1990, *Feis,* 1991, *The Astrackhan Cloak,* 1992 agus *Cead Aighnis,* 1998: **Nuala Ní Dhomhnaill** was born in Lancashire and grew up in County Tipperary, spending much time in the Kerry Gaeltacht, as well as in Turkey (more recently). Her first collection, *An Dealg Draigin* (1981), has been followed by a major corpus of innovative work. She is the most translated of modern Irish language poets. She publishes with The Gallery Press.

An Anthology of Poetry from Canada and Ireland 1175

Rugadh sa Ghaeltacht Láir, Tír Chonaill í, agus tógadh i nGaoth Dobhair. Ina múinteoir i Leitir Ceanainn. Saothar lei ar *An Chéad Chló*. **Collette Ní Ghallchóir** is from the Donegal Gaeltacht and teaches in that county. She has published two collections with Coiscéim.

Fionntrá, Co. Chiarraí. Ina múinteoir ar gach leibhéal. Cnuasaigh filíochta *Eiric Uachta*, 1971, *Leaca Liombó*, 1990 agus eile. **Máire Áine Nic Gearailt** is from the Kerry Gaeltacht and has taught at all levels. Her collection *Éiric Uachta* (1971) has been followed by several others from Coiscéim.

As Thiobraid Árainn dí; seal ina múinteoir, ina hiriseoir, ina craoltóir. *An Chéim Bhriste*, 1984 agus *Gáirdín Pharthais*, 1988: **Áine Ní Ghlinn** is from County Tipperary and lives in Dublin. She has been a teacher, actor and broadcaster. *An Chéim Briste* (1984) was the first of her collections. She publishes with Coiscéim.

Yilmaz Odabaşi, poet and writer, has worked in various positions, such as signboard painter and agency reporter. He could not continue his higher education having being arrested for political reasons. He served as the representative of many newspapers, reviews and agencies in Diyarbakir between 1986 and 1993. He moved to Ankara in 1994 and gave up journalism. He has been tried many times for his articles and imprisoned in various jails. Since 1991, he has worked solely as a writer in Urfa. His poems have been published in the reviews *Olusum, Yeni Olgu, Edebiyat 81, Sanat Rehberi, Yarin, Broy, Yeni Düsün, Çagdas Türk Dili, Yazili Günler, Düsler, Evrensel Kültür, Edebiyat ve Elestiri, Varlik, Gösteri* and *Ütopia* since 1980. He won the Temmuz Review Poetry Award in 1987, second rank in the 1989 Tayat Poetry Competition, the 1990 Cahit Sitki Taranci Award, second rank in the 1992 Union of Petrolium Workers' 4th Traditional Poetry Competition, the 1998 Sabri Altinel Poetry Competition and the 1999 Orhon Murat Ariburnu 10th Anniversary Poetry Special Award. In addition to winning international awards, his poems have been translated into various languages, and more than twenty of his poems have been set to music.

Jean O'Brien's first collection, *Dangerous Dresses,* was published by Bradshaw Books, Cork, in 2005. She has published her work in a wide variety of outlets, including *The Irish Times, The Cork Literary Review,* and *Fortnight Magazine*. She has read her work on RTÉ Radio. She lives in County Laois.

As Cill Chiaráin, Conndea na Gaillimhe dó. Ina mhúinteoir bunscoile. Dhá chnusach leis, *Uchtóga*, 1985 agus *Clocha Reatha*, 1986: **Mícheál Ó Cuaig** is from County Galway and is a teacher. His first collection, *Uchtóga,* was published in 1985. He publishes with Cló Iar-Chonnachta.

As Baile Átha Cliath dó; oibríonn sé sa Bhanc Ceannais. *Feic*, 1984. *Cambhaill*, 1987: **Aodh Ó Domhnaill** is from Dublin and has worked in the Central Bank. *Feic*, in 1984, was the first of several collections. He has been involved in amateur drama. He publishes with Coiscéim.

Bernard O'Donoghue lectures in Medieval English in Wadham College at the University of Oxford. He was born in Cork, and his poetry often reflects his place of origin. His collection *Gunpowder* (Chatto & Windus, 1995) won the Whitbread Book of the Year Award. *Outliving* (Chatto & Windus) was published in 2003. In this anthology, he translates both the work of Zbyněk Hejda and the author of *Sir Gawain and the Green Knight*. His own poetry appeared in *The Backyards of Heaven* (2003). A Seamus Heaney scholar, Bernard O'Donoghue wrote *Seamus Heaney and The Language of Poetry* (Prentice Hall PTR, 1995).

Gregory O'Donoghue lived for some years in Ontario where he taught at Queens in Kingston. Back in Cork, he published *The Permanent Way* with Three Spires Press in 1996. The Dedalus Press published *Making Tracks* in 2001. In this volume, he is the translator of the poems of Kristin Dimitrova.

Robert O'Donoghue has had six experimental plays performed. The best known of these is *The Long Night*, which was later adapted for radio. He has been writing and publishing poetry since the fifties. He collaborated with composer Seán Ó Riada on original verse and music evocation of the city of Cork. He has worked for *The Examiner* as drama critic and literary editor. With poet Patrick Galvin, he co-translates the work of Turkish poet Yilmaz Odabaşi that appears in this anthology.

Dennis O'Driscoll was born in Thurles, County Tipperary in 1954: his eight books of poetry include *New and Selected Poems* (Anvil Press, 2004), a Poetry Book Society Special Commendation. His latest collection of poems, *Reality Check*, will be published in the UK by Anvil Press and in the US by Copper Canyon Press. A selection of his essays and reviews, *Troubled Thoughts, Majestic Dreams* (The Gallery Press), was published in 2001. He edited and compiled *The Bloodaxe Book of Poetry Quotations* (Bloodaxe Books, 2006). He received a Lannan Literary Award in 1999, the E.M. Forster Award from the American Academy of Arts and Letters in 2005 and the O'Shaughnessy Award for Poetry from the Center for Irish Studies (Minnesota) in 2006. A member of Aosdána, the Irish Academy of artists, he has worked as a civil servant since the age of sixteen.

Born in Dublin, raised in County Antrim, **Gréagóir Ó Dúill** was educated in Belfast, Dublin and Maynooth, where he took a PhD in English. He has been a longtime resident in the Donegal Gaeltacht and was associated with the Poets' House there until its transfer to Waterford Institute of Technology, where he now lectures in creative writing. He has also been a lecturer in the Irish Department of Queen's University, Belfast. Author of eight collections of original poetry in Irish and editor of two anthologies, his selected poems, *Rogha Dánta*, appeared in 2001. He has also written a collection of short stories and a critical biography of Sir Samuel Ferguson and was literary editor of *Comhar* for four years. His own translations into English of a selection of his poems, *Traverse* (Lapwing, Belfast, 1998), has been recently succeeded by a selection and translations by Bernie Kenny, *Gone to Earth* (Black Mountain Press, Ballyclare, Co. Antrim, 2005.) He was the editor of *Fearann Pinn, Filíocht 1900-1999* (Coiscéim, 2000), an anthology of twentieth-century poetry in Irish. He has read from Stornoway to Palermo, from Boston to Berlin and is widely anthologised. A first collection of original poems in English, *A Vermeer Interior*, is to be published in 2008.

As Áth Luain dó agus is ansin a mhúineann sé. Roinnt chnuasach foilsithe aige, ina measc *Bláth an Fhéir*, 1968, *Saol na bhFuíoll*, 1973, *Idir Ord agus Inneoin*, 1977, *Aithrí Thóirní*, 1986 agus *Bindealáin Shálaithe*, 1989: **Seán Ó Leocháin** is from Athlone in the midlands and works as a teacher there. *Bláth an Fhéir* (1968) was the first of a number of collections. He publishes with An Clóchomhar.

Michael O'Loughlin's *Another Nation* (New Island Books, 1994 / UK Arc Publications, 1996) encapsulates work written over fifteen years. The poems offer an earned perspective within the broader European context. Colm Toibín reckons O'Loughlin to be the hidden voice in Irish writing, his exile in Europe affording him (O'Loughlin) dark insights into our own sense of exile in Ireland. Critic and novelist, O'Loughlin has also translated the selected poems of Dutch poet Gerrit Achterberg in *Hidden Weddings* (Raven Arts Press, 1987).

Mary O'Malley was born and brought up in Connemara. She has published five collections of
poetry, the most recent being *The Boning Hall* (2002) from Carcanet Press. She has written a
memoir of Connemara. She is a member of Aosdána and lives in the Moycullen Gaeltacht. Her
work has appeared in the Salmon anthology *Three Irish Poets*.

Liam Ó Muirthile was born in Cork City in 1950 and attended University College, Cork, where he
was a member of the *Innti* group of poets. He is author of two collections, *Tine Chnámh* (Sáirséal Ó
Marcaigh, 1984), and *Dialann Bóthair* (The Gallery Press, 1992). In 1984, he received the Irish
American Cultural Institute Award. He has written a weekly column in Irish, "An Peann Coitianta,"
for *The Irish Times*. A radio and print journalist, he has also specialised in prose and drama. His
latest poetry collection is *Sanas* (Cois Life, 2007). Tá CD ag gabháil leis an leabhar ar a bhfuil ceol
le roinnt de na dánta; i bpáirt le Iarla Ó Lionaird a rinneadh an taifeadach.

Derry O'Sullivan: as Beanntai, Co. Chorcaí dó agus cónaí air i bPáras. *Cá bhfuil do Iúdas?*
(Coiscéim, 1987). He is a winner of four Oireachtas poetry awards and the Seán Ó Riordáin
Memorial Prize. He made the first direct translation of the famous Irish poem *Cailleach Béara / The
Hag of Beare* into French (in collaboration with Jean-Yves Bériou and Martine Joulia) in 1995. He
co-founded the annual Festival Franco-Anglais de Poésie. He lives and writes in Paris and lectures
at the Sorbonne.

Paul Perry's debut book, *The Drowning of the Saints*, was published by Salmon Poetry in 2003. He
has been a James Michener fellow of Creative Writing at the University of Miami and a Cambor
Fellow of Poetry at the University of Houston. His second book, *The Orchid Keeper* (The Dedalus
Press, 2006), was launched at Waterford Institute of Technology in 2006.

Dana Podracká is an East European poet whose work has been translated into English by Robert
Welch to celebrate Cork Capital of Culture 2005. From Slovakia, her poetry collections include *The
Moon Lover* (1981), *Winter Guests* (1984), *Scripture* (1993), *Name* (1999) and *Catacombs* (2004).
In 2002, she entered the Slovak Parliament as an M.P. in the People's Party Movement.

Billy Ramsell is a native of Cork City where he now co-runs a small educational publishing
company. After study at University College Cork, he moved to Barcelona in 2000 to concentrate on
writing. Since 2001, his work has appeared in *The Cork Literary Review, Magma, The SHOp, The
Stinging Fly, Southward* and *The Sunday Tribune*. In 2005, he was shortlisted for a Hennessy Award
and won first prize in the Cork Literary Review's manuscript competition. His debut collection,
Complicated Pleasures, was published by The Dedalus Press in 2007.

Maurice Riordan is from County Cork. His first book, *A Word from the Loki* (Faber, 1995), was a
Poetry Book Society Choice. It was also nominated for the T.S. Eliot Prize. *Floods* (Faber, 2000)
was shortlisted for the Whitbread Poetry prize. He lives in London, where he teaches at Imperial
College and on the Creative Writing MA at Goldsmiths College. He translates the poetry of
Immanuel Mifsud in this anthology.

A major figure on the Irish-language literary landscape already, Gabriel Rosenstock is either editor
or author of over one-hundred collections of poetry and work in translation. He has specialised in
the haiku in Irish. He is a member of Aosdána and works in Dublin with the Irish-language
publishing house, An Gúm. His latest work, *Bliain an Bhandé / Year of the Goddess* (The Dedalus
Press, 2007), draws on the Indian bhakti tradition of devotional poetry. His collections begin with
Susanne sa Seomra Folctha in 1973.

Juliette Saumande, traductrice de plusieurs romans de langue anglaise d'une très grande diversité, (par exemple : Justin Edwards, le plus récent étant *La bête de l'ombre* (2006) ; Juliette Saumande a aussi publié plusieurs livres pour enfants chez les Editions Fleurus, notamment : *La véritable histoire de la princesse O'Petipoi*. D'ailleurs, elle a aussi réussi avec brio la traduction en version française de la poète irlandaise Biddy Jenkinson qui revendique la langue gaëlique et qui réfuse toute traduction de son ouvrage en langue anglaise.

John W. Sexton is variously poet, short-story writer, dramatist, children's novelist, radio scriptwriter and broadcaster. He is the author of three collections of poetry, *The Prince's Brief Career* (Cairn Mountain Press, 1995), *Shadows Bloom / Scathanna Faoi Bhlath* (a book of haiku with translations into Irish by Gabriel Rosenstock) and *Vortex* (Doghouse, 2005). His novels, *The Johnny Coffin Diaries* and *Johnny Coffin School-Dazed*, are published by The O'Brien Press and have been translated into Italian and Serbian. Under the pseudonym Sex W. Johnston, he has recorded an album with legendary Stranglers frontman, Hugh Cornwell, entitled *Sons of Shiva*, which has been released on Track Records.

Eileen Sheehan is from Killarney, Co Kerry. Her poetry is widely published in magazines in Ireland and abroad, including *Poetry Ireland Review, The SHOp, The Stinging Fly, Southword, The Stony Thursday Book, Revival, The Rialto, Staple, Pelagos, Versal* and *l'Estracelle*. Her work appears in many anthologies, including *The Open Door Anthology of Poetry* (ed Niall MacMonagle) and *Winter Blessings*, by Patricia Scanlan. She is winner of the Brendan Kennelly Poetry Award 2006. Her collection *Song Of The Midnight Fox* (2004) is published by Doghouse Press.

Peter Sirr was born in 1960. After a number of years in Holland and Italy, he returned to Dublin where he was the first Director of the Irish Writers Centre, a post he held until 2003. Now a freelance writer, editor and translator, he has been editor of *Poetry Ireland Review*. The Gallery Press has published his poetry collections *Marginal Zones* (1984), *Talk, Talk* (1987), *Ways of Falling* (1991), *The Ledger of Fruitful Exchange* (1995) and *Bring Everything* (2000). In 2004, The Gallery Press published *Selected Poems* simultaneously with a new collection, *Nonetheless*. Wake Forest University Press published his *Selected Poems* in 2006. He lives in Dublin with his wife, the poet Enda Wyley, and their daughter, Freya.

Dolores Stewart is a bilingual poet from the West of Ireland. Her *In Out of the Rain* was published by the The Dedalus Press in 1999. Her collections in Irish, *Sé Sin le Rá* and *An Cosán Dearg*, were published by Coiscéim in 2001 and in 2003, respectively.

Caribbean-American **Samantha Thomas** is currently completing her Research MA in Creative Writing at the Waterford Institute of Technology in Ireland. Her research and poems concentrate on the history of sugar and its global social and economic effects. The Bulbulia International Award in the Humanities for 2006 was recently awarded to her in acknowledgement of this work. As she says, "I write from my circumstance of never having any particular ethnic identity and the dualities that that experience incurs: namely, a continual process of recognition, rejection and forgiveness that, on this shrinking planet, is becoming more and more relevant to everyone." Thomas is also an award winner from the University of New Orleans Writing Competition 2005.

Rugadh sa Rinn, cónaí uirthi annsin. Ina múinteoir i nDún Garbháin: **Áine Uí Fhoghlú**, teacher, folklorist and former broadcast journalist from the Waterford Gaeltacht of An Rinn, published *Aistear Aonair* (Coiscéim) in 1999. She has written two plays which were performed locally. She hosts creative writing workshops under the auspices of Údarás na Gaeltachta and Waterford County Council. A fine artist also, she has exhibited with Lán Mara and won first prize in an international competition. Her lastest poetry collection is *An Liú sa Chuan* (Coiscéim, 2007).

Currently Dean of Arts at the University of Ulster in Northern Ireland, **Robert Welch** is also, by turns, novelist, poet and major literary critic. His poetry collections include *Muskerry* (1991) and *The Blue Formica Table* (1999) from The Dedalus Press. He was editor of the *Oxford Companion to Irish Literature* (1996). Among his critical works are *Irish Poetry from Moore to Yeats* (1980) and *Changing States: Transformations in Modern Irish Writing* (1993). He translates the work of Dana Podracká in this volume.

Grace Wells, who comes from London and worked there in film, lives on the slopes of Sliabh na mBan in County Tipperary, where she rears her children, Sliabh and Holly, next door to Cill Cais. She is a poet and community worker and also writes fiction for children, and, in this category, won the Eilish Dillon Award in 2003 for *Gyrfalcon*, published by The O'Brien Press. Her latest novel, *Ice-Dreams*, is also forthcoming from The O'Brien Press.

Enda Wyley was born in Dublin in 1966. She works as a teacher. She has published three collections of poetry with The Dedalus Press: *Eating Baby Jesus* (1994), *Socrates in the Garden* (1998), and *Poems for breakfast* (2004). She also writes children's Fiction. *Boo and Bear* was published in 2004 by The O'Brien Press, and her novel for 10-year olds and up, *The Silver Notebook*, was published by The O'Brien Press also in 2007.

Permissions / Acknowledgements (Ireland)

Bardwell, Leland: "Hard to Imagine Your Face Dead," "The Night's Empty Shells," "Innismurray," "'No Road Beyond the Graveyard,'" "The Horse Protestant Joke Is Over," and "Prison Poem III: For a Friend Doing Life in Portlaoise," from *The Noise of Masonry Settling* (2006). Reprinted by permission of The Dedalus Press.

Barry, Sebastian: "The Wood-Pigeons," "The Pinkening Boy," "The Owner," and "The Man Monaghan," from *The Pinkening Boy* (New Island, 2004). Reprinted by permission of the author.

Berkeley, Sara: "Strawberry Thief," "How We Meet," and "Still Life, Yellow Quilt," from *Strawberry Thief* (2005). By kind permission of the author and The Gallery Press, Loughcrew, Oldcastle, County Meath, Ireland.

Blake, Denise: "In Mourning," "*Kaiyuglak* — Rippled Surface of Snow," "Knowing the Wizard," "Early Lessons," "Letterkenny 567," and "Vows." Reprinted by permission of the author.

Boland, Eavan: 1:5 "The Dolls Museum in Dublin," from, "Writing in a Time of Violence: A Sequence," from *Writing in a Time of Violence* (1994); I "Marriage" (I "In Which Hester Bateman, Eighteenth-Century English Silversmith, Takes an Irish Commission"), II "Against Love Poetry," III "The Pinhole Camera," IV "Quarantine," V "Embers," VI "Then," VII "First Year," VIII "Once," IX "Thankëd be Fortune," X "A Marriage for the Millennium," XI "Lines for a Thirtieth Wedding Anniversary," from *Code* (2001). Reprinted from *New Collected Poems* (2005) by kind permission of the author and Carcanet Press.

Boland, Rosita: "The Astronaut's Wife," "Diamonds," "Sightless," "Gold — The Gleninsheen Gorget," "Teeth," and "Tears," from *Dissecting the Heart* (2003). By kind permission of the author and The Gallery Press.

Boran, Pat: "The Magic Roundabout," "Jupiter," and "Tent," from "New Poems" in *New and Selected Poems* (2005). Reprinted by kind permission of the author and Salt Modern Poets.

Borun-Jagodinska, Katarzyna: "Theresa at the Laundry," "Photograph of Theresa Martin as Joan of Arc," "Van Morrisson Plays Mother Goose," "Scarpia," "Mimi's Aria," "Aida," and "Scarpia's Aria," from *Pocket Apocalypse* (2005) translated from the Polish by Gerry Murphy. By kind permission of the authors and Southword Editions, The Munster Literature Centre, Frank O'Connor House, 84 Douglas Street, Cork, Ireland.

Breathnach, Colm: "Bróga Nua" / "*New Shoes*," "Scarúint" / "*Parting*," "Forlámhas" / "*Supremacy*," from *Cantaic an Bhalbháin* (1991); "An Fear Marbh" / "*The Dead Man*," "Lorgaíodh mo Shúile tú" / "*My Eyes Would Look for You*," "Seana-ghnás" / "*The Old Ways*," from *Scáthach* (1994); "Ar an Leaba leathan" / "*On the Bed Spread*" and "An Ghéag Theasctha" / "*The Severed Limb*," from *Chiaroscuro* (2006). By kind permission of the author and Coiscéim.

Brennan, Deirdre: "The Burning," "In the National Archives," "About Being Human," "'The Blue Dress,'" "Fallen Woman," "Repossession," "The Last Observance," and "The Collector," from *The Hen Party* (2001). By kind permission of the author and Lapwing Publications, Belfast.

"Sníomh"/ *Spinning,*" "Maighdeana Mara" / *"Mermaids,"* and "Is 'Werewolf' mé anocht" / *"I Am a Werewolf Tonight,"* from *Thar Cholba na Mara* (1993). By kind permission of the author and Coiscéim, Baile Átha Cliath.

Buckley, Vincent: "Hunger-Strike," from *Last Poems* (McPhee Gribble, 1991). By kind permission of Penelope Buckley.

Bushe, Paddy: "Bolgam" / *"Gulp,"* "Ag Aistriú Buddha in Der Glorie" / "Translating Buddha in Der Glorie," and "Éin i gCliabháin" / *"Caged Birds,"* from *In Ainneoin na gCloch* (2001). By kind permission of the author and Coiscéim.

Byron, Catherine: "Coffin. Crypt. Consumption," "Coco de Mer," "Egyptians," "The Getting of Vellum," "St Thomas Aquinas in MacNeice's House," "Minding You," and "After the Nuptial Mass," from *The Getting of Vellum* (2000). By kind permission of the author and Salmon Poetry.

Callan, Mary Rose: "Clean as a Wish," "Her Grief," and "Facts of Life," from *Footfalls of Snow* (2005). By kind permission of the author and Bradshaw Books.

Cannon, Moya: "Murdering the Language," from *The Parchment Boat* (1997). By kind permission of the author and The Gallery Press.

Carr, Ellie: Extracts from *Traveller Ways Traveller Words* (1992). By kind permission of Pavee Point Publications, Pavee Point, North Great Charles Street, Dublin 1.

Carson, Ciaran: Canto XV, translation from *The Inferno of Dante Alighieri* (paperback UK edition 2004). By kind permission of Granta Books, London.

Charalambides, Kyriakos: "Of the People of Olympia," from "The Tyranny of Words," "Spoon Sweet," "Death's Art," "Candaules' Wife," "Nitocris, Queen of Babylon," "Potiphar's Wife," and "Tears for Twenty-Five Years," from *Selected Poems* (2005) translated from the Greek by Greg Delanty. By kind permission of Southword Editions.

Coady, Michael: "Interview on Main Street," "Low Winter Sun," and "School Tour, Kilmainham Jail." By kind permission of the author c/o The Gallery Press.

Coyle-Greene, Enda: "Another Moon," "Grafton Street," "Handed On," "Opium," "Vertigo," "The Rooms," and "So Many." By kind permission of the author.

Cronin, Anthony: "On Seeing Lord Tennyson's Nightcap at Westport House," "In Praise of Hestia, Goddess of the Hearth Fire," and "Meditation on a Clare Cliff-Top," from *Collected Poems* (2004) published by New Island. By kind permission of the author.

Crymble, Phillip: "Tomatoes" and "Rice Lake," from *Wide Boy* (2007). By kind permission of the author and Lapwing Press.

Cummings, Philip: "Deochanna" / *"Drinks,"* "Uiscí Reatha" / *"Running Water,"* "Newton" / *"Newton,"* "Anne" / *"Anne,"* "Séamus" / *"Seamus,"* and "Reilig an Mhuine Ghlais" / *"Moneyglass Cemetery,"* from *Néalta* (2005). By kind permission of the author and Coiscéim.

de Fréine, Celia: "In Aois" / "Getting On," from *Fiacha Fola* (2004). By kind permission of the author and Cló Iar-Chonnachta.

de Paor, Louis: "Foghlaimeoirí" / "*Homework,*" "Dán Grá" / "*Love Poem,*" "Ceartúcháin" / "*Corrections,*" "Gaeilgeoirí" / "*Gaeilgeoiri,*" "Searmanas" / "*Rituals,*" "Seanchas" / "*Old Stories,*" "Didjeridu" / "*Didjeridoo,*" "Inghean" / "*Daughter,*" "Iarlais" / "*Changeling,*" and "Timpbriste" / "*Accidentally,*" from *Ag Greadh Bás sa Reilig / Clapping in the Cemetery* (2005). By kind permission of the author and Cló Iar-Chonnachta.

Dillon, Patrick: "The Crocodile." By kind permission of the author.

Dimitrova, Kristin: "Auntie," "A Lament for the Saintly Mothers," "Freight Depot," "First Blood," "Fused," "In the Train," "The Wall by the Swings," "The Local School," and "A Visit to the Clockmaker," from *A Visit to the Clockmaker* (2005) translated from the Bulgarian by Gregory O'Donoghue. By kind permission of the authors and Southword Editions.

Dunne, Seán: "The Healing Island," from *Collected Poems* (2005). By kind permission of the estate of Seán Dunne and The Gallery Press.

Durcan, Paul: "On Giving a Poetry Recital to an Empty Hall," from *Cries of an Irish Caveman* (The Harvill Press, 2001); "Golden Island Shopping Centre," "The Man with a Bit of Jizz in Him," "A Robin in Autumn Chatting at Dawn," "HEADLINES," "The Annual Mass of the Knights of Columbanus," "The Proud Cry of the Young Father," "The 12 O'Clock Mass, Roundstone, County Galway, 28 July 2002," and "Tarnowo Podgorne," from *The Art of Life* (2004). By kind permission of the author and The Harvill Press.

Ehin, Andres: "I am," "The colonels of several hostile armies," "fish livers lie scattered on the ground," "I'm a cripple with yellow, burning eyes," "Secret," "I am your Missing Car," and "deep, below ground, breathe," from *Moose Beetle Swallow* (2005) translated from the Estonian by Patrick Cotter. By kind permission of the authors and Southword Editions.

Fallon, Peter: "How frequently we've watched eruptions . . . ," from *The Georgics of Virgil* (2004). By kind permission of the author and The Gallery Press.

Fitzpatrick Simmons, Janice: "Cocoon," "Blessings," "Faith," "Making Room," "Sex," "A Year On," and "Alive, Alive, Alive," from *The Bowsprit* (2005). By kind permission of the author and Lagan Press, Belfast.

Ford, Roderick: "Giuseppe" and "First Love," from *The Shoreline of Falling* (2005). By kind permission of the author and Bradshaw Books.

French, Tom: "Touching the Bones," "Night Drive," "Asperger Child," "The Post-Hole," "Pity the Bastards," "Mending a Puncture," and "Striking Distance," from *Touching the Bones* (2001). By kind permission of the author and The Gallery Press.

Garvey, Alan: "Love," "Judge These Books," and "Poppy," from *Herself in Air* (2006). By kind permission of the author and Lapwing Publications, Belfast. "The Fields of Beaumont-Hamel" by kind permission of the author.

Gillis, Alan: "The Ulster Way," "12th October, 1994," "Cold Flow," "To Belfast," "Love Bites," "Casualty," "Niamh," "Last Friday Night" and "Progress," from *Somewhere, Somewhere* (2005). By kind permission of the author and The Gallery Press.

Grennan, Eamon: "*because the body stops here...,*" "So this is what it comes down to...," "When that great conflagration...," "Off the skin of water...," "When I saw the deer's breath...," "It must be a particular kind of grace...," "I'm trying to get one line...," "Although snow has wrapped the house...," and "Rained in all day like this...," from *The Quick of It* (2004). By kind permission of the author and The Gallery Press.

Heaney, Seamus: "Anahorish 1944," "Helmet," "The Nod," "Out of This World," "Tate's Avenue," and "The Blackbird of Glanmore," from *District and Circle* (2006). By kind permission of the author and Faber and Faber, London.

Zbyněk Hejda: "from A Stay in a Sanatorium," "A Stay in a Sanatorium" ("I was staying..."), "Some Evening," from *A Stay in a Sanatorium* (2005) translated from the Czech by Bernard O'Donoghue. By kind permission of the authors and Southword Editions.

Hutchinson, Pearse: "Fúinne" / "*About Us,*" from *The Soul that Kissed the Body* (1990). The text in Irish by kind permission of the author and The Gallery Press. The English translation is provided courtesy of Gréagoir Ó Dúill and featured in the latter's anthology of Irish-language poetry, *Fearann Pinn: filíocht 1900-1999* (Coiscéim, 2000).

Jakpa, Oritsegbemi Emmanuel: "Harmattan" and "Eden." By kind permission of the author.

Jenkinson, Biddy: "Tuireamh Marie Antoinette" / "*La chute de Marie-Antoinette.*" By kind permission of the author and translator, Juliette Saumande.

Kelly, Rita: "Beir Beannacht" / " *Fare Well,*" from *Fare Well / Beir Beannacht* (Attic Press, 1990). By kind permission of the author.

Kennelly, Brendan: "Our Place," "In Oliver's Army," "A Bad Time," "The Soldier," "Reading Aloud," and "A Running Battle" — excerpts from *Cromwell* (1992). By kind permission of the author and Bloodaxe Books, Newcastle upon Tyne.

Kinsella, Thomas: "King John's Castle" and "Pause en Route," from *Poems* (1956) *and Another September* (Dolmen Press 1958); "Chrysalides," from *Downstream* (Dolmen Press 1962); "Tao and Unfitness at Inistiogue on the River Nore," from *Songs of the Night and Other Poems* (Peppercanister 1978): all from *Collected Poems* (Carcanet Press, 2001). By kind permission of the author. "Wedding Service," from *Marginal Economy* (Peppercanister 24, 2006); Shakespeare Sonnets "29" and "30" from *Readings in Poetry* (Peppercanister 25, 2006). By kind permission of the author.

Korun, Barbara: "Stag," "Wolf," and "White Bulls," from *Songs of Earth and Light* (2005) translated from the Slovene by Theo Dorgan. By kind permission of the authors and Southword Editions.

Laird, Nick: "Cuttings," "Remaindermen," "The Signpost," "To the Wife," and "The Evening Forecast for the Region," from *To a Fault* (2005). By kind permission of the author and Faber and Faber, London.

Leahy, Ann: "A Good Rogeting," "Mince Customer," and "Cold Storage." By kind permission of the author.

Longley, Michael: "Swallow," "Laertes," and "Northern Lights," from *Gorse Fires* (Cape,1991); "Ceasefire," from *The Ghost Orchid* (Cape, 1995); "Björn Olinder's Pictures," "Broken Dishes," "The Mustard Tin," "The Daffodils," "A Sprig of Bay," "A Poppy," "The War Graves," "A Prayer," "The Horses," "Scrap Metal," and "All of These People," from *The Weather in Japan* (Cape, 2000); "A Norwegian Wedding," from *Snow Water* (Cape, 2004); all poems in *Collected Poems* (Cape, 2006). By kind permission of the author and Cape Poetry.

Lordan, Dave: "In the Model Village," "TEA," "The Longest Queue," from "Reflections on Shannon," and "Holding Chirac's Hand in Temple Bar," from *The Boy in The Ring* (Salmon, 2007). By kind permission of the poet and Salmon Poetry.

Lyons, Alice: "Thank God It's Dry" and "The Polish Language." By kind permission of the author.

Mac Eoin, Gearailt: "Deireadh Caithréime" / *"The End of Triumph"* and "Agus an Samhradh Thart" / *"Now Summer's Over,"* from *Labhraí Loingseach* (1988) and *Néalta Taistil* (1994), respectively. By kind permission of the author.

Mac Síomóin, Tomás: "1845"/ *"1845,"* from *Damhna & Dánta Eile* (Sairséal & Dill, 1974). By kind permission of the author.

Mălăncioiu, Ilena: "The Headless Bird," "The Bear," "A Dog," "Song of Joy," "You Gave Me a Long Look," "The Doctor on Duty," "Let the Grass Grow Over Her," "Laid Beside You," and "It Snowed on the Body," from *After the Raising of Lazarus* (2005) translated from the Romanian by Eiléan Ní Chuilleanáin. By kind permission of the authors and Southword Editions.

McCarthy, Thomas: "He Meets His Future Sister-in-Law, Miss Teresette O'Neill, 1811," "He Turns to His Wife, 1797," "He Watches His Wife Create a Silhouette Portrait, 1812," "He Contemplates a Stolen *Bozzetto* of Canova's *Cupid and Psyche*, 1811," "He Witnesses a Military Execution, 1804," "He Witnesses Another Hanging, 1813," "He Buries His Father, 1809," "He Goes Through His Father's Belongings, 1809," "He Writes to His Estranged Sister, 1803," "He Recalls a Letter from Home, 1771," "He Spends Christmas at Clonakilty, 1809," "He Considers the Rev. Dill-Wallace, 1817," and "He Sees a Warehouse Burning, August, 1798," from *Merchant Prince* (2005). By kind permission of the author and Anvil Press Poetry, London.

McGuckian, Medbh: "Mappa Mundi," "House without Eyebrows," "My Sister's Way to Make Mead," "The Gorgon as Mistress of the Animals," and "Woman Forming the Handle of a Cane," from *The Currach Requires No Harbours* (2004). By kind permission of the author and The Gallery Press.

McLoughlin, Nigel: "High Water" and "Bomb," from *Blood* (2005), and "A Hill Farmer Speaks," from *Dissonances* (2007). By kind permission of the author and Bluechrome, Bristol.

Meehan, Paula: "My Father Perceived as a Vision of St. Francis," "Not Your Muse," "'Not alone the rue in my herb garden. . . ,'" and excerpts from "Berlin Diary, 1991" — "5. Folktale" and "At Pankow S-Bahn" — from *Pillow Talk* (1994). By kind permission of the author and The Gallery Press. From "Suburb" — "Stood Up," "Stink Bomb," and "Sudden Rain" — and also "The Tantric Master," from *Dharmakaya* (2000). By kind permission of the author and Carcanet Press.

Mhac an tSaoi, Máire: "Mutterrecht" / *"Mutterrecht,"* from *An Cion go Dtí Seo* (Sairséal & Dill, *Bailiúchan Iomlán* 1987). By kind permission of the author.

Mifsud, Immanuel: "Confidential Reports — in the Form of a Public-Private Confession," from *Confidential Reports* (2005) translated from the Maltese by Maurice Riordan. By kind permission of the authors and Southword Editions.

Mills, Geraldine: "Blighted," "What We Understood," "Out of Old Stories," "About Lifelines," "Cutaway Philosophers," "Boy at the Window Waiting," "Poets as Magpie," and "Wednesday Women," from *Toil the Dark Harvest* (2003). By kind permission of the author and Bradshaw Books.

Montague, John: "Border Sick Call," from *Collected Poems* (2005). By kind permission of the author and The Gallery Press.

Morrissey, Sinéad: "Pilots," "Little House in the Big Woods," "Juist," "Reading the Greats," "In Praise of Salt," and sections 4 and 5 from "The State of the Prisons," from *The State of the Prisons* (2005). By kind permission of the author and Carcanet Press.

Murphy, Richard: "Kassapa" and "Sigiriya, 11 January 1987," originally published in *The Mirror Wall* (Bloodaxe Books, 1989 with Wolfhound Press Dublin and Wake Forest University Press) and re-produced in *Collected Poems* (2000). By kind permission of the author and The Gallery Press.

Newmann, Kate: "Put to Loss Because of the Snow." By kind permission of the author.

Ní Dhomhnaill, Nuala: "Na Murúcha a Thriomaigh," from *Cead Aighnis* (An Sagart, An Daingean 1998), translated as *"The Assimilated Merfolk"* by Paul Muldoon. By kind permission of the authors and An Sagart.

Ní Ghallchóir, Collette: "Antain" / *"Antain"* and "An tAmharc Deireanach" / *"The Last Look,"* from *Idir Dhá Ghleann* (1999). By kind permission of the author and Coiscéim.

Níc Gearailt, Máire Áine: "Teicheadh" / *"Fleeing,"* from *Ó Ceileadh an Bhreasáil* (1992). By kind permission of the author and Coiscéim.

Ní Ghlinn, Áine: "Teangmháil" / *"Contact"* and "Iomrascáil Oíche Leis na Mairbh" / *"Night Wrestling with the Dead,"* from *An Chéim Bhriste* (1984). By kind permission of the author and Coiscéim.

Odabaşi, Yilmaz: from "Feride," from *Everything But You* (2005) translated from the Turkish by Patrick Galvin and Robert O'Donoghue. By kind permission of Southword Editions.

O'Brien, Jean: "Severed," "Veronica's Epiphany," "Veronica," and "Yes, I can bake a cake." from *Dangerous Dresses* (2005). By kind permission of the author and Bradshaw Books.

Ó Cuaig, Mícheál: "Uchtóga" / *"Armfuls"* and "Toibreacha" / *"Wells,"* from *Clocha Reatha* (1986). By kind permission of the author and Cló Iar-Chonnachta.

Ó Domhnaill, Aodh: "Oifigiúil" / *"Official,"* from *Feic* (1984). By kind permission of the author and Coiscéim.

O'Donoghue, Bernard: excerpts from *Sir Gawain and the Green Knight* (Penguin Classics 2006). By kind permission of Penguin Books (UK) and Bernard O'Donoghue.

O'Driscoll, Dennis: "Missing God," "England," and "At the Seminar," from *Exemplary Damages* (Anvil Press 2002); "Lord Mayo" and "The Light of Other Days," from *Foreseeable Futures* (Anvil Press 2004): all published in *Dennis O'Driscoll: New and Selected Poems* (2004). By kind permission of the author and Anvil Press London.

Ó Leocháin, Seán: "999" / "*999,*" "Traidisiún" / "*Tradition*" and "Tóraíocht" / "*Pursuit,*" from *Bindealáin Shálaithe* (1989). By kind permission of the author and An Clóchomhar, B.A.C. 13.

O'Loughlin, Michael: "Latin as a Foreign Language," "Boxer," "Three Fragments on the Theme of Moving Around in Cities," "To a Child in the Womb," and "Yellow," from *Another Nation: New & Selected Poems* (1996). By kind permission of Arc Publications, Lancs.

O'Malley, Mary: "Anniversary," "My Mac," "Angry Arthur," and "The Poet's Fancy," from *Asylum Road* (2001). By kind permission of the author and Salmon Poetry.

Ó Muirthile, Liam: "When Will I get to Be Called a Man," "Basáin Mhara," "Baile an Tae," "Li Am ar Fhalla Mór na Síne," "Ringabella," "Eitseáil Bheo," "Suantraí Sarah is Asmahane," "San Aonad Alzheimer," agus "An Seanduine," from *Sanas* (2007). By kind permission of the author and Cois Life.

O'Sullivan, Derry: "Finit" / "*Finit,*" from *Cá Bhfuil do Iúdás* (1987). By kind permission of the author and Coiscéim.

Perry, Paul: "The Gate to Mulcahy's Farm," from *The Drowning of the Saints* (2003). By kind permission of the author and Salmon Poetry.

Podracká, Dana: "A Parcel from Prison," "A White Bedsheet," and "The Place of Execution of the First President," from *Forty Four* (2005), translated from the Slovak by Robert Welch. By kind permission of the authors and Southword Editions.

Ramsell, Billy: "Breath," "Middle Distance," "Complicated Pleasures," "Still Life with Frozen Pizza," "Ireland," and "Southern Shores," from *Complicated Pleasures* (The Dedalus Press, 2007). By kind permission of the author and The Dedalus Press.

Rosenstock, Gabriel: "As gach póir Díot" / "*From each and every pore,*" "Seanfhalla" / "*Old Wall,*" "Sneachta na mBunchnoc" / "*Snow on the foothills,*" "Do nochtacht" / "*Your nakedness,*" "Gustaí mhí Aibreáin" / "*April Gusts,*" "Samhradh" / "*Summer,*" "Colúr Marbh" / "*Dead Pigeon,*" "Yugapat-srishti" / "*Yugapat-srishti,*" "Coillteán" / "*Castrato,*" "Deirid gur daonnaí mé" / "They say I am human," and "Tóg Chun do Dhraenacha Mé" / "*Take Me to Your Drains,*" from *Bliain an Bhandé / Year of the Goddess* (2007). By kind permission of the author and The Dedalus Press.

Sexton, John W: "Vortex," "Frogspawn," and "Roland Gets It," from *Vortex* (2005). By kind permission of the author and Doghouse Books.

Sheehan, Eileen: "Lady in White," published in *Winter Blessings* (ed. Patricia Scanlon, Hodder Headline Ireland 2006). By kind permission of the author.

Sirr, Peter: "The Names of the Houses," from "Here and There: A Notebook," "Housesitting," from "A Journal" ("In the beginning . . .") and "The Writer's Studio," from *Selected Poems* (2004). By kind permission of the author and The Gallery Press.

Stewart, Dolores: "American Wake," "Maryville, Winter, 2001," and "Death of Socrates," from *Presence of Mind* (2005). By kind permission of the author and The Dedalus Press. "Dóchas" / *"Hope,"* "Idir Scylla agus Charybdis" / *"Between Scylla and Charybdis,"* "Ar Iarraidh" / *"Lost,"* and "Ceol Johnny Phádraig Pheter" / *"Johnny Phádraig Pheter's Music,"* from *Sé Sin le Rá* (2001). By kind permission of the author and Coiscéim.

Thomas, Samantha: "Late August, Donegal," "Man O' War," "Man-Eating Leopard of Rudrapraya," "Morne Grande," and "Verlaine." By kind permission of the author.

Uí Fhoghlú, Áine: "What's that in English?" / *"What's that in English?,"* "Sa tír" / *"In the land . . . ,"* "Íota" / *"Desire,"* "An Tine Bheo" / *"The Burning Fire,"* "I Seomra Feithimh an Dochtúra, 1974" / *"In the Doctor's Waiting Room, 1974,"* "Fiailí" / *"Weeds,"* and "An tUllmhúchán" / *"Getting Ready,"* from *An Liú sa Chuan* (Coiscéim, 2007). By kind permission of the author and Coiscéim.

Wells, Grace: "Aşure," "The Only Medicine," "Horse Fair," "The Funeral Director's Wife," "The Muezzin's Call," "The Lone Parent Does Not Write," and "The Hostage Place." By kind permission of the author.

Wyley, Enda: "Going Home," "Love Bruise," and "Master Chef," from *Socrates in the Garden* (The Dedalus Press, 1998); "Two Women in Kosovo," "Marlborough Road," "Mint Gatherers," "Emperor," and "Diary of a Fat Man," from *Poems for breakfast* (The Dedalus Press, 2004). By kind permission of the author and The Dedalus Press.

Index of Poets (Canada)

A
Akiwenzie-Damm, Kateri 3
Armstrong, Jeannette. C 7
Armstrong, Tammy 15
Audet, Martine 18
Avison, Margaret 20

B
Babstock, Ken 28
Banerji, Anurima 34
Barnes, Mike 38
Bolster, Stephanie 39
Borson, Roo 44
Bowling, Tim 49
Brand, Dionne 51
Brault, Jacques 64
Brebner, Diana 67
Brossard, Nicole 74

C
Callanan, Mark 80
Carson, Anne 82
Catalano, Francis 97
Chiasson, Herménégilde 101
Clarke, George Elliot 110
Cohen, Leonard 122
Coles, Don 129
Crozier, Lorna 147
Cuthand, Beth 158

D
Dalton, Mary 162
Daoust, Jean-Paul 169
Davis, Degan 175
Deland, Monique 176
Desgent, Jean-Marc 179
Des Rosiers, Joël 183
Dickinson, Adam 189
Dorion, Hélène 191
Dumont, Marilyn 194
Dupré, Louise 201
Dutton, Paul 205

G
Geddes, Gary 216
Gillis, Susan 219
Goh, Poh Seng 222
Goodison, Lorna 228
Goyette, Susan 233
Greenwood, Catherine 237

H
Halfe, Louise 242
Harrison, Richard 250
Hsu, Ray 252
Hunter, Catherine 254

L
Lane, Patrick 257
Langlais, Tania 262
Layton, Irving 266
Ltaif, Nadine 277
Lush, Laura 285

M
McKay, Don 295
Melançon, Robert 310
Michaels, Anne 313
Miki, Roy 318
Monette, Hélène 322
Mordecai, Pamela 328
Morency, Pierre 338
Moses, Daniel David 339
Moure, Erín 344
Munce, Alayna 355
Musgrave, Susan 357

N
Nepveu, Pierre 363
bpNichol 371

O
O'Meara, David 387
Ondaatje, Michael 398

P
Partridge, Elise 410
Pass, John 417
Pick, Alison 423
Pittman, Kyran 424
Préfontaine, Yves 425
Price, Stephen 433
Purdy, Al 436

R
Rader, Matt 450
Redhill, Michael 456
Ruffo, Armand Garnet 464

S
Scofield, Gregory 475
Senior, Olive 486
Sinclair, Sue 496
Solie, Karen 506
Starnino, Carmine 514
Steffler, John 522

U
Uguay, Marie 526

W
Walsh, Agnes 531
Ward, Frederick 534
Watts, Enos 544
Wershler-Henry, Darren 546
Whittal, Zoe 550

Y
Young, Patricia 553

Z
Zwicky, Jan 556

An Anthology of Poetry from Canada and Ireland 1189

Index of Poems (Canada)

A Berth in the Stern .... *Ken Babstock*	32
A Chinese Lantern for Audrey .... *Susan Goyette*	236
A History of Vietnam & Central America as Seen in the Paintings of Leon Golub, *Musée des beaux arts, Montréal, 1985* .... *Erín Moure*	347
A Note to the Chinese Reader .... *Leonard Cohen*	128
A Pattern of Escape .... *Frederick Ward*	538
A Sermon to the Undecided .... *George Elliott Clarke*	120
Alex Espaniel, 1920 .... *Armand Garnet Ruffo*	468
Amazon Women .... *Olive Senior*	491
Ambivalence .... *Margaret Avison*	21
"Amérique terre archaïque..." .... *Francis Catalano*	99
An Imagined Country .... *Armand Garnet Ruffo*	470
An Old Niçoise Whore .... *Irving Layton*	270
from *Anatomy of Keys* .... *Steven Price*	433
Another Version ("Look, all I can tell you is...") .... *Jan Zwicky*	562
Aperture, 1856 .... *Stephanie Bolster*	39
Aran Islands .... *Irving Layton*	275
Archie Belaney, 1915-16 .... *Armand Garnet Ruffo*	470
Archie Belaney, 1930-31 .... *Armand Garnet Ruffo*	471
Aspen in Wind .... *Jan Zwicky*	565
At Geronimo's Grave .... *Armand Garnet Ruffo*	466
At the Aching-Heart Diner .... *David O'Meara*	390
from At the Schwarzschild Radius .... *Diana Brebner*	70
from Autumn Record ("Once, early in the morning...") ...... *Roo Borson*	48
Balancing Out .... *Margaret Avison*	20
Barrens Willow .... *John Steffler*	524
Believing the First Words You Hear .... *Adam Dickinson*	189
Belvédère .... *Pierre Nepveu*	364
Berry Picking .... *Irving Layton*	270
Between Stations, October .... *Sue Sinclair*	496
Bilan / Summing Up .... *Pierre Nepveu*	370
Bill Evans: "Here's That Rainy Day" .... *Jan Zwicky*	565
Birch Bark .... *Michael Ondaatje*	409

Blind Woman .... *Frederick Ward*	537
from *Blue Marrow*	
("*Father, these robes I wear confuse me...*") .... *Louis Halfe*	248
Blues .... *bpNichol*	376
Blues for X .... *George Elliott Clarke*	119
Book Rock .... *John Steffler*	524
Border .... *Laura Lush*	288
Boswell by the Fire .... *David O'Meara*	393
Boyfriend's Car .... *Karen Solie*	506
Browse .... *John Pass*	418
Brunetto Latini .... *Lorna Goodison*	228
Bucolique .... *Jacques Brault*	65
Butter Dish .... *Leonard Cohen*	125
"c'est un soir pas..." .... *Jacques Brault*	64
Cape Norman .... *John Steffler*	523
Casson .... *Michael Redhill*	460
"Ce n'est plus le moment..." .... *Jacques Brault*	64
"Cela arrive toujours sans prévenir" .... *Louise Dupré*	203
"certains lendemains..." .... *Monique Deland*	176
Chain 1 excerpt from *The Martyrology: Book 5* .... *bpNichol*	380
Chain 10, *The Martyrology: Book 5* .... *bpNichol*	383
Chickadee Encounter .... *Don McKay*	300
Child Hood I .... *George Elliott Clarke*	110
Children .... *Laura Lush*	285
Circle the Wagons .... *Marilyn Dumont*	194
Clearing Out .... *Matt Rader*	451
Close Your Eyes and Think of England .... *Stephanie Bolster*	42
Closing the Cabin .... *Jan Zwicky*	567
Coach's Corner .... *Richard Harrison*	250
from Coming to Earth (Alzheimer Elegy) .... *Michael Redhill*	460
Contacts .... *Agnes Walsh*	533
Content .... *Paul Dutton*	212
Crossover Griot .... *Lorna Goodison*	231
Cruelty .... *Matt Rader*	450
Darkening In .... *Laura Lush*	286
"De certains rêves..." .... *Martine Audet*	18
from *de Man: a performance poem* .... *Pamela Mordecai*	328
"Début mai..." .... *Nadine Ltaif*	282

Der Poop . . . . *Louise Halfe*	242
"des fleurs sur la table. . ." . . . . *Marie Uguay*	529
Description d'un après-midi . . . . *Robert Melançon*	311
from Desert Sonnets . . . . *David O'Meara*	387
Determinism . . . . *Karen Solie*	513
Dialogue #3 . . . . *Frederick Ward*	539
Dictionary of Symbols . . . . *Lorna Crozier*	149
Dining Room, Morning after Mrs. Dalloway's Party . . . . *Sue Sinclair*	498
Distant Islands (But of course they were further apart) . . . . *Susan Gillis*	219
Dog Song 2 . . . . *Al Purdy*	440
Double Focus . . . . *Al Purdy*	446
Dream of Havana . . . . *Al Purdy*	443
Dream Thief . . . . *Catherine Greenwood*	239
Dreaming . . . . *Paul Dutton*	207
Driving Northwest . . . . *Jan Zwicky*	556
Drought 1980 . . . . *Patrick Lane*	257
Duet . . . . *George Elliott Clarke*	112
Dust . . . . *Lorna Crozier*	147
early morning variation . . . . *bpNichol*	372
Early Work: An Eclogue . . . . *Ray Hsu*	252
Elegy for the Rocket . . . . *Richard Harrison*	251
Embroidery . . . . *Olive Senior*	489
Emperor Penguin . . . . *Olive Senior*	487
"En ce temps-là . . ." . . . . *Hélène Dorion*	191
Étendue . . . . *Pierre Nepveu*	363
Essentialist . . . . *Ken Babstock*	29
Faith . . . . *Matt Rader*	451
Falling Song . . . . *Daniel David Moses*	343
Father's Old Blue Cardigan . . . . *Anne Carson*	83
Fifteen Years . . . . *Erín Moure*	350
First Kiss (Teresa) . . . . *Carmine Starnino*	514
Fishermen . . . . *Irving Layton*	267
Fishing in the Waters Where My Dreams Lie . . . . *Olive Senior*	494
fool's scold, 1.4.97 . . . . *Roy Miki*	318
For All the Settlers Who Secretly Sing. . . . . *Beth Cuthand*	159
for steve . . . . *bpNichol*	378
Forests of the Medieval World . . . . *Don Coles*	133
Fort Smith Fire Brigade . . . . *Adam Dickinson*	190

Four Guitars .... George Elliott Clarke	116
Four Lectures by Robert Lowell, 1977 .... Elise Partridge	412
Four Poems for Virginia Woolf .... Sue Sinclair	501
From Who All Was There .... Frederick Ward	540
Fun .... David O'Meara	389
Gavey H. .... Laura Lush	289
Glenn Gould: Bach's "Italian" Concerto, BWV 971 .... Jan Zwicky	568
Goldfish .... Sue Sinclair	498
Good to Go .... Carmine Starnino	521
Goodbye to Beef .... Erín Moure	348
Grade One .... Tim Bowling	49
Grey Owl, 1937 .... Armand Garnet Ruffo	467
Grocery List .... Patricia Young	554
Habitat (South elevation) .... Susan Gillis	219
Habitat (We stand here looking) .... Susan Gillis	220
Happy Hour .... Michael Redhill	458
Hard Nails .... George Elliott Clarke	113
He Was There He Was Here .... Margaret Avison	23
History Lesson .... Jeannette C. Armstrong	7
Hockey .... Degan Davis	175
Hockey .... Tammy Armstrong	15
Homage .... Erín Moure	344
Home Care .... Lorna Crozier	155
Home .... Laura Lush	288
"Homo lupus est..." .... Francis Catalano	100
Hoping to Fix Up, a Little, This World .... Lorna Crozier	157
Hour 25 .... bpNichol	381
Hover .... Don McKay	301
I Solemn .... Agnes Walsh	531
I'm Bursting to Tell: Riddles for Conception Bay .... Mary Dalton	163
Ice House .... Anne Michaels	313
Identity I .... George Elliott Clarke	110
"Il existe pourtant des pommes..." .... Marie Uguay	526
"il fallait bien parfois..." .... Marie Uguay	530
"il fut difficile de quitter..." / "it was hard to leave..." (translated by Hugh Hazelton) .... Joël Des Rosiers	187
"Il n'y a personne qui crie..." / "No one is crying..." (translated by Cole Swenson) .... Hélène Monette	325

"Il nous semblait parfois. . . " . . . . *Martine Audet*	19
"Il y a ce désert acharnement . . ." . . . . *Marie Uguay*	528
In Da Name of Da Fadder . . . . *Louise Halfe*	243
In Service to a Dream . . . . *Catherine Greenwood*	238
In These (Tough) Times . . . . *Erín Moure*	352
from "In Which Alice Poses for Julia Margaret Cameron 1872" . . . .*Stephanie Bolster*	40
from *Inferno* . . . . *Ray Hsu*	253
Influences . . . . *Armand Garnet Ruffo*	468
"J'accumule des retailles . . . " . . . . *Monique Deland*	178
Jazzstory . . . . *Paul Dutton*	208
"je ne soigne personne. . ." . . . . *Tania Langlais*	265
"Je pressens cette terre sans arbres. . ." / "*Already I see this land stripped of trees. . .*" (translated by Judith Cowan) . . . . *Pierre Nepveu*	365
"Je suis de retour dans les contrées sauvages. . ." . . . . *Nadine Ltaif*	284
"je suppose que ça va finir. . ." . . . . *Tania Langlais*	264
Je t'écris . . . . *Pierre Morency*	338
Je vois l'intelligent théâtre. . . . . *Jean-Marc Desgent*	182
Joe Hassrak . . . . *Armand Garnet Ruffo*	472
Junk Food Pastoral . . . . *Gary Geddes*	217
Kelly . . . . *Laura Lush*	290
Kingdom . . . . *Don Coles*	129
Kit-Talk . . . . *Paul Dutton*	206
Komachu's . . . . *Laura Lush*	292
"l'enfance est d'immortalité. . ." / "*childhood is immortality. . .*" (translated by Hugh Hazelton) . . . . *Joël Des Rosiers*	185
L'été. . . . . *Robert Melançon*	310
L'homme des plans / *The Plans Man* . . . . *Pierre Nepveu*	369
"la joue sur l'oreiller . . ." . . . . *Monique Deland*	178
"La nuit a rejoint la ligne . . ." . . . . *Monique Deland*	177
"la question toujours la même . . . " . . . . *Monique Deland*	176
La Simûrghiade / *Simurghiade (translated by Christine Tipper)* . . . . *Nadine Ltaif*	277
"Là, voilà ta demeure . . ." . . . .*Louise Dupré*	201
Lament for Byways . . . . *Margaret Avison*	26
from *Land To Light On* . . . .*Dionne Brand*	52
Late Drive Toward Innisfil . . . . *Ken Babstock*	31
Later . . . . *Armand Garnet Ruffo*	474
Launch . . . . *Kyran Pittman*	424

Layton's Question .... Leonard Cohen	123
"le 26 Octobre 1951..."/ "on October 26 1951..."	
(translated by Hugh Hazelton) .... Joël Des Rosiers	183
"Le cri d'une mouette..." .... Marie Uguay	528
"le désorde ça prend combien de boîtes..." .... Tania Langlais	265
Le monde dans le peau .... Pierre Morency	338
Le monde des monstres est banal... .... Jean-Marc Desgent	181
"Le monde dévore nos paupières..." .... Hélène Dorion	193
Leather and Naughahyde .... Marilyn Dumont	197
"Les arbres nus du printemps..." .... Nadine Ltaif	283
de Les cendres bleues / from Blue Ashes	
(translated by Daniel Sloate) .... Jean-Paul Daoust	169
Les dieux en décembre .... Robert Melançon	311
"Les idées fondent comme du beurre..." .... Francis Catalano	98
"Les labours blancs..." .... Martine Audet	18
Les premiers paysages .... Jean-Marc Desgent	179
Let the Ponies Out .... Marilyn Dumont	197
Letter to Sir John A. Macdonald .... Marilyn Dumont	196
Look Homeward, Exile .... George Elliott Clarke	115
Lost way Lost .... Paul Dutton	205
Magnolia .... Susan Musgrave	357
"Maintenant nous sommes assis..." .... Marie Uguay	527
"Maintenant..."/ "Now..."	
(translated by Daniel Sloate) .... Jean-Paul Daoust	169
Mama-san .... Laura Lush	292
Marram Grass .... Ken Babstock	28
Matériel .... Don McKay	303
Me Grandaunt .... Frederick Ward	542
Meditation on Antique Glass .... Don McKay	295
Meditation on Shovels .... Don McKay	301
Meeting .... Erín Moure	354
"mes mains frileuses..." .... Monique Deland	177
de Mirabel / from Mirabel (translated by Judith Cowan) .... Pierre Nepveu	364
Miss Chatelaine .... Erín Moure	353
"mon père assembla..." / "my father assembled..."	
(translated by Hugh Hazelton) .... Joël Des Rosiers	184
Monarch I .... Patrick Lane	258
More Widow Than Queen Victoria .... Susan Goyette	234
Morning on the Guitar .... Diana Brebner	71

Moth .... *bpNichol*		374
Mr. Ishigami .... *Laura Lush*		289
Mrs. Bentley .... *Lorna Crozier*		148
Murder.. *Michael Redhill*		456
"n'en pouvant plus je l'ai écrit..." .... *Tania Langlais*		265
Najean .... *Frederick Ward*		540
Navigation .... *Carmine Starnino*		515
"Neige d'un soir..." .... *Jacques Brault*		64
Néo-libéralisme à clavier (aire de rapprochement de deux solitudes) .... *Francis Catalano*		97
Nestbox .... *John Pass*		417
New Rule .... *Anne Carson*		82
Nice .... *Karen Solie*		511
Night .... *Paul Dutton*		212
Night Game .... *Don Coles*		130
Night Train .... *George Elliott Clarke*		119
No Hablo Ingles .... *Susan Musgrave*		359
No One Asks Leda to Dance .... *Sue Sinclair*		497
No One Goes with the Exhibition Boys .... *Tammy Armstrong*		16
Nōhkom, Medicine Bear .... *Louise Halfe*		246
Non-Lieu / Non-Lieu (translated by Judith Cowan) ...... *Yves Préfontaine*		428
Not All Halfbreed Mothers .... *Gregory Scofield*		479
Not the Music..................................... *Lorna Crozier*		148
Notes on Burnt Cape .... *John Steffler*		525
Nouveau monde / New World (translated by Judith Cowan).................... *Pierre Nepveu*		367
Obscure .... *Paul Dutton*		210
Ode to the Greats (Northern Tribute) .... *Gregory Scofield*		475
"Oh and one more thing..." .... *Leonard Cohen*		127
On a Maundy Thursday Walk .... *Margaret Avison*		25
On Seeing the Statuettes of Ezekiel and Jeremiah in the Church of Notre Dame .... *Irving Layton*		268
On the Obsolescence of Caphone .... *Carmine Starnino*		517
On the Road to Emmaus............................. *Elise Partridge*		410
Once Lost .... *Sue Sinclair*		499
One Calvinist's God .... *Elise Partridge*		410
One Plus .... *Paul Dutton*		205
One Year .... *Michael Redhill*		457
Pāhkahkos .... *Louise Halfe*		244

Paradise Meadows .... *Matt Rader*		452
Pardon Me .... *Leonard Cohen*		124
"Paris again . . ." .... *Leonard Cohen*		122
partridge song .... *Kateri Akiwenzie-Damm*		3
Passing Sangudo .... *Jan Zwicky*		568
Pawâcakinâsîs-pîsim / December — The Frost Exploding Moon ....*Gregory Scofield*		482
Pays Ô soudain éclaté .... *Yves Préfontaine*		426
Pays sans parole .... *Yves Préfontaine*		427
Peacock Tale, 1 .... *Olive Senior*		486
Pearl Farmer's Wife .... *Catherine Greenwood*		239
Peinture aveugle .... *Robert Melançon*		310
Peuple inhabité .... *Yves Préfontaine*		425
Pêyak-Nikamowin / One Song .... *Gregory Scofield*		483
Photograph of My Mother as a Child or Invitation to the Wedding .... *Sue Sinclair*		500
Picking the Last Tomatoes with My Uncle .... *Carmine Starnino*		516
Poem for Duncan Campbell Scott .... *Armand Garnet Ruffo*		465
Poetry .... *Armand Garnet Ruffo*		464
Poise .... *David O'Meara*		392
Poor Mrs. Lot .... *Lorna Goodison*		232
Port .... *Diana Brebner*		72
Portrait of Alice with Christopher Robin .... *Stephanie Bolster*		43
Post-Oka Kinda Woman .... *Beth Cuthand*		158
"pour Guillane . . . / "for Guillane . . ." (translated by Hugh Hazelton) .... *Joël Des Rosiers*		186
Prairie .... *Jan Zwicky*		557
Prayer .... *bpNichol*		385
Precambrian Shield .... *Don McKay*		298
Preparations .... *Matt Rader*		455
probable systems 13: ....*bpNichol*		379
"quand elle retire sa petite robe . . ." .... *Tania Langlais*		262
"Quand je pourrai écrire un chant. . ." .... *Nadine Ltaif*		283
Questions for Marcus Mosiah Garvey .... *Lorna Goodison*		231
rainstorm in volcano: eight poems for rain .... *Kateri Akiwenzie-Damm*		4
Ramsden .... *Margaret Avison*		21
Reading a Biography of Samuel Beckett .... *Don Coles*		141
Reading *Titus Andronicus* in Three Mile Plains, N.S ..... *George Elliott Clarke*		111

"Recommence devant moi . . ." . . . . *Hélène Dorion*	192
Reconnaissance . . . . *Nadine Ltaif*	281
Remembering Gordon G. Nanos . . . . *Margaret Avison*	23
de *Répertoire* . . . . *Herménégilde Chiasson*	101
Rev. F. R. Langford's Miracle . . . . *George Elliott Clarke*	120
"rien ne se raconte plus . . ." . . . . *Tania Langlais*	263
"Rien ne suffit à ton regard . . ." . . . . *Louis Dupré*	202
River . . . . *Roo Borson*	44
River (Dear X.) . . . . *Susan Gillis*	221
Rivers to the Sea . . . . *Roo Borson*	47
from *Riverlisp* . . . . *Frederick Ward*	534
Riverside Heights . . . . *Laura Lush*	290
Robert Appears Again . . . . *Leonard Cohen*	123
Robinson's Crossing . . . . *Jan Zwicky*	557
Roblin's Mills . . . . *Al Purdy*	437
from Rock Bottom . . . . *Michael Ondaatje*	401
Rocks . . . . *Jeannette C. Armstrong*	12
Rodeo . . . . *Al Purdy*	442
Romance . . . . *Don Coles*	143
Rooms Under Rain . . . . *Daniel David Moses*	339
Rough Directions . . . . *David O'Meara*	388
from *Running in the Family* . . . . *Michael Ondaatje*	404
Rural Route . . . . *Elise Partridge*	415
"s'il fallait que tu meures . . ." . . . . *Tania Langlais*	263
"sa façon, la sienne . . ." . . . . *Tania Langlais*	262
Sallie Chisum / Last Words on Billy the Kid 4 a.m . . . . . *Michael Ondaatje*	399
Sampling from a Dialogue . . . . *Don Coles*	132
Setting Up the Drums . . . . *Don McKay*	302
from Seven Rail Poems . . . . *Erín Moure*	345
Several Times Table . . . . *Paul Dutton*	213
Shadowboxer . . . . *Anne Carson*	83
Shock Troop . . . . *Erín Moure*	344
Short Talk on Defloration . . . . *Anne Carson*	96
Shy Thought . . . . *Paul Dutton*	214
"Si j'étais un homme . . . " . . . . *Nadine Ltaif*	282
Sinking . . . . *Susan Goyette*	235
Sisters . . . . *Susan Goyette*	234
Six Thoughts on a Parkdale Porch . . . . *Zoe Whittall*	551

Skid .... Karen Solie	506
Skunks .... Lorna Crozier	153
Small Gesture .... Lorna Crozier	156
Softball: .... Don McKay	295
Something Akin to Worship Now .... David O'Meara	391
Sometimes a Voice (1) .... Don McKay	296
Song for Naomi. .... Irving Layton	273
Song for the Songs of the Common Raven .... Don McKay	299
Song in the Light of Dawn .... Daniel David Moses	339
Song of the House Husband .... Carmine Starnino	520
Song of the Saxifrage to the Rock. .... Don McKay	298
Soup .... Jan Zwicky	564
South Dakota Refuge .... Lorna Crozier	153
Spree .... George Elliott Clarke	114
St. Anzas VIII .... bpNichol	371
Stiff Little Fingers .... Zoe Whittall	550
Stirring a Can of Soup on the Stove .... Mike Barnes	38
Story .... Al Purdy	447
Strata .... Paul Dutton	206
stray bullets (oka re/vision) .... Kateri Akiwenzie-Damm	3
Strays .... Laura Lush	286
Sturgeon .... Karen Solie	507
sturgeon .... Kateri Akiwenzie-Damm	6
Subsidies .... Gary Geddes	216
Succession .... Paul Dutton	209
Summer or, I Want the Rage of Poets to Bleed Guns Speechless with Words .... Anurima Banerji	34
Sundeck in Houselight .... John Pass	417
T. For .... Gregory Scofield	480
"Tell me, what is it you plan to do with your one wild and precious life?" .... Alison Pick	423
from Ten Out of Ten, or Why Poetry Criticism Sucks in 2003 (2003) .... Darren Wershler-Henry	546
"Tes morts, tu en es venue . . ." .... Louise Dupré	204
Thanksgiving .... Karen Solie	508
from The Beauty of the Husband .... Anne Carson	91
The Bench .... Karen Solie	510
The Blue City .... Al Purdy	445

An Anthology of Poetry from Canada and Ireland   1199

The Blue Light of the Neutron Pool .... *Diana Brebner*	67
The Buddhist Bell .... *Al Purdy*	444
The Cariboo Horses .... *Al Purdy*	439
The Cinnamon Peeler .... *Michael Ondaatje*	405
The Collapse of Zen .... *Leonard Cohen*	126
from *The Collected Works of Billy the Kid* .... *Michael Ondaatje*	398
The Country of the Young .... *Al Purdy*	436
The Delicate Touch Required for China .... *Mark Callanan*	80
The Diving Girls' Prayer .... *Catherine Greenwood*	237
The Dorsals .... *Sue Sinclair*	496
The Dream of the Red Chamber .... *Patrick Lane*	261
from The Edvard Munch Poems .... *Don Coles*	135
The Fertile Muck. .... *Irving Layton*	269
The Fire .... *Patricia Young*	553
The Frog Variations .... *bpNichol*	384
The Girl from Ermita .... *Goh, Poh Seng*	222
The Grandmothers of Argentina .... *Enos Watts*	544
The Green Canoe .... *Diana Brebner*	69
The Happy Little Towns .... *Patrick Lane*	259
The Last Days .... *Carmine Starnino*	520
The Last of Us .... *Laura Lush*	285
The Lesson .... *Carmine Starnino*	514
The Line .... *Daniel David Moses*	340
The Making of 'Laurence of Arabia' .... *Sue Sinclair*	501
The Memorial Wall .... *Lorna Crozier*	152
The Party Was Over Then Too .... *Leonard Cohen*	124
The Persistence of Songs .... *Daniel David Moses*	342
The Predator .... *Irving Layton*	274
The Role of Calcium in Evolution .... *John Steffler*	522
The Room Where They Found You .... *Susan Musgrave*	362
The Sermon of Liana .... *George Elliott Clarke*	121
The Session .... *Laura Lush*	291
The Siyabaslakara .... *Michael Ondaatje*	408
The Sky is Promising .... *Marilyn Dumont*	198
The Swimmer .... *Irving Layton*	266
The Unhappy Condition .... *David O'Meara*	396
The Wellesdale .... *Laura Lush*	293
The White Judges .... *Marilyn Dumont*	194

The Year My Sister Came to Live with Me .... *Laura Lush*		294
"There are no words to remember, but I do have that gaze" .... *Don Coles*		139
These Are the Days .... *John Pass*		421
Thinking .... *Paul Dutton*		207
from *thirsty* .... *Dionne Brand*		51
Thirteen Ways of Looking at Blackbird .... *Olive Senior*		487
Thirteen Years .... *Erín Moure*		350
This Contradiction of Passion .... *Susan Goyette*		233
Thomas .... *Agnes Walsh*		532
Threads of Old Memory .... *Jeannette C. Armstrong*		8
Three Mysterious Songs .... *Jan Zwicky*		566
Three Weeks .... *Anne Michaels*		313
To Be Sold .... *Mary Dalton*		162
To the Branch from Which The Robin Flew .... *John Pass*		421
To the Girls of My Graduating Class .... *Irving Layton*		272
To Train and Keep a Peregrine You Cannot Miss a Day ...... *Alayna Munce*		355
Too Old .... *Leonard Cohen*		122
"tout ce qui va suivre . . ." .... *Marie Uguay*		529
"Tout est possible à l'ombre des jardins . . ." .... *Louise Dupré*		201
Trial II .... *George Elliott Clarke*		114
Truck .... *Paul Dutton*		211
True Story .... *Michael Redhill*		459
"tu lisais l'autre nuit . . ." .... *Tania Langlais*		264
"Tu peux encore lever la main. .... *Louise Dupré*		202
"Tu refais le voyage . . ." .... *Hélène Dorion*		193
"Tu relèves ta robe. . ." .... *Louise Dupré*		204
from TV Men .... *Anne Carson*		84
Two Deaths in January, 1898 .... *Stephanie Bolster*		41
Two Scenes from Philadelphia .... *Elise Partridge*		415
Two Thousand and Two .... *Catherine Hunter*		254
Typhon dru / *Typhoon Thrum* (translated by Robert Majzels and Erín Moure) ..... *Nicole Brossard*		74
"Un arbre dans sa solitude. . ." .... *Nadine Ltaif*		283
"Un coin du jardin sans soleil . . ." .... *Hélène Monette*		322
Underberries .... *John Pass*		419
Understanding the Sky .... *Susan Musgrave*		358
"Une maison brûle . . ." .... *Hélène Dorion*		191

"Une voix sans corps annonce..." .... *Monique Deland*	178
Untitled ("Sometimes as other sums...") .... *bpNichol*	377
Variation on the Origin of Flight .... *Lorna Crozier*	151
VIA, Outside Quebec City .... *Michael Redhill*	456
"Vus d'en bas..." .... *Francis Catalano*	97
Watching the Academy Awards in the Bar of the Patricia Hotel .... *Tim Bowling*	50
Weasel .... *Patrick Lane*	257
West to West .... *Erín Moure*	351
When We Become Desirable .... *Adam Dickinson*	189
Whose Eyes .... *Stephanie Bolster*	39
Wind Chime .... *John Pass*	420
Windspeed .... *Ken Babstock*	30
Wolf Lake .... *Matt Rader*	453
Women like You .... *Michael Ondaatje*	406
Words .... *Paul Dutton*	214
Work .... *Jan Zwicky*	563
Yet Among-Us .... *Frederick Ward*	542
You're So Covered with Scars .... *Lorna Crozier*	156
You've Got to Teach White Women Everything .... *Louise Halfe*	247
Your Premiums Will Never Increase .... *Karen Solie*	512
Zen Indian .... *Beth Cuthand*	160
36 .... *Robert Melançon*	312
65 .... *Jean-Marc Desgent*	179
72 Miles .... *Karen Solie*	509
100 Love Sonnets .... *Sue Sinclair*	504
157 Islington .... *Laura Lush*	287
160 secondes / *160 Seconds* (translated by Cole Swenson) .... *Hélène Monette*	323

Index of Poets (Ireland)

B
Bardwell, Leland	575
Barry, Sebastian	580
Berkeley, Sara	583
Blake, Denise	587
Boland, Eavan	593
Boland, Rosita	604
Boran, Pat	609
Borun-Jagodzinska, Katarzyna	612
Breathnach, Colm	616
Brennan, Deirdre	626
Buckley, Vincent	642
Bushe, Paddy	649
Byron, Catherine	653

C
Callan, Mary Rose	674
Cannon, Moya	678
Carr, Ellie	680
Carson, Ciaran	682
Charalambides, Kyriakos	686
Coady, Michael	696
Coyle-Greene, Enda	700
Cronin, Anthony	707
Crymble, Phillip	714
Cummings, Philip	716

D
De Fréine, Celia	725
De Paor, Louis	727
Dillon, Patrick	744
Dimitrova, Kristin	746
Dunne, Seán	752
Durcan, Paul	757

E
Ehin, Andres	768

F
Fallon, Peter	773
Fitzpatrick Simmons, Janice	775
Ford, Roderick	779
French, Tom	781

G
Garvey, Alan	792
Gillis, Alan	796
Grennan, Eamon	805

H
Heaney, Seamus	811
Hejda, Zbyněk	817
Hutchinson, Pearse	828

J
Jakpa, Oritsegbemi Emmanuel	829
Jenkinson, Biddy	833

K
Kelly, Rita	839
Kennelly, Brendan	841
Kinsella, Thomas	845
Korun, Barbara	857

L
Laird, Nick	860
Leahy, Ann	865
Longley, Michael	869
Lordan, Dave	878
Lyons, Alice	886

M
Mac Eoin, Gearailt	888
Mac Síomóin, Tomás	891
Mălăncioiu, Ilena	893
McCarthy, Thomas	900
McGuckian, Medbh	910
McLoughlin, Nigel	915
Meehan, Paula	918
Mhac an tSaoi, Máire	927
Mifsud, Immanuel	928
Mills, Geraldine	930
Montague, John	937
Morrissey, Sinéad	950
Murphy, Richard	960

N
Newmann, Kate	965
Ní Dhomhnaill, Nuala	971
Ní Ghallchóir, Collette	975
Nic Gearailt, Máire Áine	978
Ní Ghlinn, Áine	980

O
Odabaşi, Yilmaz	983
O'Brien, Jean	987
Ó Cuaig, Mícheál	991
Ó Domhnaill, Aodh	994
O'Donoghue, Bernard	995
O'Driscoll, Dennis	1004
Ó Leocháin, Seán	1016
O'Loughlin, Michael	1019
O'Malley, Mary	1024
Ó Muirthile, Liam	1027
O'Sullivan, Derry	1037

P
Perry, Paul	1039
Podracká, Dana	1041

R
Ramsell, Billy	1044
Rosenstock, Gabriel	1055

S
Sexton, John W.	1062
Sheehan, Eileen	1067
Sirr, Peter	1069
Stewart, Dolores	1075

T
Thomas, Samantha	1082

U
Uí Fhoghlú, Áine	1088

W
Wells, Grace	1109
Wyley, Enda	1115

An Anthology of Poetry from Canada and Ireland 1203

Index of Poems (Ireland)

A Dog *(translated by Eiléan Ní Chuilleanáin)* .... *Ilena Mălăncioiu*	895
A Good Rogeting .... *Ann Leahy*	865
A Hill Farmer Speaks .... *Nigel McLoughlin*	916
from A Journal .... *Peter Sirr*	1072
A Lament for the Saintly Mothers *(translated by Gregory O'Donoghue)* .... *Kristin Dimitrova*	747
A Norwegian Wedding .... *Michael Longley*	870
A Parcel from Prison *(translated by Robert Welch)* .... *Dana Podracká*	1041
A Poppy .... *Michael Longley*	872
A Prayer .... *Michael Longley*	874
A Robin in Autumn Chatting at Dawn .... *Paul Durcan*	759
A Sprig of Bay .... *Michael Longley*	871
from A Stay in a Sanatorium ("A Poem . . . ") *(translated by Bernard O'Donoghue)* .... *Zbyněk Hejda*	817
A Stay in a Sanatorium ("I was staying. . .") *(translated by Bernard O'Donoghue)* .... *Zbyněk Hejda*	818
A Visit to the Clockmaker *(translated by Gregory O'Donoghue)* .... *Kristin Dimitrova*	751
A White Bedsheet *(translated by Robert Welch)* .... *Dana Podracká*	1042
A Year On .... *Janice Fitzpatrick Simmons*	777
About Being Human .... *Deirdre Brennan*	630
About Lifelines .... *Geraldine Mills*	932
After the Nuptial Mass .... *Catherine Byron*	672
Ag Aistriú *Buddha in Der Glorie* / Translating Buddha in Der Glorie .... *Paddy Bushe*	650
Agus an Samhradh Thart / Now Summer's Over *(translated by Gregory O'Donoghue)* .... *Gearailt Mac Eoin*	889
Aida *(translated by Gerry Murphy)* .... *Katarzyna Borun-Jagodzinska*	615
Alive, Alive, Alive .... *Janice Fitzpatrick Simmons*	778
All of These People .... *Michael Longley*	877
American Wake .... *Dolores Stewart*	1075
An Fear Marbh / *The Dead Man* .... *Colm Breathnach*	619
An Ghéag Theasctha / *The Severed Limb* .... *Colm Breathnach*	625
An Seanduine .... *Liam O'Muirthile*	1035

An tAmharc Deireanach / *The Last Look* (translated by Gréagóir Ó Dúill) .... *Collete Ní Ghallchóir*	976
An Tine Bheo / *The Burning Fire* .... *Áine Uí Fhoghlú*	1098
An tUllmhúchán / *Getting Ready* .... *Áine Uí Fhoghlú*	1105
Anahorish 1944 .... *Seamus Heaney*	811
Angry Arthur .... *Mary O'Malley*	1025
Anne / *Anne (translated by Philip Cummings)* .... *Philip Cummings*	719
Anniversary .... *Mary O'Malley*	1024
Another Moon .... *Enda Coyle-Greene*	700
Antain / *Antain (translated by Gréagóir Ó Dúill)* ..... *Collete Ní Ghallchóir*	975
Ar an Leaba Leathan / *On the Bed Spread* .... *Colm Breathnach*	624
Ar Iarraidh / *Lost (translated by Gréagóir Ó Dúill)* .... *Dolores Stewart*	1079
As gach póir Díot / *From each and every pore* .... *Gabriel Rosenstock*	1055
Asperger Child .... *Tom French*	783
Aşure .... *Grace Wells*	1109
At the Seminar .... *Dennis O'Driscoll*	1010
Auntie *(translated by Gregory O'Donoghue)* .... *Kristin Dimitrova*	746
Baile an Tae .... *Liam Ó Muirthile*	1029
Basáin Mhara .... *Liam Ó Muirthile*	1027
Beir Beannacht / *Fare Well* .... *Rita Kelly*	839
from "Berlin Diary, 1991" .... *Paula Meehan*	922
Björn Olinder's Pictures .... *Michael Longley*	869
Blessings .... *Janice Fitzpatrick Simmons*	775
Blighted .... *Geraldine Mills*	930
Bolgam / *Gulp* .... *Paddy Bushe*	649
Bomb .... *Nigel McLoughlin*	916
Border Sick Call .... *John Montague*	937
Boxer .... *Michael O'Loughlin*	1021
Boy at the Window Waiting .... *Geraldine Mills*	934
Breath .... *Billy Ramsell*	1044
Bróga Nua / *New Shoes* .... *Colm Breathnach*	616
Broken Dishes .... *Michael Longley*	870
Candaules' Wife *(translated by Greg Delanty)* .... *Kyriakos Charalambides*	690
Casualty .... *Alan Gillis*	801
Ceartúcháin / *Corrections (translated by Louis de Paor)* .... *Louis de Paor*	730
Ceasefire .... *Michael Longley*	876
Ceol Johnny Phádraig Pheter / *Johnny Phádraig Pheter's Music* (translated by Gréagóir Ó Dúill) ....*Dolores Stewart*	1081

An Anthology of Poetry from Canada and Ireland 1205

Chrysalides .... *Thomas Kinsella*	849
Clean as a Wish. .... *Mary Rose Callan*	674
Coco de Mer .... *Catherine Byron*	657
Cocoon .... *Janice Fitzpatrick Simmons*	775
from *Code*... *Eavan Boland*	594
Coffin. Crypt. Consumption ....*Catherine Byron*	653
Coillteán / *Castrato* .... *Gabriel Rosenstock*	1060
Cold Flow .... *Alan Gillis*	799
Cold Storage .... *Ann Leahy*	867
Colúr Marbh / *Dead Pigeon* .... *Gabriel Rosenstock*	1058
Complicated Pleasures .... *Billy Ramsell*	1047
Confidential Reports — in the Form of a Public-Private Confession	
(translated by Maurice Riordan) .... *Immanuel Mifsud*	928
from *Cromwell* .... *Brendan Kennelly*	841
Cutaway Philosophers .... *Geraldine Mills*	933
Cuttings .... *Nick Laird*	860
Dán Grá / *Love Poem* .... *Louis de Paor*	729
Death of Socrates .... *Dolores Stewart*	1077
Death's Art .... *Kyriakos Charalambides*	689
deep, below ground, breathe *(translated by Patrick Cotter)*..... *Andres Ehin*	772
Deireadh Caithréime / *The End of Triumph*	
(translated by Gréagóir Ó Dúill) .... *Gearailt Mac Eoin*	888
Deirid gur daonnaí mé / *They say I am Human* ....*Gabriel Rosenstock*	1060
Deochanna / *Drinks (translated by Gréagóir Ó Dúill*	
and Philip Cummings) .... *Philip Cummings*	716
Diamonds .... *Rosita Boland*	605
Diary of a Fat Man .... *Enda Wyley*	1120
Didjeridu / *Didjeridoo* .... *Louis de Paor*	737
Do nochtacht / *Your nakedness* .... *Gabriel Rosenstock*	1057
Dóchas / *Hope (translated by Gréagóir Ó Dúill)* .... *Dolores Stewart*	1077
Early Lessons .... *Denise Blake*	589
Eden .... *Oritsegbemi Emmanuel Jakpa*	831
Egyptians .... *Catherine Byron*	658
Éin i gCliabháin / *Caged Birds* .... *Paddy Bushe*	652
Eitseáil Bheo .... *Liam Ó Muirthile*	1032
Emperor .... *Enda Wyley*	1123
England .... *Dennis O'Driscoll*	1006
Facts of Life .... *Mary Rose Callan*	676

Faith .... *Janice Fitzpatrick Simmons*	776
Fallen Woman .... *Deirdre Brennan*	631
from Feride *(translated by Patrick Galvin and*		
Robert O'Donoghue) .... *Yilmaz Odabaşi*	983
Fiailí / *Weeds* .... *Áine Uí Fhoghlú*	1102
Finit / *Finit (translated by Gréagóir Ó Dúill)* .... *Derry O'Sullivan*	1037
First Blood *(translated by Gregory O'Donoghue)* .... *Kristin Dimitrova*	748
First Love .... *Roderick Ford*	780
fish livers lie scattered on the ground		
(translated by Patrick Cotter) .... *Andres Ehin*	769
Foghlaimeoirí / *Homework* .... *Louis de Paor*	727
Forlámhas / *Supremacy* .... *Colm Breathnach*	618
Freight Depot *(translated by Gregory O'Donoghue)* .... *Kristin Dimitrova*	747
Frogspawn .... *John W. Sexton*	1064
Fúinne / *About Us (translated by Gréagóir Ó Dúill)* ...... *Pearse Hutchinson*	828
Fused *(translated by Gregory O'Donoghue)* .... *Kristin Dimitrova*	748
Gaeilgeoirí / *Gaeilgeoirí* .... *Louis de Paor*	731
Going Home .... *Enda Wyley*	1115
Gold — The Gleninsheen Gorget .... *Rosita Boland*	606
Golden Island Shopping Centre .... *Paul Durcan*	757
Grafton Street .... *Enda Coyle-Greene*	701
Giuseppe .... *Roderick Ford*	779
Gustaí mhí Aibreáin / *April Gusts* .... *Gabriel Rosenstock*	1057
Handed On .... *Enda Coyle-Greene*	702
Hard to Imagine Your Face Dead .... *Leland Bardwell*	575
Harmattan .... *Oritsegbemi Emmanuel Jakpa*	829
He Buries His Father, 1809 .... *Thomas McCarthy*	905
He Considers the Rev. Dill-Wallace, 1817 .... *Thomas McCarthy*	908
He Contemplates a Stolen *Bozzetto* of Canova's *Cupid*		
and Psyche, 1811 .... *Thomas McCarthy*	903
He Goes Through His Father's Belongings, 1809 ...... *Thomas McCarthy*	905
He Meets His Future Sister-in-Law,		
Miss Teresette O'Neill, ... *Thomas McCarthy*	900
He Recalls a Letter from Home, 1771 .... *Thomas McCarthy*	907
He Sees a Warehouse Burning, August 1798 .... *Thomas McCarthy*	909
He Spends Christmas at Clonakilty, 1809 .... *Thomas McCarthy*	907
He Turns to His Wife, 1797 .... *Thomas McCarthy*	901
He Watches His Wife Create a Silhouette Portrait,		
1812 .... *Thomas McCarthy*	902

He Witnesses a Military Execution, 1804 .... *Thomas McCarthy*	904
He Witnesses Another Hanging, 1813 .... *Thomas McCarthy*	904
He Writes to His Estranged Sister, 1803 .... *Thomas McCarthy*	906
HEADLINES .... *Paul Durcan*	760
Helmet .... *Seamus Heaney*	811
Her Grief .... *Mary Rose Callan*	676
from Here and There:	
A Notebook .... *Peter Sirr*	1069
High Water .... *Nigel McLoughlin*	915
Holding Chirac's Hand in Temple Bar .... *Dave Lordan*	884
Horse Fair .... *Grace Wells*	1111
House without Eyebrows .... *Medbh McGuckian*	911
Housesitting .... *Peter Sirr*	1071
How We Meet .... *Sara Berkeley*	584
Hunger-Strike .... *Vincent Buckley*	642
I am *(translated by Patrick Cotter)* .... *Andres Ehin*	768
I am your Missing Car *(translated by Patrick Cotter)* .... *Andres Ehin*	771
I Seomra Feithimh an Dochtúra, 1974 /	
In the Doctor's Waiting Room, 1974 .... *Áine Uí Fhoghlú*	1100
I'm a cripple with yellow, burning eyes	
(translated by Patrick Cotter) .... *Andres Ehin*	770
Iarlais / Changeling .... *Louis de Paor*	741
Idir Scylla agus Charybdis / *Between Scylla and Charybdis*	
(translated by Gréagóir Ó Dúill) .... *Dolores Stewart*	1078
In Aois / *Getting On* .... *Celia De Fréine*	725
In Mourning .... *Denise Blake*	587
In Praise of Hestia, Goddess of the Hearth Fire .... *Anthony Cronin*	708
In Praise of Salt .... *Sinéad Morrissey*	956
In the Model Village .... *Dave Lordan*	878
In the National Archives .... *Deirdre Brennan*	628
In the Train *(translated by Gregory O'Donoghue)* ...... *Kristin Dimitrova*	749
Inghean / *Daughter* .... *Louis de Paor*	740
Innismurray. .... *Leland Bardwell*	576
Interview on Main Street .... *Michael Coady*	696
Iomrascáil Oíche leis na Mairbh / *Night Wrestling with the Dead*	
(translated by Gréagóir Ó Dúill) .... *Áine Ní Ghlinn*	981
Íota / *Desire* .... *Áine Uí Fhoghlú*	1095
Ireland .... *Billy Ramsell*	1050

Is 'Werewolf' mé anocht / *I Am a Werewolf Tonight*
  (translated by Gréagóir Ó Dúill) .... *Deirdre Brennan*   639
It Snowed on the Body
  (translated by Eiléan Ní Chuilleanáin) .... *Ilena Mălăncioiu*   898
Judge These Books .... *Alan Garvey*   792
Juist .... *Sinéad Morrissey*   953
Jupiter .... *Pat Boran*   610
Kaiyuglak — Rippled Surface of Snow .... *Denise Blake*   587
Kassapa .... *Richard Murphy*   960
King John's Castle .... *Thomas Kinsella*   850
Knowing the Wizard .... *Denise Blake*   588
Lady in White .... *Eileen Sheehan* 1067
Laertes .... *Michael Longley*   876
Laid Beside You *(translated by Eiléan Ní Chuilleanáin)* .... *Ilena Mălăncioiu*   898
Last Friday Night .... *Alan Gillis*   804
Late August, Donegal .... *Samantha Thomas* 1082
Latin as a Foreign Language .... *Michael O'Loughlin* 1019
Let the Grass Grow Over Her
  (translated by Eiléan Ní Chuilleanáin) .... *Ilena Mălăncioiu*   897
Letterkenny 567 .... *Denise Blake*   590
Li Am ar Fhalla Mór na Síne .... *Liam Ó Muirthile* 1030
Little House in the Big Woods .... *Sinéad Morrissey*   951
Lord Mayo .... *Dennis O'Driscoll* 1012
Lorgaíodh mo Shúile tú / *My Eyes Would Look for You* ....*Colm Breathnach*   621
Love Bites .... *Alan Gillis*   801
Love Bruise .... *Enda Wyley* 1116
Love .... *Alan Garvey*   792
Low Winter Sun .... *Michael Coady*   697
Maighdeana Mara / *Mermaids*
  (translated by Gréagóir Ó Dúill) .... *Deirdre Brennan*   637
Making Room .... *Janice Fitzpatrick Simmons*   777
Man O' War .... *Samantha Thomas* 1083
Man-Eating Leopard of Rudrapraya .... *Samantha Thomas* 1084
Mappa Mundi .... *Medbh McGuckian*   910
Marlborough Road .... *Enda Wyley* 1117
Maryville, Winter, 2001 .... *Dolores Stewart* 1076
Master Chef. .... *Enda Wyley* 1121
Meditation on a Clare Cliff-Top .... *Anthony Cronin*   710
Mending a Puncture .... *Tom French*   789

Middle Distance .... *Billy Ramsell*	1046
Mimi's Aria	
(translated by Gerry Murphy) .... *Katarzyna Borun-Jagodzinska*	614
Mince Customer .... *Ann Leahy*	866
Minding You .... *Catherine Byron*	670
Mint Gatherers .... *Enda Wyley*	1122
Missing God .... *Dennis O'Driscoll*	1004
Morne Grande .... *Samantha Thomas*	1086
Murdering the Language .... *Moya Cannon*	678
Mutterecht / *Mutterecht*	
(translated by Gréagóir Ó Dúill) .... *Máire Mhac an tSaoi*	927
My Father Perceived as a Vision of St. Francis .... *Paula Meehan*	918
My Mac .... *Mary O'Malley*	1024
My Sister's Way to Make Mead .... *Medbh McGuckian*	912
Na Murúcha a Thriomaigh / *The Assimilated Merfolk*	
(translated by Paul Muldoon) .... *Nuala Ní Dhomhnaill*	971
Newton / *Newton (translated by Philip Cummings)* ...... *Philip Cummings*	718
Niamh .... *Alan Gillis*	802
Night Drive .... *Tom French*	782
Nitocris, Queen of Babylon .... *Kyriakos Charalambides*	692
'No Road Beyond the Graveyard' .... *Leland Bardwell*	577
Northern Lights .... *Michael Longley*	869
'Not alone the rue in my herb garden ...' .... *Paula Meehan*	920
Not Your Muse .... *Paula Meehan*	919
Of the People of Olympia	
(translated by Greg Delanty) .... *Kyriakos Charalambides*	686
Oifigiúil / *Official (translated by Gréagóir Ó Dúill)* ..... *Aodh Ó Domhnaill*	994
On Giving a Poetry Recital to an Empty Hall .... *Paul Durcan*	762
On Seeing Lord Tennyson's Nightcap at Westport House ... *Anthony Cronin*	707
Opium .... *Enda Coyle-Greene*	703
Out of Old Stories .... *Geraldine Mills*	931
Out of This World .... *Seamus Heaney*	813
Pause en Route .... *Thomas Kinsella*	851
Photograph of Theresa Martin as Joan of Arc	
(translated by Gerry Murphy) .... *Katarzyna Borun-Jagodzinska*	612
Pilots .... *Sinéad Morrissey*	950
Pity the Bastards .... *Tom French*	784
Poet as Magpie .... *Geraldine Mills*	935
Poppy .... *Alan Garvey*	793

Potiphar's Wife *(translated by Greg Delanty)* ..... *Kyriakos Charalambides*	693
Prison Poem III: For a Friend Doing Life in Portlaoise ...... *Leland Bardwell*	579
Progress .... *Alan Gillis*	804
Put to Loss because of the Snow .... *Kate Newmann*	965
from *The Quick of It* .... *Eamonn Grennan*	805
Reading the Greats .... *Sinéad Morrissey*	956
from *Readings in Poetry* .... *Thomas Kinsella*	852
from Reflections on Shannon .... *Dave Lordan*	883
Reilig an Mhuine Ghlais / *Moneyglass Cemetery*	
(translated by Philip Cummings) .... *Philip Cummings*	721
Remaindermen .... *Nick Laird*	861
Repossession .... *Deirdre Brennan*	632
Rice Lake.. *Phillip Crymble*	715
Ringabella .... *Liam Ó Muirthile*	1031
Roland Gets It .... *John W. Sexton*	1065
Sa tír / *In the land* ... . *Áine Uí Fhoghlú*	1093
Samhradh / *Summer* .... *Gabriel Rosenstock*	1058
San Aonad Alzheimer .... *Liam Ó Muirthile*	1034
Scarpia	
(translated by Gerry Murphy) .... *Katarzyna Borun-Jagodzinska*	613
Scarpia's Aria	
(translated by Gerry Murphy) .... *Katarzyna Borun-Jagodzinska*	615
Scarúint / *Parting* .... *Colm Breathnach*	617
School Tour, Kilmainham Jail .... *Michael Coady*	699
Scrap Metal .... *Michael Longley*	875
Séamus / *Seamus (translated by Philip Cummings)* ...... *Philip Cummings*	720
Seanchas / *Old Stories* .... *Louis de Paor*	735
Seanfhalla / *Old Wall* .... *Gabriel Rosenstock*	1055
Sean-ghnás / *The Old Ways* .... *Colm Breathnach*	623
Searmanas / *Rituals* .... *Louis de Paor*	733
Secret *(translated by Patrick Cotter)* .... *Andres Ehin*	771
Severed .... *Jean O'Brien*	987
Sex .... *Janice Fitzpatrick Simmons*	777
Sightless .... *Rosita Boland*	605
Sigiriya, 11 January 1987 .... *Richard Murphy*	963
from *Sir Gawain and the Green Knight* .... *Bernard O'Donoghue*	995
Sneachta na mBunchnoc / *Snow on the foothills* ...... *Gabriel Rosenstock*	1056
Sníomh / *Spinning (translated by Gréagóir Ó Dúill)* ..... *Deirdre Brennan*	636
So Many .... *Enda Coyle-Greene*	706

An Anthology of Poetry from Canada and Ireland

Some Evening *(translated by Bernard O'Donoghue)* .... *Zbyněk Hejda*	825
Song of Joy *(translated by Eiléan Ní Chuilleanáin)* ...... *Ilena Mălăncioiu*	895
Southern Shores .... *Billy Ramsell*	1051
Spoon Sweet .... *Kyriakos Charalambides*	687
St Thomas Aquinas in MacNiece's House .... *Catherine Byron*	669
Stag *(translated by Theo Dorgan)* .... *Barbara Korun*	857
Still Life with Frozen Pizza .... *Billy Ramsell*	1049
Still Life, Yellow Quilt .... *Sara Berkeley*	585
Strawberry Thief .... *Sara Berkeley*	583
Striking Distance .... *Tom French*	790
Suantraí Sarah is Asmahane .... *Liam Ó Muirthile*	1033
from Suburb .... *Paula Meehan*	924
Swallow .... *Michael Longley*	869
Tao and Unfitness at Inistiogue on the River Nore ...... *Thomas Kinsella*	845
Tarnowo Podgorne .... *Paul Durcan*	767
Tate's Avenue .... *Seamus Heaney*	814
TEA .... *Dave Lordan*	880
Teangmháil / Contact *(translated by Gréagóir Ó Dúill)* .... *Áine Ní Ghlinn*	980
Tears .... *Rosita Boland*	608
Tears for Twenty-Five Years	
(translated by Greg Delanty) .... *Kyriakos Charalambides*	694
Teeth .... *Rosita Boland*	607
Teicheadh / Fleeing	
(translated by Gréagóir Ó Dúill) .... *Máire Áine Nic Gearailt*	978
Tent .... *Pat Boran*	611
Thank God It's Dry .... *Alice Lyons*	886
The 12 O'Clock Mass, Roundstone,	
County Galway, 28 July 2002 .... *Paul Durcan*	765
The Annual Mass of the Knights of Columbanus .... *Paul Durcan*	763
The Astronaut's Wife .... *Rosita Boland*	604
The Bear *(translated by Eiléan Ní Chuilleanáin)* .... *Ilena Mălăncioiu*	894
The Blackbird of Glanmore .... *Seamus Heaney*	815
'The Blue Dress' .... *Deirdre Brennan*	631
The Burning .... *Deirdre Brennan*	626
The Collector .... *Deirdre Brennan*	635
The colonels of several hostile armies	
(translated by Patrick Cotter) .... *Andres Ehin*	768
The Crocodile .... *Patrick Dillon*	744
The Daffodils .... *Michael Longley*	871

The Doctor on Duty *(translated by Eiléan Ní Chuilleanáin)* . . *Ilena Mălăncioiu*	896
The Evening Forecast for the Region . . . . *Nick Laird*	863
The Fields of Beaumont-Hamel . . . . *Alan Garvey*	794
The Funeral Director's Wife . . . . *Grace Wells*	1112
The Gate to Mulcahy's Farm . . . . *Paul Perry*	1039
from *The Georgics of Virgil* . . . . *Peter Fallon*	773
The Getting of Vellum . . . . *Catherine Byron*	661
The Gorgon as Mistress of the Animals . . . . *Medbh McGuckian*	913
The Headless Bird *(translated by Eiléan Ní Chuilleanáin)* . . . *Ilena Mălăncioiu*	893
The Healing Island . . . . *Seán Dunne*	752
The Horse Protestant Joke Is Over . . . . *Leland Bardwell*	578
The Horses . . . . *Michael Longley*	874
The Hostage Place . . . . *Grace Wells*	1114
from *The Inferno of Dante Alighieri* . . . .*Ciaran Carson*	682
The Last Observance . . . . *Deirdre Brennan*	633
The Light of Other Days . . . . *Dennis O'Driscoll*	1013
The Local School *(translated by Gregory O'Donoghue)* . . . . *Kristin Dimitrova*	750
The Lone Parent Does Not Write . . . . *Grace Wells*	1113
The Longest Queue . . . . *Dave Lordan*	880
The Magic Roundabout . . . . *Pat Boran*	609
The Man Monaghan . . . . *Sebastian Barry*	582
The Man with a Bit of Jizz in Him . . . . *Paul Durcan*	758
The Muezzin's Call . . . . *Grace Wells*	1112
The Mustard Tin . . . . *Michael Longley*	870
The Names of the Houses . . . . *Peter Sirr*	1069
The Night's Empty Shells . . . . *Leland Bardwell*	575
The Nod . . . . *Seamus Heaney*	812
The Only Medicine . . . . *Grace Wells*	1110
The Owner . . . . *Sebastian Barry*	581
The Pinkening Boy . . . . *Sebastian Barry*	580
The Place of Execution of the First President (translated by Robert Welch) . . . . *Dana Podracká*	1043
The Poet's Fancy . . . . *Mary O'Malley*	1026
The Polish Language . . . . *Alice Lyons*	886
The Post-Hole . . . . *Tom French*	783
The Proud Cry of the Young Father . . . . *Paul Durcan*	764
from The Quick of It . . . . *Eamon Grennan*	805
The Rooms . . . . *Enda Coyle-Greene*	705
The Signpost . . . . *Nick Laird*	862

from The State of the Prisons .... *Sinéad Morrissey*	957
The Tantric Master .... *Paula Meehan*	925
from The Tyranny of Words	
(translated by Greg Delanty) .... *Kyriakos Charalambides*	686
The Ulster Way .... *Alan Gillis*	796
The Wall by the Swings	
(translated by Gregory O'Donoghue) .... *Kristin Dimitrova*	750
The War Graves .... *Michael Longley*	873
The Wood-Pigeons .... *Sebastian Barry*	580
The Writer's Studio .... *Peter Sirr*	1074
Theresa at the Laundry	
(translated by Gerry Murphy) .... *Katarzyna Borun-Jagodzinska*	612
Three Fragments on the Theme of Moving	
Around in Cities .... *Michael O'Loughlin*	1021
Timpbriste / *Accidentally* .... *Louis de Paor*	743
To a Child in the Womb .... *Michael O'Loughlin*	1022
To Belfast .... *Alan Gillis*	800
Tomatoes .... *Phillip Crymble*	714
To the Wife .... *Nick Laird*	863
Tóg Chun do Dhraenacha Mé /	
Take Me to Your Drains .... *Gabriel Rosenstock*	1061
Toibreacha / *Wells (translated by Gréagóir Ó Dúill)* ..... *Mícheál Ó Cuaig*	992
Tóraíocht / *Pursuit (translated by Gréagóir Ó Dúill)* ..... *Seán Ó Leocháin*	1018
Touching the Bones .... *Tom French*	781
Traidisiún / *Tradition (translated by Gréagóir Ó Dúill)* ... *Seán Ó Leocháin*	1017
from *Traveller Ways Traveller Words* .... *Ellie Carr*	680
Tuireamh Marie Antoinette / *La chute de Marie-Antoinette*	
(translated by Juliette Saumande) ....'............ *Biddy Jenkinson*	833
Two Women in Kosovo .... *Enda Wyley*	1118
Uchtóga / *Armfuls (translated by Gréagóir Ó Dúill)* ..... *Mícheál Ó Cuaig*	991
Uiscí Reatha / *Running Water (translated by Gréagóir Ó Dúill*	
and Philip Cummings) .... *Philip Cummings*	717
Van Morrison Plays Mother Goose	
(translated by Gerry Murphy) .... *Katarzyna Borun-Jagodzinska*	613
Verlaine .... *Samantha Thomas*	1087
Veronica .... *Jean O'Brien*	989
Veronica's Epiphany .... *Jean O'Brien*	987
Vertigo .... *Enda Coyle-Greene*	704
Vortex .... *John W. Sexton*	1062
Vows .... *Denise Blake*	591

Wedding Service .... *Thomas Kinsella*		847
Wednesday Women .... *Geraldine Mills*		935
What We Understood .... *Geraldine Mills*		931
What's that in English? / *What's that in English?* .... *Áine Uí Fhoghlú*		1088
When Will I Get to Be Called a Man .... *Liam Ó Muirthile*		1027
White Bulls *(translated by Theo Dorgan)* .... *Barbara Korun*		859
Wolf *(translated by Theo Dorgan)* .... *Barbara Korun*		858
Woman Forming the Handle of a Cane .... *Medbh McGuckian*		914
from Writing in a Time of Violence: A Sequence .... *Eavan Boland*		593
Yellow .... *Michael O'Loughlin*		1023
Yes, I can bake a cake. .... *Jean O'Brien*		989
You Gave Me a Long Look *(translated by Eiléan Ní Chuilleanáin)* .... *Ilena Mălăncioiu*		896
Yugapat-srishti / *Yugapat-srishti* .... *Gabriel Rosenstock*		1059
12th October, 1994 .... *Alan Gillis*		796
999 / *999 (translated by Gréagóir Ó Dúill)* .... *Seán Ó Leocháin*		1016
1845 / *1845 (translated by Gréagóir Ó Dúill)* ...... *Thomás Mac Síomóin*		891